The Quiet

EN4CER

D1246384

The Authorised Biography of

PADDY JOHNS

Richard Bullick & Dr Fiona Neary

SPORTSWRITE

First Published 2002 by
SPORTSWRITE
Unit 2
Cromac Wood
Ormeau Road
BELFAST
BT7 2DJ

© Richard Bullick and Dr Fiona Neary 2002

ISBN 0 9544027 0 7

A catalogue record for this book is available from the
British Library

Printed in Great Britain by the Universities Press (Belfast) Ltd.

Richard Bullick, an Honours Graduate in Economics and Management from the Queen's University of Belfast, is an experienced and widely respected rugby-writer and sports columnist. A member of the Rugby Writers of Ireland, he has been Rugby Correspondent of the Belfast News Letter for the past five years, during which he has covered more than a half-century of internationals, including the 1999 World Cup, as well as reporting extensively on Ulster's famous European Cup triumph the previous season. As a regular traveller with the Ulster team, he has built up a good rapport with many of Ireland's leading professional players and administrators. Aged 27, Richard has written on rugby for every major newspaper in Ireland, including the Irish Times, Independent, Examiner, Mirror and Star, the Sunday Times, Sunday Independent, Sunday Tribune, Ireland on Sunday and Sunday People. By his own admission, a 'moderate cricketer and mediocre rugby player', he began writing and broadcasting on the summer sport at the age of 18 after leaving the Roya l School Armagh, where he was awarded an honours blazer to mark two seasons in the First XI. After graduating, he began building a successful career in tourism, marketing and management consultancy before the increasing demands of reporting on professional rugby saw him commit more time to sports journalism.

Dr Fiona Neary, was educated at Belfast Royal Academy before graduating in Medicine from Liverpool University in July 2002 and is now a Pre-Registration House Officer at Southport District General Hospital. An accomplished athlete, swimmer and hockey player, she took up rugby at the age of 15, initially with Belfast club Cooke, and currently lines out for Waterloo in the English Premiership. The winger was a member of the Ulster team which won back-to-back interpro titles in 2000 and 2001 and is currently vice-captain of her province. She has won 19 senior caps for Ireland, appearing in the World Cups of 1998 and 2002, and has played at Ravenhill and Thomond Park. Born in Australia to Irish parents, the much-travelled 25-year old has watched rugby in all of the leading southern hemisphere stadiums since attending her first international at Lansdowne Road in 1989. Dr Neary, who has worked as an assistant medic with leading Perth-based Aussie Rules team, the West Coast Eagles, has reported on European Cup and international rugby for the Belfast News Letter and Sunday People and is currently a columnist for Northern Ireland Medicine Today.

CONTENTS

of winning and losing, are common across the gender divide and unfortunately Fiona came face to face with what Paddy felt when he lost his Ireland place for no good reason, when she herself was unfairly marginalised during her second Women's World Cup in May this year. Like Paddy, she has played with a broken finger in a splint in the face of medical advice! Her medical knowledge and extensive experience of having watched rugby at all the leading southern hemisphere stadiums have also given us useful extra insight regarding various issues. Our perspectives are complementary and there is sufficient telepathy in our writing for the double act authorship to have worked fairly seamlessly.

So it's been a good team and we've also worked well with Paddy himself, who has been roped into the round-the-clock vigils of the past couple of weeks and never once complained. We're all much more aware now than when we set off on this journey, just what it entails and have even thought of setting up a counselling service aimed at all those intending to write books; advising them to get over it before they start! Meantime, we look forward to returning to leading normal lives as soon as we can make the transition.

We hope you enjoy the book and that we have managed to capture a flavour of the Paddy Johns whom we ourselves have had the privilege of getting to know so well in the course of the past six months.

ACKNOWLEDGEMENTS

The authors would like to express our gratitude to the following, without whose assistance our vision of this book would not have come to fruition:

Firstly a special thank-you to RHIAN WILMOTT, who has been a tower of strength with her tireless efforts and emotional support in riding the roller-coaster with us these last few weeks, not to mention securing our first book order in Wales! RUTH McCAUSLAND (and John) have gone the extra mile in the sort of way that only true friends will, while the efforts and enthusiastic encouragement of DEIRDRE LYNCH have also been much appreciated.

Big thanks to GEOFF MARTIN and the NEWS LETTER for agreeing to do the layout and typesetting. The personal interest and input of the Editor has been much appreciated (we wish him well in his new job in England), as has RICHARD MULLIGAN working late the night before heading off to run the New York marathon (believe us we've been hitting our own walls in this metaphorical marathon) and texting encouragement from the Big Apple. Thanks to IAN CALLENDER for working until 4am one morning (at least we hope it was good body clock acclimatisation for watching the first Ashes Test from Oz over the nights which followed, though due to us he also ended up watching the entire first session in the office!), ALEX MILLS for doing such an excellent job in designing the cover, PAUL KELLY for doing a Sunday shift after being ill, JACKIE KIDD for scanning our pics and finding us excellent staff, CHRISTIAN SCHNABEL for some scanning and CHRISTINE PORTER for sorting the cover pic when things were getting fractious that final Friday night. Finally, the cleaners, who tried their best not to waken Richard at 5.30am on the (day after the supposedly) final day as he tried to catch some kip in a chair in the office.

To HELM CORPORATION for their generous sponsorship and other practical support; directors MIKE FRAZER and SEAN SWEENEY for approving the deal, company secretary MARTIN MALLON for his input, and IT guru TONY DOGLAY for technical help and advice.

Thanks to the ULSTER BRANCH, MICHAEL REID and SIMON WALLACE for their advice and the practical support which will be so important to us in seeking to promote and distribute this book. Also to DUNGANNON RUGBY CLUB and TERRY JACKSON for promising to support us in this coming phase of the project.

To UNIVERSITIES PRESS for printing the book and the long-suffering PHILIP McCORD for cajoling us and sticking with us in an understanding and accommodating manner.

To the ISBN Agency for processing our application so quickly even though, true to form, it was received late.

To EDMUND VAN ESBECK for his warm words of encouragement and sound advice, but particularly for writing his book on the history of Irish Rugby, which we found simply invaluable as research material.

To the SUNDAY TRIBUNE for buying the rights to publishing extracts of the book in advance of publication, MARK JONES and PETER O'REILLY for working with us on that. To ALEX McGREEVY and the SUNDAY PEOPLE for the advance publicity and to all other colleagues who have promised to publicise the book ahead of publication and /or review it later.

Thanks to BILLY STICKLAND and INPHO Photographic Sports Agency for the front cover pic, to ESLER CRAWFORD PHOTOGRAPHY, to the NEWS LETTER for all pics by JOHN RUSH, MARK McCORMICK and ANDY McCONNELL, to FORMULA 1 and to the TYRONE TIMES.

A word of appreciation for all our many sources, (especially Jason Leonard, whose wife must now be suspicious that he has a female stalker!). Thanks guys for taking the time to talk to us about Paddy and share your stories, insights and amusing anecdotes.

Sincere thanks to the incomparable WILLIE JOHN McBRIDE for honouring us by agreeing to do the Foreword and humble apologies for leaving him with such an unreasonable timescale at the end in which to do it.

Talking about us being unreasonable, what can we say about ROY MEGAW, other than that he came on board at short notice when we had reached the point of no return and worked all night to finish things off. Without his intervention, you wouldn't be reading this. Cheers mate.

Obviously a big thank-you to our fellow travellers PADDY AND KIRSTY JOHNS, with whom we were conversing at all hours of the day and night by the end of the process, and MRS WANDA JOHNS for making available her photo albums and scrapbooks.

Thanks to those who will be selling the book for us and, in particular, thanks to all of you who are buying it.

Finally, thanks to our families and friends for putting up with us these last few months when we have been in book-writing mode, and to anyone else, paid or unpaid, who has contributed in any way or had their arm twisted (thanks JILL HENDERSON), ear bent or shoulder cried on, or who has worried about our health or feared for our sanity. We thank you all.

Richard and Fiona

FROM THE HORSE'S MOUTH . . .

Looking back on my rugby career, I can honestly say I have been very fortunate, privileged, and lucky and that I have no regrets. I have made many good friends, including my wife, and I have learnt a great deal about life and about myself.

I am grateful to my family for their support through the highs and the lows. To Kirsty, my wife, you have been a pillar of support and strength ever since I met you. I know I am lucky to have you walk through life by my side.

Mum, you have brought me up to work hard, aim high and persevere in everything I do.

Vanessa, Marcus and Jonny, you have backed me all the way, and I thank you for that.

To my wonderful children, Christopher, Emily, Hannah and Megan, you truly are very special and unique young people with immense capability. Believe in yourselves, follow your dreams and always make your own choices.

To Richard and Fiona, I want to thank you for writing this book. You have both put in a tremendous amount of work. I am both honoured and grateful that you thought me a fitting subject.

I recognise rugby is a very important sport to many and representing your club, province and country is indeed an honour.

Now that my competitive playing days have come to an end, I ask myself "what is important in my life now?"

Four things really. My faith, my family, my friends and my new job.

I believe in God Almighty and I know throughout my life God has been there for me. Unwisely I have not always kept that door open. Today and tomorrow it is wide ajar.

To my close friends, I value your friendship.

Finally, now that I have returned to the dental profession, my daily focus is on providing the best care that I can to my patients. Each day I wake up and say, "Life is good, Life is great."

Paddy Johns

FOREWORD

By Willie John McBride

RUGBY football has changed a lot more than Paddy Johns has changed in the 16 years since I first met him, back when he was a teenager with a broken arm at the Royal Victoria Hospital in Belfast.

In those days, I was working in marketing and PR with the bank and was up at the hospital seeing a client. I noticed this young guy with his arm up and asked him what had happened to him.

In the course of our conversation, I found out who he was and that the injury had been sustained playing rugby. That evening I rung Wilfie Wright from Dungannon and told him I'd seen Paddy. Wilfie advised me that he would go far in the game. He was right.

Because of that coincidental meeting, Paddy was a guy whose career I had an interest in from then on, though it wouldn't have been long before he came to everyone's attention anyway as he started to make a real impression.

I've always seen Paddy as my sort of player, an honest-to-God forward prepared to do the hard grind. He handled the transition from amateurism to professionalism very well, went off to England and proved himself there and also captained his country.

In spite of all that he had achieved, he was still prepared, wisely or unwisely, to come out of retirement and help Ulster in the hour of need this autumn. It was typical of Paddy in that he never shirked anything.

I admire those qualities of courage, honesty and integrity in him, and also the way in which he represents rugby's values and, like myself, holds its traditions dear.

He is respected throughout the rugby world, both among his peers and predecessors, for how he has conducted himself on and off the field.

Paddy Johns hasn't changed as a person since the day I first met him, in spite of all that he has achieved, and although the game of rugby football has changed almost beyond recognition in that period.

Rugby began as his hobby and became his career and he handled all of the challenges which came with that very professionally and very successfully.

I treasure my own years in rugby deeply, but it is an entirely different game now to the one I played and there are certain constraints now which we didn't have when we played for fun, albeit to win.

Paddy hasn't got swept away on the tide of greed and self-importance, instead getting on with the game with the honesty and humility for which he is well known.

There are some who blow their own trumpet, but Paddy always let his actions speak loudest and do his talking on the pitch.

You earn the respect of rugby people by your deeds, not by your words, and that is why Paddy Johns is held in such high esteem. He has been a good example to any aspiring young player.

It has been a pleasure following Paddy's career and I wish him well for the future.

Willie John McBride

1. GREAT OAKS...

Paddy Johns owes a lot to his mini-rugby coach for unwittingly providing the first bit of the motivation which drove him on to achieve greatness in the game. When quizzed by Mr Johns on how his three sons were getting on, the gentleman in question was quick to praise Marcus as "a good runner, strong and likes tackling", while conceding that Jonathan "messes more and isn't as serious." And young Patrick? Well, according to his first mentor, the middle of the Johns boys "cries when he is tackled and should find another sport". The rest, as they say, is history.

More than a quarter of a century later, Patrick Stephen Johns, as the BBC's Jim Neilly has doubtless referred to him countless times in commentaries in the last decade and a half, has retired from the game with 59 Ireland caps to his name, fourth on the all-time appearances list. Johnny has made occasional appearances for Dungannon down the years and symbolically came on to partner Paddy in the engineroom for an Ulster Select XV in the final 10 minutes of the charity match against a Celtic Warriors XV to celebrate his long and distinguished career. Marcus gave up the game after a back operation in his late teens.

It's hard to reconcile the picture painted by those words all those years ago with the warrior-like enforcer who never took a backward step when captaining his country on that stormy South African tour of 1998. Having said that, consider the contrast with the gentle giant happily chatting to kids as, bent double, he patiently signs autographs, the dentist with the deft touch and bedside manner to match, County Armagh's Girl Guides ambassador or the soft-spoken gentleman respected throughout the rugby world, the man described by his former Dungannon, Ulster and Ireland colleague Allen Clarke as 'a credit to mankind.'

In researching this book, we found that at grammar school he had won a Cup awarded for good manners and came across a letter from Wayne Proctor replying to one he had sent the Welsh winger after inadvertently breaking his jaw in an international. He has also been known to reply to thank-you letters! England's most capped international Jason Leonard, another gentleman of the game, recalls how Johns was the only Irish forward who showed any concern for his well-being after a match in which they had given him an almighty shoeing. But Leonard knew the same thing would happen again next time if he found himself lying on the wrong side and that Johns would expect nothing different if the roles were reversed. No quarter asked or given and no grudges held afterwards. Leave it on the pitch. Paddy and Jason will always remain firm friends. You can live in a murky world without becoming tainted.

Whatever. Paddy found the perfect balance which allowed him to give as good as he got in the jungle of the Test rugby forward battle, while remaining a nice guy off the pitch.

Both are equally important parts of his rugby legacy. The two sides of him are actually more complementary than contradictory, both reflecting his underpinning desire to honestly give his best to whatever he is involved in. In practice though that has given us the 'Pudsey and Dudsey' twin sides of Paddy Johns.

David Hands, Rugby Correspondent of The Times, once summed up the distinction. 'Pudsey . . . the bear that symbolises help for children in need; this is the normal day-to-day Johns: quiet, friendly and approachable. But his colleagues also recognise a character they call Dudsey, which is the second row forward with devil in his play and Irish fire in his limbs.'

Ireland prop Justin Fitzpatrick sums up the contrast pretty well. "There isn't a great enough quality or quantity of words in the dictionary to do justice to describing what a quietly-spoken, likeable gentleman Paddy is off the pitch. Then there's Johns the rugby player. In that guise, he's the ultimate competitor, the very force of nature almost. The stories of just how hard and how uncompromising he was on the rugby field are legendary. When he crossed that whitewash, he was totally transformed." Others grapple with contrasting the two sides of Paddy Johns in the final chapter of this book.

All told, Paddy came a long, long way from those unpromising beginnings on Saturday mornings at Stevenson Park, a ground he was to grace with enormous distinction in the decades which followed. No-one could have bounced back better from such an early put-down. Sometimes the seeds of burning desire can be planted most deeply by early slights, just as a career can be ruined by achieving too much too easily too soon. Hunger is a great attribute for any aspiring player and Paddy had it in spades from beginning to end. He would be the first to class himself as artisan rather than artist, the hard-working model professional with a cussed determination to do his best, living proof of the primacy of perspiration over inspiration when it comes to sporting success and, in particular, longevity.

When we were trawling through a mountain of memorabilia one Sunday afternoon in the early stages of putting this book together, a piece of paper floated out of one of the boxes replete with some hand-written words of wisdom. Some were like those little truisms which you sometimes find at the bottom of calendars and the one about either being part of the steam-roller or part of the pavement may have helped mould Paddy Johns into the uncompromising hard man he was on the pitch. The choice he made was clear. That was the one which tickled us most, but Johns has at least as much been testimony to one of the other proverbs on the page. Some dream of success, others wake up and work hard to achieve it, it said. No-one has worked harder at it than Paddy.

Never flashy or consciously conspicuous on the pitch for the sake of it, Johns nevertheless knew that his huge contribution would always be appreciated by the real rugby people, the connoisseurs of the game. He outlasted many a talent who let rave reviews go to their heads. But you don't win 59 caps for your country and make an impact for three seasons in the English Premiership without ability, lots of it, so as well as giving him the motivation, Paddy's old mini rugby coach must have been a little wide of the mark in his assessment all those years ago. That said, Paddy's good friend John Gamble, who played with him for school and club, can "remember him coming off the Prep pitch one day in Under 12s when we'd been playing in sleet and snow and starting to cry when he got into the changing rooms because he was so cold!"

It so often happens though. Many great sportsmen, when their tales come to be told, confess to having been considered nothing special as kids. By then, with lots of honours behind them and their place in history assured, they can laugh at having been dismissed out of hand early on, but doubtless it wasn't as funny at the time. Sport is full of highs and lows and fluctuating fortunes and those who go furthest tend to be those who respond best to the inevitable setbacks which will occur along the way, work on the weaknesses and counter the threats head-on. When the going gets tough and all that. Providing the person is made of the right stuff, adversity can bring out the best in them and, to a self-styled stubborn sort like Paddy, brickbats in the early days would have done more for him than bouquets.

In many ways, there is nothing as character-building as sport, and it may say as much about the personal qualities of those such as Johns who came through in spite of damning verdicts being delivered almost before they had started as it does about their first coaches not being able to spot supreme talent. Considering Paddy's tender age at the time, it would be wrong to read too much into the fateful comments of the Dungannon mini-rugby coach of almost three decades ago and they now stand mainly as an amusing anecdote.

And yet. Fast forward to when he lost the Irish captaincy for the tour Down Under a few months ahead of the 1999 World Cup. The main reason he was axed as skipper seemed to be the growing clamour for a 'dream ticket' second row pairing of Jeremy Davidson and Malcolm O'Kelly. It never really materialised. In the event, Paddy was the one lock who started both Tests against Australia, but again the tendency had been there to write him off and look elsewhere. It wasn't the first time and it wouldn't be the last, but confounding the critics had become second nature to him. From those earliest days he had been used to having to prove a point. It didn't take him long to make his mark either. In spite of the 'can't play, won't play' slur, Johns came through quickly and certainly wasn't a late developer in the Davy Tweed or Jeff Probyn sense as the coming chapters will relate.

But what was Paddy Johns like as a kid? He was the third of four children, the middle of three sons, and grew up in Ireland's 'Orchard County', Armagh, having been born on 19th February 1968 in the Carleton Home, Portadown. The name of that town has become synonymous with the strife surrounding the issue of traditional marches in Northern Ireland, given the Drumcree dispute on its doorstep, but although Johns was born just as civil unrest was starting to beset the country, his young life was, like many others, largely unaffected by the 'troubles'. He played soccer with, amongst others, future Tyrone county gaelic football star Plunkett Donaghy in sheep-soiled fields round the village of Moy where he attended the local primary school.

The friendship with Donaghy has been an enduring one, with Paddy supporting Plunkett in pursuit of All Ireland gaelic glory but, sadly and inevitably, Paddy was to get more than a glimpse of what the consequences can be of living in a sick society stained by sectarianism. One of his best buddies at grammar school, Adam Lambert, was cruelly cut down by loyalist paramilitaries in a botched attempt to reap random revenge for the

IRA's infamous 'Poppy Day massacre' in Enniskillen on Remembrance Day, November 1987. Paddy would visit the grave at Christmas time and putting a picture of his tombstone in the book was even considered, such is the very real sense of loss which he still feels.

"Adam was a very good friend right through school, both on and off the rugby pitch. He was such a great buddy, there wasn't a bad bone in his body. We'd have spent a fair bit of time at each other's houses and were really good mates. I went off to Newcastle to do dentistry and he stayed in Ulster to study architecture at Queen's University in Belfast. The day after the Enniskillen bomb (in which 11 civilians lost their lives), he was out on a building site as part of his work experience. The firm that he was working for was Catholic-owned, which is probably why they were targeted, in blind retaliation at a time when feelings were naturally running very high. Adam was simply in the wrong place at the wrong time.

"His wasn't the first futile death of an innocent person in the province and it wasn't the last, but Adam was my friend so it was simply that much closer to home. We all came back from universities across the water for the funeral and I remember thinking what a waste it all was. Adam was a young guy with everything to live for, but his life was just taken away in an instant. A lot of people here have been touched in some way by what has gone on and, sadly, his death will always remind me of the problems which this country has had."

Mistaken identity. Paddy knows a little about it himself. Many people in Northern Ireland like to be able to work out what religious background those who they meet are from and will treat them at least a little differently depending on whether or not they adjudge them to come from their 'side of the house' and thus be more likely to share similar religious or political views. With his first name, Johns was always a bit of a confusion to those anxious to attach sectarian labels and of course he also encountered some of the issues directly when, as an Ireland player, he stood silent along with his Ulster colleagues as the anthem was played before home internationals.

An Irish captain called Patrick not feeling able to sing the Irish anthem sounds, er, a bit Irish alright. Just as a matter of interest, how come a lad ostensibly of Ulster Protestant stock was given such a stereotypically Irish Catholic name in the first place, especially in a society where perception is everything?

"I was christened on St Patrick's Day and both my parents, although Protestant, came from southern Ireland, my father born in Monaghan and my mother born in Dublin" explains Paddy. "My mother liked the name and saw no reason why a name like Patrick should be the preserve of only one section of the community. Some people would have been a bit confused though and assumed that I was a Catholic. There aren't many Patricks playing rugby in Ulster I suppose."

On one occasion, during his A-level resits year at Armagh College of Further Education, Paddy was called a 'fenian' on the stairs by someone who quickly made off after he looked at them rather intently and, on another occasion, a fight broke out during a match between Dungannon and Portadown for the same reason. Ironically, he and other northern Protestant players have experienced occasional abuse from southern counterparts, though he insists that sectarian slagging is not prevalent in Irish rugby.

"I've been called a few things recently as well, but that's one medium which I have never used as an insult, even in matches where there is a bit of talk going on or where I may have been called something myself. There are a lot of things which go on when you cross the white line but, in this country, abusing people on the grounds of religion, is beyond the pale in my view. When it has occasionally happened to me, I've been able to pass if off as a case of it being the other person who has the problem. It doesn't go on much, but does happen occasionally. It would be an individual thing I'd say, rather than being institutionalised. I was abused in an AIL match last year, but have also heard of an inverse case involving an Ulster player, so the problem, such as it is, wouldn't be exclusively on one side or another.

"To my mind, rugby in Ireland actually does a fair bit to break down barriers. At school, we went down to play southern schools such as Templeogue, St Munchin's and St Gerard's and then would have hosted their players in our houses on return visits. That would have helped alleviate misconceptions about other people being unrecognisably different to ourselves."

When Paddy was 19, he spent a summer playing rugby in Canada as one of six Irish lads, the only northern Protestant alongside five southern Catholics, but they all had a great time and the religion factor never cost him a thought.

Another very good friend is the inimitable Irish team baggage master, 'Rala', whose real name, Paddy O'Reilly, might attract upon him some adverse attention in certain parts of the north. Mrs Johns, Paddy's mum, recalls Rala arriving in Dungannon for her son's last home game for the club earlier this year and taking him over to a nearby village, which would have strong loyalist leanings. "He is a devout Catholic and was telling me about having met the Pope on the Ireland team's recent visit to Rome and how he had even learned a few lines of Polish for the occasion" she says. "I was just hoping we wouldn't be overheard!

"Rala has been a tower of strength for Paddy around the Irish team, a man with a heart of corn who any player could go to with any difficulty and get a reasoned and sympathetic response. Their friendship is also indicative of how there are really no borders or barriers in Irish rugby. Terenure College conferred a special honour on Rala recently and he asked Paddy to be guest speaker at the dinner. Religion doesn't really come into the rugby."

The Peace International in 1996 and the lack of crowd trouble at games between Ireland and England are also indicative of the positive, even healing, powers of rugby, which has itself been touched by the Troubles, notably when Ulster flanker Nigel Carr was forced into premature retirement ahead of the 1987 World Cup when caught up in a republican bomb blast. Like Paddy's friend Adam, Carr was in the wrong place at the wrong time; it could have been anyone. In his time as Ireland captain, Paddy again came face to face with the effects of terrorist violence on innocent young lives when Omagh bomb victim Alastair Hall was chosen as team mascot for the international between Ireland and England in 1999.

Alastair was 12 years old and looking forward to starting to play rugby in a fortnight's time when a republican bomb killed 29 civilians and two unborn babies in August 1998.

He lost a leg below the knee and had to have an artificial limb fitted, but the prospect of acting as Irish mascot helped strengthen his courage and resolve to walk again.

"He hadn't walked before that match" reveals Paddy, "but was determined that he didn't want to be pushed out in a wheelchair. He managed it and we were able to walk out slowly together. It was a poignant and emotional moment for all concerned. People in the stand were crying. He's a very brave boy. The Omagh bombers may have taken his leg but they couldn't take his spirit and I'm sure he'll continue to be an inspiration to many." Paddy didn't mention it himself, but he also gave Alastair his match jersey after the game. The following May, Paddy played in a match at Stevenson Park where Dungannon beat a star-studded invitation team containing many ex-internationals including Zinzan Brooke, 89-64, with all proceeds going to the Omagh bomb victims' fund.

Compared to losing his friend Adam Lambert, or seeing at first hand the affliction which has befallen Alastair Hall, other things pale into the inconsequential category, but Paddy has other little regrets about what was lost as a result of growing up in a deeply divided community. "In our part of Ireland, you will tend to do different things depending on which side of the community you are born into and, while I'm admittedly generalising a bit, in sporting terms that means that you'll play either rugby or gaelic games." Maybe, to inject some typically black Ulster humour, that's what they mean when they talk about 'which foot someone kicks with', but Johns readily admits that, from a sporting point of view, he'd kind of have liked to have a go at the football, gaelic style.

Contemporary Irish internationals from other provinces such as Mick Galwey and Eric Elwood made their mark in inter-county gaelic football before switching their main focus to the oval ball game, the former even picking up a coveted all-Ireland winners medal with Kerry. Ulster, by contrast, essentially only draw their rugby stars from one section of the community, which these days constitutes little more than half of the province's population and, while the northerners have been remarkably successful considering that, the growth of the game in rural areas of Munster for example could exacerbate the disadvantage.

Up until recently, some of the rural hinterlands surrounding rugby-mad Limerick and Munster's second city in rugby terms, Cork, have largely been the passionate preserve of gaelic football and hurling, but parish pioneers like Galwey and Ireland prop John Hayes have proved rugby role models in far flung outposts. Add in the glorious European Cup runs of the magnificently supported Munster team in the past few seasons and it is no surprise that rugby is thriving in the south and south west.

Ulster can't afford to continue to draw from only half of their potential player base and Johns rightly muses on how good rugby players the likes of Donaghy – "he'd have made a good blindside I reckon" – might have been, given the chance. The converse also applies, for no doubt plenty of rugby players below the tied-up professional level would be capable of making a contribution to their county's bid for all-Ireland gaelic football glory in the summer months. It is ironic that the Brooke brothers, Zinzan and Robin, of All Black fame have played gaelic football, with the former also having savoured the atmosphere as part of a 70,000 plus crowd on all-Ireland final day, yet there are cultural barriers for those like Johns.

That's just the way things are. The man isn't a bigot, he's even got as Irish a name as they come and no doubt he'd relish the physical, competitive aspect of gaelic football as well as appreciating the fitness and commitment of his counterparts in the other code. But things in Ulster have never been that straightforward. The good news is that the degree of sporting cross-fertilisation is slowly picking up, helped by IRFU Development Officers taking the game into what would have been regarded as non-traditional schools, a generally improved political climate and the enthusiasm of the likes of Willie Anderson for reaching across the divide. Anderson, Johns' second row partner, captain and later coach at Dungannon, not to mention a predecessor as Ireland skipper, has always embraced the gaelic form of football, encouraging co-operation between his own club and their counterparts in the other code. Anderson's own son also plays the sport.

A slow growth in integrated education may also impact on the range of sports open to young boys and girls in the future, while the cross-code challenges which now take place annually at a few clubs, including Dungannon, are giving some players the chance to try their hands and feet at a new game. These matches, which generally feature one half gaelic football and one half rugby, are largely for fun and fund-raising purposes in a commendable cross-community context, but both sports could also reap the benefits of closer co-operation.

In Ulster, the wider the appeal of rugby the bigger the base of potential support and there is still a belief that the famous European Cup triumph of January 1999 has played a part in reaching out, including across the religious divide, to those who would not previously have been Ravenhill regulars. While no-one would want to even get into suppositions about crowd composition in terms of backgrounds or beliefs, the attendance figures have certainly increased dramatically in the 14 years from Paddy's first Ulster game to his last, a phenomenon which will be reflected upon in more depth later.

Ulster rugby, like South African rugby, may have tended to draw its players and supporters from a particular group, but while the exclusive tag may apply in both cases, there is clear evidence that the sport has not been as exclusionist in the northern Irish province as in the rainbow republic. Unlike in post-apartheid South Africa, Johns reasonably believes there will never be any need for quota systems when selecting Ulster teams at any level. "I think a large part of the problem has been the Catholic schools historically refusing to play rugby, so they must take their share of responsibility for any imbalance at adult level. But the situation is improving and that is to be welcomed."

Rugby has actually played a positive part in bringing people together rather than deepening divisions and, in contrast to the riot which threatened to wreck Lansdowne Road when the Republic of Ireland played England a few years ago, there is no need for segregation when the Irish and English do battle at the same venue in Six Nations rugby. That is perhaps largely a reflection of the civilised values traditionally enshrined in rugby, but the fact that the oval ball game features an all-island Ireland team including northern Protestants born and brought up under the UK jurisdiction adds another ironic twist.

Paddy admits that those in other rugby nations are fascinated by the nuances of the Irish situation and that he has been asked to explain the apparent anomalies on numerous occasions to outsiders. He himself, however, sees no contradictions, as will be discussed in chapter six.

But let's leave the rest of the politics for later. Back to boyhood, when such weighty and wearying matters simply washed over him, and primary school memories of "playing football every spare minute." With all three Johns boys being born in the space of three years, Paddy was very close to his siblings in age, so the same applied to some extent at home, though the oval ball code was also on the agenda with the trio attending mini-rugby at Dungannon RFC where, believe it or not, Paddy initially found himself being groomed as a back as his former school and clubmate John Gamble reveals further on.

Among his childhood likes were 'playing football, mini rugby and winning', while on television his favourite programmes included Dr Who, Match of the Day and, inevitably, Rugby Special. He disliked 'getting up early, my mum used to open the curtains to get me up faster, being called names and having my face washed in public by my mum, using her hanky with spit on it to dampen it!' He also seemed to dislike his third name, Charlston, and so it was duly dropped, rendering him Patrick Stephen Johns for those commentators with a penchant for using middle names! "It was actually supposed to be Charlton, after a previous generation, but was spelt wrongly on the birth certificate" he explains.

"As a child, Paddy was very placid, contented and happy" says his mum, Wanda. "He could amuse himself and wasn't demanding. I have four totally different children and can honestly say that he was the most placid. He also seemed to be good at most things, which didn't make life easy for the other three.

"That said, he got into the usual scrapes too. I remember him and Johnny getting into a big margarine tub thing at the top of the stairs and sliding down like as if it was a bobsleigh ride. Paddy was in the front and, at the bottom, Johnny flew out over his head and through a glass door. The accident has left a scar over his left eye. There was another time when Paddy climbed up a 40-foot conifer tree and we had to try and coax him down. He then proceeded, to our great consternation, to go out onto a branch. He was all feet and hands."

Sister Vanessa says: "Paddy and I used to gang up on the other two because we were bigger and stronger and I would have got on best with him. He was a good buddy and support through the teenage years when we were both going to Dungannon rugby club on a regular basis. I really lived the rugby circuit with him in those early days, going on Dungannon weekends away and the like and also got going to occasional functions with him until his own Mills & Boon story took off. I attended every Irish match he played in up until the birth of my first child."

It would be fair to say that Paddy has given a lot to his rugby and it has given a lot back, not only to him, but to those around him.

2. LEARNING THE TRADE

Some dream about success. Others wake up and work hard to achieve it. That old truism again. Paddy Johns remembers vividly the day he decided he wanted to play for Ireland. Most of us, in a vague, notional, indulgent sort of way will have fancied pulling on the green jersey or of playing for our country in our chosen sport. Every kid has sporting heroes and sporting dreams, but we generally grow out of it and settle for an awful lot less. It is all wishful thinking as the vast majority of us would never have had either the ability or the application to make it a reality. There is a world of difference between childhood fantasy and genuine aspiration.

In Paddy's case it was different. Dream alright, but then believe and ultimately achieve, with unstinting dedication and relentless hard work providing the foundation and the cement which allowed it all to be turned into something tangible. We all remember the excitement we felt when attending our first international, but in Paddy's case that maiden visit to Lansdowne Road had a much more profound effect. He decided there and then that one day he would be back, taking that field in one of those green jerseys. Or at least would have left no stone unturned (a phrase so many of our sources in this book have used to describe how he approaches his rugby) in his quest. The experience sparked something deep inside him and the fire burned bright for the next two decades. He was to represent his country 30 times in the old stadium, leading them out as captain on six of those occasions.

"I was about 14 at the time" he recalls. "We'd gone down to Dublin with the school and played against Templeogue College in the morning before being taken to the international in the afternoon. One of the abiding memories of the trip is the food: the beef soup and the corned beef sandwiches. In the end, we scoffed them because we were so hungry, but I still get the horrors. It probably put me off corned beef sandwiches for life!"

Put him off corned beef sandwiches maybe, but switched him onto rugby big-time. Without unnecessarily wishing to conjure visions of the British Prime Minister of the time, Paddy Johns too is not one for turning. The corned beef sandwiches may have lingered in his mind for longer than they sated his hunger, but he took away images and visions from that afternoon which he was to feed off in the years ahead and which were to sustain him through all the effort needed to make his dreams come true.

"We were standing in the schoolboy section on the south terrace. It was the biggest crowd I had ever seen and what I saw and felt when the Irish team ran out made me want to be there myself one day. I made a conscious decision there and then." Paddy admits he didn't know the names of the Irish players that day and that, at the time, he was "in no way hung up with individuals. There was no-one in particular who I aspired to be or regarded as a favourite player."

So it wasn't about heroes then, but something more nebulous, the sense of occasion perhaps, the honour and the glory. But, while it was abstract in that sense, it was nonetheless real and Johns also knew just what would be required if he was to get there himself. It may surprise some who know this man, who is modest to a fault, that he was so caught up, even at an impressionable age, by what, in a sense, was a yearning for the fame and spotlight, but doubtless some of it was a desire to compete and win in such a charged environment.

Paddy's other confession in relation to how his rugby ambitions were honed and nurtured suggests that he had discovered transcendental meditation even before the yogic flyers of the Natural Law Party had tried to make it mainstream! "I cut pictures out of the programme that day and stuck them on my bedroom wall, so they were there before my eyes first thing in the morning and last thing at night, though strangely enough it still wasn't about individuals, like kids having posters of their favourite footballer. It was still more generalised, more about what they represented than who they were."

In his collection, we found 12 programmes from internationals between 1981 and 1988, some autographed. The games included Ireland's 17-0 victory over England in 1987, England's romp in the following year's fixture and Will Carling's first game as English captain, against the Wallabies that autumn.

"We also did Art at school and I used to paint rugby pictures, again I suppose because that was what captured my imagination at the time. Some of those were on the walls as well. There's also that time, when you're kind of in a hypnotic state just before you really go to sleep, and again rugby would very much have been present, hardly surprisingly in that I'd have been looking at the pictures on the walls as I drifted off." Visualisation techniques are all the rage these days for some players, coaches and sports psychologists, but trying to imagine himself in the environment he aspired to certainly seems to have played a part in helping pull Paddy through towards realising his rugby dreams.

Only a small part though. The visions may have driven him and sustained him, but what turned Paddy Johns from terrace teenager to pitch protagonist was the steady and inexorable progress being made down in Dungannon. From mini-rugby, he had moved on to the Royal School, a traditional boarding and day-boy grammar school whose younger pupils had to wear caps when outside school, and a bit of a bastion of the game among the mid-Ulster academical institutions, but never quite able to give the Belfast big boys more than the occasional bloody nose.

"We weren't a great Schools Cup side" recalls Paddy, who spent three years in the First XV, firstly under Ken Armstrong, a man who gave two decades of service to Ulster and Irish Schools rugby, and then, for both Sixth Form seasons under the tutelage of Keith Patton, still at RSD and, in the intervening years, an extremely successful Irish Schools' supremo. Prior to that, Patton had made him Medallion captain in Fourth Form, recalling that "at first, captaincy appeared to affect his game, but after early season hesitancy, his game went from strength to strength."

"The highlights were always beating the big Belfast schools like Methody, Inst and Campbell" says Paddy. "We seemed to manage to beat at least one of them each season, but not in the Cup. In the Cup, as a rule, we seemed to get to the quarter-finals and lose there to the team which went on to lift the trophy or at least reach the final. I suppose my most memorable would be, in fifth year, my first time around, when we beat Bangor Grammar after two replays, saw off local rivals Portadown College away and then lost a replay to the eventual winners Methody in the last eight at Pirrie Park after drawing with them at home."

The following season, RSD reached the quarter-finals with 15-6 and 15-9 victories over Cambridge House and Strabane Grammar respectively, before their injury-disrupted team agonisingly went down 3-0 at Belfast Royal Academy in the last eight. In his final year, as captain, Dungannon Royal drew with and then lost to RBAI in two low-scoring ties at the second round stage.

Paddy was always tall for his age so, not surprisingly, it was as a willowy lock that he had made his Schools Cup bow in Fifth Form, later alternating between the engineroom and the middle of the back row as Dungannon sought to make the most of a player now starting to show he was destined for greater things. At the end of his maiden First XV season, his coach refers to "a gentle giant" but also his lineout prowess, adding that Johns' selection for the Ulster Country Schools XV "augured well for the future." He had thus stepped onto the first rung of the representative rugby ladder and kept moving upwards relentlessly until he reached the top. In the school magazine, Patton looks forward to the day when "we are arranging a coach to Lansdowne Road (to see him in action for Ireland)."

"The pressure wouldn't have been as intense as for the boys at the biggest Belfast schools, where there are huge burdens of expectation but, as well as enjoying the rugby, we were always very keen to do well" says Paddy. "Keith Patton's track record in coaching schoolboys at representative level speaks for itself, but we never really had the numbers to rule the roost. We probably did quite well for a school of our size. Dungannon Royal always seemed to have a good pack, which people maybe put down to the fact that we were country boys, with a good few farmers' sons, and some decent enough backs, but inevitably not quite enough depth. He was realistic but ambitious, which meant we were able to both enjoy our rugby and achieve as much as we were capable of. I enjoyed those years playing under Keith and we thought he was very good, both technically and in terms of his overall influence."

The no-nonsense Patton played his part in ensuring Johns would stay on the straight and narrow for the rest of his career by actually stripping him of the school captaincy, albeit just for a day, as punishment for a night on the town in his final year! "Myself and Adam Lambert (his friend who later died at the hands of terrorists) came in late one night from a party. I suppose there's no harm in admitting now that we'd had a few beers, though obviously it was frowned on at the time. When Keith became aware of the situation, he wasn't best pleased and actually took away the captaincy from me for that weekend's game against Bangor Grammar. I must say I was a bit annoyed at the time, but he gave it back to me on the Monday and things ran smoothly thereafter!"

Maybe it was more because of his pledge to ruthlessly pursue the vision he had had earlier, but that short, sharp shock of being stood down as RSD skipper also probably helped shape the model professional about whom such a story now seems almost incongruous. By his own admission and as others will testify in coming chapters, Paddy's single-minded dedication throughout his career was legendary with nothing being done by half measures and nothing deflecting him from his desire to be the best. Lesson learnt.

Those were the drinking days alright though it seems, judging by a couple of other stories of similar exploits from the same period, including another rugby-related one from future Ireland centre Mark McCall. "We were on an Ulster Schools' tour and were due to play Cumbria Schools' the next day, but when the selectors were coming back from the pub or restaurant or wherever they were late that night, they came across Paddy lying in the road outside our hotel!" reveals McCall. "He'd obviously overdone it, but maybe it was a reflection that he wasn't too used to drinking at that stage."

He grew into it though! One of his best buddies from school, Andy Oliver, recalls a holiday which he and Paddy took in Donegal in the summer of 1986. "It was when we were waiting for our A level results and I think that Adam Lambert and John Gamble were supposed to be going too, but it ended up just being me and Paddy. I got the lend of our estate car and Paddy's side of the deal was to supply the beer. He packed five crates even though the two of us were only going for four days, but by the time we came back there was only one can left and the only reason it escaped was because it had wedged under the seat and we couldn't find it! We also drunk in the local pubs at night, so our supplies were just for the daytime!

"We had a wee camping fire thing but never got round to getting it lit until the last day. We slept in the car, which was fine until one night Paddy had a nightmare that he was being chased by some guy with a pitchfork. Thinking he was being murdered, he woke up and went mad, starting to wreck about and lay into me. I'm glad I survived without permanent damage!"

Talking of damage and cars in the same breath, Gamble recalls a couple of scrapes where firstly Paddy was amused at his predicament and then found himself in similar hot water within 24 hours. "Again it was just after we'd finished A levels. I'd borrowed my da's brand new car, picked up Paddy and Andy, and we were heading back to Paddy's house for a couple of beers and a swim. Anyway, I hit another car in the middle of Armagh, turning through 180 degrees in the process. Had it been now, with all the extra traffic, we'd probably have been killed.

"Anyway, we got the car to the garage and Mrs Johns came and picked us up. My brother came later to lift me at her house. After a while the jokes started and the boys were tittering away at my expense. I was laughing along superficially, but inside I was thinking about facing my father when I got home. But, by an amazing stroke of fate, the very next afternoon, Paddy was driving his mother's Nissan Sunny and hit a motorcyclist, sending him flying. The guy he hit was alright, but suddenly my mishap the previous day didn't seem so funny anymore."

"Those were the days and we all had a great time" said Oliver. "The likes of myself, Paddy and Adam Lambert were great mates and got up to a fair bit of messing around, all pretty harmless stuff but a lot of fun. I remember us being over in Bradford on a school rugby trip and being allowed out for the night. Keith Patton checked our dormitory, removed contraband (poured brandy and whiskey down the sink), did a count, found that Adam was missing and then gave us all a bollocking.

"Keith then looked out of the window and, conjuring a scene from St Trinian's, spotted Adam systematically coming up the tree-lined school path, hiding behind each tree in turn to avoid detection. The only problem was that the tree trunks were only about six inches wide but with a few beers on board, Adam thought he was invisible!

"Adam's death was a great shock to all of us, for it can't be stressed enough what a nice and decent fella he was and what a good friend to all of us. We came back from universities in Britain when we heard the news and were invited to the house, but hardly knew how to react. Paddy and I had talked before we went and I wasn't too keen to look at the body, so when Adam's mum asked us if we wanted to come up and see him in the coffin, I said no, but Paddy was strong and said 'come on, we should'. So we did and I think it helped. The funeral was a very, very sad day for all, but the nobility and courage of the family left a lasting impression."

When Paddy and Adam had broken that curfew a few years earlier, Patton's stand-in skipper had been none other than Allen Clarke, the future Ulster and Ireland hooker, something which took on a great irony some 15 years later when the roles were reversed and Johns was asked to fill his old schoolmate's boots. When injury forced club captain Clarke into retirement just before the Foot-and-Mouth outbreak in the Spring of 2001, big Paddy took over as Dungannon skipper and steered them to All Ireland League glory.

The pair had made history as the first Royal School Dungannon pair to represent Irish Schools in the same season and went on to play together in the first ever Under 21 international which Ireland undertook, against Italy at Lansdowne Road in the autumn of 1988. Seven years later, Clarke came on as a replacement for Terry Kingston to win his first senior cap the day Johns scored his second Test try on the same ground against Fiji. The first time they started an international together was 12 months on, on that miserable night when Ireland lost to Samoa, but on the second and final occasion when the pair took the field together for their country, Johns was captain as the men in green beat Romania in a World Cup qualifier.

But perhaps the most poignant image of these two great 'Gannon men came in a club context when they held up the All Ireland League trophy together in Lansdowne Road in May 2001. It was an emotional and unforgettable moment for two good guys who go back a long way and have respected each other ever since schooldays. "Sniffer was a very talented player and we were both very competitive, so it was great when we were on the same side for the school, but there was no quarter asked or given when, for example, we were on opposing sides for the internal house matches. I was in Mountjoy and he was in Beresford. It was always a good tussle."

Clarke had captained RSD Under 14s before giving way to Johns the next year at Medallion level, but coach Patton's notes from the time record: "Clarke's contribution to the side was considerable and his personal determination, fitness and eagerness were an example to everyone."

Two great competitors, they must have been a formidable force in harness and Clarke recalls: "By Upper Sixth, Paddy and I virtually lived together, not only in travelling to Irish Schools' stuff and so forth, but also spending all our free periods out on the pitch, practising our jumping and throwing. Those were the days before lineout lifting was legalised, so timing was everything and, as hooker and main jumper, we were a unit in the team. We became very close and would have talked each other through games, especially at representative level. Mainly because of how much time we were spending on the rugby, we both flunked our A levels first time around, but it was a great honour for us and Dungannon Royal that we both represented Irish Schools in the same year.

"We were both very dedicated and competitive, so when we were on opposing sides in House matches, our good friendship was very much left on the sidelines. I can remember all those matches and there would definitely have been a few handbags. We used to come off almost embarrassed about it. We were the blues and they were the reds and you could almost use the boxing imagery of 'blue corner' and 'red corner' for the scraps. He beat me in the school badminton final, though I still get him going by bantering him that I won, probably because I want to believe it myself. If even that match could have been physical, it would!

"Years later, we played against each other two or three times in the English Premiership and it was like the old House matches re-enacted on a grander scale. We were polite before kick-off and then knocked lumps out of each other on the pitch before returning to being best buddies afterwards. It was great playing together though for the school team, where we had an excellent pack and loved scrumming whenever we were allowed to. Everyone apart from me was big and I was very combative!" Clarke laughs.

It is fascinating that, in the RSD Under 13 coach's notes in the 1981 school magazine, he comments: "In the forwards we had outstanding players in Clarke, the hooker, and Johns, the No 8. Their workrate was an example to any rugby forward." Start as you mean to go on obviously. The following year, third-former Johns alternated between the Under 14s and the Medallion XV, an indication of how good he already was. Little wonder that the coach of the former rued the loss of Paddy's "enthusiasm" on the occasions he had to step up. Other notable rugby contemporaries at RSD included Ashley Blair, who was to become a long-serving club stalwart, talented midfield man Paul Archer and scrumhalf Richie Weir.

Those of us who played the game at school will recall that, in those early years from Under 13 to Medallion (Under 15) every team had its very own Lomu, the lad who had grown that bit more that bit sooner than everyone else and who used to, well, simply run over or through people. In Dungannon Royal in the Johns era, that player was John Gamble, a prop who went on to alternate between the town's First and Second XVs and was a useful enough campaigner at club level. But at school, he was THE man . . . amongst boys.

"The main memory of coming up through the age group teams at school was us giving all the tap penalties to John" says Paddy. "He was simply massive for his age and everything went through him." In his school magazine notes on the season, Clarke as Under 14s captain refers to "the pack competing effectively with any they met. One very successful tactic employed was the so-called 'Gamble drive'."

"I did have a certain amount of size in the early days, but by the age of 15 I'd say we realised that Paddy was going to go further than any of us and go a long way in the game" says Gamble. "That was when he started getting really good and, after 16, we knew he'd play for Ireland, that he was a bit different, something special. What marked Paddy out and set him apart was his preparation, his focus, his drive, even in those early days. Even at the age of 13 or 14, he'd have sat on his own on the bus going to away matches, not speaking to anyone, staring out the window and getting himself psyched up for the game ahead. Then, when he was actually running onto the pitch, his face would've been all contorted.

"His determination, his desire to succeed were phenomenal and, even back then, he was trying to approach rugby like a professional. By Sixth Form he gave up summer sports and went and trained on his own, doing weights and so forth. He was the sort of guy who really knew what he wanted and once he set his mind on something, nothing would have distracted him. It was the same with his dentistry too when he decided that was the career he wanted to pursue. But he really stood out in rugby. I'd say we had one of the best schoolboy packs in Ulster ever but Paddy was head and shoulders above the rest."

Great pack, shame about the backs. Actually in other circumstances, Paddy might have been one himself but for the wisdom of Ken Armstrong (though it was hardly rocket science come to think of it) in plucking him from the fantasy world of wannabe winger in his formative years, as Gamble recalls

"In First Form, we had Games on a Monday afternoon and, in the first week or two, we were allocated to our respective Houses and then asked 'who wants to be a forward'. Paddy went and stood with the backs and I remember Ken Armstrong saying 'Johns, boy, you're going to be a forward, you'll enjoy yourself much more'. Paddy was politely protesting 'Sir, I'm a winger', but in the end commonsense prevailed. Can you imagine how frustrated he'd get on the wing and not being involved!"

One back who Johns does remember from the school side was a centre called Derek 'Willball' Willis, primarily because he 'used to win absolutely everything on Sportsday.' A mix of long jump and the 800 metres was Paddy's poison when it came to track and field and, outside of rugby, he also played a bit of basketball but old habits died hard. Forgetting himself all too often as to what sport he was playing, the big fella got over-physical and kept getting thrown out of the game for fouls. The leopard couldn't change its spots, so he quit.

His most sedentary sporting activity came as a member of the school snooker club. Few details of his chalk and cue exploits exist, but the RSD 86 magazine casts limited light on this subject. "In the break-time Pot Black competition, P Johns managed to overcome the slick opposition of A Curran in a tremendously unexciting match", it reports. Apparently, also "Mr Edgar put his career on the line with a four point win over Paddy Johns." Perhaps Paddy saved his best potshots for South Africa 1998!

Like every lad, Johns played his share of soccer, taking his turn as a goalie in between predictable enough roles as a tall centre half and a tall centre forward. You can't imagine opponents getting much change out of him in the air, though he claims his control on the deck wasn't the worst either. He considers it an unfortunate coincidence that the first place he played football, in the village of Moy as a primary school kid, rejoiced in the name of 'Duff's Park'! Paddy didn't excel at cricket, but captained the school badminton team and among his other extra-curricular pursuits, he had a good time in the Army Cadets. "We did some shooting and, although it's probably not very politically correct to say it, I enjoyed that" he laughs.

"Paddy was the sort of guy who could turn his hand to any sport" says Gamble, who refuses to pour cold water on Johns' soccer skills. "Paddy was pretty decent at football, captained the school badminton team and was very good at tennis before phasing other things out to concentrate on his rugby and make sure it always came first. He was also a great artist, very talented."

Although he did well enough academically to ultimately be accepted to study dentistry at Newcastle University and also became a sufficient pillar of the school community to be made House Captain, serve on the Charities Committee and be awarded the Deputy Head Boy-ship in Upper Sixth (and Gamble suggests he might have been Head Boy had he not left the school for a week in Lower Sixth and gone to Portadown College, which was closer to the new family home but where he didn't settle), he got into his share of scrapes along the way. Before poacher turned gamekeeper, Paddy's visits to the Headmaster's study had been to receive the odd whaling for misdemeanours, which tended to be administered for trivial enough things in those days.

"One of the exam halls at school was an old gym and the ropes were tied back for exams. We used to go in at lunchtime and pull the ropes out to do Tarzan jumps from table to table. Obviously if you didn't quite get your landings right, a few desks got scattered and unfortunately the Headmaster came in one day when the place was like a bomb site. That was one of the canings, but there were plenty of others."

Another occasion was a snowball fight at the bus stop between RSD pupils and their counterparts from St Pat's Academy, the local Catholic school. Surely something as mild would virtually constitute good community relations in Northern Ireland? Snow better than stones. "You don't know what was in those snowballs" he grins mischievously. "No, seriously, there was no bitterness towards the pupils from the other school, but as they were walking past on the other side of the road, they were good moving targets!"

Those were the days of catapults constructed from coat-hangers, pea-shooters improvised from biros and magnifying glasses nicked from the science labs to start little fires and burn unsuspecting classmates' flesh. Those were popular pastimes, for they were still around when the authors of this book got to other grammar schools a few years later. Paddy also remembers the farmers' sons "bringing in crow bangers and flogging them at Halloween." Oliver describes another regular lunchtime activity which sounds like it would have been right up Johns' street, the 'big drive'. "It took place along a narrow corridor. Some of the bigger lads like Paddy and John (Gamble) would charge at each other and whoever was left standing at the end was the winner," recalls Andy.

Life 'was great' at RSD. Lots of larks, and a little learning too. "At school, if I was interested in something I'd have studied it keenly, but I certainly wouldn't have been studious for the sake of it. For example, I didn't really go in for the Latin or the French at all!" Paddy reflects wistfully. "The French might have been useful later though for understanding their lineout calls!

"I wouldn't have been naturally exceptionally bright or anything but, just like the rugby, if I was interested in a subject or wanted to do well in it, I would really apply myself and put my mind to it. My best subjects were probably Biology, Geography and History, but my mum would have encouraged me to try and concentrate on the sciences, with a view to doing something like dentistry, so that was the route I took for A levels."

His mum says: "Paddy was always very conscientious at school. When he came in, his first trip would be to the fridge, then he made himself a hot drink and then it was off to do his prep. As I worked in education, I was pretty strict but, although I used to have to shout at the others, I never had to tell him. When it was done, he'd have gone out and kicked a ball around."

Ironically, the science labs also threw up some of the best stories of Paddy's schooldays and some of the exploits of what, if not exactly a mis-spent youth, was certainly a reassuringly roguish existence. "Biology was maybe my best subject of all, though I have to admit now that some of my results were not quite all that they may have seemed at the time. This might come as a bit of a shock to my old teacher, Jimmy Napier, for I don't think he ever caught on what we were up to. We used to have Biology the period after lunch in Room 22 and, on the day of a test, he'd have it written out on the overheads before going off to get his dinner. There was a dodgy Yale lock on the door and you could open it with a ruler, so we used to get in at lunchtime and check out the questions! No wonder I did alright in the tests.

"I can also remember our history tests in that there was a little sporting theme to them. The teacher, Mr Teddy Edgar, used to ask a football score from the previous night's games as the last question in our weekly test. Every Wednesday morning I would go to the shop for mum and get the News Letter and memorise the midweek scores and scorers. I would always get that question right!"

His main memory of Physics is that a Bunsen Burner tube was that subject teacher's favourite form of corporal punishment in a school where "each teacher had their own preferred method and a lot had their personal cane. There were different types of cane, but other masters used alternative tools of the trade so to speak, including metre rulers, gym shoes and, in the case of one teacher, a cricket bat! He certainly wielded it more effectively than I ever did at the wicket.

"I remember in second form, our first season as a rugby team, playing an Under 13 match against Armagh Royal, our rivals from the next town. One of our players gave the referee a mouthful and, not surprisingly, a sending-off resulted. Unfortunately, there was a case of mistaken identity which meant the culprit escaped and that, not only did Alastair Ross get ordered off wrongly, but he got the cricket bat back at school on Monday as punishment for swearing when he hadn't opened his mouth.

"We won by about 70 points I think, but it taught us all a useful early lesson about respecting referees and the game was also memorable from a personal point of view for a lucky let-off. That was the first match I had ever worn anything under my shorts, which was just as well for I got them ripped off that day. I'd swimming trunks underneath and I remember thinking 'how lucky was that'. You can imagine how scundered a 12-year old would be to be caught with no cacks!"

Chemistry class? "We used to do experiments in groups of four and I was always with my best buddy Andy Oliver, who is still a good mate, a laidback lad called Gary Stewart and Richard Kavanagh, who'd have been more the studious type. The problem was that ours used to go horribly wrong. I'd blame Andy and he'd blame me. One day the teacher, Mr Ronnie Irvine, tried an experiment of his own, swapping me with a guy from another group. I was put into a very studious group, who always used to get the experiments done without any problem, but after I joined, theirs started going wrong and my old group's improved. I was indicted as the common denominator in lab disasters from then on!" Oliver's memory differs slightly; he recalls the old gang of four ultimately being re-united so that two groups wouldn't suffer mishaps!

So Paddy's schooldays, as for all of us, were a bit of Billy Bunter meets Tom Brown and, surprisingly enough, there was almost a hint of bullying too, though you suspect the perpetrator may have come off worst had he persisted. "There was this fellow in my year called Mark Wilson, a big, big lad who really sticks in my mind because of the way he used to wind me up, massively. We had a few battles, though I didn't fight much at school. I was quite tall and skinny and he used to really get at me by calling me lanky and stuff. I used to crack, and scrap with him. He usually came off worse, so I'm not sure why he didn't drop it. I haven't seen the guy since we left the Royal, but would like to apologise now I'm wiser and have more sense. I believe forgiveness is the key. As Ghandi said, 'The weak can never forgive; forgiveness is the attribute of the strong'."

Maybe those jousts were what prepared Paddy for looking after himself in the jungle of Test rugby forward play in the years to come. From Mark Wilson, he moved up to Springbok lock Mark Andrews and the like, never taking a backward step. His philosophy, particularly in South Africa in 1998, was very much 'an eye for an eye' and 'a tooth for a tooth' (or should that be two eyes for an eye and two teeth for a tooth!), yet these days a mellowed and more religious Johns is trying to teach his son Christopher to turn the other cheek rather than seeking to create a real chip off the old block.

3. DESTINY CALLS HIM

Never mind Tony Blair's remark about what he felt on his shoulder when he came to Northern Ireland at a key moment in the peace process. The hand of history really did touch Paddy Johns. He holds the distinction of being the first man to represent Ireland at almost every conceivable level and, considering that sense of occasion which he felt on that first ever visit to Lansdowne Road as an impressionable adolescent, it was appropriate that most of Paddy's debuts seemed to have a notable backdrop. Hard work may have got him where he was and no man did more to earn his chances, but often his timing appeared perfect in terms of where and when he made his various breakthroughs.

It is a function of the durability of Paddy's playing career and a reminder of how relatively recently most of the subsidiary international fixtures were introduced that he had the distinction of appearing in the first ever Under 21 international Ireland played. To this day, that game, against Italy in September 1988, remains the only such match to be played at Lansdowne Road, while he also got to make his B international debut at Murrayfield, an equally unlikely scenario in terms of the use of a national stadium. For good measure, his first green jersey was worn at Ravenhill, with Australia providing the showcase opposition for his first Irish Schools international on the very first day of 1986. It is a remarkable hat-trick of firsts and the Irish sides didn't do too badly in all three cases, the Schools only going down narrowly to the Wallaby wannabes, the 21s getting the Italian job done successfully and the B boys sharing the spoils away to the Scots.

Incidentally, his Under 25 international debut was also at Ravenhill and ended in victory over Italy. As at Under 21 level, he had the distinction of playing in Ireland's first ever Students international.

For a boy and young man who had so strongly empathised with his predecessors when watching matches at Ravenhill and Lansdowne Road, his provincial and national meccas respectively, it was entirely fitting that he should make his own bows there. His Irish Schools debut at Ravenhill came little more than a year after being inspired by watching Ulster's famous ambush of the 1984 Test Grand Slam Wallabies there, while running out for the 21s reminded him of the Dublin day when seeing others do the same had lit an unquenchable fire. Now it was time to live it out for himself and Johns ended up coming back for more time after time after time, that initial desire never waning. He was available to answer his country's call right to the day of his retirement, always disappointed when it didn't come.

Murrayfield too, looking back, was an appropriate venue to launch himself as an adult international, with that drawn B game back at the end of the 1980s. Just under a decade later, it was at the same Edinburgh ground where, as captain, he ran out well ahead of his team-mates, to mark his 50th Test cap. His full international debut was also at that theatre of his dreams, Lansdowne Road, his overseas Test debut in that most worthy of rugby lands, New Zealand, and he played his first Championship game at Murrayfield, the middle of a hat-trick of milestone occasions there, though admittedly it hasn't overall been a happy hunting ground for Ireland.

Jonah Lomu was in the opposition when he finally appeared in a World Cup match, at the famous Ellis Park in 1995, after missing out on the previous tournament, and his first Test as captain was in South Africa against what he has always regarded as the hardest rugby nation in the world. In what proved to be his final Ireland match, the guys in green romped to a record rout of Japan just as they had done previously against Georgia in his first home game as captain. Remarkably, his last 'Gannon game was also at Lansdowne Road, a victory over the host club, by then coached by his first Ulster mentor, Harry Williams!

His farewell fixture before hanging up his boots brought a last gasp victory for Ulster over fierce rivals Munster, a team led by his old adversary Mick Galwey, at his beloved Ravenhill. He even got two for the price of one when briefly coming out of retirement this autumn and again tasting victory against the southern province. Yeah, although never the dramatist or the showman, Paddy's had a sense of occasion and timing alright.

Honours or lack of them at Schools level don't always translate into senior success or failure, but Johns came right through the system and made the grade at each level en route to the top. Indeed, the things that came closest to denying him schoolboy honours were a dodgy automobile and a leg wound rather than any lack, or failings, in terms of ability, attitude, aptitude or application.

"I remember, when I was 17, my dad bringing me down to my first Irish Schools Trial and the car breaking down on the way to Dublin. When I got there, both teams were already changed. How much it counted against me, I don't know, but anyway I didn't get selected. The following season, I played in the Trial with nine stitches in my knee. The doctor said it didn't make good medical sense and I'm sure he was right, but I knew what I wanted and wasn't going to let a few stitches stop me. Only two of them opened during the game."

Paddy's representative career began with selection for the Ulster Country Schools XV when he was a fifth-former at RSD and progressed rapidly to the full provincial schools panel. On New Year's Day 1985, the year Ireland were to win what remains their last Triple Crown to date at senior level, Johns had his first taste of tackling the Kiwis when he played for Ulster Schools in their defeat, (after actually scoring first), by New Zealand Secondary Schools at Ravenhill. Johns was in the second row of a side which featured Mark McCall at flyhalf, another Bangor Grammar boy who was to become a good mate of Paddy's, Michael Webb, on the wing and his RSD schoolmate Paul Archer at centre. Future club colleagues Jeremy Hastings and Davy Millar were at No 8 and on the bench respectively. No less a figure than future Wales and Lions supremo Graham Henry was coach of the New Zealand Secondary Schools, with the programme notes prophetically stating that he was "widely tipped to go on to higher coaching positions." The visitors featured Steve Bachop and Rhys Ellison, who wound up at Shannon many years later, in the centre, with a famous name of the future, Robin Brooke, opposite Johns in the second row. Jon Preston was on the bench.

Paddy was one of four Dungannon Royal boys invited to the Ulster Schools trial when First XV captain in his final year, with both himself and fellow future full international Allen Clarke coming through to make the core squad. Johns was an Ulster Schools regular that season but, such was Clarke's impact when he finally did get his chance against Leinster, both were picked in the Probables team for the Irish Schools trial and duly selected to face the Australians at Ravenhill. The fixture was on New Year's Day 1986, a fitting start date for an international career which was to last almost 15 years until he trotted off to let Gary Longwell on for a first Test cap in the Japanese game in November 2000.

It was the first time that two RSD boys had played in the same Irish Schools team which was, incidentally, captained by McCall, who was to have a long association with Johns in various capacities in the years ahead. Room-mates on Ireland's senior tour of New Zealand in 1992 when McCall won his first Test cap and Johns established himself at international level, the pair played together many times for Ulster down the years and, in Paddy's second stint with Ulster, Mark, by then prematurely retired due to injury, was the province's assistant coach.

"The first time I saw Small was when he was playing for Bangor Grammar Under 13s against Royal School Dungannon Under 13s. He did everything for them from kicking the goals to jinking round the pitch, sidestepping people and scoring tries. I remember the feeling of frustration that we couldn't contain this tiny guy with the bright blond hair. Not surprisingly they won the game and the world was to hear a lot more about Mark McCall."

And of Paddy Johns. "As a 13-year old, there weren't many as big as him" says McCall. "We didn't know the name then, just the frame. You know what it's like in the early days at school, when you eye up the opposition side as they get off their bus or come out of the changing rooms. As the years went by, I obviously got to know him much better through Ulster and Irish Schools and found him the most polite guy you'd ever come across, very well mannered. Bangor Grammar and Dungannon Royal played each other in the Cup when we were both Fifth Form, but as that was our first year in our respective school's senior side, neither of us would have been quite as influential as in subsequent Sixth Form seasons."

Clarke was joined in that Irish Schools front row by Ballymena Academy prop Simon Booth, with RBAI flanker Davy Todd, who was to be tragically struck down with a brain haemorrhage when studying Medicine at Edinburgh University and is now confined to a wheelchair, being the fourth Ulster representative. The others from that side to make it to senior international status were Nicky Barry, Jack Clarke and Ken O'Connell, while fullback Charlie Haly and No 8 Barry Walsh went on to play at provincial level for Munster and the Irish Exiles respectively.

"We popped the Aussie frontrow in the very first scrum and in response their loosehead gouged Simon Booth, who had to leave the field for treatment. Simon's eye closed straight away and he couldn't return. It was a close game and, although Ireland lost 13-9, we could be well pleased with our effort. Ricky Stewart, who was to make a name for himself in rugby league, was their captain and he actually stayed at our house as part of a hosting arrangement."

Johns played three more Schools internationals in April of that year, a 13-6 defeat by the English in Nottingham, the 16-6 victory against Japan at Lansdowne Road three days later and, finally, a 17-3 win over Wales at the Sportsground in Galway. Inst pair Philip Pollock, on the wing for all three matches, and Robin Semple, at loosehead against the English and Welsh having come on as a replacement in the Australian match, were involved, while Methody fullback Ian Gallagher was in the team for the Japanese game. "That was my first match at Lansdowne Road, making it a very special occasion, but one memory that will always stick with me from that day is of four players getting stuck in the lift at Tara Towers when we were going down to get the team bus to the ground and Noel Murphy calling the Fire Brigade and going crazy about the situation!"

In between the Australian clash and the April programme, Paddy had been on his first real rugby tour, a five-day jaunt to Yorkshire as captain of Dungannon Royal. Described as "dominant" as the visitors came back from 7-0 down to draw with Bradford Grammar School, skipper Johns then led by example in bagging a brace of tries in a 31-16 triumph over Woodhouse Grove. Legend has it that the trip also featured at least one memorably inspirational team-talk by the young leader, but more of that later!

Although Paddy didn't go to university until the autumn of 1987 as a result of retaking A levels to obtain the grades he needed to study dentistry, he was at Armagh College of Further Education the following academic year and ineligible to play for Irish Schools on the grounds of age. Hence he missed out on the successful Irish Schools tour of Australia in August and September of that year, when the squad, coached by Davy Haslett, won all 10 warm-up games before losing the only Test, 20-11.

In addition to some of those whom Johns had played with the previous year, including squad skipper Nicky Barry, that party included Paddy's fellow future Ireland captain, Rob Saunders of Belfast Royal Academy, lock Gabriel Fulcher, who was to be his national team nemesis for a period, and Angus McKeen, a colleague at the 1999 World Cup. Touring Australia would have been a great experience for young Johns, but it was far from a wasted summer. Instead, he spent three months playing rugby in Canada, an enjoyable experience in itself but a trip which was to have far further-reaching consequences as a later chapter will reveal.

When he left RSD, Paddy joined Dungannon RFC, a decision which didn't require any soul-searching. "There was never any option of going anywhere else," he confirms. "It was the natural thing to do and I never regretted the decision from that day until I hung up my boots. Dungannon is a great club and players have always been well looked after at Stevenson Park. There were guys there in those days who, as senior players, took young lads like me under their wing, men like Willie Milligan, Kenny Wright, Stanley Turkington and Will Taylor. I enjoyed those early days with the club and it was a good rugby education.

"In my first season, when I was 18, I sustained the first fracture of my career, breaking my wrist in a local derby against Armagh at Stevenson Park. My arm slipped down in a tackle and a guy fell on it, snapping the bone. I was in the Royal Victoria Hospital in Belfast for a week with my arm up in the air, but at the time it almost seemed worth it because I received a visit in hospital from Willie John McBride. Wilfie Wright, who was PRO for the club at the time, was a good friend of Willie John's and he had organised for him to come in and see me to cheer me up. I wasn't expecting him, obviously, and was absolutely chuffed at meeting such a legend."

He actually wouldn't have got to the RVH had it not been for the decisive intervention of his mother. "We'd brought him into the local hospital and some young surgeon chap, who I assume was fully qualified but didn't exactly inspire confidence, said he would need a plate inserted" recalls Mrs Johns. "I ran downstairs and phoned my mother's cousin, Dr George Irwin (father of the then Ulster captain, David) who advised me to get him to the RVH. When I went back up, Paddy was ready for theatre, but I said 'you're coming with us' and got the car driven to the door. The hospital wasn't too impressed and the registrar met us on the stairs but I simply said 'We're taking him, he's our son'. Every bump on the road that evening was agony for Paddy, but it was worth it for, when we got there, George had everything organised and, in the end, neither a plate nor even an operation was needed. Their techniques were more sophisticated and manipulation did the trick instead."

Both before going to Newcastle University and during his time on Tyneside, Paddy represented Ulster at age-group level as well as coming home to play for Dungannon. In his second season across the water, now attached to Newcastle Gosforth, Johns made another Lansdowne Road appearance, as a member of the first ever Irish team to play in an Under 21 international.

Captained by Haly, this Ireland side featured some of Johns' colleagues from that Irish Schools debut against the Australians almost three years earlier, including Clarke and Booth. His second row partner was Jim O'Callaghan, a provincial player of the future, while Garryowen back-rower Paul Hogan emulated Johns, Clarke and Barry in reaching Test level. Ards winger Graham Copeland and CIYMS centre Ricky McLean were the other Ulster representatives in the side, while Gallagher came on as a replacement. Ireland won 22-13 in what was to be Paddy's first and last Under 21 international. He was too old when the next fixture at that level, also against the Italians, this time in Treviso, came round some 53 weeks later.

"I don't remember an awful lot about that match either, but was fortunate that Under 21 and B internationals and the like were starting to feature on the fixture list as I was coming through, especially as there was no European Cup rugby in those days or even, at the start, an All Ireland League. Apart from helping to bridge the gap in terms of standard between club and full international rugby, those games got you used to the environment of meeting in Dublin as a squad, preparing and playing a match. The greater the frequency and familiarity of that routine, the less the culture shock of finding yourself involved in the senior set-up. It was also a chance to play against other countries and something I valued both at the time and with hindsight."

Italian jobs were regular assignments in those days it seemed, for three months after that Under 21 international, Johns was again facing the azurri in a green jersey, this time for an Ireland Under 25 team. Subsequently discontinued in the face of regular Under 21 and A fixtures at international level, Johns was coming through at a time when the Under 25 concept was briefly in fashion and ended up appearing in three of the four such games Ireland have ever played. His Under 25 international debut, at Ravenhill three days after Christmas 1988, ended in a formidable Irish team, most of whom, naturally enough, were older than Paddy, beating the touring Italians 21-16.

"That was a very physical game and I can recall getting my eye closed. Partly out of frustration the Italians can be pretty illegal, but back in those pre-professional days the French were always the dirtiest. Anything went with them!" Johns was partnered in the engineroom by Connacht man mountain Aidan Higgins, his opposite number on his senior Ulster debut, also at Ravenhill, earlier in the season, and one of only a handful of this Ireland Under 25 team not to win a full cap. Captain Michael Bradley and Terry Kingston already had. Jim Staples, on the wing with Fergus Dunlea at fullback, Bradley, Nick Popplewell, Kingston and Peter Clohessy were all to become regular Test colleagues of Paddy's, while he toured New Zealand with both Peter Russell and Mick Fitzgibbon a few years later.

If Paddy's main motivation in switching from Newcastle University to Trinity midway through his dentistry studies was to put himself more in the shop window for selection for Irish teams, the move was an unqualified success. He decamped to Dublin in the autumn of 1989 and that season represented his country at no fewer than four levels, Students, Universities, Under 25 and Ireland B. It is now taken for granted that aspiring Test players will have the stepping stones of Celtic League, European Cup, Under 21 and A international rugby, but Johns admits he was fortunate to arrive on the scene at a time when the gap between club level and the national senior side was just beginning to be bridged. Apart from playing in the first ever Under 21 and Students internationals undertaken by Ireland, Johns won his first B cap in the first shadow international to be played by the Irish for five years.

In winning a century of caps between them at senior level as front-jumping second rows in the same era, Paddy Johns and Mick Galwey cast fairly lengthy shadows over each other's careers in every sense, a theme which will be returned to later. But as well as having careers which lasted longer than most, finishing up with more honours to their names, sharing the distinction of captaining their country and each being looked up to by others, both also made early marks on the lower rungs of the ladder. They played with, against and instead of each other at various levels for over a decade, Johns just winning the race for a Test debut and ending up with more caps, but Galwey gaining favour during what has amounted to a golden autumn to the Kerryman's career, something which rankles with Paddy as will be revealed in a subsequent chapter.

Johns and Galwey initially ran across each other as opponents and first featured on the same side, or almost, when Paddy came on as a replacement for Mick during that B international against Scotland at Murrayfield in December 1989. Considering both locks had their lineout jumping credentials questioned earlier in their career, what each has achieved over such a long period is a testimony to their strength of spirit and it is no surprise that these two determined men of character have enjoyed a fierce rivalry down through the years. Opponents at provincial level and competitors for national team honours, the pair have also packed down together, significantly on some of Ireland's greatest days, not least for the two great victories over England in the early 1990s. When

Galwey's memoirs are written, some of the same ground will be covered and, while sometimes one man's highs corresponded with the other's lows, those games will feature prominently in both tales.

Although Johns beat both Galwey and Brian Rigney to a first senior cap, the two future Shannon colleagues were paired in the B team engineroom against Scotland in successive Decembers, firstly in 1989, and then just after Christmas the next year at Ravenhill, following which they leapfrogged Paddy to appear together in the 1991 Five Nations. When Johns ran on to make his first appearance at B level, there were five Ulster colleagues already on the pitch, including two who never got a senior cap in centre John Hewitt, then with London Irish, and Instonians prop Brian McKibbin More than a dozen years later, McKibbin, as head of the PR firm contracted by the Ulster Branch to handle their media relations, was to preside over the press conference called to announce Paddy's retirement from professional rugby. Back that day at Murrayfield no-one could have envisaged the changes in rugby which would produce such a scenario as part of a professional set-up at Ravenhill, though McKibbin says forecasting that Johns would have a big future in the game wouldn't have been as difficult.

Like Johns, Russell and Brian Robinson went on to play for the full Ireland side, while John McDonald, a veteran of the inaugural World Cup in 1987 had already done so. The captain was loose forward Paul Collins, who also appeared in that tournament, while Clohessy, who has emulated Johns in reaching a half-century of senior caps, joined McKibbin and McDonald in the front row. Blackrock pivot Alain Rolland, who like Johns was to make his full Ireland debut against Argentina within 12 months, was at the base of the scrum and another feature of the Ireland B team that day was the presence of three natural fullbacks, Kenny Murphy wearing the No 15 jersey with Staples and Pat Murray on the wings. "It was an absolutely freezing December day and very wet. We were all inside, sat way up in the stand behind the screens. Mick Galwey got injured and I went on, probably about halfway through the second half. We ended up drawing 22-22. I was thrilled to get on."

Paddy's first game for the Irish Universities ended in a 34-18 defeat by the English at Sunbury and then, during a mad March of representative rugby, he almost made an unexpected Five Nations debut as will be revealed later, and appeared in two games against the USA in between playing his second and third Universities internationals. Irish Universities lost 19-13 to their French counterparts at Rheims on a weekend that Johns still remembers vividly and almost could never have forgotten and, in the course of the next eight days, took on the Americans twice at Thomond Park.

On the Tuesday night, the Irish Students team sneaked home 19-18 and another fine performance by the US Eagles on Saturday saw them hold a considerably stronger Ireland Under 25 line-up to almost as close a victory margin, the game finishing 12-10. Brian Glennon, Simon Geoghegan, Barry, Saunders and Johns were the future full internationals in the Students side, which also included the entire Trinity front row. By contrast, no fewer than 11 of the Under 25s went on to Ireland senior status, the exceptions being Shannon stalwart Murray, halfbacks Paul Hennebry and Paddy's schoolmate Ashley Blair, and Cork Con hooker James O'Riordan. But that didn't save a side captained by Phil Danaher and containing such eminent names as Staples, Jack Clarke, Cunningham, Popplewell, Halpin, Johns' engineroom partner Galwey, Ken O'Connell, Robinson and McBride from having to be grateful to squeeze the win.

Paddy's representative season ended on a high when, 13 days later, he was a member of the Irish Universities team which crushed their Welsh equivalents 25-4 at Trinity's own ground, College Park. The following season, in addition to his October Test debut against Argentina, he again played six matches for four subsidiary Irish representative sides, three for the Universities and a game apiece for the Under 25, Students and B teams.

So, by playing for each of those intermediate national teams, progressing to the senior side at the age of 22 and going on to win 59 full caps, Johns has been the perfect product of the Irish system. But none of it came about by chance. He never saw any of it as his right, but realised that destiny is something which has to be delivered upon, fate something which has to be fulfilled. You get out what you put in. Ever since he saw the vision and dreamed the dream, Paddy pursued it in a practical way, determined to make the most of his talents. What he describes as God-given ability has always been backed up by honest hard work and the sort of thorough, meticulous approach which leaves nothing to chance and no room for regrets about not making the most of oneself, as similarly driven colleagues like Denis McBride will readily testify. He says simply: "I have made mistakes, but I am a fast and willing learner."

Willie Anderson, his mentor as captain and coach at Dungannon and Ulster, adds: "Paddy obviously had a very distinguished career at school and I saw him coming through. He had raw talent and also slotted into the club set-up very well. His background was conducive to coming through the excellent Irish system, for which he is an perfect advert and it is also to his great credit that he has set an example in terms of loyalty to his school, club and parish. The most important thing about Paddy in the early days was that he was so meticulous and took his rugby so seriously, a professional in the wider sense of the word. He was always keen to get, take and apply advice. With his attitude and ability, I knew he'd certainly play for Ireland."

Paddy has literally trodden on a fair few bodies on the rugby pitch, but never tramped on enough metaphorical toes to be regarded as anything other than a decent human being, liked and respected by those who have had the privilege of getting to know him. Paddy Johns is much more than what he has done in the past or will do in the future. There is a risk of simply becoming a parody, a walking list of one's own accomplishments, but Paddy has never fallen into the trap. It may be nice to be important, but it's even more important to be nice. Johns recognised that truth without ever disingenuously using it as an excuse to be soft, weak or cowardly. He has achieved more than most, but being a good guy also leaves a lasting legacy and Paddy is living proof that the two are not incompatible.

4. CUTTING HIS TEETH

Everything comes full circle and after a long and distinguished hiatus into the world of pro rugby, Paddy has turned once more to his first profession, dentistry. He's glad to have it and all. Many of the first crop of rugby professionals are now reaching the end of their time as full-time players, either by choice or otherwise, and some have very little tangible or worthwhile to return to by way of alternative career.

Apart from getting to sample the amateur era, leading players in Paddy's age-group will have had some experience of working outside the sport, but inevitably future generations will include those who went into the pro game as young stars straight from school without even going to university or college. Relocation and programmes of parallel education for young professional players aimed at ensuring they have meaningful qualifications when they finish as full-timers are issues which will be considered later. But, back when Johns was growing up, professional rugby wasn't even a pipe-dream. Never mind any chance of the sport offering a full-time job, the whole notion of pay-for-play was anathema in the old strictly amateur era.

"I always casually thought that I'd like to be able, as an adult, to concentrate on my sport day in, day out. But unlike young guys who aspire to be professional footballers, the option simply didn't exist in my sport. To be honest, I never dreamt it could happen. There was, of course, rugby league, but that was never a serious option either. Apart from the taboos in those days, there was no rugby league culture here or even a pattern of Irish guys going that direction, unlike say the Welsh, some of whose biggest names were crossing the divide when I was in my late teens. It also seemed to be a very closed community, a working class game concentrated in the north of England and, anyway, I don't think I necessarily had the right attributes for rugby league, where the players have traditionally been more of a generic size and shape than union."

The caricatures of the podgy prop, the lamp-post lock and the wing waif in the union game have also become less relevant in the pro era with loose forwards and midfield backs increasingly indistinguishable but, in any case, Johns saw his future firmly in the 15-man code. Therefore in Paddy's day, so to speak, no matter how much playing potential you had in rugby, you needed a day job to pay the bills. As Johns progressed through the years at RSD, there was never any particular path he tended towards, however. Rugby came first, second and third, and the real world could wait. But it wasn't going to put bread on the table. Eventually, career decisions had to be made. As indicated, Paddy's mum was always keen for him to continue with the sciences, with a view to entering a medically related type of profession.

Despite the odd disastrous experiment, Paddy did actually enjoy them, so A-level choices were made accordingly. His future was still not certain when the time came to do work experience but, encouraged once more by his mother, Paddy undertook several days in a dental surgery in Dungannon with local practitioner, Philip McCarter. "I never had a lifelong ambition to be a dentist the way some people do with whatever profession" Paddy freely admits. "I didn't know what I wanted until I did my work experience and thought 'hey, I'd like to do this'. It was something I thought I could be good at and would enjoy."

So the decision of 'what' had been made, no doubt to his mother's relief, with enough of a sense of 'why' to sustain him in his subsequent studies, both before and during university. The next question was 'where'. "I didn't want to stay at home and thus didn't even apply to Queen's. I was looking forward to getting away from the Troubles, of being able to get out and look in from the outside, though I knew I would eventually come back."

Paddy's first choice of location was the historical Trinity College, Dublin, established in 1854, but unfortunately for him, he failed to secure a place. However, Newcastle University knew a good thing when they saw it and in the autumn of 1987, having improved his original A-level grades in two subjects, Physics and Chemistry, Paddy traded in Guinness for Newcastle Brown Ale en route to becoming a dentist. Why Newcastle specifically? "I didn't want to go to London, which I thought would be bigger than I would like. We had about five or six nominations to make and I think I applied for Leeds, Newcastle and Edinburgh. I went for an interview to Leeds, but didn't get an offer, so Newcastle it was. It worked out well and I really enjoyed my time there.

"Living away from home was good experience at that stage in my life, though I was back over a lot for rugby and would, like many students I suspect, have brought a load of dirty washing over and taken plenty of food back with me. I remember mum packing loads of tins."

Yes, the food. It has always been something close to Paddy's heart. His friends speak of his insatiable appetite and several can recall being on the receiving end of Johns' quest to fill his considerable frame. Greg Lynch was always popular with Paddy as a near neighbour at table, given that he "ate like a sparrow" and Johns got most of his portion as well as his own. Andy Oliver though seemed to suffer more than most.

"Paddy was very fond of his food and the one thing which gave him more pleasure than eating his own food was eating someone else's, often mine it seemed" laments Andy. "He was over at my house once when my parents were away, but we'd been left these steaks and had managed to cook them up. They were fantastic and we were really enjoying them but, when I was about halfway through mine, the phone rang. When I came back the steak had gone; Paddy had had it and I was raging. But I got my own back last Christmas, some 15 years later, when a few of us were out for a meal at a hotel in Dungannon. Again we both had steaks and were eating away when I says to Paddy 'look, there's Paddy Green (an old Dungannon stalwart), maybe you should go and have a word'. When he got back to the table, I'd whipped his steak. Now it was his turn to be furious, but he did remember his misdeed all those years ago!"

There were also spin-offs though of having a mate as big as Paddy. "One time we were up having a drink in a pub in Dungannon" relates Oliver, "and I knocked someone's beer over. I apologised and said it was an accident, but the guy started to get quite unpleasant about it and nothing would satisfy him even though I was offering to buy him a drink to make up for spilling the other one. But then his attitude started to change and he went from being very upset and hostile to calming down, to actually being friendly . . . as Paddy rose to his feet! By the time Paddy was half standing, the guy wanted to be best mates and, when he stood up fully, this fella bought us both drinks. Being around Paddy definitely gave one a bit of licence for mischief and was a real get-out-of-jail card sometimes."

The price of having a big bodyguard was getting your grub scoffed sporadically as the giant Johns had an appetite to match. "I was at university in Edinburgh along with another RSD old boy Richie Weir and Paddy and three of the other guys, Alastair Ross, Ian Stewart and Rodney Davison came across to see us" says Oliver. "Our mothers had packed off goodies with them, four big boxes which were to last us the whole term. But of course the big gulpin couldn't resist the food and, when he got on the boat, ripped open the parcels and got stuck into the buns, chocolate cake and the rest. The other lads might have had a bite or two, but I'd say he had most of it. By the time they arrived, there were literally only a few crumbs left in the bottom of the boxes."

The next year, Paddy was off to uni across the water himself. "Northern Ireland will always be home, but getting out of the wee country for a while did me good and broadened my horizons" he says. "I think university in general does that, which is why you hear it said that the benefits of third level education go beyond the degree you get. Young fellas who go straight into professional rugby from school these days without either going on to further education or getting a bit of work experience are definitely missing out on something."

Introduction to university life included the traditional compulsory initiation, via ritual humiliation, of the freshers into the rugby team, in time-honoured fashion. "Basically all the freshers had lots of pints thrown at them and had to play lots of games which involved the downing of lots of pints in the Agriculture bar in the Students Union, where all the tables and chairs were nailed to the floor" he reminisces with a slightly rueful grin. "There was one game called a three man lift where three guys were in a row tied together by the arms and legs, with a fresher as the middle one. A rope was tied to the fresher's belt and a member of the First XV came forward and tried the three man lift. He then had three attempts to try and lift the other two guys up. After the third attempt, a few people would rush in, pull down his trousers and fill his boxers with chilli, eggs, custard - whatever crap they had, and then the poor guy was left with everyone laughing and his trousers round his ankles. Thankfully it didn't happen to me!

"Another of the games the freshers had to do was a stage dive with two rows of four people to catch you. Sometimes the freshers fell, and I always wondered whether this was done on purpose for some guys." Luckily for Paddy, he made it through the initiation relatively unscathed. "I generally kept my head down. I don't know if it was my size or that I never really drew attention to myself, but I was glad that I was left alone!"

Not surprisingly, alcohol continued to provide an underlying theme in university rugby as Paddy recalls. "For every away game, everybody in the team had to buy a bottle of port, which we all did on the Saturday morning. You then had the bus journey back home after the game in which to drink it, be it half an hour or three hours. The bar staff at uni quickly realised that all the glasses should be packed away by the time we got back at around 7pm, as any found lying about always ended up being thrown across the room and broken, with the odd glass being hurled across the Union men's bar." Actions which perhaps contradict the 'quiet man' image, but evidence of a pretty typical student, albeit with a bit more rugby talent than your average freshman.

There was indeed some actual rugby played in Paddy's first year which he describes as, "great craic, but not too serious." So, still armed with visions of green jerseys as he fell asleep at night, Paddy decided to join a club side in his second year. The two real choices available to him were Newcastle Gosforth and Northern and, at the time, the former was the stronger of the two. Hard though it is to believe now and indicative of the pace of change in the game during the course of Paddy's own adult career, league rugby had still to be introduced in England at that stage, so a club's fixture list was comprised of friendlies and Cup competitions.

There he was exposed to a higher level of rugby, playing alongside people such as British Lion Steve Bainbridge, who was in the second row while Paddy tried his hand at No 8. He describes the Newcastle set up as "serious, but fun - everyone was friendly" and appeared to fit in well, but problems arose initially with the language barrier. "I couldn't understand a word half of those Geordies said" he laughs, "but at least most of them were in the backs!"

Of course rugby in Newcastle was later transformed totally by the advent of professionalism and the pioneering project run by Rob Andrew and John Hall which came, in ways, to symbolise both the good and bad of the new era and new order in the game. Certain advances were made and other important things sacrificed, all in the pursuit of progress and overnight success, with a range of high profile players parachuted in in an attempt to turn Newcastle from a second division side to trophy winners. It worked and it didn't. In ways, there may have been a world of difference between the Gosforth of Paddy's day and the Newcastle Falcons entity engineered by Hall and Andrew, but Johns says that, even back then, the club was 'very professional' in its approach. "It operated on a bigger scale than Dungannon and was on a par with Ulster in those days."

Another drawback with Newcastle was the amount of travelling necessary. Firstly most of Newcastle's away games were some distance removed, requiring the players to leave Friday afternoon and stay over. That did have a silver lining though for the opportunistic student! "For away matches, which were generally a fair bit away, we would travel on the Friday evening and have dinner. That was my biggest eating time of the week, for we also got a big breakfast the following morning. Naturally, as a student, I was glad of a good free feed and used to look forward to those away weekends from one fortnight to the next! The other big perk was that, as a student, there was also a free bar after the home games. Such considerations were very important in those days!"

Paddy was also fairly regularly travelling back across the Irish Sea for Dungannon league games, especially during his first year, and commitments with various Ulster and Irish teams throughout his stay on Tyneside. "Although there was an airport in Newcastle, there either weren't flights to Belfast or it never worked out for some reason, so I had to get the train to Leeds on a Friday afternoon and fly home from there, making the same return journey on Sunday. Sometimes I'd have got the train to Edinburgh, stayed over with Andy Oliver on the Friday night and flown home Saturday morning. I'm sure I was back and forwards more than a dozen times in the year. But it was my own choice and I never felt burdened by it. The incentive was always there, for I knew that, if I had any representative ambitions, it was crucial to play on Irish soil. Every time I could come home and play reasonably well, it was going to help my cause."

Oliver recalls the Johns stop-overs in the Scottish capital. "When Paddy was at university in Newcastle, he'd sometimes come up here to fly home. Being into his health, he was trying to convert Richie (Weir) and I to a more healthy diet. At that stage he was onto the bran flakes for breakfast but, being cash-strapped students, we decided we'd buy cheap cornflakes instead and sprinkle them with bakers' bran.

"So this weekend Paddy comes up on the Friday evening and, as usual, we went out for a few beers, though he'd never have too many because of the match the next day. Anyway, we came back in and there was nothing to eat, so we got out the cornflakes and the bran. He had to be up at 5.00 the next morning for his flight, so I got up too and we had some more. I went back to bed and got up again at 10.00 and had a third helping. In my match that afternoon, I made it into the second half and then my guts knotted up and I had to be subbed. I was still on the toilet when the boys were leaving the changing rooms a couple of hours later!"

This was all against the backdrop of Paddy keeping his head above water regarding dentistry, making for a hectic schedule and an ongoing juggling act. Rugby took up most of the weekend and, apart from training during the week, there were often university matches on Wednesday afternoons. "The first semester was always the worst. Rugby was its most intense and the dentistry came second to it. As the academic year went on and the rugby calmed down, my marks always improved, but the link was pretty obvious."

Clearly whilst combining an all-consuming course with an all-consuming hobby, sacrifices had to be made if success was to be achieved. Even the young find they can't do everything. "I had to give up most of my socializing, especially during the week. My friends were out about three times a week while I was either training or studying. But I have no regrets. I saw my close friends in my class and had friends on the rugby team who I saw at training and matches at the weekend."

It was quite a juggling act and, when you're running yourself into the ground or snowed under, it can be all too easy to feel the immediate sacrifice and lose sight of the long term reward, but Paddy knew what he wanted and never wavered from pursuit of his goals. As well as chasing his vision of Irish honours, he also loved the game in general and was having a ball simply playing the sport. That underlying sense of enjoyment helped make him strong enough to continue making the sacrifices even when the wider goals seemed distant.

Paddy remembers his time at Newcastle Gosforth as "happy" and also recalls, with fond nostalgia, his humble student digs at the time. "We lived in an area called Benwell where the Newcastle riots were a few years later. Our house stood out because it was the only one in the street with purple curtains, so we christened it 'the Purple Palace'. It was a typical student house with a one inch gap between the skirting board and the floor, the shower leaked into the kitchen, mould everywhere and it was so cold that you had to dress up to go to bed!" Not exactly prime conditions for producing an international athlete, but Paddy soldiered on. There was nothing else for it in those days though, as will be considered later, being spared the temptation of turning pro before he had his qualifications was perhaps a blessing.

His three closest friends from his course in Newcastle were Jeremy Wynne, Kevin Higgins, both of whom were housemates, and Anil Shrestha. Anil was Nepalese and a black belt in several disciplines. He may well have taught Paddy a few moves to use on the pitch, not in front of the ref of course!

There were also some culinary ventures. "I remember Anil being over and he and Paddy doing curry. I could smell it coming up the avenue and was washing dishes for a week" says Mrs Johns. Kev was a Scouser who fanatically supported Everton, and Geordie Jem, the Peter Beardsley look-alike, made up the foursome.

Not surprisingly, Paddy didn't have an awful lot of time for organised extra-curricular activities or interests outside of rugby, though he does recall joining a kick-boxing club and making more of an impact than he had bargained for! "My good mate Anil was a black belt, but I knocked him out one day. I gave him a front kick and down he went, but the problem was that, when he fell back, he banged his head. He lost his short-term memory and started talking rubbish and the situation was compounded by the fact that he was going back home to Nepal the following day. Thankfully he came round later that night, but not before I had visions of him permanently turning into a vegetable!"

Johns was enjoying student life and, to a large extent, his rugby, yet at this stage frustration was beginning to set in. Irish selectors didn't regularly travel to England, so Paddy felt he was missing out on the chance to be seen and, without suitable exposure, how could he ever progress and achieve his goal. He was involved with Ulster at various levels, including making the senior side in his second year in Newcastle, but the provincial team had obviously less games in those days so he had a limited shop window. Ideally he should be on Irish soil.

Therefore, Paddy made enquiries about a transfer to his original choice for tertiary education, Trinity. They were now keen to have him and Newcastle University were receptive to his request for a switch, so half way to being Patrick Johns Bachelor of Dental Science, he moved to Dublin. That was for his third academic year and coincided with the start of the 1989-90 rugby season, an early highlight in which was playing for Ulster against the touring All Blacks at Ravenhill. His mum was "thrilled" as she and seven other members of the family had themselves attended Trinity.

At time of writing, Brazilian World Cup winning football star Rivaldo has recently supposedly turned down a move to Newcastle United, while Italian Ravanelli and others have allegedly been disparaging about life in Middlesborough. But Paddy insists he loved life in the North East of England and, apart from rugby considerations, was in no rush to leave behind the place or the people. You might have had Gazza's 'Fog on the Tyne' and all that but he recalls Dublin as "having its smog and grime as well. I liked Dublin though too. The people were very easy-going, laidback and friendly. Trinity had, after all, been my original choice of university and I knew it was a good move for my rugby.

"When I moved to Dublin, the only person I knew there was Michael Webb, a friend from Bangor Grammar who had played with me for Ulster Schools. I rung him up to find out the story about Trinity and so forth before I went there. He said I could bunk in with them for a few days until I found somewhere, but I ended up staying about six months! We lived out in Clontarf near a big park. It was only a couple of minutes away and I used to go and train out there, doing all my sprints and the different runs. Later we lived on the North Circular Road for six months and during that time I used Pheonix Park.

"I also bought a mountain bike when I first came to Dublin and got an awful lot of stick over it. It was a way of getting about, but also counted as training so I got to burn a lot of calories at that time. Michael made up a stupid song about 'Pat the Baker on his bike' and, for a while, I got called Pat the Baker. There was a bakery in Dublin called Pat's Bakery and, just by coincidence, they happened to advertise at Lansdowne Road a few months later. Michael was well amused! The bike was actually a quick way to get about town, providing you could manage to dodge the traffic and stay on it. Michael had a car and he used to leave way later than me, but catch up with me going into town and beep and roll down the window and sing his song. The usual slagging. I preferred to have my own wheels and independence. When I got involved in the Irish squad, I'd have used the bike to get to training sessions. Most of the players were arriving in company cars and I was cycling in, probably soaked to the pelt a lot of the times, but I was just delighted to be there."

So Paddy initially had to adjust to living in a new city, while dentistry a la Trinity also proved to be something of a culture shock. "It was like going from modern to medieval. The dental school at Newcastle was very new and up to date. All the patients had individual cubicles and the equipment was state of the art. In Trinity, by contrast, there were rickety wooden floorboards, creaky stairs and about thirty chairs per room for the patients, though in the past few years it has been modernised. It was still a very good dental school" he is quick to add, "although we did have a few lectures that were in the style of Father Ted!"

"Paddy was always very single-minded when it came to rugby," recalls Michael Webb. "He drank a lot less beer and ate a lot more healthily than the rest of us! He wasn't a killjoy by any means and, when he did occasionally let his hair down, he knew how to do it properly, but his attitude was one of a professional long before Paddy actually was one. I think he was tailor-made for the job as he always loved training and the athletic lifestyle."

As well as several sterling performances in the green jersey, the Irish public may well have Paddy to thank for saving the Book of Kells! "Paddy was studying in his room," Michael remembers, "when he thought he smelt smoke." He came out of his room, and sure enough there seemed to be smoke coming from underneath the door of the room opposite. Paddy being Paddy, he called in another guy for a second opinion. Between the two of them, they confirmed that there was in fact smoke coming out from underneath the door, so the fire brigade was called and the whole building was evacuated. Unfortunately for Paddy the firemen hatcheted down his door before realising it was the wrong one! The fire had been started by a cigarette catching fire to a mattress and was quickly extinguished, but this was of little comfort to Paddy who was left with a ruined wardrobe and a carpet covered in sooty footprints! I don't think he was too impressed."

His best mates from the Trinity dental class included Philip Hardy, Frank Gallagher and Kevin O'Boyle "all of whom kept me right when I transferred into fourth year BDS."

Rugby wise, Trinity were guided by coach Roly Meates and although all the matches were friendly in name, the side was very competitive and could hold their own against the bigger club names like Blackrock and Old Wesley. It was no longer a case of out of sight, out of mind as Paddy regularly earned rave reviews in the Dublin papers for his performances, including one Leinster Senior Cup tie against Blackrock when it was noted that he "led the final onslaught by stirring example." He was, by a long way, the biggest name in the team, and Trinity were well outside the net of the All Ireland League when it started with only two divisions in 1990. But the be-all-and-end-all was the Colours match against bitter rivals UCD. Bragging rights were at stake.

"To lose the Colours match simply wasn't an option and, fortunately, I never tasted defeat against UCD. We drew 6-6 with them in my first year and then won in my second. We also won the Dudley Cup, which was a wider achievement as it involved all the big Irish universities, but there was nothing could beat the Colours match." Being awarded the 'Pink', which took the form of a scarf, was the Trinity equivalent of an Oxbridge 'Blue'.

That second Colours match, at Donnybrook, came less than a month after Paddy had won his first Ireland cap against Argentina and, remarkably, was Meates' 25th in charge of Trinity, who had won 11, lost 11 and drawn two under his tutelage in the quarter century until that point. "Roly is a very nice fella and all the players loved him" says Paddy. "He'd been there so long and he and his wife had no kids, so the Trinity team was essentially like a family to him."

Meates, like another of Paddy's mentors, Willie Anderson, ultimately found himself burned by the blazers of the IRFU and, although Leinster have recently availed of both men's services, Irish rugby has appeared to cut off its nose to spite its face by refusing to make more of what are, arguably, the country's best scrummaging and lineout coaches respectively. "Roly might have annoyed a few people because he is such an honest guy, while Willie seems to have suffered for speaking his mind. That's the problem with the IRFU, if someone's card gets marked, they all turn against them. Committees do good work and certainly had a place particularly in the amateur days, or still at club level, but there is a case for professional set-ups being run by professionals. From Will Carling's comments about the '57 old farts', I guess the problem isn't unique to Ireland though.

"It is a pity though if someone like Roly Meates is marginalised just because people don't like them, fairly or unfairly. Props such as Nick Popplewell and Justin Fitzpatrick would swear by him as a superb scrummaging guru. He has also played a significant role in the early careers of guys who, between them, have won hundreds of caps."

For that 1990 Colours match, Johns was joined in the back row by Michael Webb, and another housemate, Gavin Ellis, another former Bangor Grammar pupil, was at outside centre. The team was captained by fullback Ian 'Moggie' Morgan. A young Niall Woods, the future Ireland winger, was on the Trinity bench, while another two men who were to wear the green at the highest level, pivot Steve McIvor and lock Gabriel Fulcher, featured in the UCD team, but Paddy was the only guy on the pitch to already have earned senior international honours. Trinity did well to win, for the opposition also included several other names who were to make a mark in club rugby or higher, wing Dave Hernan, flanker Stephen Rooney and hooker Andy Donovan.

The match programme listed Johns' height as 9'6" and Paddy's penpic is worth reproducing verbatim. Never mind the Canadian sprinter referred to: let's just all have some of whatever the guy who did the programme notes was on! It said: "Having received a 'Dear John' letter from his fiancée, Kirstie is now actively involved with Ben Johnson. Pat the Baker set off on his shiny new bike to ding-a-ling his way to Peekers and was later heard to use his famous chat-up line 'Hello Mrs Dumas, I see you've cut your grass!' on a chancey oul one. His second Colours today."

Right from his first term at Trinity, Paddy was enjoying his rugby and, most importantly, was back in the Irish game. He knew that good performances would be more likely to filter back to those who could make his dream come true. The amount of representative rugby he played in the next couple of years seemed to prove the point. He had the satisfaction of playing for Irish Universities in a handsome win over their Welsh counterparts at College Park and, by the time he left Trinity, graduating in December 1991, Johns was a full Irish international, the first forward to be capped while at the university in living memory.

"Graduation was a very formal affair. Lots of pomp and circumstance. Trinity was very traditional like that. It was great that I was finally graduating. We all wore black robes with a red trim and mortar boards which annoyed me no end!" The interim between student and working life was short for Paddy. He began work on 5th January in the field of general practice in Carrickfergus with Jimmy McDonald. "I'll always be grateful to Jimmy for giving me my first job and he was a great help as I started out in the big world of work.

"I was glad to get stuck in," Paddy recalls. "You spend so long pretending to be a dentist at university and I was also looking forward to earning some money and being able to pay off all those student loans. I stayed in Carrick for one year. Although I was really glad to be a dentist, I was finding the workload very frustrating. The practice was too big for one person, but not big enough for two and I was keen to work, not sit about. After that, I decided to take an opportunity to move into community dentistry, a post in Newry, and loved it. I enjoyed the variety within the job and found it very rewarding. At this time I knew community dentistry was for me."

At the age of 24, Johns had realised his dream of playing for Ireland and was armed with his dentistry degree. He was ready for the world of work and also about to make the big breakthrough in the Test rugby arena on the tour of New Zealand.

5. MEETING THE MISSUS!

Every cloud has a silver lining. It's an ill wind and all that. If Paddy hadn't been sent off for the first and only time of his career playing for Newfoundland Under 19s against Newfoundland senior side in Quidi Vidi 15 summers ago, he mightn't have been married to Kirsty today. Well, he might, but it's a good story, as is the notion that, in a club that same night, he only grabbed her in panic as the first girl he could lay hands on in order to dissuade a guy who propositioned him thinking it was a gay bar!

The first tale at least has enough of a ring of truth to it to justify not letting the facts get entirely in the way of a good story, but the second could be considered a scurrilous suggestion only it's being thrown in by way of a first strike before she turns the tables and ridicules the romantic notion of her falling in love with this gentle giant from Ireland. Listening to the light-hearted banter and the gentle chiding as they cut across each other to put their own side of the story as we sit around the table, both giving as good as they get, one thing is clear: still crazy after all these years.

'How Paddy met Kirsty. Discuss' is tonight's topic and Pudsey goes in to bat first as Mrs Johns serves up some homemade damson crumble to the all-ears authors. That gives him the chance to get his retaliation in first before Kirsty hits back with her version of events and we gradually piece together the history of a relationship which has now clocked up 10 years of marriage and produced four lovely children. What started that summer in Canada lasted through the long-distance phase when both were students, sustained them in the early days of marriage when funds were tight and later took them to London and back as Paddy pursued a professional rugby career. It's been eventful, but it's been fun.

They've been at this banter before. In an interview with the Irish Examiner in 1998, Paddy's reported version of events is that he 'had to move house and change numbers several times to avoid being harrassed', while, for Kirsty, it was a case of 'finally deciding to come to Ireland after four years of begging letters and phonecalls'!

But what was Paddy Johns doing in Canada anyway in the summer of 1987? He had been contacted by Irish Schools fullback, Charlie Haly, who later went on to play for Munster and London Irish, regarding a summer trip to Newfoundland. The link here was two Irish doctors, Pat Parfrey and Noel Browne.

"Pat was a nephrologist (kidney specialist) from Cork who got one cap for Ireland on the wing, and a very, very funny guy. He was the only person who managed to use the word f*ck as a noun, verb, adjective, adverb, anything" Paddy laughs. "His best ever was, 'The f*cking f*ckers f*cking f*cked it!' For a southern Irishman, he had a very British address, Regent Street, Prince William Estate! Noel was a GP who looked after the police. He had played No 8 for Connacht and the two of them really got rugby going there in the 1970s. There were plenty of good, hard, physical players around, but skills were generally basic and there wasn't much depth of talent."

The deal on the table was free flights and jobs working in a timber yard in exchange for services on the pitch. In the end, six Irish Schools players took the plunge and headed across the Atlantic. These included Paddy, future full international scrumhalf Steve McIvor, Finbarr Griffin, Fergal O'Bierne, Keith Higgins and Haly. Of his five fellow pilgrims, Paddy developed the closest friendship with Haly, who later followed him into dentistry. He also spent part of a summer up north with the Johns family. "Charlie had never been up north before" recounts Mrs Johns. "I sent him and Paddy in to sign on for benefit, which you could get in the summer in those days. Some boy asked Charlie if he'd think of joining the territorial army and he was afraid to open his mouth to reply because of his accent!"

"We were going over with the attitude that we were going to teach them how to play rugby, and to be fair, Paddy was a hero out there" says Charlie. "They'd never seen anyone his size before and he played fantastically. At the time though, Paddy fancied himself as a tennis player and he thought he was good at it, but it's just as well he was so good at rugby! Tough, ruthless and athletic, there was no doubt in his mind that he was going to play for Ireland."

These Irish boys had to be greeted into the bosom of Newfoundland's fishing community in the traditional manner. This took the form of a 'screeching-in ceremony'. Each individual had to stand with one foot in a bucket of saltwater, a sou'wester on their head and chant a rhyme which went as follows:

'Up the harbour
Down the shore
Come on Bay Roberts
Score, score, score!'

This poetry was followed by kissing a cod, which was "fairly putrid and could be tasted all night", and necking a tumbler of screech, hence screeching ceremony. This beverage is a very potent local rum, which apparently lives up to its name.

The boys were welcomed into Noel Browne's house as a short-term measure until they found more suitable accommodation. This meant that there were 11 in the Browne's home, including children Greg, Noel Junior (also on the U19 team) and Nancy. However, Noel's wife Christina made the fatal mistake of cooking steak or salmon every night and seeing to it that all the boys' washing was done, so they did very little towards actually moving out. Eventually, several weeks down the line, the Irish contingent did branch out, but not for long. "We were meant to stay for a few days which ran into weeks until we finally sorted out a rented house, but we only managed to stay there for a couple of days!" Paddy chuckles. "The Brownes went away for the weekend and we moved back in to 'keep an eye on the place' and just never moved out again! The skinny Irish boys certainly got well fattened up!"

The Brownes' house backed on to the Stokes' house," recalls Charlie Haly. "What was great about this was that the Stokes family had a pool and we used to all sneak over the fence and go skinny dipping. However Mrs Stokes came out a few times and we had to leg it over the fence naked!" On another occasion, the six Irish lads spent a week in Charlie's aunt's one-bedroom apartment in New York!

In return for the excellent hospitality, the Irish boys certainly did their bit in helping to put Newfoundland on the rugby map, though their success didn't exactly make the province popular in Canada, with resentment bubbling away about Newfoundland's use of so many non-nationals, even though there was nothing in the rules to say they couldn't.

"Newfoundland were always getting hammered in the Canadian national junior championship, but we helped them to the final for the first time ever and were only beaten in extra-time by British Columbia in St John's" explains Paddy. "During the match, which was televised live, a fist fight broke out in the crowd; the BC supporters were so angry that these imported paddies should be playing for Newfoundland. The cameras swung away from the action on the pitch to follow the action on the sidelines. Even though we lost in the end, it was a very successful season for Newfoundland and we all enjoyed the rugby."

There were also other attractions about Newfoundland for the Irish boys, not least the favourable ratio of females to males. "One of the things Charlie told me in advance was that there wasn't much work apart from fishing, that unemployment was fairly high and that a lot of the young fellas tended to leave the area. It sounded promising!" And how. Paddy got his girl alright, though the circumstances in which the initial connection was made are sufficiently unlikely to be well worth recording.

"We, the juniors, were playing against the seniors and stuffing them in one of the first games of the season. They were hitting back with sly digs in the lineouts and so forth to try and put us young pups in our place. Needless to say us Irish guys were the first to retaliate and when everything had calmed down the ref sent off four players, two from each side, and I was one of them." Every cloud has a silver lining, however, and this sending off seems to have been what kick-started the Kirsty-Paddy romance. Not that it was the bad boy image which appealed to her. "I'd gone with friends to see the game," explains Kirsty. "One of them had a brother who was playing. I must admit, I knew nothing about the game and when Paddy stormed off the pitch, I thought it was just like American Football and he'd been subbed! Paddy then stripped his shirt off at the side of the pitch and I thought, 'that looks like a bit of alright!' Then later on he came searching for me at the bar."

"Absolutely not!" interrupts Paddy. "It was all a bit of a fluke really. We were out celebrating one of the guy's, Finbar's, birthday at a place called Club Max which is now a strip joint! Me and my mate saw Kirsty and her friend. Both of us wanted to dance with Kirsty, so we flipped a coin for it and I won. So I went over to her and ended up giving her my number, but she never rang'."

"It took a while to meet up again" Kirsty admits. "A couple of weeks later I went with my friend to pick up her brother from the rugby club and after several elbows and nudges in the back I invited Paddy to a party we were going to. He got in the car with us and after that we saw each other every day and night for two weeks solid, after which he turns to me and says, 'Are you seeing anybody?' to which I replied, 'I think I'm seeing you, Paddy!'"

Six weeks later it was time for Paddy to leave Canada with the usual holiday romance promises of keeping in touch. However, there were regular phonecalls made and letters written, and by the time Christmas 1987 rolled around, Kirsty was preparing to spend it in Northern Ireland with Paddy. He was now at Newcastle University doing his degree in dentistry, while Kirsty was a biology undergraduate back home in Canada. The pair would write to each other "once or twice a week", with phonecalls every fortnight. In the summer of 1988, Paddy returned to Newfoundland for another season with the same club and found time to cause some confusion with Kirsty's car.

"It was the strangest thing," Kirsty remembers. "I had this little Renault 5 which went perfectly well unless I was driving Paddy somewhere, when it would always break down, without fail. So Paddy was going round telling everyone that my car was rubbish and I couldn't drive, yet whenever anyone else was in the car there were no problems at all. Anyway, as it turned out, Big Feet here," she says nodding in Paddy's direction, "was hitting the wire under the dashboard every time he sat in the passenger seat!" "Size fourteen," Paddy smiles ruefully.

Christmas was again spent together in Northern Ireland and, in summer 1989, Kirsty travelled over to work on the 'chickstick' line in the Moy Park factory whilst Paddy was employed in the flavouring department. Paddy also managed to persuade Dungannon that their tour of Canada in August of that year should include Newfoundland. At this time, rugby there had really taken off and Newfoundland was in the top three or four teams in Canada at both junior and senior level. Rod Snow, the future Canada and Newport front row forward, was playing for them then, incidentally at No 8, as was Denis Clark, the international centre.

"Newfoundland has this backwater image, so when we were coming in to land, I told the players that there was no runway at the airport, just a gravel track, and one of the guys actually broke out into a sweat! There's a big Irish community in Newfoundland, so we were all well looked after and there was great hospitality. Afterwards all the guys said it was the best stop on tour."

"It was a great stop," agrees Greg Lynch, formerly coach of Wanderers and Bective. "I think I was the only guy on tour with an Irish passport, but was welcomed into the tour party with open arms. Paddy sat beside me on the plane because he knew I wouldn't eat any of the food, so he could get double! When Paddy was at Trinity and we used to meet up, his Mum would send me down from Dungannon with loads of food to make sure he was ok. Never mind playing rugby for Ireland, that guy could eat for Ireland! He must have a very high metabolism or else he'd be about 30 stone the amount he packs away." Incidentally, Kirsty recalls Paddy's first meal at her family home; twice the usual quantity of potatoes were cooked, yet none was left over!

After completing a hat-trick of Christmases in Ulster, the following summer saw Kirsty make the trip to Dublin, bribing cleaning ladies with biscuits and sweets to keep quiet about the fugitive in uni halls, where Paddy was now based having relocated to Trinity. Then, a year later, the inevitable happened. "I decided to pop the question," recalls Paddy. "I had one year left at Trinity and Kirsty had a year left of her biology degree. She was coming to the end of her course and I made the decision that I had to make a decision! Her dad had also had a 'talk' with me. He took me out in the car and basically said, 'Don't mess with my daughter's head,' but I had decided what I wanted anyway.

"We were in Newfoundland after spending part of the summer in Ireland and I took Kirsty for a meal at a place called Victoria Station. It used to be Kirsty's mum's house, but had been turned into a restaurant. Afterwards we went to Signal Hill, where Cabot Tower was, the site from which Marconi sent his first radio message across the Atlantic."

"Local make out point," interjects Kirsty. "I thought it had a nice view!" claims Paddy. "It looked down over the harbour. So, I got down on one knee and promptly dropped the ring. After some groping around, I found it and asked Kirsty to marry me. Happily, she said 'yes'." Paddy was staying with Kirsty's family, so when they arrived home he officially asked her dad, a professor at Memorial University, who was very pleased to see that young Mr Johns was indeed not 'messing with his daughter's head'!

Paddy's mum wasn't surprised at the development. "When Paddy was in Canada that first summer, he'd written home to say he'd met a 'very special girl', which was a whole new departure. I remember thinking 'what has happened here'. Between studying and rugby, he'd never had a lot of time and wasn't the sort of young fella who was out to discos every weekend. Marcus by contrast had a 'special girl' every week and I recall one day two different cars landing on the street at the same time, one which had come in the back avenue and one the front; two different girls calling to bring him to school. Paddy was looking out the window and going 'Huh, he's in a right fix now; wonder what he'll do'.

"Kirsty is the only serious relationship that Paddy has ever had and once they got together, that was it, in spite of the distance. She's shown tremendous commitment, coming over to Newcastle and Dublin and then basically jumping on the first plane for a move to Ireland after completing her degree. I remember him going off to the airport for her first time she came and then her arriving in. Her parents were nearly out of their mind with worry because of the civil unrest here. She has been very supportive throughout his rugby but I think, like myself, has enjoyed it all immensely too."

The summer they got engaged the couple had rented a flat on the North Circular Road in Dublin. After another year apart, Kirsty tried her hand at waitressing in Fat Freddies restaurant, located in the trendy Temple Bar area of Dublin. "I had a great time working there. It was very hip and they were filming some of the Tom Cruise/ Nicole Kidman film 'Far and Away' at the time. I didn't get to meet anyone famous though!

"At that point, I was pretty much here to stay. I'd finished my biology degree and had secured a place in Jordanstown to study physiotherapy. It had been between there and Halifax University in Nova Scotia. I'd had my interview with Halifax conducted on a payphone in Dublin city centre! But I was always going to come here if I got a place. It wasn't a very hard decision to make."

In 1991, Paddy took up his first post as a dentist working in Carrickfergus under Jimmy McDonald. He was living in a flat above a headstone sculptor's whilst Kirsty, in her first year at University of Ulster, Jordanstown, was in halls. This time it was Paddy who almost got her kicked out for stretching visiting regulations! The couple then moved in together with a friend from Dungannon, Gareth McKee, to a house in Whiteabbey, in a development called The Firs. "We had one crummy little bedroom and there was a baby upstairs crying all the time. We were looking for a house to buy as we'd both hated our places."

It was at this time that Kirsty's mother rang to ask if they had any idea when they were getting married as everything had to be booked a year in advance. So the date was set then and there for 28th August 1992. At this point Paddy was juggling community dentistry in Newry and an international rugby training programme. This meant leaving home at 07:30 and not returning until 23:30 which didn't allow much time to plan forthcoming weddings. "I basically did everything," says Kirsty. "Paddy was three thousand miles away and then he went on tour to New Zealand. He finally showed up three days before the wedding! His role was to generally prove agreeable to whatever I arranged and turn up for the big day itself.

"Ultimately I had a week to find a church when it turned out the one I'd picked, the university church, had to go under construction. There was scaffolding round it and we were told we could come along and sweep up the night before. No thanks. Then, on the actual day, the cake wasn't ready. Luckily this was kept from me and my brother managed to sort it out between the ceremony and the reception."

"We all trooped over for the wedding" recalls Paddy's mum. "We were staying in an apartment and the first morning we were there we walked down into St John's, towards the harbour and saw a tricolour hanging on one of the boats. We shouted in 'are you Irish?' and they shouted back to come on in. The boat was skippered by a chap called Michael Coleman and a great time was had by all. He ended up hiring a tux and coming to the wedding, and we still keep in contact."

Unsurprisingly, Paddy's best man Andy Oliver also had a ball. "We went over for the wedding, myself and his friends from Newcastle" says Andy. "We were supposed to be staying at Kirsty's house, but had arrived a day before Paddy, so I didn't want to be imposing on the family and stayed instead with these other Newcastle uni guys in a caravan in the centre of town. We spent the whole week out on the town partying.

"Two nights before the wedding I still hadn't written my best man speech. We were at Kirsty's house that evening for a meal and her granny came up to me and asked about it. I was making light of it, telling her it wasn't done (which was true) but was promising her that I'd a few juicy stories. I think the poor woman was petrified from that to the wedding that I'd lower the tone of the occasion.

"Anyway, when I finally decided to get down to it, the only thing to write on in the caravan was a cornflakes packet, which I tore up and used the insides of to do out the speech. The night before the wedding, Paddy, Greg Lynch and I were staying with Noel Browne, who gave me these nice little proper cards to write my speech out on. My whole focus was on getting him to the church on time. I wouldn't be the most organized person in the world, but I knew that I couldn't mess up. I was nagging Paddy from early morning and, in fact, he was relaxed and it was me who was stressed.

"My temperature rose when I couldn't find my cufflinks, which we searched for for about 20 minutes without success, until Paddy suddenly 'found' them under the pillow. I put them on and we were just ready to go when I went to check my jacket pocket.

No speech cards! I started ransacking the caravan, but the taxi was arriving and we simply couldn't be late, so I had to grab the big pieces of cornflakes packet (which, luckily, I'd kept) and stuff them into my pocket. But that meant I was bulging out the front like I was pregnant so, when we got to the church I decided 'I can't go in looking like this'. So I went round the back of the church and hid the pieces of cardboard behind a stone. Inside the church it dawned on me what happened and I turned to Paddy and said 'you've stolen my speech'. He burst out laughing and handed it over."

The biter had been bit and the tables turned on the practical joker. And an insight into Paddy the prankster provided. "After I'd done my speech, the first person to congratulate me was Kirsty's mightily-relieved granny" continues Oliver. "There was a huge party that night which lasted until 9.30 the following morning. Both Paddy's brother, Johnny, and I had said we'd play rugby for St John's that day, but we'd got split up by early morning. As we had to be at the ground by 10am, I just grabbed a taxi in my full regalia and, as we drew up, Johnny was stepping out of another car. We were supposed to be playing for the Seconds, but their game was cancelled and we were asked to play a half each for the Firsts instead. I lasted about five minutes and Johnny about three, before puking up. That shattered any illusions which they may have had that we'd be like Paddy!"

After the dramas of the unbuilt church, the unmade cake and the unwritten speech, all went smoothly for the happy couple and the wedding night was spent in Victoria Station, "very old, typical St John's", with the honeymoon up the country in the cabin of Mick Maguire, a dentist from Ireland who, incidentally, was also married to a physio. "At that stage we were fairly skint, in fact in massive debt. Kirsty's fees were a big ongoing commitment at that time" says Paddy. "We were happy to take up Mick's offer of the country cabin and also, when we came back, did a week in Donegal, splashing out £12 per night on B&Bs!"

However, married life mustn't have been all it was cracked up to be, for after three days at the cabin, Kirsty wanted to go home! "Sounds awful, doesn't it?" she acknowledges. "We were meant to stay for a week, but I got really homesick. I was leaving Newfoundland and didn't know when I was going to see my family again." Any regrets leaving Canada?

"Oh no," Kirsty says assuredly. "Obviously I missed my family, but rugby is so important to Paddy, I could never have asked him to give that up and as I could have done my physio degree in either country, it just would have been selfish. There are definitely similarities between the two types of people, and I'd been spending a lot of time here. My mum was born in Britain and all her family is English, plus she studied in Coventry and my dad studied in Scotland and at Cambridge. They'd been over in 1969 to see some Irish relatives. Mum would have been pregnant with me at the time. They were never going to stop me, but secretly they were sweating buckets because of the troubles. My mum got a map of Northern Ireland and used to put pins in it wherever there were bombs or violence, just to make sure I was nowhere near it!"

The new Mr and Mrs Johns moved into their recently purchased marital home in Abbeyville Street, Whiteabbey. The area gave good reason for Paddy's in-laws to worry.

"The house only cost £23,500 but was nice enough," remembers Kirsty, "but there were two shootings on the street in our first six months of living there, so it wasn't the best of areas. There was a gate attached to the house that led into an alley. The kids would swing on it and bang on the house, so I took it off and put it in the back garden" says Paddy. "Then the next door neighbour came banging, looking to know why it had been taken off. She used to throw her kids in there."

There were a few other problems for Kirsty. "At Jordanstown, I was considered a foreign student and that my marriage was one of convenience, or inconvenience, depending on how you look at it!" she laughs. "The fees were astronomical, just too much, so 18 months into the course, I ended up taking a year out until it was all sorted. I did some voluntary work at Daisy Hill Hospital when Paddy was based in Newry."

After the second shooting, the couple then moved to a three bedroom semi in Sandyknowes Park, Glengormley, near Belfast in 1993, where they remained for three years until the move to Saracens. "We'd seen about 10 places and didn't like any of them" Kirsty recalls. "The photo of this one was poor and I didn't really want to try it, but Paddy did. We ended up taking it." Whilst living here, Paddy was working for the Northern Board in Larne and the move to England included one new addition.

Christopher Patrick Adam Johns was born on 13th May 1995 at the end of Kirsty's third year, in the City Hospital, Belfast. Weighing in at 6lbs 6oz, Johns Jnr was induced so Dad could be present before leaving for national duty in South Africa. Kirsty's obstetrician, Mr Houston, was an unashamed rugby fanatic and decided that the decision to induce was "for the good of the country". Christopher was induced on a Friday morning, but had "no desire to enter the world", so didn't appear until the Saturday evening.

"Kirsty's sister had flown over and she came in with us" recounts Paddy. "There was nothing happening on Saturday afternoon, so I went home to Glengormley for something to eat. But the Middlesex Sevens was on the TV and, when the call came to get back, I hadn't got any tea! The main thing though was that there were no problems with the birth." Christopher's middle names are after his dad and Paddy's close friend Adam Lambert who, as has already been related, was randomly murdered whilst working as an architectural student on a building site at the age of 19. To add to this futility, it had been a case of mistaken identity, and left a major mark on Johns.

Two years later, Emily Kirstine, the heaviest of the Johns babies, was born late on 23rd June 1997 at Enfield Hospital, London, weighing 7lbs 6oz after a rushed journey in late at night. Kirsty's mum was over to help out, and whilst she was timing contractions and tending to her daughter's needs, the expectant dad was practising his lineout jumping in the back garden, with a skittle fixed to a tree! He further ingratiated himself by falling asleep in the waiting room and when awoken was very groggy and irritable and suggested to the nurse that Kirsty needed an epidural to calm her down! Dad reports that his eldest daughter is "not very into sport; her interests and abilities lie elsewhere - in animals and the arts."

After returning to Ireland in June 1999, Paddy and Kirsty decided to have one more baby. "Couldn't even get that right!" Kirsty says, rolling her eyes. "Paddy was at the World Cup when I found out it was twins. It was three days before the opening match against the United States. I just said, 'You'd better sit down' which he did - 'You've got two!'"

The twins were delivered by Caesarean section on 23rd March 2000 in the Royal Victoria Hospital, Belfast, just three days after Ireland had famously won in Paris with that late David Humphreys penalty. Quite a week for Paddy. "They were getting distressed, so it was decided to be safer to deliver them then and there, even though they were six weeks premature" explains Kirsty. "One wasn't growing as well as the other and the consultant decided they'd better get them out."

Megan Wanda (after Paddy's mum) was born first weighing 4lbs 12oz, and Hannah Jennifer (after Kirsty's mum) followed two minutes later at 3lbs 15oz. "I was given steroids before the deliveries to help their lungs and luckily they didn't need ventilation or incubators, which were on standby" reveals Kirsty. "They were so tiny though - smaller than Paddy's hands. We got home in three days"

"Technically they're identical and the pair have never been separated. They sleep in the same bed, and will be in the same class at Waringstown Primary School. Incidentally, there are triplets in the same class, in the year below Christopher."

Although when they came home from England, Paddy and Kirsty had no set ideas about where they wanted to live, they feel fortunate enough to have ended up in their current location outside Dromore, County Down, which has been home for the past three years. There is a Canadian connection in that they call their house Cabot Lodge.

"I had Keith McGarry, a friend and former Dungannon team-mate, looking out for a place for me. He's a solicitor, but one of the firm's branches shares premises with an estate agent's, so I asked him to keep his eye out. This place had been on the market for some time, but they couldn't get it sold with land attached, so decided to split it and sell the two separately. We came home a week early when Ireland played Italy in April 1999 and had a look. It seemed right, so we signed up." McGarry recalls "going out there one Saturday morning to look at the house. I'd an awful hangover and was stinking of drink, so it's a wonder Paddy got it, for the previous owner was quite a religious man who couldn't have been impressed!"

"The geography was a complete accident, but it has worked out well" says Paddy. "Funnily enough, my mum is a senior educational welfare officer for the Southern Board and Waringstown Primary School was one of her schools. She always thought it would be a good school for her grandchildren and it always gets listed by the Sunday Times as one of Northern Ireland's top five primary schools, but all the family were away at the time, so it was hardly likely it would work out that way. We ended up here by accident rather than design" reveals Paddy. A bit like getting together really.

6. RED HAND HERO

"Huh, that would never have happened with Ulster." That was Paddy's reflex response when the fact that there were 14 Canterbury players in the All Blacks side to face Ireland in the Auckland Test came up in conversation one evening in June. We'd just been casually discussing the 2002 Irish tour, 10 years on from his own participation in a similar series in New Zealand, but the statistic triggered a thought which reflected a long-held grievance. The sense of Ulster being under-represented in the national team has rankled throughout his career.

At face value, Irish rugby seems to function smoothly enough on an all-island basis regardless of the country's deep divisions, but scratch a little below the surface and the odd fissure will appear. Perception is reality and, if you look hard enough, a certain paranoia can be detected in Ulster about whether the northern province gets fair treatment, especially when it comes to national team selection, but also more generally. Parochialism is by no means the sole preserve of Ulster rugby, for fans of any club or provincial team in any sport will inevitably promote the claims of their own players for higher honours but, in Ulster, more tends to be read into selection snubs and slights.

Whether the claims are real or imaginary is, in ways, missing the point. The belief that there isn't a fair deal has been there and held by more than the politically prejudiced or the conspiracy theorists. Rightly or wrongly, and however controversially, Paddy Johns bluntly states that "there was always a perception in Ulster that we needed to be a fair bit better than our opposite number from another province to get picked for Ireland."

He'd say that sense of inherent disadvantage was a major factor in driving the likes of himself and Denis McBride to take as professional an approach as the day jobs allowed back in the old amateur era. They felt it would take it all to level up the playing field and counter the dice being weighted against their claims. McBride was a little ahead of Johns in chronological terms, but both were around the Ulster team to witness at first hand the scapegoating of, and witch-hunts against, men like Jimmy Davidson, Willie Anderson and David Irwin at national level. There was a trio who had put the province on a pedestal through the unprecedented success of the Ulster side, yet people seemed to be queuing up to vilify and pillory them at national level at the first opportunity.

All too often, there also seemed to be a nasty undercurrent to it all and, in the circumstances, it was hardly surprising if a siege mentality resulted. Selection is subjective and condemnatory comparison draws more on circumstantial than empirical evidence and applying logic or the law of averages rather than specific, forensic analysis, but a case can certainly be made by those who wish to make it. Johns arguably lost out to Mick Galwey late in his Ireland career largely because of the bandwagon effect which had built up round the Shannon stalwart and Munster as a result of that province's domestic domination.

At the start of the new millennium, Munstermen have made up up to two-thirds of the Irish team on occasions, yet Ulster were hardly ever anywhere near as well represented when the boot was on the other foot. In spite of the magnificent 10 interpro titles in a row achieved between 1984 and 1993 during a decade of domestic dominance, Johns asserts, with a hint of bitterness, that "we would never really have got more than five or six players into the Ireland team, generally less." Ulster, reasonably enough perceived to be the 'third province' in the past few seasons in spite of, against the odds, finishing no lower than second in the interpro table in that period, have currently slumped to a negligible representation in the national team, most recently two in the regular match 22. In the current circumstances, no-one would expect the Ravenhill ranks to be backboning the Irish squad, but Johns doesn't recall Munster or Leinster ever providing as paltry a contingent as Ulster do now.

It was never something you could afford to allow to eat away at you though or, like a cancer, it would have destroyed you. Undermine morale, ruin your rugby and sully your soul. Better, especially for those given to thriving on adversity, to use it as additional motivation like Johns and McBride. That was feasible as the situation was never hopeless. The door was never actually closed. But there was a nagging feeling in Ulster that some men would always be more equal than others.

The other politically related controversy which rears its head from time to time, particularly when Ireland are losing or an Ulsterman is captain, or, arousing the great wrath of redneck republicans in the south, when both coincide (and the witchhunts really begin), is the thorny anthem issue. Damned if they do and damned if they don't. There's no easy answer. You can't please everyone. For a while the IRFU decreed that Amhrain na bhFiann, the Soldier's Song, be played at Lansdowne Road, with nothing by way of an anthem played to represent the Irish team at away games.

The logic was that the Soldier's Song was acceptable in Lansdowne Road, due to the stadium being in the Republic of Ireland jurisdiction, with the quid pro quo that God Save the Queen would be played before any internationals at Ravenhill in good old British Belfast. Problem of course is that, with a standard capacity of only 12,500, there will be no full Test matches involving Ireland played at Ravenhill as currently constituted and no anthems are played before subsidiary internationals at, for example, A or Under 21 level. So the compromise is all a bit hypothetical.

Then along came Phil Coulter with Ireland's Call, the song so many seem to love to hate, but something which can at least be played in lieu of an anthem before away internationals without it causing controversy or offence. That isn't to say that embarrassing situations still don't arise. It now means that two 'anthems' are played before kick-off at Lansdowne Road and how often do we see the visiting team break away after the first and start shedding their tracksuit tops, only to have to link arms again for the second. The television cameras still, as they do for any international, pan in on each player down the line of the Irish team, invariably featuring the handful of Ulster representatives with mouths tight closed in what almost seems like silent protest. It needn't be such a big deal. Some of the Republic of Ireland soccer stars at the recent World Cup in Japan and Korea were spotted not singing, which has raised another old chestnut, the infamous 'does your granny come from Ireland' syndrome, as it appears to have involved the contingent of second generation Irish.

Glasgow Celtic footballer Neil Lennon, under the spotlight for various reasons from sections of the Northern Ireland soccer support at Windsor Park, was criticised for not singing God Save The Queen when that sorry saga was at its height last year. Taken in conjunction with his reported declaration, slightly taken out of context, that he would prefer there to be an all-Ireland soccer side like there is in rugby and his perceived nationalist background, people got hot under the collar at the thought he had a problem singing the national anthem of the United Kingdom. And yet, many of the English football team aren't seen moving their mouths at the appropriate time at Anfield, Old Trafford and so forth while the world awaits the new Wembley. The Italian soccer side were blasted by some of their own media for the same offence at this year's World Cup. But in general no-one gets too bothered, because their loyalty or allegiance or identity is not called into question.

When times are hard for the Irish rugby team, the murmurings of disquiet among the ultra-green gombeens kick in pretty quickly. They lament the absence of the Soldier's Song and blame it for a lack of spirit when Ireland lose on foreign fields. They lambast the two-tune 'farce' which pertains in Dublin and ask how a team which cannot embrace its own nationality can expect to do well against 'united' opponents. They generally look for Ulster scapegoats and start to question whether the team really needs the northerners, suggesting the price of 'diluted national pride' is too high to pay.

It isn't just the anthem debate; flags and emblems enter the equation as well. Those of us who were at the 1999 World Cup final in Cardiff couldn't help but cringe during the closing ceremony before the game when all the competing nations were represented by one of the huge national flags carpeting the pitch of the magnificent Millennium Stadium. Ireland, er, had an anaemic duck egg blue blanket with the IRFU crest on it. Irate sections of the southern press who spotted it ludicrously blamed watered-down identity for the relatively poor tournament which the team had, culminating in that disappointing early exit at the hands of Argentina in Lens some 10 days earlier.

Even in the 2002 Six Nations, with the new phenomenon of website discussion forums adding fresh fuel to tired old fires, David Humphreys, by then the only Ulsterman in the starting line-up, was berated in some quarters for not moving his lips during the Soldier's Song in the Championship opener. Never mind that Humph then had a blinder as Ireland romped to a record rout of the Welsh, winning 54-10, or that young Limerick lad Paul O'Connell, apparently too nervous and emotional on his first cap, didn't sing either. Those who wanted to put the boot in, did.

At the other end of the scale, some fundamentalist politicians in the north have demanded that Ulster players refuse to represent Ireland because of having to 'play under a foreign flag and antagonistic anthem.' Both are wrong. Rugby is played on an all-island basis, so representing a 32-county team is what the guys in every province aspire to. That's simply the way it has been and is. Yet Ulster players may find themselves depicted as unworthy unionists, unworthy Irishmen or both. In reality, private political allegiance is left at the door when the ethos of the team environment kicks in. You play for yourself, your family, the team, the coaches, the jersey, the country, whatever.

Patriotism comes with the territory, but there's also personal and professional pride in the culmination of what you've worked for and the burning desire to achieve and to win, which has helped get you this far. Ulster boys dream of pulling on the green jersey at Lansdowne Road just as much as lads from other provinces. Ask Paddy Johns. David Tweed, yet another Ulster second row, is another classic case in point. Firebrand Orangeman and Councillor for Ian Paisley's DUP in the Ballymena bible belt, but he marched down the Dublin road without a murmur when he finally won his handful of Test caps as a grizzled veteran in 1995. Not only does wearing the green mean as much, there is also that feeling that the Ulster boys have to work harder to achieve their ambition and are under special scrutiny from those who would, outrageously, question their commitment to the cause.

Johns grew up in the generation which saw men like his first two Ulster captains, Irwin and Anderson, persecuted in spite of being such ferocious competitors and rightly revered on their own patch. He has also, at times, found himself fed up with the carping and sense of being disadvantaged, if not institutionally, at least all too often believing it to be the case in practice. The black north. As for the anthem, Johns was among the silent brigade even during his days as captain, but he sees no contradictions in playing and giving 100 per cent but not singing something which is not only alien to his culture but which is sung in a language he never learnt.

"Rugby started as an all-Ireland game through the clubs and universities in the 1800s and that is how it always has been. That is the sport's history and heritage on this island, so having an all-Ireland rugby team is not a political statement. It would, however, be political to split it in two. Sometimes people in other countries are a bit confused by it all. Over in France, the first question is 'why do you not sing?'. They find it hard to understand that you're Irish but British. Personally, I never took any abuse about not singing the anthem even when I was captain. I wouldn't think other guys in the team would have been offended or that they would have expected someone from my background to sing.

"There were classes brought in by Warren Gatland for us to learn it, so I suppose that was indirect pressure, but there was certainly no direct pressure. Anyone who has grown up in this country, north or south, pretty much knows the score. The Soldiers Song is the Republic of Ireland's national anthem and is sung in a language which the likes of myself would never have learnt. So it wouldn't have been a part of my culture. I identified with it inasmuch as it always, to me, symbolised the build-up to kick-off as an international whether I was watching from the terraces as a schoolboy or standing on the pitch as a member of the Irish team. It always will.

"Coming from Ulster, singing the anthem was never really an option. You'd only have been singling yourself out for trouble. The other boys knew we had to go back home afterwards! I didn't want to become politicised and, without a doubt, it would have been a bigger talking point if I had started singing it at any stage instead of remaining silent. As an Irish player, I naturally didn't sing God Save the Queen either when it was being played at Twickenham before we played England. It may be the United Kingdom anthem and I live in the United Kingdom, but it was being played for the English team on those occasions, so it wouldn't have been appropriate for me to sing."

Although there is no official Northern Ireland team, the Ulster team is a de facto national side to some people and, when Paddy Johns first came into the Ulster team, they were going for their fifth successive interpro title, Harry Williams having taken over from Davidson as coach due to the latter's elevation to the Irish post. Those were the days when, in spite of Ulster's remarkable run of success and the fact that there were only a handful of home matches every season, interpros would only have attracted a few hundred people. It was a far cry from the fashionable floodlit Friday night affairs of the modern era when Europe's finest are subjected to the now famous Ravenhill roar when they come to what has become one of the Heineken Cup's most intimidating venues to visit.

But pulling on that white jersey with the red hand was always a huge honour for any young player and, for Johns, making his Ulster debut alongside his heroes at the tender age of 20, was a dream come true. Four years earlier he had watched many of the men who were now his team-mates play their part in famously conquering the Grand Slam Wallabies of 1984 and was keenly aware of the standards that had been set.

The names from that great Ulster era still resonate: Rainey, Wilkinson, Ringland, Crossan, Hooks, Irwin, Hewitt, Harbinson, Field, McCall, Brown, Russell, McAleese, Brady, the Matchetts, Blair, McKibbin, Reynolds, Elliott, McCoy, Millar, Bell, Smith, McDonald, Adair, Anderson, Rogers, Morrison, McCall, Tweed, Matthews, Carr, Morrow, Whittle, Duncan, McBride, Robinson, Hamilton, McKinty and any number of useful bit-part players from the likes of McMaster and Cowan through to the fringe squad members at the latter end of the era. Different characters, different abilities, but all very proud indeed to represent the province.

As the Irish provinces now become de facto club teams in the European Cup and employ outsiders, both those classified as overseas players and others who conveniently have qualifying passports, care must be taken that identity and heritage does not become dangerously diluted. A dozen of Ulster's core-contracted squad of 30 full-timers for the 2002-03 season were not born in the province and, although most of the imports have fitted in pretty well, the genuine local links remain vitally important, especially if and when the team should hit hard times and need the public to really rally behind them.

It is also crucial that young local players can aspire to following in the footsteps of men like Johns and Humphreys who, in their time, had been inspired by the deeds of a previous generation of heroes. On the night that Ulster beat Stade Francais at Ravenhill in last season's European Cup, delighted young hooker Paul Shields recalled how, three years earlier, he had been a terrace steward for the famous semi-final victory over the same opposition there. Now it was his turn and those magical memories helped him savour the success.

When Johns came into the Ulster team, he was keenly aware of the standards that had been set in the previous few seasons and was determined to play his part in keeping the flag flying. Right from the start, he made an excellent impression. It wasn't purely his impact on the pitch which struck the old hands; indeed, Paddy was left out again for the next match after making his debut against Connacht in the autumn of 1988. He did alright, especially considering he was only 20, but, importantly for his long-term prospects, he showed all the right signs, of having the attitude and the aptitude, the appetite and the application, to make the most of his undoubted ability. "Even when Paddy was very young, just starting out with Ulster, he was so precise about everything and wanted his preparation to be perfect" recalls Denis McBride. "You knew he would do whatever it took to make the most of himself and fulfil his potential"

As befitted a guy who had won an award for good manners at school and typical of the man who was then emerging, Johns didn't go round shouting his mouth off in those early days in the Ulster changing room. "That was a great Ulster side and it was a dream come true for me to be involved with so many of the players who had beaten Australia. I knew my place and didn't really say too much. There were some really strong characters in that side, great leaders of men like David Irwin and Willie Anderson and other very distinguished internationals, but they were very good, very welcoming and supportive.

"I was studying in Newcastle when I made my debut against Connacht. I remember the flight across and being taken to Holywood Rugby Club. The media were there and I suppose that was the first time I'd had any attention of that nature. It was a very proud occasion, but I don't remember all that much about the game now, other than that we won and that I was jumping against a real man mountain of a fella called Aidan Higgins (who also played prop during his career), who later went to London Irish.

"He was a real character and could do brilliant impersonations of a cow when he'd about 10 pints of Guinness in him. You'd have sworn it was the real thing. My main memory of playing against him that day is of him flicking his hips and knocking me out of every lineout. Up until then, I'd been mainly playing Schools and age-group rugby, but that game taught me that I'd need to jump more aggressively when up against big, powerful guys. There would be no uncontested lineout ball any more and no easy rides."

Coach Williams clearly recollects Paddy's arrival on the Ulster scene. "Yeah, he'd have been about 20 and was over in Newcastle at the time. He came down to Holywood to the school where I was Headmaster at the time. This big gangly fella arrived in with his mummy. She had a cup of tea in the school while we went outside and John McDonald threw a few balls to him. One thing I certainly remember is what a modest young fellow he was."

Left out for the next game against Leinster, Johns returned for the final interpro with Munster, when he found himself opposite the then Ireland captain Donal Lenihan, a wily old campaigner and one he was to encounter in various capacities in the years to come. "Donal had a lot of experience and was good in the set-pieces" recalls Paddy. "Apart from being younger, I would have been lighter across the pitch, but he definitely knew what he was about. At that time he was on the Irish team and had been for years, the sort of player you want to test yourself against as you're coming up. He was a great lineout forward, good in the loose and generally made the most of his experience. He was coming toward the end of his career when I faced him and wouldn't have been quite at his peak, but made up for that by being a real battle-hardened campaigner and, as they would say in his native Cork, a 'cute hoor'."

Former England captain Bill Beaumont tells the story of how, as a young thruster, he fancied his chances against an ageing Willie John McBride in the Six Nations match between England and Ireland in 1975, his first international season and the Irish legend's 14th and last. Beaumont remembers eyeing up McBride standing opposite him as the first lineout formed. Next thing he knew he was coming round from a daze and play was on the far side of the pitch. Being hard and streetwise is a big help when it comes to dealing with the young pretenders. McBride, Beaumont, Lenihan and Johns all proved that in their turn. From both sides.

There was no shortage of good second row contenders around Ulster in those days, even though Gary Longwell, the man who finally won his first Ireland cap as a substitute for Johns the day he earned his 59th and last, self-deprecatingly tells the tale of making his provincial debut by default in 1991, "when even the coach bluntly admitted to the press that there was no-one else." Exile Brian McCall, like Paddy a county Armagh man, was drifting out of the picture, but the likes of Colin Morrison and John Rogers, though never capped by their country, were worthy contenders to partner the inspirational and inimitable Dungannon firebrand Anderson. Late developer Tweed, a brute beast of a man, was also to assert himself in the early 1990s, so competition for places was always intense, but Johns practised what he preached in "always seeking to make it impossible for selectors to leave me out."

Selection is out of a player's hands so, while being picked to play is the be-all and end-all, it isn't part of 'controlling the controllables' and is ultimately in the gift of others. But that doesn't mean that the ball isn't in the individual's court. By leaving nothing to chance and giving his all every time he stepped on the pitch, Johns knew he would never have anything to beat himself up about. There could and would be disappointments, blows and even feelings of injustice at times, but no regrets, no need to blame himself. Some infuriatingly enigmatic players squander their god-given gifts but Denis McBride, himself an embodiment of the same philosophy as Johns, says: "Paddy had enormous talent, obviously, but there were guys with even more who didn't achieve half as much. His determination and dedication were phenomenal and his approach to the game was always very thorough."

"I was honoured to play alongside Paddy for Ulster in his early days" says Willie Anderson. "It was a privilege because he fitted in well and was a perfectionist; you knew that you would get 110 percent. He came into the Ulster team in another era, but the best aspects of the Jimmy Davidson idolism and approach which were handed down in the days of the likes of myself and David Irwin have been carried through by Paddy and he is now handing the baton on to Jeremy Davidson so the tradition will be maintained and hopefully continue to be passed on."

Apart from natural ambition, being dedicated by nature, facing formidable competition for his place and the pressure which every player who came into the Ulster side at that time was under to play his part in help maintaining the high standards which had already been set, Johns and others also had that little extra edge as a result of feeling like Irish rugby's second class citizens.

"We felt we had to be top of the interpro tree to get people into the national team at all. There was a belief that, even if we were interpro champions, we wouldn't get more than five. Not a lot was said about it, but the feeling was always there. Ulster used it as extra motivation and we went out to prove ourselves the best season after season. At the very least, we hoped our success might be a bit of an embarrassment to the powers-that-be, though to be honest I wouldn't say it ever shamed them into redressing the balance.

"The selection system has obviously changed since then and Ulster are no longer doing as well relative to the other provinces, but I still think our guys suck the hind tit. During most of my last season, there were only two Ulster players regularly involved in the Ireland senior squad. I'm convinced, for instance, that our two young frontrow forwards, Paul Shields and Simon Best, would have been in New Zealand this summer with Ireland but for the fact that they wear the wrong colour of jersey at provincial level. That's the bottom line" he insists defiantly.

In his second season playing for Ulster, the highlight for Paddy was the game against the touring All Blacks at Ravenhill, three days after Anderson had, famously or infamously depending on your viewpoint, faced down the haka before the Test at Lansdowne Road. The images of the fiery Anderson eyeballing the fearsome All Blacks skipper Buck Shelford as the two sets of players converged in the middle of the pitch are etched into rugby folklore and the incident was still a talking point when the tourists took the field in Belfast. "The haka thing on the Saturday had been totally unexpected. It had never been done before, but it really got the adrenalin pumping, even for those of us sitting watching at home never mind the guys on the pitch."

Ironically, in light of this chapter's theme of Ulster under-representation, there were no fewer than eight northerners in the side for Ireland's 6-23 Dublin defeat on the Saturday and seven of them were on provincial duty on Tuesday night. The exception was winger Kenny Hooks, who at the time happened to be both the Maths teacher and Medallion XV rugby coach of one of the authors, as he had been concussed in the international. But fullback Rainey, who in the Test had belatedly won what proved to be his only Ireland cap following years of understudying Hugo MacNeill, leaders Irwin and Anderson, winger Keith Crossan, frontrow forwards Stevie Smith and Jimmy McCoy and blindside flanker Phil Matthews all lined out in the white jersey against the men in black. "I can remember that three of the Irish guys, Anderson, Irwin and Smith, all had black eyes from Saturday going into the Ulster game. But none of that trio were exactly shrinking violets so, who knows, maybe they had been as much sinning as sinned against!"

There were only three All Blacks, however, who appeared in both matches, loosehead prop Steve McDowell, hooker Sean Fitzpatrick and lock Gary Whetton.

The last two selections meant, respectively, that reserve hooker and future Ireland coach Warren Gatland, who had worn the No 2 jersey against both Leinster and Connacht, didn't get to play at Ravenhill, while young Johns was up against one of the tourists' top men. "I was jumping opposite Gary Whetton and barging him as best I could. It must have been having some effect, because he told McDowell, who then had a swing at me. He was a blackbelt in karate, but I took my chances and had a swing back at him anyway."

Hooks' place on the right wing was taken by Malone's Stuart Porter, a Scotland A international, with the experienced John Hewitt of London Irish, unlucky never to win a senior cap for his country, as usual partnering Irwin at centre. The halfbacks were Paddy's Dungannon club colleague Ashley Blair and Peter Russell of Instonians, who made his Test debut in Ireland's next international, the Five Nations opener against England at

Twickenham and was first choice No 10 on the New Zealand tour of 1992. Hooker Smith and tighthead McCoy were joined in the front row by Malone loosehead Mark Reynolds, Johns partnered Anderson in the engineroom and Matthews, a young Brian Robinson at No 8 and Denis McBride formed a more than useful loose forward unit.

The All Blacks' two tries in a 21-3 victory were scored by two men who went on to become cult heroes of the global game, Zinzan Brooke and Va'aiga Tuigamala, while future rugby league star Frano Botica, tour understudy to Grant Fox, converted both and kicked a hat-trick of penalties. Alan Whetton, along with his brother Gary, McDowell and Fitzpatrick, was one of four members of the World Cup winning team of 1987 to play at Ravenhill that night, along with two others who were part of that squad, Brooke and centre Bernie McCahill. Ulster's points came from a solitary Russell penalty and they never seriously threatened to topple the tourists, but put up an extremely spirited fight and had the satisfaction of restricting the All Blacks to their lowest points tally of the Irish leg of the tour.

"That was the Barry McGuigan era and, just like his fans used to do, the big crowd at Ravenhill that night were singing 'Here we go' and really getting behind us. Jimmy McCoy had a try disallowed, but we fought hard throughout. We couldn't understand why the rucking hurt so much until we realised that the All Blacks were wearing tapered rugby league studs. They really cut us up badly, very sore indeed."

That Ulster game against the All Blacks then had been Paddy's biggest to date and further whetted his appetite for playing with and against the best. Full international honours were to follow within the next 12 months and, although there was then a brief blip in the upward curve, the next time Ireland took on New Zealand in a Test, Johns was there in the green jersey.

7. IRELAND'S CALL

The night before he almost won his first Ireland cap at Parc des Princes, a champagne-charged Paddy Johns went to bed at 5 o'clock in the morning and some 10 hours later sat on the bench against France in the 1990 Five Nations. Eh?

As the veteran Irish rugby-writer Sean Diffley later wrote in the Irish Independent, that sounds like 'the stuff that Irish rugby legends are nearly made of. And reminiscent of those more leisurely days when we couldn't even spell commitment and haematomas were still bruises and half the Irish team would drop into Sean Lynch's pub the night before the match for a couple of relaxing pints.'

But surely the story doesn't square with the image we have been building of a driven, dedicated young man, utterly committed to striving for continuous improvement in his quest to realise that early dream of playing for his country.

If Labour's slogan before the last British General Election was 'Education, Education, Education', Paddy's motto throughout his career was 'preparation, preparation, preparation'. And for something so auspicious as a senior Ireland debut, he'd have wanted it to be perfect in every regard. Even in those more hedonistic days of the amateur era, rolling home hammered as the dawn broke on the day of an international would have been a bit much for anyone and utterly inconceivable for Johns, a player who strictly shunned the social side when the Irish panel met up on Saturday nights for Sunday squad sessions. Yet the above is a true tale. Better explain.

Actually, Ireland's call came all of a sudden and, although it turned out to be a false alarm in that he didn't ultimately win his first cap on that occasion, the circumstances of his emergency elevation to the senior bench that weekend in Paris remain vividly etched in his memory. Now based in Dublin at Trinity College, Johns had already represented Ireland at several subsidiary levels in that 1989-90 season and played for the Irish Students XV in the defeat at the hands of their French counterparts at Rheims the night before the full Five Nations game.

"Rheims is a major champagne region in France and the champagne was flowing in abundance at our post-match reception. After dinner, the French players took us to a club. It was a long night and a late one. The craic was mighty and it was about 5.00 in the morning by the time we got back to our hotel and hit the sack. A couple of hours later we were up again and on the coach to Paris. I can remember a stray bottle of champagne from the night before being opened and passed around the back of the bus along with a few bottles of French lager. As you can imagine everyone was in high spirits, hungover from the night before but looking forward to watching the big game at Parc des Princes."

Unknown to them, however, a crisis had developed in the Ireland camp ahead of the main match of the weekend, which Johns and his Irish Students colleagues were due to attend as spectators. Championship defeats against England and Scotland had caused typical chopping and changing in the senior side by the selectors and nowhere was the musical chairs syndrome more pronounced than in the second row, albeit that the situation was exacerbated by injury. Former captain Lenihan was ruled out of the Five Nations opener against England, so Neil Francis partnered skipper Willie Anderson, but the Leinster lock lost out to the fit-again Munsterman for the Scottish game. Although he had led the side in all previous internationals that season, Anderson was, in turn, axed for the French match along with provincial colleague David Irwin in a double whammy ditching which incensed many in Ulster and fed the persecution complex which existed in northern circles.

Johns' Dungannon and Ulster mentor was dropped to the replacements panel, with Lenihan and Francis paired in the engineroom, but Anderson cried off sick on the morning of the match in Paris, leaving Ireland with no second row cover. The fact that the Irish Students were due to attend the game offered a solution and Johns, who had been making a good impression with Ulster and various Irish representative teams, was the obvious man to call up. If they could find him, that was.

"Willie had had a dodgy steak and had been up boking all night" explains Paddy. "Apparently the IRFU people were out looking for me in the bars in Paris and they also had the gendarmes stopping every coach on the way into town to try and intercept our team bus. In the end I was told by a couple of UCD players in a bar outside the ground that the IRFU officials had been in the bar looking for me earlier and that I was to go to the team changing room in the stadium. Of course I took a while to be convinced."

Diffley, more colourfully, writes: "It was like the Day of the Jackal, Inspector Clouseaus in their white trenchcoats bristling with authority. "M'sieu Johns? Non? For Jasussake has anybody seen Paddy Johns? Where the heck are you Scarlet Pimpernel now that we need you?" Up and down the Champs Elysses the patrol cars whined and roared "Patrick Jean? Irlandais?" And all of the time . . . (he) . . . was draped over the counter of a bistro a few hundred metres from the Parc totally unaware that he was the most wanted man in Paris. And . . . it took a fair bit of persuading to dispel the notion that it was a bit of taking the mickey. But eventually the penny, or rather the centime, dropped and using his hoi polloi ticket . . . he gained primary entrance to the ground. But could he get any further?"

"I spent about 20 minutes looking for a steward or somebody who could speak English" Paddy recounts. "And when I did, he wouldn't believe my story." "Which, or course, was incredible" writes Diffley, with a huge dose of irony. "A rather dishevelled student, in untidy jeans and well-worn sweater, with the minimum value ticket, trying to talk his way into the Irish dressing room with the story of being one of the players." In the end, Paddy ran into former Ireland second row Jim Glennon, who whisked him off to the changing rooms.

"Of course, I had no kit and Willie's boots were too small for me, so a gendarme was sent back to the hotel to get my own boots. I remember though that he returned with absolutely everything from the room, so something must have been lost in translation! I was rooming with Ray Ward and the policeman took all his clothes and mine and brought them to the changing room. At least we'd known where to send him for, luckily enough, I had brought a little card with the hotel's contact details so that we'd be able to show the taxi-driver where we were staying when it was time to go back to base that night after what we anticipated would be another evening on the town."

Instead, following chaotic scenes and a mad scramble to get ready in time, Johns spent the afternoon sitting on the Irish bench as the guys in green lost 31-12 to a French team which had itself, just like the visitors, been coming off the back of two defeats in the first half of their Championship campaign. That was, of course, before the days of substitutions and neither Lenihan nor Francis had to come off injured, so Paddy was not called upon to make what would have been one of the more unlikely entrances to the Test arena. "I felt fine at the start, swept up with all the rush and excitement when Jimmy Davidson told me I was on the bench but, as the game went on and the adrenalin wore off, the effects of the alcohol and lack of sleep started to register. It was just as well I didn't get on, for it could have been ugly. Noel Mannion went down injured with about 10 minutes to go and I got up from my seat and went into the tunnel to stretch and warm up. My Irish Universities team-mates, who were on the other side of the ground told me afterwards that they thought I got such a shock when Mannion went down that I had gone into the tunnel to be sick!"

His full international debut was to come before 1990 was out but, not surprisingly, the circumstances were less dramatic. There was almost an uncanny parallel with what happened in the next year ending in nought, 2000, if we take a little bit of poetic licence regarding the details being slightly different. If Johns had indeed won his first cap that day in March 1990, it would have been as a result of coming into the Ireland match panel in place of his senior Ulster colleague Anderson who, as it happened, was never to appear in another international. Some 10 and a half years on, Gary Longwell did win his first Ireland cap when he came on against Japan as a substitute for his senior Ulster colleague Johns who, as it happened, was never to appear in another international!

Paddy's day, the one he had dreamt of as a schoolboy and worked assiduously ever since to bring about, came on 27th October 1990 when he finally realised his ambition of playing for his country at full international level. The call-up for the one-off autumn Test against Argentina genuinely came as a surprise to young Paddy, who obviously held strong aspirations, but felt that his time may not yet have arrived. "I had no idea. Really didn't see it coming, even though I had played for the B and Under 25 teams in the previous season. I guess the selectors saw it as a chance to blood somebody new, especially with the World Cup the following year."

Johns was not the only new face against Argentina. He was one of three new caps along with Bective No 8 Phil Lawlor and Blackrock's scrum-half with French antecedents, Alain Rolland, who incidentally was to be the referee at Paddy's farewell testimonial match. By the time the Dungannon lock hung up his boots, Rolland was well on his way to becoming one of the most respected whistlers in the international game. Lawlor these days is a Provincial Development Manager with the IRFU.

Paddy admits that a lot of the details surrounding his international debut are lost to him now. "I've had too many knocks to the head since" he concludes with a grin when asked for chapter and verse on the days and hours leading up to taking the field at Lansdowne Road where he had been so captivated watching others do so a number of years earlier. For example he cannot recall when or how he was actually told of his selection, but does remember that the team was announced publicly two weeks prior to the game. The resulting barrage of media hype was on a much bigger scale than anything with which Paddy had previously been involved, both because of the superior standard of rugby and, as a new cap, he received more than his fair share of attention. It was a novelty then to some extent, but never a part of the game he was to particularly relish.

"Obviously it was a much bigger stage than I'd been part of before, with many more interviews. It was much, much more intense and I suppose being asked about my feelings and to dissect and analyse the whole thing kinda added to the pressure. In ways, I feel I had too long to think about the upcoming game. It's like when you are about to do a bungee jump" he analogises. "You just have to decide you are going to do it and then jump. If you take too long to think about it, it gets harder and you end up chickening out."

A total contrast then to the frenetic French experience when he came within an injury on the day of winning his first cap. But did the relatively long wait from hearing he had been picked make Paddy feel he was losing his bottle as the moment actually approached? "Absolutely not" he retorts. "I felt my preparation before the game was good and I was itching to get started, to get out there, get on with it. This was what I had been working for and playing would be the bit which came naturally, the thing I could get stuck into."

The players had gathered at their traditional match base of the Berkeley Court Hotel in Dublin on the Wednesday evening the week of the match, as was customary in those amateur days. No meeting up in the Glenview in Wicklow the previous Sunday back then. The fellow Ulstermen were obviously well known faces to Paddy, but he was not so familiar with the representatives from the other three provinces. He would have played against most of them and with some of them for other representative teams, but many were essentially strangers. That illustrates a major difference between the amateur and professional eras, with many more squad sessions and sporadic training camps familiarising the country's leading players with each other before they break into the Test team. The one exception should be the British and Irish Lions, given that they are a composite touring team which only comes together once every four years, but even they managed a week-long crash course in team-building exercises and bonding stuff before leaving for Australia last summer.

Johns was one of five Ulstermen in the starting line-up for the Argentinian game, being joined by wings Kenny Hooks and Keith Crossan, and the Malone pair of hooker John McDonald and Denis McBride, who was to be his tried and trusted comrade in many battles down through the coming years. His engineroom partner Lenihan, who had taken over from Anderson for that game in Paris during the previous Five Nations, continued as captain while, as well as the other two new caps, Greystones prop Nick Popplewell was getting a second chance nearly a year after a rough baptism against the touring All Blacks. He too was destined for a long and distinguished Test career but, like Johns, not before a period in the wilderness. Experienced Lansdowne tighthead Des Fitzgerald was actually to be the only forward to start the next international, while the pack was completed by Connacht No 8 Noel Mannion, who had switched to blindside to accommodate Lawlor.

Popplewell for John Fitzgerald, McDonald for Terry Kingston, Johns for Francis and Lawlor for Pat O'Hara in a reshuffled loose forward unit were the four changes from the pack which had started in the closing Championship clash with Wales at Lansdowne Road seven months earlier, when Ireland avoided a whitewash by winning 14-8. There was only one alteration behind the scrum though, Rolland taking over from Michael Bradley, so Kenny Murphy remained at fullback with the 1985 Triple Crown winning centre combo of Michael Kiernan and Brendan Mullin in harness as usual. Kingston, John Fitzgerald, Bradley, Cork Con outhalf Ralph Keyes, Vinny Cunningham and the uncapped Mick Galwey made up the replacements panel.

After old acquaintances were rekindled and introductions made, the pack had a scrummaging session on Wednesday night and further squad sessions on the Thursday and Friday. "It was probably too much training in terms of overdoing the heavy work" Paddy reflects, "but we didn't train as much together then or as regularly as we do now, so I guess we had to pack it all in and make the most of the time." Surprisingly, in a way, Paddy can't actually remember now who he roomed with, but feels he fitted into the general environment reasonably easily.

He was also conscious that his second row partner would be the captain. Lenihan was a player he had already come up against at provincial level and who had won 46 Ireland caps and a couple of Triple Crowns as well as having been the midweek skipper on the previous year's Lions tour. The best part of a decade later, Johns was to pass Lenihan's mark as the second most capped Irish second row of all time behind the legendary Willie John McBride but, back then, the Cork Con man had very much been there and done it, whereas Paddy was relatively untried and unknown. "Donal was the first big name I came up against directly when playing for Ulster and then two years later he was my captain and second row partner when I won my first cap for Ireland. Many years later, he was manager of the Irish team when I was captain, so we've had a long association in one way or another.

"I first got to know Paddy when playing against Ulster," says Lenihan. "My first impression was of how committed and single-minded he was. He was going to play for Ireland and that was it. Despite this, when he came onto the international scene, he probably didn't have as much confidence as he should have. I've always had huge respect for him on and off the pitch, though it would be fair to say that, after the performance of the pack that day, if you'd said he was going to get 50 caps I don't think anybody would have believed it.

"I remember the training session on the Thursday. He was jumping in the middle of the line and he'd never jumped there before. He was incredibly nervous and I remember staying back at the end of the session, going through the whole thing with him. He wanted to get it right, which was typical of him both then and throughout his career. Paddy is the type of fella who is totally methodical. Everything had to be written down for him and explained to him and then he'd go through the whole game in his mind."

Everyone has the ambition in them somewhere to represent their country. For Paddy Johns, this would be the realisation of a goal, which had begun as faceless green jerseys on the verge of sleep, through weekdays spent at training grounds and not in the pub, weekends at airports and making sure rugby always came first. "The day of the game was a huge big day for me. I felt emotionally charged; my childhood dream was coming true. This was it. When we went to internationals, my friends and I would always meet at the Berkeley Court and then go on to Lansdowne Road from there. But this time I was taking a different route! I remember, however, seeing Andy Oliver, who had come over from Edinburgh, as the bus was driving in through the back gate of Lansdowne Road. It gave me a huge lift to see him."

Oliver recalls: "Paddy had asked me if I was coming across for his first cap, but I didn't get a flight until the last minute so he didn't know I'd be there. When I was walking up to the ground, the Irish bus was arriving and I saw him sitting about the middle, looking as white as a ghost! He was always very good at getting his friends tickets for the big matches. Even when he was captain, he'd ring up from the team hotel in Dublin to see if you were coming down for the game. He never changed, never forgot about his friends. I spend a lot of time travelling abroad and had been away for about a year before the 1995 World Cup. Paddy told me that if I could make it to South Africa for the tournament, he would make arrangements. I arrived in from India just before it started and found that he had organized everything for me: accommodation, match tickets, the lot. It was just as well, for I'd picked up a dose of the sh*ts and was relieved to find all my plans were in place."

Support seemed to come from all over the UK to see Paddy in action on the occasion of his first cap. "I also had about eight or 10 friends from Newcastle who'd hired a mini bus and come over to see my play. Amazing. Again, it was great just to know they were there, along with all of my family."

Once on the bus, time seemed to slow down and Paddy found himself watching the seconds tick by until it would finally be time to hear the whistle for kick-off and get on with the task in hand. "To be honest, I found the whole build-up a bit of a drag. I just wanted to get started. We walked into the changing rooms and our jerseys had been left on the pegs. I can't remember much about who said what or what the general mood was. I did feel nervous before the game. Nervous, but not sick. Some guys throw up before games, Paul Wallace virtually every week! But I've never been like that. I've never been physically sick." But nerves gave way to something else come anthem time. "When the band played, I felt like I've always felt since when it's been played, like I always feel now even when I just hear it, because of the associations it holds with my international matches. It was just like someone had stuck adrenalin intravenously into my arm. The waiting was over, the nerves were forgotten. I was just ready to play."

"The media attention was huge," agrees fellow debutant Alain Rolland. "You felt as though everybody should know you walking down the street. For me though, there are some painful memories. My friend John McDonald was killed a few days beforehand and it put it all in perspective and took away a lot of the fuss that would have been there. As a result, I didn't have too much time to dwell on pre-match nerves."

Paddy and Alain were far from the only new boys on the field that day for, apart from other Irish debutant Lawlor, there were no fewer than nine new caps in an Argentinian side captained by legendary flyhalf Hugo Porta, then 39 years of age and in the twilight of a most distinguished career. Among the newcomers were four of the tight five, including the two locks, Perdo Sporleder, still only 19, and the 22-year old German Llanes, both of whom were to become all-time Puma greats. A lot more was also to be heard of debutant teenage prop Federico Mendez, who had been a very late call-up for the tour. Another leading name in that Argentinian team was centre Diego Cuesta Silva, but most were unknown back then, including two teenage bench backs who were to be part of the side which ended Ireland's 1999 World Cup hopes almost a decade later, Lisandro Arbizu and Gonzalo Camardon.

Argentina, although rugged, formidable and dangerous were a less heralded force in those days and, given Ireland's home advantage against such an inexperienced team from one of the lesser nations, the public expected a convincing, maybe comfortable, win from Lenihan's team. It didn't work out that way. Johns' Ulster colleague Hooks scored a try, as did Kiernan, who also kicked four penalties, but it took the last of them deep in a seemingly interminable period of second half stoppage time to give Ireland a 20-18 victory and spare their blushes. It wasn't to spare a lot of that side from the selectorial axe though.

"The game itself went in a flash. I don't remember any specifics. I don't remember my first contribution, or a lot about the game as a whole. There was a definite step up in pace and Argentina had a strong pack. They gave us a lot of trouble in the scrums and with their mauling. We won, but we were lucky to win." And afterwards? "I felt exhausted, but exhilarated. Like I had run hard all day and given it all I had. When all's said and done, that's all you can do and all anyone can ask of you is that you give it your best shot."

An attitude which those who have played both with and against him know is characteristic of Paddy Johns. He was to be uncompromising throughout each and every one of his 59 caps, though the second had to wait. Unfortunately for Paddy, despite achieving his dream goal, topped with a winning result, the fairytale was put on hold for almost two years, when for the next game, against France in the following Spring's Five Nations, he was dropped. Ecstasy to agony within what seemed like a few short weeks.

"Eight of us were dropped, so I wasn't on my own, but that was no consolation and I was gutted. It wouldn't have mattered whether I was the only one or whether it had been all 15 who got the boot. That was just how the selectors were in those days, very fickle. One bad result or disappointing performance, or if there was criticism of the team, they just took the head staggers and made sweeping changes. Instead of looking at what had gone wrong, they just got the guillotine out and went mad. To some extent we were victims of the mindset which prevailed at that period, but the number of fellow casualties in no way eased the blow. I went from the biggest high to a massive low. I'd never really been dropped before in rugby and it was hard to get used to."

After the game, Lansdowne prop Des Fitzgerald, who was to be the only forward retained for the next Test, is alleged to have briefed one or more members of the media that Johns was largely to blame for Ireland's setpiece struggle, mainly on the basis that he had proved a weak scrummager.

"I felt I'd done alright in the game" insists Paddy. "I don't really remember how we did in the scrums, except that their pack was big and strong, a typical Argentinian outfit really. Myself and Donal Lenihan were both natural front-jumpers but, as he was the established player and captain, he wasn't for moving so I, as the young guy who had come in, had to jump in the middle of the lineout which I'd not really done before. But I thought I'd got round the pitch well and my work rate was high. In any case, there was no real feedback for players in those days, so you didn't really know how those who picked the team felt you had done.

"And, back then, it wasn't purely the coach who picked the team, but a panel of selectors. Apart from the horse-trading between provinces, that also allowed people to hide behind the 'it wasn't my team' defence and answers would have been hard to obtain. I think the current arrangement of one man picking the team and the buck stopping with him is a much better system, though obviously you're screwed if that particular coach doesn't really rate you, or doesn't like you for some other reason. In principle though, that has been a change for the better in terms of how the Irish team is picked, even though I'm sure there were some worthy enough people who served as selectors down through the years."

Perhaps international honours had come knocking too early, before he was really ready? After all, Paddy himself confesses to having been surprised to be brought in against Argentina. "I was a young guy who they wanted to have a look at. I thought I was ready and I so wanted to play, but unfortunately after the Argentina game, the selectors obviously disagreed." There had been a lot of media interest, especially in the debutant Johns, in the fortnight leading up to the international, and it was a novelty for the young man to read about himself in the papers. In the couple of days after the game though, as some of the papers were sharply critical of Ireland's display, was his attitude to reading about himself thereafter affected?

"Not really. I suppose as time goes on, players take less notice of what's written, partly because it's less of a novelty after a while and also because there'll be a degree of disillusionment. Most players won't mind constructive criticism or whatever, but you'd get annoyed at times with inconsistency, ignorance or unfairness. Journalists are like punters, selectors and even coaches in that each will tend to see things differently and you will inevitably end up valuing and respecting the opinions of some more than others. In general, my attitude to being criticised in the papers would be the same as being left out of a side. At one level, I learnt to largely dismiss it as 'simply someone's opinion', but it also served to just increase my determination to do better, to prove the doubters wrong."

Willie Anderson had no doubt his star pupil would bounce back. "Paddy started very early for Ireland, maybe too early, but he learned a lot in that period out and developed a very strong 'the next time I get in, I'm staying there' determination. He was durable because he came through the Ulster system and was influenced by the team loyalty and oneness and work ethic which he had seen there from the start of his adult career. The other big factor which would have convinced me that when he got back in he'd be there for a period was his own application and consistency. The guy never missed an opportunity to learn. He was always keen to leave no stone unturned and would spend as long after sessions as he did during them in order to get whatever it was right, be it blocking, rucking, mauling. He ultimately reaped the rewards."

You could argue that he'd made it, albeit briefly and was now Patrick Stephen Johns, Irish international rugby player, so even though he was rightly disappointed, the dream goal could be ticked off the list and it didn't matter so much if he was never selected again. Yes? No. Not on your nelly.

"There's a standing joke round clubs about being a one-cap wonder, and I was determined not to be one. It just made me all the more determined, and when the second one came, I was relieved I'd got a second chance and I didn't want to wait another two years for the next one."

8. DON'T CRY FOR ME ARGENTINA

On the outside again, picking up the pieces. Autumn internationals and Ireland have never seemed to mix all that readily and Paddy was one of those to pay the price for the team's close call against Argentina. Unlike in Lens 10 years later, or indeed a young Federico Mendez on Paul Ackford at Twickenham the following Saturday, the Puma punch hadn't been a knockout blow, but there were certainly consequences in the form of collateral damage.

Although Ireland had finally sneaked a victory over the visitors thanks to referee Colin Hawke's largesse with his calculation of just how much time should be added, the country wasn't impressed by the performance and neither, it seemed, were the selectors. In one of the most dramatic clearouts in Irish rugby history, there were, to put it mildly, sweeping changes for the first Five Nations match of the season just over three months later. Lansdowne prop Des Fitzgerald was, remarkably, the sole survivor from a pack pummelled by the Pumas and there were no fewer than four new caps among the forwards when Ireland faced France in Dublin at the start of February. There were a further three changes behind the scrum, including the switch of Kenny Hooks from right wing to left to accommodate a newcomer, one Simon Geoghegan, on what at that stage was his preferred side.

It was a dramatic changing of the guard, with the ushering in of half a dozen new caps, one of whom, the London Irish scrum-half Rob Saunders, was sensationally named as the new captain. That was the first time a man had captained Ireland on debut since Jim Ritchie had led the side against Scotland in 1956, the former Queen's University pivot taking over at the tender age of 22 from Lenihan, skipper against Argentina, who had been ruled out of the entire Championship with a shoulder and neck problem.

Saunders' nomination among such drastic changes was probably symbolic of the selectors' over-the-top mood swings and whimsical decisions of the time, though Johns did rate him highly. "I played with Rob for Ulster Schools and he was an excellent prospect" recalls Paddy. "People were talking about him as the next Colin Patterson, which was high praise indeed and I think he would have done very well but for deciding relatively early that he would put his business interests before rugby. He was a very jovial guy, very confident and, he'd probably say himself, would have been quite cocky in ways. I'd imagine the selectors quite liked the way he was so assured and they pitched him straight in as captain at the start of that Five Nations."

Lenihan and veteran Ulster winger Keith Crossan were ruled out of the French match by injury, but that still left a lot of scapegoats to be culled by the wielding of the selectorial axe as neither the old hands nor the young guns were spared. Not for the first or last time in his distinguished international career, diminutive Ulster flanker Denis McBride was among the victims as was his Malone clubmate John McDonald, both men whom Johns played under at provincial level. Connacht No 8 Noel Mannion, who had been deployed out of position at blindside to accommodate a debut for Phil Lawlor in the middle of the back row, lost his place as did the latter and the other two debutants against Argentina, pivot Alain Rolland and Johns.

Paddy's cause was, admittedly, not helped by the fact that he had been suffering from injury in the lead-up to the Championship, though he is far from convinced that he would have survived the cut anyway in the circumstances. While mercifully not finishing up as one-cap wonders, a dubious distinction normally reserved for those Irishmen unlucky enough to make their Test debuts in that green graveyard, Parc des Princes, Lawlor and Rolland were to make little future impact at international level. They ended up with three caps apiece, but Johns and future Lions prop Nick Popplewell, still a novice at that stage too having gone into the Argentina game with just a truncated and traumatic first cap against the All Blacks a year earlier under his belt, were to bounce back emphatically. Popplewell got back in on the following summer's Namibian tour and made the 1991 World Cup squad, scoring two tries in the tournament opener against Zimbabwe but, although Johns had to wait a further year for a second chance, he also lasted longer, ultimately making 59 Test appearances to the frontrow forward's 48.

Joining backline boys Saunders and Geoghegan, the half dozen new caps for the French game included two Ulster loose forwards in Brian Robinson and Gordon Hamilton, along with a couple of relatively short, solidly built locks who were later to join forces at Shannon, one Mick Galwey, and Brian Rigney, then with Greystones. Paco Fitzgerald returned at loosehead for Popplewell, Phil Matthews, who was to succeed Saunders as captain for the summer tour and World Cup at the end of the year, was back at blindside for Mannion and big Stevie Smith took over again from his smaller provincial colleague McDonald in the middle of the front row.

Many of those who came in did so on the strength of Ireland's 16-0 victory over their Scottish counterparts in a B international at Ravenhill a few days before Christmas 1990. Some staked very strong individual claims in Belfast and others did well enough to be swept into the senior side on the back of what was a good result set against the disappointing display by the main team against Argentina back in the autumn. The four new caps in the pack to face France, namely Galwey, Rigney, Robinson and Hamilton, had all featured in that B game, as had Saunders, though in fact the second string Irish team at Ravenhill had not been captained by the pivot but by Wanderers flanker Kelvin Leahy.

It all seemed like a brave new world as Ireland earned themselves a 10-6 interval lead, including a Smith touchdown, but a Saunders mistake let the French in for a try and, although Michael Kiernan kicked the hosts ahead again, the gallic geniuses got back in front with a penalty and added a late converted try to make the final score 13-21. When Ireland went to Cardiff for their next game, half of the six survivors from the Argentinian game were dropped, with Kenny Murphy, Hooks and Kiernan all biting the dust. This paved the way for the inclusion of a further trio of new caps, fullback Jim Staples, versatile three-quarter Jack Clarke and David Curtis, the Zimbabwean-born centre who was plying his trade with London Irish. The last two had both played in that B game against the Scots.

An exciting game at the Arms Park ended in a 21-21 draw, Staples and Clarke both getting tries on debut and Geoghegan making his mark with a super score which pointed to his great potential. If the game contained a glimpse of Geoghegan's genius though, it also featured another recurring theme for another of Irish rugby's top talents of the 1990s. Staples, like the wing wonder to be plagued by injuries throughout his international career, damaged an elbow and had to go off.

For the visit of England, there was a change in the second row, Galwey being dropped for the first of what was to be a remarkable 14 times in his Ireland career, but that didn't mean a call for Johns. Instead, the selectors returned to the enigmatic Neil Francis, who had been a regular throughout the previous season's Five Nations, as they looked for some lineout presence. Crossan returned for Clarke on the left wing. Ireland competed reasonably well before going down 7-16 and an unchanged team then displayed some now customary flair at Murrayfield, where three of the visiting three-quarters scored tries.

Geoghegan make it three in his first three Tests, while centre Brendan Mullin went over for the 15th time in an international, breaking George Stephenson's 61-year old record to become his country's leading try-scorer. But Ireland lost 28-25, giving them a record of three defeats and a draw in the 1991 Five Nations. In spite of the results, there was a bit of a buzz about how Ireland had played, but any sense of optimism was soon to be dissipated on the disastrous summer tour of Namibia. Meantime, Brian Smith's brief and unsatisfactory flirtation with Irish rugby ended on a sour note with a defection to rugby league back in Oz amid accusations of duplicity and double-dealing following denials that he was about to change codes.

But what of Paddy Johns? Part of that rather ill-fated, if ultimately victorious, 90-odd minutes against Argentina and then left to wait and wonder if and when the call would come again. Bypassed by two even newer kids on the block in Galwey and Rigney, who by the end of the Championship had got in and established themselves. Time was on his side alright, but being young meant he also had to contend with the impatience of youth, exacerbated by the frustrated desire to show what he could really do. To be sunk without trace for what was not so much a poor performance personally as collective under-achievement by the team would have been cruel indeed. Given his natural work ethic and a horror of the one-cap wonder stigma, it wasn't that big a challenge for Johns to continue plugging away trying to improve and develop his game, but how easy was it to keep believing?

Once you've got a taste of Test rugby, you don't want to step back again. He didn't feel he had done badly, things were still going well with Ulster and subsidiary Irish teams and he was learning all the time from the likes of Anderson. All he needed was another chance. "Playing for Ireland added to my confidence more than the blow of being dropped knocked it. There had been no-one capped at Trinity for a long time, so that was a real honour and I just wanted to go on and achieve more. I certainly continued to work very hard and there were games that Spring for Irish teams at various levels, so that helped keep me involved in representative rugby."

Seven weeks before making his full international debut against Argentina, Johns had started the season by playing for Ireland Under 25's in a 36-17 victory over Spain at

Thomond Park, when he partnered Galwey in the engineroom. Rolland and Lawlor had also appeared in that game, as had Staples, Clarke, Geoghegan, Paddy's old Irish Schools colleague Nicky Barry, and a trio of full internationals in Vinny Cunningham, Terry Kingston and Gary Halpin. Leahy skippered the side. The following Spring, instead of being on senior side duty, Johns found himself representing the Irish Universities on the first two Five Nations weekends, being part of victories over the French, 9-7 at the Mardyke in Cork, and Welsh, a thumping triumph by 27-3 at Newport, respectively. He missed the Universities' notable 17-16 win against England because of being involved in the Spring's only B international fixture, which resulted in an excellent 24-10 success for the Irish shadow side at Donnybrook.

With Francis now back as Rigney's Test team partner, Galwey dropped down from the senior side to link up again with Johns in a B outfit led by experienced pivot Michael Bradley. Michael Kiernan, now usurped in the main team by Curtis, also played as did Popplewell, Pat O'Hara, John Sexton and Jack Clarke, thus adding up to nine full internationals in all, while Colin Wilkinson, Richard Wallace, Barry, Paul McCarthy and Mick Fitzgibbon were later to play for their country at the highest level. The sole exception was Cork Con hooker James O'Riordan. England fielded a very strong side, especially the backrow of Dean Ryan, Tim Rodber and Neil Back, with other notables including Graham Dawe, Nigel Redman, Tony Underwood and Ian Hunter. "In those days, the England B side would have been more of a national Second XV if you like than more recently, when they have tended to use their A team more for development purposes." Paddy had the satisfaction of scoring a try that evening and well remembers "having a great night after that win!"

A week later, Johns was brought back down to earth when the Irish Universities team was humbled 3-22 by their Japanese counterparts at Ravenhill and his representative season ended with another defeat the following weekend, when the Irish Students lost 16-12 to Scotland in Edinburgh. The Students team was captained by Oxford University No 8 Mark Egan, featured Barry at flyhalf and included a quartet of Johns' fellow Ulstermen in Queen's winger James Harley, his future Dungannon colleague centre Alan Burns, hooker Michael Patton and pivot Andy Matchett, who went on to be a European Cup winner with Ulster in 1999. A young Doddie Weir was playing on the blindside flank for the Scots, with Carl Hogg at No 8, Stewart Campbell in the second row and Rowan Shepherd at outhalf.

In those days, with no regular extended squad get-togethers and no contact with the coaches, there was no real feedback either on performance or where you stood. You waited until the team was picked for the next game and, if you weren't involved, found out through the media. "No-one was in touch with me after the match against Argentina, so as well as Roly Meates at Trinity, it would have been people like Willie Anderson who I would have turned to and talked to about my game and what I needed to work on. As a second row himself, he would have helped me with the basic skills, but also in terms of my whole approach, mental attitude and so forth. He would have been a sort of mentor for me I suppose."

"I was disappointed for him at the time" says Anderson. "He mightn't have been quite ready, but if you're going to bring in a young fella who is thought to be good enough, it is silly not to persevere with them. Paddy probably also suffered from the tendency to make sweeping changes which existed in those days and the fact that, back then, Argentina weren't rated as highly as now. But it served to make him much stronger and more determined to achieve. As I'd say to any international, it's harder to stay there than to get there, but Paddy showed then and throughout his career that he's made of the right stuff. I gave him what help and support I could, but he was strong himself."

That season brought a new departure for the Irish squad in the form of what was supposed to be a warm-weather training camp in Portugal over the festive period and Paddy was pleased to be involved, but any notions of a spot of winter sun were badly misplaced. "It rained every day we were there. Really torrential rain too. The drainage seemed to be poor so, when we were training, we were simply sliding about on top of the water. There might have been better conditions back home at the time, but the concept was a step forward. Funnily enough, the weather was also dreadful when we were in Atlanta on a similar exercise a few years later."

Paddy didn't feel the need to work on any specific skills after being left out of the Ireland side following his debut, but continued to strive for improvement in his general game. "There were no particular technical areas that I focused on, just worked on all aspects and, of course, the natural response was to just train harder and develop myself physically. I set out to improve my fitness, putting in extra training, extra work in the gym."

Johns has no retrospective sense of any silver linings to being axed or of it doing him any particular good in terms of his long-term career, but getting in had certainly whetted his appetite and then being out again gave him a real hunger to get back for a greater taste of Test rugby. Touring Namibia may not, at first thought, be the stuff of dreams for players from the established nations, yet it was deeply disappointing for Johns to miss out on that July 1991 trip as he sought to get his foot back on the bottom rung of the international ladder, especially with time running out ahead of the second World Cup. The three locks chosen for the African adventure were Francis and the pair who had come in after him during the season, Galwey and Rigney. When the last-named tore cruciate knee ligaments on tour, ruling him out of the World Cup, the selectors summoned former captain Lenihan, now fit again after missing the Five Nations.

Disappointed not to be chosen, Paddy went off with Kirsty "on a cheap holiday to Bilbao in Spain", perhaps fretting that others would become even more established in his absence. But, for Ireland, the tour was a complete disaster. Admittedly, Namibia weren't the worst side in the world, having beaten Italy twice and Zimbabwe, while the tourists did suffer from stomach upsets and struggled to cope with playing at an altitude of over 5,000 feet. After beating the Namibian second string 45-16 in the tour opener, Ireland lost the first Test 15-6 without the ill Keith Crossan. St Mary's centre Cunningham wore the No 10 jersey in the absence of the departed Brian Smith, leaving Fitzgerald's team effectively without either a genuine outhalf or a recognised goal-kicker. The other changes from the final Five Nations match saw Popplewell make the first of 22 Test starts at loosehead in the next 23 internationals and O'Hara play at openside instead of Hamilton. Brendan Mullin was the unlikely converter of a penalty try, but that was the extent of Ireland's scoring.

For the second Test, Crossan was fit again but Geoghegan ruled out, while both flankers, tour captain Matthews and O'Hara, were unable to play due to illness, so Mannion made a return to Test rugby in the No 6 jersey with Hamilton coming in at openside. Lenihan, who had played in the 35-4 midweek win only 24 hours after arriving in the country, came straight into the second Test team to take over from the injured Rigney as engineroom partner for Francis ahead of original tourist Galwey. In the event, the future Munster captain entered the fray a quarter of an hour into the second half when Francis had to go off, while Crossan left the field at halftime which meant a first cap for Barry in a backline reshuffle. With Matthews missing, Saunders resumed as skipper. But Ireland went down 26-15 to complete an embarrassing 2-0 series defeat, surely leaving everything up for grabs in terms of places in the World Cup squad that autumn. Being beaten in both Tests in Namibia might have been adjudged considerably worse than being pushed by the Pumas in Dublin.

Ireland's struggles in Africa held out hope for the fringe players who hadn't made the trip, but life is all about timing and the imminence of the World Cup at the start of the next season militated against the chances of change. "The fact that Ireland didn't go well in Namibia gave me a boost in terms of thinking that I'd got a chance, but I knew that time wasn't on my side with the World Cup coming up so quickly, so I didn't build up that much hope. When I missed out on the warm-up games, against Gloucester and Malone, it was a bad sign and there was little time or opportunity for outsiders to stake a claim even though the Irish team didn't exactly impress.

"In those days too, you were either in or you were out and there was no-one contacted me to say that I was in their thoughts, or on standby or anything like that. While, by that stage, I wasn't really expecting to be involved, not being in the World Cup squad was still disappointing. Playing in a World Cup is such a huge goal for any player and, although I was young enough to stand a chance of going to the next one, four years is a long time. Anyway, when you're young you want everything here and now and there's maybe also a tendency to think that you're better than you actually are."

So he spent the tournament looking on from the outside, an Irish fan like the rest of us, but, by his own admission, understandably enough picking a few holes and feeling he could have done more than the men in possession. "Absolutely, you're sitting there thinking that you could do better, it's human nature I suppose" says Paddy. "If you have the necessary levels of self-belief, then naturally you would back yourself to do a good job. I think if you see people perform exceptionally well, you've hopefully enough honesty to recognise that but, if that isn't really the case, then it's frustrating. I was looking at the guys in my position and not seeing they had much to offer that I didn't."

Those were the days when World Cup squads only numbered 26 rather than the modern day 30 and, even with Rigney ruled out, there were still three locks ahead of Paddy in the pecking order. Former captain Lenihan was there, as was the much-vaunted Francis and, unlike for most of the rest of the decade, Galwey got the nod over the Ulsterman for the tournament, which took place in the northern hemisphere during October. In contrast to the clearout after the Argentinian game, the unsuccessful Namibian tourists were collectively given another chance with few exceptions, in a squad captained by Ulster flanker Phil Matthews. There were no uncapped players included.

Ralph Keyes, who had earlier been denied by the dubious presence of Smith, was fit-again after missing the Namibian tour due to injury and came in for Barry to enjoy a good World Cup as first choice outhalf. The Cork Con man had his limitations, but did a satisfactory job in the No 10 jersey and his presence meant that Ireland had a reputable and reliable goal-kicker, who contributed no fewer than 68 points in the four matches.

Terry Kingston and Gary Halpin, both of whom were to feature prominently in the next World Cup in South Africa four years later, joined John Fitzgerald in the reserve frontrow which took the field for the second match against Japan. Mannion, with two touchdowns, and O'Hara both came into the backrow for that game as Ciaran Fitzgerald rotated his resources, scoring three tries between them in a not entirely convincing 32-16 victory. That followed a 55-11 annihilation of Zimbabwe first up, No 8 Robinson making history by touching down four times, a feat to be emulated by Keith Wood against the USA in the 1999 tournament opener at the same venue, with prop Popplewell bagging a brace of tries and Geoghegan and Curtis claiming one apiece. Keyes' haul of 23 points broke Ollie Campbell's previous record of 22 as Ireland served up their Sunday best in the first ever Lansdowne Road international to be played on the sabbath.

Galwey had also got a go in the Japanese game in place of Lenihan, but Ireland fielded what was perceived to be their strongest side for the crunch group game against Scotland at Murrayfield three days later. Victory would have given the guys in green a quarter-final against the still little known Samoans, who had shocked Wales, with the losers facing the much-fancied Wallabies in the last eight. The game will forever be remembered for the appalling challenge on Staples by Scottish flanker and captain Finlay Calder and the fullback's failure to fully recover his composure was to prove costly.

In a tight affair, the trusty boot of Keyes had edged the Irish into a 15-9 lead, but Staples' failure to hold a hoist from Scottish pivot Gary Armstrong allowed 1990 Grand Slam winning hero Tony Stanger to put replacement Graham Shiel over for a try which was to turn the tide. Gavin Hastings converted to level the scores and then kicked a penalty. He also added the points to a late try from Armstrong and, although the Scots, who were to go on to lose to England in a dour semi-final, weren't really worth a 24-15 victory, it left a slightly deflated Ireland to tackle Australia.

Never mind about where you were when the news of Princess Diana's death came through or, for the older reader, the assassination of President Kennedy. All Irish rugby fans will surely hold vivid memories of a certain try as long as we live. North flanker Gordon Hamilton will forever be remembered as the man who raised the spirits of a nation with his famous gallop to glory, only for Ireland's dreams to be dashed in the cruellest circumstances in the dying seconds.

Australia, who had beaten Ireland on home soil at the same stage of the inaugural tournament in 1987, a game featuring five of those on Dublin duty in green jerseys in Mullin, Fitzgerald, Lenihan, Francis and Matthews, took an early lead with a try from the wing wizard of Oz, David Campese, converted by Michael Lynagh. But two Keyes penalties made it 6-6 at the break and the same player dropped a goal to again peg the Aussies back to level terms in response to a Lynagh penalty early in the second period.

That man Campese scored another converted try, but Keyes kicked another penalty to keep Ireland in touch and then came the magical moment six minutes from the end. The mercurial Campese went from Australian hero to villain as he failed to deal with a kick down the line from Staples and Jack Clarke, filling in for the injured Crossan, was up to gather the ball. He offloaded to the supporting Hamilton, the openside doing superbly to reach the corner and Keyes' magnificent touchline conversion doing justice to what looked likely to be the most memorable try ever scored at the world's oldest international stadium.

Ireland led 18-15 with time fast running out, but a bad call by Saunders when he fielded a kick ahead and returned it downfield instead of putting it out of play allowed the Aussies to counter for one last time. Winger Rob Egerton kicked back down and a touch by Brian Robinson in the Irish 22 gave the Wallabies a scrum five which led to a match-winning try for Lynagh, who had just spurned the more conservative option of going for a drop goal which, if successful, would have levelled the scores. The last twist of a dramatic tale was heartbreaking for the gallant greens and Ireland were left to watch from the sidelines as Australia returned to Lansdowne Road to knock out holders and neighbours New Zealand in the semis before beating England in a low-scoring final at Twickenham.

"I remember that Australian game, watching on a portable television in my rooms at Trinity, thinking I could have been there as a player, but then being caught up in the whole excitement of the thing. The noise would virtually have carried from Lansdowne Road to where I was. It was stirring stuff for anyone watching but, for me, it added petrol to the fire that was burning in me to get back and made me even more determined not only to earn a second cap but to make an impact when I did. My feeling that afternoon was 'I'll be back'. I wanted that second cap very badly, though when I got it, I then found that I was just as keen to get the third and the fourth and so on. I was always very hungry for the next cap no matter how many I won. Maybe that's what kept me going for so long."

One of Paddy's frustrations in relation to the 1991 World Cup was the feeling that Lenihan was now past his best, even his sell-by date, and that he was being picked mainly on reputation. Lenihan did finally reach the end of the road at Test level after a distinguished international career spanning 11 years in which he garnered 52 caps when Ireland lost their opening Five Nations fixture against Wales in the Spring. World Cup hero Hamilton missed the match due to injury, meaning a first cap for Mick Fitzgibbon of Shannon, while there also changes on both wings from the line-up for the Australian quarter-final. Crossan returned for Clarke, while Garryowen's Richard Wallace, who had been blooded as a sub in the first Test in Namibia the previous summer and was the first of three brothers who were to play for Ireland, came in for Geoghegan, who was absent due to a family illness.

Wallace, a future team-mate and close friend of Paddy Johns during their time together at Saracens, scored a try on his Championship debut after Ireland had turned around with only three Keyes penalties and a 9-6 interval lead to show for their dominance of the opening period. But Neil Jenkins, that points-machine who has punished Test teams throughout the intervening decade, kicked two penalties to keep Wales in touch and they ultimately snatched a one-point victory with an unconverted try.

The defeat was the end of the line for two great stalwarts, Ulster winger Crossan bowing out along with Lenihan, while Saunders was another never to be seen again. Veteran prop Des Fitzgerald, who was selected for the next match only to withdraw due to illness, never started another international. Johns pays tribute to Crossan, a real stalwart in the great Ulster 10-in-a-row team, as "an inspirational player when you consider all the size of him. He really bounced off people and was a fierce tackler."

After the Welsh defeat, Ireland took a 38-9 hammering at Twickenham, blown away after a Keyes try, conversion and penalty had given them early hope and serving no notice of the heroics which were to be produced on their next visit. Halpin, Galwey, Fergus Aherne and Geoghegan were the quartet who replaced Des Fitzgerald, Lenihan, Saunders and Crossan respectively for the game in London. Kenny Murphy and Phil Danaher, making his first Test appearance at centre having originally won a few caps as a fullback in 1988, then took over from the injured Staples and Curtis for the next match, at home to Scotland, but Ireland again played poorly, not least in the lineout and lost 10-18.

Paris was hardly the ideal place to go for a team seeking to avoid a whitewash and the record rout in a Spring setting at Parc des Princes was hardly surprising, particularly considering the body blow of the ridiculously premature retirement from international rugby prior to this match of one of Ireland's few world class players, Brendan Mullin. The international careers of Ballymena outside half Derek McAleese and Garryowen back-rower Paul Hogan began and ended that miserable afternoon. Curtis returned to fill the vacancy left by Mullin's bombshell, while Rigney came back in for the injured Francis. France scored seven tries in winning 44-12, McAleese contributing all of Ireland's points with four penalties. Assistant coach John Moloney was sacked in the wake of that match as Ireland counted the cost of picking up a deeply disappointing wooden spoon.

Johns felt he was still in the picture, having played for Ireland B in a 47-15 defeat by the English second string at Richmond just before the Five Nations at the end of January and then for the Irish Students side when they lost 28-19 to the same country at Waterloo after the Championship had ended in April. The English Students team included future Saracens team-mates Kyran Bracken and Steve Ravenscroft along with Jon Sleightholme, John Mallett and Eric Peters, plus Harvey Thorneycroft, who was to feature in Johns' testimonial game just over a decade later. Future Ireland scrumhalf Christian Saverimutto was on the English bench. By now Paddy had decided that his future lay at No 8 and duly played in the middle of the Ireland B backrow at Richmond, flanked by Leahy and Ballymena's Dean Macartney in a side skippered by John Fitzgerald and featuring Paddy's Dungannon clubmate Ronnie Carey, Mark McCall, Ballymena prop Peter Millar and Instonians hooker Andy Adair.

The natural follow-up to the game against English Students at Waterloo, when Johns again played in the backrow with Macartney, was the Students World Cup in Italy in the summer but Paddy missed out on a World Cup appearance for the second time in the same season. This time though he was happy to miss out. Paddy wasn't part of the Italian job because he had bigger fish to fry that summer. He spent a month of it in New Zealand with the Ireland senior squad. His second chance had come.

9. THE SECOND COMING

Touring New Zealand shredded the reputations of more than a few Irish players in 1997, but five years earlier Johns had made the most of an unexpected visit to the land of the Long White Cloud. Paddy had waited long enough to get a second chance and, when it came, he grabbed it with both hands, taking advantage of a late call-up to the tour party and establishing himself in the Test team.

New Zealand. Make or break. Intimidate or inspire. Steam-roller or pavement. Well, Paddy Johns went out as a late call-up, a fringe player, still a potential one-cap wonder with his international career prospects in the balance. It may be over-egging the pudding to say that he went out a boy and came back a man, but even as understated a guy as Paddy wouldn't seek to downplay the importance of that tour in shaping his rugby fate. It was a watershed alright.

Donal Lenihan had departed the scene and Neil Francis pulled out of the trip, leaving a bit of slack among the second row competition, but Johns had asked to only be considered as a No 8. So uncapped locks Richard Costelloe and John Etheridge were in the party as back-up to Galwey and Rigney, but Johns found himself operating in a more cut-throat area and originally lost out to Mannion, Lawlor and Robinson.

"Phil Lawlor was in the original squad, but withdrew due to back trouble, so although I wasn't initially picked for the tour, that let me in" he recalls. "There were a lot of cry-offs and some suggestions that one or two people didn't fancy it, but to me it was just the opportunity I wanted. Getting the call was a real bonus after not being picked originally. The previous 18 months had been spent bursting to get back in and getting a chance to tour New Zealand was a very exciting prospect, given the rugby reputation of that country. I'd probably never been away for more than a week with Ulster in rugby terms prior to that, so it was by far my longest tour at that point and, naturally, further away than I had ever been in life. Before that I'd been to Canada those summers and also to the Hong Kong Sevens, but New Zealand really is a long haul."

There are legendary tales of Australian cricketer David Boon downing dozens of tins of beer en route to England for Ashes series, but the Irish rugby players did not indulge in similar exploits. "It was all fairly serious stuff. There was definitely no drinking on the plane. Things were a bit different in those days alright, but most of the excesses would have been after games. I remember us getting there at around 8.00 in the evening after 36 hours of travelling, dropping our bags off, getting our gear on, these luminous lime green rainsuits, and going out to run for about three-quarters of an hour in the freezing rain. That had Gary Halpin saying he wanted to go home!

"Everyone realises that it just takes a lot of time to get to New Zealand, but what was really annoying about that tour was the crazy itinerary, which had us hopping back and forwards between north and south island for no good reason. That, more than anything, contributed to us being jaded and weary by the second Test coming round and, while that might sound like a lame excuse for the hammering we took, I still maintain it was a ridiculous way to organise a tour. Only the IRFU would have agreed to such an illogical and draining schedule, but back then the authorities didn't really give a damn about the players, or at the very least, give too much thought regarding them. Travelling knackers you, but nobody cared. If something like that had happened with the Ulster team in my last season, Phil Mack our fitness coach would have gone ballistic and it just wouldn't have been tolerated by a professional set-up. Thankfully, players' needs are a bit higher up the priority list now, but in the dark days that was just the itinerary thrown at Ireland and no-one objected."

Talking of fitness coaches, Ireland actually had one on that trip for the first time, none other than Eddie O'Sullivan, head coach of course on the men in green's next Test tour to New Zealand a decade later. The rest of the non-playing element of the 1992 party comprised head coach Ciaran Fitzgerald, his assistant and successor Gerry Murphy, who had taken over from Moloney, manager Noel Murphy, medical officer Dr Donal O'Shaughnessy, physio John Martin and masseur Joe Doran.

Absenteeism and a 30-man squad, captained by Phil Danaher, allowed for the inclusion of eight uncapped players, including Johns' Dungannon clubmate Ronnie Carey, fellow Ulsterman Mark McCall, locks Costelloe and Etheridge, Connacht winger Neville Furlong, Munster prop Paul McCarthy, Leinster flanker Kelvin Leahy and his provincial colleague, centre Martin Ridge. A further two, Clontarf winger Damien O'Brien, a domiciled Kiwi, and Wanderers wing forward Pat Kenny were called up during the tour, the latter a replacement for Leahy and the former summoned after Richie Wallace had his jaw broken by a punch in the second game, against Canterbury. Etheridge and Ridge were to remain uncapped. As well as Francis and Lawlor, the season which had just ended's first choice flankers, Ulstermen Phil Matthews and Gordon Hamilton, both missed the tour, while Brendan Mullin's retirement continued to leave a void in midfield.

The experienced Michael Bradley, in Matthews' absence the sole survivor from the 1985 Triple Crown winning team, was recalled after making only one appearance in the previous four seasons and, along with hookers Steve Smith and Terry Kingston, was one of only three squad members who had been in Australasia for the inaugural World Cup five years earlier. Ireland faced a tough eight match itinerary, with six provincial games in addition to the two Tests and the other big difference compared with the tour a decade later was that the opening match was as early as May 13, which would now be a fortnight ahead of the European Cup final!

In their hop around the islands, Ireland started off by beating a fairly anonymous South Canterbury side 21-16 in Timaru, which was also to be the location for O'Sullivan's tour a decade on. A young Brendan Laney, now one of Scotland's kilted Kiwis, was at outside centre for the hosts that day. Next up, Fitzgerald's team disappointingly went down 38-13 at Lancaster Park to a Canterbury side featuring Graeme Bachop at scrumhalf and Andy Earl at blindside as well as hooker Matt Sexton, who was to be a team-mate of Johns in his final game for Ulster almost exactly 10 years later. Todd Blackadder and Jon Preston were on the bench, along with Steve Cleave, another player who briefly flirted with the prospect of donning the white jersey with the red hand alongside Johns. Ironically Earl, the man whose punch broke Wallace's jaw, has recently been appointed coach of Dungannon.

Frustratingly for Johns, he had not made the team for either match and, although only on the tour as a late call-up and although enjoying the country, he was, naturally enough, bursting to play and disgruntled not to be getting his chance. "After those first two games, we flew to the north island for our third match, which was against Bay of Plenty in Rotorua. I was rooming with Mark McCall and we were the only two guys who hadn't had a game by that stage. When the team was named, we were both in, but he was delighted and I was absolutely raging, for I'd been picked in the second row, having taken a very firm decision that I didn't want to be considered there and made my position clear on that. Mind you, by that stage, while I wasn't happy about where I'd been selected, I was just desperate to get out and play. Touring is tough when you aren't actually in the team, so by the time the third match comes around, you're pretty hungry if you haven't started up until then."

McCall, who usually tends to be conservative in his comments, is actually more dramatic in describing Paddy's despair. "I was over the moon, but he was almost suicidal" reveals Mark. "He was talking about going home, giving up rugby, everything. He'd been bursting to play all tour, but was dead against playing second row at that stage."

A decade has since passed so, a bit like the rule that allows Government papers to be published after a certain number of years have elapsed, Paddy can now make an admission about his preparations for the game. Pudsey Johns and Small McCall: no more Mr Nice Guys! "Ireland had been on the receiving end of some fancy footwork in the opening couple of games and been subject to intimidatory tactics, not to mention the Richie Wallace incident in the Canterbury match, so a few of us decided we'd give them a taste of their own medicine. So we went out the evening before the Bay of Plenty fixture looking for rugby league studs, y'know the long ones with the tapered ends. We actually cleared a local sports shop of their entire stock of them" laughs Johns. He was, incidentally, pulled up by the referee over his studs before his final away match for Ulster, against Connacht in April 2002, but the inspection must have been less rigorous in Rotorua.

Armed with their new studs and a resolve not to take another backward step, Ireland got the show back on the road by beating Bay of Plenty 39-23, the Dungannon man performing well on his unexpected return to the engineroom. "I think I partly went out and unleashed all my frustrations that day, but there was probably also a subconscious sense of wanting to book myself pitch-time in the coming games as I had so hated not being involved" says Paddy. Johns was to play in all but one of the remaining tour games, including the first Test cliff-hanger 10 days later, and go on to be an Ireland regular in the following years.

A 62-7 annihilation by awesome Auckland at Eden Park the Saturday before the first Test did not augur well for Ireland's prospects in the internationals and Johns still vividly recalls the culture shock inflicted by one of the world's greatest provincial teams of all time. That Auckland team, with whom future Welsh coach Graham Henry gained his reputation, dominated provincial rugby and national selection in much the same way that Canterbury Crusaders are doing a decade on. They had a side which, on paper, would have been the equal of many national teams and, when their advantage of playing together regularly was added, Ireland were always going to be massively up against it.

Led by lock Gary Whetton, who was partnered in the engineroom by a young Robin Brooke, the Auckland tight five was completed by a formidable frontrow of All Black captain Sean Fitzpatrick with Steve McDowell and Olo Brown either side of him, with a youthful Craig Dowd on the bench. The loose forward unit boasted both Pat Lam and Zinzan Brooke along with Mark Carter, with the points machine Grant Fox at first five-eighth and two all-time greats in John Kirwan and Va'aiga Tuigamala on the wings. Scrumhalf Jason Hewett, second five Eroni Clarke, fullback Shane Howarth, the All Black who later defected to Wales, and powerful islander Waisake Sotutu made up the rest of a very useful backline which had no room for either pivot Ant Strachan or 1987 World Cup winning centre Bernie McCahill.

"Those guys were awesome that day" he still marvels. "It was rugby at a level most of us hadn't experienced before. They were just bigger, stronger and fitter than we were and, coming off, there was an acute sense of what a stuffing we had taken and it wasn't only measured by the one-sided score. I think we actually got on the board first, but us scoring early on was just like a red rag to a bull and they tore us apart. I remember Tuigamala and, to some extent, Sotutu, running through us. It was a great Auckland side and, boy, they played well that day.

"When we got back to the hotel, Michael Bradley got everyone into the players' room. We were all convinced that we were about to get a serious dressing down, especially with the Test the following week and, being one of the youngest on tour, I think I was particularly nervous. Michael then gave everyone a can of beer, at which point we were really confused. He then stood at the front and said, 'Ok lads, only one thing for it'. We then had to all shotgun our beers and headed off for some more. So it wasn't quite the telling off we'd been anticipating!"

Ireland had to pick themselves up for a midweek game against Poverty Bay-East Coast in Gisborne, a fixture which Johns remembers as "involving another tiresome and tiring trek", and which they won 22-7. And so across the water again to Dunedin, for the first Test in Carisbrook's 'House of Pain', but, rather than the match featuring the torture which most pundits were predicting for the understrength Irish, depleted and reeling from the Auckland result, it was the All Blacks who were tormented by the tenacious tourists. Remarkably, this was only the second international Ireland had ever played on New Zealand soil and it almost resulted in the greens' first win anywhere in the history of the fixture but, as was to prove the case a decade later, it was to be a tale of so near and yet so far.

Skippered by Fitzpatrick, New Zealand fielded relatively few other Auckland players in a team featuring regular centre Walter Little in the No 10 jersey instead of Grant Fox, who was left on the bench, as the home side sought to play more of a running game. The All Blacks side in full read: G Cooper; J Kirwan, F Bunce, E Clarke, V

Tuigamala; W Little, A Strachan; S McDowell, S Fitzpatrick (capt), R Loe, I Jones, B Larsen, J Joseph, A Pene, P Henderson.

Every time the Irish players visited a new part of New Zealand, they were treated to a traditional Maori ceremony including a haka, followed by a customary Maori greeting. This involves rubbing noses with your hosts by way of welcome. However, after much haka-ing, it usually translated into rubbing sweaty noses which was "not the nicest way to say hello." So, by the time the first Test had arrived, the players had already been exposed to the haka on several occasions, which may have diluted some of its ability to intimidate. "It definitely always has an air about it and always gets your heart-rate going, but after the first time, it doesn't quite have that edge."

Sentiments like this may have helped Ireland get off to a dream start, going 12 points up in as many minutes and it could have been even better had Peter Russell not missed with a good dropgoal chance, while Carey intercepted an opposition pass but, agonisingly, couldn't quite hold on. Carey was one of four new caps in the starting line-up, along with fellow winger Furlong of UCG, Cork Con prop McCarthy and Wanderers flanker Leahy. Danaher, who had been injured in the opening game of the tour, was passed fit to partner Cunningham in the centre, with Jim Staples at fullback, Russell wearing the No 10 jersey and Bradley getting the nod at the base of the scrum. Incidentally, Bradley and reserve hooker Terry Kingston had played against Canada at the same Carisbrook ground five years earlier to the very day in the first World Cup. Coach Ciaran Fitzgerald had captained the Lions there in the third Test in 1983.

New boy McCarthy joined Popplewell and Smith in the front row, with Johns and Galwey paired in the engineroom. Robinson was at No 8, flanked by Leahy and Mick Fitzgibbon. On that tour, Johns formed a close friendship with the two Micks from Shannon, Galwey and Fitzgibbon. "We became good buddies out there and they made me an honorary Shannon man and taught me to sing The Isle."

The All Blacks gradually gained the ascendancy, helped by a try resulting from an error by experienced Aussie referee Sandy McNeill, but the gallant greens simply refused to lie down and fall away in spite of more injury problems. Staples, who scored a try to go with Cunningham's two, all of them converted by Russell, was replaced by Kenny Murphy, McCall came on for his first cap in place of the skipper Danaher and the impressive Leahy broke his ankle, meaning the introduction of Brian Rigney in a forward reshuffle. Popplewell and Robinson stamped their class on proceedings and Ireland trailed by just three points going into the closing stages, but Carey couldn't gather the ball as the tourists tried to launch a raid from deep and the last chance was lost. It finished 24-21.

"I'd been waiting for a second chance for more than 18 months and was determined to take it if it came, whenever it came, wherever it came. You could choose less tough places than New Zealand and I didn't expect to be playing in the second row at the start of the tour, but you can't pick and choose. It wasn't quite like winning my first cap over again, but there was definitely a sense of a fresh start and that 'the future starts here'. Playing for Ireland meant a lot to me and I was determined not to blow the chance.

"After being stuffed out of sight by Auckland, we reckoned the All Blacks might take us for granted and, as a team, were well up for that first Test. We knew we couldn't afford to be anything below our best or it would end up a total humiliation. The first lineout was thrown long to me at the back, which kind of seemed to surprise them and set the tone for a great first quarter. They were certainly rattled and we could have won it, but in the end we didn't.   One or two little bits of luck, like if Ronnie (Carey) had been able to hold onto the ball and the outcome would have been so different." But at least, even in defeat, Ireland had exceeded expectations unlike in Johns' only previous full international, against Argentina.

The penultimate game, in which he played No 8 for the only time on tour, was lost 58-24 to Manawatu at Palmerston North before the tired and weary tourists were swamped amid a deluge of All Black tries at a typically wet and windy Wellington in the second Test. New Zealand, whose press and public had been unimpressed by the Dunedin display, made half a dozen changes, Matt Cooper replacing his namesake Greg as the last line of defence and John Timu taking over from a benched Tuigamala on the wing.

Flankers Joseph and Henderson gave way to Mike Brewer and the magnificent Michael Jones, Robin Brooke was brought in to join the other Jones, Ian, in what was to prove an enduring engineroom pairing and Olo Brown was at tighthead for Loe. Tall timbers Johns, Jones and Brooke were all to tower over Test fields for most of the next decade, but Paddy admits to having had no real sense at that stage of just what the two opposition locks would go on to achieve, never mind himself. "We didn't know much about them then and I remember thinking Jones was physically a bit on the light side, but his Test record speaks volumes about his ability to play at the highest level for such a long period."

An article in the match programme was ominously titled: 'Irish eyes are smiling but . . . beware of a wounded All Black side'. A prophetic warning indeed, if not exactly rocket science. A mighty relieved Fitzpatrick had come into the Ireland changing room after the previous Saturday's Test in Dunedin to offer his congratulations on the visitors' performance. "Thanks fellas; well played" he said simply, before adding a trifle ominously: "See you next week in Wellington." Indeed.

Again Ireland got the perfect start with Furlong, who was actually playing with a broken bone in his foot, scoring a try which Russell converted, but it amounted to little more than the condemned man spitting on his executioner on the way to the gallows. Danaher had been ruled out by injury, McCall filling his centre spot and Bradley taking over as captain, with Galwey moving to blindside to replace Leahy and Rigney starting alongside Johns in the engineroom. The appalling chapter of misfortune continued during the game, with Fitzgibbon bowing out in the first quarter, thus handing a first cap to Paddy Kenny, only called up to the tour as a replacement for leg break victim Leahy. Kenny had been on the non-cap tour of Japan seven years earlier. Then Ireland were hit with a double whammy early in the second period, losing the luckless Staples, for whom they at least had a straight replacement in Murphy, and outhalf Russell, which required a juggling of backline resources, with Jack Clarke coming on.

It was hardly a huge surprise that Ireland slumped to a record defeat, New Zealand piling up the points to run out winners by 59-6, a miserable end to a memorable enough tour, certainly for Paddy Johns. "By the time the second Test came round, we were basically running on empty and everyone was looking forward to getting home" admits

Paddy, with a great degree of candour. A combination of that fatigue and our wretched luck with injuries left us very vulnerable and New Zealand duly exploited that. It wasn't nice to be part of a record defeat, but the tour as a whole certainly increased my confidence."

There was undoubtedly more of a social side to tours in those days than in the professional era and their longer duration also helped facilitate a bit more off-task time than under the typically tight Test-only schedules of more modern times. But it still was far from a holiday camp for a team which played itself to a standstill and also suffered from the rigors of a tortuously convoluted itinerary, which Johns contemptuously dismisses as "an absolute joke. We took things very, very seriously on the pitch but, it was very good craic as well. In the amateur days, there was inevitably more craic. I suppose there was less pressure and more sense of release. Back then rugby was a break from the day job; in years to come it was the day job and that makes a difference."

Although New Zealand is rugby mad, the Irish visitors found time to try their hand at another sport under the guise of team bonding. "We all went duck shooting near Christchurch" Paddy recollects. "It got quite late in the evening, dusk really, and the light wasn't so good. There were some decoys on the lake to encourage the real ducks, and as some flew past, others took off from the water. I just kinda aimed and shot. Unfortunately I managed to kill one of the plastic ducks! Needless to say, the others thought this very amusing." Ireland should be thankful Paddy's rugby-playing abilities far outshone his duck-shooting ones. "I was rubbish," he freely admits. "Some of the boys were good though. Ronnie Carey was very good. Then again he is in the police!"

The other difference with more modern times was that, with eight matches and the best part of a month in New Zealand, Ireland got a great chance to see the country, meet its people and experience its culture. "I really enjoyed it, touring there was fantastic. The whole thing was great, very exciting and varied and a lot more relaxed than the shorter in-and-out Test tours which nations generally undertake these days." Like the great New Zealand outhalf Andrew Mehrtens, speaking in Belfast in November 2001 as the All Blacks prepared for what, remarkably, was their first midweek match in four years, Johns feels something has been lost as a result of longer tours going out of fashion.

"Touring has always been a great part of rugby's heritage and it is definitely sad in ways that the longer tours, and I don't mean the six month go-on-the-boat trips of the early days, don't seem to be happening much any more at international level. I suppose it is a consequence of the packed schedule in each hemisphere with competitions like the European Cup and Super 12, not to mention so many Test matches, but I'm glad to have been around when they did happen. Professional rugby has been progress and I have experienced at first hand the benefits it has brought, but I also enjoyed the good times of the amateur days and feel privileged to have had a part in both eras. Playing international rugby through the 1990s gave me the best of both worlds, I suppose."

Touring New Zealand really is what it's all about and, like so many others, Johns found himself consumed by the all-pervading passion for rugby for which the country is justifiably famous. Current Ireland prop John Hayes, who spent two seasons playing in Invercargill in his formative years, and Paddy's fellow Ulster lock Gary Longwell, a tourist in 2002, have been among those to try and put into words what rugby means to the New Zealand nation, but it isn't that easy to encapsulate for anyone who hasn't actually experienced it at first hand.

Hayes did not take up rugby until the age of 19 but, having taken a crash course in the best finishing school in the world, has graduated with international honours. The time he spent there was the making of him and gave him an insight into the unique rugby culture in a country where the game is pretty much everything. "What really opened my eyes was seeing the way that rugby just takes over, the way young fellas from the age of maybe three or four years upwards aspire to play for the All Blacks as the greatest thing they can achieve" stresses Hayes. "In many ways there's more pressure being their coach than being New Zealand Prime Minister. That's how important it is to people there. No matter where they go, there's a certain aura about the All Blacks, something special. For me, they just epitomize what rugby is all about." Longwell adds: "The thing about New Zealand is that they really know their rugby, no matter where you go, any restaurant or you could be talking to people in the street and they know the game inside out. You want to go over there and do well. You really want those people to rate you."

Paddy too picked up that sense of real worth which goes with proving yourself on New Zealand soil and, as much as what he did on that 1992 tour, it was where he was doing it that gave him both satisfaction at the time and confidence for the future. "You were just continuously aware of how big rugby is, even from the sheer number of kids who are playing in the streets and any bit of space they can find, hundreds and hundreds of them, some very tiny indeed" Paddy recalls. "Where you'd find children in other countries kicking a football around, in New Zealand they'd have a rugby ball." Longwell's comments about the people of New Zealand knowing their rugby are supported by a tale which O'Sullivan tells from the 1992 trip, when he and the assistant coach were apparently accosted by a lady in a shopping store and asked why Ireland had thrown so much to the tail of the lineout in their last match!

Rugby is how each Kiwi defines his or herself. Never mind foreign affairs and financial markets, if the All Blacks are on top, everything must be alright. Each time the All Blacks line up to play, every New Zealander believes they can win and, beyond that, expects them to win. A newly hired radio broadcaster in New Zealand reportedly did a very thorough overview of the status of all the major sporting events ongoing at that time including hockey, tennis, athletics and netball. After what he had thought had been a very comprehensive report, his boss burst into the broadcasting studio and shouted, "What the f*ck was that?! In this country the only sport there is is f*cking rugby and that's it!" The poor fella never made the same mistake again.

In many ways, it wasn't a bad tour for Ireland, especially if remembered for the first Test heroics, when the guys in green came within a whisker of a victory which would have rewritten the history books and shocked the rugby world. Apart from a few anoraks, being asked to name the two Ireland wingers who played in the internationals on that tour would be a trivia question which would stump many casual rugby fans, but both Carey and Furlong did their bit and did their best.

The diminutive Carey, a Crossan clone in terms of size, had only made his Ulster

With brothers Marcus (left) and Johnny, holding cousin Calum Shaw

Paddy (back right) with his siblings

As a toddler in the garden at home   *Dungannon mini-rugby team*

**RSD First XV 1985-86 including captain Paddy (holding ball), Allen Clarke
and future golf star, Darren Clarke (middle row, third player from left)**

Paddy on dental duty ahead of his first cap and (inset) with his proud grandmother Mrs Florence Shaw

A spot of whitewater rafting on Dungannon's 1989 Canadian tour

Ashley Blair clears for Dungannon watched by Paddy, Willie Anderson and Gary Longwell (back left) of Queen's

Picture: News Letter

debut against Leinster the December before that New Zealand tour, but bagged a brace of tries in the next match against Munster, also scored against Connacht and ran them in regularly as Dungannon won promotion to the top flight of the AIL. "Maybe in ways Ronnie was in the right place at the right time in terms of getting his chance on that tour, but he certainly did himself proud and it will always stick in my mind how well he dealt with Va'aiga Tuigamala in spite of being so small. Compared with Carey, Tuigamala was a real man mountain and, in many ways, the All Blacks' most formidable player at that time, but whenever he got the ball, Ronnie was there snapping at his heels. He was very brave and tenacious."

People may also remember little about the relatively brief and unsuccessful international career of Peter Russell, Ulster's outhalf through a significant stretch of the province's decade of dominance, with that unfortunate early fumble on his Twickenham debut in 1990 being what sticks in many minds, but he was another unsung hero of the trip. The tour was the end of Ciaran Fitzgerald as coach, but really hadn't been that bad an exercise from an Irish point of view and, for Johns personally, it was much better than that.

"Yeah, I suppose that tour made me in ways. I was more mature than when I had played the first time, had gained more experience and worked very hard on my game. Being picked against Argentina gave me a taste of Test rugby and fuelled my ambition and then being left out for the best part of two years meant that, when the chance came again, my hunger was huge. Even on tour, I had to wait for my opportunity but, when I got in, I made it count and the fact that the tour was to New Zealand was very important psychologically. You don't get much higher benchmarks that that, so to have come through reasonably well out there was going to do more for my confidence than say if it had been Namibia or somewhere. On tours like that, being named in the side for the Saturday game a week before the first Test is generally a good indicator that you're in the frame to play in the international and, although as a team we were heavily beaten by Auckland, so it proved.

"Although I was annoyed to be picked in the second row earlier in the tour, by the time the Test came round, I was happy to be in the side and of course I was desperate to play against the All Blacks." The positional issue was to remain a recurring theme and will be considered in more detail in a later chapter, but Johns came home from New Zealand not only convinced that he could cut it at Test level, but also knowing that he didn't need to limit himself to competing for only one jersey.

10. FINDING HIS FEET

When you've done it in New Zealand, you can do it anywhere. Having taken on the All Blacks in their own backyard and lived to tell the tale, Johns now felt properly part of the international scene. He returned having trebled his tally of Test caps and exorcised the ghosts of Argentina, and much more relaxed about what position he was prepared to play. Just as well, for he was to be an ever-present in the Irish engineroom throughout the following season.

In the autumn of 1992, Johns partnered Mick Galwey in the second row as Ireland were well beaten in the eagerly-awaited rematch against Australia at Lansdowne Road, but helped Ulster claim a ninth interpro title on the trot after coming out on top in a competition which now involved an Irish Exiles team. Ciaran Fitzgerald had been reappointed Ireland coach for the new season, but there were changes in the selection committee, with Frank Sowman of Leinster and Munster's Pat Whelan replacing Kevin Flynn and Jerry Murray respectively.

In his definitive history of Irish rugby, Edmund van Esbeck records that, in a complete about-turn from previous policy and practice, a national selector could no longer sit on a provincial selection committee. In the past, doing the latter was a prerequisite for being the former. Either way, the old system, the flaws in which have already been discussed, was essentially retained. Of greater and wider import was the change in the laws of the game to allow for the temporary replacement of a player who needed a wound attended to. A try was now worth five points and Patrick Stephen Johns was a newly married man.

The Wallabies won comfortably against Leinster in the first match of their October tour, though a 38-11 victory was clouded somewhat by the injury which ruled captain Michael Lynagh out of action for the rest of the trip. A memorable match against Munster followed, a controversial Cork contest ending in a famous 22-19 triumph for the Irish province who therefore followed up their legendary lowering of the All Blacks flag in 1978. Galwey and Wallaby lock Garrick Morgan were both sent off in a stormy game, but were no more culpable than many of their colleagues and afterwards Australian coach Bob Dwyer angrily accused Munster of all sorts of malpractice. He also suggested that Young Munster prop Peter Clohessy, who already had something of an unfortunate reputation, had been provocatively selected by the Irish province to take out opponents. Not surprisingly, Munster, whose team included Paddy's old mate Charlie Haly, in turn felt Dwyer's attitude smacked of sour grapes.

The midweek team may have fallen to Munster and were glad to get out of Galway with an unconvincing 14-6 win over lowly Connacht, but the Saturday side proceeded to beat Ulster by a similar margin to the Leinster victory. "We started well against them at Ravenhill, but they were a good team and eased away in the final quarter. One incident that sticks in my mind from that game was Mark McCall chasing a high ball from Peter Russell and hitting their fullback Marty Roebuck slightly late. Roebuck took exception to that and started smacking Small on the head with his elbow."

Paddy was never the sort to see a team-mate in trouble and not go to his aid. Anyway, he and McCall went back a long way to their Ulster Schools days. And, hadn't they kept each other's spirits up as roomies in Rotorua that summer when feeling surplus to requirements early in the New Zealand tour. Blood brothers and all that. "I saw what was happening and ran in and retaliated, which then brought two or three of their forwards piling in to help Roebuck. I quickly had a sense that I was on my own. When the ref stopped it, I looked around. There was Small, halfway up the pitch. He'd legged it. That was the thanks I got for rescuing him" he recounts with a chuckle. Incidentally McCall admits that the tackle was "high and late" and that he did leave the scene as soon as possible!

So any Ulster dreams of repeating their heroic giant-killing exploits against the 1984 Wallabies were well and truly buried and, likewise, any hopes that Ireland could go one better than their agonisingly near miss in that dramatic World Cup quarter-final 12 months earlier quickly disappeared. First choice wingers Geoghegan and Wallace, both of whom missed the Tests in New Zealand, were restored to the wide berths in place of their gallant deputies, Carey and Furlong, while Danaher was back at centre for McCall and resumed the captaincy from Bradley, who gave way to Fergus Aherne at the base of the scrum. Up front, Greystones hooker Johnny Murphy, the only new cap in the team, made his Test debut and Galwey reverted to the engineroom alongside Johns at the expense of Rigney, with Robinson switching from No 8 to blindside and Lawlor coming into the middle of the backrow. A fit-again Hamilton returned for Fitzgibbon as breakaway.

The Wallabies played extremely well and, several days after Ireland's 17-42 defeat, Fitzgerald stood down as coach, citing the best interests of Irish rugby allied to increased business commitments as the reasons for his decision. Like Graeme Sounness at Liverpool, this was a case of a man who had become a hero by leading a side to success on the pitch but proved unable to emulate it when he returned in a managerial role. Fitzgerald will be remembered for captaining his country to Triple Crowns in 1982 and 1985 rather than anything achieved in his capacity as coach.

"Ciaran's army background certainly came through in his approach and I personally liked him. He was the guy who gave me my second chance and we were all aware of how inspirational he had been as Irish captain. The best players or even best captains don't necessarily make great coaches as has been proved and what a guy achieved on the pitch himself will only count for so much if he hasn't got the necessary attributes to develop players and get the best out of them. Someone like Alan Solomons, my last Ulster coach, did not play at a high level, but certainly quickly earned the respect of everyone in the squad and no doubt the same applied when he was assistant coach of the Springboks. The short-term advantage a guy who's been there himself will have is that he'll be guaranteed automatic and instant respect when he first comes in to take over a team, but in the long run every coach has to cut it as a coach to be a successful one."

Fitzgerald's resignation pointed up the flaws in an archaic, anomalous and ridiculous rule of the IRFU's whereby the Ireland coach had to come from those nominated at the end of the previous season. Gerry Murphy, Fitzgerald's assistant on the tour of New Zealand, was firstly appointed on a caretaker basis and then as the fully-fledged successor to the former Lions captain and, more importantly, better provisions were put in place should similar situations arise in the future. So it was Murphy's law for Ireland, in that Noel was continuing as manager, but some things never changed it seemed. Just like two years earlier when Johns had made his Test debut, there were wholesale changes in the wake of a disappointing autumn international. Some of them didn't make much sense either.

Between the Australian Test at the end of October and Christmas, Ulster had won their eighth outright interpro title in nine successive seasons as champions, this time having had to win four matches rather than three to complete a clean sweep, given the advent of the Exiles as participants. A honeymooning Johns had missed the three warm-up matches against Cornwall, Yorkshire and Cumbria in early September, but returned to face London Counties and Australia. Injury caused him to miss the famous 12-11 Thomond Park victory over Munster which was inspired by the boot of young supersub David Humphreys, who came on for Peter Russell and kicked two penalties and a drop goal. But Paddy was back for the hat-trick of victories over Connacht (19-6), the Exiles (16-13) and Leinster (12-8), partnered on each occasion by Davy Tweed.

Yet the northern province only had four players in the Irish team for the Five Nations opener against Scotland, a side showing no fewer than eight changes from the Australian match as the selectors again wielded the axe with devastating effect. This time Johns survived the cull which cleared out more than half of the team, an indication of how he was beginning to cement his place and a reassuring retention given the number of casualties all around him.

"That Australian match was a big game for me at the time. This was the World Cup winners coming back to Dublin where Ireland had almost beaten them 12 months earlier and the chance to play against the Wallabies is a big thrill for any young guy in any era. At a personal level, it was my first chance to play at Lansdowne Road since my debut against Argentina two years earlier and, given that I had been dropped following that one, I wanted to make a good impression and cement the place I had gained on the New Zealand tour. I feel that I did reasonably well in the Test and holding my place for the start of the Championship was a good confidence boost. In those days of five selectors, it was a bit of a lottery and you didn't need to be playing all that badly to be dropped."

There were three new caps for Murrayfield, New Zealand tourist Richard Costelloe in the second row, cavalier Malone fullback Colin Wilkinson, who had by then replaced Philip Rainey as Ulster's regular last line of defence, and young stand-off Niall Malone. Ulsterman Malone had been catapulted into the limelight as a result of his virtuoso performance for Oxford in the Varsity match in December and was thrown straight in by selectors who had decided to cut their losses with the likes of his fellow northerners Russell and McAleese in the No 10 jersey. Many doubted that Malone was really ready to play international rugby and so it proved, while the mercurial Wilkinson was asked to adopt a conservative approach which was totally alien to him and failed to make the most of his talents.

Not surprisingly, Ireland went down 15-3 with barely a whimper, essentially failing to fire a shot in a poor game after falling 10 points behind before they even looked like getting out of their blocks. Scotland fielded three new caps in the pack in prop Alan Sharp, lock Andy Reed and openside flanker Iain Morrison. Gavin Hastings was the captain of a side which included his brother Scott in the centre and already established halfback stars, Gary Armstrong and Craig Chalmers. In the Irish team, Smith was back for Murphy, who was to be condemned to life membership of the one-cap wonder club, Costelloe took over from Galwey and Lawlor was, surprisingly, deployed at blindside as Mannion returned to the backrow for the injured Robinson.

McBride reclaimed the No 7 jersey from fellow Ulsterman, Hamilton, and Bradley was recalled at the base of the scrum. Paddy compares the rivalry between McBride and Hamilton to the earlier outhalf scenario involving Ollie Campbell and Tony Ward. "You could have either in and know they would do a good job. They were slightly different players who brought different things to the party. Both of them was very competitive and both made significant marks in the history of Irish rugby, Gordon with that try against Australia and Denis by winning so many caps."

Although Johns suddenly found himself as the more senior of the two second rows, given that Costelloe was winning his first cap, it was the last thought in his head. After all, he himself was making his Five Nations debut, playing his first game in a competition with great prestige and history. "The Five Nations, or Six Nations as it now is, has a huge heritage and, certainly before the advent of the Tri-Nations and Super 12, would have been the envy of the southern hemisphere and people in New Zealand, South Africa and Australia would have watched it avidly. That may have diminished a bit, but it remains special and will always have its long history and great social dimension for the fans. Stadiums will continue to be sold out comfortably for Championship games."

He has particular views, which will be discussed later, on why Ireland have struggled so much at Murrayfield in the period immediately before, during and after his international career, and understandably recalls few games there with much affection. "That was the first of many disappointing days at Murrayfield and a frustrating afternoon. Wilkie was over the moon to be there and so pleased to be picked, but it was a bit annoying that he was given orders not to counter-attack and so forth. The qualities which had got him there were not actually utilised and it ended up being his only cap. I know he was determined to enjoy the experience come what may and probably wasn't expecting a long international career, but it was a pity he had to go away feeling he could have done more."

So Ireland had made another bad start to a Championship campaign and there were a further half dozen changes for the next game, though again Johns was unaffected. He and Popplewell were now the only forwards to have survived since the Australian game and, along with the entire three-quarter line, among only six in the side. Indeed the pair were to start every Test together thereafter up until, ironically, the first Test against the Wallabies on the 1994 tour, when Popplewell was injured. As for Johns, he had embarked upon a run of 17 consecutive caps and he played in 27 of Ireland's next 28 Tests.

It can be argued that Ireland finally got the right men on the pitch, judging by the two wins over Wales and England in the second half of the Championship, and so the end justified the means, but the causal linkage could be disputed. To some extent, it all too often seemed a case of musical chairs or change for change's sake. Or, if the selectors can be credited for getting it right in the end, they can equally be criticised for not getting it right earlier.

"Selection was very reactionary in those days, not massively well thought out or anything" says Johns. "Instead of a guy maybe getting one or two caps in those days, they would now get say five or six to prove themselves. Some might then go on to 30 caps and others would drop out, but at least there should be enough evidence on which to make a decision as to whether a particular player has what it takes. But previously, by discarding so quickly, there were probably babies thrown out with bath-water, if you like."

The hapless Wilkinson joined the one-cap wonder brigade by being jettisoned for the French match a month after Murrayfield, Terenure's Ciaran Clarke being handed his full international debut in the No 15 jersey. The other new cap was Clohessy at tighthead, while the enigmatic Francis returned to partner Johns in the engineroom. Kingston came in at hooker for Smith, who never played for Ireland again, and the same applied to Mannion, who gave way to Galwey at No 8. Pat O'Hara made a welcome return at blindside, where he was a much better bet than Lawlor and Ireland made a great game of it before France pulled away at the death. Olivier Roumat and Abde Benazzi were the visiting locks that day, both already seasoned internationals.

Malone put Ireland into a 6-0 lead with a pair of penalties and although they were pegged back to level terms by the break before falling behind for the first time when France kicked a penalty early in the second period, the hosts were still in it until near the end. Two tries in the final seven minutes gave France a 21-6 victory which, if not exactly underserved, was certainly by a flattering margin. Unsurprisingly, the selectorial surgery was relatively minor for the trip to Cardiff. Young Malone, who had scored all of Ireland's paltry nine points in his two Tests, was discarded in favour of Eric Elwood, an emerging Connacht player from a gaelic football background who was to become a stalwart in the green jersey after a dream start to his international career with victories in Cardiff and over England on his first two outings. Brian Robinson was fit again and predictably returned to the middle of the backrow, Galwey being pushed forward to partner Johns at the expense of Francis in the resulting reshuffle.

Ironically the two men who had come into the team, Elwood and Robinson, between them accounted for all but three of the visitors' points in a 19-14 Arms Park victory which extended Ireland's unbeaten run there to five visits. Remarkably, it was Ireland's first win in the Championship since they had beaten the Welsh in Dublin in 1990 and came as a great relief after two wooden spoon campaigns, with the draw on their previous visit to Cardiff being the only punctuation in a tale of defeat after defeat. It was a good season for Irish teams against the Welsh, with victories at Schools, Under 21 and A international level also.

Ireland, for whom a Clarke dropgoal cancelled out an early Welsh penalty, led 13-6 at the break, the assured Elwood sandwiching his conversion of Robinson's try with a couple of penalties. The Connacht man and Jenkins then traded three-pointers early in the second period, but the ace Welsh marksman was to fail with his attempt to level the scores by converting a Ieuan Evans try. Elwood landed one more penalty and Ireland held out. "It was great to win in Cardiff and that was a very enjoyable match in spite of it being a muddy old day. Eric was very authoritative on his debut and kicked very well. He played a big part in the victory." Johns did though spare a thought for Malone, who he remembers at the time as "a quiet young guy, who I didn't really know as he wasn't involved with Ulster" and defends as having done reasonably well in difficult enough circumstances in his two games. But Elwood certainly took the big stage by storm.

The famous home win over England which followed rounded off the season in the best possible way, yet Popplewell and Galwey were the only Irishmen to make the Lions squad for the summer tour of New Zealand. In April, Johns played his part in an exhilarating Irish challenge at the inaugural Sevens World Cup and, not required by the Lions, was also excused from participation in the Irish Development tour of Africa, taking in Zimbabwe, Namibia and South Africa. Considering that several capped players were asked to make that trip, this reflected Paddy's increasingly secure senior status in the set-up. He agrees that, by now, he was beginning to feel at home in the international arena, having played two Test matches in New Zealand, won in Cardiff, tasted victory against England and, most importantly, had a run of seven consecutive games in the green jersey.

Ireland didn't set the world alight by winning 25-3 against Romania at Lansdowne Road in their only autumn international of 1993, while Ulster's crown was also beginning to slip as they ended up grateful to secure a three way tie at the top of the table with Munster and Leinster. The men in white started their 10th successive interpro title defence by beating the Exiles, but were then soundly thrashed, 25-0, by Leinster, ending Ulster's amazing unbeaten run in the series which had stretched to 32 matches. Munster came to Ravenhill, an unhappy hunting ground for them, needing only a draw to take the title, but a late drop goal and then an injury-time penalty gave Ulster a thrilling 24-21 victory.

"I suppose at times, especially towards the end of the 10-in-a-row, we just made it and had a few close shaves, but that team had the knack of winning and knew what it took. We were probably a bit like Munster have been in recent seasons in that we had great team spirit and also a kind of aura about us which might have meant that, on occasions, other sides choked against us at the crucial moment. There was pressure on us to maintain our position, but we definitely did have a psychological advantage over the opposition in those days. I remember that match against Munster in 1993 and Mick Galwey giving away the crucial penalty right at the death. They had been leading until very near the end and only needed a draw to take our title, but we sneaked it. The game took place a week before Christmas, so another interpro title was a nice early present."

Earlier that autumn, Paddy had had his first game against South African opposition when Ulster lost to a SA Barbarians XV, captained by current Springbok coach Rudolph Straeuli and including such notable names as Adrian Garvey, Japie Mulder, Gavin Johnson, Jannie de Beer, Pieter Hendricks and Dick Muir, with Kyrauw Otto on the bench. Lansdowne fullback Conor O'Shea won his first cap against Romania in November at the expense of Clarke, Neil Francis returned to a reshuffled pack in place of the injured Pat O'Hara and Gary Halpin took over at tighthead from Peter Clohessy, who was serving a carried over suspension following an incident in an AIL match earlier in the year.

Available again, Clohessy returned for the Five Nations opener against France in Paris, a game for which Ireland made one other change, uncapped Munster blindside Ken

O'Connell being picked out of position at openside on the very questionable premise that McBride was too small for such a game. One of McBride's predecessors as Ulster openside, Nigel Carr, had similarly lost out in a horses for courses selection for the corresponding fixture eight years earlier, but it didn't really work on either occasion and suggested Ireland were more concerned with the French than with what they were aiming to do themselves.

Mind you, in those days, that was probably true, as Johns would concede. Back then, before the advent of the European club competitions, the only time Irish players set foot on French soil was every other year for the traditional Paris pasting. "Travelling there with our record was always a daunting prospect. We always found Parc des Princes very tough and the away games against France were the toughest matches we would play, the hardest physically, and that includes the few meetings with the big southern hemisphere nations.

"There was a belief that Ireland could be intimidated, physically and particularly psychologically, so they invariably rolled out the biggest guys and simply sought to beat us up. What often went on certainly wasn't too pleasant at times. I remember them once bringing back Mark Cecillon, who everyone thought was retired, to have another go at us. It was perhaps no wonder that our selectors looked for big backrows, but we would have paid a price at the breakdown. One of the great things about the European Cup was that playing French club sides more regularly got rid of the myth and associated fear factor. The more close games and wins we got under our belts, the less hang-ups we had."

Elwood, who had kicked six penalties and converted Simon Geoghegan's try in the Romanian match, accounted for all of Ireland's 15 Paris points courtesy of five penalty goals, but France scored twice that tally in a slightly flattering result. So Paddy's first visit to Paris wasn't actually as painful as some of Ireland's other pilgrimages there in the last two decades of the 20th century, the greens only trailing 16-12 at the break and, in spite of a couple of near misses by Elwood, still being in touch until a late French try finally put the issue beyond doubt.

Elwood again kicked five penalties in the next match against Wales at Lansdowne Road, but the game will be remembered for a sixth strike which came back off the post as Ireland went down 15-17. "My last ever away game for Ulster, eight years later, was against Connacht and afterwards we went to Eric's pub in Galway, the Goal Post. I couldn't resist asking him if it was named after his 1994 miss!" Typical of Paddy's propensity for the odd outbreak of schoolboy humour and mischief-making in his own quiet and droll way.

A source in the Ulster camp recalls how, also in his final season, the big streetwise second row had been involved in an incident which had resulted in a yellow-card for an opposition player. It was team policy to fine any Ulster player who got sin-binned, so Johns, a methodical man of perfect logic, naturally wondered what applied where the situation was reversed. "Hey, Solly, how much do I get paid for getting that fella carded?" he piped up from a corner of the changing-room afterwards.

Paddy's old mucker McCall had got back in at centre for the Welsh game due to the dreadful leg break sustained by Cunningham in an AIL match, but the only other change from the French fixture directly affected Johns. For the first time at international level, he was handed the No 8 jersey, which he had coveted a couple of years earlier but was no longer bothered about, having settled in the second row. He and Galwey, who had previously been playing blindside, switched rows, though it wasn't a straight swap as the change also meant a move for Robinson from the middle of the backrow to the No 6 jersey. Scott Quinnell was winning his third cap at No 8 for Wales.

Within one game of the move, Johns had tasted victory over England at Twickenham so, just like doing well in New Zealand two summers earlier had relaxed him about playing second row at Test level, he quickly gained confidence in his new berth, a position with which, in any case, he was well familiar at lower levels. After the high of beating England though, Ireland ended their Championship campaign on a low note with a dreary Dublin draw against Scotland. All 15 Twickenham heroes had been retained, but it was a major anti-climax.

"Yeah, it was disappointing, especially after Twickenham" admits Paddy. "The 6-6 scoreline gives a fairly accurate reflection of what the game was like. I'm not sure if we were, subconsciously, hit with some sort of hangover effect, but the game was there for the taking and we didn't take it."

By the end of that season, Johns had played 12 Tests on the trot and, although he claims no-one could ever quite feel secure in that environment because of the selection system and mentality of the time, he was starting to feel more at home at the highest level. "Naturally, I was a better player than when I made my Ireland debut in 1990, though not because I had changed all that much or because my skills were dramatically superior to what they had been.

"But you learn with every game and there is no doubt that experience is experience. The more times you do something or be in a situation, the more comfortable you become and the better you deal with it. By being there, you gain confidence and self-belief, especially with results like those against England in 1993 and 1994. You do have to get better though to keep your place, for more will be expected of you with every match and the onus is on you to put your growing experience to good effect."

So onwards and upwards then for Paddy as he headed Down Under for the first of his two Test tours of Australia.

11. DERAILING THE CHARIOT

For the celtic cousins, there's nothing quite like beating England. It doesn't happen that often these days, but what's seldom is special. There has been a lot of talk about Brian O'Driscoll tasting victory in his first two Tests against France, but Paddy's proud record after his first couple of encounters with the English was just as impressive. Played two, won two.

Being part of what we can have licence to grandly call the Lansdowne landslide to round off the 1993 Five Nations was a wonderful feeling, his best day in a green jersey to date. But the even greater Twickenham triumph some 11 months later, beating a much-vaunted and vengeful English side on their own (Billy Williams' cabbage) patch, was the most brilliant birthday present imaginable. Paddy will never forget the day he turned 26.

It's always harder second time round, especially when you're trying to emulate an achievement above normal levels of expectation. Lightening doesn't strike twice and all that. Just ask Ulster's European Cup winning heroes. The surprise element has gone, the opposition are gunning for you and some of the pressure switches to those who may previously have rejoiced in an unfancied underdog role. Providing an encore isn't easy.

So beating England back-to-back was a great feather in the cap of Irish rugby and both of the wins were high points in the careers of Paddy Johns and the other players who were involved. Those two glorious giant-killing acts and the attendant sense, even though at the end of the day these were only rugby matches for goodness sake, of the Irish thumbing the nose at the English rather than tugging the forelock fed fans on the emerald isle for long enough.

Whether Dublin 1993 and Twickenham 1994 had a slight negative spin-off of covering a multitude of sins and sweeping general Irish under-achievement in that era under the carpet is something which will be considered later. But, just like the high of Ulster's European Cup triumph being followed by a spectacular slump, few would have traded those famous victories over England for a bit more boring consistency throughout the decade. The joy of sport lies in its unpredictability and ability to inspire, for its magic moments like that Simon Geoghegan try in Twickenham. Days like those make the memories and create the legends. It was a bit of everything. Apart from the traditional national rivalries between the Irish and English, there was the sheer satisfaction of beating one of the world's top teams twice in a row. All the more so considering the arrogant attitude of elements of the opposition, their public and their media.

"In 1993, our game against England was the last in the Championship and they seemed to be coming over expecting to walk en bloc onto the Lions tour which was coming up that summer. Psychologically they had their bags already packed for that trip and we felt they could be vulnerable if we really got in amongst them and put it about a bit. Our victory may not actually have changed a lot in terms of Lions selection, but it definitely did dent a few reputations."

Yet another victory in Cardiff a fortnight earlier sent Ireland into the England game in good heart and, while the guys in green have never needed any motivation for facing the old foe, Johns accepts that beating Wales did boost confidence. "Until that Welsh win, Ireland hadn't tasted victory in the Championship for about three years so it was definitely a factor going into the England match. It all helped create a positive feeling."

Unsurprisingly, the Irish team was unchanged, led by Michael Bradley on the day he became his country's most capped scrumhalf by making his 29th Test appearance. Like Johns the following year, the Cork Con pivot was to have double cause for celebration. "Michael Bradley was a great guy to play with and to be around. A lovely fella with a big heart and, although he had a lot of critics he also had a lot of qualities and, in spite of the highs and lows, would still have a smile on his face."

England brought a star-studded line-up, captained by Will Carling, who was joined in the three-quarter line by his regular centre partner Jeremy Guscott and the Underwood brothers on the wings. Jonathan Webb was winning his 33rd cap at fullback, while the mercurial Stuart Barnes had recently displaced the more conservative Rob Andrew as Dewi Morris' halfback partner. The familiar front row of Jason Leonard, Brian Moore and Jeff Probyn was on duty, with skyscraper Martin Bayfield partnering veteran Wade Dooley in the engineroom and a youngish Ben Clarke being flanked by Mike Teague and Peter Winterbottom in the loose forward unit.

It was a stereotypically Irish performance, the home country relentlessly taking the game to England from the start with a real relish. The pack went about their work with an intensity and ferocity which knocked the visitors out of their stride and the big guns behind the scrum saw little ball. "We got stronger and stronger as the game went on" Paddy recalls. "They were really rattled and panicking as they found they were getting nowhere. And yet most of their players didn't really seem to want the ball either and we got the impression that they were always keen to move it on before the next big hit came in. I remember Pat O'Hara almost cutting Winterbottom in two and that set the tone." What others remember more is Johns being penalised right at the outset by referee Sandy McNeill for flattening the mighty Dooley as he ferociously followed up Elwood's kick-off. Ireland meant business.

With only Mick Galwey as a real alternative jumper to Johns, Ireland were short of options out of touch and Paddy, self-deprecatingly and a little ruefully, recalls that "we didn't win many lineouts that day! I remember jumping against Bayfield, who's a good 6'10" and has these extremely long arms. In the days before legalised lifting, it was very difficult to compete with that. We used some shortened lineouts, but I'd say England got most of ours as well as their own." But Johns and his colleagues certainly more than made up for any shortcomings in that area with a great first half display which they then took on to an even higher level after the interval.

The teams turned round with the score at 3-3, Elwood and Webb kicking a penalty apiece. Another penalty and then an excellent dropgoal by the Connacht outhalf raised the Irish spirits and England's best chance of a try went begging thanks to a knock-on. From ruck possession, Elwood crucially dropped a second goal to put Ireland two scores ahead with five minutes remaining and then came the unforgettable coup de grace. England threw caution to the wind as they sought to attack but, fittingly, captain Carling spilt possession when hit with yet another big Irish tackle and Elwood fed Galwey, who surged over for a crowning try as the ground erupted.

"The crowd were absolutely unbelievable too. I would still say that that was the best crowd I've ever played in front of and, when Galwey scored, it was just incredible altogether. Sometimes in a really tight game you get crucial tries which maybe put a team back in front or whatever, but the tension is so great and the game still so much up for grabs that everyone is almost afraid to celebrate scoring. But Galwey's try that day put us well and truly out of sight. We all knew then, the players and the fans, that there could only be one result and the feeling was amazing. I'll never forget that atmosphere.

"Not surprisingly, Dublin went absolutely mad that night. I remember us being handed champagne as we got off the bus back at the Berkeley Court. Beating England was quite something, not the sort of thing that happened every day. It was a fantastic feeling. It wasn't just England; there was a genuine sense of having beaten a great team. They had so many excellent players and, while we might have grumbled about the number of them who were subsequently picked for the Lions, they had proved themselves over a period and you can't judge just on one game. Ireland had a great day, but that was a superb English side and that made beating them even sweeter. To go on to win twice in a row against them was very satisfying indeed."

His mum vividly remembers the champagne celebrations too. "The butlers were out with the silver salvers serving the champagne. I've never seen the like of it before or since. Paddy handed me his glass of champagne so he could sign autographs, but I was taking photographs, so I handed it to my brother-in-law. When I got the glass back it was empty, but I've kept it to this day" she says. "I will never forget seeing the English team going past before the match, looking so arrogant, so that made it even sweeter. Dick Spring, the former rugby international and politician was simply flying round the foyer in the Berkeley Court that evening."

"It wasn't just the Irish public, or even the other Home Nations supporters who were delighted" recalls Richard Wallace. "The sevens team went to Hong Kong two days later and when we got there everyone congratulated us from all over the world. It was huge for Irish rugby. We weren't meant to be celebrating out there, but taking the Sevens as a serious competition. If anyone was caught drinking they would be sent home. So we decided either we played by the rules, or all ran the risk of getting caught, and that way they couldn't send all of us home. We opted for the latter," he grins. "The rule was that we weren't allowed to go home until the last person wanted to go and then we all left together. As it was, we had a really good tournament and only lost to Australia in extra time in the quarter-finals. We were just so high after our win against England."

Barnes took a fair bit of stick in the wake of that Dublin drubbing and his chances of ever taking over properly from Andrew seemed to suffer irreparable damage that day, but Johns says it "wouldn't be fair to single him out as a scapegoat. To be honest, there were a few English players who didn't seem to want to know that day when the going got tough. We didn't really target Barnes as an individual and in fact weren't too bothered which outhalf they picked."

When the Lions squad was named a few days later, prop Nick Popplewell and glory-grabber Galwey were the only two Irishmen included, a tiny fraction of the English representation. "One game wasn't going to change everything and, although we beat England, I would never have had any thought of making that Lions tour. It didn't really cross my mind. Nick was always a banker, while the game against England would have helped Mick inasmuch as he played well and scored a try. We went to the Hong Kong Sevens together just after the Lions squad had been announced. There were two big bronze lions outside the Bank of China and we got Mick to pose for pictures in front of them. But I didn't feel hard done by or anything like that. I actually roomed with him on that trip."

In 1994 compared with 1993, the Scottish match was the last of the four Five Nations games instead of the first, but Ireland again played France and Wales in that order in the two fixtures immediately before facing England. They put up a reasonable performance in Paris, but lost narrowly to the Welsh in Dublin and had only 10 Eric Elwood penalties, split evenly between the two matches, to show for the tryless first half of their Championship campaign. It didn't augur all that well for going to Twickenham to surely reap the wrath of an English outfit still smarting from what had happened 11 months earlier in Dublin. Paddy wasn't expecting a relaxing birthday, but he and his colleagues weren't planning for their hosts to have a pleasant afternoon either.

An important decision had been made shortly before the previous year's England game to bring former Irish captain Willie Anderson into the set-up to work with the forwards and the move was reaping real dividends. He made an immediate impact and deserves some credit for the Dublin display against England, but Johns and others best remember his massive influence in the build-up to the Twickenham rematch.

"Willie was obviously a man who had a very major effect on my own career, both in terms of skill-building and how I approached my rugby, so naturally I was delighted when he got involved with Ireland. I would imagine that the Munster boys in the Irish squad now would feel much the same about Niall O'Donovan. If you've been working with someone and are comfortable with them, you know you can go and have a chat at any time and ask some advice. I had benefited from playing with him for both Dungannon and Ulster, often with him as captain and, by this stage, he was also my club coach.

"He was always good at instilling self-belief and encouraging you to go for it, but the real secret of his success as a forwards coach was that he drilled you and drilled you and drilled you. Sure, Willie was good at getting people whipped up, but he was far more than a coach who just relied on roaring and shouting and sending sides out to get wildly stuck into the opposition. The thing which struck me even in the early days was how precise he was when we were going through drills, with how you set the ball back and how you hit the ruck and so forth."

Accuracy is a word which is common currency in rugby parlance these days, but Anderson seems to have been a bit of a pioneer of preaching its importance. It comes as no surprise, however, that he was also into the psychological stuff, the mind games. "The night before that Twickenham game, he called all the Irish forwards in. It was pure Willie, vintage Willie, Willie at his best. Kyran Bracken, who was just starting his England career at that stage, had been named in their team at scrum-half and, as everyone knows, he'd been born in Dublin. Willie decided it was worth making a big deal out of it. It was, like 'Kyran Bracken. Irishman. Playing for England. Traitor'. That was the theme and, apart from the expletives, it could have been fire and brimstone preaching.

"Even by Willie's standards, he was surpassing himself, with the fury of his talk and I'll never forget the way his eyes were popping out of his head, face as red as a hot iron and the sweat pouring off him in bucketfuls. He implored us to climb all over Bracken the first time he found himself on the floor and I'm sure there were eight enthusiastic converts by the time we left the room that night! Sure enough, the game got underway and, within the first five minutes, England tapped ball back untidily from a lineout and poor old Kyran had to go down on it. I think every Irish forward had the same flashback at once and we all went over him with a real relish, churning him out the back of it and leaving as many studmarks as possible. He had to change his shorts which were ripped to shreds and, if I remember right, was dropped by England for the next game. I kinda felt sorry for the guy, for he'd also got rough treatment on his Test debut against the All Blacks the previous autumn when Jamie Joseph had infamously stamped on his ankle.

"But I suppose newish halfbacks, fullbacks and the like have always been on the receiving end of a bit of what we could euphemistically call character-testing in the early stages of games. You want to see what they're made of, what stomach they have for it, and whether they are the sort to be easily knocked out of their stride. It's all about trying to get a bit of psychological advantage and to gain the upper hand. In Kyran's case, that was heightened by Willie's sermon about his Irishness and he got such rough treatment that day that I was still a bit sheepish when I met him as my one of my new Saracens team-mates a few years later!"

Neil Francis, who played in the Irish second row in that Twickenham game, joins Johns in telling the tale of Anderson's exhortations regarding Bracken, but also recalls that "the training session on the Thursday had been the worst at international level which I could remember. "Every ball was dropped and it was just one of those shambolic sessions which happen sometimes, but Willie Anderson came over to me afterwards and pointed out that England had injury problems and so forth. He said we were going to win" said Francis.

Being part of the Twickenham 1994 victory was also a proud moment for Anderson, who cites Johns as being one of those who carried out to the letter what he was asked to do. "I can still see Paddy doing the things we'd worked on before that game" says Willie. "Paddy was one of those people who knew that practice makes perfect and I always admired the way he worked tirelessly to get something right. He was an easy guy to coach in that he never got tired going over and over things in an effort to get them right; in fact he would have insisted on it himself. Those were innovative times and Paddy was right on the mark with how he played that day, keeping the ball alive, driving low and so forth. In that second win over England, we managed some great continuity play and Paddy was central to that."

While the forwards were feasting on what Anderson had served up, others in the Irish camp were finding Friday evening was dragging a bit with little to settle the nerves as they awaited the morrow. One such was Maurice Field. Field, the Ulster and Malone centre, a fire-fighter from Belfast, was over the moon to finally be winning his first full Irish cap only five days before his 30th birthday, having been brought into the side at the expense of his provincial partner Mark McCall. Having waited so long, presumably it was a quiet, early night on the Friday? Not quite. A fair bit of relaxation maybe, but not quite as much rest as you'd have imagined.

"We were staying in Chelsea Harbour and, after dinner, I remember having a walk out and us wandering into a local pub. Pat Whelan, who was one of the selectors then, was there at the bar and, if we'd just ducked out again, it would have looked like we were naughty schoolboys with a guilty conscience. As far as I was concerned, I was a grown man working in a day job in which I see some awful tragedies and rugby was always a welcome diversion, a form of escape, something I enjoyed. Anyone who would have seen my play could never have criticised my hunger or commitment and, although I enjoyed the social side of the game, I always went out on the pitch to be the best I could be and wanting to do myself justice. And an international debut at Twickenham is about as big as you'll get.

"Anyway, Pat says, 'What are you having' and I replied 'Mine's a pint, Pat, if you're buying'. It was a pub which was familiar with having the Irish team next door and the next thing we knew, there were a few drinks sent down the bar. I suspect it was more a case of genuine hospitality than shades of the legend about the West Indies cricketers being filled full of Guinness the night before they lost to Ireland in that match back in the 1960s, but whatever it was, we were there for long enough. About eight pints later, we headed back to the hotel, nice and happy and relaxed and ready for a good night's sleep. I remember Phil Danaher wakening up when I came clattering back into the room after midnight. He told me it was up to me to do what I liked, but just hoped that none of the press had seen me that evening, or it would be a story.

"I slept like a top and there was none of the tossing or turning which there probably would have been if I'd stayed in and gone to bed too early, before I was ready to sleep. Next morning, I wasn't up too early and, being a bit on the tired side, didn't suffer from the sort of nerves which would have been likely otherwise. We were back in the same pub that night celebrating a win over England and I think I'd a lot more than eight pints this time!" Such a scenario, except inadvertently on the occasion he was called up to sit on the Irish bench against France in Paris, would have been unthinkable for Johns, though his admiration for the fiercely committed and combative Field is unqualified. Every man is different and Maurice never let anyone down on the pitch, not least that day.

Paddy was rooming with Galwey, while the other second row, Francis, was sharing with Clohessy. Apart from the latter's smoking, the pair fed their faces with burgers and chips and flicked fretfully through the channels as they too found sleep hard to come by. When passing Sky News, the Young Munster prop spotted the English captain Carling, who was spouting on about his own team without as much as a reference to the men in green in spite of the result 11 months earlier. "That was typical of the English arrogance and really riled the Claw" says Francis.

The direct revenge element was diluted slightly by the fact that there were no fewer than nine changes to the line-up England had fielded in Dublin, that result having taken its toll in bringing a few illustrious Five Nations careers to an end even though it came too late to really affect selection for the 1993 Lions tour. Jon Callard took over at fullback from retired Bath predecessor Webb, while another Recreation Ground player, Phil de Glanville, was at centre in place of his injured clubmate Guscott. Rob Andrew and relative newcomer Bracken, winning his third cap, had usurped Barnes and Morris, both of whom were on the bench, at halfback, while Leonard, Moore and Bayfield were the only survivors up front from the loss at Lansdowne Road.

Stalwarts Probyn, Dooley, Teague and Winterbottom had all gone, replaced by Victor Ubogu, a young Martin Johnson, Tim Rodber and Neil Back respectively. That quartet had only 11 caps between them while, with Clarke injured and Dean Richards out of favour, the uncapped Steve Ojomoh of Bath was brought into the middle of a backrow between an allegedly less than fully fit Rodber and Back, who had been a little under the weather with flu symptoms. That was good news for Ireland's all-Ulster loose forward unit of Robinson, Johns and McBride, while the other bonus was having a French referee with an Irish name for good measure, Patrick Thomas. He was, incidentally, officiating in his first international.

"Never mind his name, which sounded like a good mix of Irish and Welsh, the great thing was that Monsieur Thomas was French, so we knew we'd have carte blanche. It would be a case of 'jouez, jouez', basically "play on, play on'. Having French officials was ideal for Ireland in situations like that and the other thing we looked for in those days was wet weather, for our basic aim was to make mayhem and anything which helped us in that regard was welcome."

In contrast to England, Ireland only had three personnel changes from the meeting in Dublin, one of which was enforced by the serious injury sustained by Cunningham in an AIL match. McCall had played against Wales a fortnight earlier, but Field came in now in Ireland's only alteration from that team. The other variations from the line-up which had claimed England's scalp the previous season saw O'Shea at fullback for Clarke and Francis in the pack for O'Hara with both Johns and Robinson having moved in the consequent reshuffle.

This time, as well as doing very well in the loose and being solid at the scrummage, Ireland did manage to effectively disrupt England's supply of lineout possession in spite of the presence of Johnson and Bayfield. England led 6-3, two penalties to one from Elwood, but Ireland applied impressive pressure and it was ultimately rewarded with a great Geoghegan try. Richard Wallace came off the blindside wing to take the ball from Danaher after Ireland had won possession on the right and he released Geoghegan, who did the rest with what Johns describes as "a bit of brilliance."

"Simon was a very exciting player, unpredictable but capable of moments of magic. I actually played in his first ever Irish game, for the Students against the US Eagles. He showed fantastic acceleration in scoring a great try in that match, yet he'd been running the wrong way in training the day before and dropping balls all over the place. That Students international demonstrated though that he definitely had considerable raw talent. Before internationals, you had to put your head out of the hotel room door before venturing out in case he was running past. You needed to apply your green cross code and look both ways and all that. He used to do his sprint training in the corridor outside the rooms. Simon was also a real character in many ways. Jim Staples and he were very good friends and they were very much the terrible twins in terms of always talking in Cockney slang. They also had this thing, which seemed to amuse them greatly, that every time they got a taxi to the airport, they used to ask the driver where Blake's restaurant was as they passed it and then be amused when he would point it out. I'm not quite sure why, but it always tickled them."

Elwood landed a superb conversion from wide on the left to stretch Ireland's lead to four points and, although England pulled back three with a penalty, superb defence by the visitors saw them largely withstand the third quarter onslaught. As the English continued to press, Ireland took great heart from a rapid raid which brought them three points out of nothing, with that man Geoghegan again playing a crucial role. Running out of defence, he kicked deep into the English half and followed up to nail a flustered Andrew, who was whistled up for not releasing in the tackle and Elwood landed the penalty.

There was still a lot of time for England to win the game and Ireland faced a long last quarter of an hour when Callard's fourth penalty again reduced the arrears to a single point. That set up a frenetic finish, but the greens gloriously held out. It was, remarkably, the first time a visiting side had won at Twickenham in six years, a statistic which speaks volumes about Ireland's achievement.

"No-one expected us to win that game, especially after Dublin and given England's record at Twickenham. It was, perhaps, less convincing than the previous year and there were bits of controversy, but beating England at HQ is a fantastic feeling. For Irish rugby at the time, it was a huge result, and definitely ranks right up there for me in any list of career highlights. I can remember us having a scrum at the end and me keeping the ball in at No 8 for what seemed about five minutes as we looked to run down the clock. It was incredibly close throughout. There was a lot of energy and emotion expended that day.

"There were a lot of Irish people there and we could hear Molly Malone ringing out from the stands, which gave us a great boost as we just tried to keep going and keep going. At the final whistle, Philip Danaher ran to me and jumped onto me to hug. He was a very heavy centre and it nearly knocked me to the ground I was so exhausted."

His mum was to be mortified though after the match. She wasn't there in person, but had sent him a telegram to wish happy birthday and good luck, and watched the match on the television. "Someone had put a green cap on Paddy at the end of the game and I suddenly saw him walking up to meet Prince Edward and the Prime Minister John Major with this thing on his head. I cringed at such a show of bad manners, but he was so excited, he didn't even realize he had it on" she says. The Irish really had taken over Twickenham and Paddy was set for the mother of all birthday parties.

"When we got back to our hotel, Noel Murphy had organised a birthday cake. They also gave me a bathroom robe out of the hotel for a present, but I'd already had the best present I could have had" he smiles. "And, from what I can remember, it was a fantastic night!" The Twickenham heroes slumped to a disappointingly drab draw with Scotland in a dire Dublin denouement to the 1994 Championship campaign, but Irish eyes were still smiling and the memories would last forever.

12. MAGNIFICENT SEVENS

Ireland just don't do Sevens these days it seems. Not seriously anyway. And more's the pity according to Paddy Johns. The big man got a lot of pleasure out of the slimmed down version of the game and was at the heart of the halcyon days when the Irish side sensationally stormed the inaugural World Cup Sevens in 1993, only knocked out in the semis by an Aussie try in the last minute.

He's got this dream of a modern Irish team featuring the likes of Keith Wood, David Wallace, Eric Miller, Peter Stringer, David Humphreys, Brian O'Driscoll and Denis Hickie taking on and beating the best in events like the Hong Kong Sevens. Throw in the likes of Geordan Murphy, young Brian O'Riordan and Donnacha O'Callaghan, maybe Alan Quinlan, and it's easy to get excited at the prospect. It ain't going to happen though. Professional players at the top end of the game are overworked already and the governing bodies in most of the leading nations are, understandably, placing sevens tournaments well down their list of priorities or barely mapping them at all. Ireland, not surprisingly, perhaps aren't the only nation who send players to Sevens tournaments primarily for development or rehab purposes, with a few specialists thrown in and relatively journeymen then making up the numbers.

At a lower level, the toll which longer seasons take on players means that many clubs no longer send strong senior sides to the traditional end-of-term tournaments which used to coincide with the April showers or those which used to act as curtain-raisers to the new season in September. The fixture list is so packed these days that something has to suffer and, more often than not, Sevens is getting squeezed though it's hardly a conspiracy. Many traditional events and friendly fixtures have also had to be sacrificed in the name of progress in the modern era.

Paddy had played a bit of Sevens here and there in his youth and enjoyed it. He still recalls his first visit to the Omagh Sevens with Dungannon with a rueful grin. "I was a young cub at the time and was handed a bottle of Ouzo. It was knocked back with no apparent problem and I thought I was a great fella but, when we walked outside into the warm air, I just hit the ground (John Gamble recalls him 'going down like a sack of spuds'). They had to bundle me into one of the cars and I lay there in a very delicate state the whole way home. The guys made a stop-off halfway home, but I couldn't get out of the car. Sevens tournaments have always had a very pronounced social side!"

But he was really bitten by the bug of the abbreviated form of the game when representing the Irish Wolfhounds in the famous Melrose Sevens of 1991. The only non-Scottish side in the field surprised everyone by winning the event, even though skipper Denis McBride reputedly had to be introduced to the squad's two wingers, David Beggy and Brendan Hanavan, just before the tournament started. McBride was joined by fellow full internationals in Johns, Neil Francis, Rolland, another of the discarded debutants against Argentina, and Kenny Murphy. The nine man squad was completed by cavalier Ulster fullback Colin Wilkinson, a future full cap, and Skerries hooker Billy Mulcahy, who played for many years at provincial level and was to be a member of the Irish squad at the inaugural Sevens World Cup two years later.

Defending champions Randwick provided an Aussie flavour, while the other visiting side, Loughborough Students, featured Ulsterman Niall Malone. All of Scotland's big clubs were represented in a 20-team tournament, the sides liberally sprinkled with past, present and future internationals from the home country. These included the likes of Kenny Milne, Iain Paxton, Iwan Tukalo, Finlay Calder, Derek Turnbull, Tony Stanger, the Hastings brothers, John Jeffrey, Kenny Logan, Craig Chalmers, Doddie Weir, Bryan Redpath, Sean Lineen, Gary Armstrong, Gregor Townsend, Rob Wainwright and Rowan Shepherd. Jeffrey, Scotland three-quarter Roger Baird and future Test loose forward Adam Roxburgh were in the Kelso squad beaten 28-12 by the Wolfhounds in the final, their second loss in successive deciders.

In the following year's Melrose Sevens programme, the Wolfhounds were described as "highly popular and worthy winners . . . their preparation uniquely Irish, nevertheless conjuring up a potent winning combination of pace and guile which proved irresistible." "We went over there in 1991 without having trained as a group or anything" Paddy reminisces. "On the morning of the tournament we had a runout, but we were absolutely terrible. Craig Chalmers and his team came walking past and couldn't stop themselves laughing when they saw what a seemingly hopeless mess we were. Honestly, we really were awful."

In explaining his own selection for Irish Sevens sides, Johns points to the general tendency of nations to use such forums to give promising young players experience and exposure. "I would have been in that category at the time in terms of my stage of development but, more specifically, I suppose my height was also an asset in that I brought a real lineout presence in Sevens. Most guys in Sevens squads would be no more than about 6'2", so I had a few inches on them which was useful at lineout time and for trying to win the ball at kick-offs. Apart from the lineout and the kickoffs, my role in Sevens would generally have been to stay in the middle of the field and tackle, maybe cause a bit of chaos too!" he adds with a knowing look.

In another article for the 1991 Melrose Sevens programme, a former Scottish international, Leslie Allan, talks up the merits of the shortened version, and effectively argues that it should have a useful purpose in the evolving modern game which requires all players to be better athletes and more multi-skilled. "Definitely" agrees Paddy. "Sevens was always attractive to me from a fun and fitness point of view. It was a fast game and helped make you flexible and hone your general skills. I played for enjoyment and had no specific Sevens targets like playing in that first World Cup, but being part of that Wolfhounds success at Melrose in 1991 helped push my name forward."

The Wolfhounds, another tradition to be squeezed in the professional era, is a concept remembered with fondness by Johns. "At the time, it was an outlet, a sort of Irish Barbarians, and it was always an honour to represent them. You always had great names on the Wolfhounds committee like Karl Mullen, Tony O'Reilly, Tom Kiernan and Fergus Slattery."

In an article for the 1992 Melrose Sevens programme, 1950 Lions captain Dr Mullen reminisces about his own visits to the tournament in yesteryear and praises the virtues of the short version of the game. "I am of the firm belief that its contribution towards improving the timing of passes, the organisation of defence and the practising of elusive running is all of great benefit to the full 15-man game" he wrote. "In short the equation goes something like this. Rugby to the power of seven helps to eliminate the 10 and expand it to 15!" A cleverly perceptive perspective indeed.

That summer, Paddy returned to the Test arena on Ireland's tour of New Zealand and established himself in his country's 15-a-side team, but that didn't mean turning his back on Sevens. The following Spring, having played for the Wolfhounds in monsoon conditions the previous year, he made the second of what were to be four appearances at the Hong Kong Sevens and then, a fortnight later, took part in the inaugural World Cup Sevens tournament at Murrayfield. Rolland skippered in Hong Kong at the end of March, where Ireland beat Italy 7-5 and the host nation 24-0 before going down only 17-12 to Australia. Better was to follow on Scottish soil, when McBride had taken over the captaincy of an unchanged 10-man squad.

Eight of the 10 were full caps, including Eric Elwood, the Connacht outhalf who had starred in the recent wins over Wales and England in his first two Tests, and Lansdowne utility three-quarter Brian Glennon, who had won what proved to be his only senior cap as a replacement that Spring against France. The exceptions were Mulcahy and Wanderers flanker Jon Garth, an Irish cricket international all-rounder, who had played with Johns in Melrose 1992. McBride, Johns and Mick Galwey completed the complement of five forwards. Rolland, Elwood, Vinny Cunningham and Richard Wallace were the best backs combo with Glennon in reserve, while Johns, McBride and Garth ended up as the first choice forwards, supported by Galwey and 'Wigs' Mulcahy.

Those well known workaholics and fierce competitors Johns and McBride need no introduction, but Paddy is quick to praise Garth, a man better known for his prowess in the summer sport. "Jonathan had good hands, maybe reflecting his cricket background, and was a very intelligent player. He was strong enough to be a forward, but also genuinely quick, able to score tries from the halfway line. Wigs was around the provincial scene for a long time, but I suppose his great loyalty in sticking with Skerries right down through the years didn't help his chances of getting a cap. I admired his loyalty.

"Alain Rolland was our scrumhalf, Eric a great goal-kicker, Vinny Cunningham was a well-rounded and versatile player and Richie Wallace our speedster. I suppose it proved to be a fair combination, but no-one would have known what we were capable of in advance of the tournament, not least because we didn't know ourselves! Things like our strengths and weaknesses or possible permutations or team tactics wouldn't have been that much discussed among us. Even though we had done pretty well in Hong Kong and surprised a few people there, we weren't expected to make much of an impression."

There was an extensive qualifying competition, stretching back to May 1992, to determine who would take part in the inaugural Sevens World Cup. This involved as unlikely nations as Latvia, Lithuania, Poland, Portugal, Sweden, Belgium, Morocco, Spain, Sri Lanka, Czechoslovakia, Tunisia, Taiwan, Germany, Malaysia and Kenya. Ireland were seeded 10th in a 24-strong field, behind favourites Fiji, New Zealand, Australia, England, Western Samoa, Scotland, France, South Africa and Wales, with Argentina and Canada completing the top half of the rankings. The remaining dozen, in order of seeding, were Namibia, Italy, Romania, Japan, Korea, Tonga, Spain, USA, Hong Kong, Taiwan, the Netherlands and Latvia.

"I didn't even know at the time that we were seeded 10th and would probably have been surprised that our ranking was as high as that" admits Paddy. "We'd probably have been more fancied as a leading light in the entertainment stakes! Sevens was always a fun thing to do in Ireland, with the tournaments being a big part of rugby's social calendar. Even though this was a World Cup, we'd have gone down as a team to the Rutland Bar in Edinbugh for a few pints the nights leading up to the tournament, which started on a Friday. It was very relaxed. The other teams would all be in their hotels, but there we'd be in the Rutland every night.

"That accounted for the Monday, Tuesday and Wednesday nights, but we decided we had better start to get a bit more serious and so we stayed in on Thursday night. We were watching Question of Sport in our rooms when suddenly a photograph of me appeared on the picture board. You could hear the shouts coming out of the rooms up and down our corridor, the boys having a laugh. It was a real coincidence that I should be on that evening, for it's the only time I'm aware of ever having featured on the programme. I was pleased that Bill Beaumont was able to identify me alright to save a lot of stick. My fingers were all taped up in the picture and I remember him commenting 'that guy's a dentist and look at the state of his hands'."

The tournament was a wonderful collection of exciting players, a compelling combination of established Test stars, up and coming prospects, sevens specialists and a few flambuoyant relative unknowns, mainly from the minor nations, who were to make their own mark. Among the youngsters were teenagers Townsend and future French fullback Ugo Mola, while a trio of 20-year olds, Lawrence Dallaglio, Matt Burke and Matt Dawson, were all to become household names in the sport. Neil Jenkins, Todd Blackadder, Lisandro Arbizu, Brian Lima and Glenn Osborne were all 21 at the time of the tournament. Two of the younger brigade who were to become team-mates of Paddy's were 21-year old Australian Ryan Constable and South African Dion O'Cuinneagain, 20, who later declared for Ireland and played firstly under Johns and then as his captain at international level.

"It's funny how the paths of myself and Ryan have crossed, right down through our careers, from the time he came to Dungannon with an Australian Outback Barbarians team. By remarkable coincidence, he was also in Newfoundland with Emerging Australia one summer I was there and years later became a club colleague at both Saracens and Dungannon. We've also obviously had a couple of seasons together for Ulster."

Constable was joined in the Australian squad by two world famous names in David Campese and another future clubmate of Johns, Michael Lynagh, who already had 132 Test caps between them. Their squad also featured Burke and formidable forwards Willie Ofahengaue and Ile Tabua. Perhaps not surprisingly in light of that nation's relatively recent return to Test rugby, O'Cuinneagain was one of eight uncapped players in the South African squad, along with Joost van der Westhuizen, Chester Williams, Reuben Kruger and Dick Muir. Andre Joubert and Jacques Olivier had three caps between them.

Ireland opened up on the first day by beating the South Koreans 21-12 and then had an excellent 17-9 win against a formidable French outfit featuring Laurent Cabannes, Eric Bonneval, Philippe Bernat-Salles, Christophe Deylaud, David Berty and Mola. "France was very close and we just about beat them after not having had all that much to spare against the Koreans. Anyone watching that game probably wouldn't have given a lot for our chances of going too far. I suppose it would be fair to say we started off slowly and then it kind of snowballed."

Captain Denis McBride cites Paddy as a major influence over Ireland's unexpected progression after meeting France. "France had Philippe Bernat-Salles playing for them and we all knew he was a flier. At one point Paddy found himself put on the wing marking him. Bernat-Salles got the ball and tried to chip over Paddy's head, after which he would have had a clear run to the line. Paddy pretended to be concentrating very hard on the ball and just cleaned Bernat-Salles out by running into him! He kept us in the tournament."

On Saturday, Ireland scored 38 points without reply against a United States squad starring Brian Vizard and then rounded off their Pool B campaign with a comprehensive 45-0 thrashing of the Netherlands. Between the American and Dutch matches, the guys in green lost their only group game when going down 24-7 against second seeds New Zealand. New Zealand could call on two men, Pat Lam and Junior Paramore, who were to mainly make their names in the Samoan backrow along with sevens specialists in Blackadder, Eric Rush and Dallas Seymour. Established All Blacks Frank Bunce and John Timu were involved, as were the young Osborne and Stu Forster. Those results put Ireland into Sunday's second phase of the competition, when the eight surviving teams were split into two groups, McBride's men being bracketed with the three sets of south sea islanders, Western Samoa, Tonga and Fiji, as Johns recalls only too well!

"I remember when we found out the group we were in on Sunday, everyone thought 'oh f**king 'ell'. Those countries revel in sevens because they've always got big, strong guys with a bit of flair and to have to face all three one after the other was quite a prospect! Samoa were seeded well above us, but we got them at 10.00 on a miserable wet morning when they maybe didn't fancy the rain and cold that much and probably wished they were still in bed. I'd have to admit the conditions did favour us. They looked frozen and we took advantage with a real guerrilla raid. We also beat Tonga, which was close, and although we got stuffed by Fiji, still went through to the next stage."

On Fijian Waisale Serevi, arguably the greatest and probably the most famous Sevens player of all time, Johns enthuses: "He was just a maestro on the pitch. Serevi had incredible skill, but the thing that really struck me about him was his nonchalance. He could produce moments of breathtaking brilliance and still look as cool as ever. You'd hardly ever see him look out of breath. He wouldn't have been the bravest in the world, mind, but I suppose that's allowable when you can do what he could!"

Cross-overs between the island nations and New Zealand were common at that stage so, just as the latter featured Lam and Paramore, Western Samoa were able to call on future All Blacks Alama Ieremia and Junior Tonu'u in this tournament. But Ireland secured an excellent 17-0 victory against the joint fourth seeds and then edged past a Tongan team backboned by the Vunipolas on a 14-12 scoreline before going down to 31-7 to the Fijians and the incomparable Serevi. Again though, a team could afford to lose a game in this round and still progress, so Ireland were through to face the Aussies in the semi-final, an achievement way above their seeding.

"The semi-final was very exciting and we did well, but the decisive, final turning point came with two minutes to go when Vinny Cunningham was wrongly adjudged to have knocked on. He picked up and kicked to touch way downfield, but play was called back for a scrum and they scored from it. I'm not sure who got the try, whether it was Lynagh or Willie O, but that levelled the scores and Lynagh then kicked the winning conversion, making it 21-19. It was heartbreaking to miss out on the final but, overall, we'd had a great tournament. No-one could have expected us to still be in it at that stage on the Sunday afternoon."

Constable says: "Ireland gave us two very close games that year, in Hong Kong and at the World Cup, but thankfully I was lucky enough to largely avoid Paddy! In fact, I count myself very fortunate to have played most of my rugby with him, not against him!"

England's largely untried squad, whose 10 players only had three caps between them, two for Tim Rodber and the other for skipper, Harlequins winger Andrew Harriman, had also done well to reach the last four, albeit that they had been seeded to do so. But they then really made the world sit up and take notice by knocking out hot favourites Fiji in the semi-finals and went on to be crowned inaugural champions with victory over Australia in the decider. Not surprisingly, that success helped launch a number of English players on the big stage, with Dallaglio, Rodber and Dawson in particular going on to have very distinguished Test careers. The versatile Nick Beal became a Lion, while Damien Hopley would have made more of an impression but for the presence of Will Carling and Jeremy Guscott followed by the injury problems which cut short his career. Adedayo Adebayo also played 15-a-side for England as did sevens specialists Harriman and Sheasby, leaving Wakefield pivot Dave Scully and the little-known JPS Cassell of Saracens as the only two not to be capped by their country at Test level.

Scotland fielded Weir, Townsend, Nicol and Turnbull, while the Welsh squad contained the men who were to be their two main halfbacks of the 1990s in Jenkins and an as then still uncapped Rob Howley. They also had Stuart Davies, Emyr Lewis, Wayne Proctor and Rupert Moon. Some of Paddy's Argentinian opponents on his Test debut in 1990 were present in Edinburgh that weekend, while an experienced Canadian squad included the likes of Al Charron, Gordon Mackinnon and Dave Lougheed. The Argentinian-born Diego Dominguez, Paolo Vaccari, Marcello Cuttitta and the late Ivan Francescato were among the Italian contingent.

That almost endless roll of honour from the 1993 World Cup Sevens serves to illustrate just how seriously that inaugural tournament was taken, leading to an exciting three-day festival of rugby. But Ireland, in particular, have failed to build on that excellent top four finish, either in terms of future sevens success at international level or in increasing the popularity of this version of the game back home.

"The tournament as a whole was a success and an exciting event. Anyone who was in Edinburgh that weekend would have come away with a positive view of the concept of a Sevens World Cup. We had done well too, but it didn't really change anything in Ireland or get the nation enthused about the idea of serious Sevens. The rugby public at home and elsewhere probably got a bit of a shock that we reached the semi-final, but it was never really built upon in any way. One problem too was that the televising of the tournament by UTV was very poor indeed, which didn't help in terms of reaching out to a wider audience."

A number of traditional Sevens competitions remain, such as those in Ulster where Paddy cut his teeth at Carrick and Omagh, and, most high profile in Irish terms, the wonderfully appointed Kinsale Sevens by the Sea on the coast of west Cork, famed for the craic and camaraderie to be enjoyed by all. Such tournaments bring together teams of varying abilities in a range of categories and some good rugby is played, though they are primarily important elements of the very fabric and soul of rugby, high points of the social calendar. That is how it has been, how it is and how it seems set to remain. Paddy is convinced Ireland could have a decent Sevens side right now, but accepts that the demands on the leading players are too high already.

Other countries, notably New Zealand, which has a genuine Sevens culture, and Australia, contract specialist Sevens players at national level, treat it like a sport in itself and make heroes of their star turns in the shortened game, the likes of Eric Rush. But it is doubtful, even if the will was there, whether Ireland have the depth of real talent to go down that route, so the current trend of low-key and relatively poorly-prepared sides making relatively little impression in tournaments around the world looks likely to continue. It is a vicious circle. Murrayfield in April 1993 was memorable because it was a World Cup tournament and for Ireland's exhilarating performances and unexpected degree of success, but Hong Kong has long been a Sevens mecca and Johns also treasures his four of appearances there.

Paddy was back in 1994 and again in 1996, both times under the captaincy of Ulster colleague McBride. Paddy, Denis, Rolland and Elwood were the only members of the Murrayfield panel to go in 1994, being joined by Ulster pair Brian Robinson and Innes Gray, Shannon flanker Eddie Halvey, Rolland's Blackrock halfback partner Alan McGowan and Munster centres Phil Danaher and Cork Con's Ireland A international Brian Walsh. On that occasion, the greens started by beating Singapore 40-0, but then lost 22-7 to the President's VII and disappointingly went down 14-12 to the USA.

In 1996, the spirit of Edinburgh was represented by captain McBride, Johns, Cunningham, Wallace and Garth, who were joined by Cork Con pair Paul Burke and David Corkery, Blackrock flyer Niall Woods, Ballymena wing James Topping and national 15-a-side captain Niall Hogan. But, even with nine full internationals supplemented by an experienced exponent of Sevens in Garth, Ireland were hammered 49-0 in the quarter-finals by New Zealand after getting out of their group by beating Malaysia 43-5 and Namibia 21-15 before drawing with the Samoans.

Hong Kong. Ah yes, Hong Kong. That place that dare not speak its name in the Johns household. Paddy got his permission to go every time in the end, but whether Kirsty gave in with good grace or not is another matter entirely! "The first time it was 'this is a once in a lifetime opportunity', second time it was 'I'll never be asked again', third time it was 'you come too' and, by the fourth, it was, like, 'feck off Paddy, just go'," Mrs Johns relates with a shake of the head as a grin spreads over hubby's face.

"Ach, Hong Kong was great" he reminisces. "The first night was always initiation, about getting to know your team-mates, even though you knew them already anyway! We'd get there about 1pm and want to sweat the journey out of us, so we'd go to the gym and do cycling or weights, then have a shower and get something to eat before heading out to the Bull and Bear. The first evening would be spent playing drinking games and then we'd end up in Joe Bananas. My first time there was pretty bad and I got violently sick. I'll never forget the first training session.

"Denis McBride was captain and his policy was that everyone trained, no matter what. I was the only one not down to breakfast next morning and I remember him coming up and dragging me out of bed, green and as sick as a dog. We had to get the tube to training and then walk for a distance. It was hot and humid and I wasn't feeling a bit like it at all. Mick Cuddy was our President and, in the end, my training that day consisted of walking round the edge of the pitch with him, getting air into my lungs. I asked the groundsman if he had anything for a headache and he went away and brought back tiger balm. It was the first time I had ever used it. I put it on my temples and experienced a wonderful burning menthol fragrance which made my eyes water and took my mind off my headache! Great stuff!

"I was still in a bad way when we returned to the hotel and was back in bed when the tournament doctor came in in the middle of the afternoon to administer treatment, most notably an injection in my backside." Although sweating beer, Johns did his best to explain to the medical man that he'd been eating dodgy shellfish and, Kirsty recalls, "he phoned me later and tried to fob me off with the same sort of story. The penny quickly dropped though and he got no sympathy from me!"

It wasn't the only time in Hong Kong that Paddy found himself seeing stars or feeling helpless, thanks to the dazzling displays and fancy footwork of the likes of Waisale Serevi and a young Christian Cullen. "In my last Hong Kong Sevens, we were on the New Zealand line and gave away a penalty. Cullen took it quickly, ran at me, sidestepped and ran the length of the pitch to score. I swear, his lateral movement seemed like it covered about six yards! It was a long jog to behind the posts for the conversion."

One of the highlights of the Melrose Sevens for Paddy was meeting the legendary Bill McLaren for the first time at the scene of the famous commentator's final stint behind a BBC microphone just over a decade later. "As is well known, Bill used to come down to the stadium the day before internationals and chat to the players so I got to know him quite well in later years. Like everyone else, I've sampled the striped humbug sweets which he is famous for dispensing. It was always nice to see Bill and he was someone whom players respected and had a genuine affection for. We ended up both retiring in the same year but, even though people might reckon I was around for ever as a player, I think his commentary career was just a little longer!"

13. THE BACK ROW MOVE

There is no doubt that, when it comes to casual classification, Paddy Johns will be remembered as a second row forward. Yet no fewer than 17 of his 57 Test starts for Ireland were made in the No 8 jersey. He was in the middle of the back row for one of Ireland's greatest triumphs in the past decade, the win over England at Twickenham which rocked the rugby world, and featured there throughout the 1995 World Cup.

Changes in the laws literally gave him a lift in terms of lineout prowess, but backrowers being obliged to stay bound slightly devalued his currency as an international No 8 and he ultimately reverted to the second row to prolong his Test career. At his best, he was good enough to play either position at the very highest level and, although at times being a jack of all trades could be a double-edged sword and the constant prospect of being moved was a little irritating, he ultimately wasn't too bothered where he played.

Indeed, it was a tribute to his versatility that the selectors always knew they could pick him where their need was greatest, depending on whether at a particular period they were better served for second rows or loose forwards. The horses for courses criteria was also applied on certain occasions, depending on what type of game the coach wanted to play and whether he wanted more size or more mobility. In any case, Paddy was such a good forward at his prime that there was generally little real danger of him falling between two stools and losing his place altogether. It usually wasn't a case of whether he played, simply a question of where.

The season after he had made his international debut against Argentina, Johns had made quite a big deal of the fact that he saw his future as a No 8. Came out publicly and said that was the only position he wanted to be considered for by Ireland. At the time, it seemed to some a bit of a foolhardy statement for a young player still trying to make the breakthrough into regular international rugby. He had made his name up to that point mainly as a lock, so there was a possibility that this decision could set him back a bit as he started almost from scratch to climb up a new ladder. There were also several significant No 8s on the scene at that stage, including Noel Mannion, Brian Robinson and Phil Lawlor. And anyway, if you could have two arrows to your bow, why restrict yourself to one, especially as a young player trying to make his way?

"I'd had trouble with my back at Trinity and had lost a degree of confidence in my physical ability to survive longer-term in the second row at the top level. So I made it known that I only wanted to play No 8. It was something which I felt that I had to do at the time, but circumstances changed and I ended up winning another 40-odd caps as a second row!"

Injury to Lawlor gave Johns an unexpected opening with the late call-up to the New Zealand tour of 1992 but, as already related, when he finally saw some action on that trip, it was as a second row, a management decision which had him seething at the time. But successful outings in the position and Test selection thawed his frostiness to the extent that, when he returned home, he was easy about where he played in the future. From then on, he was generally cool about it.

His first international outing at No 8 came after nine consecutive appearances in the second row, starting with that first Test in New Zealand and he then packed down in the middle of the back row on seven successive occasions. A brief flirtation with lock during the 1995 Five Nations was followed by another nine Tests on the spin at No 8 including every match at that summer's World Cup. Then came the lean period in the middle of his international career when he alternated between positions and was in and out of the side, before bouncing back to really blossom and, from then on, all his Test appearances were in the green No 4 jersey.

"Although I'd made the strong statement at one stage that I only wanted to be considered as a No 8, being picked in the second row in the Tests in New Zealand in 1992 and feeling comfortable enough there meant that the issue wasn't pushed thereafter. Following that tour, I was setting my stall out as an international second row and, although I was still playing No 8 quite a bit for Dungannon, that was my role in the Ireland team for most of the next two seasons. But then, in the middle of the 1994 Five Nations, the selectors decided that they would like to try me at No 8 in the interests of playing a bigger pack and having more height. That was what they thought at the time and I was happy enough to go along with what they wanted to do, though I suppose there was always a concern of getting caught between two stools, of ending up as a jack of all trades and master of none.

"But I really enjoyed playing No 8 for Ireland, just as I have done for any team for which I have filled that position. It's a place where you have more influence, more control and so forth. To a large extent, Nos 8, 9 and 10 decide where it goes and I liked that responsibility. I also enjoyed, in games like Twickenham 1994, working in a unit with my Ulster colleagues Brian Robinson and Denis McBride.

"Overall, I feel that I did well enough in the middle of the back row for Ireland and, although there was criticism from certain quarters, the selectors or coaches obviously felt that it was the best option for the team at the particular time. It seemed to me that most of the scrutiny or criticism of my perceived limitations as a No 8 came at times when the team as a whole was struggling or had had a bad result. Those were the times that it became a talking point, about me being supposedly out of position. It was a simplistic solution to scapegoat me and gloss over the wider malaise. I was only playing where I was told to and, while sticking to one position may have been simpler in a way and, while I was predominantly a second row taking my career as a whole, I've no regrets about the period at No 8.

"Versatility is a double-edged sword and, although I probably did suffer to some degree in that regard, refusing to play where you're asked will not endear you to those who are picking the team and believe you can do a job in that position. Willie Anderson would always have said to me to 'play where you're picked and you don't know what doors will open'. Later, when the law changes came in, he advised me to think about going back to the second row and, in both cases, I think his counsel was wise. Moving forward again undoubtedly prolonged my international career, but the attributes which had enabled me to play No 8 and the skills acquired there continued to serve me well as a general forward even though I now had a No 4 on my back. I always knew that I didn't really have the pace to be a world class No 8, but my handling was quite good and I feel I read the game fairly well and made my share of tackles in open play.

"Maybe it was because the spotlight of some detractors always tended to be on me as a No 8, but one of the things which gave me considerable satisfaction during that period was an article which my sister had cut out of one of the English papers at the end of the 1995 World Cup. In it, Rob Wainwright had picked his World Cup XV comprising players from all the countries and had chosen me at No 8. Alright, it was just one guy's opinion but, coming from a fellow international loose forward and Test captain, it was a pretty gratifying endorsement. Before that World Cup, I'd been in the back row for the win over England at Twickenham and a Test series in Australia, so the experiment, if that's what some people saw it, must have been considered something of a success by those who picked the team."

In another newspaper article, which described the 'emergence of Paddy Johns as a world class No 8' as 'one of the largely unsung successes' of Ireland's 1995 World Cup campaign, one of Ireland's greatest ever players in the position, Willie Duggan, speaks of a 'Johns-dominated' back row and refers to his 'control at the base of the scrum.'

On the positional issue, Willie Anderson says: "Paddy was always destined to be a front of the line jumper at the lineout and he could best be described as a grafting, mobile second row, but he certainly gave No 8 a good shot and reminded me in a roundabout way of a player from a previous era, Harry Steele. Both men were prepared to do the hard yards. Paddy worked very hard to develop the finer points of No 8 play and I think having that knowledge and skills definitely gave him an edge over his second row rivals. Whatever number he had on his back though, it was appropriate that he should be termed a 'forward', in that every time he got the ball, he went forward."

Johns headed Down Under for his first tour of Australia in the summer of 1994 firmly ensconced at No 8 in a team still on a high following that second successive victory against the English. There was, however, room also in the squad for a significant infusion of new blood, including several players who were to have a major impact for Ireland either immediately or over the coming years.

The men who became the biggest names were Keith Wood, who had sat on the bench at Twickenham but was still uncapped when he went on the tour, and his fellow 1997 Lions tourist Jeremy Davidson, who was only 20 at the time and didn't play in either Test in Oz. Those newcomers who made the greatest impression of Johns at the time, however, were another young Ulsterman, three-quarter Jonathan Bell, who was the same age as Davidson, and abrasive young Cork Con flanker David Corkery. In total, there were a dozen uncapped players in the party, four of whom, centres Brian Walsh and Martin Ridge, Cork Con prop Philip Soden and Instonians No 8 Roger Wilson, were destined never to appear at Test level.

St Mary's No 8 Victor Costello didn't make the big breakthrough on tour, but the man who had competed in the shotput for Ireland at the Barcelona Olympics of 1992 became a regular for his country several years hence, while Blackrock outhalf Alan McGowan, who had been on the bench at Twickenham, won his only cap later in the year against the United States. Like Wood, Bell and Corkery, Blackrock wing Niall Woods made his senior international debut in the first Test at Ballymore, while Cork Con lock Gabriel Fulcher, a man who was to become Paddy's nemesis for a period, made his bow in the second. Of the team which had beaten England, Richie Wallace and Nick Popplewell, a big loss, were missing. Others who weren't on duty at Twickenham to make the trip included Jim Staples, Rolland, experienced prop John Fitzgerald and backrower Paul Hogan, who had been capped in Paris.

Tours of Australia may not have quite the same mystique as of New Zealand or South Africa where rugby union is more of a religion, but going to any of the southern hemisphere big three is still a daunting prospect for Ireland. All the more so back in 1994, according to Johns, given that those were the days when Ireland were still amateur in every sense of the word whereas their opponents were powerful, progressive and innovative.

"Furthermore, Australia were world champions at that time and were now getting the upper hand over New Zealand by winning regularly in the Bledisloe Cup. They'd thrown that monkey off their backs. It was a great Australian side and one which, although they had a close shave in Dublin en route to winning the 1991 World Cup, had beaten us comfortably enough at Lansdowne Road the following year. The Wallabies had lost both Tests at home to the last Irish team which had toured there in 1979, so there was also a need for them to set the record straight and avenge those defeats.

"By the end of my career, it was commonplace for sides to analyse the opposition and plan everything precisely but, back then, the Australians really were before their time in that regard. They had a file on each one of our players and really did their homework on us. They may have been firm favourites in most people's eyes, but their preparations were still meticulous and nothing was left to chance. It was a fact that, in those days, the Australians were fitter than us and also more skilful. They benefit from a climate which delivers hard grounds and a dry ball, which helps teams at all levels play constructive rugby. For us going over there, it was always going to be a war of attrition for us, the old story of Ireland seeking to stop the opposition playing. In those days when the gulf was there, that was more or less what it came down to."

With Noel Murphy unavailable to travel, Frank Sowman took over as manager for the tour and Willie Anderson was on board as forwards coach, working under Gerry Murphy. Michael Bradley was tour captain but, even though he had now played a dozen Tests on the trot and in spite of the number of uncapped players in the party, Johns insists he didn't feel anything even approaching senior status. "Yes, I was more comfortable now in the international environment and had picked up a fair bit of experience, but was still only 26 and didn't feel entirely secure or established, especially with the way selection worked in those days. You were just hoping to be in for the next game."

Ireland's opening two tour games ended in sharply contrasting results against opponents who varied vastly in standard. Murphy's men began by beating Western Australia 64-8 at the WACCA in Perth but were brutally brought down to earth when walloped 55-

18 by the New South Wales Waratahs four days later. It was a sobering experience for an Irish side which featured eight of the heroes of Twickenham, namely Geoghegan, Danaher, Elwood, captain Bradley, Robinson, McBride, Francis and Kingston.

Although the two great Wallaby centres of the 1990s, Tim Horan and Jason Little, were both missing due to injury, it was still a most distinguished Waratahs outfit which had the luxury of leaving Willie Ofahengaue, Tim Gavin and Ewen McKenzie on the bench. Captained by renowned Wallaby hooker Phil Kearns, the New South Wales pack also included 1991 World Cup winning prop Tony Daly, while David Campese was the star of the backline. In the absence of Little and Horan, a young Matt Burke was paired with Richard Tombs in midfield. The other internationals in the side were seasoned prop Mark Hartill, lock Warrick Waugh, loose forward Michael Brial, right wing Darren Junee and fullback Tim Kelaher. "I played in the first game against Western Australia, which was a very comfortable victory against a side which seemed to consist mainly of ex-pat Kiwis. The second match, which thankfully I didn't play in, was a very different story and Ireland got stuffed."

From Sydney, it was on to the capital Canberra for a clash with ACT which the tourists disappointingly lost 22-9. The ACT team was not as powerful as the modern day Brumbies, with captain Matt O'Connor, hooker Marco Caputo, future Wallaby captain George Gregan and utility back Rod Kafer, these days an assistant coach with Leicester Tigers, being the only four names from the home line-up to mean much to the wider world eight years on. Joe Roff, then a teenager, was on the bench, having played outside centre for an ACT Under 21 team, which also featured fellow future Wallaby stars Stephen Larkham and Justin Harrison, against Sydney Under 21s in a curtain-raiser to the main attraction.

Blackrock hooker Shane Byrne, finally capped by his country seven summers later, had now arrived on the tour because Kingston was injured and started the ACT game, for which Clohessy, Galwey, Johns and Field, none of whom had played against the Waratahs, were back in, with the Shannon lock skippering the side in place of the rested tour captain Bradley. The quartet of Blackrock backs, Rolland, McGowan, Ridge and Woods featured in an inexperienced backline which also featured Walsh out of position on the right wing and Field, who was still a relatively new international. Staples at fullback was the only old hand. Johns' young Dungannon clubmate Davidson partnered Galwey in the engineroom, while Paddy was flanked in the back row by Hogan and the uncapped Corkery.

"My main memory of that ACT game is of us trying to catch Gregan. He played very well and, to some extent, it was that match which helped to really put him on the map. We got a real lift from our next game though when we only lost to a very strong Queensland side because Michael Lynagh kicked a penalty in injury-time at the end." Ireland did field a strong side and Queensland left John Eales on the bench, but the hosts still fielded a formidable line-up packed with internationals headed by Lynagh, so it was a decent effort by the tourists.

Having suffered a hat-trick of defeats after that facile first win against Western Australia, Ireland were now at the mid-point of the tour and had retreated to Mount Isa for a game against an Australian XV and to prepare for the following weekend's opening Test. Paddy remembers the place well. "Mount Isa is a small mining village, town if you're being charitable, in the middle of the Queensland outback which happens to have the biggest Irish Association in the whole of Australia. There's not much happening in Mount Isa and the Irish club is the heart of the community.

"It was there that I got my revenge on Peter Clohessy for a prank which he and Mick Galwey had played on me when we were in Paris for the Five Nations match earlier in the year. On that occasion, we'd been staying in a place with a square courtyard and the pair of them were rooming next to me. They got a binful of water and Clohessy went round to the room the other side of mine. Anyway, Galwey called me from his room so I went out onto the balcony and was looking in his direction when Clohessy poured the water over me from the other side.

"I got my own back with a vengeance in Mount Isa though, when I was rooming with Peter. My chance came one day when he was fast asleep on the bed. I got the wastepaper bin, filled it with water and threw it all over him. It hit him about waist level as he lay there and went up over his stomach and chest and into his face. He woke up in a panic, struggling and kicking. Apparently, by sheer coincidence, he'd been dreaming that he was swimming and so, as the water came up over him, his dream turned to an instant half-awake nightmare that he was drowning. He was in a right old state. Don't think I've ever seen the Claw so terrified" Paddy chuckles.

It could also either have been advance or retrospective revenge for another moment of indignation provoked by the same two Munster stalwarts, recalled by Mark McCall. "One of the things we used to do when we were in Dublin on a Thursday night was go to the cinema in Tallaght" explains Small. "A favourite party piece of Mick Galwey and Peter Clohessy was to pull someone's tracksuit bottoms down in public when they were off guard. Paddy was standing there in the middle of the queue, very straight and tall and regimental looking and totally unsuspecting what was coming. So they did the usual, with Paddy the victim, but what they couldn't have realised was that, as well as wearing a very short T-shirt that evening, he also happened to have no boxers on! As the public dived for cover, I donít think I've ever seen Paddy as embarrassed . . . or annoyed!"

"The Munster boys were awful messers" agrees Paddy. "I remember also on that trip being out one day playing golf with Clohessy and Keith Wood. We had hired buggies largely because we needed so much water with us, but ended up riding round squirting it at each other. The course had these really high tee boxes, so it was kind of standard to go up one bank and down another at 45-degree angles. Anyway, we lost control going down this bank and took out a sprinkler, completely demolished it. It looked like a tap with a big round head and was solid enough to leave the buggy the worse for wear. The buggy also turned over in the process and the axle was completely buggered. We threw it away into the bushes, but it wasn't long until the damage was discovered and the culprits chased. The manager Frank Sowman called us in for a chat to find out what had happened, but the problem was fairly quickly and quietly sorted out."

By the standards of room trashing tales of old Lions tours and rugby trips right down to social side level it was pretty tame stuff, though Wood now regularly refers to that tour as being the last hurrah of the amateur era in many regards. As for the match in Mount Isa, what essentially amounted to a second string Irish, captained by the fit-again Kingston, were thrashed 57-9 by their Australian counterparts, a strong side skippered by Wallaby prop Dan Crowley. It featured Willie Ofahengaue and Brett Robinson on the flanks, with Joe Roff in the centre and Ryan Constable and Alastair Murdoch out wide. Pat Howard, Owen Finegan, Richard Harry and Marco Caputo were on the bench.

Not surprisingly, only two of the Irish side which played in Mount Isa were picked in the team for the first Test against the Wallabies four days later, Galwey in the second row and young Bell, who had played on the wing in midweek, as Danaher's centre partner. In addition to the versatile Bell of Ballymena, who had burst on the scene as a schoolboy star, primarily as a fullback, there were first caps for hooker Wood, who had been an exciting prospect for a couple of years and sat on the bench throughout that Spring's Five Nations, winger Woods and Corkery at openside, in preference to McBride.

Australia went into the game at Ballymore in Brisbane as red hot favourites even though, preposterously, Ireland had won all three previous internationals against the Wallabies Down Under, the one-off Test of 1967 and both in the series of 1979. Compared to the side which won at Twickenham, non-tourists Popplewell and Richard Wallace were replaced by John Fitzgerald and Woods respectively, with Geoghegan reverting to the right wing. Up front, new boys Wood and Corkery had usurped smaller men in Kingston and McBride with Bell displacing Field behind the scrum. Clohessy, Galwey, Francis, Robinson, Johns, Bradley, Elwood, Danaher, Geoghegan and O'Shea continued in the side.

For the first time at international level, seven players could be named on the bench and Ireland's reserves that day included the axed Malone pair of McBride and Field, both of whom came on as replacements. The other five were Kingston, prop Gary Halpin, young Davidson, reserve outhalf McGowan and Niall Hogan, who had been called up to the tour because of injury to Rolland.

Australia won comfortably enough in the end, but Ireland didn't disgrace themselves in going down 33-13, in a game marked by the first of four Test tries scored by Paddy Johns in his international career. The Wallabies went in at the break 13-3 ahead thanks to a try in the corner on 39 minutes by Ille Tabua following good handling by the forwards, Lynagh converting. Tries by Lynagh and Campese, who was driven over by the pack, followed by Burke's brilliant scoop up to score had already put Australia out of sight when Johns' big moment came. Elwood made a good break and, when he was hauled down deep in the Wallaby 22, Johns showed his instincts as a backrow forward by being there in support to crash over. Winger Damien Smith rounded things off with Australia's fourth try of the half right at the death to confirm the world champions as clear winners. The tourists' other points came courtesy of a penalty apiece from Elwood and O'Shea and the former's conversion of Johns' try.

"Nice to score, even if it was from all of about three yards out" says Paddy, who moved to the second row when McBride came on for Galwey, self-deprecatingly. "But you'd always trade a try for a win and, as I've said, we were a fair bit off the likes of Australia in those days. The odds were stacked in their favour and it would have taken something fairly remarkable for Ireland to cause an upset, but we did battle pretty well and they didn't really take us apart in either Test. I've kept a tape of that match, probably because of the try, but any time I watch it, the striking thing is just how much the game of rugby has changed in the intervening years. The pace was so slow back then and all the players look about three stones lighter than their modern equivalents!"

It is interesting to note from the match programme some stars of the future who played for a Brisbane Under 21 side against a Country Under 21 XV in the curtain-raiser to that first Test, David Giffin, Toutai Kefu, Pat Howard and Nathan Grey. In the penultimate tour match, the midweek side beat New South Wales Country 20-18 in Lismore and Ireland then confounded the doom merchants by giving Australia a good game in the second Test at the Sydney Football Stadium. Unlike two years earlier in New Zealand, where an admittedly depleted and fatigued Irish side collapsed a week after running their hosts close in the first Test, Bradley's boys actually came closer second time round.

Fulcher won his first cap in the engineroom in place of Galwey, while Australia also made one change, with Daniel Herbert winning his first cap at centre alongside Burke who, at time of writing, has recently returned to the Wallaby midfield after making his name as a world class fullback in the intervening years. Matt O'Connor of ACT, who had won his first cap in the opening Test, dropped out altogether, with Herbert earning promotion from the bench, where his place was taken by Constable, Johns' future team-mate for Saracens, Ulster and Dungannon, who was to come on and win what proved to be his only cap. It really was a formidable side with Daly and McKenzie supporting Kearns in the front row, John Eales and Garrick Morgan paired in the engineroom and Gavin packing down at No 8 between the Queensland duo of Tabua and David Wilson. Captain Michael Lynagh was partnered at halfback by his Queensland colleague Peter Slattery, with Damien Smith and the inimitable Campese either side of the makeshift centre pairing necessitated by the injury-enforced absence of Horan and Little. Fullback Matt Pini was making his debut in the first Test.

The writing seemed to be on the wall for Ireland when Australia led 21-6 at half-time in Sydney, but the guys in green came out after the break determined to finish the tour with a flourish and duly scored tries through Clohessy and Francis. O'Shea kicked one conversion to add to his penalty and dropgoal in the first half. Lynagh's 17 points, which took him past 800 in international rugby, proved to be the difference between the sides, though Wallaby coach Bob Dwyer graciously acknowledged after the match that the 32-18 scoreline had flattered his team.

"There has often been a bit of a second Test syndrome not only for ourselves but other northern hemisphere sides whereby we do pretty well in the first international of a tour only to get soundly stuffed in the second" reflects Paddy. "I suppose that is due to a combination of things, the removal of the surprise element, the home country not being as rusty as in what would generally have been their first Test of their season and the touring team being hit by injuries and fatigue and the like. But we held up very well in Sydney in 1994 and it was certainly an encouraging tour, especially with a few young players like Wood and Bell and Corkery emerging as real prospects. The tour was useful for Irish rugby and it was good to get playing Australia and measuring ourselves against them, but at that stage we still weren't good enough to beat sides like that. There was still a big gulf and it was a case of give it our best shot and hope the Australians had an off-day. Damage limitation was always the basic objective and winning was never really an option if the other team performed to the level they were capable of.

"From a personal point of view, I enjoyed the tour and, by the time I came back from Australia that summer, I had won 15 caps and gained a fair degree of experience and confidence. Experience provides you with practical benefits and also adds to your self-belief so, in that sense, apart from skill and strength and fitness levels, I would by then have been a better player or, if you like, a greater force, than when I made my debut against Argentina. That said, more is expected as you go on in terms of being able to take responsibility and really contribute and so forth, so you must keep developing and never rest on your laurels. In any case, with the selection system which pertained at the time, and radical team changes still being pretty much par for the course, you could only try to make sure you were there for the next game and that ensured you took things one step at a time."

That autumn, Ulster's long stranglehold on the interprovincial championship was broken as they lost their opener 17-16 to their successors Munster and also went down 6-12 to Leinster at Ravenhill later in the competition. Ireland beat the USA 26-15 at Lansdowne Road in November, McGowan winning his only Test cap at outhalf in place of the injured Elwood and a fit-again Popplewell returning at loosehead for Fitzgerald. Pat O'Hara was recalled on the blindside in place of Robinson, who had sadly been forced into early retirement by a knee injury at the age of 28, but Brendan Mullin, who had also quit the international scene prematurely, albeit by choice in his case, a couple of years earlier, reversed his decision and returned to the side. That meant Bell switching to the wing at the expense of Woods, but the young Ulsterman at least stayed in the team along with three of the other finds of the Australian tour, Wood, Corkery and Fulcher.

Captain Bradley and Geoghegan each scored tries, while O'Shea landed a penalty and McGowan contributed 13 points on debut courtesy of two conversions and a hat-trick of penalties. "Typical autumn international with Ireland struggling to put away an inferior side everyone expected us to take to the cleaners" admits Paddy. "Ireland have never been good favourites; being underdogs brings the best out of our psyche, but I think we've got better in that regard in the professional era, showing greater efficiency and consistency, helped by superior fitness levels."

For the 1995 Five Nations opener at home to England, the selection of former England Under 21 flyhalf Paul Burke and the call-up of Niall Hogan following the withdrawal of Bradley meant Ireland went into the game with two debutant halfbacks and a new captain, Mullin. Galwey was back again as engineroom partner for Francis at the expense of Fulcher, while young Shannon loose forward Anthony Foley, son of former Ireland lock Brendan, came in at blindside and marked his first cap with the hosts' only try in an 8-20 defeat, Burke getting the other points with a penalty.

"The score was very close until near the end but, with Dean Richards back, England were always in control. He was a dominant figure who typified their ability to keep it tight and grind teams down. Perhaps significantly, he wasn't in the team for either of the two previous meetings when we beat them. The English forwards have always been big and strong and, to be honest, we didn't make much of a dent in them that day."

With Francis injured and Galwey dropped, neither occurrence being for the first or last time, there was a new engineroom pairing for the next game, with Fulcher coming into the side and Johns moving forward after a run of seven successive Tests at No 8. Bradley returned at the base of the scrum and resumed the captaincy. McBride was recalled at openside for Corkery and Ben Cronin came in for a dreadful debut at No 8 as Ireland had to endure more Edinburgh anguish, "the usual great expectations" giving way to a familiar empty feeling thanks to a 26-13 defeat. Ireland had flattered to deceive, going 8-3 up with a Mullin try and, although two more penalties from Gavin Hastings left them behind at the break, the visitors produced a great score early in the second period, with Bell touching down. But a fortuitous try from Craig Joiner got the Scots' noses in front and they never looked back.

Johns had to withdraw from the next game against France with an appendicitis scare, frustratingly breaking a run of 17 Tests on the trot stretching back to Dunedin in May 1992, thus handing Ulster colleague Davy Tweed a full international debut at the ripe old age of 35. Cronin also cried off, so Foley moved to No 8 with another Shannon player, Eddie Halvey, coming in to win his first cap at blindside. Kingston and Staples displaced Wood and O'Shea respectively, Elwood was back for Burke and Woods took over from the injured Bell.

It was only 3-0 at the break and, although Geoghegan scored a second half try for Ireland, the French pulled away to win comfortably, 25-7, sending Ireland to their old happy hunting ground, Cardiff, needing yet another win on Welsh soil to avoid a Five Nations whitewash. Johns, back in the team at No 8, was under the weather for the match at the Arms Park thanks to a bad flu, but played his part as Ireland, now captained by Kingston as Bradley had lost his No 9 jersey to Hogan, won 16-12. Richard Wallace was back on the right wing with Geoghegan switching to the left and McBride was the man who lost out to accommodate the return of Johns to a reshuffled backrow with Halvey taking over the breakaway role and Foley moving to blindside.

Elwood, a hero on debut on Ireland's previous visit to Cardiff, was forced off as a result of a shocking high tackle from Richie Collins, but replacement Burke really did the business, first dropping a goal to cancel out Neil Jenkins' early penalty. He then kicked a penalty to put Ireland ahead and converted a great Mullin try, making it 13-6 at the interval. Two Jenkins penalties had the visitors' nerves jangling, but another Burke strike gave them a little breathing space and the greens held on for a four point victory. Thanks to his flu symptoms the game left Johns more drained than most, but he recovered in time to fulfil his World Cup dream that summer.

14. A FIRST WORLD CUP

Playing in a World Cup is the pinnacle and life couldn't have felt much better for Paddy as he boarded the plane to South Africa in May 1995. Now a proud father following the induced birth of first child Christopher a few days earlier, Johns had a spring in his step as he set off for the rainbow republic about to realise another of his rugby dreams.

Back in 1987, just finished school, he followed the inaugural tournament with great interest from afar and then, four years later, had been disappointed to miss out on the squad himself. This time he could look forward to being well and truly involved, as an established international who had now played in 19 of Ireland's last 20 Tests, a run broken only by the appendicitis scare which had forced him out of that Spring's Five Nations match against France.

And there is no doubt that the 1995 World Cup was bigger and better than the two that had gone before, helped by extra marketing and more media hype and the fact that it was all being held in one country. That that country was South Africa meant extra interest being taken in the tournament by the wider world as well as the rugby fraternity and Johns agrees that even the players were aware of being part of an historic event. Great efforts were made in the hope that the World Cup could make a positive contribution to the emerging 'new South Africa' and help with the healing and unifying process which was underway.

Rugby had always been a fairly elitist and almost exclusively white sport during the apartheid era but, with Chester Williams in the side as something of a black icon, a liberal captain in Francois Pienaar, a new anthem and President Mandela ostentatiously supporting the Springboks, attempts were being made to widen ownership of the sport. It wasn't entirely successful, however, for not everyone was converted as Johns readily recalls: "From our experience, a lot of the blacks would have been behind whoever was playing the Springboks. That wouldn't have been true of all of the black population, but I'm sure it was a sizeable element.

"I suppose we have parallels in our own country, with some Catholics in Northern Ireland not supporting the Northern Ireland soccer team, and some Ulster Protestants supporting England in rugby rather than Ireland. There wasn't a real sense of ownership of the Springboks among many people and in some cases that would have extended to resentment and a wish for what was obviously a predominantly white South African team to lose. You'd have also had considerable apathy towards the rugby in that, without wishing to generalise too much, soccer is the big sport for blacks in South Africa, so some would simply have been fairly indifferent to the rugby."

Coming from what has, in simplistic shorthand, perhaps also on occasions been branded a bit of a warzone by the world's media, Johns was maybe better placed than most to empathise with the security situation in South Africa. Northern Ireland people are no strangers to armed patrols, polarised communities, a sense of unease and deaths as a result of conflict. Yet Paddy admits that he was a bit taken aback by what he saw in Johannesburg in particular.

"There were a couple of heavily-armed policemen attached to every team and they would accompany us everywhere. Each team had a minibus for any time we had to go out an errand and they would come with us. I remember driving in the van one day and, when we'd stop at traffic lights and there'd be a few black guys standing around, the policeman would take out his gun and cock it. Apparently it would be common practice in situations like that for guys to smash windows of vehicles and try to steal things, so this was his way of warning them off. At one level, it was a bit like Belfast and because of that you wouldn't be as bothered in ways as if you weren't used to that or hadn't experienced it, but even though we were conditioned to some degree to a sort of militarised environment back home, I still saw things which shocked me.

"Our opening match against the All Blacks in Ellis Park was a night match and I remember being taken to the hospital for an X-ray on my wrist afterwards, so it would have been pretty late. There were flashing lights up ahead of us and, when we got there, we could see a young black man lying in the middle of the road in a pool of blood, obviously dead and although there was a bit of commotion, the police didn't seem to be making much of a fuss. The cops who were with us gave the impression that it wasn't a big deal either, almost a routine occurrence. Life seemed fairly expendable. That incident has stuck with me since as an indication that we never quite reached the same level of indifference in Northern Ireland no matter how bad things got at particular points.

"While we were in Jo'burg, I remember there were a couple of policemen shot by local black guys with AK47s while sitting in their patrol car. It was the sort of thing which could have happened in Northern Ireland. Both societies probably got conditioned to violence to some degree, but back home there would have been much more of an appearance of life going on as normal. Bad as we've been, they were worse than us even in terms of fortifications, for all houses in Johannesburg seemed to have high walls and fences and security cameras and the like."

In spite of the backdrop of a country torn by racial tensions, a degree of civil unrest, crime and the legacy of apartheid, there was a real sense of excitement at being part of a World Cup being held in such a hotbed of rugby. "There's a massive rugby culture in South Africa and it would be hard not to have a sense of the history and heritage of the game there. The Springboks had only got back into the international arena a few years earlier and there was still a huge hunger around among the rugby fraternity following the international sporting famine.

"As a player, you felt part of a huge event, and were conscious that the whole rugby world was watching. Whatever the sport, a World Cup really is the biggest stage of the global game and has something special about it. You've got all the world's best teams in one place and the spotlight falls on each match regardless of what countries are playing. It's just like the football World Cup this summer. Costa Rica might have been playing China or whatever, but players and fans from the other countries would have been interested because it was all part of the same tournament that their team was in and that they were swept up by. We'd have been lying in our rooms watching the other games and knew it would be the same with the other nations when we played."

As with four years earlier, Paddy didn't really face a selection sweat and an anxious wait to see whether he would make Ireland's World Cup squad, albeit for the opposite reason. In 1991, he had been pretty much resigned to his fate before the panel was announced and four years later the case was even more cut and dried. This time though it was because he was by now a real banker in the squad, having been picked for 20 Tests on the trot leading into the tournament. "Naturally, I'd have been confident of making the squad, but it's still nice to get formal confirmation that you're going to a World Cup and even though by then it would have been expected, it was still going to be the fulfilment of a big personal goal."

Terry Kingston, who had led Ireland to victory over Wales in their final Five Nations match of the season, was asked to skipper the squad of 26, which was split along predictable lines with 12 backs and 14 forwards. A stark reminder of the days of the day jobs is the fact that both former captain Philip Danaher and prop Peter Clohessy were unavailable for the tournament due to business commitments, but the rest of the team who had finished the Championship by winning in Cardiff were included.

Blackrock prop Paul Wallace, younger brother of wing Richard, joined the seasoned Gary Halpin as the two tightheads in Clohessy's absence, while the experienced John Fitzgerald was due to understudy first choice loosehead Popplewell. But the Young Munster prop tore a calf muscle at the team's pre-tournament training camp in Kilkenny and had to withdraw from the squad to be replaced by Leinster's Henry Hurley, who was to spend a second successive summer abroad with Ireland without winning that elusive first Test cap. Keith Wood was the second hooker and, with Johns being regarded as one of five loose forwards along with Anthony Foley, Eddie Halvey, David Corkery and Denis McBride, there were three specialist locks chosen in Neil Francis, Gabriel Fulcher and Ulster veteran Davy Tweed.

Niall Hogan, Bradley, Eric Elwood and Paul Burke were the halfbacks, with Ulstermen Maurice Field and young Jonathan Bell joining Brendan Mullin as the centres. The injury problems which had afflicted Johns' former Dungannon colleague Tyrone Howe gave Darragh O'Mahony his chance as back-up winger to Simon Geoghegan and Richard Wallace, while Jim Staples and Conor O'Shea were two quality fullbacks.

As part of their preparation for the World Cup, Ireland played Italy in Treviso some three weeks before the tournament started and, typical of such warm-ups, things didn't really go according to plan for the men in green. Both pivots, Bradley and Hogan, were unavailable, while Geoghegan was injured. Their absences meant new caps for the O'Mahonys, Darragh on the wing and David at scrumhalf, with Alain Rolland on the bench. Bell and Halpin came into the side for the unavailable Danaher and Clohessy. Burke kicked the first pair of his four penalties to put Ireland 6-0 up, but those were cancelled out by Diego Dominguez and the visiting outhalf had to repeat the dose to ensure Kingston's side led 12-9 at the break. But Italy managed 13 unanswered points in the second period to claim a prized scalp, though Johns says a game which he recalls with little relish didn't have much bearing on Ireland's mood or prospects going into the World Cup.

"I think you could definitely call that one a bit of a botched Italian job" he says. "We flew over and had an absolutely massive training session the day before the match, really running the legs out of each other. I remember thinking 'what are we doing this for', but I suppose in those days when we weren't full-time and didn't have that much time together, there was training to be got in ahead of the World Cup. It wasn't ideal preparation for the Italian game, but it was only a means to an end.

"The other disaster was the team bus not turning up to take us to the match. Noel Murphy our manager was standing out on the road trying to flag down buses and taxis. In the end we only got there 15 minutes before kick-off. It was all a bit of a shambles. It was disappointing to lose, but I think the main purpose of Treviso was to get a match under our belts and, once it was over, we didn't dwell on it a great deal but focused on the World Cup opener against the All Blacks. They were going into the tournaments as favourites and had a big reputation, so that was what we were thinking about rather than getting too hung up with the Italian friendly."

Apart from seeing son Christopher coming into the world, Johns recalls spending a few days at Ireland's pre-tournament training camp and attending a large lunch in London in the lead-up to the big World Cup adventure. "We trained at Kilkenny RFC and I remember us going to a pub quiz down there one night. Gary Halpin is from that part of the world and his father was the quiz master. The squad were flown over to London for a big Farewell Lunch thing at the Grosvenor House hotel the week before the tournament started. We stayed overnight and went to the dinner the following day. I think it was mainly for the benefit of sponsors and was a bit of a drag for the players at the time."

It wasn't the only occasion on which the players were wined and dined ahead of the action getting underway. "We were staying in Jo'burg before our first game and were flown down to Cape Town for a big banquet which was attended by all the teams. The banquet was held in a vineyard in a massive marquis. It was absolutely lashing out of the heavens that day and the water started gathering in various parts, resulting in the tent springing a few leaks. The rain started coming in in places and then, all of a sudden, part of the canvas just gave way and opened up, almost drowning the Japanese team! The water had been lying in puddles up there, so it was as if someone had poured bucketfuls of water down on them."

So the tournament may have got off to a soggy start, but nothing could have dampened Paddy's enthusiasm for the challenge ahead, even though the All Blacks would, to say the least, be formidable first opponents. "We knew it would obviously be our toughest group game and there was some talk about this big new guy, Jonah Lomu, on the wing. I think we were pleased to get them first up, maybe hoping to hit them hard before they really got into their stride. Our aim was to go out and give it a blast and we did get off to a very good start before the Lomu factor began to dominate the game. He scored two tries and had a very big influence even though he'd just turned 20 a couple of weeks before.

"That was the first time he changed the course of an international, but it certainly wasn't the last. He announced his arrival in style that night and by the end of the tournament had become a complete sensation, especially with his four tries against England in the semi-final. I just couldn't believe his performance that night. There was one time he simply bounced the whole of our backrow." One of the authors also recalls McBride being asked after the game how Lomu could be stopped. Looking straight into the camera, he hilariously produced a classic Ulsterman response: "You'd need to bring a baseball bat!"

"Back then, no-one really knew how to defend against him and, although teams are now better prepared, he can still do major damage" insists Paddy. "He has consistently proved himself the hardest fella in the world to put down and has achieved an awful lot. Jonah has won so many caps already in spite of missing out for a while through illness and yet he's still only 27. People thought at the time that the Irish simply couldn't tackle, but Lomu showed up other sides later in that tournament. When the match was over, we just wanted to forget about him" he says, shades of Will Carling's comment following the semi-final about Lomu being a 'freak' and wanting him to go away.

"New Zealand won fairly well in the end, but it was an encouraging enough performance by us with a view to the rest of the tournament. We scored three tries and certainly put it up to them for a while." Flankers Corkery and McBride scored a try apiece for Ireland, whose great opening had been rewarded by an early touchdown for Gary Halpin, followed by the prop's infamous one-fingered gesticulation to New Zealand skipper Sean Fitzpatrick. The incident spoke volumes about how pumped up and emotional Ireland were that evening and was no more than a case of Fitzpatrick, no shrinking violent, getting a taste of his own unpleasant medicine, though Johns admits to a grudging regard for the All Blacks legend even if he could be a nasty bit of work.

"Fitzpatrick was one of the all-time greats and you have to give him due credit for what he achieved in the game. He was a hard man, not afraid to either give it or take it. The closest I got to him was in the second Test in Wellington on the 1992 tour when he went to smack me one. I was lying on the ground and he ended up on top of me. I was pinned and he had his fist raised but, luckily for me, Stevie Smith came in and smacked him as hard as he could just as he was about to hit me. Fitzpatrick got up, spat some teeth out and put his mouthguard back in. He had to get some dental work done after that game. As for Stevie, he'd hit him so hard he tore a tendon in his hand. His finger dropped and he needed an operation when he got home."

Incidentally, had Halpin needed to, he could have got himself further fired up by taking umbrage at the inaccuracy of the World Cup programme, which dubbed him Barett Halpin. Ireland's other two secret weapons in the pack that took on the All Blacks were Sean Corkery and Denis McBridge! Paddy reveals that the other players spotted and, inevitably, made mischief out of the misprints. "The nickname has stuck with Denis to this day."

Lomu had already picked up a couple of caps before the World Cup, while the other young winger, one Jeff Wilson, had made three Test appearances to date, but the tournament really launched both along with another pair of new boys who were to have a huge impact, first five eighth Andrew Mehrtens and openside flank forward Josh Kronfeld. The team was an excellent blend of youth and experience, with the likes of Fitzpatrick, centres Walter Little and Frank Bunce, pivot Graeme Bachop and lock Ian Jones there to guide the young guns. They easily accounted for Wales in their second group game before rounding off the Pool phase with a record 145-17 rout of Japan, for whom both Bachop and flanker Jamie Joseph were actually to play in the next World Cup. By the time Lomu had trampled all over Mike Catt and Tony Underwood in the semi, Johns and his colleagues had returned home but, as he watched the final from afar, Paddy would not have argued about New Zealand being favourites to lift the trophy.

"Especially after the way in which they beat England in the semis, the All Blacks seemed virtually unstoppable, so I was pretty surprised when they lost to the Springboks, very much so in fact. South Africa countered New Zealand fairly effectively that day, but you can't discount the possibility the All Blacks were got at. One of their players, Mike Brewer, who was later our Ireland forwards coach, was certainly pretty convinced."

On whether, as an international player himself and conscious of how being even a little off-colour can massively affect your performance at that level, is Johns more likely to believe that something untoward happened than Joe Bloggs the ordinary punter? He shrugs. "I don't know. I wouldn't be a conspiracy theorist, but they did seem off their game on the day and do appear to believe themselves that something was amiss. If so, as for why, well who knows? They were playing the home nation, so I suppose it could have been a 'patriotic poisoning' if you like, or you can't rule out the possibility that a betting syndicate was involved and that a considerable amount of money was at stake."

Former Welsh centre Mark Ring and others have claimed that attempts have been made to bribe players to throw big rugby matches, a depressing thought following on from the match-fixing allegations which have dogged both soccer and cricket. If people cannot have complete belief in the outcome of games, all sport is sullied, but Johns is adamant that he has never either had any personal experience of such approaches, or been aware of any having taken place. Considering the length of time he has spent in high-level rugby, including as a national team captain, that is reassuring, though he doesn't feel the game would be automatically immune to the threat of corruption. "It mightn't be that easy for individuals to act on their own to influence the outcome of rugby matches, but getting sinbinned in a tight game, which the biggest ones usually are, could make a big difference. It's common for a couple of tries to be scored by the other team when a side is a man down."

Next up after the All Blacks opener, Ireland faced a very different challenge in the shape of the small and elusive Japanese, against whom they would also, obviously, be favourites rather than underdogs. The men in green had struggled a bit to despatch Japan at the previous tournament and again Ireland's oriental opponents had their moments as the tempo at which they played caused problems, especially in the extreme heat of an afternoon game in Bloemfontein.

"Japan rely on pace, movement, variation and workrate, but will always lack size and physical presence. They pose a genuine threat and I believe could, on their day, turn over a side like Ireland, Scotland or Wales. In general though, they can be countered effectively by a bigger team keeping it tight and wearing them down. If you throw the ball around against them, that will play into Japan's hands, though in my last game for Ireland we did get on top to the extent that we were able to become more expansive as time went on without having to worry. But on that hot day in Bloemfontein, it was really all about making sure we won the game. We found we could do them real damage when we took the ball down at the lineout and drove them or kept it in at the back of the scrum and pushed them around. They put up a good fight and scored plenty of points but, although it was a tiring enough afternoon, we were never in any real danger of losing the match."

In what seemed like a horses for courses selection, the solid and experienced Bradley had been picked to do battle against the All Blacks, but Niall Hogan was restored to the base of the scrum for the Japanese clash and remained there for the rest of the tournament. The New Zealand match was Bradley's 40th senior international and to prove his last, but he went out with his head held high, having played his part in a brave Irish rearguard effort. A nice touch during the tournament was the graduation ceremony held in South Africa for the newly qualified Dr Hogan, who was missing out on the formalities at his university back home.

Ireland made a total of eight changes for the Japanese game, one of them enforced by the broken hand sustained against New Zealand which had forced the luckless Staples out of the rest of the tournament. Danaher, originally unavailable for the World Cup but now able to commit for what would be a shorter period, was flown out to replace him, though he didn't get a chance to set foot on the field. Field got a game at centre as Mullin's partner in place of his fellow Ulsterman, Bell, while Elwood was rested and Burke was given a run in the No 10 jersey. Half the pack was changed, with uncapped prop Paul Wallace, reserve hooker Wood, veteran Ulster lock Tweed and Shannon flanker Halvey coming in for captain Kingston, Halpin, Fulcher and McBride respectively. Popplewell, Francis, Johns and Corkery remained.

Tweed, who had done well in the final two Five Nations matches and played against Italy, had lost his place to Francis for the World Cup opener, the enigmatic Leinster lock returning to partner Fulcher after missing most of the Championship with rib trouble. Foley and Halvey had been the flankers for the win in Cardiff but, come the World Cup opener, Corkery was in for his first Irish outing at blindside after bursting on the scene as a breakaway in Australia the previous summer, with McBride restored to the No 7 jersey. With Kingston rested, experienced prop Nick Popplewell had taken over the captaincy for the Japanese game, but the squad skipper was to be on the pitch within 10 minutes of the start as Wood's World Cup sadly ended almost before it had begun.

The young Garryowen hooker dislocated what, by now, was seen as a suspect shoulder and took no further part in the tournament, Shane Byrne being sent for as Kingston's new understudy. It was, however, to be another six years before the long-serving Leinster hooker finally won his first cap. "I remember Keith going off in that Japanese game. It was a very worrying time for him in that the shoulder problem wouldn't seem to go away. So it wasn't just the disappointment of his World Cup only lasting nine minutes, but the concern for a young player that his career might be going to be ruined by injury."

Just like England cricket captain Nasser Hussain, who at one stage seemed destined to break a finger every time he batted in a Test match, Wood looked doomed to having a dodgy shoulder for the rest of his career, with the danger that it could even cut it short, but thankfully he was able to shake off the problem. "There was a time when you'd have thought his body just couldn't cope, but he's obviously had good operations and, in the past few years has held together very well in spite of all the punishment he takes and the very vigorous way he plays. Rugby is more a collision sport these days than a contact sport, so his shoulder must be alright."

For the second World Cup match running, Paddy's two backrow colleagues, this time Corkery and Halvey, were on the scoresheet, as were Francis, Geoghegan and Hogan. There were two penalty tries as Japan couldn't contain Ireland's calculated attempts to bully their way over and were forced to infringe. Burke converted half a dozen of the tries and also kicked a penalty in a 50-28 victory, setting Ireland up for their final group game against Wales, a match which had always looked likely to be their pivotal fixture of the Pool phase.

"We were expected to lose to New Zealand and beat Japan, as were Wales, so there was always a good chance that it would come down to the match between us as to who would be going on to the quarter-finals and who would be on the next plane home. It was like the knockout stages starting a game early, so the pressure was on, but we responded well, having prepared well in the lead-up to the game. We had beaten them in Cardiff a couple of months earlier, but that had happened before the 1987 World Cup when the result was turned round in a group game, so we knew it would totally come down to who performed on the day and who really wanted it most." Bell, Elwood, Halpin, Fulcher and McBride returned for Field, Burke, Wallace, Tweed and Halvey respectively as Ireland reverted to their strongest side. Skipper Kingston was back in the middle of the front row, but Hogan held his place at the base of the scrum.

The game was in the refurbished Ellis Park, scene of Ireland's opener against the All Blacks, venue for the final and a famous name among world rugby grounds. "Ellis Park is fantastic, definitely one of my favourites grounds anywhere" he eulogises. "We played New Zealand there in a night match and the floodlights made for a great atmosphere, as we've witnessed at Ravenhill in recent years. When you play well somewhere or win, it makes you much more likely to remember the place with fondness and Ellis Park, as well as being an awesome stadium, was both the venue for my World Cup debut against the All Blacks, which I'll never forget, and then the win over Wales which put us into the quarter-finals and was, in my opinion, one of my very best games for Ireland at a personal level." Willie Duggan concurred, describing it as the day that Johns "came of age" as a Test No 8.

An audacious try by McBride rewarded Ireland's early enterprise and pressure and they continued to take the game to the Welsh in a very positive fashion which reaped its rewards against a team captained by Mike Hall, who was partnered at centre by Neil Jenkins with Adrian Davies in the No 10 jersey. Popplewell got a try, as did Halvey during a brief period on the pitch while a bloodied McBride was attended to. Elwood landed all three conversions and also kicked a penalty to give Ireland a comfortable cushion and leave Wales really chasing the game. They finished with a flourish, ultimately ending up only a point adrift, but it was all too little too late for the Welsh as Johns recalls and, even though they were flattered to get so close, the scoreline was academic.

"It was a very pleasing performance and we thoroughly deserved to win. Wales did get late scores, but we had got ourselves into a very healthy lead and it proved enough.

I remember their backrow forward Hemi Taylor scoring right at the death. He was jumping up in the air very pleased with himself. One of our boys went 'relax Hemi, you're on the next plane mate' and it just suddenly hit him that it wasn't going to matter; they'd be going home. Reality dawned and he quickly went very quiet. We were relieved and delighted to be going on to the quarter-finals."

So Ireland had emulated the achievements of 1987 and 1991 in reaching the last eight, something the Welsh had now missed out on for the second tournament running. Their basic objective having been achieved, some of the pressure was now off and anything from here on was a bonus but, naturally, the squad fancied a crack at the French even though, unlike in later years, there was still something of an aura about the gallic lot.

"We were going into a World Cup quarter-final as underdogs, which was what we wanted and we felt we had a very good chance, especially if it stayed cool and overcast like the day before the game, which was in Durban. The Irish players were hoping it stayed that way, but come match day there was a real change and it was absolutely roasting hot. King's Park was like an oven, with the heat just sitting on the pitch. I will never forget the heat that afternoon, the worst I have ever played in. It was simply unbelievable and we struggled in the temperatures to even breathe. I guess the French would have felt more at home in the heat. We couldn't really wreak the sort of havoc we would like to have and, although it was 16-12 at one stage, with Eric kicking four penalties to keep us in touch, they pulled away in the final quarter and got another 20 points.

"Thierry Lacroix punished every offence, some of them caused by our weariness, and ended up with eight penalties. They finally got a couple of tries, which gave the scoreline a lop-sided look, though the contest was over by then anyway. Our fitness as a team wouldn't have been nearly as good back then as it became a few years later so, especially taking into account the conditions that day, it was hardly surprising that we weren't able to hold them for the whole 80 minutes. One other factor was that they maybe, when we looked back with hindsight, got their preparation more right than we did in terms of when they arrived in Durban.

"After the win over Wales, Noel Murphy decided we'd all earned a trip up to Sun City. Noisy doesn't drink, but he's a man who knows how to enjoy a party without it. So we all got the bus up there and the IRFU Gold Card came out. It turned out that the girl in charge of marketing for the Palace was from Cork and Noisy really turned on the charm with her. The hotel was unbelievable and we got into these really, really nice rooms and spent the next few days in luxury. It's a real man-made paradise in a barren land; there's a mountain with slides and a lake with a wave-maker. We had a great time.

"But the thing was, we flew into Durban two days before the game whereas France only arrived there the day before. Normally it would be best to get in as long as possible in advance to get settled in and so forth, but we were coming down from altitude and, apparently, by arriving as late as possible France minimised the negative effect." It was, in ways, a disappointingly tame end to a brave bid and Johns had also suffered the misery of a corneal abrasion, sustained when Abde Benazzi's finger scratched his eye.

But France were, it must be remembered, a strong side starring Jean-Luc Sadourny, Emile Ntamack, the legendary Philippe Sella, Thierry Lacroix and skipper Philippe St

Andre behind the scrum and mighty formidable forwards. From loosehead Louis Armary to No 8 Marc Cecillon, now 35, there was a typically hard edge to the French pack which included household names in Laurent Cabannes, Benazzi, Olivier Roumat, Jean-Michel Gonzales, the emerging Christian Califano and the thoroughly unpleasant Olivier Merle. Not much fun to face.

So Ireland went home reasonably satisfied with their overall campaign, which had seen them put it up to the All Blacks, run up a half-century of points against Japan and triumph in the shootout with Wales. "The feeling would have been that we had a respectable World Cup and that Ireland had largely maintained its place in the pecking order. We hadn't enough gas to upset the French, but getting to the quarter-finals was a fair effort. It was a great tournament, especially with South Africa winning and the great story which that was, but there were a lot of other highlights, not least the excitement generated by the new phenomenon that was Jonah Lomu. The Irish support out there was fantastic, which was great for us, as was the fact that every hotel seemed to have their own Irish bar!

"I thoroughly enjoyed the experience and it was great to feel part of it all. At a personal level, I was on the pitch for every minute of all four of our games, which is what every player wants. Yes, the whole World Cup thing was, on reflection, pretty much all I could have hoped it would be. Sometimes when you've set your sights on something for such a long time, it can be a bit of an anti-climax, but that definitely wasn't the case with South Africa 1995."

So Ireland proved very human, reduced to mere mortals in the heat against France, even though it looked like they had Superman in their ranks that day in Durban thanks to one of Paddy's more embarrassing experiences on the field. "In that tournament, my jerseys seemed exceptionally long for some reason and I was forever tucking my jersey back into my shorts during the matches. So before that French game, I decided I would solve the problem by tucking them right into my swimming trunks. As fate would have it, that would, of course, be the very day that I should get my shorts ripped off after about five minutes of play. Olivier Merle, their second row ripped them right off and ended up standing there with them in his hands. I was left standing there like Superman and had to make my way across the pitch over towards the touchline to get a new pair. It must have been quite a sight, but there was nothing I could do to hide it. I'm sure my face was pretty red at the time!"

At the moment when Francois Pienaar held the William Webb Ellis Trophy aloft with Nelson Mandela amid those famous scenes at Ellis Park, Johns was thousands of miles away back in Ireland. Paddy didn't know it then, but he and the Springbok skipper were to spend a lot of time together in the next few years.

15. JUGGLING ACT

The World Cup had been an exhilarating experience but, when the show was over, Paddy found himself facing up to a punishing personal schedule as a new season loomed large. Straight after his return from South Africa, there had been a bit of time for some early bonding with baby son Christopher but, when a new campaign got underway, he certainly had his hands full with the demands of being a father, full-time dentist and representative rugby player.

Some of the more garish trappings of the new era which was to emerge may have led to the odd traditionalist accusing professionalism of turning rugby into a circus. Considering, however, the juggling act which Paddy and others were now facing in the dying days of the amateur era in a sport which was making ever greater demands on their time, it is little wonder that far-reaching discussions were well underway which would transform the face of rugby forever. Change was inevitable and everyone embraced it sooner or later but, to keep the circus analogy going, Paddy initially chose to continue trying to keep all the balls in the air rather than step straight onto the untested high-wire of full-time rugby before anyone even knew whether there was a safety net or not.

So although the game 'went open', which was partly a euphemism used to ease the blow for the traditionalists but also a reflection that what had happened was more the authorisation of pay-for-play than a proactive embracing of professionalism, at the end of August 1995, things went on pretty much as normal for Paddy. He stayed in Ulster and kept working as a community dentist, while continuing to represent Dungannon at club level and also his province, including in the inaugural European Cup, a competition still very much at the embryonic stage. Several Irish players had turned professional with clubs in England but, at that stage, it was still a trickle rather than a torrent and the sport was still very much in a state of flux.

In light of the huge revolution taking place in the global game, changes which would transform the face of rugby forever, the IRFU had decided to, for the first time, appoint a full-time coach to take charge of the Ireland team. The names of existing coach Gerry Murphy, Ulster's Harry Williams and John O'Driscoll of London Irish had all been in the frame prior to the Union's decision, but the entire trio were to withdraw from consideration as was Dungannon's Willie Anderson, who also threw his hat in the ring. Discussions were held with Australians Bob Dwyer and John Connolly but, ultimately, neither was available and the IRFU turned to former Garryowen coach Murray Kidd, a New Zealander who by then was in charge of Sunday's Well. He became not only the first full-time coach of Ireland, but also the first foreigner to fill the role. Pat Whelan replaced Noel Murphy as manager.

The relationship between Kidd and Ireland was short-lived and ended in tears, and the period of his reign did not provide Paddy Johns with any great degree of success or satisfaction. Yet the Kidd era had begun brightly enough with an impressive 44-8 Lansdowne Road victory over Fiji, whose touring team was captained by prop Joeli Veitayaki, later to play alongside Paddy for Ulster.

There were eight changes from the line-up which had taken the field for the summer's World Cup quarter-final against France, including the return of a fit-again Jim Staples, who took over from Conor O'Shea and was appointed captain. Richard Wallace regained his right wing berth from Darragh O'Mahony, the rookie surprisingly preferred to him in Durban, and Maurice Field came into midfield for Brendan Mullin, who had retired permanently this time. Burke was at stand-off and partnered at halfback by a new cap in Christian Saverimutto, the Sri Lankan born Sale scrum-half with an Irish mother, while Davidson was the other Test debutant. Although seen as an out-and-out second row, Davidson was chosen at blindside, with Johns at No 8 and Corkery again switching flanks resulting in McBride's latest exclusion from the Ireland side.

Paul Wallace made his home debut at tighthead, replacing Halpin, but the rest of the tight five which faced France, Popplewell, deposed captain Kingston and locks Fulcher and Francis, were all retained. The only backline survivors from Durban were Bell and Geoghegan. Bell, still a student at Loughborough, had joined Northampton after the World Cup and his clubmate there, Paddy's old school chum Clarke, was one of three Irish players to win their first caps that afternoon as replacements. He came on for Kingston, while the other two, Old Wesley prop Henry Hurley and Sean McCahill of Kidd's club Sunday's Well, picked theirs up as a result of Popplewell and Field leaving the pitch for running repairs. McCahill, predominantly a centre, was born in New Zealand and his older brother Bernie played for the All Blacks in the inaugural World Cup of 1987, but their parents were Irish. The run-on against Fiji was to prove Sean McCahill's only cap.

Clarke stresses how "having Paddy there made it very easy for me to fit into the environment", while Davidson already had huge respect for Johns, who had taken him under his wing down at Dungannon, laying the foundations for what has become a very strong and close friendship between the two big second rows. As a mutual admiration society, you couldn't top it and, best of all, both are genuine guys so you know it's real.

"The first time I heard of Paddy Johns was on the Irish Schools tour of New Zealand in 1992" says Jeremy. "He'd been on the Ireland senior tour there earlier that summer and some of my friends who were from Dungannon were saying "you'll never play for Ireland for we've got Paddy Johns". That was a bit daunting and the boys were proved right about how good Paddy was, so it was a great privilege to go on to play with him for Dungannon, Ulster and Ireland.

"A few months after that tour, I had joined Dungannon and, although Paddy was away with Ulster the first time I was down at Stevenson Park, I soon got to meet him at training. For me as an 18-year old, he was a huge man and very physically imposing, though by character he is shy and very polite. He was extremely nice to me off the pitch, but when you were training with him, he had a real no-holds barred attitude and was 100 percent professional. I quickly developed an awful lot of respect for him both on and off the pitch.

"For a player coming through, he was the perfect role model. You can look at a lot of good second rows, but no-one had such commitment and determination. His combination of sheer aggression and determination on the pitch and remarkable modesty off it in spite of his achievements are qualities which any young player would do well to aspire to. When you're playing in the same position as someone, it would be easy to see each other as competition, but I had never any doubt that Paddy had my interests at heart, and would like to think that I also had his. Because we rated each other, I think we felt, all things being equal, that there should be room for both of us in an Ulster or Ireland team and for that reason we didnít need to be rivals. It shouldn't be a case of either/or.

"I've played with quite a few good second rows, but Paddy'd be the one that I would pick as my best partner. You never had any doubts or worries and simply knew that he'd be there, with you and for you, throughout the game. I think that we both have the same determined attitude deep down and had a lot of trust in each other when the going got tough.

"I remember playing Wales one year at the Arms Park. Paddy and I had been ill all week, both bed-ridden with some bug, but I'd got over it a bit better than him. He was still rundown by the Saturday, but played, and during the game he said to me 'I'm f*cked'. I can remember thinking 'right, I'm going to go even harder here to compensate, to try to take a little extra of the load' for he'd have done the same for me, but in the end Paddy lasted most of the game through sheer determination. That do-or-die spirit is probably his greatest asset and serves him well off the pitch as well as on it.

"My girlfriend back in my early days at Dungannon was from Greenisland and Paddy lived in Newtownabbey, so I used to get lifts up and down to Stevenson Park. He'd a white Nissan and we needed to have the seats well pushed back! Paddy was always the ultimate pro and I remember that he always used to have a packed lunch with him to eat in the car going home after training. Even though this was set aside for him to recover and get some carbs in, he always shared it with me. From there, it wasn't long until we played together for Ireland and luckily we always seemed to get rooming together in the Irish set-up.

"I trained a bit with him on a rowing machine in his garage before the 1995 World Cup, which I almost got called out to, and then made my debut against Fiji that autumn. One of the Fijians came up to me at the end and asked me to swap jerseys. Theirs was a lovely white shirt with a palm tree on it and I'd have given a lot to have one, but naturally I wasn't going to part with my first Ireland jersey, so I said no. In the changing room afterwards, Paddy came over and handed me a Fijian jersey; he'd swapped his Ireland one with his opposite number so I could have both my own Irish debut jersey and a Fiji one. It was a typical gesture and I know that he has been generous on so many occasions down the years without making a fuss about it. He also does a lot of unseen work for charity.

"Paddy is one of the most gentle and considerate individuals who you'll ever meet and is very thoughtful and full of little acts of kindness. When my mum died this summer, he and Kirsty were more than good in trying to help me through what was a very difficult time. He'd arrive at the house one night with a loaf of bread and a poem about grief on another. You meet a lot of people through life, but there are very few who you can really depend on. Paddy Johns would be one of them though.

"When I was injured last season, even though by then we were, I suppose, rivals in the Ulster squad, he would show me the exercises which he did to get back after knee surgery and invited me down to his house to do recovery sessions. Recently, when I was injured again, he wrote me this lovely letter which finished up with his own motto 'PWP – play with pain'. He certainly was an example in that regard."

Apart from being pleased for Clarke and Davidson, Johns has happy personal memories of that Fijian fixture, for it brought his second Test try. It was also a good day for Ireland, in welcome contrast to many an autumn international. "To some extent, you could argue that we may only have done the job that the public would have expected and demanded in putting away a lesser nation by scoring a few tries, but the fact that that hadn't always happened on previous occasions made it pleasing. I think it was actually better than that, a genuinely good performance which was an encouraging start to a new four year cycle following the World Cup. Everyone, both inside the set-up and the pundits, seemed fairly satisfied and felt it augured well for the season ahead.

"We knew we had to be aggressive and hit very hard against a Fijian team which would be quite physical and certainly dynamic or it could be a very long afternoon for us. It turned out to be quite an open game, to which Ireland contributed impressively but, as always, it was laying a solid platform up front which enabled us to dominate the match and play more expansively as time went on.

"With myself and Jeremy in the back row, we essentially had four locks in the side and, with David Corkery at openside instead of Denis, there was a great deal of height in our pack that day. It was a very big back five and proved fairly effective but there's no utopia either, for you always get a trade-off. Jeremy did well that day but it was clear his future lay in the second row while Corkery wasn't a natural openside. David was always a good ball-carrier and very destructive, but being good on the ground would not have been one of his strengths. McBride was much smaller but, like Neil Back with England, whenever he didn't play, you sacrificed his good work at the breakdown."

There is no hard and fast template or formula for picking a backrow and each coach will have to make what he feels to be his best balanced selection for each particular game based on the unique attributes of the individuals at his disposal. He may take into account what type of game he wants his team to play, the nature of the opposition, the relative degrees of experience of the players concerned, the need for at least one credible lineout option and so forth. At a later stage, for example, Ireland had to choose between the power of Victor Costello and the pace of Dion O'Cuinneagain at No 8 and, for long enough, had the dilemma of whether to pick McBride or a bigger man in the No 7 jersey. The Ulster team which won the European Cup in 1999 used Andy Ward heavily as a ball-carrier because of his explosive qualities and, in general, his role for the province has seldom been that of a pure openside. He has also, in more recent years, been used as a more than occasional lineout jumper.

But, in a classic backrow, many, including Johns, see a big-hitting blindside as the dream ticket and Ireland have had a few during his career, with Corkery as effective as most in succession to the likes of Phil Matthews and Pat O'Hara. He could be a bit of a loose cannon and gave away more than his share of penalties but, perhaps, suffered less from the red mist than his provincial successor Alan Quinlan or Leinster loose cannon Trevor Brennan.

Ireland's back three of Staples, Wallace and Geoghegan were among their try-scorers against Fiji, as were Richie's brother Paul, Paddy himself and Francis. It was a case of six of the best and the half dozen tries were supplemented by 14 points from Burke's boot. After Christmas, Ireland went to Atlanta for a training camp and international against the United States. It is a trip which Johns will always remember for the dreadful weather conditions and the hard work done under the auspices of John Mitchell. Mitchell, who had been a regular midweek All Black without ever winning a Test cap, spent a season playing for Garryowen before captaining Waikato to victory over the 1993 Lions. Now concentrating on a coaching career in which he was to progress to Clive Woodward's assistant with England before taking charge of his native New Zealand in late 2001, Mitchell was brought in to work with his compatriot Kidd.

"John Mitchell was so New Zealand" Paddy recalls. "He was very big into his rucking and into really beating us up in training. We used to do endless down and ups, y'know where you run 10 metres, go down on your stomach, get up and go back again. The Irish players weren't used to that sort of thing then and some people actually resented being pushed that hard. It was to become a way of life in the professional era, but things were done differently in those days. Mitchell was quite ruthless and clinical, a very determined guy and it's easy to see why he's gone a long way. In general the players respected him, for he was hard himself and had been around the All Blacks.

"I suppose him and Gatty, who were team-mates and good friends in their Waikato days, had frustrations in their playing careers with being around the All Blacks for so long but never winning a cap due to the presence of Fitzpatrick and Brooke. But they obviously learned a lot, probably including patience I guess, and the experience of missing out as players maybe helped make them determined to make their mark on the sport as coaches. They've certainly done that."

It was a tough regime in Atlanta, with the Irish players "training flat out every day with fitness training at the end. It was all done at a level which was higher than anything which we had experienced before. For example, we'd do maybe 10 sets of 200 metre sprints. Victor Costello in particular got it very tight. He'd been an Olympic thrower and was very strong and explosive, but he was very much a power athlete rather than a stamina athlete." For years afterwards, Costello's career was dogged by question marks against his fitness, workrate and attitude, with accusing fingers continually being pointed and regular omissions from the Irish set-up resulting. Ironically, it is only now in the past couple of seasons since his regular senior Ireland days have appeared done, that he has managed to largely silence the critics and make a more rounded contribution. So what was Victor's problem, Paddy? That he couldn't or he wouldn't?

"Victor went to London Irish after professionalism came in, but he didn't settle. I think he was a bit homesick and missed Dublin. He went back to Ireland and maybe dropped into a comfort zone for a short time. Victor was built for power not stamina, but over the last few years he has worked very hard to improve his aerobic fitness. He was vital to Leinster when they won the Celtic League last season."

Ironically, in light of the fitness concerns and the fact that they had been highlighted at that training camp more than previously, it was in the blindside berth that Costello won his first Ireland cap against the US Eagles at the end of that trip. Following McCahill's brief appearance in the Fijian fixture, Ireland blooded another Kiwi centre in this game, Kurt McQuilkin of Bective Rangers, whose father coached the club and was to be in charge of the Divisional XV which faced the Irish on the New Zealand tour of 2002. He and Costello, in for Field and the injured Davidson respectively, were the two new caps, while there was one other change with Elwood replacing Burke at outhalf, though the latter did come on to kick three penalties. Before his departure, Elwood had also landed a hat-trick of penalties and converted Ireland's only try, scored by Richard Wallace. Ireland came away with a 25-18 victory and Johns credits the Eagles with being "a good side, much stronger than the one we played previously in Ireland. They played well on the day and pushed us hard."

But, in what was to be a recurring theme under Kidd, the pre-match preparations were not to Paddy's liking. "We had really busted ourselves all week, training really hard right up to the game. To some extent you could argue that, because the match was there at the end of a training camp, the context was slightly different to other Test matches. Although it was a capped international, our approach made it seem like the USA game was more of a practice match slotted into the main business of a training camp rather than being a proper Test match and prepared for as such. The trip wasn't geared that way and, to some extent, our poor preparations for that American match could be justified on the basis that being in Atlanta was not just about the game, but mistakes were definitely made in relation to future internationals when there was no such excuse."

One thing which couldn't, however, be blamed on the management was the weather. "It rained and snowed all week and, on the day of the game itself, the sleet and rain were simply torrential. We were playing in a kind of open field with the spectators huddled round the sides. The surroundings were hardly inspiring and the pitch barely playable, but we just about got the win and then just about got out of the country. Conditions were so bad that the whole of the eastern United States was closed down by snow. We were the last flight to get out for days."

If conditions were atrocious and awful in Atlanta, it was to be a dark and dismal Dublin day on which Ireland opened their Five Nations campaign against Scotland a fortnight later. By the end of the afternoon, that grim greyness matched the mood of public and players alike after the same old story of great expectations against the Scots not being met and another miserable Irish start to the Championship. The sense of hope and purpose and feel-good factor which the win over Fiji had generated on a sunny autumn afternoon had been thoroughly dissipated as two tries by an unlikely hero, winger Michael Dods, gave the Scots a 16-10 victory. Clohessy, recalled in place of Wallace as one of two Irish changes with Davidson being brought back at the expense of Costello at blindside as the other, scored the host country's try, Elwood converting and adding a penalty.

"The same old thing" sighs Paddy. "We always felt we were much better than Scotland and that we were going to beat them, but it never happened. They were a very dogged side and coped better with the conditions on what was a dreadful day for a game." There were two main casualties of Ireland's defeat, with Elwood being dropped to accommodate a debut for Ulsterman David Humphreys and the international career of Neil Francis, which had begun at the 1987 World Cup, coming to an end. Francis was an enigmatic and frustrating figure, an immensely talented player who finished with 36 caps but, many felt, could have won more and done even better in the green jersey with greater application.

"Franno was a fantastic player and, like everyone else, I rated him as a great lineout forward, with an exceptional natural leap and good hands" says Paddy in tribute, before adding the qualifications which so many people have felt obliged to do. "He was immense when he was switched on and had 60 caps plus in him.

"Even now, as a newspaper columnist, Franno is a colourful and, in ways, controversial character, but I must say I have always got on well with him both on and off the pitch. In the early days, when he was well established and I was in the A team, I remember doing a lineout session at Lansdowne Road during Ciaran Fitzgerald's time as coach. I climbed all over him at the first few lineouts and punches were thrown. At the next lineout, Phil Matthews, my Ulster team-mate and very experienced international, floored me with a punch I didn't see coming. End of lineout training!"

For the trip to Paris, the dropping of Francis saw Johns moved into the second row with Costello coming in at No 8. Humphreys and Hogan usurped Elwood and Saverimutto at halfback, with Niall Woods replacing an injured Geoghegan on the wing. Humphreys had been turning on the style for Ulster, with one dazzling display against New South Wales sticking in the mind to this day, but it was his virtuoso performance for Oxford in the Varsity match just before Christmas 1995 which had finally made his Test claims irresistible. In general he was further on in his career and had done more than Niall Malone had done when his fellow Ulsterman had been catapulted into the Irish team by a Varsity match performance three years earlier, but it was still going to be a baptism of fire.

"France in Paris, particularly in those days, was a daunting debut for anyone, not the ideal place for your first Test" says Paddy. "During my lifetime, there have been a number of Ulstermen who won their first cap there and never got any more. David didn't do badly that day, but if you look at him now compared with then, it's chalk and cheese. He's very confident and composed and a great decision-maker these days, but it takes experience to make you a really commanding international outhalf." The point has recently been echoed by current Ulster coach Alan Solomons in discussing the merits of Humphreys and young pretender Paddy Wallace. "Paddy is a smashing player already, but David has been round the block and that is invaluable. It's the same with the All Blacks at the moment. Aaron Mauger is very good, but Andrew Mehrtens brings great maturity and experience to the New Zealand No 10 jersey" says Solomons.

Apart from Ireland's 45-10 defeat and the fact that it was to be their last ever game at what, in light of traumatic experiences there down through the years, would be the little-lamented Parc des Princes, that match will always be remembered for the infamous incident involving Peter Clohessy. It was an undistinguished day for Irish rugby in terms of the result and the Young Munster prop's much publicised stamp on the head of French lock Olivier Roumat ensured that disgrace was added to humiliation. The referee missed the incident, but it was caught on camera and the damning evidence resulted in a suspension of 26 playing weeks being imposed on Clohessy, effectively putting him out of the game for the best part of a year. That he was a player who already had an unfortunate reputation and something of a bad disciplinary track record added to the vilification which Clohessy received in the press and elsewhere at the time.

What was the perspective of Paddy and the other Irish players? In sport in general, there is an understandable tendency to close ranks round a team-mate who is under fire, almost regardless of the offence. Like sheltering the family member who has committed a crime. But rugby is a sport which holds out the potential for a reckless or malicious player to do untold damage to an opponent and, for that reason, the game must police itself and draw certain boundaries which are seen as unacceptable to cross. Not only can the solitary referee not see every incident; they certainly can't pre-empt and prevent acts of thuggery and, at lower levels where no television or video cameras are present, there is certainly no guarantee that culprits will be caught. So, as a protective mechanism, the sport has to shame offenders as part of an attempt to deter those who might think of causing serious and deliberate damage to an opponent.

"I didn't see a thing at the time, but we obviously watched the incident on television later and the evidence of what he did was pretty conclusive." Given that he and others had been on the receiving end of persistent foul play and unpleasant behaviour from the French for years, did Johns take the view that they were good for whatever they got or that a line of acceptable behaviour had been clearly crossed?

"When I was in New Zealand, I learnt a painful lesson that, if you're on the ground, you're part of the ground. But, having said that, the head has always, rightly, been seen as out of bounds because of the damage which you could cause to the brain. So something had to be done about it, but the ban was certainly a long one considering other suspensions which have been handed out both before and since and that so much stuff from the French went unpunished in those days. As a team-mate, we also felt for Peter with all the press attention and criticism, and sort of knew what he was going through. He had done wrong and certainly paid the price for it."

Of much more pressing personal concern to Paddy, however, was the fact that, when the team was announced for the next match, his name was missing as well as Clohessy's. Dropped after having been selected for 28 Tests on the trot, including the previous year's Five Nations game against France when he had been a late cry-off due to the appendicitis scare. It was a big blow and a real culture shock.. I was absolutely gutted to only be on the bench. I can't remember exactly how I heard, or whether there was any degree of dialogue or feedback from the hierarchy at the time, but it was a big disappointment." As on the occasion of his first and only previous axing, following his debut against Argentina in 1990, Johns was part of a major clearout, but again that was little consolation and, this time, it was harder to take as an established player.

The Birkenhead-born Simon Mason, a future Ulster colleague of Paddy's and renowned as a prolific goal-kicker in the English leagues, came in at fullback for Staples, so Hogan, who still had only half a dozen caps to his name, assumed the captaincy. A fit-again Geoghegan was back on the wing, though at the expense of Wallace rather than his replacement for the previous game, Woods, while Field took over from McQuilkin as Bell's centre partner. Up front, Clarke, so long in Paddy's shadow, was handed his first Test start, thus keeping the RSD flag flying, while Wallace was recalled in place of the suspended Clohessy. Johns' place in the team was, ironically, taken by his old friend McBride, who won back the No 7 jersey in a reshuffle which saw Davidson and Corkery move to their more natural positions in the engineroom and at blindside respectively.

"It's no real consolation how many guys have been dropped, but I suppose when there are plenty of others you feel that less individual blame has been attached to you personally for the previous defeat or poor performance or whatever. It also looks like the selectors had made a conscious decision to ring the changes." So how was it, being a bench boy after such a long stint in the team? "In ways, funnily enough, it felt fantastic that week" is his slightly surprising response.

"There isn't the same pressure or worry during the build-up of knowing that, come 2.30 or whatever on Saturday, you'll be out there with the spotlight on you and needing to deliver the goods. That might sound bizarre, considering that every player wants to be on the pitch for every minute of every game and that representing your country is what you crave and what you've worked for but the initial disappointment of being dropped was briefly replaced by a sense that being on the bench wasn't too bad a state of affairs. When you're standing holding the bags as opposition in training, there's less weight on you and, in a strange way, I felt good that week though, not surprisingly, the feeling didn't last too long. The novelty quickly wore off! Come Saturday, it was actually terrible sitting on the bench, helplessly watching the clock. It just ran down so quickly, an hour left, 40 minutes, 30, 10, down to five and just hoping in vain that someone would twist an ankle or something. It never happened.

"Afterwards, you're pleased that Ireland have won because it's your team and the guys are your mates and all that, but gutted you didn't get on. Although you had given your best in training, been pushing the man hard who was playing in your place and so forth and had had to be prepared to come on in the first minute of the match in the event of an injury, the fact was that you hadn't actually contributed on the day. So it was hard to feel part of the victory or have any sense of ownership. There are mixed emotions and you can't honestly celebrate in the same way as if you had been on the pitch, even briefly. Then the reality sinks in that the team has won well without you and that that won't help your cause. Whether or not the guy in your position played especially well, changes are less likely on the back of a victory and that had been a pretty good one for Ireland."

Wingers Woods and Geoghegan, the latter's 11th and last touchdown at international level, had scored Irish tries, as had Fulcher and Corkery, with new boy Mason converting two of them and also kicking a couple of penalties. Unsurprisingly, it was an unchanged

Irish team which went to Twickenham a fortnight later, when harsh reality hit Paddy very hard indeed. Being on the bench was no fun after all.

"I remember getting off the bus and walking though the Irish crowd. The fans had surrounded the bus and it was just a sea of Irish flags and faces, full of expectation and all wishing us well. It would have been uplifting but for the thought that I couldn't really do anything to influence the game. The likelihood of someone in my area of the team getting injured, which was basically what you needed in those days in order to get on, seemed remote. I felt really gutted and could hardly lift myself to make my way through with my bags. It was a real low feeling. I remember sitting in the changing rooms with my head in my hands before the game and feeling a bit sorry for myself."

As Ireland again did reasonably well, keeping in touch with England through four penalties from Mason supplemented by a Humphreys drop goal until a Jon Sleightholme try gave the hosts breathing space, Kidd's team could be considered to have had a decent second half to the Championship. Johns couldn't help realising that he had been associated with the disappointing first half, through playing in that depressing Dublin defeat against a moderate Scottish side and taking part in the Paris pasting, but had had no hand in the revival represented by the win over Wales and respectable margin of defeat at Twickenham.

"You think, 'hold on a second here, where do I stand'. Things weren't looking that healthy, but I had a choice of either going into freefall or getting the finger out and training even harder, fighting tooth and nail to get my place back. I chose the latter." So Paddy's international career was at something of a crossroads and, indeed, his whole relationship with rugby was about to change. Within a few months, he had packed in the dentistry day job to become a fully-fledged professional sportsman.

16. TURNING PRO

As the sun set on South Africa, a new day dawned on the rugby world. Professionalism was now an official part of the sport and for many clubs and players alike it truly was a case of learn as you go. This new ethos had been simmering beneath the surface south of the Equator for some time. In the north, clubs were being reinvented with multi-millionaire backers, and players were calling their whole lifestyle and reasons for playing into question. For those like Paddy, it was a case of turn pro, or get left behind.

In fact the game had already been 'open' for a season when Paddy took the plunge in the summer of 1996, but the putative professional rugby world was so confused and uncertain that it was still something of a leap into the unknown when he signed for Sarries. Certainly he never seriously considered going full-time straight after the ground-breaking bombshell dropped by the IRB on Sunday 27th August 1995, a day before Johns' wedding anniversary.

For some years, the IRFU had had an Amateur Status sub-committee which sought to manage the blurring of the edges that was occurring in the sport and it was thought that the IRB's two day Paris meeting would bring a further relaxation of the guidelines governing the global game. Allowing the appointment of professional coaches and permitting players to benefit financially from the game and their status courtesy of indirect earnings from commercial activities was as far as many predicted that things would go at this stage. Some saw professionalism as inevitable further down the line, but expected a longer transition phase and more halfway house arrangements before any move was made to formally abolish amateurism, a cherished state of affairs which had pertained for well over a century.

Instead, the IRB surprised most people by going the whole hog and giving birth to professional rugby with no real idea of how it would be nurtured or whether it could become the trojan horse which would destroy many traditions which the game held dear. There seemed to be no strong sense of how professionalism would work out in practice. Ireland's representatives on the IRB, Syd Millar and Tom Kiernan, apparently opposed the drastic move but, although professionalism was not being imposed on any country, it would have been suicidal for the leading nations to opt out. Indeed, while in many ways the Irish structure is now the envy of other countries, with the three tiers of clubs, provinces and national team functioning in relative harmony compared to the conflict elsewhere, the initial resistance and reluctance of the IRFU had a price.

Perhaps their caution and financial prudence at the advent of professionalism has helped deliver the stability which exists in Irish rugby today but, even by the second season after rugby going open, little was done to stem the flow of leading players across the water. Only a handful had signed up for English clubs right away and, in the early days,

Irish players were generally released to play for their provinces, which were still seen as representative teams then, in competitions like the new European Cup.

Admittedly, it would have been hard to compete with the lucrative deals being tabled by English clubs who, bankrolled by wealthy benefactors, were gambling heavily on immediate success. While the IRFU is relatively well off, it had to behave as a governing body, the custodians of the game in Ireland, whereas the English clubs had, essentially, become businesses run by entrepreneurs and could take what risks they saw fit. Furthermore, once a few players went, others felt obliged to follow in the hope of improving their own game in an English Premiership into which household names from round the world were flooding. By the autumn of 1996, moving was the obvious thing to do for ambitious Irish internationals and, when Brian Ashton became Irish coach a few months later, he displayed a blatant preference for English based-players.

"It seemed to happen all at once," remembers Richard Wallace. "Before I went on holidays that summer, I was definitely staying put, but in those two weeks, all the top players signed contracts in England. I thought that the competition back home would be seriously diluted. Also the IRFU were acting like ostriches in embracing professionalism."

Paddy's employers, the Northern Health and Social Services Board, had always been sympathetic to his circumstances and releasing him for international duty, but it really wasn't going to be enough if Paddy decided to embrace this new philosophy. Throughout the amateur era, rugby players had always relied on the flexibility and goodwill of employers in facilitating them to represent their country. Sometimes the profile which went with having a rugby international in the workforce made it worth the employer's while and many players worked as sales reps for example, with their status and easily recognisable image being used to promote the given product. Bank jobs also seemed to be popular among international players. Other employers, recognising how big an honour it obviously was for the individual to be picked for their country, were simply sympathetic to their requests for time off. Working in jobs, as in Paddy's case, where leave could be taken rather than holidays being set, was an advantage.

But it had now come to a stage where even the most sympathetic employer or flexible job would not really be able to accommodate a player trying to keep step at the upper end of a game in which other players were now full-time and both fixture lists and training schedules were becoming more demanding. It was not just about being available to play and train, but also having the time to take the necessary rest in order to optimise performance and not become run down. The option to go full-time was now there so, at one level, grasping it was the glaringly obvious thing to do.

But it wasn't quite as simple as that. The concept of a professional game was still very new and represented a very significant cultural change for rugby people. As already recorded, Johns the schoolboy could never have envisaged becoming a full-time paid player. Getting paid to pursue a hobby sounds like a job straight from heaven, but it was not a decision to be taken lightly. Issues such as being good enough for long enough, getting injured, where to go and so forth each equated to several sleepless nights.

"I often lay awake thinking, 'am I doing the right thing? What if I fall flat on my face?'. It would also mean giving up a job I liked and enjoyed. However, once I decided I was going for it, that was it" Paddy states. "My attitude changed. I wanted to do a good day's work in rugby just like I had in dentistry and quickly realised I had to look after myself extremely well to do it. Because of my somewhat medical background, I knew the basics of nutrition and the differences between carbohydrates, proteins and fats. We also got a lot of advice from dieticians working with both the Ulster Branch and the IRFU. I'd always trained hard and put in 100 percent, but now I was getting paid to perform and in my head each day I had to justify my wages." Such an attitude gives an insight into why Johns coped so well and thrived in the professional environment.

So too do the words of Willie Anderson. "Because of the meticulous and committed approach which he had always had, Paddy was prepared for professionalism and thus able to draw the benefits" says his former Dungannon coach. "The result was that he went from being 'just an international' to a very good international, respected and renowned throughout the world. Just like as a coach I knew at that stage that England was the sharp end, Paddy did the right thing going to Saracens at the time, for it was there that he learned the roundedness of professional rugby and had the most conducive environment, whereas back then Irish rugby was still in a state of dabbling and resisting."

However, it wasn't a total dream ticket for Paddy, not least because his move into the paying arena meant he had to once more leave his beloved Ulster. "My first decision was whether or not to go full-time. Once I'd decided that, my second decision was whether to stay at home or go away. It was a hard decision to leave, but at that stage I would have been the only full-time pro in Ulster" he rationalises.

"I was one of the last Irish ones to go. Most of them had already signed up for Harlequins, Bath, Saracens or London Irish. There was just a better system set up in England and I thought it would be better for me to train with other full-time players rather than stay in a semi-pro limbo in Ireland. The previous year it hadn't really been an issue. Professionalism had only been rushed in five minutes earlier so to speak and only a couple of Irish guys went over initially. It certainly wasn't something I even considered at that point. The notion of a professional game and its implications was still sinking in and, even before that second season, people were still very uncertain." Syd Millar had been among those to publicly urge caution for players thinking about giving up the day job.

In addition, Paddy did not have the luxury of just considering his own playing future and general well-being and happiness. He also had a wife and son to think about. "I definitely had quite a few reservations" admits Kirsty. "The whole professionalism thing was just so new. What if it all collapsed? It was a big risk. The safer option was to stay put. Paddy had a good permanent job, which he enjoyed, while I had just finished my physiotherapy. We had a child and financial commitments to worry about and we were going to have to move into the unknown, both in terms of professionalism and relocating our family to somewhere where essentially we knew no-one.

"However our adventurous side told us to go for it. We were young and we saw it as a challenge. An adventure. Paddy was in a profession he could go back to, as he has now, and would not be burning his bridges jobwise. Plus I knew it was what he really wanted and, I suppose, needed to do for the good of his rugby career."

But, while Paddy, unlike some players, had the responsibility of a family, he was in a better position than many others, both at the time and since, when it came to the level of risk he was taking. As an established international player, albeit one who had lost his place in the Ireland starting line-up by the end of the 1996 Five Nations, Johns knew that, at the very least, he was good enough not only to break into, but sustain himself in, the professional game, providing it itself survived. In fact, he was good enough, to have real options about where he would go and would not be restricted to staying there longer term if it didn't work out. He also could command a good salary, though these were still modest relative to soccer even in the early days of English extravagance.

It had also come along at the right time for him and he was in an ideal alternative career for taking a sporting sabbatical. Paddy had got his qualification and five years work experience under his belt before having to make what would, earlier, have been an even harder choice. Also, as a profession, dentistry was a career which he could fairly readily resume at any stage whereas some other guys were faced with the agonising decision of whether to risk stepping out of a company structure into which there was no way back, effectively jumping off a ladder they had already spent time working their way up.

Three of Ulster's European Cup squad of 1999 who ultimately chose not to turn professional, Stephen McKinty, Andy Matchett and Gary Leslie, were all essentially in that boat and, furthermore, by the time the chance came for them, they were of a certain age and no longer had any realistic international aspirations. Just as that trio's choice to stay out would appear to have been the right one, Paddy's decision both to turn professional and to go to England, looked entirely logical to the outside observer at the time, not least in light of the mass exodus from the emerald isle which was taking place and the fact that he had the incentive of an Ireland career to safeguard.

Again the question of 'where?' had to be answered, and for a while it looked as though Bedford would benefit from the Irishman's 6'6" frame. A Mr Ian Bullerwell had spotted Paddy whilst refereeing Ulster against the All Blacks in 1989, an occasion of which he recalls that "I thought I played quite well." Well 'quite well' was good enough to have Johns headhunted years later by Bedford, where Bullerwell was the chairman of contracts.

They were the first club to contact Paddy and prompted a visit to meet key officials and check out what facilities were available. Bedford had a good pedigree and was currently a solid second tier team with first division aspirations within the next two seasons. The town seemed friendly and was very rugby-orientated, and the Johnses liked the atmosphere. So Bedford it was. By the start of August, stars like Paul Turner and Martin Offiah were signed up to the Bedford cause and things for Paddy started to change. Every week a contract was 'coming', but never actually came and Ian Bullerwell was on holidays and not contactable during the first two weeks of August.

The press had announced that Johns had signed for Bedford, so he wasn't even in the running for any other clubs, and with his job in dentistry due to finish at the end of the month, Paddy's 'professional' career looked to be over before it had even started.

Thankfully, the luck of the Irish saw to it that London club Saracens happened to hear that Johns hadn't actually signed on the dotted line and invited him over to the capital. Again Paddy liked what he saw and, perhaps more importantly at this stage, a contract was faxed over the very next day.

"I was starting to panic a wee bit," says Kirsty. "Paddy had given up his dental job and suddenly he had nothing lined up. It was a relief when Saracens came in. Admittedly their offer was the only one on the table at that point, but I was happy to go there. I'd been over and seen that the set-up and environment was a place where we could survive as a family. I wouldn't have gone just anywhere, though if we'd had an offer from a French club, for example, I would have been happy to go there too if it had been right for us. Anyway, it all worked out for the best."

When Bedford's boxing backer Frank Warren heard of these developments, his advisers contacted Paddy straight away with promises of doubling contracts and pandering to every need, but as the player explained, "It wasn't really about the money. Basically Bedford hadn't kept their word and I wasn't about to uproot my family and take a chance with people I couldn't trust. I told Warren's representative all this and there it was, I was going to Sarries."

At that time there were no agents involved and the only professional input Paddy received was from his brother-in-law Robin Fletcher, a 6'8" second row from Scotland who had attended Oxford with Victor Ubogu and who, acting in his solicitor's role, went through the contract from Saracens checking the small print. One autograph later and there was one more professional rugby player in the world.

At Saracens, Paddy would be one of a trio of Irish internationals which included the elder two Wallace brothers, Richard and Paul. Like Paddy, Richard had chosen Saracens only after looking around other clubs. "Being Irish, perhaps London Irish was the natural move" says the former Ireland winger. "I met a guy from the club, but had mixed thoughts about the move. London Irish would be a home away from home, which could be good, but I worried, perhaps unfairly, that it would be like living in a comfort zone. Paul had already decided to go to Sarries and told them that I might be interested. I liked the set-up and there were rumours that Lynagh and Sella were joining. Also, Paddy and I had had many conversations worrying about going to England, and the fact that we both rated Sarries gave me more confidence about the move."

Mrs Johns Senior also approved. "Paddy discussed with me the issues around turning professional and I supported him fully" says his mum. "I didn't like the idea of him leaving Ireland, but knew that he would be back. I saw it as a great opportunity for him and, when I went over and saw the set-up and met Nigel Wray, I knew he'd made the right decision. Nigel is a delightful man, looked after everyone well and really got the families involved in the club. Playing for Ireland has always been the ultimate for Paddy and there is no doubt that Saracens raised him to a new level, working with the likes of Francois Pienaar and Michael Lynagh.

"Francois had a very good relationship with Paddy and was inspirational regarding his captaincy, but I'd have known Michael better. Paddy brought Michael over in 1997 to be a guest speaker at a Royal School Armagh dinner and I had him and his wife for next day, he went to Roe Valley and, when stopped by the police and asked ... was doing, he replied 'You'd better ask Paddy Johns'!"

With more money, time, research and resources being pumped into union, could it still be the game that Paddy loves? "Definitely" he enthuses. "You couldn't be a successful professional rugby player if you didn't enjoy it. I always loved both training and playing, so there wasn't really any risk of over-kill as far as I was concerned. My only problem was that I trained too much in that first season. I was used to training twice a day and still fitting in work, so when I had all day to train, I did too much. By the end of the season I was burnt out. It was a steep learning curve for both players and clubs in that season and I think across the board nobody really got it 100 percent right, but there was definitely more structure and knowledge on both sides as time wore on."

At the start, there was probably a sense that, if guys were employed full-time and that this was now their day job, they should be visibly seen 'working' throughout the working day. But players and coaches alike have progressively realised that the advantage of professionalism is not that it allows people to be flogged to death all day every day, but that it enables their training to be planned in a way which maximises its efficiency, effectiveness and quality and permits that essential commodity, rest.

"Obviously there have been changes. The main one I think is the pace of the game. Players are fitter, faster, stronger and more powerful than before. Skill levels have massively improved, especially aspects like handling amongst the forwards. But we have the time to do it now. Professionalism has allowed players to concentrate on their game and to develop physically, mentally, technically and tactically. Everything is analysed these days and put out there for public scrutiny, not only by coaches but by an expanded and increasingly involved media. Then again, it's your job so you should be accountable for what you do at the 'office'.

"Something I'm not sure about in the modern game is player physique. It used to be that every size had a position in rugby and now players are often interchangeable. Although it's good that everyone on the pitch can pass and kick and ruck, I do wonder if a standard size and shape of player is being developed, which would be sad. However, at the moment anyway, you do still need to have bulk, for example, to be a prop. Across the board however, players have definitely filled out – even David Humphreys! I've put on about 10lbs and I noticed an increase in the Ulster guys when I came back home. I've taken protein powder and tried creatine for a while. Creatine made me put on weight, but I felt it was all water retention, so I tried it only for a short time."

Being at the top of the rugby tree now had the added attraction of sizeable financial gains along with publicity and accolades. Was there a temptation and exposure to the darker side of performance-enhancing supplements, namely illegal drugs, something which his former team-mate Neil Francis claims infiltrated the Irish game during his career?

"Not for me personally. Absolutely not. To be fair, it was never in the culture I grew up in. You hear rumours, but I certainly never saw anyone shooting up in the changing room! I think the sport's pretty clean, but then again people do get caught, so it is out there. I can understand the temptation, but it was never an option I considered. I guess," he muses, "it's more tempting if you're at a lower level trying to break into the professional arena or get noticed by the big clubs than if you're already in a professional environment."

With so much free time compared to the amateur days, was there ever a problem with filling his day, and does this leave players susceptible to pitfalls like gambling and other snares into which certain young footballers have infamously fallen? "I never had a problem keeping busy. I have a lot of interests and my family were always there. They give me stability and kept me very grounded. Regarding gambling, some of the guys would play card games like hearts between morning and afternoon sessions, but I never saw any evidence of gambling as such. I guess rugby isn't a glamour sport like football and we don't get wages like they do, so it's not as though we have so much money we don't know what to with it, though it is true professional rugby players do have a fair bit of time on their hands and it could be spent unwisely.

"Conscious of this and the fact that some of the younger guys now may have come into the game early with little qualifications, many professional set-ups are proactively helping players find suitable courses to further their education. Harry Williams, who was a Headmaster himself, was very aware of this and organized computer and French classes for Ulster players in 2000. There are good opportunities there to be availed of, especially with the concept of flexible learning these days being embraced by most universities and colleges, and part-time studying should help reduce the incidence of guys leaving the game with nothing to fall back on.

"Now that professionalism is here long enough for people to have dropped out again, be it through retirement, or injury, or not getting a new contract, the issue of player welfare is coming to the fore. On the same basis that I've just said about rugby players not having so much money they simply don't know what to do with it, equally guys don't make enough out of the game to not have to work again, so planning your life after rugby is important."

Wages in professional rugby are vastly inferior to football, while Paddy's old Dungannon Royal schoolmate, top Irish golfer Darren Clarke, is a multi-millionaire, but he philosophically accepts the reality of those differentials. "You could argue, for example, that rugby training is harder, or certainly heavier, than what footballers apparently do, according to our old Irish fitness trainer Andy Clark, who was fitness trainer at Liverpool FC. I was surprised at that, but maybe it's because they don't want footballers to put on bulk and correspondingly lose agility. Anyway, it's all about market forces and, if the money is there in those sports and the guys can cash in, good luck to them. Golf or football are such that you can make a fortune in them, whereas rugby isn't. Some of the bigger wages paid in English rugby in the early days of professionalism, which were still nothing like football, simply weren't sustainable. Clubs were overstretching themselves and their revenues couldn't support the wage bill."

Johns insists that he has never really enviously compared his lot in life with that of Clarke, who was one year below him at Dungannon Royal and played flanker for the First XV in Paddy's season as captain. "Darren was a very good rugby player at school" recalls Paddy, before adding, a touch mischievously, "and a lot slimmer then than he is now! He wasn't quite as well-built in those days, but we all fill out. He could easily have played for Dungannon at club level and probably Ulster. Darren was a lively wing forward, an excellent support player with good hands, good at taking the ball on and breaking the first tackle." Incidentally Clarke says he would have preferred to have played No 8 than flanker, but that clearly wasn't an option with Paddy in the side.

"I didn't actually know at the time that Darren played golf seriously, but he has obviously done extremely well for himself in the intervening years. Physically, golf may not be as tough as rugby, but you need the skills and the mental toughness and he's had to fight his way through to the top of the professional game to earn the rewards he's getting now.

"Before he was famous, Darren would come to a lot of Dungannon's games, both home and away, but he's not back very often these days, so I never see him now. Good guy though. When he started to win big tournaments in the golf, he'd phone back to the local golf club and order a round for the regulars. I've never really compared our situations. I was crap at golf, still am, so I could never have been him! Rugby was my thing and I achieved a fair amount, got a lot of satisfaction from it and enjoyed playing both as an amateur and a professional. I've no complaints."

Looking back, Paddy has absolutely no regrets regarding his decision to turn professional and the hobby becoming the day job didn't take the fun out of rugby. "It's like being on an extended tour and it suited me. I liked the training and discipline. It never stopped my enjoyment of the game. I've always enjoyed training as well as playing. It does grate though when you're injured."

Keeping a sense of perspective is presumably harder in the professional game when rugby is what you do every day and, if it really takes over your life, can become the only barometer of general happiness. Being out of the professional team you are attached to, either through injury or non-selection, can make life fairly depressing and, even as a mature man with a family and other interests, Paddy found that situation tough when it happened from time to time in the last couple of years of his career.

You have to accept those ups and downs though and, what he regrets more has been the virtual sacrifice, in the professional era, of one of rugby's great traditions, that of the sides socialising together after beating each other black and blue. "The drawback now is that you don't get to bond with the opposition after games the way you used to and that's sad. Sometimes it's due to logistics whereby one team or other has to get out of town pretty sharp after a match, but it's definitely a pity.

"I've enjoyed the professional game and it has been good enough to me, but you must remember that, although rugby's great, you have to put your other career on hold, so you're at the bottom when you eventually go back into it and everyone else has passed you by." Apart from falling behind your contemporaries in the alternative career, some players at lower levels of the professional game may actually earn less in the sport than they could do in another job.

At least one fringe player in the present Ulster squad who was an academic high-flyer but is only on a basic provincial contract to play rugby has had to give serious consideration to his future before committing to another year in professional rugby. Being paid to play seems like a dream, but to some, it can actually cost them in the pocket.

Paddy on his Ulster debut, against Connacht at Ravenhill in 1988 (above) and with the Ireland team on the occasion of his first Test cap, versus Argentina at Lansdowne Road two years later

Pictures: Esler Crawford

Wedding day August 28, 1992 and (bottom right) Victoria Station, St John's, Newfoundland where they spent their wedding night

Celebrating Saracens' 1998 Tetley Bitter Cup final victory in the changing rooms (above) and relaxing at home next morning

Above pic: Formula 1

Paddy and Mick Galwey celebrate an Irish victory over England

Paddy's mum, Wanda (right), with Mrs Wray, mother of Saracens owner Nigel

Wallaby great Michael Lynagh and wife Marianna with Paddy's son Christopher and Mrs Wanda Johns

Paddy with Omagh bomb victim Alastair Hall who was Ireland team mascot for the game against England at Lansdowne Road in 1999 and (inset) captain Johns just before kick-off against South Africa the previous year

Pictures: John Rush

Marking his Ulster return with a try against Glasgow in Stranraer on July 31, 1999 (left) and on the charge in his first competitive game since moving back from Saracens, against Connacht at the Sportsground in Galway a week later

Pictures: Esler Crawford

Paddy and Kirsty with their new-born twins Hannah and Megan and (left) the Johns family at home in Co Down

Top picture: Belfast Telegraph

On the attack for Ulster against Stade Francais, supported by Paddy Wallace and (left) with Eric Miller, coach Harry Williams and Gary Longwell

Pictures: Mark McCormick & Brian Little

An international cricketer in New Zealand recently pulled out of the professional side of that sport for similar reasons at the age of 28. Rugby may not pay quite enough across the board to ensure that it will recruit and retain every single talent for the entirety of their useful playing life, especially when you consider the opportunity cost of taking time out of the alternative career. This raises the question of problems facing young men, no more than boys really, fresh out of school and keen to wear green jerseys of their own. What if Paddy's son, Christopher, was offered a professional contract aged 18?

"That would be hard," he sighs. "I was lucky in that professionalism came in at the right time for me, after I'd finished uni. I was also lucky that I'd done dentistry in that it's something I can go back to now. My gut feeling with Christopher would be for him to try and get some professional qualifications under his belt. In hindsight, I'm really glad I did my exams and got the qualifications I did. If I had been offered a contract at 18, I'd like to think I would still have got my degree, but it would have been tough to turn it down and, realistically, I don't think I would have, but it would have been the wrong decision. Especially as a forward. I think forwards develop a bit later and need a few more years to mature. I also firmly believe that if you are good enough you'll come through in the end."

Although still a full-time dentist, Paddy received his first financial reward for playing rugby in the 1995-96 season, when the IRFU started paying match fees and win bonuses in relation to international matches. In other countries, there had been rumours of breaches of amateurism and innuendo about a culture of used-fivers-in-brown-envelopes. Especially in the southern hemisphere, players were believed to be 'well looked after', under the euphemism of expenses payments.

Paddy had heard stories of what might be going on elsewhere, but insists that the Irish system had, up until the announcement of August 1995, remained strictly amateur, virtually to a fault in the sense of too many people being amateur in their approach, never mind simply not being paid. "We all knew about Wales, where they were trying to stop more players going to rugby league, but that was never really a factor in Ireland. I certainly never received any material benefit from the game until after the 1995 World Cup." A year later, he was about to start earning his living from the sport, courtesy of a Saracens salary and, during his time in London, also continued to receive match fees and win bonuses from the IRFU in relation to his Irish appearances.

17. BRIGHT LIGHTS OF LONDON

Once more Paddy was heading east to England, but with a few differences. South instead of north this time, family in tow and as a fully qualified dentist and now professional rugby player. Although Kirsty was very supportive of Paddy's decisions, the issue of accommodation was something she would not compromise on. "We went over for a few visits to see some houses Saracens had lined up for us" Paddy remembers. "Some we walked into and straight away Kirsty said, 'No. We're not living here'. So we didn't!" he laughs.

In their days of more modest means, the couple had lived in some less than luxurious surroundings but now, as parents, they were much more selective about what they deemed suitable. "With Christopher now on the scene, our priorities had shifted slightly. Some of the houses didn't have a garden, or were on a busy street, or were just generally rundown. We had sold our house in Sandyknowes and, when the time came, moved into 61 Connaught Avenue in Enfield. It had a good Irish name, so I was happy with that, and it was in a nice leafy suburb only three miles from training."

The Johns family didn't really expect to meet anyone there that they knew but, during their time in Enfield, were to bump into Gareth Robinson, who was later to be Paddy's physio with Ulster but, back then, was better known to Kirsty. "Gareth had been on Kirsty's physiotherapy course at Jordanstown and then moved on to Trinity. When we were at Saracens, he got a job working as a physio for Spurs. It was a surprise meeting him in Enfield High Street. After that, he'd have come over to our house the odd time for a bite to eat."

Robinson, a former scrumhalf for Armagh Royal First XV and keen rugby fan, can tell a tale of how having a temperamental David Ginola on the Tottenham treatment table thwarted him from watching part of the 1999 European Cup final on television. But, by later that year, he and Paddy had both joined the Ravenhill ranks and Johns recounts the story of the message which Ulster coach Harry Williams left on Robinson's phone when the province were selecting a successor to John Martin. "Before the beep which lets you leave a message on GG's phone, you have to listen to Jim Neilly's commentary of the final few seconds of the European Cup final. I'm sure Harry enjoyed listening to that. Anyway Gareth must have returned the call, for he got the job!"

At the time Paddy joined, Saracens had a Second XV who were not on professional contracts, although most of the Firsts were full-time professionals. So for that first season the players trained morning and evening to accommodate the part-timers. It was a familiar enough scenario in those days, with other clubs also trying to find a way of facilitating existing star players who, for whatever reason, didn't want to go full-time.

Harlequins, for example, worked around former England captain Will Carling and

Irish fullback Jim Staples for a while, but it became apparent that players could not satisfactorily serve two masters and would either become too detached or else be holding the full-timers to ransom in terms of the scheduling of training. Ulster's dramatic European Cup glory run in the 1998-99 season began almost immediately they switched to a proper day-time training regime and players such as Ireland prop Justin Fitzpatrick would swear the change was the biggest single factor in the team's success. Paddy himself continued to work part-time in the afternoons for that first season away in order to 'keep his hand in' as a dentist, whilst still managing to thrive in his new rugby environment. "The rugby was faster than interpro level. Players were bigger, hits were harder, the standard was higher. I was injury free and really enjoying it."

The money behind the London club was businessman Nigel Wray, with whom Paddy has always enjoyed a good relationship. "We met before I'd actually joined Sarries and got on very well. He was always very friendly and enthusiastic and made himself known to the players. He was an effervescent type of character. Very down to earth and genuine fun. It made a big difference that he was not a John Hall type figure but a genuine rugby fan and not just in it because it made business sense. He went in with the right motives and was always very approachable. The main reason that he put his money in was because he loved Saracens and the game in general, but obviously he also sought to use his business acumen to build a successful club both on and off the pitch. We still keep in touch through the odd letter or postcard or phone call and it was good to see him when he came over to Belfast for my retirement match in May of this year."

"I have played rugby all my life," says Wray, "and when it went professional, I thought it would be great to get involved with a club and Saracens as my local club became the obvious choice. By happy co-incidence, the club also approached me at this time with a view to sponsorship. I declined this avenue, but agreed to become a substantial shareholder. I've often said that if I had known form the outset what a financial burden it was going to be, I never would have got involved! But I love rugby and now that I am involved, I wouldn't change a thing. Except the mistakes of course!"

Wray's millions allowed for a First XV teamsheet which read like a who's who of rugby. World Cup winners Michael Lynagh and Francois Pienaar, French legend Philippe Sella, Argentine prop Roberto Grau and the Wallace brothers and Paddy from Ireland were joined by a sprinkling of native talent in the likes of Kyran Bracken and Richard Hill. In wonderful Wallaby Lynagh and the silky-skilled Sella, Saracens had Test rugby's record points-scorer and most capped player respectively, while former Springbok skipper Pienaar would always symbolise South Africa's success in the 1995 World Cup.

"I was approached by three English clubs, Saracens, Leicester and Richmond," says the South African. "Saracens was actually the first offer I received, but I turned them all down. I wanted to stay in South Africa. However my wife was all in favour of an adventure to the UK, and I discussed it with my long-term coach and mentor Kitch Christie who encouraged me to go. He told me, 'In South Africa you have achieved everything, why not try something new?' So I met up with Nigel Wray, who I liked immensely and two weeks later we were in London.

"When I got there I was shocked. I couldn't believe the conditions we were training in. I had been so spoilt in South Africa, both in terms of weather and facilities. In an attitude sense, not necessarily a financial one, South African rugby was so much more professional, but then again at home I had been playing in front of 50,000 people every week. In a lot of ways this made me respect my team-mates more. There must have been a real love for the game and a desire to be the best. At one training session, I remember looking down the pitch and the weather was so bad and the lighting so weak that I couldn't see my fullback!"

That was a tremendous trio for Saracens to sign, but they were by no means the only notable names to play for the club during Paddy's three-year sojourn in London. He had a couple of Irish international colleagues in the Wallaces, Richard, with whom he had agonised over the move, and prop Paul, who was to go on the Lions tour to South Africa at the end of that first season. In contrast to his compatriot Lynagh, Wallaby World Cup winner of 1991, Tony Daly, was one of the first wave of recruits who perhaps contributed to the Premiership being branded an expensive retirement home for overseas internationals in the twilight of their careers. Johns doesn't dispute that assessment of the Australian, agreeing that "he was not the Wallaby I remember and probably came over to enjoy himself and earn some money", but adds that "he did play well enough and was a lovely fella, very funny. Tony pulled a hamstring at his first training session, which was pretty hilarious. He'd never suffered that sort of injury before in the pre-professional days!"

After Daly's departure, Grau and Wallace regularly filled the propping positions, while in the early days Johns was partnered in the engineroom by Welshman Tony Copsey before the arrival, from Coventry, of future Lion Danny Grewcock. Eddie Halvey had gone back to Ireland before Johns arrived but, in Pienaar, Hill and Tony Diprose, who captained them in the 1998 Tetley Bitter Cup triumph, Saracens had a superb backrow with hot prospect Ben Sturnham and Alex Bennett as useful back-up.

Bracken was, for a period, pushed hard for his place as Lynagh's halfback partner by Brad Free who, along with another Australian, exciting utility back Ryan Constable, was to follow Johns to Ulster in the summer of 1999. The three-quarters on the books included Sella, Wallace, Kiwi sevens star Brendan Daniel and under-rated centre Steve Ravenscroft, with Springbok Gavin Johnson initially first choice in the No 15 jersey. Guys like Matt Singer and Andy Lee helped provide squad depth. Later, following Lynagh's retirement, French outhalf Alain Penaud was among the new recruits and since then Saracens have continued to make big name signings, including Thomas Castaignede, Tim Horan, Jannie de Beer, Scott Murray, Abde Benazzi, Christian Califano and Craig Quinnell.

"I didn't know enough about individual players to pick and chose who to chase," admits Wray. "Obviously many were household names, and I did think that we should bring in some high-profile players to put us on the map. We were just extraordinarily lucky that Lynagh, Sella and Pienaar joined because they did exactly that and were outstandingly good characters as well as players."

It must be difficult for such a variety of individuals with differing cultural backgrounds to mix harmoniously at the best of times, but what if you have been used to ёhating' these players when they kitted out for opposition teams?

"It was like the United Nations," Paddy acknowledges, "but I think overall we all got on well. I certainly felt I got on with everyone. Most of the foreign guys could speak good English. Roberto Grau had a few problems at the beginning, but he caught up pretty quickly. I taught both Roberto and Philippe Sella a bit of English, but a lot of the boys joked that they couldn't understand my English either, so I'm not sure if it did them that much good, though Roberto also went to private English lessons. He used to always nod and say 'yes, yes' even when he didn't understand!" Constable confirms: "It really was like the United Nations, but the fact that so many players had left their family environment to be there, men on a mission if you like, bound us all together and helped us achieve what we did. There was a great blend of characters."

"In a lot of ways it was surreal to be at training and playing with some of these players, either because I'd only ever seen them in the white of England or the blue of France, or because I had so much respect for them" muses Paddy. "I never dreamt I'd play with the likes of Pienaar or Lynagh. I remember going to the first training session worrying that Kyran Bracken would remember that I had been one of the guys tap dancing on his back at Twickenham in 1994. Whether he did or not, nothing was said and we were team-mates after that!"

Apart from that intentional fancy footwork of Paddy's and some unintentional fancy footwork at a Christmas party years later as Constable relates further on in this chapter, poor old Bracken was later to find himself on the receiving end of some slagging thanks to Christopher Johns and the youngster's faltering attempts to pronounce the player's name. Johns Junior spent a lot of time around the Saracens set-up as he learned to walk and talk, the fact that most of the players were not natives of the area creating a virtual village environment and ensuring that Kirsty and the other partners gravitated towards the club.

"There was a team picture at the start of the season with 40 people in it and Christopher probably knew about 30 of them by the time he was two, but he got the pronunciation of Bracken's name wrong and called him 'Broken'. Of course, with Kyran always seeming to be injured, it was quite apt and, when the Wallaces and the other boys heard Christopher at it, they were tickled by it and thereafter tried to convince him that 'Broken' really was his name. Y'know what a team is like so, from that point on, Kyran was kind of stuck with 'Broken' as his nickname. There was actually an article in the 2002 England versus Ireland Twickenham match programme entitled 'Bracken not Broken' and, in it, he explains how Christopher was responsible for getting him called that."

Paddy may have felt a little more sheepish about linking up with Bracken at the beginning than he needed to, but any advance idolising of Pienaar proved thoroughly justified. Johns names the South African World Cup winning skipper as his all-time best captain. "Francois was amazing. He led from the front by example" Paddy enthuses. "A complete player on the pitch and the consummate ambassador off it. One of those guys who has an aura about them and just inspires you."

The feeling is somewhat mutual. "I have nothing but the utmost respect for Paddy," enthuses Pienaar. "He is a great bloke: honest and open, with strong opinions. He would always do his best for his team-mates. My epitomising memory of Paddy is when we played Swansea and we'd put a load of youngsters on the field and left Paddy on the bench. We were losing when Paddy went on the field at half-time. He turned that game around for us practically single-handedly. That's Paddy Johns."

With inspirational teammates all around him, Paddy was quick to settle in and loved his new club. But how were things for wife and son? "Kirsty worked as a physio for the first six months, so she had her own social network through that. Then she fell pregnant with Emily, so she gave up work and stayed at home with Christopher, who was now two. I think Kirsty found it a bit difficult at the start. She is very close to her mum and missed her whole family, but she coped very well. We just treated it like a big experience, an adventure.

"There was a possibility at the start of Kirsty doing some physio work for the club, but was put off very quickly when a rather large, spotty forward came into the physio room wearing nothing but a jockstrap and asked the then physio to put some cream on a stud mark on his butt cheek!"

"Because there were so many of us foreigners at Sarries, there were a lot of wives and girlfriends in the same position. They would have all met up each week after the game and Kirsty soon made new friends through that. She and Roberto Grau's wife, Marianna, got on particularly well. They had several things in common, like not having their family around and being mothers. The pair of them just hit it off. Myself and Roberto would have been good mates too; I'd probably have been closer to him than anyone. He'd have been completely lost though without his wife, who had better English than he did. I used to ring her to tell her what time training was to make sure he'd be there." So soon the whole Johns family had bought into the Saracen way of life and settled in their new surroundings.

Paddy's first outing in red and black was against Stirling County on a pre-season tour to Scotland. Sarries were victorious and Paddy bagged a hat-trick of tries for himself. Not bad for the new Irish boy, until recently an amateur. The team still called Enfield ëhome' and Paddy's debut here was against Leicester in the league, the Londoners triumphing over a team which was to largely rule the roost of English club rugby for the next number of years.

Another big game was against London Irish. "It was important for all sorts of reasons, including the fact that I knew the selectors were watching." In front of such influential spectators, Sarries impressed with a victory and once more Paddy was on the scoresheet. "I was really happy to have scored, and it was great to have won. Great for us Irish boys on the team in particular."

"We were very lucky to get three Irishmen who were so completely committed to Saracens," says Wray. "They were crucial in creating that absolutely intangible feeling of camaraderie or team spirit, or whatever we call it, which is so difficult to capture." "There was a tremendous team spirit," agrees Pienaar. "We gelled together very well and earned the respect of each other and our opposition."

Apart from the club's historic ties with the old sod, London Irish now featured a number of old acquaintances of Paddy's including coach Willie Anderson, Mark McCall, Jeremy Davidson and David Humphreys. In Davidson, Gabriel Fulcher and Malcolm O'Kelly, London Irish had Johns' three main rivals for Test selection so any game against Big Willie's team was a bit of an Ireland trial. Apart from those five, Niall Woods, Victor Costello and Ken O'Connell had also joined the club, while numerous more leading Irish players were now attached to other English teams. Indeed, during the Brian Ashton era, which began in the Spring of 1997, Irish-based players in the national squad were the minority, even the exception.

For Paddy's old friend Charlie Haly, now on duty for London Irish, one particular incident stands out during his encounter with the rival capital club. "Paddy had just joined Saracens and we were playing them away from home. I was at the bottom of a ruck when I felt this huge boot. I got up and turned to my teammates saying, 'Who the heck was that who just kicked me?, to which they replied 'It was Paddy'. I wouldn't ever want to cross him on the pitch!"

Mark McCall also recalls being on the receiving end in one of those games. "We were playing Saracens; it was a very important match and a big thing for me personally playing against Sella. I remember being on the ground and getting an awful shoeing. I grabbed the foot of the assailant and held on as tight as possible in the hope of identifying who it was, because I was so angry after having had my chest stood upon so many times. There was Paddy grinning down; I should have guessed!"

Apart from playing with and against many of his compatriots in the English Premiership, Paddy was not totally cut off from Irish rugby below international level during that first term in London. It was the second season of the European Cup and Johns travelled home for Ulster matches in this tournament. The English league had incorporated European Cup rugby into its fixture list and so these matches did not conflict with Paddy's commitments to Saracens and gave him an opportunity to catch up on old friends. "It was like I'd never left" he recalls. "It was great to see the guys and good to get home, albeit for a very short time. I always enjoyed playing for Ulster and was always welcomed back. We also came over, of course, to train with and play for Ireland."

Saracens didn't appear in the European Cup until its sixth season, 2000-01, when, ironically, they were in the same group as an Ulster side now featuring Johns again, but took part in the European Shield in Paddy's second term at the club. They won five of their six group games, including doing the double over Narbonne and Neath, but were pipped on points difference at the top of their Pool by Castres and hence didn't make the quarter-finals. They did beat Castres 26-21 at Vicarage Road, Saracens' first ever home game in Europe and a match which Johns recalls for an amusing incident.

"We had this little car that used to bring the kicking tee on for Lynagh to take penalties or conversions. I think the idea came from some of the Super 12 teams. Anyway, we were playing Castres at home in a European game and Lynagh had already had some kicks to take, so the car had come on and obviously the French team had seen this. Then their kicker had to take a pot at the posts and he stood there for ages wondering where the car was with his kicking tee. We were all saying, 'you'll be waiting for a while, mate, the car only comes out for us, get your own tee!' I think he was quite disappointed!"

Paddy believes that during his first year as a professional, his own game improved tremendously, which was something he was able to carry through from the English league to the European Cup. "There was a general increase in my confidence. When you play with better players you play better. Just look how Jeremy Davidson blossomed on the 1997 Lions tour of South Africa. It also helps because you get to see these 'great' players make mistakes in training or during matches and think, 'so they are human after all', or 'I would have caught that ball'. It all makes you believe in your own ability more. I also felt that some specifics of my game improved. My lineouts came on really well. My technique improved and again confidence was high. Again it helps when you are playing with quality players because you know the throw will be accurate, the lift will be good and the drive will be strong."

Over that season and the next couple of seasons, both Saracens and Paddy became more professional. As an individual, his approach in the amateur era had been more committed and thorough than most. The desire and the dedication were there, but now he had the scope and the support to really make the most of himself.

"Professionalism would have been less of a culture shock for me than most guys in that I had always taken my rugby extremely seriously and trained very hard and looked after myself. I remember in the early days, when the Irish players would meet up on a Saturday evening in Dublin after the afternoon's AIL matches. We'd have a big meal, maybe a team meeting, and then a lot of the boys would head out down Leeson Street and go on the beers even though there was a training session on the Sunday morning. I would have stayed in and gone to bed early to be prepared as best I could. After all we'd had a club game a few hours earlier and made the trek to Dublin.

"I could never quite understand the mentality of the others. I had gone to Dublin for rugby business and that was all I was interested in. There'd be other opportunities to go out. This was the time to make the sacrifices, but not everyone was prepared to. It's amazing Ireland competed even as well as we did pre-professionalism because attitudes were poor and the approach of too many players was sloppy. No wonder Ireland used to blow up after an hour. The fitness levels just weren't good enough, compounded by the fact that there were no substitutes allowed in those days."

Two men after Paddy's own heart before rugby went professional were the Malone pair of Denis McBride and Maurice Field. "At one stage the IRFU offered the players a couple of hundred quid each to join gyms or fitness clubs or whatever. The three of us, with the Union's blessing, pooled our money and invested in weights and other equipment. We trained in each other's garages. The three of us worked very hard and tried to be professional in our approach although the game was still amateur. We were each very competitive. I travelled a lot to the Irish stuff with those two and, in many ways, we shared the same outlook as well as car journeys."

"Maurice nearly killed all three of us" says McBride. "We had had an absolutely knackering weekend in Dublin with the Irish squad and Maurice was driving us back up north. He was wearing sunglasses, so you couldn't see his eyes, and must have fallen asleep at the wheel. The barrier on the passenger side started to drift closer and closer and then we realised what must have happened. Paddy was in the front, because of his long legs, and grabbed the steering wheel. Unfortunately he overcompensated and nearly sent us into the oncoming traffic!"

"Maurice was a real pusher and took every break which came his way and everything Denis achieved was against the odds because of his lack of size or, more accurately, other people's hang-ups about it" reflects Paddy. "If he'd been put off by the first knock-back, he wouldn't have won all those Irish caps. I remember using Cavehill Country Park for workouts and also running up and down steps at those reservoirs up behind Carrickfergus. We've got a picture up on the wall at home which always reminds me of that" he says, grimacing slightly. "Earlier, when I worked in Newry, that meant leaving home at 7.45 in the morning, doing my day's work as a dentist and then, two nights a week, driving to my mum's house and getting a bite to eat en route to a couple of hours training with Dungannon, not getting in until maybe after 11.00."

"Paddy's technique with weights was appalling!" laughs Maurice. "Denis was spot on and I wasn't great, but at least I was better than Paddy. He was all limbs and couldn't quite co-ordinate it all. I used to joke that Kirsty could lift more than he could!" Field's Ulster and Ireland centre partner Mark McCall corroborates the claim: "I remember us going to the gym and Paddy being embarrassed that he wasn't able to lift 60kg."

"To be fair though, as players we didn't really receive any input as to what we should do when it came to individual training" reflects Field. "We were all given fitness programs from Eddie O'Sullivan in 1991, but no expertise or techniques. I don't think we were ever taught what to do until Andy Clarke, who is now the fitness advisor for Liverpool FC, came along."

Professionalism meant no corner had to be cut anymore or the candle burned at both ends and, rather than resenting the hard work, for Paddy, it was a pleasure to be able to do everything properly and at a civilised time of day. Especially as part of an increasingly sophisticated Saracens set-up. "Initially there was just a head coach and assistant coach, but then came fitness coaches, defence coaches and video analysts and every base was covered. We also had easy access to physios and the like, so although I'd always looked after injuries, there was more opportunity to get them seen to immediately with more intensive treatment. I gave up work totally after that first year when training moved to morning and afternoon, so it really was a proper job now."

At the beginning of the 1997-98 season, Saracens moved grounds to share the spotlight with Watford FC at Vicarage Road. This meant vastly superior facilities and a much larger crowd capacity. "Professionalism brought enormous changes," says Wray. "I can remember early on discussing if we needed a full or part-time coach! The move to Vicarage Road was essential for the economic survival of the club. In today's television age, you have to have a proper ground with four stands etc to generate the theatre that television requires.

"The pitch was fantastic. It had artificial fibres in it, so it didn't cut up" Paddy explains "and the stadium had a really good atmosphere. I don't think there was a better ground in the Premiership." Saturday games for Watford and Sunday clashes for Sarries meant that the two codes were never vying for crowd support, but how aware was Paddy that spectators were now needed to pay his wages? "I never thought of it like that," he claims.

"We wanted people to watch, but only because we wanted the support. I never looked round and thought, 'Oh no, there's hardly anyone here to watch.' I was more conscious of playing well and winning games, and if you do that eventually people will come and watch."

Considering the star-studded sides involved, the crowds for English Premiership games in London have generally been disappointing in the professional era, with a degree of geographical and social dislocation being seen as a negative factor. The fact that, in the case of Wasps, Saracens and, latterly, London Irish, the professional Premiership outfits share soccer stadiums and play their home games at what may be a significant distance from their clubs' old base and natural catchment area for fans should add to that syndrome. Furthermore, if clubs aren't careful, the professional layer can become detached from the grassroots, who may feel little real affinity for a group of paid performers, largely outsiders, who never become fully integrated, not least because even their home games are 'elsewhere'.

But Paddy insists that he never felt it was an issue at Sarries and, although he and his colleagues didn't get to know the bulk of the players down the club, that there was a genuine feeling of attachment to Saracens on the part of himself and others. This extended to an ability to identify with the wider club beyond the narrow confines of group loyalty to the professional entity which played at Vicarage Road.

That said, there was a particular closeness within the group of full-timers and the forging of friendships which extended beyond the guys themselves and into the circle of partners and families. Everyone got on pretty well. There were some great characters in the group, not least Brendon Daniel, the exciting but unpredictable Maori, whose extravagant and exuberant wing play often left his own team guessing as well as the opposition.

"Brendon loved diving spectacularly to score but, one day, he actually managed to leave the ball behind. At our next training session, Francois made him do 20 dives in the mud. He was a young, happy-go-lucky guy who played the way he lived. He was a bit of a rap artist, nicknamed Cuzzie-Bro, and always wore a wee hat. One night he had an accident going home from a fancy dress party at Saracens at which the theme had been 'bad taste'. Brendon had gone as a woman. As luck would have it, he crashed the car on the way home that night, so it was a bit embarrassing when the local constabulary arrived. He had to go down the police station in his dress!"

Constable recalls: "Another year, the theme at our Saracens Christmas party was fancy dress. Paddy had left it until the last minute to get sorted out, by which stage when he went into the costume shop in Enfield, the team had already taken the best options and most of those outfits left didn't fit him. So he ended up having to go as Dr Spock from Star Trek! I also remember that he had this little bottle of some drink, 'Goldslanger' I think it was called, and he was going round forcing people to partake. Whatever happened anyway, Paddy managed to stamp on Kyran Bracken's foot. Kyran later walked in a puddle on the way home, with the result that his toe got infected and he missed the next couple of games. For a player who seemed to be sidelined so often by injury, it was a bit of an unlucky blow."

"Kyran was always very funny and witty and loved practical jokes" says Paddy. "He was an excellent mimic and poked plenty of fun at people, though in fairness he could also take a joke. Our hooker Greg Botterman, one of the real Sarries clubmen, was the chief card shark. He was a bit of an Arthur Daly character and probably doubled his salary playing cards.

"The Samoan prop Brendan Reidy was very laidback. He was nicknamed 'The Chief', but also got called 'Pineapple' after he got his hair braided with a little tuft at the top. Tony Copsey was always the judge for any of our kangaroo court sessions. He was coming to the end of his career, but I played with him in my first season at Saracens before Danny Grewcock arrived. I suppose his age counted against him at that stage and he went through something similar to what I did a few years later with Ireland and even Ulster. He was, in a sense, the hard man of the team and also liked his partying, but we got on well and it was nice to see him coming over for my retirement game this year. Tony Diprose was a Saracens man through and through, a laidback sort of guy and another who was big into his cards. He loved a game called 'Grass' and was the squad's undisputed champion of it. I better point out that, in spite of the name, it was money that was played for, not marijuana!"

Another player who came to the fore in the latter stages of Paddy's Saracens sojourn was Kris Chesney, a fairly remarkable utility player who featured in as diverse positions as wing and second row at Premiership level. "Kris was incredibly quick for a big man and, as a result, could play in both the backs and the forwards, but he would never have been the sharpest tool in the box. A chef by trade, he was an Essex man and just a touch gullible. The first time that he went on tour with Sarries, the boys told him that he would be dirt-tracking, a well known rugby term for not being in the first team on tour. But rather than being downcast, he was excited by the news, declared that he loved BMXs and asked where the track was!"

There are a few stories about Paddy too. Sometimes the laugh was on him. "I remember we were playing Bath at The Rec, in a crucial league game," tells Pienaar. "We'd stayed in the Hilton the night before and after breakfast had walked to the ground in our tracksuits. We were all warming up and running around, when two teaspoons fell out of Paddy's tracksuit pocket! He was so embarrassed and everyone took the mick out of him for ages afterwards, bearing in mind we were literally about to kick off! We said that wherever Paddy went from then on, someone would have to ring ahead and warn the hoteliers to watch their cutlery because Paddy was coming to stay!" Constable adds: "Francois joked Paddy that he should come and see him in his office on Monday if he really needed more money so that he wouldn't have to be stealing cutlery!

18. COMINGS AND GOINGS

Sometimes things have to get worse before they get better. In the autumn of 1996, Paddy was liking his new life in London, enjoying the new world of professionalism and settling in well at Sarries. But regaining his Ireland place was never far from his thoughts. He had felt very low at Twickenham back in March, on the bench, feeling peripheral and wondering where his next international start was coming from. Young Jeremy Davidson had burst onto the scene and Gabriel Fulcher's lineout prowess was tipping the scales in the southerner's favour as first choice front-jumper.

Ireland had done much better in the second half of the 1996 Championship without Paddy in the team than in the opening two games. Hardly a clear case of cause and effect, but these things don't look good. Your bottle is half-empty at times like this and, in that frame of mind, you expect others to draw negative conclusions from such spurious evidence. But, helped by a good performance against the Barbarians in the Peace International in May, the clouds seemed to have lifted when Johns was back in the Ireland team for the opening Test of the new season, Lansdowne Road's first floodlit international, against Samoa on a Tuesday night in early November.

It was, however, to be an inauspicious evening for Irish rugby, Paddy's last ever Test at No 8 and lead to another short period out of the national side. Like the floodlights, the Samoans made history that night with a 40-25 victory. Although Irish rugby didn't know it then, wing wonder Simon Geoghegan had played his last international at Twickenham the previous Spring thanks to the arthritic condition which was progressively afflicting his feet. Richard Wallace returned in his place, while there were first caps for Ballymena's James Topping on the other wing and London Irish powerhouse Rob Henderson at centre. Up front, Henry Hurley got his first start in place of Popplewell, while Galwey was back in the second row for Fulcher and Johns took over from Costello at No 8.

Ireland were outscored by five tries to one by the rampant Samoans and only achieved some semblance of respectability on the scoreboard thanks to 20 points from the boot of Simon Mason who, however, paid the price for a poor performance defensively and was never picked again. Henderson disappeared for a year following a disappointing debut, though the long-haired Topping buzzed about and looked fairly lively. The totality of the defeat rocked Irish rugby as much as the result, for the hosts were comprehensively outplayed by their dynamic and abrasive visitors.

Including positional switches, there were no fewer than 11 changes for the next game, with Johns being one of nine men from that team who didn't feature in the side for the Australian game 11 days later. Topping moved to his preferred right wing berth with Garryowen's Dominic Crotty winning his first cap wide on the left rather than at fullback, where Staples was restored in place of Mason. Bell moved to outside centre at the expense of Henderson to facilitate a recall for his fellow Ulsterman Mark McCall, who had played very well for the northern province against the Wallabies the previous weekend, in the No 12 jersey. McCall had come on as a replacement at Twickenham, but not started an international since February 1994. Halfbacks Humphreys and Hogan were axed in favour of Paul Burke and another new cap from Garryowen, Steve McIvor, while Popplewell and Fulcher returned to the tight five in place of Hurley and Galwey respectively. Keith Wood was back for Allen Clarke and made captain for the first time, taking over from the dropped Hogan. Johns made way for the recall of Foley in the middle of the back row.

Paddy was one of those to pay a personal price for their part in a poor performance by Ireland but, in his case, it was also clear that his versatility was now proving a double-edged sword. Picked at No 8 because that gave the selectors what they believed to be their best balanced side for the Samoan game, he was then duly dropped for the next match because in the words of manager Pat Whelan at the time he "has not got the required skills for basic No 8 play!" Whelan prefaced that remark by praising Paddy's general play in the Samoan match as "outstanding" and went on to describe him as "most unfortunate" and declare that he felt sorry for him, but those platitudes were not enough to save Johns' bacon or see him selected in the engineroom at the expense of either Fulcher or Davidson for the next game.

Interestingly, Paddy doesn't actually feel that he did play particularly well against the Samoans and angrily cites ill-devised preparation as being a big factor in the team's poor performance that night. "That wasn't the only match in those days where we fell flat on our faces because of the way we trained. There just wasn't the concept of rest back then. They simply seemed to think that the harder they trained you the better you'd play.

"Take the Samoan match, which was on a Tuesday night. We probably met on Friday night and had two sessions on Saturday and two on Sunday, double sessions with contact. It was madness. You leave it on the training pitch. When the adrenalin at the start of the match wears off, there won't be a lot left. But that was Murray Kidd. He just couldn't see that. I doubt that even any of the senior players had much input into how sessions were organised. We definitely over-trained before Samoa. I remember we talked afterwards about how we'd felt before the game. We had really knocked the sh*t out of each other and everyone was knackered.

"Francois Pienaar didnít believe in a lot of contact in weeks which had games at the end of them. The contact came on matchday, be it Saturday or Sunday. He realised that bodies had to be managed and could only take so much battering." Allen Clarke, who started alongside his old RSD schoolmate in a senior international for the first time that night and is now a coach himself, agrees. "If contact is good on the Saturday, it isnít needed on the other days. As for that Samoan game, put it this way: I can distinctly remember no-one could get a spot to get a rub before that game because the guys were so beaten up."

"It was a disappointing result and Samoa were a good enough side who played pretty well" Paddy continues, "but I don't think we'd have been beaten in that manner if we'd have been fresh. Losing like that would have felt worse if we'd known we were at our best, but even though a flawed training regime may have been largely to blame, that didn't save lots of players from losing their place for the next game. It was very annoying. I realised that I didn't play well against Samoa. I under-performed and was very disappointed with how I played. To use a Big Brother analogy, I wasn't surprised to be nominated for the chop. But, because I blamed the physical preparation for affecting my performance, it was frustrating to be dropped."

Johns didn't get on the pitch against Australia, but came on for the last 10 minutes of the next game. Although it ended in another disappointing defeat by Italy which effectively cost Kidd his job, Paddy believes that brief outing was very positive and did his cause no harm at all. "I felt that, even with so little time on the pitch, that I did well and made an impression. I had decided I was going to clatter everything that moved and that's what I did. Whether it was because of that or more due to a new coach coming in, I was delighted to be back in the team for the first Five Nations match against France a fortnight later."

For that Italian game, which took place on the first Saturday in January, there were two changes from the team that started against Australia. O'Shea returned at fullback, while there was a first cap in the back row for the 21-year old Eric Miller. Miller, who was to be chosen for the Lions a few months later, was an exciting talent who had been making a big impression for Leicester, but was deployed out of position at openside on his debut. It proved an abortive appearance as injury forced him out of the game in the early stages, with McBride, who had been dropped to accommodate him, coming on in his place to give Ireland a better balanced back row. But even that made little difference as Ireland found themselves outscored by four tries to one and it was only the record eight penalties by Paul Burke which restricted the final margin of defeat to 29-37.

Kidd seemed to have lost the confidence of his players, among whom morale appeared poor and motivation relatively low. Johns and others were critical of his methods and it was time for a change. Sensing that he was likely to be sacked, Kidd agreed severance terms with the IRFU and his resignation was announced a week after the bungled Italian job. "I think it would be fair to say that the players were pleased to see him go" says Paddy. "There was no compromise with him to the point of it being a weakness. He didn't train us right for games and too often during his time in charge we'd have gone into an international without a full tank."

Ireland's Championship campaign was due to start a fortnight after the Italian fixture, so the Union had to move quickly in putting new arrangements in place. Brian Ashton was brought in in a caretaker capacity. Seen as a visionary, Ashton had been a very successful supremo with Bath before departing the club in controversial circumstances. He had very little time to work with the players before the French game, but Ireland certainly performed much better than against Italy. Field, Elwood and Hogan were recalled to the backline at the expense of McCall, Burke and McIvor, with old mates Johns and McBride displacing Fulcher and Foley up front, as Miller stayed in the team with a move to his more natural position of No 8. In spite of losing captain Wood early on with yet another shoulder dislocation which was to rule him out of the rest of the Five Nations, Ireland started promisingly and competed well throughout but could only manage five Elwood penalties to set against 32 French points.

"We were in touch for most of that game" said Johns, who produced a storming performance to thoroughly justify his recall and put down an early marker for the Lions selectors. "One of the things which I will always remember about the match is their hooker, Tordo, hitting rucks with his head." Miller too had a good match, but France did ultimately outscore the Irish by four tries to none, with winger David Venditti getting a hat-trick.

Ashton and Ireland could not have hand-picked their next fixture better. Wales in Cardiff had been a bit of a banker for the guys in green for over a decade and the long run of success there was duly extended thanks to a 26-25 victory. Staples was recalled in place of O'Shea and took over the captaincy in the absence of Wood, whose hooker spot went to Ross Nesdale, a Kiwi with Irish ancestry who, like Gatland, had seen his route blocked in New Zealand by the presence of Sean Fitzpatrick. Topping had to cry off with injury, handing a Test debut to young St Mary's winger Denis Hickie, who confirmed himself as an exciting talent by showing a clean pair of heels in scoring one of Ireland's three tries, a superb score from long range set up by the new skipper and good hands from Corkery in putting him away.

The other two touchdowns came from Miller and Jonathan Bell, who managed to push the ball against the post to register a score after Neil Jenkins had failed to deal with an Elwood garryowen. "We'd practised that one in training" grins Paddy, whose lineout steal on the Welsh 22 had led to Miller's try before the Hickie effort which sent Ireland into an unbelievable 20-7 lead considering that Wales had got the perfect start with a converted try in the very first minute of the match. Jenkins and Elwood traded penalties either side of the break and did so again after Ieuan Evans' second try of the afternoon had pulled Wales back to within eight points. With four minutes left, Scott Quinnell crashed over and Jenkins goaled, but Ireland deservedly held out.

It was a good team performance featuring some great rugby and left the Irish rugby fraternity hopeful that there were better times ahead with Ashton at the helm, but the visit of England to Dublin a fortnight later brought everyone back down to earth with a bump. A fit-again Topping returned to the wing, but at the expense of Crotty rather than Hickie, in a line-up which, unsurprisingly, was otherwise unchanged. Ireland were thrashed 46-6, England taking full toll of their hosts' kamikaze attempts to play catch-up rugby from deep in their own half in the final quarter, the situation being compounded by the fact that the yet again injured Staples was virtually operating on one leg by that stage.

"That was a chastening experience, especially for me in that we had beaten England those first two times that I had played against them. They did get a couple of soft scores at the end when we were caught out trying to attack, but I suppose there's no point in going for damage limitation. You have to keep trying to score."

Discussions had been ongoing between the IRFU and caretaker coach Ashton about a more concrete contract, but it was more than a touch of unfortunate timing that the deal was done between the crushing Dublin defeat by England and a real Murrayfield mauling. People were prepared to give Ashton time and not read too much into immediate results, but what did cause many raised eyebrows was the astonishing length of his contract, six years. The IRFU also announced a key structural change in the selection process with the old panel being slimmed down to feature only the coach, manager Whelan and one other selector.

But some things didn't change. Ireland still stayed in Princes Street for the Murrayfield match and, as usual, fancied their chances of beating Scotland only to suffer another depressing defeat, losing 38-10. The visitors had conjured a great try early on, scored by Hickie after a brilliant break by Staples, but the skipper did his hamstring and had to be relieved by O'Shea. By the end, the backline was a mess with Brian O'Meara and Kurt McQuilkin also having had to bow out injured, replaced by McIvor and Burke. Both O'Meara and McQuilkin had come in following the annihilation by England, with Bell moving to the wing and Topping dropping out along with Hogan. Humphreys was recalled at outhalf for Elwood. Popplewell and Miller were injured, leading to a first and last international start at loosehead for Paul Flavin and a recall for Ben Cronin two years after winning his only previous cap in the corresponding fixture. Cronin never played again, left to reflect on how he managed to fit double Murrayfield misfortune into such a brief Test career!

"We thought we were the better side going into that game but ended up getting stuffed" Paddy reflects. "That was a strange Five Nations for Ireland in a way. Traditionally we would start the Championship slowly and do better towards the end, but in 1997 it was the other way round. To suffer record defeats by both England and Scotland in our last two games was very disappointing indeed but, looking on the bright side, I had started all four matches and re-established myself in the team."

Paddy had been one of Ireland's successes in the Championship, but being part of a team which was sunk without trace in their final two matches would have done little for his Lions prospects. To rub salt in the wounds, three Scottish second rows were to make the tour party at his expense. But he had certainly cemented his place in the Ireland team. There were a staggering dozen changes for the next international eight months later, but Johns was one of the three survivors along with Paul Wallace, who had had such a good Lions tour, and the find of 1997, Hickie.

The game was against the awesome All Blacks touring team at Lansdowne Road and Ireland fielded a remarkable five new caps from the start, with two more introduced from the bench before the afternoon was out. Three of them were clubmates of Hickie at St Mary's, including his rookie back three colleagues, fullback Kevin Nowlan, unkindly described by one hack as a 'Fourth XV player who had hit a purple patch' and a wing wild card in John McWeeney, a converted second row. The third was pivot Conor McGuinness, Connacht halfback partner of Elwood, who was restored to the No 10 jersey in place of Humphreys who, like axed scrumhalf O'Meara, had been buried in the Murrayfield malaise. McCall and Henderson took over from McQuilkin and Field at centre.

Popplewell and Wood, who reassumed the captaincy from the absent Staples, were back from injury to form a formidable front row with Wallace, while Johns had a new engineroom partner in athletic young London Irish lock Malcolm O'Kelly. The enigmatic Eddie Halvey, who hadn't featured for some time, was brought back at blindside, Lions tourist Miller reclaimed his No 8 place from Cronin having missed Murrayfield through injury and the fifth new cap was London Irish openside Kieron Dawson. McBride had bowed out of international rugby at the end of the previous season so Dawson, a promising former Ireland Under 21 player, was thrown in at the deep end and, by the end of the game, had been joined in the back row by another exiled Ulsterman, David Erskine, who had come on for Halvey to win his first cap. The seventh player to earn that distinction was Bath three-quarter Kevin Maggs, English-born but Irish-qualified and one of the few successes of the disastrous Development tour of New Zealand that summer. He was sent on when a floundering McWeeney was called ashore.

Ireland put up a fantastic fight in the first half against a super side being talked up by some as potentially the best rugby team ever to take the field. Two tries by the inimitable Wood meant Ireland went in at the break only a couple of points down, but the pressure eventually told and the floodgates opened towards the end as New Zealand piled on the points in storming past the half-century mark. It finished 63-15. "We'd a good first half, including Woody's tries, and were pretty pleased at the interval with how we were doing, but they really took off in the second half and the last 15 minutes were fairly traumatic. I remember them throwing long passes and running in some tries which may have looked a bit soft but were essentially a product of the platform which they had laid."

The game marked the start of a long and successful Test career for O'Kelly, who was to partner Paddy in the second row in the next nine internationals. "It was clear that Mal had a lot of talent and that, with the right application, he could have a long career at the highest level. His athleticism and ability were readily apparent and he didn't show a lot of nerves either. I roomed with him and found him very laidback off the pitch. Although Kieron Dawson came from Ulster, he'd been away from the province since he was quite young, so I hadn't really played with him, but he was obviously an exciting prospect and a player of whom a lot was expected."

Next up was a match which, at face value, could have caused divided loyalties in the Johns household, with Kirsty's country, Canada, taking on Ireland at Lansdowne Road 15 days after the All Blacks visit. Apart from being married to a Canadian, there was an other usual connection with the opposition for Paddy, in that Canada were being coached at that time by Pat Parfrey, his old mentor in Newfoundland a decade earlier!

"Kirsty was obviously supporting Ireland because of the fact that I was playing while, although Pat was a good Corkman and had played for Ireland, he was naturally totally committed to the Canadian cause and devastated by the outcome. They had hoped to at least push us fairly close, but never really looked like winning even though it wouldn't have been our best performance by any means. Pat probably felt that we hadn't seen the best of Canada either."

It was a dead Dublin day with the Sunday lunchtime kick-off and relatively unattractive opposition creating a bit of an after-the-Lord-Mayor's-show feeling in the wake of the fare served up by the All Blacks in front of a full house crowd a fortnight earlier. That wider lethargy seemed to infiltrate Ireland's performance, but the men in green won 33-11, with Nowlan bagging a brace of tries and two of the other November new boys, Maggs and McGuinness, getting a touchdown apiece. Ireland crossed the line five times in total, the other coming from Costello, at No 8 in place of the injured Miller. Maggs had been brought in on the wing for McWeeney while, with Wood ruled out, Popplewell took over the captaincy and Nesdale played at hooker. Erskine got a first start at blindside, pushing out Halvey.

The Canadian clash proved to be a last Test start for Popplewell, who was replaced in the second half by new cap Reggie Corrigan, missed the next match with the injury, and didn't regain the No 1 jersey in subsequent matches. He and Paddy went back a long way. "Poppy was a character, a very funny guy. We had first played together for Ireland seven years previously and got to know each other pretty well over that period. He was the Arthur Daly of the team in the nicest possible way, a very likeable fella. He was a very strong, stocky prop, very solid and powerful in the legs. Packing down in the second row, you wondered if you were making any impression on him at all at scrum time."

A third successive Test defeat by Italy, 37-22 in Bologna, just before Christmas meant the year ended as it began and didn't exactly do much for getting the Irish rugby fraternity into the festive spirit. If losing to Italy in January proved the final straw in relation to Kidd's demise, doing so in December marked the beginning of the end for Ashton, a mere nine months into his six year contract. Maggs was moved to centre at the expense of Henderson leading to a recall for Darragh O'Mahony, who of course had made his Test debut in the first of the three Italian defeats, en route to the 1995 World Cup. It was a considerably changed side, in that Humphreys and Hogan replaced Elwood and McGuinness at halfback, the fit-again Wood returned as captain, Corrigan got his first start at loosehead as Popplewell was still injured and Clohessy played his first Test since his suspension, taking over from Wallace in an all-changed front row.

Miller, recovered from injury, was back at No 8, while there was a first and, as it proved, only cap for Dylan O'Grady of Sale, who had played for the Irish Exiles when they featured in the interprovincial championship, at openside. O'Grady was a nightclub bouncer who later ended up spending time in jail, but Paddy has nothing but good to say about the back row forward. "I found Dylan a very likeable fella. We knew he was a doorman and he had a reputation of having a hard background, but he fitted in fine. In the Irish squad he was close to David Erskine, who also played for Sale. He was a big Man United fan.

"We did well in the first half of that match in Bologna, but there was an incident around halftime which I feel was crucial to the outcome. I remember us being on their line and we were driving them over when Eric picked at the back of the scrum and went. It was a bad decision because, if he didn't make the line, it was almost certain to be a turnover as the flankers had been down pushing as we went for the try and weren't going to make the breakdown. I feel we lost a real choice of points in that incident. If we'd scored then, it might well have made quite a difference, but Italy got off the hook and they ended up pulling away in the second half with Dominguez calling the shots and kicking a lot of points."

Around that time, a lot of media attention was focusing on alleged tensions between coach Ashton and manager Pat Whelan. It was something which the players were also aware of. "We didn't see any bust-ups between them, but there was definitely a feeling in the squad that they weren't getting on. I couldn't actually point to any incidents which would have confirmed that view, but it seemed to be the case." Ask Paddy about his view of Whelan, considered by many to be a somewhat surly and abrasive figure, and his answer is sufficiently laboured and hesitant to suggest that, at the very least, he is not inclined towards effusive praise of the former Ireland hooker.

"To be honest, y'know, I found Pat very hard to work out at first. To my mind, everyone involved in the IRFU or in rugby must have their own particular motivation or plan or agenda or what they're getting out of it. Pat would be . . . what's the best way of putting this . . . I was vary wary of him initially and wouldn't say that I got on that well with him at the start. My view changed though and, towards the end of my career, I had time for him. I can now see a good side to Pa but, to sum up, basically I would have been very guarded in Pa's presence. Donal Lenihan who took over from him would have been easier to talk to, more approachable, but then again I played with Donal and there was less of a generation gap. Coaches and managers tend to be younger these days, closer in age to the players, and that can be a good thing."

Paddy's best Pa anecdote relates to the Five Nations match in Paris in 1996, the day Humphreys made his debut, Clohessy was banned for stamping on Roumat and Ireland lost 45-10. "Emile Ntamack was due to be playing on the wing for France and, as manager, Pat was giving us a bit of a pep talk. But he didn't get the name quite right. He said 'these boys have a guy called Nattermack'. People were looking at each other, about to piss themselves laughing. He said it about three times and it got harder and harder to keep a straight face. Little things like that can tickle you, especially in a group and when it's supposed to be a serious time.

"He'd also decided that self-belief was the buzz word or phrase for the day, so had written it up on the board in the team-room, but unfortunately had left out the 'e' in belief, so it was belif. Pat was getting into his motivation bit, pointing at the board and emphasising 'you've got to have . . .'. This was about two hours before kick-off and it all seems rather silly now, but it was funny at the time in a schoolboy humour sort of way. You needed to be there to appreciate it. I suppose, on a more serious note, we did lack self-belief in Paris in those days."

The sense of dislocation between quintessential Englishman Ashton and Irishman Whelan was the backdrop to Ireland's 1998 Five Nations opener against old nemesis Scotland at Lansdowne Road. In a press conference following a training session at Suttonians RFC prior to that game, Ashton was pressed about his supposedly poor relationship with Whelan. His reply, 'Pat is an Irishman and I am an Englishman; he is an amateur and I am a professional', seemed to signal, at best, an uneasy truce. In the event, both men were gone from their posts by the end of the season.

O'Shea, Paul and Richie Wallace, Corkery and Dawson were all back in the Ireland side, while O'Meara was at scrumhalf in place of Hogan, thus reuniting the halfback pairing which took part in the Murrayfield mauling the previous March. It was to prove an ill omen and, in the wake of a deeply depressing defeat, Ireland found themselves looking for a third coach in the space of only 13 months.

19. GATLAND'S GREENS

Brian Ashton's reign ended abruptly and with barely a whimper courtesy of another dismal defeat by Scotland, the sting of the thistle proving as painful for the little Englishman as the bout of shingles which accompanied his departure. There is always admiration for gallant losers in the face of overwhelming odds, while history is forever kind to the team which sneaks a scrappy win like Scotland did at Lansdowne Road on this occasion. But for Ireland's failure to finish off the Scots, there could be nothing but opprobrium for losing a dreadful match which they so evidently had the opportunity and resources to win. By the end, however, they had forfeited any right, which their extra creativity may have afforded, to a first triumph over the tartan terrors for a decade.

This low quality contest looked every inch the wooden spoon decider it was dubbed in advance and most people would have left the ground expecting a hammering in Paris a month hence to bring Ireland half way to claiming the booby prize. If the men in green were going to turn over possession with the inexcusable regularity they did through basic errors in this Championship opener, the gallic geniuses would undoubtedly punish them in a way which Scotland's own glaring limitations prevented them from doing.

It was accepted at both press conferences that Ireland had had the winning of the match. But the Scots, for whom Jim Telfer had just taken over as coach from Richie Dixon, who departed after a defeat by Italy, felt no guilt at the result and none of the home representatives dared to suggest that Ireland were robbed. Although it would have been remiss not to acknowledge Ireland's superiority in many facets of this game, that counted for little when set against the harsh statistical reality of Scotland's 10th victory in the last 11 encounters as the tartan torment continued.

In terms of the mathematics, Ireland lost by a single point because Paul Wallace gave away a needless penalty in front of his own posts when they were leading 16-14 with only 10 minutes remaining, but Craig Chalmers' straight-forward kick was really only one link in a sequence of failures which condemned Ashton's team in the crucial final quarter. When a period of sustained pressure on the Scotland line around the hour mark was finally wasted when that same man Wallace was penalised at the last of an interminable series of scrums, there was a sense that a turning point had been reached, and so it proved. Scotland surged straight downfield and immediately their emergency place-kicker Chalmers had a simple shot at goal, with which he reduced the arrears to a precarious two points. Five minutes later he had repeated the dose and, although there were 10 minutes remaining, incoherent, panicking Ireland spent most of them in their own territory until Humphreys' desperate, late attempt to drop a goal from the proverbial mile out, fell well short. Even though Rowan Shepherd missed with four shots at goal, Scotland had still led 11-10 at the interval thanks to a clinical retaliatory try on the half-time whistle.

South African referee Andre Watson had just awarded Ireland a penalty try, converted by Humphreys - albeit one scrum after Gary Armstrong's more blatant interference as yet again the green juggernaut shunted towards the line - to restore the lead his earlier penalty had given them. But, true to form, Scotland hit straight back, as Shepherd released British Lion Alan Tait on the right and the veteran centre showed great strength and awareness - of the sort Ireland lacked close to the line - to twist out of a tackle and ground the ball in textbook fashion. Humphreys gave the capacity crowd hope with a penalty and neat drop goal in the third quarter, but McCall's failure to exploit an overlap followed by the series of barren scrums was a critical sequence.

Three statistics also told their own story. Scotland won 65 rucks to Ireland's 30, crossed the gainline 62 times compared with 37 and won the contest for loose ball 71-36. Johns and his second row partner O'Kelly, both lineout efficiency personified, were two of Ireland's successes, but it was a most unhappy afternoon for his old friend McCall, who failed to do himself justice, and Small's anonymous fellow centre Kevin Maggs. Humphreys marred an otherwise satisfactory performance by failing to discharge his basic duties consistently well. Paul Wallace destroyed George Graham on the Scot's Championship debut, but gave away costly penalties.

The assembled hacks had begun Irish rugby's latest post-mortem long before the chief protagonists arrived to be grilled but, when they finally showed up, manager Whelan wasn't even given a microphone and it was left to Ashton and Wood to offer whatever explanations they could. To his credit, the under-fire coach displayed his usual courtesy, openness and honesty as he described with clarity where Ireland lost the game and neither he nor the skipper sought to make excuses.

Ashton said: "We made an unacceptable number of technical errors in the first half. Then we got penalised at the last of that series of scrums on their line. After that we lost our way tactically and Scotland, recognising this, stepped up a gear to take full advantage. It is a disastrous start to the Five Nations . . . losing a game we should have won, to a team who arguably didn't play as well as us. We scrummaged exceptionally well, improved at the lineout from the Italy game, produced most of the sharp backplay in the second half and can claim that, on balance, we were the better side. But all that is meaningless if a side makes the number of errors we did today. Some of the mistakes seemed to result from a lack of absolute concentration. I also found it quite remarkable the way in which we kicked away possession at critical times."

If that comment put a little distance between Ashton and the debacle, it was nothing to the infamous disowning remark with which he will forever be associated. "I don't know whose gameplan that was, but it most certainly was not mine" he declared. Much was made of that comment, both at the time and subsequently, not least because it seemed disloyal and a breach of a coach's etiquette, but how big a deal was it for Paddy and the Irish players? Did they find his outburst offensive?

"I don't think we took all that much notice of it or that it affected us much. The prevailing mood was one of deep disappointment to have lost again to Scotland and in that way. We felt we had let ourselves down, so what was said was only a side issue. In hindsight, maybe a coach has to be careful with words, because anything he says will naturally be held up to scrutiny, but he was probably emotional and feeling the strain by that stage."

The remark was indeed the strongest sign yet that Ashton was losing his way and that his affair with Irish rugby was turning sour. In a 12 month period, the initial enthusiasm and vision had been replaced by exasperation and pessimism as the coach found himself on a different wavelength to his players. By trying to introduce a culture of personal decision-making within an all-singing, all-dancing gameplan, Ashton misjudged where Irish rugby was at and, in spite of evidence that he was trying to make his charges run before they could walk, he persisted and refused to cut his cloth to suit. He was also roundly criticised for his failure to really buy into the Irish rugby culture, even with a view to trying to change it, never relocating properly to the country and exhibiting a strong preference for picking English-based players.

"Brian did have a house in Ireland, but I think it would be fair to say that he found it difficult understanding the Irish psyche" reflects Paddy. "Things didn't move as quickly as he wanted and he got frustrated. He had a lot of innovative ideas about backplay in particular, but some of the things he was trying to introduce were probably ahead of time. Four years on, Ireland's horizons are now a lot wider, but back then people may not quite have been ready for his approach and he ran out of patience."

Within a fortnight of the Scottish defeat, Ashton had informed the IRFU of his decision to resign, citing personal reasons. The doyen of Irish rugby writers, Edmund van Esbeck, provides a clear and concise summary of the sorry saga in his definitive history, 'Irish Rugby 1874-1999'. "A fortnight later Ashton had resigned" records van Esbeck. "He got an attack of shingles and informed the IRFU that he had decided to resign. In his resignation letter he made no mention of any disagreement with Whelan, but in all the circumstances said that he no longer felt he could continue as coach." His next sentence is a stunning indictment of the whole Ashton episode: "So the man who had been given the longest contract in the history of the game by any country, ended up having the shortest tenure of any Ireland coach. Ashton subsequently stated that he had made a mistake in taking the Irish coaching position. He also intimated that he did not understand the Irish character and had probably made an error in not attending All Ireland League matches. He was probably right on all three counts" adds van Esbeck. "But it would have been better had he stated that earlier and it would have avoided an unpleasant situation. He had been given a very lucrative contract, was supplied with a car and an apartment in Dun Laoghaire just outside Dublin."

"I think he expected the atmosphere and attitude to be like it was in England," Paddy adds. "Not that we couldn't be serious, but all the Irish boys knew how to have fun and Woody and the Claw are awful messers. Brian rated the English league far above the AIL and interpros, and so only picked players from England. He still managed to keep a pretty good relationship with the players and the IRFU, but none of us thought he saw eye to eye with Pat Whelan. He would probably fit in better today, as the Irish set-up is definitely more professional now."

So Ireland found themselves rudderless less than a fortnight away from a daunting trip to face France in Paris. The Parc des Princes had been an unhappy hunting ground for the men in green and they had leaked over 40 points there twice in their last three visits. This time the game would be at the new Stade de France, but this wasn't considered likely to offer much respite for Ireland, who went into the match as out-and-out underdogs to the extent that the bookies were quoting France at 33-1 on, remarkable odds in a two-horse race. Some newspapers in France were speculating that their side could even challenge New Zealand's world record Test win of 145-17 against Japan at the 1995 World Cup. To say the least, Ireland's prospects were considered bleak!

The man to whom the IRFU turned to lead Ireland into the lions' den was Warren Gatland, a former hooker for the All Blacks midweek team who never won a Test cap for New Zealand due to his career coinciding with that of the great Sean Fitzpatrick. Unlike Ashton, he had a real feel for Irish rugby, having fallen in love with the emerald isle and was settled in Galway, where he was proving an extremely successful coach of Connacht, whose fortunes he had transformed that term. He had spent several seasons as player-coach of Galwegians but, ironically, the opportunity to coach Connacht arose because of the resignation of Eddie O'Sullivan, the man who was to ultimately replace him in the Irish post at the end of 2001.

It was lowly Connacht who led the way in Irish sides becoming competitive on French soil and that season, as well as winning at Begles, they had also beaten Northampton both home and away, a magnificent double, in the European subsidiary competition. The timing was bad for several other more established contenders, but perfect for Gatland who, along with Leinster's Mike Ruddock, was already involved with the Irish set-up given that the pair had stood in for Ashton when he missed a session due to the shingles just before his resignation.

"Warren got a lucky break in that the job came up at the time when Connacht were going so well, but all credit to him for being in that position and then proving himself in the post. To be honest the change of coach didn't mean that much to the players in that you get used to people coming and going and it isn't really your business or in your interests to get too caught up in the whys and wherefores. It was pretty much a case of 'he's gone, someone else will be coming in' and you just get on with it, making sure you're professional and that you're trying to maintain your own level of performance. I got on well with Brian and was sad for him that it didn't work out. As for Warren, I knew of him and that he'd been doing very well with Connacht, but didn't know him personally. There was good feedback about him though from Eric Elwood, who had been playing for him in Connacht and, from my own point of view, I felt that, as a former All Blacks forward, he would be well equipped to help the Irish forwards. It was also hoped that he'd have more idea of the Irish psyche than Brian and so it proved."

Gatland made five changes and a positional switch for Ireland's apparent mission impossible, though to many tinkering with the team seemed merely akin to rearranging the deckchairs on the deck of the Titanic. McCall gave way in midfield to a fit-again Henderson, with Maggs moving to inside centre, while Gatland brought in his two Connacht halfbacks, Elwood and McGuinness, and handed a surprise first cap to fellow Kiwi Andy Ward. Married to an Irish girl and settled in County Down, Ward had been doing well for Ulster, but was playing in the lower reaches of the AIL for Ballynahinch, hardly ideal preparation for facing the French in Paris. The final alteration saw Costello take over from Miller at No 8.

Apart from his work on the training ground, Gatland's big innovation ahead of the game was to appeal to the Irish public to send their messages of support to the team hotel. It may have sounded like a bit of a gimmick, but seemed to have the desired effect. "There was a degree of hype surrounding the whole concept" admits Paddy, "but it certainly did allow us to tap into a rich vein of public support and see that the people were still behind us in spite of the Scottish result, which was a huge disappointment to both ourselves and the fans. I think several thousand faxes were received and it was very encouraging for the players to go into the teamroom and read through dozens and dozens of messages of support. It did give us a lift in the days just before the game. After yet another Scotland defeat there had been a bit of a feeling of 'not again' and 'just when is our luck going to change'. We were seen to be going to Paris in disarray and people expected us to be hammered."

In the event, Ireland raised their game sensationally and almost came away with a famous victory which, if they'd managed it, would have been one of the great shocks in rugby history. Apart from the faxes, Paddy recalls that the Irish team were preparing for the game in an ideal environment. "We stayed in the Trian Palace in Versailles and had a look round the palace on the Friday. It was nice to be out there away from it all and then just come into town for the game, totally the opposite to our arrangements every time we went to Edinburgh.

"France had the first lineout and Mal took it on their throw after we had stood there initially looking like we weren't even going to compete for it. That was the catalyst which helped us start quickly and really get in their faces. The crowd soon got on their backs and we just did better and better." The new Kiwi coach had rekindled all of Ireland's traditional pride and passion, but his team were also extremely effective in snuffing out the natural French threat for most of the game.

Gatland's greens led 13-6 at the interval, courtesy of two Elwood penalties and his conversion of Denis Hickie's intercept try from halfway. Elwood kept Ireland's noses in front with another penalty to counteract a French try from winger Philippe Bernat-Salles, but then Gatland made what proved a fatal blunder with a double substitution in the unbearably tense closing stages as his team hung desperately onto their narrow lead. Paul Wallace was replaced by Clohessy but, more importantly, Johns gave way to Mick Galwey who immediately lost a crucial lineout deep in the Irish 22 and French hooker Raphael Ibanez scored what proved a match-winning try from the resultant maul. There were seven minutes remaining and Ireland mounted one threatening attack, but a poor option was taken and the chance was lost. Irish pride had been restored in Paris but, naturally enough, Paddy was gutted. So near and yet so far. Oh what might have been.

In the changing room afterwards, others reported that, a bit like Galwey when Munster agonisingly lost the 2001 European Cup semi-final in Lille, Johns had said that being beaten by a bucketful of points would have felt less wretched. "I basically said that, when you're well beaten by a better team, you can accept it more easily but when you lose a game which you know you should have won, it is harder to accept. Nobody likes to lose by 30 points, but you play the All Blacks and you get beaten by 30 points and you tried everything and you can stand up and say 'yeah, they were the better team'. But I couldn't stand up after either of those matches against Scotland or France and say they were the better team.

"On reflection, Paris was a very encouraging performance, but it was bitterly disappointing to lose in those circumstances, to do so well and get so close to what would have been an incredible victory and then to see it snatched away. There was a sense that justice hadn't been done. It was also very annoying to have come off just before the try was scored. You go over and over things in your mind and wish you'd still been on, but who knows what would have happened one way or another. Afterwards it did knaw at me a bit and there was a sense of frustration, a feeling that the substitution was a direct factor in France scoring and us losing, but then hindsight is a wonderful thing."

Johns gave an emotional address in the changing room before the next game to mark his 40th cap, but Ireland couldn't match their Paris performance and were rather flat in going down 21-30 at home to Wales, a result which was all the more disappointing in light of the heroics against France. Gatland unsurprisingly made only one change and it was enforced, injury to Conor O'Shea meaning a recall for Ciaran Clarke, who had played in the 1993 win over England, at fullback. It was to be an unhappy day though for the big Terenure player.

Ward, watched by his parents who had come over specially from New Zealand, scored a try on his home debut following a lineout take by Paddy, while his fellow loose forward Costello also crossed the Welsh line inside the opening 24 minutes. But then Clarke spilled a high ball, handing a try to Allan Bateman and, although Ireland led 15-12 at the break, Wales found the better form in the second period and Neil Jenkins' late try and conversion, taking his personal tally to 20 points, finally confirmed their victory.

Johns, who typically fought hard to the end, was one of the few Irish players to maintain or enhance his reputation that day, along with engineroom partner O'Kelly, David Corkery and Rob Henderson, the only member of a painfully pedestrian backline to impress. But he confesses to remembering little about a game which sent Ireland off to Twickenham, hardly the easiest place to go trying to avert a whitewash, on the back of a hat-trick of Championship defeats.

However, in an interview with the London Evening Standard a few days ahead of the English match Paddy pointed out that Ireland had only lost by single figure margins in their opening three games and that, contrary to what some may have expected, morale in the camp was relatively high. That said, he had been quoted in the Irish Times ahead of the Welsh game outlining that sense of despair which he felt after Ireland's first two Five Nations defeats against Scotland and France. "After the last two defeats against Scotland and France, I don't think I've every felt as angry after a game as I did then" he is on record as saying at the time. "It was soul-destroying, very, very difficult. It's frustrating to look back over the tapes, so disappointing. You don't play to perform, you play to win and I think it's even more annoying that we didn't win those games. Yes, you can take performance as a positive, but you can't be satisfied."

So Ireland went to Twickenham seeking to make some amends for a disappointing campaign and, although well beaten, in many ways they didn't make a bad fist of it against a side which had put 60 points on Wales earlier in the Championship. Indicative of the consistency in selection which was to be Gatland's trademark in the job was that, just like after Paris, the only change to the side to face England was an enforced one, with McCall returning to midfield in place of the injured Henderson.

England, who had brought in Paddy's Saracens captain Tony Diprose at No 8, were clearly the superior side, but Ireland hung in there and made it as difficult for them as possible in spite of leaking a try in the first couple of minutes. "England were much better than us on the day, but the pleasing thing was that it looked like being a cricket score and we pulled it back" says Paddy. Another intercept try by Hickie five minutes before the interval lifted Ireland's spirits and he scored again in the second period after being brought through by Elwood's trademark reverse pass.

The match will also be remembered for an incident in which the outhalf crashed into McCall, with the clash of heads resulting in the latter having to be carried off, thus handing Killian Keane his first cap. There was also the feud between Corkery and Lawrence Dallaglio, culminating in the infamous refusal to shake hands after the game. Humphreys got a first run at fullback, coming on for Clarke, while England brought on an 18-year old Jonny Wilkinson for his first cap near the end. It finishing 35-17, giving England the Triple Crown for the fourth year running, while whitewashed Ireland were left holding the wooden spoon. But Paddy had a happier time on his return to Twickenham a few weeks later, winning silverware there with Sarries, and, when he next played for Ireland, in South Africa that summer, he was captain of his country.

20. THE LION THAT NEVER ROARED

To the rugby fraternity in these islands, 1997 will always be the year that the British and Irish Lions took on world champions South Africa on their own soil and beat them 2-1 in the Test series. For Paddy though, this tour was to be remembered, with a degree of anguish, as the time he should have been one of those Lions but for the saga of a broken finger and badly timed op.

Having been included in the preliminary squad of 64 as a second row, when the Lions left for the rainbow republic, Paddy was not in the touring party even though five locks were chosen. In his stead were captain Martin Johnson, the Scottish trio of Doddie Weir, Damien Cronin and Andy Reed, and young Jeremy Davidson, his former Dungannon clubmate and now regular partner in the Ireland engineroon.

Naturally enough Johns was deeply disappointed. Selection for a Lions tour is a big goal for top players from England, Ireland, Scotland and Wales but, now he wasn't going, it was a chance to get his finger fixed. Over a period of several matches that Spring, Paddy sustained a fracture of the ring finger of his right hand, but had soldiered on until the end of the season, even playing with a splint. It hurt every time he caught the ball, but he simply hated missing matches and, with both Saracens and Ireland, a place forfeited wasn't certain to be regained easily. Now though, at the end of term and with a rare free summer on the cards in that he hadn't made the Lions and wasn't roped into the ill-fated Irish Development tour of New Zealand, Paddy decided this would be a good time to undergo the surgery his finger required.

This involved two operations. Firstly, pins were placed perpendicular to the back of his finger to try and stretch the shaft of his bone and get the broken bit back into the right alignment. "I looked like I had small, metal rugby posts growing out of my finger. It was really awkward to do anything. The pins were meant to be in for three weeks, but I accidentally pulled them out when I was taking my T-shirt off one day at the gym only two weeks into it. I can't say I was too gutted!" Next, the finger was actually opened up and the dislodged piece of bone was pinned internally to the main part. With all this ahead of him, Paddy wrote to the Lions management explaining that he wouldnít be available for selection.

At the time, the chances of him being required seemed rather remote, so he went ahead and had the operation but, as he recuperated, fate was to deal him a cruel blow. "I remember watching the game when Doddie got injured. He was standing at the side of a ruck and got kicked on his knee. Ultimately he had to go home early. Gareth Archer and I were the next second rows in line, but Gareth had been out of contention because of his own surgery and now I was in the same boat. Next thing Nigel Redman was called away from England's tour of Canada and was on his way to join the Lions. 'I was gutted', recalls Paddy. "The Lions tour had been a big target for me, and it was awful to realise I had been so close, but I had made my decision and had to live by it. You can't keep second guessing what's going to happen in the future."

As it happened, one Irish second row made his name in South Africa. With his protégé Davidson taking the spotlight, did Paddy feel a trifle hard done by, having so much experience and then seeing this young kid taking his place? "No, I didn't begrudge him at all. There was a big press build-up before his selection, so I had had time to get used to the idea long before it actually happened. I knew Jeremy's strengths and had always enjoyed playing with him. We have always been good friends and I'd rather have him selected than someone from England, Scotland or Wales. You have to remember that selection comes down to personal opinion and sometimes you're in and sometimes you're out."

There is no doubt that Paddy was particularly unlucky to lose out to two long-serving but relative journeymen Scots in Cronin and Reed, both of whom by then were past their best. "Jeremy certainly justified his selection though and winning Players' Player of the Tour proved that. I thought he was absolutely outstanding on that tour. Watching the first Test I couldn't believe it was the same player I'd played with at Dungannon. When your team are playing well, you can do your bit and look good, but he definitely came of age in South Africa. Jeremy's a big game player and in that Test he shone. He had most of the ball thrown to him in the lineout and won it quite easily, plus he played well in the loose."

It rankles with Paddy that he never became a Lion. That cherished status is one of the few things missing from the record of a long and distinguished career at international level. He runs restlessly through the list of Ireland's most capped players, on which he is fourth, and sorrowfully notes that his is the only name near the top of the chart with no Lions tag alongside it. While he wouldn't say so himself, there are less worthy players who have pulled on that famous red jersey.

There is no doubt that timing counted against him. Had the tours of New Zealand and South Africa been in 1994 and 1998 respectively instead of a year earlier in each case, he might well have made both. As it was, the four year cycle fell badly for him. In 1993, he had only been back in the Ireland team for 12 months and being in and out of his national side between the 1995 World Cup in South Africa and the Lions trip there a couple of years later didn't help his cause. Neither did alternating between second row and No 8. That's the way the cookie crumbles though. The history of sport is littered with stories of star names missing out on big stages such as World Cups, Olympics or Lions tours. If you lose out once through injury, it's a long time to stay at the top until the next one comes round.

It isn't quite the same of course but, in lieu of the Lions, Paddy did at least have the honour of representing the Barbarians on three occasions, against Leicester on Boxing Day in 1993, against New Zealand at Cardiff Arms Park and in the Dunblane international at Murrayfield.

On the first of these two outings, the Baabaas were on the wrong side of the full-time scoreline, but the Dunblane match resulted in Paddy's only ever victory against

Scotland, thanks to his injury-time try. "It was a fantastic game," Paddy comments. ìIt was great to win a Murrayfield and to score the winning try was just the icing on the cake. Barbarian rugby has always had a special camaraderie with its ërun everything' attitude. You had only one training session together, but there were always players with a bit of magic to shine through. In the amateur days, it was strange to play with other nations, so I was very lucky to play with guys like Aaron Pene, Rob McCall and Olivier Roumat. Players who were number one or two in the world."

He also played for Ireland against the Barbarians in one non-cap match, the Peace International organised by Trevor Ringland and Hugo MacNeill in May 1996 but missed out on the IRFU's 125th anniversary game four years later. Johns had lost his place midway through the 1996 Five Nations and was only on the bench, but injury forced flanker Eddie Halvey off early in the game and, with Davidson moving to blindside, that allowed Paddy to come on and he made the most of his opportunity. Campese and Pienaar, the latter soon to become a clubmate of Paddy's, were present, while a very strong Baa-Baas line-up included another man he was to link up with at Saracens later that year, Philippe Sella and various household names including Rory Underwood, Laurent Cabannes and Dean Richards. Ireland featured a few new faces, including Rob Henderson and James Topping, both of whom won their first caps against Samoa later in the year, and the game was a fine spectacle with plenty of free-flowing rugby.

The Barbarians won 70-38, with Jon Callard converting all 10 of their tries, but Ireland did well in crossing half a dozen times themselves and played more enterprising rugby than they normally would in the more stultified surroundings of an entire Championship campaign. Paddy's performance was lavishly praised by former Ireland coach Mick Doyle who, writing at the time in the Sunday Independent, said he had a 'superb game' and then went further. "Johns, as Ireland's best player, was the spearhead of almost Irish attack and must feel huge personal satisfaction." No wonder Paddy has kept the cutting!

"Rugby is one of the few all-Ireland sports, so it was ideal for something like the Peace International," Paddy explains. ìI was disappointed to be on the bench, but actually played most of the match. I remember it was a hot day with lots of running and lots of tries. Unfortunately we were playing catch-up for most of the game, but there was a brilliant atmosphere. Like all Baabaas games, it was about putting on a show." By the time Ireland next took on the Barbarians, in that IRFU anniversary match in May 2000, moves had already been made to consign Paddy to the international scrapheap and he took no part, even though Galwey was unavailable due to the previous day's European Cup final.

While the 1997 Lions tour may have been the blow that hit him hardest, it wasn't the first time that Paddy had missed out when he 'could have played'. Ireland were taking on France at home in the 1995 Five Nations and he was in the starting line-up for the 17th time in a row. Preparation was going well until dinner-time the night before the game. "I was sitting there eating my dinner with no problems, when suddenly I got really bad abdominal pains. The team doctor, Mick Molloy, examined me and decided that it was probably appendicitis. I then went to the hospital where I had an ultrasound scan and they agreed with the diagnosis."

With a heavily-pregnant Kirsty waiting at home across the border, Paddy didn't want to be admitted in Dublin and so got a private ambulance the 100 miles north to the City Hospital, Belfast. Fortunately for Paddy, the cost of the ambulance was picked up by the IRFU. Here he was monitored overnight, although his pulse was so slow it couldn't be recorded on the chart! With no further drama, he was subsequently released on the Saturday morning and ended up frustratedly watching the game on television at home in Glengormley.

"It was a strange situation, surreal really. One minute I was eating my dinner, thinking about playing against France and suddenly I'm back home watching it on telly having been through all the drama, for nothing it seemed. If I'd had to have the op, I'd have been out for ages but instead there I was at home without much wrong with me. I was absolutely gutted. The fact that I'd been there with the squad preparing for the match made it worse than if I'd been ruled out days in advance. I hadn't missed an Ireland game for ages and it was very disappointing."

This turn of events allowed regular Ulster engineroom partner Davy Tweed to win his first cap at the ripe old age of 35, a real fairytale for the big Ballymena lock, who did well enough to retain his place for the next match at someone else's expense and make it to that summer's World Cup. "Despite everything, I was delighted to see him win his first cap. Davy was always a big honest player. What you saw was what you got. He was very aggressive and took no prisoners." Unlike Johns, who had been capped at 22, Tweed was a late developer and, although not good enough to be chosen by his country earlier in his career, became such a hard, strong figure at provincial level that he finally forced his way in.

Although following doctor's orders on this occasion, Paddy has been known to play despite medical advice. He started at an early age when he played in an Irish Schools trial in 1986 with nine stitches in his knee. "I was told by the doctor 'don't play' and I was thinking 'hang on, this is Irish Schools trials, I'm playing'!" Luckily for Paddy this gamble paid off in that he came through relatively unscathed and, more importantly, was subsequently selected to face Australian Schools. So the end justified the means. And so much for the 'cries when tackled' tag he had got at mini-rugby! That criticism had been well and truly confounded. In the future, he was to play with both a splint on a finger and also a thumb brace, though he found it more of a help than a hindrance around the fringes of rucks, when it occasionally came in contact with a few opponents!

Any sportsperson worries about injuries and, as a professional, they can result in a premature end to a career and a serious dent in your bank balance. Paddy himself took out personal insurance to protect his family from financial worries if he couldn't play either because he was dropped or because of injury. "I've always managed my injuries well, even before professionalism. I've been a religious icer and I'm lucky in that I tend to heal very quickly. I used to sleep with phone books under the feet of the bed if my legs were sore which meant that Kirsty had to too! Joe Doran, our masseur with Ireland, used to have this great treatment for heavy legs. You'd put about two to three inches of warm water into a bath and get in. Then you'd fill the bath up with cold water and sit in it for 10 to 15 minutes. The theory was that you wouldn't notice the cold as much because you had this layer of warm water on top. After that you put on warm tracksuit bottoms and sat with your legs elevated for 10 minutes. I was also very lucky to be married to a physio, so I could get plenty of rubs!"

Being a contact sport, knocks, bumps and bruises are all in a day's work when it comes to rugby, but with it now being a day job, livelihoods being at stake and bigger, stronger players putting in harder hits in a faster game, professional players have sought various forms of physical protection. Many are now using prophylactic padding, while the wearing of headguards has mushroomed to the extent that they are now commonly being sported by a significant number of backs as well as a great many forwards.

Paddy first embraced the idea of cranial protection in 1998 when he became concussed two weekends in a row playing fellow Londoners, Richmond, in both the league and the cup back to back. He was due to be on Irish duty against France the following weekend, decided enough was enough and purchased his first scrum-cap to mark the occasion. That one was actually bought, but later he was paid by the manufacturer to wear their product. It does though beg the question, should he have been playing at all in either the second Richmond encounter, or against Les Bleus if he had been concussed? "Ach sure, they were only little concussions!" Paddy laughs. "But the second one was worse, so I decided to get a scrum-cap." He noticed the benefits straight away. "They do take a bit of getting used to, but wearing it definitely increased my confidence."

With rugby now becoming a feasible livelihood and matches with increased intensity and becoming more and more physical, there is the worry that players could become more reckless and gung-ho regarding contact because they felt safe whilst padded, thus paradoxically causing the injuries they were trying so hard to avoid. "I never found that" Paddy disagrees. "Although I was more confident, I wasn't about to lead in with my head. You still have to follow basic techniques, but it just meant that I didn't get a phobia about my head." The headguard was the last piece of protective clothing Paddy acquired. He already wore shoulder pads because of sore AC joints, including partial dislocation of the left one in a match between Ulster and Munster at Musgrave Park, and had worn shin guards from about the age of 23. "Basically I was just fed up of getting kicked in the shins!"

So, surely all these measures meant that Johns had a long and injury-free career. Alas for him it was not to be and being right in the middle of the fray on more occasions that not resulted in probably more than Paddy's fair share of injuries. He has gone under the knife a total of eight times, each one the consequence of damage sustained on the pitch. The first was at the tender age of 18 when he broke his right wrist playing for Dungannon against near neighbours Armagh. The outcome of this was that he had to do his A-level resits using a scribe. However, it mattered not, for, as we know, he got the grades to study dentistry in Newcastle.

Next came a series of four knee operations at regular intervals of two years from 1992 to 1998. All these were partial lateral left menisectomies which, in layman's terms, means removing bits of cartilage on the outside of his left knee. The initiating event occurred whilst playing for Dungannon against Cork opponents, Dolphin. Paddy's left foot became trapped in a ruck and his knee felt the force of his upper body turning whilst his lower leg and foot remained stationery. After his final operation in 1998, doctors told Johns that he would be very lucky to make it to the following year's World Cup. But Paddy worked hard to make his own luck and was there to take the field against the USA in Ireland's tournament opener at Lansdowne Road.

In between knee operations and one on his elbow, Paddy found the time to suffer a corneal abrasion and detached retina courtesy of Frenchman Olivier Merle in Paris in 1994. He also managed to break the ring finger on his right hand in 1997 which caused him to miss out on the highest possible accolade for a player from the Home Nations and tore thumb ligaments when his hand, er, came in contact with Kyrnauw Otto's head in the second Test of the stormy South African tour of 1998. If that injury comes into the self-inflicted category, one which could be classified under the heading of 'friendly fire' occurred in the victory over England at Twickenham in 1994 when both Paddy and Mick Galwey were so anxious to rough up Kyran Bracken that the latter broke the former's nose!

On the basis that they say it is good to give as well as to receive, Paddy dished out a few blows in his time too, though the exchange of letters between himself and Wayne Proctor after inadvertently breaking the Welsh winger's jaw in an international in 1994 point to his lack of desire to deliberately damage. Proctor's note of reply to Johns says: "Dear Paddy, Thank you for your kind words. The injury is indeed recovering very quickly. I suppose that will teach me for putting my head the wrong side. Hopefully if we are both in the position to do so next year we can have a drink together in Cardiff. Once again thank you for your kind thoughts. Yours in sport, Wayne Proctor."

Another major pitfall for professional athletes is illness. You just need to look at Jonah Lomu to see how such a powerful body can be rendered helpless. Although Paddy has never suffered from anything as serious as nephrotic syndrome, the common flu can still have devastating effects. After France and the appendicitis scare, Paddy was back again to take on Wales in Cardiff in the final Five Nations match of 1995, and again his health let him down.

"I took the flu and had it really bad on my chest. They did a stress test on a treadmill in the hospital to see if I could play. There was someone else who had to have a test too. I played, but I probably shouldn't have. I was very tired for the next few months, like I'd hit a wall. I was in some kind of post-viral state. People find it hard to believe that something like that can really set you back for weeks. Playing top level sport is very demanding and requires you to be in peak physical condition. If you try to play when not quite right, it can take a great deal out of you. It's like running a car battery down. I probably did feel alright at the start of that Welsh game, but the action soon took its toll and I felt fairly drained in the next couple of months leading into the World Cup."

Something similar happened five and a half years later when Ulster played Leinster in a Celtic League/interpro double-header at Donnybrook at the end of August 2001. The Ulster camp was struck down with a stomach bug, with players dropping like flies.

Having a big squad, most of the vacancies could be filled, but the second row berth was caught short, being hit with both illness and injury. Johns wasn't fit to play, but bravely agreed to do so as Ulster were desperate. Leinster won convincingly, 31-9, and as a consequence, Paddy didn't recover to full fitness until Christmas. He was given time off by coach Alan Solomons after that game, but didn't readily regain his place in the following months and there is no doubt that his courage cost him a lot and blighted his final season in the game.

"I really shouldn't have played that night," Paddy says, shaking his head, "but I didn't want to let the team down when we were so short on numbers. I've always found it very hard to pull out of matches and I guess it was a case of damned if you do, damned if you don't. I went out not letting myself worry beyond half time, and to be honest at the break I thought I felt ok, but I felt rough towards the end, and after it having been a close game up until that point, that's when they started to pull away. The sinbinning of my fellow second row, Mark Blair, compounded the situation. I couldn't have said no to starting. It really would have taken someone else to pull me out. Sometimes you mightn't feel great, but you go out and play alright.

"It's easier if you have an actual physical injury and a physio says you can't play, because you have to accept that and no-one expects you to take the field, but when it comes down to how you feel and you've to make a judgment call, it's so hard. I may have said no if the rest of the squad was full strength, but I couldn't on that occasion. Often it comes down more to desire, adrenalin or a sense of the team needing you than an entirely rational calculation. Sometimes playing when you aren't quite right can be selfish, in terms of you just wanting to play even it risks letting the team down, but on that occasion at Donnybrook, I believe it was selfless."

Injuries in rugby and, indeed, most sports, are a fact of life, but that doesn't make them any easier to bear. There's the pain and suffering when you sustain them, the hard work of rehab and, for certain injuries, the confidence issue when it comes to taking contact again. Occasionally, players can even dice with death on the field of play and Paddy has been there, having swallowed his tongue in a floodlit Premiership match against Orrell in his first season at Saracens. "I ran into their flanker Alex Bennett, a player who later came to Saracens. My head hit his shoulder and, as I fell back, I swallowed my tongue. I was gurgling, trying desperately to breath. Luckily Michael Lynagh was nearby, realised what was happening and got the game stopped quickly so that I could be attended to. It could have been serious, but I suffered no long-term effects, though I did have memory loss for quite a while afterwards. And, naturally enough, Kirsty got into a bit of a panic at the time."

Generally though, injuries aren't sustained so dramatically and the worst thing of all, even more than the physical pain, is the frustration of inactivity and the disappointment of missing out on the action. Although, fortunately for his own sanity and that of his long-suffering wife, Johns has never had an injury which has sidelined him for a whole season or missed many internationals, Kirsty reveals that, whenever he can't play, "Paddy isn't a pleasant person to be around."

Missing matches through injury or illness is not only frustrating, all the more so for u full-timer, but also has financial repercussions in the modern professional game. "I found it very frustrating to be sidelined. There was also the issue of money and missing out on match fees and win bonuses, but my contract always guaranteed me a certain amount and I reckon if you went into a game thinking 'I have to win this to get my win bonus', you wouldn't be a very good player. It's the same with missing games due to injury or not being picked. Not playing hurts the heart more than the pocket in my experience. Maybe some of the younger players these days would be more mercenary, I don't know, but having played in the amateur era, I was never used to money being a motivation."

As retirement arrives, thoughts of the long-term effects, in terms of his future health, comfort and mobility, of what rugby has put Paddy's body through must cross his mind. "Sure, I know things like arthritis are going to happen. When I was younger I had that 'I'm invincible' attitude and never thought I'd be injured or arthritic. Even now it doesn't really bother me. Although players are, in general, much fitter than they used to be, with bigger hits in the game these days there's an increase in injury intensity and you get wear and tear problems more quickly. Players aren't going to last at representative level for 12 years anymore."

It is a staggering statistic that some 14 Lions required knee operations when they returned from last summer's Australian tour, many of them players who had soldiered on, stuffed with pain-killers, perhaps against medical advice and possibly risking longer-term or even permanent damage. Longer seasons featuring heavier collisions between ever more bulked up bodies in a faster game will surely add up not only to shorter careers at the top level but, without putting too fine a point on it, a generation of partially crippled ex-players. Eh, Paddy?

"But I once read something that I thought was very true. I think it was some fairly famous poet who said it, though I'm not sure who exactly. The expression was 'I want to be well used up when the candle goes out. There's no point in dying healthy.' I liked the turn of phrase and would concur with the sentiment. I would like it if someone could invent a knee replacement that lasted forever or a cure for arthritis though!"

Well used up. Paddy'll be that alright. In the latter days of his career, Johns was so patched up and kitted out with body armour that you couldn't decide which he resembled more, a robot or a mummy. When he retired, frequent reference was made in interviews by both himself and Alan Solomons to the amount of traffic which his body had taken during all those years at the top of the game. So what sort of state is Paddy's body really in?

"It's probably much better now that he's retired!" laughs Dr David Irwin. "In the main, his injuries would be to the fingers, hands and wrists – all from lineouts, and maybe a few fists! Paddy was always very conscientious about injuries and did exactly what you told him. It probably helped that, being a dentist, he had a good general medical knowledge. Also, he was very determined to get back fit as soon as possible. "Paddy was a model patient," agrees Ulster physio Gareth Robinson. "His body's taken a lot of traffic over the years, but he's managed his injuries very well and always did anything you asked of him."

"With players playing more games, there has been an increase in the number of injuries," admits Dr Irwin. "There are bigger hits and more high impact collisions. Also, although protective gear has its place, it does mean that some players have a false sense of security and think that it means it's a licence to lead in with your head, or whatever. The laws are constantly being changed to reduce the number of injuries, especially at the scrum where refs are much harder on collapsing nowadays. However, because the emphasis is on a tackling and running game, this lends itself to more injuries, especially to midfield and back row players who are involved in most of the clashes and are first to breakdowns. Making players stay on their feet at rucks does reduce the risk of injury, but it's a fine line between keeping the players safe and keeping the paying public happy."

"I don't think the innate risk in rugby has changed," says Robinson, "but it is a quicker game with bigger hits, and because it is now people's livelihood, the medical set-up has to be more professional. We have tremendous support from various consultants in the Royal Victoria Hospital and a good relationship with the MRI and X-ray department in Musgrave Park Hospital. We are now more accountable for avoiding injuries and getting players back on the pitch. Therefore, it's in our interest to keep ahead of developments and to pick little niggles up before they progress to bigger problems."

Another rugby medic to have worked closely with Paddy is former Ireland team doctor, Dr Donal O'Shaughnessy, who is full of praise for how meticulous Johns was in looking after himself. "I've never come across anyone like him in my lifetime in sports" he said in an Irish Times feature on the day of Paddy's 50th cap. "He's a model professional. He does everything he's told and he's on time for every appointment, be it massage or physio or medical. He's so well versed on his own body that he can work the machines himself."

And finally there's his motto. PWP. "Whenever I was in Canada with Pat Parfrey and Noel Browne, two hard men, they had this phrase which I took up, 'play with pain'. At the end of the day, pain is only a sensation; you CAN block it out."

He put those words into practice according to Ireland prop Justin Fitzpatrick. "One thing that has always struck me about Paddy is his mental strength. He'd come in battered and bruised from a match or training and you'd say to him 'Paddy, are you not going to take tomorrow off?' and he'd look at you quizzically and reply 'it's only pain . . . where your mind wants to go, your body will follow'."

In the early days of professionalism when I was coming into the upper end of the game, the way Paddy managed his body was phenomenal. When he'd come down for breakfast or dinner, he'd have ice packs all over his body and also wore all sorts of pads in training. When he went out for a match, he'd have so much body armour and be so taped up that he looked a bit like a mummy. I'll never forget the comment made from the stand during a hush at Ravenhill one Friday night. Paddy ran on as a sub with his shin pads, knee pads, elbow pads, shoulder pads, helmet, the lot. Next thing you hear is this lone voice: 'Paddy Johns, skate or die!'

21. SILVERWARE WITH SARRIES

It took just three seasons of professional rugby to transform Saracens from also ran status to Tetley Bitter Cup winners. They delivered on Nigel Wray's dream in glorious fashion on 9th May 1998, with two of the world's greatest players, Michael Lynagh and Philippe Sella, signing off the big stage in stunning style as Saracens romped to a record rout of Wasps in the final.

That tremendous Twickenham triumph against their London rivals, who they had never beaten by so much in over a century of playing them, capped a remarkable journey from the time, a mere three years earlier, when they were using municipal facilities in Southgate. The win gave Wray a tangible return on the millions which he had invested in the club, while the manner in which it was achieved exhilarated players and fans alike. Ironically, three years later, Johns was also to be part of a Dungannon side which rewrote the history books by destroying their opponents in a domestic decider. Finals are typically tight and tense affairs, but for Paddy, they have been processions.

Saracens supporters had been starved of success for, remarkably, the club had never won a major trophy before, but Johns refutes the suggestion that the club was now under huge pressure to win silverware in light of the presence of superstars like Lynagh, Sella and Pienaar and the money which had been spent. "If we'd been professionals for 10 years, possibly that would have been the case, but the side which I played in was really only in its second season together when we won the Cup, so I don't think we were seen as under-achievers or expensive flops or anything like that. We also had a good set of supporters whose instinct was to really get behind us and enjoy the rugby rather than be critical or begrudging. There was a good feeling round the club and it was great to win the Cup and do so in the way we did."

Although having lost only a few games that season, Saracens defied the odds to even make the final. As a curtain raiser to their semi-final battle with Northampton, they first had to take on Newcastle in a Wednesday evening Premiership clash. This was a hugely physical encounter which left both sides drained and Newcastle two points better off in the league. "Everyone was fairly knackered after that one," remembers Paddy. "Personally I felt very drained going into the semi, but it was a Cup game, a one-off and we knew that we were just 80 minutes away from the biggest game in Sarries' history. I think that's what got us through, even though we were almost running on empty. Although we were away from home, which nobody wants in a semi-final, Franklin's Gardens has plenty of atmosphere, especially for Cup ties, and we always seemed to play well there."

At Franklin's Gardens, Saracens were hungry in attack and solid in defence. Their appetite was rewarded with a 10-3 lead at the break thanks to would-be Ulsterman Ryan Constable's try, sandwiched between a Lynagh penalty and conversion. Scrumhalf Kyran

Bracken left the field at half-time, not knowing if he would return due to a shoulder injury. But return he did, and was instrumental in the two tries which resulted in a 10-25 scoreline in favour of the London outfit. The way in which Saracens scrapped for that result convinced many sceptics that they were not merely a menagerie of mercenaries and that such a cosmopolitan collection of players could still tap into a sense of club spirit. To win in a hostile environment and on the back of that energy-sapping epic against Newcastle said a lot for their resolve and strength of character.

Bracken and Lynagh totally dominated English internationals Matt Dawson and Paul Grayson in the halfback battle, while Pienaar and skipper Tony Diprose were rampant against a home pack which was without the highly influential Tim Rodber. Constable's score was a superb team try, with Springbok Gavin Johnson, Lynagh, unsung centre Steve Ravenscroft and Sella all having a hand in the lead-up, but the quarter of an hour of wonderfully defiant defence which followed in the face of a Northampton siege also played a huge part in determining the outcome.

Sarries survived and Lynagh tagged on another penalty with half an hour remaining to take the lead out to double figure proportions and then a double whammy of tries by Matt Singer, a sub for Sella, in the space of five final quarter minutes, sealed victory. Both were created by Bracken, the first coming from his break and chip ahead, the second from an attack initiated by another break of his, carried on by Ravenscroft, Richard Wallace, George Chuter, Diprose, Constable and Johnson. That was game, set and match to the visitors, rendering Jon Sleightholme's subsequent try for Northampton too little, too late.

The Northampton side included Allen Clarke, thus re-enacting on a rather bigger stage the house rugby battles which had taken place at Dungannon Royal many years earlier, while there were enough other internationals in the Saints' line-up to make this a really distinguished victory. They also had Dawson and Grayson, Scot Gregor Townsend, Sleightholme and Ian Hunter, Springbok prop Garry Pagel and Scottish tighthead Matty Stewart, with Budge Poutney in the back row.

Sarries were in the Cup final. "It really hit us – bang! We were going where Saracens had never been before. The fezzes went wild and the crowd started chanting 'We're going to Twickenham!' as we did a lap of honour to acknowledge the travelling support. There was a huge buzz about everyone involved with the club." The only thing standing between Saracens and cup glory were London rivals, Wasps, who had beaten Sale in the other semi. "We knew they were a good side with players like Dallaglio, Rees and Henderson, but they knew we had good players too."

In their last league game ahead of Twickenham, Saracens had again shown their spirit and tenacity in coming from behind to take the points at London Irish and remain at the top of the table, three points ahead of Newcastle, but with two extra matches played. Ultimately the double proved beyond them, but it was another notable result against a London Irish team containing several friends of Paddy's and plenty of his compatriots. These included David Humphreys, Mark McCall, Conor O'Shea, Niall Woods, Gary Halpin, Malcolm O'Kelly, Kieron Dawson and two men who were to make their Test debuts under him in South Africa that summer, the two Justins, Bishop and Fitzpatrick.

The London Irish game was the fourth in a row in which Sarries had overturned a deficit to win, an indication both that they weren't firing on all cylinders but further evidence that this was no team of uncaring mercenaries. When Ireland scrumhalf Niall Hogan scored for the hosts, Saracens were 21-6 down with under half an hour remaining, but a burst of 23 unanswered points in as many minutes totally transformed the situation. Brendon Daniel got over for a try as did replacement back-rower Ben Sturnham soon afterwards and, although neither was converted, two penalties from Johnson edged Saracens in front with seven minutes remaining. As London Irish tried to respond, they were picked off by Daniel, who pounced on a spilled pass on halfway and showed both Bishop and Humphreys a clean pair of heels en route to the line, with Johnson converting this time to give his team a two-score cushion.

It was a morale-boosting victory before Twickers, but both coach Pienaar and captain Diprose admitted that, while scraping results, they were not playing particularly well. That was all to change, and how. It all came right on the night or, to be more accurate, afternoon.

One of Nigel Wray's business partners owned the Disney Channel and had his own cinema. So, the Thursday evening before the final, the team met and went to what they thought was going to be a private showing of a latest release. Instead they were treated to a three minute motivational video organised by Pienaar and the management team. The video was a compilation of the team's tries and big hits throughout the season. It certainly had the desired effect. "It was very inspiring," says an emphatic Johns. "With the big screen and surround sound, it was like reliving it all. Although it was only three minutes long, when the lights went up everyone had glazed-over eyes. We were ready to play. I think we won the final then and there."

That season Saracens had used a 'Men In Black' theme and the Wil Smith hit accompanied the players running onto the pitch. This theme continued throughout Cup final day. "It was a sunny day and we all wore sunglasses and had black suits with button holes. Everyone looked really well. Although Wasps were dressed smartly, we were treating the occasion like FA Cup final day, so we dressed like it was a Cup final. I think that just added to the sense of occasion and strengthened our resolve to win."

Paddy was no stranger to playing at Twickenham, and had famously won there with Ireland in 1994, but it was his first time to do so in a club context, and wanting certain Englishmen, like Bracken, to play well! "It was a bit different because, although there was a big crowd, almost capacity, I knew more of them than I usually would and more of them would have been supporting the side I was playing for than when I'd be there with Ireland. About eight of my best buddies from Dungannon came over, including Keith and Neil McGarry, Andy Oliver, Hugh McCaughey, Kenny Wright, Wilfie Nelson and Brian Smith.

"We found them accommodation above some pub in Enfield, which I'm sure they made good use of!" he laughs. "They wanted to be fully-fledged members of the Saracens support that was there, so they all went off to buy fezzes, but they couldn't find any anywhere, as they were probably all sold out by then, so they bought these flower-pots and wore them instead! That's the Dungannon sense of humour for you. But it was great to know they would be there. Kirsty was watching, of course, along with my mum, my sister and her husband, and my two brothers."

As per usual with Pudsey, he doesn't remember much about this big game itself, although the way Sarries went about their task that day did warm the hearts of all who watched. "All I really remember about the match is that we drove the first lineout 20 metres and after that Wasps didn't really come back at us. It was largely a one-sided affair which Michael Lynagh controlled from start to finish. It definitely helped having big match players with big match temperament on our side. Plus it was Lynagh and Sella's last final, so there was no way they were going to lose it. It was the biggest game in the club's history and there was that 'winner takes it all' vibe you get with cup rugby. We weren't going to miss our opportunity. There was simply too much at stake."

Predicting the outcome of Cup finals is notoriously difficult, especially when you add the extra spice of a local derby, and a decent Wasps side probably went in as favourites due to Sarries' faltering form. Wasps were disadvantaged by the fact that Lawrence Dallaglio was hampered by a damaged shoulder, yet they still had a good enough pack to leave Samoan hooker Trevor Leota and Scottish Lion Andy Reed on the bench, where they were joined by useful backs in England pivot Andy Gomarsall and the exciting Paul Sampson. Canadian general Gareth Rees was at fullback behind a three-quarter line featuring Paddy's fellow Irish international Henderson. The Wasps pack featured top prop Will Green, man mountain lock Simon Shaw and the emerging Joe Worsley.

For Saracens, Ireland winger Wallace lost out to Wallaby wizard Constable and another arch-entertainer Brendon Daniel in the battle for the wide berths, while Singer, the two-try supersub hero of the semi was again left on the bench, playing second fiddle to Springbok Johnson. Ravenscroft and Sella were, as usual, the centre combo, with Bracken and Lynagh at halfback. George Chuter had the No 2 jersey ahead of Greg Botterman between regular props Roberto Grau and Paul Wallace. The engineroom pairing was, predictably, Johns and Grewcock while, in the absence of Richard Hill, the promising Ben Sturnham was at blindside, with Pienaar wearing No 7 and skipper Diprose completing the team in the middle of the back row. Wallace was called upon to replace Daniel before the half hour mark, while four more of the bench boys, Singer, reserve pivot Olsen, Botterman and prop Andy Olver, were thrown on for the final few minutes to share in the glory. By then Sarries were well out of sight and it had become a victory parade.

Sarries ran out victors 48-18 in a game they dominated throughout. In the opening 12 minutes, Wasps yielded 15 points, which serves to illustrate Saracens' intent. Lynagh showed his class early on with a drop goal after Sella had marked the beginning of the end of an extraordinary career, which had brought him 111 international caps, in fitting fashion with the opening try of the game. Wasps did manage a mini uprising just after the interval with 12 points in three minutes, but it was too little too late and, with their lineout in disarray, Wasps left a Cup final for the fourth time clutching runners-up medals. At the final whistle, Nigel Wray's 4.5 million dream had come true.

"It was fantastic, just fantastic. Although we'd led through the whole game, it's still a relief to hear the whistle and know you've won. It was also brilliant that I'd had so many friends and family come to watch, and holding the Cup up at Twickenham I just felt so elated" Paddy sighs. Among all the matches and honours Paddy has won over the years, where does this Cup victory rank? "It's definitely up there, but I think winning the AIL with Dungannon three years later surpassed it. With six games to go in the AIL, Dungannon had been written off. Although to win the Cup with Sarries was very special, we were an in-form team that whole season, whereas I think it was a greater relative achievement for Dungannon to be AIL champions."

Winning, of course, is everything in a Cup final but, in celebrating the victory, Saracens could also feel euphoric and exhilarated about the manner in which it had been obtained. To shake off the weariness and turn in such a dazzling display on the big stage on a hot early summer afternoon not only made them worthy winners, but captivated a wider audience and did justice to Wray's vision. Sella was superb and Lynagh lordly, both bowing out while still at their best, an example which Johns later chose to follow as he too ended his career on a high and capable of earning his opponents' respect right to the last.

Sella's try, on six minutes, came following a Grewcock lineout take, a good driving maul and some fine approach play by Johnson, but it still took all his class to turn the opportunity into points. Lynagh converted and, although Rees opened Wasps' account with a penalty, the Wallaby dropped a goal to cancel out those three points. Constable, with his trademark trick of squaring up to his opponent and then burning him on the outside, left Lawrence Scrase transfixed to scorch away and score on 13 minutes from a super Sella pass after Saracens had firstly taken the sting out of a Wasps attack and then relieved their opponents of the ball for good measure.

Rees landed a second penalty on the half hour, but the buzzing Saracens swatted down any hopes Wasps had of a revival by stinging them with two scores between that and the interval. Within two minutes of the second strike by Rees, Lynagh went blind from a lineout and Diprose made an intelligent intervention to put Johnson over, with the Australian legend adding the points. He repeated the dose six minutes later to give Saracens an astonishing 29-6 lead at the break after Grewcock had charged over to make the most of a rampaging raid by the storming Sturnham.

Rather than relax, Saracens pressed on in the second period and extended their lead seven minutes after the resumption, the score being set up by Lynagh's top class touch-finder followed by Johns' superb steal on the Wasps throw. Sella stretched the Wasps defence and Lynagh cleverly chipped ahead, judging it so well that either Constable or Ravenscoft could have comfortably claimed the try. In the event, the honour fell to the latter. Entering the final half hour, Paul Volley and Shane Roiser touched down in the space of three minutes for Wasps, but Rees inexplicably failed to convert the second from in front of the posts and Sarries were still three scores clear.

They finished with a flourish, the brilliant Bracken and Wallace, set up by Sella, both bagging tries to complete Saracens' magnificent seven haul and Lynagh landing two conversions to take his personal points tally for the afternoon to 13 points and bring his team close to the half-century mark. For the legendary Lynagh, it was a remarkably dominant display in light of the cancer scare with a non-malignant growth in his groin which had kept him out of action for the previous three weeks.

Lynagh said: "This was a wonderful way to go out and, although I was fine once I got on the pitch, I'd been very nervous all week. It was a very big game and to have one chance at it, knockout, and my last one meant that it meant an awful lot. People get surprised at the fact that I got nervous, but the fear of failure and not performing drove me throughout my career and, I believe, contributed positively in helping me achieve what I did."

One paper afterwards, in comparing Johns and Lynagh's contribution, likened the big Irish lock to a 'hewer of wood and a drawer of water', whereas Lynagh was 'the engineer who built the dam and controlled the flow which washed Wasps away'. It was no doubt a pleasure for Paddy to play that less glamorous but nonetheless essential role in facilitating the supreme craftsman in their midst to fashion such a handsome victory.

Sella afterwards spoke of his love both for the game and for Saracens and Johns vouches for how the superstars all mucked in, blended well with the long-serving clubmen, gave their best in the cause and contributed to the superb spirit in the squad. The players had proved their commitment to the cause even in times of adversity and ultimately won some silverware for the sizeable following of genuine fans, whose support was the cement which held it all together.

"There was a certain geographical divide when we moved to Watford, but you could definitely compare Saracens to Dungannon. The players and supporters did mix together and there were no barriers between us. After the final was over, there were all the usual formalities, aftermatch speeches and stuff, but then we got buses back to Vicarage Road and were able to parade the cup in front of all the fans who had gathered there. The support was tremendous and there was a big family feeling. Then we all went to this dodgy night club called Eros and really started to celebrate!" "I was very, very proud," says Pienaar. "The club had not won anything for 127 years and it was a superb achievement for the club, the fans and of course, the players."

"That Tetley Cup win was definitely the highlight of Paddy's time at Saracens" recalls his mum. "Nigel Wray, with typical thought and generosity, organized a champagne breakfast for the players' relatives and buses to the game. When we got to Twickenham, he had arranged for a free bar to be laid of for us. That was the day that Paul and Richard Wallace's mum, Greta, introduced me to Pimms, so I was in high spirits! I remember pulling Nigel Wray's mum, a wonderful lady of 80 years of age, onto the pitch at the end and us dancing around together on the Twickenham turf. It is a day which I will never, ever forget. Nigel then threw a wonderful party the following day attended by all the players and those close to them. We all enjoyed ourselves immensely."

So was this Saracens outfit truly a great side, or a good side with a great Cup run? Even though he denies that the fez boys had to win a trophy that season to justify their existence and the whole Wray project, Paddy plumps for the former. "I think it was a great side" he answers. "We lost only a couple of games that season. We won a lot of close games, came from behind to win matches and weren't far off doing the double. Then if you've got players like Lynagh...."

Talking to him, you get the impression that along with Pienaar, Lynagh would quickly find himself in the Johns rugby Hall of Fame. "He was brilliant" Paddy agrees. "He could control a game so well. A world class player. Another big game for us that year was against Newcastle in the league. Lynagh won it for us in the last minute with a drop goal. He could just turn a game on its head. Michael was the best player I've ever played with. His amazing stats speak for themselves. He directed the show and did everything with a great composure. People found him hard to tackle. But, in spite of all the assurance he showed on the pitch, he was in no way arrogant off it. Like everyone else, he fitted in very well."

When Johns speaks of his fellow Sarries stars of that era, it is clear that he is discussing friends as well as assessing some of the world's finest players of his generation. The warmth with which he remembers his colleagues and the grin on his face as he relates anecdote after anecdote tells a tale about the happy days which Paddy spent at Saracens. As well as being superstars, it is reassuring to know that this was a group of ordinary guys who played the same sort of pranks as go on in any other team.

"Michael always tried to make fun of me when we played games of touch in training, but anytime I did manage to get close enough when he had the ball, I really made him pay. I'd drag him into the mud, especially on cold, wet days. He used to hate the rain and snow and was always pleased when Francois suggested that we train on the astroturf or in the gym rather than go on the pitch. We'd always meet at 9.50am for training at 10 and he would sit beside the window looking out at the weather and dropping hints that the pitch would be unplayable."

The other Aussie ace Constable got the same treatment as his illustrious compatriot Lynagh. "I managed to survive a very muddy night at Stevenson Park without getting a spot of mud on me in training" relates Ryan. "I was standing at the side of a ruck inspecting the forwards when suddenly someone came in, flattened me and then rolled me around a bit. It was, of course, Paddy and, as he got up and left me in a fairly sorry state he said 'mate, I thought you were looking a little too clean there'! "There is no doubt that Michael worked very hard at his game though" Paddy continues. "He practised his kicking religiously after every session. Often I'd have stayed behind to field the balls, which would have helped improve my catching at kick-offs and so forth." Two model pros then. Sella was another.

"Philippe had a lot of natural ability, speed and aggression. He wasn't big, but was very wiry and committed, a great tackler. The man was simply a great competitor. He was 35 when he finished with Saracens and he could have eased up earlier, but he didn't. No-one could suggest that he came to England for an 'easy pension'. Both he and Michael went out with victories in the Cup final at Twickenham and then in their final home game, against Northampton in the Premiership. That was fitting, but it wasn't just fate which ensured it. They played big parts themselves in those games being won."

As with Bracken, Johns was initially a little sheepish around Sella as a result of past misdemeanours, but this pair also became good friends. "It was the match between Ireland and France in 1993 where we first ran across each other" Paddy reveals. "Philippe was at the bottom of a ruck and I went to ruck him out, but he caught the sole of my foot. He's quite a strong man for his size and the result was a sort of freeze-frame situation, with him looking up and me looking down. I'd already caught him with one foot though, so I was a bit nervous meeting him at Saracens for the first time, just like Bracken!"

Johns' admiration for Bracken too is clear. He is at pains to point out that, whenever the injury-prone Sarries pivot went head-to-head with his perennial England rival Matt Dawson, "Kyran came out on top every time." Indeed his enthusiasm for talking about members of that Saracens side reveals how highly he rated his colleagues. The previous chapter contains his warm insights into some of them as people and he also has no shortage of praise for them as players.

"Our fullback Gavin Johnson used to get really pissed off with the weather and he could afford to be very laidback at training because he was aerobically very very fit. But when it came to matchday, he could certainly perform and also proved a very good place-kicker when Michael wasn't there. Richie Wallace was a very elusive runner, very quick and quite under-rated. He got injured in his last year at Saracens and unfortunately his career was cut short. Nice fella too, probably the sort of guy you'd introduce to your sister.

"His brother Paul really came through to make a big mark on the 1997 Lions tour and playing in England probably helped his game a lot as it did for the rest of us, but perhaps in the end he stayed on a bit too long at Saracens. In my time there, he was always in the team, but subsequently found himself in and out of the side, competing with up and coming English players in Julian White and David Flatman. He'd also lost his Ireland place after Twickenham 2000.

"Then he got his bad ankle break playing against Ulster at Ravenhill and spent most of last year on the sidelines either side of finally returning to Leinster. He has also become something of a marked man with referees and tends to get penalised very readily at the scrummage. Referees undoubtedly talk among themselves, so I'm sure he's very closely watched at scrum-time. The media have also highlighted the issue which further increases the scrutiny. But Paul is still fairly young for a prop and I wouldn't write him off yet. I think he still has a chance of getting more involved again at international level. I was surprised at the way he came through on the 1997 Lions tour in that, being Irish, he was probably more at the back of the management's minds than the front when he went to South Africa.

"Paul had a reputation of being scatter-brained and was always late for training. He loved to socialise off the field, but got so nervous before games that he'd be sick. But he was a very strong prop and has often had bigger opponents in trouble in the scrum. Our other prop, Roberto Grau was a typical Argentinian in that he simply loved scrummaging. He'd have done it all day if he could. He was very strong, with a real Latin temperament and was fiercely patriotic. Playing for his country was a huge source of pride to him."

Paddy's second row partner in the Cup winning team, Danny Grewcock, has become a bigger name in the intervening years than in his early days with Saracens following a move from Coventry, but Johns says he could always see his potential. "Danny was naturally very strong and worked very hard at his game, so those were two good ingredients for success. He came on well at Saracens and I think we were good for each other. I've been lucky down through my career in terms of the type and calibre of second rows I've played with."

One man after Paddy's own heart in terms of not being an attention-seeker and one whom, consequently, he has a lot of time for is Lions flanker Richard Hill, so often and for so long the unsung member of the England back row. "Richard's a West Country boy and has never been affected by the limelight. A real grafter, he did an awful lot of unseen work for us but he also has huge ability. He is definitely good enough to play all three backrow positions at the highest level, which says it all. Personally, I liked him at No 7.

"Pienaar and Hill were top flankers, but even in such distinguished company, Tony Diprose also managed to make his mark on the backrow and as captain of the team. He's a very skilful No 8 with great hands, almost unnaturally good hands in fact. He was a Saracens man through and through and captained the England A team for years. If he'd been Scottish, Welsh or Irish, he might have had a lengthy international career, but he came along in an era with some very strong contenders for the English back row."

In addition to Diprose, there were other unsung clubmen who represented the old Saracens soul and, Johns admits, were the cement which helped hold the whole multi-national package together. "Take Steve Ravenscroft. Very consistent, very passionate about Saracens. He knew the club inside out before any of us came. People like him played a big part in integrating us into the ways of the club. Matt Singer, Greg Botterman and Andy Lee were other good players who contributed to us having a strong squad."

It was always going to be difficult for a side shorn of Lynagh and Sella to maintain the high of Twickenham and Paddy admits that things did tail off a little in his third and final season at Sarries. One man who in ways came to symbolise the slide was temperamental French flyhalf Alain Penaud, the player given the unenviable task of trying to fill the void left by Lynagh's retirement.

"Alain was typically French, in that he could be very fired up one minute and simply shrug indifferently the next. He had big boots to fill and I think both he and his wife missed France. He did seem to play well though any time his parents were over! It was going to be a season of consolidation for Saracens, but in the end we didn't do too badly, finishing high enough in the Premiership to qualify for the following season's European Cup."

As always, Paddy gave his best, but had plenty on his plate as Ireland captain through a busy international season. And, long before it was over, he had also begun to negotiate a return home to the emerald isle.

22. CAPTAIN OF IRELAND

When Kirsty answered the phone in her Enfield home one April evening in 1998 and heard Donal Lenihan's voice on the other end of the line, her heart sank. The Ireland manager would only be ringing if there was bad news to impart. Such phonecalls have a purpose and, more often than not, the outcome would not be a happy one. Could he speak to Paddy, please? She handed over the phone with trepidation.

This was how you'd hear you were dropped. Didn't make sense though as Paddy had just had his best ever season in the green jersey and was looking forward to a Cup final appearance with Saracens. His place in the national team seemed at its safest in a long time. But Kirsty had been around it long enough to expect nothing, to fear the worst. For once, she needn't have worried. Paddy's first Ireland captain and now the national team manager was not, on this occasion, to be the bearer of bad tidings. Quite the opposite in fact.

"Donal explained that Keith Wood wouldn't be going to South Africa and that they'd like me to be captain. Not the sort of thing you're asked every day. Naturally, I was delighted to accept. I'm not sure if I even knew that Woody was unavailable but, if I did, it certainly didn't cross my mind that I would be chosen as captain. Although it was a massive honour, the Ireland captaincy was something which I had never aspired to as such.

"There are things which you can directly influence in rugby, like how well you play and then, by extension, selection for the next game by making it virtually impossible for the selectors to leave you out. But captaincy is not like that. It is completely in the gift of others and is something which is granted rather than achieved. You can set your sights on certain targets in the game and work towards them, but it would be madness to ever say 'I intend to become captain of Ireland within the next three years' or whatever. That will always come down totally to the opinion of others and depend on factors outside your control. Things which will come into the equation include the calibre of the other contenders and what the coach or selectors are looking for in a captain."

"At the time, Paddy was a senior player" explains Lenihan. "He was someone we knew we could rely on to lead by example. He had the experience and the respect and his commitment and workrate were an example to every player. He justified our faith by proving a fantastic captain for us both on and off the pitch."

The chance may simply never arise if your peak period happens to coincide with that of an established captain who has become a virtual institution in a set-up by virtue of their distinguished leadership. Mick Galwey, for example, has been the undisputed main man in Munster for years, while with David Irwin and Willie Anderson around, no-one else was going to get a look in with Ulster in their halcyon days.

"So, while I dreamt of playing for Ireland and had that as a very definite goal, I never dreamt of captaining Ireland. When it came, I hadn't been waiting for it or hoping for it, but obviously I was pleased to be asked and honoured to accept. I was fairly hyper for the rest of the evening and couldn't readily get to sleep that night. Donal had asked me to keep it to myself for a couple of days until it was announced, which was difficult, but soon it all came out and the phone then started ringing."

So Paddy was pretty chuffed and, as well as being proud and pleased for him, Kirsty felt that, although the Irish captaincy would, obviously, be a challenge, it would also "bring out the best in him. It would be something which he would take very seriously and I felt he would thrive on the responsibility." His mum agrees: "I remember him ringing and being all thrilled to bits. I was surprised, but we were all on a high. It was a tremendous honour and responsibility, one I knew which he would take very seriously. Pienaar had been a great role model for him at Saracens so I thought that would help too."

There was some surprise in the media at Johns' appointment, largely because he had never been the type to push himself forward into the limelight and, consequently, was not, in some quarters, considered to be cut out for captaincy. He and the extroverted Wood were certainly chalk and cheese in terms of people's perception of how they handled themselves and, perhaps, their wider public profile. In any case, however, Paddy would dispute whether what could, for want of a better term, be dubbed the charisma factor, should really come into the equation anyway when considering a captaincy contender's credentials. Johns accepts that we live in a media age, that the Irish captain is largely the public face of the team, that certain responsibilities go with the job and that interviews are, at worst, a necessary evil.

"Whoever is captain will automatically have various duties off the pitch and that includes going to press conferences and doing interviews, but I don't believe that how well a guy is perceived to do that side of things should ever be a consideration when picking a captain. I wouldn't have been chosen for my public relations skills but mainly, I suspect, because they needed a new captain as Woody wasn't going on tour and I was one of the senior, established players at the time.

"Luckily for me, they decided that I was the man to do the job, but it's up to Warren Gatland to really explain the reasoning behind my appointment. It had been a good season for me, both in terms of how I played for Ireland and as part of a successful Saracens side which, by then, had reached the Cup final. I had captained teams up through school, including the First XV, and had done the job the odd time for Saracens, so it wasn't as if I had never skippered a side, but equally I hadn't a huge amount of adult experience at it."

With Johns, aged 30, now the senior statesman in the side following Nick Popplewell's retirement, Gatland had no hesitation in turning to the Saracens lock after regular skipper Wood had been given permission to miss the tour due to fatigue. "He has honesty, great experience and is very well respected by the players" said Gatland at the time. "Every time Paddy has pulled on the Irish jersey, he's given 100 percent of total commitment, and that's the sort of quality I'm looking for."

Johns too had had a long taxing season with club and country, but there is no doubt that the move to England had helped him mature from the decent international who left the emerald isle into a world-rated all-round forward fit to lead Ireland into the backyard of the world champions. Even his lack of captaincy experience at adult level didn't count against Johns as he got the nod over the likes of London Irish skipper Conor O'Shea, Eric Elwood, who had taken over in several matches during the season when Wood left the action early, and Munster's Mick Galwey. Like Popplewell and Wood, the latter's immediate predecessors as Irish captain, Jim Staples and Niall Hogan, were not in the tour party.

A rugby captain lies somewhere between a soccer skipper and a cricket captain in terms of the importance of the role and the level of responsibility or degree of decision-making which goes with it. In association football, you'll get the odd inspirational leader, but generally the captaincy is no big deal, whereas in cricket, the captain has to be strategist, tactician and mathematician as well as Mr Motivator and man-manager. The rugby captain is more of a revered figure than the soccer skipper and they have more weight to carry, from responsibility for all liaison with the referee to deciding whether or not to go for goal from a particular penalty award.

"My view is that a captain should lead from the front, more by what they do than what they say. They should set an example by working harder than anyone else, try to instil a positive attitude in the team and motivate others. You also have certain decisions to make like, for example, whether to kick at goal. That will be influenced by the scoreboard situation, the amount of time remaining, where the penalty has been awarded and how good your kicker is. To some extent, the kicker will also have an input as to whether they fancy it or not. Occasionally, if a guy misses a couple and there's another capable kicker in the side, you may have to make a call on whether you give someone else a go."

Johns values the presence on the pitch of a few tried and trusted lieutenants to turn to, especially because "you can't control the game from the second row or see all that goes on. I've always said that Nos 8, 9 and 10 are the key decision-makers and, although you must take into account the credentials of the individuals both in those positions and elsewhere in the team, I feel that, in an ideal world, the captain would be one of that trio.

"The outhalf is your general and, in my opinion, should theoretically at least be an obvious captaincy contender but, on the other hand, some people would say that the outhalf, particularly if he also takes the place-kicks, has enough on his plate and that the load should be shared around. You can argue either way and, as I say, it does also depend on the individuals involved. Anyway, whatever position the captain comes from, he is likely to have a confident and capable figure in at least one of those positions, No 8 or halfback, to act as his eyes and ears. The guys in those positions are used to making decisions and controlling a game, so the likelihood is that they won't be afraid to contribute. Chances are that at least one of them will also be fairly experienced."

Although Paddy was not afraid to consult his colleagues, he would equally recognise the danger of captaincy by committee and, retrospectively, caution that a captain can even undermine themselves by adopting too democratic a style of leadership. A players' man to a fault, Johns never became even a little semi-detached from the rest of the team in spite of his status as skipper.

"I always felt that I didn't want to distance myself from the rest of the team and tried to ensure that there would be no gap develop between the captain and the other players. At the time, I felt that that was the way to go but, with hindsight, maybe sometimes that approach allowed too much licence for people to speak, not necessarily out of turn as such, but too many too often and not just when they had something worthwhile to say."

Paddy never believed in talking for the sake of it or being long-winded in either his pre-match team-talks or his post-match press conferences, which, in the words of one journalist, used to contain plenty of 'pregnant pauses'. In both arenas, he preferred to be a man of relatively few, but well-chosen, words. There are some captains who would be bouncing off the walls, using colourful and emotive language to get their team pumped up, but his approach would have been more quiet and under-stated than that of the classic whipper-uppers. He generally spoke quietly, in a considered manner, and then went out and led by example. No-one would have been in any doubt that he was prepared to go out and run through brick walls for the team.

"I always planned what I wanted to say and when, not just immediately before the match, but at other stages of the build-up, for example mentioning particular players we wanted to target or whatever. I tried not to say stuff just for the sake of it, or fall into the habit of empty rhetoric."

One time when other players recall Paddy speaking movingly before a match prior to his stint as captain was the occasion of his 40th cap, against Wales at Lansdowne Road in 1998. He read from a piece of paper, on which he had painstakingly pieced together what he wanted to say. But, although the words were written down in advance rather than spilt out spontaneously, this was no empty sermon. Silence fell and hardened international forwards were moved to tears as Paddy told the tale of how, as a terrace teenager, this was what he had dreamt of and aspired to. There was hardly a dry eye in the house as this intensely private man bared his soul.

"Pat Whelan the manager had asked me to say something, so I spent around half an hour thinking about it and jotted a few things down. I didn't want to leave anything out and I knew I would have to read it out. I chose not to stand up. It was harder than expected and I struggled to get the words out, but in the end I did manage to say what I felt. Most of the players in the dressing room could relate to what I was saying, for they felt exactly the same way. There was a common theme they could empathise with and I just wanted the guys to understand what it all meant."

Interestingly, Wood, a man who has both captained and played under Johns and, with his extrovert manner is himself seen as an inspirational leader, is quick to point to how Paddy also inspires those around him, albeit perhaps in a different way. "If ever there was a guy whose Irishness shone through in the dressing room, it's Paddy" insists Wood. "If you were ever in any doubt about just how much the whole thing means, all you needed to do was just look at Paddy and listen to him. He was always totally up for it and afterwards his body would just be a mass of ice packs. He put himself through incredible work. I have all the time in the world for Paddy Johns."

On a lighter note, an early insight into Paddy's facility for rallying the troops is provided by the Dungannon Royal magazine's report on the school First XV's tour to Yorkshire in 1986. The tour notes record: "The first match of the tour, against Bradford Grammar, took place at 4.00pm. Patrick Johns delivered a rousing and uplifting team talk, the closing speech of which I feel I must quote: "I see you standing like greyhounds in their traps, straining to get going. The game's about to start. Follow your captain and when I give the signal cry 'God for Harry! Dungannon and Saint Keith!'. Thus uplifted the Dungannon boys took the field in high spirits." Uh huh. It's all about knowing what makes your team tick!

A good guy for looking after individuals in the pastoral care aspect of the captaincy and loyal to his players, but Paddy was always a reluctant public face of Irish rugby. It just wasn't his style to seek the limelight and he generally felt uncomfortable in it. Apart from feeling that he perhaps occasionally allowed a bit too much of a free-for-all environment with people chipping in their views right, left and centre, Johns is reasonably content that he did a fairly good job and generally got things more right than wrong during his time as captain. Reasonably enough, however, he points out that it is for others to pass objective judgement on his style of leadership, his strengths and weaknesses as a captain and his success or otherwise in the role.

"As a captain, Paddy was outstanding," Lenihan enthuses. "I think he was influenced by Pienaar and Saracens which was a very close knit unit with a family atmosphere."

"Paddy knew just what was needed," asserts David Humphreys. "When you are a captain with other captains on the team, they can help you make the decisions. You have the benefit of their experience and obviously he sees things differently in the second or back row than I do at 10. As captain, Paddy could say the necessary quiet word, or gee people up. Whatever was required."

"He was meticulous as a captain and concerned himself with every aspect and detail of the job" says Allen Clarke. "He was also a good integrator between the players and the management. Both of those things were particularly evident on the South African tour of 1998 and helped make it such a good environment."

"When Paddy was captain of Ireland, he was one of the best captains I ever played under" insists Jeremy Davidson. "The amount of respect which he commanded was incredible and no-one dissented from his wishes. He had a real aura about him. He was a man of not many words but, when he spoke, he meant it. No-one had to be told twice. If he called everyone into a huddle, we'd almost break into a run to make sure we didn't get there last. He wouldn't ask anyone to do anything he wouldn't do himself but when he did ask, he wanted action."

"Paddy is great from a ref's perspective," adds Alain Rolland. "It's a totally different game from player to ref, and your job is so much easier with good captains. If players were getting narky, you could always speak to Paddy and he'd have the necessary words."

He is content that he always did his best in leading the team and is also adamant that, overall, he dealt fully and fairly with the media and, while not perhaps enjoying them, always carried out the duties required of him in that regard. At the very least, they were accepted as a necessary evil. One thing which he would do differently if he had his time over again, however, would be making himself more available for flash interviews straight after the final whistle of internationals.

"There were a few times that RTE tried to get a word with me as captain as we came off the pitch and I pushed them away because, at the time, I was just so disappointed or emotional or couldn't have thought of anything to say. One of them was the Five Nations game against France in 1999 when we lost in such agonising circumstances. I thought it better to say nothing than maybe go on and make a fool of myself by saying stupid things. But, on reflection, I should have done the interview. Television is a pretty powerful medium and, these days, people expect to hear reaction from those involved in a big sporting event as soon as it is over. You have to find a way of dealing with that particular responsibility even though some days it will be harder than others. It's never much fun to have a microphone stuck under your nose straight after a defeat, though players can handle it better the more mature they become and, as captain, it's something which you should be able to do."

Paddy has always been seen as a good guy of the game so, in general, people were pleased for him and it would be fair to say that, at the time of his appointment, the media were no exception. Even the traditionally hard to please and occasionally controversial Dublin Sundays. "The bulk of the squad picks itself as does its captain" wrote the Sunday Times Irish rugby correspondent ahead of the South African tour. "Paddy Johns is an outstanding player and a splendid individual and deserves the honour."

Although he was never first in the queue of volunteers to be interviewed and seldom provided a juicy soundbite or controversial comment, Johns had a reputation of being civil, courteous and obliging enough. At times though during his tenure, the relationship with the media became slightly strained and prickly, with the natural suspicion which governed Paddy on one side leading to a degree of frustration and resentment on the other. Sure, press people recognised that he was a modest man and a reluctant hero, not the shallow and self-seeking sort who saw himself as a superstar and would take every opportunity for personal promotion. It wasn't in his nature to fill notebooks and talk until the tape ran out in the dictaphone. He didn't talk for the sake of talking, and never used a sentence where a syllable would suffice, but what occasionally annoyed the hacks was the perception that he was exceptionally wary and cagey and guarded, rather than simply not having a lot to say.

On occasions, some felt that he hid behind the quiet man image to avoid getting into debates which he didn't want to, calling the bluff of the journalists by deliberately interpreting questions at face value and giving a more simplistic and narrow answer than was being sought. One example is the first press conference on that tour of 1998, when he was asked by a South African journalist about 'your record against the Springboks'. Instead of reflecting on the weight of history and Ireland's failure to ever win an international against South Africa down through the decades and getting into the whys and wherefores, Paddy simply pointed out that he hadn't faced the

Springboks before and was looking forward to it. Pressed again, he conceded there was room for improvement in Ireland's record.

The travelling Irish press corps loved the bit of devil in his answer, but it wasn't the only instance of him fielding a question in that sort of way and he occasionally made journalists want to wring his neck. They were never quite sure whether he was simply answering in good faith, or actually being evasive and trying to be that bit cleverer than them. Johns was seen by many in the media as lacking charisma, but the odd conspiracy theorist would have gone further and considered him calculating, cussed and contrary, a man who viewed the press with a degree of distaste and the interface with them as a battleground. Although guarded in what he said and deliberately diplomatic at one level, he could occasionally be argumentative or slightly awkward by not simply going along with a question which he didn't see as particularly relevant, or not just providing a trite answer and moving on.

There was also an unfortunate perception that Paddy managed to attend a lower percentage of press conferences after internationals than some of the other Irish captains of the modern era. It got to the stage that one or two disaffected hacks used to speculate while waiting for the Irish delegation to arrive for their interrogation as to whether there'd be a captain as well as coach and manager. Perception is a powerful force and, in the small and perhaps conceited community which the Irish rugby media constitutes, whispers and rumours and accusations can grow legs and spread relatively easily. Some were determined to portray Paddy as being reluctant to front up and face the music.

At the best of times, neither he nor Gatland were all that talkative so, compared to the modern Wood-O'Sullivan regime, Irish press conferences could in those days, be fairly barren territory for disgruntled journos with space to fill and deadlines to meet and looking for an angle. Once or twice, Johns' absence was explained on the grounds that he had been selected for the random drugs test. To one or two it all seemed too cosy and convenient. Maybe he was even in cahoots with the doping people?

"You guys are impossible" a pained Paddy chides, shaking his head sorrowfully, but with a trace of mild amusement. "No wonder a player would be wary! It was never that big a deal one way or other. If I had to do a drugs test, I trotted off to do that and the same with the press conferences. I can't say I ever really looked forward to them or enjoyed them, but nor did I seek to avoid them or lie awake at night worrying about them. One thing I can say is that my number seemed to come up for the drugs test more than most guys. I never got the luck of the draw. People might think I wasn't fussed on the press conferences, but going off to try and provide a urine sample was hardly an exciting alternative!"

In Paddy's defence, this writer can point to at least two instances, as the preface to this book records, where he acted beyond the call of duty in furnishing me with quotes in advance of internationals, the first of them at a stage when I had never even spoken to him before.

It was the night before the All Blacks match of 1997, my first game as Rugby Correspondent of the News Letter, and he even delayed or interrupted dinner to take my call at a time when he was under absolutely no obligation to do so and could easily have refused. At a personal level, this writer has always found him obliging when it comes to interview requests and both authors are very pleased with how forthcoming he has been with us in the course of writing this book.

That said, Paddy is the most meticulous of men and he has been painfully precise throughout the process, and it was trying at times to get chapter drafts back heavily annotated with minor adjustments in tiny handwriting in several colours of ink. It may or may not surprise some that he has proved more fussy to write for than David Humphreys, a loquacious and immensely articulate man with a precise legal mind and very clear sense of how he wants to come across. One of the authors has ghost-written 1,200-word columns for Humph during the latter stages of Ulster's European Cup run and, although that was a different exercise to this, the propensity of the player to seek small changes has been greater in Paddy's case. Much of it though has related to his sensitivity to the feelings of others.

How come though, given the respect and affection in which he is held by many journalists as well the wider rugby fraternity, that problems may have arisen, with some suspicions on one side and perceptions of awkwardness, even evasiveness, on the other? A leading rugby-writer, who has covered Ireland at home and overseas for a good number of years, differentiates between the private and public sides of Johns with an exaggerated example.

"Paddy Johns is the sort of guy who would always be civil enough and polite enough to say 'good morning' to you, but then add 'and that's off the record'. He was always paranoid about being misquoted and never gave too much away in an interview" says the journalist. "There was a recurring joke among some of the press corps that if you asked Paddy Johns how he was feeling he would politely refer you to the manager of the day. An exaggeration, perhaps, but nevertheless he will never be numbered among rugby's great interviewees. He would sooner remove his finger nails with pliers than face the tape recorder."

It isn't just the media though; he simply isn't one for strutting the stage. Invited back to his old school, Dungannon Royal, where he became the youngest ever main speaker at Speech Day, he "got on fine" according to his mum, "but would rather have being going out to face the All Blacks!"

Part of it is simply a reflection of the way Paddy is, essentially a person rather than a performer. But being stung in his earlier days when, by his own admission, he was probably too open and genuine for his own good, taught him to be wary. "Once you've been misquoted, or misrepresented, you learn to always choose your words carefully and leave as little room as possible for anyone seeking to pursue some agenda or make mischief."

You reckon he wouldn't care much for the notion of journalistic licence. One article we came across in his scrapbook, a preview of Ireland versus England in 1997, started "England's giant pack were warned last night: 'We'll beat you up in 80 minutes of Lansdowne hell'." Wonder what the chances are that those were genuine verbatim quotes! Much of the confrontational language being used in the article as a whole seem a step removed from the Johns way.

"I suppose the first time that I suffered at the hands of the media was back in 1989 when some inaccurate reporting cost me any chance I might have had of making Ireland's summer tour to North America. That was when I was still in Newcastle and my mum was sending over all the food, including big whopping horse tablet vitamins. Through taking too many of those and too much protein powder to try and keep weight on, I developed vitamin-induced hepatitis, known as hyper vitaminosis, a condition which caused jaundice. But it was reported in at least one paper that I had Hepatitis B, which is contagious. It wasn't the case and we had even been vaccinated against that as dental students, but once that appeared in the press, any hopes of me going on the tour were gone."

"I'm sure it was ignorance rather than anything more sinister which led to what appeared in the paper but, even if it was just a mistake, it still had the same detrimental effect for me and I was angry about it" says Paddy. As such a thorough and precise guy himself, professional in all that he does, sloppy and inaccurate journalism annoys Johns as much as vindictive or malicious journalism. If doctors or dentists are careless and make mistakes, people suffer physical consequences, which may be grave or even fatal. Journalists may not, by contrast, be dealing with matters of life and death, but they should still be mindful of their potential to cause hurt and do damage to careers and reputations. Check the facts at least.

"I think first and foremost that players want the truth. You can generally accept constructive criticism, particularly if you respect the knowledge and integrity of the person making it, but if something is deviated or twisted or inaccurate or downright untrue, that is a different matter. As my career went on, I probably read less stuff in the papers, though a lot of cuttings were kept to have for when I hung up my boots. The fact that I do have scrapbooks and boxes of cut out articles is probably an indication that I by no means regarded the entire media with contempt. Men like Ned van Esbeck were always very honourable indeed. But players are human and can be hurt. A lot of the rugby-writers are decent guys with whom I feel that I got on pretty well at a personal level. You get the odd one who would give the profession a bad name, but people generally find out who they are and steer clear of them."

Although there are now more and more ex-players popping up in the media, either as analysts or as frontline correspondents, Paddy declines to make a distinction purely based on the level to which a person has played the game. "Sure, a rugby-writer who has played at international level may have a better idea of what it feels like to be there, but I don't see it as a pre-requisite. Respect still has to be earned and qualities such as integrity and writing ability, thoroughness and a good knowledge of the game are important. Players have also been shafted by ex-players, who are sometimes perhaps trying to be controversial to justify their fee, so you really just have to take each writer or broadcaster as you find them. Sometimes past players are actually less readily forgiven by present players on the basis that they should know better.

"One thing which taught me not to take too much to heart what was written was looking at the ratings which some papers give players after internationals. The scores vary so widely from paper to paper for the very same match. Of course giving players marks out of 10 can never be an exact science, but to do it properly, you would need to watch the tape 15 times and track each player. So it's all a fairly superficial exercise."

Given that Johns instinctively shunned the spotlight and given the higher profile which would inevitably come with being Ireland captain, did he or Kirsty have any fears that their lives could become a bit of a misery as a result of his appointment? Rugby is far removed from football in terms of media intrusiveness into players' personal lives and, anyway, Johns was hardly a guy who was likely to have too many skeletons in the cupboard, but still. It was going to change things even a little, surely? "I didn't notice much difference in the lead-up to the South African tour apart from, obviously, a few more interviews in the aftermath of my appointment. There weren't really any other pre-tour appearances which the captain had to make as far as I can remember."

Quite a few biographical type features appeared at the time, with references to Kirsty and the kids, some rehearsing of the story of how he and his future wife had met in Newfoundland and at least one picture with Christopher on his shoulders. But none of it was intrusive, all nice cleancut stuff about the family man, the gentle giant. There was no desire for dirt-digging on behalf of the press or the media and Paddy never got the sort of rough ride which English captains Will Carling and Lawrence Dallaglio were subjected to on occasions.

"I'm not saying that anyone is fair game for whatever they get in the press, but Carling and Dallaglio would have courted attention more than someone like Martin Johnson who, apart from a few incidents on the pitch, has never really featured much in the media, certainly not in terms of his personal life.

"An Irish captain in England would, obviously, be very little noticed compared to the English captain, and the Irish media is substantially different in that there isn't that tabloid mentality which builds sportsmen up into celebrities and then knocks them down. In any case, rugby isn't a big tabloid sport. I wouldn't have been high profile enough to sell papers so, thankfully, was always left alone. No-one had any real reason to go out to get me and there wouldn't have been too much to interest the papers anyway. I was never a big party animal or anything, pretty boring really in their terms!" he adds, with a wicked grin.

So there was never any danger for Paddy and Kirsty of fame and fortune making life unbearable. He still didn't seek the spotlight, or even go out of his way to cash in on the captaincy by using his new status to chase money-making promotional appearances. In spite of being an Irish international, becoming captain of his country and ultimately getting to 50 caps and beyond, Johns never became conceited and often struggled to come to terms with any notion that he was an icon, a hero, a role model.

Before going to Saracens, Richie Wallace had regaled him with stories that pin-up players like Kyran Bracken were bombarded with knickers in the post. Paddy remains sceptical about the veracity of those tales to this day and assures us that he has still to receive his first pair!

23. CIRCLING THE WAGONS

Bruising battles. Trials and tribulations. Under siege and battening down the hatches. Claim and counter-claim. The uncompromising captain who never took a backward step. Ugly scenes and damage limitation. Grudge games and grudging respect. And yet, in spite of the defeats and adversity, the happiest and most united of touring parties and a trip remembered with great affection by all who were on it because of the superb spirit in the camp. Ireland's South African tour of 1998.

What a baptism for Johns as captain of his country. It was a tough tour in so many ways and big Paddy was never far from the heart of the action. He saw it as his responsibility to be in the frontline and never shirked. Whether he caused some of the trouble is a matter of opinion, but he certainly didn't run away from any of it. If anyone wanted to hit an Irish player, they had to hit the brave warrior in the No 4 jersey first. Those who did generally regretted it.

Right from Ireland's arrival in the country, Paddy's insists that they felt despised, isolated and under siege. The South African media showed little respect and saw them simply as cannon-fodder for what was a very strong Springbok side. "We got off the plane in Cape Town and went straight into our first press conference. I remember all the squad sitting at the back of the room, with myself, Warren and Donal at the front. My first impression was that they were very patronising and dismissive, that they saw Ireland as a bit of an irrelevance in international rugby rather than a team to be treated with respect. I resented their attitude right from the start. To some extent, that set the tone for the tour.

"In general, when it came to rugby, I found the South Africans to be very arrogant people. They were quite insular, but perhaps that was partly a consequence of the years of sporting isolation. The ban during the apartheid era may have had an effect in turning them into a very tight-knit community with a bit of a siege mentality and they did have a very good team when we went there in 1998, but I certainly found a lack of humility.

"It was a difficult tour in many ways. What with the security situation and so forth, we had a fairly restrictive environment. Prison wouldn't be quite the right word for it, but the constraints didn't make for the most pleasant of existences. On top of that, the South African media seemed determined to get on our backs, one way or another. At the start, they were patronising and wrote us off, then after the first Test they called us cheats and labelled their own team soft. Naas Botha, the former Springbok outhalf, had a rugby programme on one of the South African television channels and I remember us being laid into on it. We were being attacked on all sides it seemed and there was a feeling of needing to circle the wagons. I was determined we weren't going to be pushed around and should stand up to any attempted intimidation on the pitch. I think we did that alright" he concludes with a grim smile.

Perhaps the South African rugby community had itself been feeling the heat with the critical eye of the world being back on it for some time in light of the failure to build on the opportunities which had been offered by the World Cup and the Mandela-Pienaar alliance. The tour had actually been in considerable doubt thanks to the antics of controversial South African rugby supremo, Louis Luyt, as the progress made towards a more inclusive regime in Pienaar's time seemed to dissipate by the day.

Pienaar was long since in exile in England having been disgracefully burned by the rotten rugby regime back home and South African rugby was in something of a state of turmoil off the field, again finding itself ostracised in the wider world. Paddy says that he and Francois spoke little and seldom about the rugby politics of the rainbow republic, but acknowledges that the World Cup winning captain felt he was pushed out. Things were volatile in South Africa at the time and we were aware that the tour was in some doubt. It had been a long hard season at home, but it would have been a big disappointment for us if it had been cancelled.

"When we got there, there still seemed to be no great degree of integration and we were quite shocked by the fact that the (black) people who helped with our bags and drove them from destination to destination a day or two ahead of us making the same journeys by air, who chose to sleep in their vans to save some money for their families, were quite nervous and reluctant about coming into the hotels. Rala would have gone out and brought them in for breakfast, lunch too by the end of the tour, and they virtually became part of the party. He'd also have given them drinks, Mars bars, bananas and so forth for the long drives. There appeared to be little real interest in the rugby among the black community and most who did take an interest appeared to be supporting us."

But, following Luyt's resignation, the trip was finally given the green light by South African Sports Minister, Steve Tshwete, and, when the tour party of 34 was announced on the same day that Johns was revealed as the new captain, the names of three of the four Irishmen who had made such a contribution to the Lions triumph in South Africa the previous summer were missing. Paddy's former Dungannon second row partner Jeremy Davidson had elected to miss the tour even before suffering another setback on the long road to recovery from a serious knee injury while, like Wood, a jaded Eric Miller had been excused duty. The fourth, Paddy's clubmate Paul Wallace, was in the squad along with both his brothers, fellow Saracen Richard and the versatile and extremely promising Garryowen loose forward David, one of seven uncapped players in the squad.

The youngest Wallace was actually one of three backrow rookies, along with St Mary's hitman Trevor Brennan and former South African Sevens star Dion O'Cuinneagain, who had earned a trip to his homeland courtesy of some eye-catching performances for Sale. Terenure pivot Derek Hegarty and Clontarf hooker Bernard Jackman have remained uncapped, but both new props taken on the tour came through, Justin Fitzpatrick making his Test debut during the trip and John Hayes proving a great investment for the future. Like Hegarty and Jackman, Hayes was taken on the tour as third choice in his position but was still seen as something of a wildcard selection given that he had only recently settled down to regular propping having previously alternated between the front and second rows.

Johns had six fellow Ulstermen in the party, including Jonathan Bell, who was making a welcome return to the colours following an injury-ravaged season and winger James Topping, thrown an international lifeline after having been out in the cold. Andy Ward was travelling as a likely Test starter, with David Humphreys and Allen Clarke tipped for bench duty in the big games and Mark McCall competing with Rob Henderson, Kevin Maggs and Bell for a centre spot in the internationals.

Apart from the rested Lions pair of Wood and Miller, the match 22 on duty at Twickenham was selected en bloc and supplemented by the return of several established players in Bell, Henderson, O'Shea and Ross Nesdale, all of whom were fit again following injury. There were recalls for London Irish lock Gabriel Fulcher and Anthony Foley, who had impressed in the inaugural AIL final a few days earlier, but the latter's Shannon backrow colleagues, Eddie Halvey and Alan Quinlan, both missed out in the ultra-competitive loose forward department as did exiled Ulstermen Kieron Dawson and David Erskine. Topping's selection in the squad helped ensure that three full international wingers of relatively recent vintage, Niall Woods, Darragh O'Mahony and John McWeeney, missed out on the trip.

For Johns, the captaincy was a brave new world, but a challenge that he was relishing. He was going on the tour with no particular pre-conceived ideas, or specific hopes and fears, but with the aim of "doing the jersey proud and making the most of the tour." In pursuit of those goals, he left no stone unturned and history will judge him to have been successful in achieving all that was possible, considering Ireland still had their limitations and were up against a better side who were playing on home soil and in the middle of a long run of world domination. He gave everything himself, got the best out of those around him and ensured that, in spite of the defeats and adversity, the men who were on that tour thoroughly enjoyed it and look back on it with fond memories. Scrapbooks compiled for him by Neil Garrigan, a friend of Rala's from Terenure, are a tangible reminder of the trip.

In putting together this book, we have talked to Paddy himself, coach Warren Gatland, manager Donal Lenihan and a considerable number of the players in Justin Fitzpatrick, Mark McCall, Allen Clarke, David Humphreys and Andy Ward and all agree that the spirit in the squad on that tour was second to none. Both management and players are adamant that Paddy's personal touch and single-minded embracing of all aspects of the captaincy, with attention down to every minute detail, played a big part in creating that excellent atmosphere and ensuring things ran as smoothly as possible. Gatland reveals that even Denis Hickie, in spite of his first Test nightmare, singles out that trip as a treasured memory of the Kiwi's period in charge.

"If you ask any of the senior people who would have toured before and had enough past experiences to compare with, I'm sure they'll tell you that that was one of their most enjoyable tours ever, at any level" claims McCall. "The management were very good and Paddy, as captain, devoted every minute of every day to making it the best that it could be. He threw himself into the role in every conceivable way, totally getting involved in all the minutia, from organising the social activities to helping to plan the training sessions to making sure everyone was happy.

"Everyone totally respected him and was 100 per cent behind him because of his great honesty and the way in which he led by example, especially in the Tests. I remember before the first Test him lecturing us on discipline and then him going out and getting a yellow-card for flattening Gaffie du Toit in the opening minute of the match! But most of what went on was provoked by the South Africans, who were as arrogant as anything and were guilty of an awful lot of off-the-ball stuff as well as constant comments and niggling. Paddy saw what they were doing was wrong and decided that he would stand up to it.

"If he hadn't been captain and brought the attitude he brought and set the example he set in terms of preparation, commitment and so forth, the scorelines in the Tests would have been a lot worse. I think outsiders did expect us to lose by more and, of course, the Springboks came out the week after our series was over and beat Wales by 98 points. In spite of being stung by all the criticism in their media and coming out with more purpose in that second Test, South Africa only scored four tries against us, so we came out of the tour with considerable self-respect."

Fitzpatrick says: "I've been on several tours and the striking thing about that one is that we came back very, very tight as a group, partly because we were treated so badly and really had to stick together. We encountered a huge siege mentality among the South African public and media and, by the second Test, even their players. Wherever we went, we were like gladiators thrown out to be bated. It's hard to put into words the hostility we encountered. South Africa has a very proud rugby culture and all that, but this went beyond ordinary fanaticism.

"You can't tar the whole country of South Africa or all of its people, and I used to live with a South African guy with whom I got on well, but as a tour party we definitely did feel that we were up against it and you only have to look at some of the extremist reaction to the attack on (Irish referee) David McHugh this summer to realise that some attitudes there are over the top and have no place in rugby. The fan who attacked him received quite a lot of sympathy in some of the newspapers it seems, there was one phone-in poll which apparently came out in his favour and three lawyers even wrote in to offer him a free defence! That's crazy, but there were several incidents on our tour which just weren't rugby and really opened my eyes.

"We beat Boland in the first match and Jimmy Topping scored a very good try, but took a late tackle and broke his collar-bone. As he was being stretchered off, a group of South Africans were shouting abuse at him, even though he was obviously in a lot of pain. They were shouting things like 'go home, you're not hard enough, not tough enough to be here'. That's simply not sporting behaviour. That little episode stuck in my mind, but I'm sure if you talked to every guy who was on that tour, each one could relate an incident which left a bitter taste.

"When our bus pulled up at the gates of the stadium for the first Test, which was also my first cap, they wouldn't let us in. They could see that it was the Irish team and it wasn't a case of keys not being able to be found, but we were made to sit there for 15 or 20 minutes. It was clear that they were trying to throw us off our stride. Hundreds of supporters surrounded our bus and it struck me that this must be what it would be like to be an away team in football whose bus gets caught in a sea of hostile home supporters.

To be honest, it was bloody ugly. They started rocking the bus and cursing and swearing at us. It was almost like being in the middle of a riot situation. I've been all around the world playing rugby, but never seen that sort of thing before or since. Rugby just isn't like that.

"So it was a tough tour in many respects, but the environment was very enjoyable and it was great having such a strong but sensitive captain for my first Ireland tour. Paddy really took me under his wing and made sure that I was ok with everything. He knows his own mind and wants to be the best he can be at the things he commits to."

One of the things which Paddy committed to on that tour, on the basis that he would fully exhaust the possibility of something being useful before discarding it, gives rise to arguably the best anecdote of this entire book. Gatland spontaneously bursts into laughter when reminded of the tale, as told here by Fitzpatrick. "As you know, there isn't as much sun in Ireland as there is in South Africa, so we looked like sickly children playing against these bronzed provincial players" explains Justin. "The effect was exacerbated by the bright sunlight, which showed up just how pasty white we were and, when we were watching the tapes of the first couple of games, someone made a comment about how much fitter the opposition looked.

"It was suggested, perhaps half-jokingly, that we should use fake tan to eliminate this visual effect, but anyway Warren Gatland got some brought in and said that any player who wished to could use it. Of course Paddy, who never dismissed any idea which may be of use, got stuck into it. He must have come down before a session, got on his gear and then spent some time applying it to the 'seen' bits. Basically, he'd have had his shorts on, socks pulled up and sleeves cut to mid-arm, so it would only have gone on his thighs and forearms. Later when he took off his jersey, the contrast between the 'orange' bits and his pale Irish skin was hilarious. He wasn't the only one to make the mistake, but it was certainly a moment of levity on a tough tour and added to the camaraderie in the group" concludes Fitzpatrick.

Johns claims: "The fake tan was Warren Gatland's idea. I remember people at home saying 'they're a great colour, must be having great weather'. The routine was: down to Rala's room, get boots cleaned, get jerseys and shorts and get fake tan on. I think most people bought into it. I'd never used the stuff before, nor have I used it since. The gaelic boys in the squad dubbed it a 'Pat Spillane tan' after the famous gaelic footballer, who apparently had really freckly arms and a very, very white torso."

Paddy, who had taken his role as tour captain extremely seriously from the day and hour he was appointed, had met up with his fellow Saracen Pienaar at Heathrow Airport just before the Irish team were due to fly out to South Africa. "He was flying out too, so we met for a coffee and a chat at the airport, though we would have met up somewhere even if that hadn't coincided, for I was keen to have a talk with him. Naturally he was still very proud of his roots, but was talking to me as a clubmate and a friend. He wished both myself and the Wallaces well and also gave advice, which I can't specifically remember now." Whether Pienaar would actually have liked Ireland to give South Africa a bloody nose is largely irrelevant, given the extent to which the odds were stacked against Gatland's greens.

Gatland says that Paddy's hardness and experience and the fact that he commanded the total respect of his own players were going to be important qualities for leading Ireland through a tough tour. "It was a very simple decision to have him as captain in that he had the sort of qualities which I personally was looking for" says the coach, while manager Lenihan adds: "Paddy made an ideal tour captain because of his inclusive style of captaincy which makes everyone feel involved." At that stage, Gatland was wanting some degree of the control and direction to come from the senior players and trying to get the team to take responsibility itself for the discipline, work ethic and motivation required. Johns was an ideal man to both lead and drive that process.

"It was a very enjoyable tour and everyone was very supportive, so what we were doing must have worked quite well" Paddy acknowledges. "I didn't set out to be any particular 'type' of captain, or to model myself on anyone. I did my own thing and, I suppose, subconsciously applied the bits and pieces which I had learned from other captains in the past. I always tried to motivate people by how I played, so perhaps 'leading by example' would sum up my approach. I also got these motivational quotes from various sources and got them onto laminated A4 sheets to put up in the physio-room and team-room, so that when players were in getting treated, or playing table tennis, or whatever, they could read them."

On the customised concern that he showed for each and every player in the party, Johns says: "We're all different and some players are mentally tougher than others. It is up to the collective management of any team, especially maybe on tour, to be aware of each guy's make-up. Some players are mentally tougher than others, but the bottom line is that every sportsman or woman needs confidence to play well so it is important to keep everyone's head up. Some heads would go down more easily than others, so you have to watch for that."

So taken up was Paddy with his captaincy duties and little extras beyond the call of duty, that even his mum, who had come to South Africa to follow Ireland and support him, had to settle for fleeting visits with her son. "I saw him a certain amount, but he was very involved in everything that was going on and I'd never have wanted to intrude on his time" says Mrs Johns.

"But I was with a group including Justin Fitzpatrick's parents and George and Ruth Humphreys, and had a fantastic experience all told. Visiting Ellis Park was great and we also went to Kruger National Park. I was in a shop there with Colm and Mary O'Kelly (Malcolm's parents) when someone from the group came to the door and shouted that the bus was going on. I'd bought something and was waiting to pay for it, so the O'Kellys went on while the girl in the shop went to get some change for me. As luck would have it, Jim Sherwin the RTE commentator had joined the party just at that point, so when the guide on the bus did a headcount, she still got the right number of people, 17, even though I wasn't there. The backs of the seats were very high so it was literally a headcount and just an unlucky coincidence. I was left on my own and ran up the hill after the bus, but fell and put the knees out of my trousers. In the end I was able to contact the hotel and the bus came back for me, which was a great relief. I'm not easily intimidated, but was never as glad to get back to base."

She recalls touring a goldmine and visiting the township of Sowetto, "a stark contrast of appalling poverty and extreme wealth. The deprivation there was incredible and my dogs live better." Mrs Johns was also conscious of the siege mentality the whole Irish party felt, simply from her own experiences as a supporter.

"There was very much a siege mentality and a certain amount of anxiety. In that sense it wasn't the most comfortable tour" she observes. "I also found some of the South Africans patronising. When we arrived at the stadium for the first Test and took our seats, there were a couple of South Africans sitting behind us who said 'we feel so sorry for you ma'am'. I told them 'I appreciate your concern, but you needn't bother your heads'. There was a great build-up to the match with all sorts of smoke going up, parachutists arriving and what have you. I will always remember the very proud moment when Paddy led the Irish team out amid all the smoke and dramatic effects. The hype is just amazing compared to back home."

Mention the stormy scenes in the Test matches, especially Pretoria, and Mrs Johns defends her son for playing it hard, right on the edge. "Paddy isn't a softy and he was very aggressive in that series. I remember him and Teichmann coming to blows. Teichmann's mother was actually sitting right in front of me at the time, but didn't know who I was. Incidentally, there were two Irish Catholic priests sitting behind us who had driven 600 miles to be there to support the team."

Lions prop Paul Wallace and lock O'Kelly were both ruled out of the tour opener against Boland at Wellington, 50 miles from Cape Town, a game for which Gatland fielded a very strong line-up and saw his strategy reap dividends in the shape of a morale-boosting 48-35 victory against a side featuring Marius Goosen, McNeill Hendricks and veteran Springbok prop Tommy Laubscher. In a free-flowing, high-scoring game, the clear-headed captaincy of Johns was praised by Irish Times correspondent Gerry Thornley, who remarked on the way that he had 'slowed it down and asked Eric Elwood to kick penalties at key moments' rather than just get swept along on the tide of the game's openness.

"The world will be watching and there'll be no hiding places" said Johns in an interview before the game, conscious that everyone was writing his team off. "We are representing our country and that will be our motivation. We face a big challenge but I'm looking forward to it." In the event, Ireland hit their hosts for half a dozen tries, with Topping bagging a brace and O'Cuinneagain, Hickie, O'Shea and McGuinness also crossing the line while Eric Elwood's boot contributed 18 points. "It was a very open game, but as a win was vital, and as we hadn't played for a while, I made sure we always took any points when they were on offer in the form of a penalty."

The only downside was that Topping's dislocated shoulder and Bell's hamstring tear would rule both men out of the remainder of the tour, as indeed Corrigan was as the result of a knee to the back. London Irish winger Justin Bishop and Clohessy's younger brother, Des, were called out as replacements, while Wood, who had agreed to make himself available after all for the last five games of the trip, was due to arrive in the rainbow republic shortly. The manner in which Corrigan had received his injuries incensed the Irish management and Gatland warned publicly that his team would not lie down in the face of attempted intimidation in either the provincial matches or Tests.

For the second tour game, against South West Districts in George, Paul Wallace and O'Kelly were not rushed back into action, being left to bench for a side showing 13 changes from the opener, with only Clohessy and Fulcher being retained. Foley was made midweek captain. In the event, O'Kelly played due to the withdrawal from the side of Munster skipper Mick Galwey with bad bruising to his lower back. Less than a quarter of an hour from the end, Ireland led 20-14, but SWD hit back with a try and Jacques Benade, who was later to become Malone player-coach in Belfast, converted to edge the hosts in front. Benade added a penalty and late drop goal to take his personal tally to 17 points in a 27-10 victory.

"The game was on a knife-edge and, had the ball bounced our way, we would have won" says Johns, who had been brought into the match 22 when Galwey withdrew, and came on as a sub right at the end. "We failed to score from a threatening situation and then they went up and scored at the other end." Gatland, meanwhile, blamed himself for introducing Hayes and Corkery in place of Clohessy and Brennan at a critical stage.

Paddy singles out Brennan as the real character to emerge on that tour. "Trev's a bit of a character and loves his singsongs. He's known as the milkman because of the job he used to do and he came through well on that trip. There are no back doors in Trevor and I'd have had no hesitation about having him in the trenches with me. A pretty useful fella to have around if trouble broke out."

From George it was on to Cape Town and a game against Western Province, for whom it was future Ulster coach Alan Solomons' first match in charge. Ireland showed six changes from the Boland fixture, with Bishop, Maggs, Fitzpatrick, Paul Wallace, O'Kelly and Corkery all coming into the side. Humphreys was later drafted into the team when Elwood cried off injured. O'Cuinneagain was chosen at No 8 against his old provincial team in preference to Costello. Western Province were without Percy Montgomery and Pieter Rossouw, but could still field the likes of Chester Williams, Robbie Fleck, Breyton Paulse, Louis Koen, Toks van der Linde, Cobus Visagie, Selborne Boome, Bobby Skinstad, captain Andrew Aitken and Paddy's future Ulster team-mate, Robbie Brink.

Ireland went down 12-6 in dreadful conditions in a match marred by the referee's refusal to recognise the legitimacy of a 13-man lineout at the end, Gatland's trademark tactic being rendered null and void by whistler Jonathan Kaplan, much to the disgust of the Irish team as they went for the pushover try which could have delivered victory. Collared after a half-break, Humphreys drilled a penalty into touch and Allen Clarke's throw was taken by O'Kelly, but then Kaplan intervened much to the annoyance of the visitors.

Clarke refused to shake hands with Kaplan at the final whistle a few minutes later but, although the referee publicly extolled Johns' discipline and revealed that the Irish captain had 'thanked' him afterwards which "wasn't a feeling shared by the Irish players on the pitch" Paddy was seething like everyone else in the touring party. The referee continued: "Until that last decision when Johns obviously disagreed, he was exemplary. If I made a mistake, it was a genuine mistake. I wasn't trying to rob the Irish. If I made a mistake, I would offer them my sincere apologies. I'm not trying to create a scene. I'm disappointed at the attitude after the game when Ireland were so disciplined during the game in accepting a decision. I like the Irish. I don't have anything against them because if there's a favourite people in the world, it's the Irish and this is all a little bit sore for me."

Paddy says: "Newlands was very, very wet that day and it was a very tight, low-scoring game, as you'd expect with heavy conditions and a slippy ball. We were exerting good pressure at the end and were in a position to win the game until that baffling decision. The referee was adamant that he was right, but the overall penalty count (19-9) was also very frustrating. All the referees for the provincial matches were South African and at times it felt like we were playing against 18 people."

As captain, how did Paddy get on with referees in general? "I wouldn't have licked up to referees or sweet-talked them, or tried to manipulate them in the way that you'd see Munster doing, with maybe five or six players around the guy at the same time, but obviously I'd have sought clarification from them regarding decisions, for a team needs to know what it has got penalised for exactly so I could communicate that to my players. Rugby is a game of interpretation, so you need to know where a particular referee is coming from. I'd say that I got on fine with most of the ones I encountered."

Speaking of communication, McCall will never forget Paddy's on-field teamtalk just before kick-off that day at a saturated Newlands. "We were out on the pitch, which was in bad condition and there was just about a minute to go before kick-off. The referee had called us, but Paddy decided he needed to say something at that stage, something which he had written the night before, so he got this little folded piece of paper out of his shorts pocket, opened it up and read from it." For lack of spontaneity, that sounds like rugby's equivalent of a real passion-killer, but the players knew Paddy's methods and listened intently. "It is important to choose your words carefully, even at that stage, rather than just using meaningless emotive language and talking for the sake of it" Johns insists. "If people expect what you say to mean something, they will listen."

Ireland's fourth tour game was a midweek match against Griqualand West, a team rumoured to be strong enough to have been more fitting opposition for the tourists' Saturday side and so it proved. The hosts won 52-13 in Kimberley, with manager Lenihan expressing his doubts that even a Lions dirt-tracker team would have come close against them. Griqualand, coached by disgraced former Springbok supremo Andre Markgraaf and fresh from hammering Golden Lions 57-0 in the Vodacom Cup final, also had a reputation of being on the itinerary for a touring side a few days before the first Test in order to soften them up. So Ireland expected a rough ride and got one.

Paddy remembers well that visit to Kimberley. "As most people would know, Kimberley is famous for its diamonds and almost as much so for the massive big hole beside the town. It is an old diamond mine and I've no idea how wide or deep it is, but it is definitely massive. On the field, the Griquas were a very strong side, powerful in the upper body in particular and not used to losing. They overwhelmed us." Young centre Lourens Venter starred for the hosts, while the best performers in an Ireland side showing four changes from the previous midweek match were Henderson, Brennan and Bishop.

The two London Irish Justins, wing Bishop and prop Fitzpatrick, were handed Test debuts against the Springboks in Bloemfontein at the end of the week, with O'Cuinneagain also being given his first cap, against the land of his birth. Wood, who had got half an hour's tour action under his belt in Kimberley, displaced Allen Clarke in the middle of a front row completed by Paul Wallace with O'Kelly predictably joining Johns in the engineroom. O'Cuinneagain was chosen at blindside with Costello at No 8 and the in-form Ward as breakaway. Behind the scrum, the Connacht pair of McGuinness and Elwood were confirmed as the halfback pairing, with McCall and Maggs at centre, Hickie on the left wing with Bishop preferred to Richie Wallace on the right, and O'Shea at fullback. An experienced bench included Humphreys, Clohessy and Fulcher.

South Africa had two debutants, wing Stefan Terblanche and flyhalf Gaffie du Toit, in a backline completed by Montgomery, Rossouw, centres Andre Snyman and Pieter Muller and the great Joost van der Westhuizen. Up front, a great back row of Rassie Erasmus, skipper Gary Teichmann and Andre Venter was operating behind a useful tight five comprising Ollie le Roux, James Dalton, Adrian Garvey, Mark Andrews and Kyrnauw Otto. The bench included Skinstad, future Ulster player Robbie Kempson and Naka Drotske. One thing was for certain: if Ireland didn't perform, they could expect a pasting.

In the event, Ireland succumbed to a four-try freak show by debutant Terblanche on a nightmare afternoon for Hickie, but emerged from the Free State stadium with their heads held high in spite of a 37-13 defeat. They actually led 7-10 at one point in the first half courtesy of Bishop's try from an Elwood bomb which Montgomery couldn't hold, and only trailed by three points at the break. Terblanche kept widening the gap in the second period, but Ireland still kept the Springboks' victory margin to such respectable proportions that the South African media got stuck into their own side in the week leading up to the second Test.

While South Africa were lambasted for being too soft, Ireland came in for some criticism for roughhouse tactics, most particularly a short-arm challenge by Wood on Teichmann and the Irish captain's reported alleged comments afterwards which appeared to indicate he may have intended it. Paddy, who had an excellent game and won a lot of lineout ball, had set the tone by clattering du Toit late after the rookie Springbok flyhalf had cleared from the recycled opening kick-off and admits now that targeting the newcomer was part of Ireland's plan. Left groggy by that challenge, the new boy then had to depart to the bloodbin with a gash a few minutes later.

"We did target du Toit because he was a new cap and I did hit him a bit late, but by then was kind of trying to pull out of the tackle. I can't remember how he got cut soon afterwards. The point was that, the only way to get them to respect us was to really put it up to them and we did that, getting off to a very good start indeed. It was very frustrating Terblanche scoring all of those tries and a bit of a nightmare situation for Denis to have to come to terms with. If your opposite number scores three or four against you, mostly one on one, you won't feel too happy. No-one was hard on him about it, but he'd have had to deal with a lot of wounded personal pride.

"But the upshot of the first Test was that South Africa realised we were better that they thought, so that focused them even more for the following Saturday as did the slurs in the local media that the Springboks were too soft. There was quite a furore about us being abrasive and them not standing up to it. For them that was like a red rag to a bull and stoked up the fires, ultimately contributing to the second Test boiling over." It was reported at the time that Johns had been "severely reprimanded" by the Irish management for indiscipline during the first Test, but neither he nor Gatland have any recollection of that having occurred. "We probably talked about the importance of discipline and not giving away penalties, which would be counter-productive, and that would have been pointed out to Paddy like everyone else. We had to be aware of discipline and it was probably primarily a reinforcement of that message" suggests the coach. "It may also, in light of the late tackle on du Toit, have been talked up to placate opinion in South Africa."

Between internationals, the Test team stayed in Pretoria while the dirt-trackers completed their programme with a game against North West Districts in Potchefstroom, where a redemption-seeking Hickie was the only starter from Bloemfontein to feature in the Irish midweek side. Galwey captained the tourists in the absence of Foley and Ireland won 26-18 against relatively anonymous hosts, though Johns confirms that "there was a fair old gulf by this stage between the Test team and the midweek team."

With Teichmann hinting darkly at retribution against Wood, "it will catch up with him", the second Test (which was lost 33-0) at Pretoria's Loftus Versfeld was always likely to be combustible, as the then Springbok assistant coach Alan Solomons, later to become Johns' coach at Ulster, admits. "We felt that the players allowed Ireland to take advantage in the first Test with, for example, Andy Ward being regularly allowed to block the path of Rassie Erasmus and we couldn't allow that to happen again. Terblanche's four tries meant the first Test scoreline was comfortable enough but Ireland had done well and we were too gentlemanly. After our video session and in light of some of the coverage during the week in between, it was fairly predictable what was going to happen in Pretoria.

"It was one of those games. I don't know of any Irish rugby guys who lie down; there is never a lack of courage and Paddy epitomises that. He was seen as a very aggressive individual who took no prisoners and there'd be huge respect for him in South African rugby. There were obviously a lot of incidents in the game and Ireland were going to cite Joost, who was very lucky not to be sent off for kicking O'Kelly. Nick Mallett asked me to go through and sort it out with the Irish, so I talked to my opposite number Phil Danaher, who I knew a little through David Curtis, his former Ireland centre partner, who was born in Zimbabwe and who I had coached at uni in South Africa. In the end we realised that citings could mean a lot of guys not playing any rugby for quite a few weeks, so discretion prevailed."

Gatland points out that "it didn't bother us; we'd finished for the season whereas South Africa had big matches coming up but, ultimately, we let it drop. There were a couple of off-the ball incidents which the touchjudges completely bottled, especially one where James Dalton was blatantly punching. I put Trevor Brennan and Peter Clohessy on with 15 minutes to go because we needed fresh legs. The last thing I said to Trevor was 'whatever you do don't get sent off', but I was asked afterwards if the introduction of those two players was intended to intimidate and provoke. Brennan was standing near where I was doing the interview, so I just said to him 'Trev, come here, what did I say to you'."

Afterwards, amid claim and counter-claim, both sides tried to absolve themselves of primary responsibility for the shameful scenes which occurred during an encounter of "sustained brutality . . . an incessant stream of punch-ups" in the words of Tom English of the Sunday Times.

More sinned against or sinning? Just like both sides sought to get their retaliation in first on the field, likewise they were quick afterwards to point the finger. Mallett claimed that 'we were trying to play rugby and Ireland were trying to keep the score down by any means', while Lenihan was slightly more gracious, saying that 'the tone was set when their No 9 kicked Malcolm. However we were not blameless'. Most analysis of cause and effect and what sparked what was subjective, while there was clear circumstantial evidence against both sides. Ireland, as the lesser team and aiming for damage limitation, would surely have had more to gain from the game descending from a rugby contest into a brawl, yet South Africa were known to have been smarting for revenge on Wood and keen to restore their macho credentials in the eyes of the public following a week of criticism for being too 'soft'.

Before turning to Paddy's case for the defence, it is perhaps instructive to quote from a piece by Gerry Thornley in the Monday morning's Irish Times. "You have to admire Ireland's defiance if not their rugby" he wrote. "They met fire with a volcano and then bade good luck and good riddance to South Africa. Perhaps it was a game too far. After a month of being dismissed at every turn, at having little obstacles constantly put in their way; heck, after just living inside a bubble, which in turn was inside a bubble of a country, one could understand where their defiance came from. Keith Wood was clearly targeted before the game and during it and the Irish were not going to roll over and die.

"One imagines," continues Thornley's article, "that back home there was a certain amount of admiration for Ireland's fighting spirit, a cliche readily applied on this day of all days, if mixed with a degree of shame at the way the match degenerated." The journalist also launched a scathing attack against the match officials for sparing van der Westhuizen a red card on the grounds of "who he is." On Johns himself, Thornley suggested in his report that Paddy "seemed a little too pumped up for his own good, especially given he was setting an example."

The South Africans claim that, prior to the disgraceful van der Westhuizen assault on O'Kelly, who was viciously kicked as he lay on the ground, Johns had started the rot by punching opposing captain Teichmann. But there is no doubt the Springbok scrumhalf's kick was the worst single offence of the match and Paddy is also at pains to point out that "Francois Pienaar attributed the first three acts of foul play to South Africa. Mal getting kicked was the worst, but they had at least a couple before that.

"Going into the game, we didn't really focus on the possibility of things turning ugly, partly because we didn't think they'd quite have taken the approach that they did and, secondly, because we actually were keen to have a rugby match rather than a boxing match. We had tried to take the positives out of the first Test and felt that, if we didn't give away soft scores, we knew we could improve. Although South Africa were a good side and used to winning, there was no fear factor on our part. It was disappointing not to get any points in Pretoria, but it wasn't until the last 20 minutes that we knew we weren't going to win. Then we were still determined to defend our line as ferociously as we could."

For the record, South Africa led 19-0 at the interval and added two converted tries in the final 15 minutes from Teichmann and Rossouw, but couldn't top their previous biggest margin against Ireland, contrary to most people's expectations. One writer did though observe that Ireland were 'lucky to get nil'. Franco Smith, in for the injured du Toit as the one change in either side, seemed to have set up a try for Andre Venter in the early stages but it was disallowed and, by the time van der Westhuizen did get the first touchdown on 16 minutes, he should have been having an early bath. Montgomery missed a penalty and had a try disallowed as Ireland hung on by their fingertips, but the floodgates finally opened in the five minutes before half-time when Erasmus and Dalton both crossed the line.

A fight between Maggs and Teichmann early in the second period was followed by a mass brawl just before the hour mark which ended with Otto and Johns standing toe to toe trading punches. There is no doubt that, wherever the scuffles were taking place, Paddy was always in the frame, eager and willing to stand his ground and fight his corner. In Tom English's end of tour player ratings in the Sunday Times, he says: "(Johns) went about his work well but, to the team's cost, he lost the run of himself on a number of occasions in the Tests."

So did you lose it, Paddy? "The only stage that I was really out of control was that Otto incident. He hit me and I didn't see it coming, so I was pretty annoyed. I hit him back so hard that I damaged my thumb. There was a lot went on that you could see and a lot you couldn't see. As a player you can either lie down and take it or you can stand up to it. It wasn't planned, but the way the thing went early on, it was going to happen. They clearly came out to intimidate us and we weren't going to let them."

Would he have got as involved if he hadn't been captain? "It would probably have been similar" he muses. "We were in a foreign country and been forced into a siege mentality. We felt on our own in a hostile environment. I was frustrated, incensed actually. After van der Westhuizen kicked Mal so blatantly, you were thinking 'what does a South African have to do to get sent off?'. It wasn't easy to keep our cool. There was also a lot of mouthing went on between the teams, a lot of stuff being said. There's a bit of sledging in the game, but more than usual in that series, especially the second Test. The insults were flying, with Fester and the Claw excelling themselves from our side. I think a few aspersions were cast about Joost's mother after the O'Kelly incident - you know how it is.

"Relations between the sides actually weren't good off the field either. We didn't mix and the atmosphere in the post-match reception was the worst I've seen in rugby. There were no formal dinners as such after the Tests out there, but I talked to Teichmann at the dinner after the Dublin match in November and he was dead on. That game itself had been more of a normal rugby match than the one in Pretoria. By the Dublin dinner too, we knew that we wouldn't be playing each other again afterwards in the foreseeable future, so there was less looking at the other captain down the gun barrel."

"We took a battering on that tour but never a backward step" says Gatland, while Fitzpatrick reflects: "There was lots of stuff going on. In the changing room guys were being stitched right, left and centre. It certainly wasn't all one way or we wouldn't have had so many war casualties. There were lots of cheap shots going in. We certainly didn't go out to do anything untoward, but weren't going to be walked over and the whole nature of the place and how we'd been treated were aggravating factors.

"And yet we came home with good memories from that tour. Paddy was to the fore of a tight-knit team ethos on the trip. There were no cliques, no-one felt excluded, no-one was bigger than the team, no-one more important than anyone else." Andy Ward adds: "That was the best rugby tour ever. Everyone got on really well and were keen to do things for each other. It hasn't always been like that, but Paddy set such a great example and worked tirelessly to ensure everyone was happy. Those of us who were fortunate enough to be on his tour will always treasure the memories."

24. ULSTER ON HIS MIND

You pays your money and you takes your chance. It's a pity for Paddy that he missed Ulster's famous European Cup triumph in January 1999. He'd love to have been part of it. Of course he would. But there are no real regrets. The life choices he had made which resulted in him being exiled at the time were carefully thought out and, in his mind, the right ones. They didn't become the wrong decisions just because Ulster became incredibly successful that season. He will admit to watching a little enviously from afar, but there was no dog in the manger begrudgery. What the boys back home were doing made Paddy one very proud Ulsterman indeed.

Thankfully, while there had been feedback from home about how the remarkable roller-coaster ride of Humph's heroes was capturing the public's imagination, he was far enough removed from it to not be choked by a sense of loss. It would have been worse to be Jimmy Topping, his fellow international who missed out on the glory run through injury, but had to live in the middle of the hype and see at first hand what he was missing. Paddy had his own life in London and his own team of the time, Saracens, to focus on.

"I was sent over tapes of the quarter-final and semi-final and, although you can't fully pick up an atmosphere from television, it was obvious that they were wonderful occasions and the final was simply amazing. But we weren't saturated by it over there, not forced to come face to face every day with the fact that something special was going on that I could perhaps have been part of, but wasn't. To have been at home and injured would have been much harder.

"Obviously, with my own commitments at Saracens, I couldn't get over to attend the final at Lansdowne Road and in fact I didn't even get to watch it live on television, which I must say I was a bit annoyed about at the time. Saracens were playing a Cup game on the Sunday and Francois Pienaar wanted us all to go to the pictures together on the Saturday afternoon. I wanted to watch Ulster against Colomiers but, in the end, the cinema was a team thing and it had to be done. You can't have exceptions in a team environment and I had learned throughout my career that 'the team' had to come first. So I got over it. They agreed to tape the game and we watched it when we came back.

"It was very exciting for me, very emotional to see Lansdowne Road that amazing sea of red and white. I'm sure anyone who was there that day will never ever forget it. The way Ulster simply suffocated the French was fantastic. There was definitely an air amongst the English players that the competition was devalued by the fact that the English teams weren't taking part that season, but I didn't care. It was great to see the place where I was from being on top of Europe.

"Even though Saracens had qualified for that season's European Cup and would have fancied their chances against Ulster, I don't believe that the boycott of the English clubs should be allowed to take away from Ulster's achievement or used as an excuse to talk down what they did. The English clubs made their own choice not to take part and Ulster could only beat what was in front of them. That included winning twice against Toulouse and seeing off Stade Francais in the semi, so it wasn't as if they didn't face decent competition. It was an absolutely remarkable achievement and a credit to all of those involved. No-one can ever take away from Ulster what they did and anyone who tries to diminish it misses the point."

That said, Paddy is open and adamant in stating his belief that either the great Ulster team which beat the Wallabies in 1984 or the Sarries side which won the English Cup at Twickenham in 1998 were better than Ulster's European Cup winning outfit. "I think that, nine times out of 10, the Saracens side of 1998 would have beaten the Ulster team of 1999, though it might have been a different story if we'd have been taking on Harry's boys either at Ravenhill in a Euro semi or Lansdowne Road in the final."

We? Saracens was Paddy's side at the time. If they'd played Ulster, he'd have been in the frontline of trying to beat his beloved province. Two seasons later, the role was reversed and he was giving his all against the London club. Er, a case of black and white really. "You have total loyalty to whatever team you're playing for at a particular point and any talk of divided loyalties is nonsense. When you're part of a team, everyone else becomes the opposition, especially if you're playing against them. Your allegiance is not an issue."

Ulster, the provincial side which represents the region in which Paddy was born, which he grew up watching and which he will grow old watching, is undoubtedly his team. He made his name with Ulster and finished his career with the province. "Ulster will always be my team. If Ulster play Saracens in future European Cups, you don't even need to ask who I'll be supporting, though Saracens holds special memories for me and would always be my second side. I'd want them to do well in English club rugby or, if Ulster were out of Europe say, I'd be wanting Saracens to go all the way. It isn't surprising that, during what were three happy years there, I developed real feelings for the club. People may talk about a sense of dislocation between the top, professional end of some of the English clubs and their grassroots, but I did genuinely feel part of a club at Saracens rather than simply an employee of some sort of nomadic rugby franchise."

Although Paddy will defend, as vigorously as anyone, the value of Ulster's European Cup win in 1999, he does not subscribe to gushing, unthinking eulogies about it being the 'best Ulster side ever'. The chances are that, if you held a Ravenhill referendum some Friday night in the current season, a majority of the attendance would vote the Euro heroes of 1999 as Ulster's finest. That would be understandable given the presence of many young fans, not to mention the 'new Ravenhill crowd', the thousands who only started to follow Ulster seriously in the latter stages of that European Cup winning run. The magical memories of the Stade semi and the final at Lansdowne Road are persuasive and intoxicating.

The authors, for example, are too young to remember Ulster's win over the Grand Slam Wallabies of 1984 and the Sarries success at Twickenham in 1998 would naturally have meant little to most rugby fans in the province. By contrast we have put Harry's heroes on a permanent pedestal and rightly so. They gave many of us our greatest sporting memories. No-one would seek to take away from that, but men like Johns and David Irwin try to maintain a sense of perspective. Dr Irwin points out that his Ulster team, which beat Australia and launched the 10-in-a-row interpro title run, didn't have the chance to compete in a European Cup or, for that matter, have the advantages of full-time training and so forth.

"When Ulster won the European Cup, they got on a great roll and had fantastic team spirit. They got home draws, drew on wonderful support and had a simple gameplan which they executed to superb effect" says Paddy.

"The return from England of quality players like David Humphreys, Jonny Bell and Allen Clarke as well as the signing of Justin Fitzpatrick and Simon Mason gave Ulster a real boost and, along with Andy Ward, those key men all performed very well. There were a lot of unsung heroes too, guys who were inspired and played above themselves game after game. Harry handled it all very well and managed to make the most of the momentum which was building up with each game.

"The organisation was good, the defence, built around Jonny Bell, was very sound and whenever Ulster got into the opposition half, there was always the chance of coming away with points thanks to Simon's superb place-kicking. Ulster were good at hassling the opposition into giving away penalties and he did the rest. He was capable of knocking them over from everywhere. Humph also produced a few moments of real magic like the semi-final try. But, while it was a remarkable achievement, if you go through that Saracens team I played in which won the Cup, or the line-up which Ulster had in 1984, in my opinion they were better man for man than the European Cup winning side" he insists.

It is hard to disagree with that viewpoint. If you were picking a composite team from the Saracens class of 1998 and Ulster's Euro heroes, Bell and Clarke might be the only two men who would get in from the Irish province. Even Humphreys would miss out due to the presence of Lynagh in that Sarries side while, in spite of their great contributions to their team's success, it would be hard to make the case for picking Mason or Ward ahead of Gavin Johnson or Richard Hill.

Assuming Grau edged Fitzpatrick for the No 1 jersey, Clarke would be the only Ulster player in the tight five, with Paul Wallace, Johns and Danny Grewcock preferred to Rab Irwin, Mark Blair and Gary Longwell. Saracens skipper Diprose would get the nod over Ulster's McWhirter in the battle of the Tonys at No 8, with Francois Pienaar obviously chosen ahead of Ulster stalwart Stephen McKinty to complete the pack. Andy Matchett and Humphreys proved an effective halfback pairing for Ulster, but wouldn't get in ahead of Bracken and Lynagh, while comparing Sella with converted centre Jan Cunningham further confirms the gulf in class between these teams on paper. On the wings, most people would pick two from Brendon Daniel, Ryan Constable and Richard Wallace ahead of Sheldon Coulter and Andy Park, leaving Ulster's only representatives as Bell and Clarke, with Steve Ravenscroft and George Chuter being the two Saracens players to miss out.

When comparing the Ulster teams of 1984 and 1999, more of the latter lot might make a composite line-up than would have got into the Saracens Tetley Bitter Cup winning side, but again it would be a minority. Bell, Humphreys and Fitzpatrick look the best bets, but there would be a good number of other close calls, at fullback, scrumhalf, hooker, one second row spot and No 8. Far from being a criticism or a belittling of the Ulster team which won the European Cup, these comparisons simply serve to illustrate the sheer enormity of their achievement given the resources at Williams' disposal. The reality is that Toulouse, who they beat twice, and Stade Francais also looked much stronger on paper, yet Ulster eliminated France's finest and so thoroughly deserved their continental crown.

Paddy wasn't there, so we can't dwell on the detail too much, but he's Ulster through and through and so are the authors, so brief indulgence reliving that roller-coaster ride to a once in a lifetime triumph is permissible. Williams' warriors had actually got their campaign off to a disappointing start, drawing 38-38 with Edinburgh at Ravenhill before being trounced 39-3 in Toulouse. They were then well beaten by Munster in an interpro in Cork and found themselves languishing at the bottom of the interpro table.

For a side now sporting stars like Humphreys, Bell, Clarke, Fitzpatrick and Mason, all of whom had been signed that summer, it was an unacceptable state of affairs and Williams had to do something to turn things around. Up until then, Ulster had tried to schedule their training to suit the part-timers in the squad, but now they moved to a more realistic regime and it reaped real dividends. They scored 60 points in winning their next match, a European Cup group game at Ebbw Vale, sparking a run of eight straight victories, culminating in the crushing of Colomiers in the final. Toulouse lost the Ravenhill return 29-24, Ebbw Vale were defeated 43-18 in a scrappy, ill-tempered affair and Connacht were beaten in Belfast in an interpro. Then came the final Pool match in Edinburgh and Coulter's famous intercept try which gave Ulster a 23-21 victory.

That was enough to put Humph's hopefuls into the last eight, but the big bonus was getting a home quarter-final thanks to the remarkable result at Eugene Cross Park the previous day when Toulouse unbelievably slipped up against Ebbw Vale, having put 100 points on them in France earlier in the competition. The upshot was that Ulster ended up as group winners and found themselves hosting Toulouse at Ravenhill in mid-December, a game which will always be remembered for the crowd's cult hero Ward leaving the field during the second half to a rapturous ovation to attend the birth of his first child. Ulster won 15-13, courtesy of a hat-trick of penalties by Mason and a brace of dropgoals from Humphreys, who badly damaged his shoulder making a match-saving tackle right at the death and faced a race against the clock to be fit for the semis.

Again fortune favoured Ulster in the form of a home draw, albeit against the cosmopolitan collection of big names which money had brought to Paris to play for Stade Francais, and Humphreys had recovered in time. Extra stands had been erected to bring the Ravenhill crowd capacity up to the stipulated 20,000 for this stage of the competition and a full house was treated to a magnificent match under the brilliant blue sky of a Saturday lunchtime. McKinty was driven over for a first half try and the metronomic Mason was at his sharpshooting best, with one monster drop goal from near halfway over towards the terracing as he shaded his eyes from the low winter sun sticking in the mind.

The other big hero was Captain Marvel Humphreys and no Ulster rugby fan will ever forget his dramatic dash to glory down the stand side early in the second half after he had chipped out of deep defence and exchanged passes with Coulter before showing the French a clean pair of heels. He won the personal battle with Diego Dominguez that day and Ulster won the match 33-27 to put them into the final which, as luck would have it, was played at Lansdowne Road, ensuring that Harry's heroes would command the vast majority of the support.

Ulstermen and women descended on Dublin in their thousands that final weekend in January 1999 and the rest of the country united in willing a happy ending to this fairytale of fairytales. Fate seemed to be with the team and they duly delivered on their destiny. It was another French outfit, Colomiers, which stood in Ulster's way, but they never got a look-in as the red-jerseyed red handers were in almost total control throughout the game, roared to the rafters by a capacity crowd. Defensive brick Bell was man-of-the-match, while the skipper dropped yet another goal and ace marksman Mason rattled over six penalties, taking his points tally for the competition to a remarkable 144.

With the pitch at Lansdowne Road a sea of red and white, Humphreys and Mark McCall proudly held the European Cup aloft amid amazing scenes of euphoria and elation. It was an unforgettable evening and the team toured Belfast in an open-top bus on their return the following day. McCall had been captain earlier in the season before suffering a neck injury and, although he recovered from it, couldn't get insurance to play again and was reluctantly forced into early retirement. But the team made sure he was part of the occasion, there to share in Ulster rugby's finest hour.

It will remain one of the great anomalies that Johns, one of Ulster's leading players of all time, should be so far removed from a glorious chapter in the province's history in spite of it coinciding with the peak period of his career. "Yeah, just one of those things and you could glibly say that I was in the wrong place at the wrong time inasmuch as I missed out on such a memorable Ulster success, but I was satisfied at the time that it made absolute good sense for me to be at Saracens that season. It was the right decision to move to England when I did and, although the option was there to come home a year earlier than I did, I made my choice to stay on in a careful and considered manner. No-one could have known what would happen with Ulster either."

There had been some speculation in the late Spring of 1998 that Johns might relocate to Ireland after only two terms at Saracens. Unlike Ashton, the new national coach, Gatland, was keen to pick home-based players rather than exiles and the IRFU were now proactively trying to bring Ireland's leading lights back into the increasingly professional provincial set-ups. Many of Johns' fellow internationals did make the move that summer, including the return to Ulster of a number of the province's prodigal sons, headed by Humphreys. How close was Paddy to joining the migration?

"The IRFU tried to talk to all the players each year about coming home, so the possibility was there, but I didn't feel that it was the right time in spite of knowing that a number of the other guys were going back. Things were going well with Saracens on the pitch and life was good for us there. Saracens were keen to keep me too, so it wasn't that hard a decision. It didn't come down to money. I'd gone there with a view to staying at least two years, maybe three so we were still within that timescale."

It was thought at the time that Dungannon's relegation from the top flight of the All Ireland League might have militated against the chances of Paddy returning home in the summer of 1998, the reasoning being that he wouldn't have wanted to either drop from the English Premiership to AIL Division Two or join his old club's arch-rivals Ballymena. "That didn't come into it to be honest" says Paddy, knocking the theory on the head. "I was looking at a wider picture and made a positive decision to stay at Saracens rather than it being a case of not wanting to come back to Ireland."

His final Saracens season was to be a leaner one for a club which had now lost both Sella and Lynagh to retirement and couldn't emulate the heights of that tremendous Twickenham triumph of May 1998, but the Irish captaincy gave him an extra lease of life.

The elation and pride which Johns felt at seeing his good friends McCall and Humphreys hoisting the European Cup aloft amid those incredible scenes must have been tempered by a human hankering after a part in it all, but Paddy had plenty of consolations at that stage of his career. He had, of course, won silverware with that great Sarries side the previous season and, a couple of years later, completed a memorable club double by captaining Dungannon to victory in the All Ireland League final.

A couple of months before Ulster had stolen the show, Paddy had skippered Ireland to a record-breaking win over Georgia in a World Cup qualifier and, a mere three weeks after Ulster's Lansdowne Road triumph, he had the thrill of leading Ireland out at Wembley and to a fine victory there over Wales. Johns knows that, if he hadn't left Ulster originally, at least some of those other magical moments may never have happened for him or his career as a whole been so successful. So he certainly didn't begrudge happy Harry and his Red Hand Heroes.

Although the English clubs had boycotted that season after taking part in the previous two European Cups, the full house for the final at Lansdowne Road indicated just how far the competition had come from its humble beginnings a few months after the 1995 World Cup. Paddy had played for Ulster in the inaugural European Cup, which featured only 12 teams from France, Wales and Ireland, split into four Pools of three sides in each, with the group winners qualifying for the semis.

Ulster, who not long since had enjoyed a decade of dominance in the Irish interpros during which they also fancied themselves against outside opposition, made a most inauspicious debut in the competition, being thrashed 46-6 by Cardiff on a Tuesday night at the Arms Park. Johns missed that one due to a knee injury, but returned for the other group game, also a midweek match, in which Ulster put up a fair fight before going down 16-29 to Begles-Bordeaux under the lights at Ravenhill.

"The European Cup was much smaller scale and lower profile at the start than it is now and no-one could have said with certainty that it would become so big. It has built up very well over the years. But, right from the start, I felt the concept was very good. Playing against sides from different countries was an exciting prospect. I know that the Ulster team which I came into at the start of my career would have relished the competition, for back in those days the only time we faced external opposition was in the odd one-off friendly or when touring teams came to town. Getting used to playing against French clubs for the provinces and, hopefully, in time, starting to beat them, could also only be good for

Ireland's prospects in the longer term as it would remove that fear factor."

Saracens didn't actually appear in the European Cup until 1999-2000 due to a combination of the English clubs twice declining to take part and their own failure to qualify in the other two of the first four seasons. But Paddy recalls that, perhaps more so than some of their counterparts, Saracens were enthusiastic about the concept of European club competition, while adding the proviso; "on the right terms of course." "Saracens hadn't qualified for the 1996-97 European Cup, but they were keen for me to get experience in the competition and so readily released me to play in it for Ulster."

Paddy partnered Jeremy Davidson in a high-scoring opening win, by 41-34, away to Scottish district side Caledonia and then in a narrow home defeat by Harlequins, who were glad to get out of Ravenhill with a 21-15 victory. He missed the third match, when Scottish referee Chuck Muir had a huge hand in Ulster going down 15-13 at Neath, but was back in harness alongside Davidson as the Irish province gave eventual winners Brive a brave Belfast battle before losing 6-17.

The following season, Saracens were in the Shield themselves and although they didn't progress from their group in the secondary competition, "it got us into the way of playing in Europe. Anyway, with qualification for the European Cup being based on what happened the previous season, some of the English and French clubs playing in the Shield in any given autumn could be as strong at that particular point as some of those in the Heineken Cup."

The English boycott in 1998-99 left Johns watching from the sidelines as Ulster won the European Cup, but he was back at Ravenhill the following season for what was to prove an ill-fated attempted trophy defence. His old club Saracens didn't make the knockout stages either, their first attempt floundering thanks to two agonising single point defeats in high-scoring matches against Munster, both games being lost to kicks right at the death.

In between Ulster's big day in Dublin and his own Euro return for them, however, Paddy captained Ireland to a Wembley win, gained his 50th cap, lost the captaincy, toured Australia and played in his second World Cup. He had little time to brood over what might have been. The move back home had been in the pipeline from very early in the year, when the IRFU began their regular round of trying to persuade what was now a dwindling band of exiles to return to the old sod.

"The IRFU were trying to get the players home and would have talked to us each year, making a concerted effort to persuade us to come back. We had discussions with Warren Gatland and Donal Lenihan, who would have been supportive in terms of trying to get us the right deals. They were naturally proactive in the attempt to get the guys to come home, but I think those behind the scenes, the committee people, also realised that it wasn't ideal to have leading Irish players controlled by the English clubs. I remember having a meeting in the Glenview Hotel, which was attended by Keith Wood, Malcolm O'Kelly and myself. Kevin Maggs was there as well, although he didn't ultimately move to Ireland and there must have been someone else for we were dubbed the 'Glenview Five'.

"From about Christmas 1998, I was of a mind to move back to Ireland at the end of the season. I had enjoyed Saracens and all that went with it, but the reality was that I had gone there purely for the rugby and not to settle in that part of the world. It was now time to set up a proper, more 'permanent' family home and I wanted to do that back in Ulster. Christopher would be ready to start school the following autumn so it was time to put down roots in the right place. Apart from the rugby, there wasn't a lot to leave behind and we knew it wasn't the place where we wanted to bring up our children.

"That was my third season at Saracens and my contract was up at the end of it. If I hadn't returned to Ulster, I would have stayed there rather than move anywhere else and could have done so even though things hadn't gone quite as well for us as the previous year. Following on from our Twickenham triumph was always going to be difficult, especially without Sella and Lynagh. Lynagh in particular was a very hard act to follow and his replacement Alain Penaud blew hot and cold. He was very French and didn't really settle.

"When you're winning, everything is happy, but when you aren't, life isn't so good for the professional sportsman. That was essentially a season of consolidation and, helped by a good run towards the end, we did well enough, most notably qualifying for the European Cup for the first time by finishing sixth in the league. Things weren't bad by any means, so it was more a case of the time being right to move back home than wanting away from Saracens. A lot of the Irish guys had gone back the previous summer, so apart from personal circumstances, the trend was now a reverse of what it had been when I went and, just like then, the move made sense."

There was one other theory though why Paddy moved back to Ulster. "There was a rumour round Saracens" insists a grinning Constable, "that Paddy was heading back home because Christopher was picking up a Cockney accent and he wasnít too keen on it!" Either way, his mum was delighted. "We were over the moon" says Mrs Johns. "I missed the grandchildren, so it was wonderful when he decided to come back."

So who was in the stronger bargaining position, the players who were on bigger salaries in England than were on offer from the IRFU, or the Irish management who were making it clear that they preferred home-based players? Were Paddy and others in a position to really haggle over money or, because of knowing the individuals concerned would want to safeguard their Ireland prospects, did the Union have them over a barrel? Was there any degree of brinkmanship and playing hard to get?

"Basically the players in England had to be enticed home and I think, in overall terms, there was compromise on both sides. Guys saw it in their own rugby interests to play in Ireland, but naturally wanted things to be right contractually rather than just jumping into it. The IRFU realised they had to make an effort to make the packages reasonably attractive, but at the end of the day most people, myself included, who came home took a pay-cut of significant enough proportions."

Half-jokingly, Paddy likens the negotiations with the IRFU Contracts Committee, headed by Billy Lavery, to "the Orangemen trying to get permission to march down Garvaghy Road", but Ulster Branch Chief Executive Michael Reid identifies Johns, along with fellow former Saracen Ryan Constable, as one of the easiest people he has had to deal with contractually in the professional era. Another analogy which is hard to resist because of Johns' dentistry links is the 'pulling teeth' one, but the deal was finally concluded over a period of time and Paddy signed a contract with the IRFU which would commit him to Ulster for the next three years.

25. WEMBLEY WINNER

Winning at Wembley is a dream realised by precious few footballers and even fewer rugby players. Captaining your country to victory there is a mighty special feeling and one which will stay with Paddy Johns for as long as he lives. The 21st of February 1999 is a day which Paddy will never forget as things all gloriously came right in the afternoon after a sartorial faux pas by his other half in the morning had been headed off. Kirsty had dressed up in her best for the big occasion and was ready to proudly support hubby when a friend pointed out that a full length red coat was hardly the most appropriate colour for the Irish captain's wife at a match against Wales!

The Twin Towers and Wembley Way are about much more than English football, of which the now sadly derelict and crumbling edifice was the world famous home. It was a soccer stadium first and foremost, but the name was simply synonymous with sport. The round ball game, of course, is all-pervasive and, like most young fellas, Paddy, a Leeds United fan for his sins, grew up on a diet of FA Cup finals on the box, enthralled by the footballing fairytales, captivated by the colour and drama of the occasion. He certainly never expected to play there though, to emerge from that famous tunnel, to tread that hallowed turf, to strut his stuff in front of a big Wembley crowd.

Even after he vowed to become a rugby international, playing at Wembley was never an ambition or aspiration. It simply wasn't an option. The place was the preserve of football. Winning at Twickenham, the home of English rugby, in 1994 would do him nicely! But then came the change in Cardiff, the demolition of the old Arms Park and the building of the magnificent new Millennium Stadium. Wembley became the Welsh team's adopted home during the transition. That was to give Paddy the opportunity to do something which no Irish rugby player had ever done before or ever will again. The chance to lead their national team up the famous Wembley tunnel and out onto the hallowed turf.

At one level, he had mixed feelings. The old Arms Park had been a happy hunting ground for Ireland in that they had not lost there in seven visits from 1983, with Paddy already having been part of a hat-trick of Irish victories at the ground. Would the charm work at Wembley? The answer was yes, Ireland steaming well ahead and then holding off the Welsh rally to record a 29-23 victory which, remarkably, was the first time Keith Wood had tasted victory in the Championship in spite of having been around the Irish squad for six or seven seasons. His personal performance played a big part in the triumph.

Ireland's international season had begun back in November without the Lions hooker, who was in a contractual dispute with the IRFU and consequently missed the World Cup qualifier against Georgia at Lansdowne Road. Wood's loss wasn't felt on the pitch as, under Paddy's captaincy, Gatland's greens romped to a facile 70-0 victory, Eric Elwood converting all 10 tries, one of which was scored by the skipper himself. Even if Wood hadn't been at loggerheads with the IRFU, Gatland made it clear that Johns would have remained as skipper, a clear endorsement by the coach of Paddy's performance in the role on the South African tour.

The absence of Wood meant a start for Ross Nesdale at hooker in a front row which also featured Peter Clohessy wearing the green No 1 jersey for the first time at Test level. There were five survivors from the pack which had taken the field in Pretoria, Johns being joined by his engineroom partner Malcolm O'Kelly, Lions prop Paul Wallace, No 8 Victor Costello and flanker Andy Ward. Eric Miller was at blindside for Dion O'Cuinneagain. Behind the scrum, Elwood and McGuinness continued at halfback, O'Shea at fullback and Bishop on the right wing, but a three-quarter line reshuffle resulted in Maggs being moved out to the wing to facilitate a new midfield pairing of Bell and Australian-born Connacht centre Pat Duignan.

Denis Hickie was out of the picture after the trauma inflicted by injury and Stefan Terblanche in South Africa, while Ulster captain Mark McCall was sidelined with the neck problem which was to prematurely end his career. Substitutions were now in vogue and, with his team romping home, Gatland made a record number of replacements with all of the bench boys except David Humphreys, surprisingly so in light of Elwood's unimaginative play, getting a taste of the action.

Paul Wallace got Ireland's opening try from a lineout early on, with Johns following suit near the end of the first quarter before the backs got in on the act late in the half with two tries in as many minutes, scored by Maggs and O'Shea. Costello opened the second half account and it was 42-0 with half an hour remaining after Johns had stood in at scrumhalf and sent out a fine pass which enabled Elwood to put his Connacht colleague Duignan over on debut. The seventh try, from Bell on 58 minutes, brought Ireland close to the half-century mark and they immediately cruised past it on the hour courtesy of a touchdown from Girvan Dempsey, who had come on at fullback to win his first cap. Reserve pivot Ciaran Scally of UCD, on for McGuinness, emulated Dempsey's feat by announcing his arrival with a try, but the Terenure man went one better and had Ireland's last word by claiming the 10th touchdown five minutes from the end.

At the post-match press conference, Johns famously made the statement that "they wouldn't have beaten the All Blacks" when asked to sum up the Georgian challenge or lack of it as Ireland had romped to a record win in front of a paltry crowd of 11,400. Looking back he points out that Ireland were on a real hiding to nothing in that "anything less than 50 points would have been seen as a disaster, but we were never going to get much credit no matter how much we won by.

"From my point of view it was a potential banana skin, if only inasmuch as we knew absolutely nothing about Georgia before that game. Our objective was to get points on the board early on and just keep going. I think we did it fairly successfully. At a personal level, it was nice to get the chance to captain Ireland at Lansdowne Road. Even though I had skippered the side in South Africa, I assumed it would be a temporary arrangement and didn't really expect the opportunity to lead the team on home soil.

Even though, in a sense, it was 'just Georgia', and although there was only a small crowd there, it was still special. Winning by a record score is always a good feeling and the fact that I got a try myself put the icing on the cake. So it was a nice one, but as a team we weren't getting carried away by the result."

Fitzpatrick, Davidson and O'Cuinneagain all got a run-out in the second half, while Clarke had come on in the opening period for Nesdale, who had a hamstring strain and was ruled out of the second qualifier against Romania a week later, thus allowing a now reconciled Wood to return to the match 22. The Lion was made to wait though for a recall to the starting line-up, Clarke being handed the No 2 jersey in recognition of the fact that, unlike Wood, he had originally been in the squad for the World Cup qualifiers. Gatland made two other changes, Scally getting a first start at the base of the scrum instead of McGuinness and Darragh O'Mahony, who was in prolific try-scoring form for Bedford, gaining a go on the left wing at the expense of Maggs.

Romania had a much more formidable team in late 1998 than the decimated and demoralised outfit which was annihilated 134-0 by England a few years later, but few expected them to run Ireland as close as they did. The Irish might have eventually registered their hoped-for half century of points, but to leak five tries in a game like this was simply shocking and, although the final margin was 53-35, it would have been much closer had the spirited visitors not had a better place-kicker than the otherwise excellent pivot Petre Mitu.

Both teams crossed each other's line the same number of times and while, as Johns claimed afterwards, Ireland's two penalty tries may well have been justified, for Romania did spend much of the afternoon killing the ball, they spent the rest of it playing some pretty exciting open rugby and were well worth their handsome points haul. Ireland only played to their potential in very short bursts, leaving serious questions to be asked about their collective performance both in defence and attack, where they threw possession away like confetti, ahead of their rematch with South Africa. The main consoling hope was that Ireland, traditionally more comfortable being underdogs than favourites, might be lifted by the challenge of the Springboks, though in the modern professional era, as Wood said after the game, full focus is required in every international.

Perhaps though, until the past couple of years with the advent of Brian O'Driscoll, the problem was not as much one of finding proper motivation for lesser games as the old accusation that Ireland played better without the ball. That line has always been an indictment of Ireland's inability to be constructive and creative, which was proved, to a degree, by their embarrassing attempts to use the ball against Romania or reflect on the scoreboard their dominance in most of the possession stats.

To concede more points than they had in Pretoria to a Romanian side beaten 60-0 and 25-3 on its two previous visits to Dublin seemed like so many steps backwards, particularly considering that the visitors had only beaten no-hopers Georgia 27-23 three days earlier. But the straw to clutch was that Ireland probably wouldn't have conceded some of the tries had South Africa been the opponents, primarily because most of them originated from the breakdown of Irish moves which they would not have been attempting - or had the ball to attempt - against the Springboks.

Romanian captain Catalin Draguceanu insisted that the referee had awarded the hosts their brace of penalty tries "too fast and too easy" and, when asked what was good about Ireland, he eventually volunteered the old cliché about the men in green "playing with heart." Apart from his limited English, he could hardly have truthfully come up with much else. But talk about damning with faint praise. So how concerned was Paddy ahead of the Springbok showdown?

"We knew that South Africa would be a totally different sort of test and I never felt that the two World Cup qualifiers would have much bearing on that one apart from giving us match practice. The Romanian game is not one which I remember with any great affection, not least because of being subbed at halftime even though I was captain. It was a bit of a surprise to me at the time, but I suppose the idea was to give Jeremy Davidson a half. I was never too concerned about losing, but Romania certainly did play a lot of rugby and we didn't help ourselves. We probably tried too much too soon without getting the basics in place and dropped a lot of ball in the process, which played into their hands."

In many ways, the two World Cup qualifiers were mere warm-ups for the third Test in as many Saturdays and the third that year against the Springboks, a Lansdowne Road sequel to the summer showdowns on South African soil. Maggs returned to partner Bell at centre, giving the midfield a more solid look, with Dempsey getting his first start, on the wing, and McGuinness restored at the base of the scrum for young Scally. Unfortunately, Paul Wallace was absent through injury, so Clohessy switched to his old position of tighthead while Dion O'Cuinneagain started at blindside against the land of his birth with Miller missing.

Most significantly, Wood was back at hooker and had an absolutely outstanding match as Ireland took the game to their illustrious visitors, only trailing 6-7 at the interval as a result of giving away a try through a defensive blunder. The Boks began to pull away early in the second period and, although the inimitable Wood gave Ireland faint hope with a try which Elwood converted to close the gap to 11 points, the gallant greens couldn't score again and the South Africans had the last word with another penalty.

Victory meant that this superb Springbok side, coached by Nick Mallett and future Ulster supremo Alan Solomons, had equalled the world record of 17 successive Test triumphs, a mark set by Colin Meads' All Blacks between 1965 and 1969. Defeat at Twickenham in their next game prevented Mallett's men from becoming a neat single entry in the history books, but by emulating the All Blacks of three decades earlier, they had earned the tag of true greatness.

No fewer than 11 of the South African starting line-up had featured in both battles a few months earlier, while the same applied to a dozen of the Irishmen, so it really was like a third Test of the same series in spite of the time gap. Fullback Percy Montgomery, wingers Stefan Terblanche and Pieter Rossouw, centre Andre Sunman and pivot Joust van der Westhuizen were the five ever-presents behind the Springbok scrum, with Henry Honiball's return at outhalf actually strengthening the side. The backline was completed by centre Christian Stewart, who had won his first cap against Scotland the previous Saturday. Gaffie du Toit and Franco Smith, both of whom had featured in the summer series, were on the bench along with reserve scrumhalf Werner Swanepoel. Up front, there were six men starting against Ireland for the third time that year in hooker James Dalton, prop Adrian Garvey, locks Kyrnauw Otto and Mark Andrews and loose forwards Rassie Erasmus and Gary Teichmann who, like Johns, was continuing as captain.

A glance at the forward replacements, Ollie le Roux, Naka Drotske, Andre Venter, who had been usurped by Bobby Skinstad, and the still uncapped Corne Krige, indicates just how strong a squad South Africa had at the time. The tour party also included a number of other uncapped players later to make their mark for the Boks in Breyton Paulse, Deon Kayser, Robbie Fleck, Braam van Straaten, Selborne Boome, Philip Smit and Andre Vos. Willie Meyer, another reserve, had already made his Test debut. It was an awesome array of talent, comparable with the star-studded All Blacks party which had visited Ireland a year earlier in late 1997 and vastly superior to the present day Springbok squad as the drain of top South African players to Europe continues.

Ireland emerged with their heads held high from this eagerly-awaited encounter, which could easily have ended up even closer on the scoreboard than the 13-27 result in favour of the Springboks. Until South Africa's devastating burst of two cracking tries in two minutes early in the second half, it was actually all a bit confusing at Lansdowne Road. Ireland didn't look like Ireland in their unfamiliar white jerseys flecked with green and navy shorts, but because they produced such a typically Irish response to a monumental challenge, the Springboks weren't allowed to look like the world champions they were either.

With the game being in Dublin, this wasn't just the negative, however necessary, backs-to-the-wall spoiling exercise which Ireland had had to employ to contain South Africa in that last, ill-tempered, meeting between these nations in Pretoria back in June. In that first half, the Irish enjoyed a huge territorial advantage but, for those wanting to be critical, yet again the problem seemed to be that the hosts could work themselves to death, get into good positions and then not quite have the wherewithal to make it count. What distinguished South Africa was their ability to conjure seven points from brief raids and relatively unthreatening situations, and that killer instinct was exemplified in Erasmus' try on 27 minutes, which gave them an undeserved lead.

The home team had started so promisingly, with one early trademark run from Wood the perfect way to get a packed house buzzing, but unfortunately Elwood pulled the first of three penalty attempts wide after six minutes when Ireland caused classic mayhem which led to South Africa losing the ball and then infringing. The Irish scrum was characteristically solid and the Springboks conceded several penalties there. From one such award, Elwood kicked to touch in the visitors' half, and then O'Cuinneagain launched a devastating break, ended only by a van der Westhuizen ankle tap.

It was a pity that South Africa lost Dalton with injury after only 11 minutes, for his clash with Wood had been eagerly awaited, but nowhere near as disappointing as Elwood's second missed penalty on the quarter hour as more swarming Irish pressure went unrewarded. But the team's response was a great attacking phase straight from the dropout with a characteristic charge from the colossal Costello supported by good link play from Clohessy, and when Paddy set up the ruck, the Boks handled on the deck and Elwood popped over the three points.

Ireland, still in the ascendancy, got very close in midfield after Elwood kicked a penalty to the corner, and then O'Kelly almost released Bishop after more furious Irish tackling again turned over South African ball. And still the hosts came in waves, either side of a first fracas of an afternoon which never saw the ugly scenes of the summer, but after the ball went dead when Elwood charged down Montgomery's clearance, the Springboks swiftly struck. Bishop was left isolated close to the touchline, but got cracked on the head as the South Africans swept over him, and the ball rolled out their side for wing Rossouw to float a long pass which Erasmus took to the posts, Montgomery converting.

But South Africa were playing mainly in their own half and the result was that another huge midfield hit by Maggs on Rossouw led to the Boks killing the ball and Elwood landing a second penalty. As Honiball's restart failed to go the requisite 10 metres, the first strains of Molly Malone filled the old ground, and Elwood launched a great diagonal to the corner to keep up the pressure, but missed a penalty in stoppage time, so a great spell of pressure in which both Wood and Ward went close went unrewarded.

It was a devastating start to the second half by South Africa though, Montgomery kicking a penalty to reward early pressure before Skinstad showed why he was picked ahead of the mighty Venter by scoring one try and creating another. He touched down under the posts following a swerving run at pace after Honiball had broken in midfield and then, from a second break when Ireland lost possession soon afterwards, he repaid the compliment by flipping inside to his stand-off who released van der Westhuizen with a perfect pass.

At 24-6, the floodgates were poised to open, but Ireland responded brilliantly and Wood ripped his way over like a man possessed, with Elwood converting. Montgomery responded with a penalty just before the hour mark. Ireland were unlucky not to be awarded a penalty try going into the final 10 minutes, considering the two they were given against Romania the previous week, as the Boks repeatedly infringed close to their own line, and more than deserved a score for their sustained pressure. A moment of indecision by Elwood just before the final whistle may have been a reminder of Ireland's underlying limitations, but at least the proud defensive credentials had been restored after the debacle of conceding 35 points against Romania seven days earlier.

From the summer series, the three changes in the Irish line-up saw the return of a fit-again Bell in place of his sidelined Ulster colleague McCall, Clohessy deputising for the injured Wallace and Dempsey appearing on the left wing in place of the damaged Hickie. In spite of the animosity which had been simmering from the summer, this contest thankfully didn't boil over. The game had been billed as another bloody battle but, in the event, an absorbing rugby match broke out and Ireland gave a good account of themselves therein.

"I suppose, subconsciously, we realised that the world would be watching and that there was an onus on players from both sides to be on their best behaviour, but it wasn't something which was specifically discussed in advance of the game. If it had started again, we were ready. We weren't going to look for trouble, but equally we wouldn't have walked away. In the event, I think South Africa approached it differently and weren't looking to start stuff this time. We also may have had less of a siege mentality on home soil.

"Considering that we hadn't left South Africa on the greatest of terms, we were determined to make a major impression, but it is good that people can remember that game for how competitive we were in rugby terms rather than for unsavoury incidents. Their first half score was very soft and we had a lot of pressure which went unrewarded in the second half, but it was definitely an encouraging performance and a reasonable result against a team which were in the process of writing themselves into the history books. It set us up nicely for the Five Nations."

Ireland's Championship campaign opened on the first Saturday in February when France visited Lansdowne Road where, the previous weekend, Ulster had famously conquered French club Colomiers in the European Cup final. That success had created a feelgood factor among the Irish rugby fraternity, while the near miss in Paris the previous year provided grounds for hope that the French could be taken and, in the event, Gatland's team again came agonisingly close. But, ultimately, it was to be another case of heartbreak for the gallant greens on a dirty Dublin day which played a big part in ensuring that it would be a tense low-scoring affair, ultimately settled by two late penalties, one at either end, one on target and one missed.

There were several changes from the side which had taken the field against South Africa, with two Lions returning, a fit-again Paul Wallace in place of Fitzpatrick with Clohessy reverting to loosehead and Jeremy Davidson starting in the engineroom for the first time in nearly two years. He took over from the injured O'Kelly, who had partnered Paddy in the previous dozen Tests since being one of the seven new caps against the 1997 All Blacks. O'Cuinneagain moved to openside at the expense of Ward to accommodate the return of Miller to the back row which, in spite of the South African-born captain's great pace, was not particularly well balanced given that he was by no means a natural No 7. But the most talked about change was the return of Humphreys, in red hot form and fresh from lifting the European Cup as Ulster captain in the same stadium a week earlier, at the expense of Elwood at outhalf.

Three Humphreys penalties pushed Ireland up to a 9-0 lead, but the French eventually conjured a try which was converted to set up a fraught and frantic finale. Not for the first or last time in his international career, Paddy's Saracens clubmate Paul Wallace gave away a penalty and from it, with time running out, flyhalf Thomas Castaignede gave the visitors the lead for the first time. But there was still enough left on the clock for Ireland to get down the other end and force the French to infringe, giving Humphreys the chance to snatch victory back from the jaws of defeat right at the death. With the final whistle about to blow, everything rested on the kick but, although it was well within range, about 10 metres outside the 22 and around halfway out towards the left touchline, the prevailing conditions meant Johns was not particularly confident and certainly didn't envy his fellow Ulsterman.

"It was teeming with rain and the ball was like a bar of soap. I was beside David when he took the kick. I was praying, but I was not optimistic because of the wind. There was a helluva change in the wind that afternoon. It was swirling and would blow up, then die down. The kick was on target but the wind took it out. It was one of those things. I felt we deserved to win, but I didn't see it as David's fault that we lost. It should never have come down to that last kick.

"I think, because of not having beaten France for over a quarter of a century and having come so close the previous year in Paris, to have victory snatched away like that was especially hard to take. That said, I was always one for trying to take the positives out of any defeat and the fact was that we deserved to have won and, a few years earlier, would readily have settled for one or two point defeats against the French. We knew we weren't far away and that the gap was definitely closing. Victory in Paris the following season proved that point."

As well as Humphreys' miss, the match will be remembered for the blue paint plastered over the players and, most memorably, Wood's pate, from the sponsors' logo which had been decorated onto the pitch. The rain had caused the paint to run. For the Irishmen, it was a case of the blues, Les Bleus in every sense.

And so down Wembley Way and the chance to bounce back with a victory which would extend to 16 years the remarkable run of not losing away to Wales. By a strange quirk of fate, Dempsey was ruled out of the game by injury, leading to a recall on the wing for Niall Woods, who had been in great form for London Irish and was instrumental in Ireland A's victory over the French in the opening round of the shadow Five Nations. Woods had been enjoying great success as the frontline marksman at London Irish, so his presence in the team allied to Humphreys' miss against the French and perceived unreliability with the placed ball based on past record, made him a credible alternative.

At the time, although Ulster captain, Humphreys was not kicking regularly for his province because of the presence of Simon Mason, so speculation was rife all week in the build-up to the game that the duties could pass to Woods. In the lead-up to the match, Johns came out in support of his under-fire flyhalf. "David is a very strong character and a dedicated professional" he was quoted as saying. "Wembley will be a good opportunity for him to silence all those critics. I have absolutely every confidence in him."

Humph exclusively revealed to this writer the night before the game that he would indeed be taking the first pot at goal the following day and keeping the faith in him proved an inspired decision by Gatland. Apart from Woods replacing the injured Dempsey, Ireland's only other change saw Ward return to a reshuffled back row at the expense of Costello, with Miller moving to No 8 and O'Cuinneagain going back to blindside.

Humphreys silenced his critics in glorious style with a man-of-the-match performance which enabled Ireland to realise their dream of becoming Wembley winners. It may have taken a slightly fortuitous try to set the ball rolling and the men in green were guilty of panicking a little as Wales hit back strongly in the second half, but in this case winning was all that mattered and Ireland thoroughly deserved their success.

There was no bread of heaven for a Welsh team forced to rely on scraps of possession for most of the afternoon as King David led the slaying of the dragon and steered Ireland to a first Five Nations win under Gatland. For the coach and his players, victory against a major Test nation after 12 months of progress and near misses had become the holy grail and it was the man the coach had kept faith with who led them to the promised land at the expense of the Great Redeemer, Graham Henry.

Humphreys directed operations from outhalf with confidence, efficiency and vision to build on his encouraging display against the French, but this time he also had his place-kicking boots in good working order. An early strike from an almost identical spot to his crucial final penalty miss of a fortnight earlier set the tone for a productive afternoon which brought him a personal tally of 19 points as well as creating a try for Maggs. Undaunted by a disgraceful crescendo of whistles, Humphreys split the posts confidently from 27 metres out, on the left, giving Ireland the perfect start to a first half which they went on to dominate as undisciplined Wales struggled to compete. The Ulster captain was guilty of one wild long pass in the opening 10 minutes and was unlucky with a second penalty attempt after 13, but any Irish mistakes were drowned in a flood of Welsh errors.

Deadly marksman Neil Jenkins levelled matters when Ireland went offside with a quarter of an hour gone and a scrappy spell ensued until the men in green went back in front with a snatch and grab try. Humphreys charged down Jenkins' attempted clearance, scooped the ball up and slipped it nicely to Maggs, leading to the great scene of a posse of five Irishmen bearing down on the posts at Wembley's famous tunnel end with not a Welshman in close pursuit. With Woods and Bell either side of him as cheerleaders, Maggs gleefully claimed his first try for his country and Humphreys knocked over the simple conversion. To this day Gatland remembers it "as a wonderful moment within a great occasion."

From the kick-off, Ireland went straight back on the rampage, immediately forcing another penalty which the outside half, now doffing his scrum-cap for each shot at goal, turned into points, and Wood tore through on the next restart to set up Humphreys for an exquisite rolled kick into the Welsh 22. The position was wasted with the concession of a free kick, but Ireland continued to dominate and a dreadful high tackle by Scott Gibbs on his fellow Lion, Wood, after half an hour saw Humphreys kick a penalty to the corner and duly add another three points when Wales offended in midfield following the lineout. Jenkins cut the deficit to 10 points five minutes before the interval, but things got worse for Wales before they got better, as mighty Ireland extended their lead despite a complete aberration by O'Shea, who somehow let Welsh wing Daffyd James beat him to the touchdown of his kick ahead.

When the try did come two minutes later, it resulted from several great Irish phases, when O'Cuinneagain linked well with Woods, who slipped elusively into the 22 and Ireland won the ruck. McGuinness fed Wood who came through in the outhalf position with a perfectly timed and angled run which saw him bounce one tackler and sidestep another to bag a score which again underlined his credentials as a world-class performer. Again Ireland countered from the restart and when Wood thundered to the 22 after Davidson had towered at a lineout, the ball came back for Humphreys to strike a sweet drop goal.

Now 20 points in arrears, Wales were stung into an immediate response with Craig Quinnell brutally bulldozing his way over from a lineout and, as a red sea of attackers lashed the Irish defence in the period that followed, everyone realised there was still enough time left for it all to slip away. Debutant wing Robinson was superbly bundled into touch by O'Shea near the corner flag as that hauntingly melodious Welsh singing started to reverberate round Wembley, but Ireland continued to survive, with Bishop pulling off one great tackle on James.

O'Shea almost became the villain by missing touch from a penalty and it led to another Welsh try after Humphreys was wrongly adjudged to have kicked straight to touch from outside his 22. A long Jenkins pass to Robinson led to Kiwi fullback Shane Howarth crossing in the corner and when the outhalf converted to leave one score between the sides with more than a quarter of an hour remaining, the force was now with Wales. Worse was to come when a terrible unforced handling error by Woods near his own line gave Wales a scrum from which Ireland blatantly went offside and Jenkins punished them to make it 23-26 after 68 minutes.

It was reminiscent of Cardiff in 1997 when Ireland had to withstand a Welsh fightback after opening a huge lead, and again it would come down to who had the nerve and who wanted it most. But Ireland crucially struck next when a penalty gave them a good position, the imperious Davidson won the lineout cleanly, O'Shea was used on the crash ball like London Irish were wont to do so effectively, and when the ball came back from the ruck, Humphreys calmly slotted his second drop goal. He missed with another attempt two minutes later which would have given Ireland a two score cushion, but Gatland's greens were not to be denied, with one brilliant O'Cuinneagain cover tackle summing up their resolve, and after five tense minutes of injury time, the celebrations which had been on hold for 12 months began in earnest.

"It was great to win at Wembley, of course it was. Just to play there was great, but winning naturally made for an awful lot better memories of the place than losing would have done. But it was also a very important result for Irish rugby at the time. We felt we had been making progress since Warren took over, but hadn't been getting the wins in the big games. After a number of moral victories, it was time for an actual one.

"The whole occasion was fantastic. There I was, captain of Ireland and about to win my 48th cap in a big Five Nations match against Wales, but I still felt a bit like an excited schoolboy when the team bus was pulling up at the ground for I'd never even been there before as a spectator. I've played at some great rugby stadiums, but it was a real novelty to be playing at Wembley, just like Georgie Best! We also knew that, as a one-off, it was an historic appearance. No Irish rugby team had played there before or ever would again."

Paddy doesn't recall playing up the Wembley factor in his teamtalk in the famous changing-room or evoking any great footballing deeds which had been done under the shadow of the Twin Towers, but admits that leading his team up the legendary tunnel and out onto the hallowed turf was "absolutely awesome. It's very hard to put into words what that felt like, but I'm sure every individual was inspired by the surroundings and sense of occasion. Wales had played there before, but for us it was new and wonderful. We got a big start, helped by Welsh indiscipline, which gave us a few penalties and, consequently, momentum. It was nice for Humph to get some early chances and I'm sure seeing a few kicks go over helped him play very well."

A marked feature of the match was how the Irish, in marked contrast to the previous summer in South Africa, repeatedly turned the other cheek in refusing to respond to Welsh provocation. Craig Quinnell's fists were flailing at Johns within a couple of minutes of the start, but didn't draw the sort of response the Springboks had done, while Gatland revealed hardman prop Clohessy's dressing room remark to him afterwards: 'I took a punch for you today, boss, and it hurt not giving one back'. Both Quinnell and Young were sinbinned for indiscretions in that first half while Ireland simply focused on the rugby and piled up the points.

"That was a deliberate tactic" he reveals. "We knew that the Quinnells would 'lose it' and, although they were a real physical presence, the indiscipline of Craig in particular cost Wales dearly that day. Our plan was to not retaliate, or at least to not get caught. The idea was to draw the penalties, let the lead mount up and leave them chasing the game. It worked very well and, although they came back at us, we had enough in the bank. In a game between two teams that are fairly evenly matched, each will have its period of pressure and it would have been unrealistic to expect us to remain totally dominant throughout."

Davidson was Ireland's main source of possession out of touch, but Paddy's mobility and workrate had been crucial in such a loose contest as this one, with his ferocious fringe tackling in support of the back row being a major factor in his team's success. The way in which he fought a dead leg until almost the end before giving way to Mick Galwey underlined his commitment to the cause and desire to see Ireland home.

"It was a fantastic experience and a remarkable rugby occasion" says Jeremy. "Wales had been going well so it was an important win for us and made for an unbelievable day. Paddy was outstanding and thoroughly deserved to have the unique honour of being a winning Irish rugby captain at Wembley. At that time, it was seen as much more profitable in the game in general to be throwing to the middle or tail, so he didn't have a massive lineout role that day, but was right at the heart of everything else."

It was clear what this meant to him from the unusually demonstrative way in which he exultantly saluted the very vocal contingent of Irish supporters as the victorious visitors strode towards the tunnel after the game and his colleagues speak of the emotion which he showed when back inside. "Paddy dedicated the victory to the people of Ireland" said Wood, who was celebrating his first ever win in the competition. "He said it was for all those who had supported us." "We could hear the Fields of Athenry ringing out around the ground" recounts Paddy. "The Irish supporters stayed on forever afterwards, celebrating the win and soaking up the Wembley occasion. They just didn't want to leave. I was genuinely delighted for them as well as ourselves."

For once, the post-match press conference would have been a pleasurable enough affair, with the Irish hierarchy chewing the cud in reflecting on victory rather than being part of a post mortem into another depressing defeat. But poor old Paddy missed out. "Yes, as luck would have it, that was one of the occasions on which my number came up for the drugs test" he reflects ruefully, before adding with a grin: "At least you guys couldn't have claimed that I would have been wanting an excuse to not turn up on a day like that!"

You have to enjoy the good times while they're here. When Ireland next returned to London for a Championship match, against England at Twickenham the following February, Johns wasn't even part of the 22. He was almost history. But memories of Wembley will warm him long into his dotage.

26. HITTING THE HALF CENTURY

Paddy could have picked a few happier hunting grounds than Murrayfield for winning his 50th cap. You play international rugby to win, so he never really enjoyed Edinburgh apart, perhaps, from Ireland's good run at the inaugural Sevens World Cup in 1993. In the course of his long career at Test level, Johns never tasted victory over Scotland in seven lean meetings. His only consolation was scoring the winning try for the Barbarians in the international organised to raise funds following the Dunblane disaster.

Some of Paddy's career milestones came at Murrayfield, including his Ireland B debut, first Five Nations appearance and the 50th cap which was also, though he could hardly have foreseen it at the time, to prove his last start in the Championship, so the ground is very much part of his rugby history and, of course, his sister is married to a Scotsman. Although Scotland are traditionally hard to beat on their own patch and teams visiting Murrayfield get a hostile reception, the stadium was not the problem. Paddy has strong views on why Ireland always seem to struggle in Edinburgh. "I never particularly enjoyed going our Five Nations visits to Murrayfield and they got more and more depressing as the years went by. The result never went our way in my entire career, even though we always travelled with a fair degree of hope and never felt we were an inferior side.

"This might sound like a bit of an excuse, but I could never understand why, throughout my career, when Ireland were in Edinburgh, we always stayed in a hotel in Princes Street, which was invariably noisy and guaranteed plenty of distractions. It would have been far better for us to have stayed in a hotel somewhere out in the country where it would have been much easier to focus. Murrayfield was always a real graveyard for Irish teams and I genuinely believe where we stayed was partly to blame for that.

"My first Five Nations start was at Murrayfield in 1993 and, by the time I made my final one six years later, we were still staying in the same place, because it was nice and handy for the Blazers being right in town. I never cared whether the IRFU committee men were in the same hotel as the players or not, it didn't bother me, but their convenience should never have been the priority. But, with Edinburgh at least, it sadly seemed to be and the players were disadvantaged as a result. By contrast, with Cardiff we used to stay more in the middle of nowhere and, when we almost beat France in Paris in 1998, we were well out of town and it was ideal. The environment you are in in the lead-up to an international is important in my view."

Before rounding off their 1999 Championship campaign at Murrayfield, Ireland had entertained England at Lansdowne Road a fortnight earlier. The fit-again Dempsey returned for Woods on the wing, Henderson took over from Bell in the centre and Costello replaced Miller at No 8. It was a game in which Ireland did reasonably well, but not one which Johns remembers much about other than the fact that his team lost, 15-27.

That Lansdowne Road was so flat after watching Ireland come within inches of snatching the lead in the dying minutes against England was not just down to the immediate sense of disappointment at the result. A packed house, some paying up to £600 on a thriving post-Wembley black market for their ticket, had seen a match where unlikely victory had remained a possibility for so long finally slip away after the men in green had outrageously produced several good chances to steal it and keep Triple Crown hopes alive.

The English chariot rode on in pursuit of the Grand Slam as three Johnny Wilkinson penalties and a late try finally carried them home to a victory which should have been secured earlier, after the visitors had totally dominated a first half which Ireland could never get into. But the real frustration was that this steadily improving Ireland team had not played to the level now expected of them, particularly up front, where Jeremy Davidson alone enhanced his reputation.

Even though Ireland were seldom able to assert themselves, they remained in contention on the scoreboard into the closing stages, when fine individual breaks by both home halfbacks almost brought tries which would have levelled the scores at 20-20 with a conversion to come. Had that happened, it is probable Ireland might have held on and not conceded the late try to Tim Rodber. It would certainly have been daylight robbery, but after what France did in Dublin a month earlier, the team would have felt entitled to take it.

England laid the foundations for victory in a turgid first period when, although a combination of their own mistakes and determined home defence kept the scoreboard fairly even, they strangled Ireland deep in their own territory and thus snuffed out the special Lansdowne factor. It would have needed a few furious Irish surges early on to get both the team and the crowd going, but England kicked off and then had a penalty to the corner from where they spent five minutes laying siege to the home line. Humphreys actually give Ireland the lead with his first of five penalties and two more meant England only led 11-9 at the break, having scored a try through Matt Perry which was supplemented by a penalty by the teenage Wilkinson and a Paul Grayson drop goal.

Ireland, who were very fortunate to go in only two points down, could surely only improve in the second half and they began it perfectly when a charge from Wood in the first minute led to a penalty from which Humphreys put his team back in front. But Wilkinson kicked England into the lead again and after major pressure by the visitors added two more either side of the hour mark, though Ireland responded well and could have scored in the lead-up to Humphreys' fifth penalty. The Ulster captain scorched round a big blindside with five minutes remaining, but Bishop was squeezed out and eventually Ireland were penalised in attack and the pressure evaporated. Back came England to tighten the screw, and although Luger knocked on with the line at his mercy and Dempsey pulled off a great tackle on Martin Johnson, the latter's second row partner Rodber powered over in injury-time and Wilkinson's conversion made the final score more reflective of the balance of play.

So Ireland went to Edinburgh with reasonably high hopes at the end of an encouraging enough Five Nations, but it was to be the same old story. Déjà vu all over again. For Paddy the match brought the milestone of 50 caps, making him only the ninth Irishman to reach this great landmark. He agrees that it was a very special occasion and an achievement to be proud of.

"As captain I would have been doing a few interviews anyway, but there was a fair bit of extra attention before this game because of the 50 caps. It isn't the sort of thing which happens every day. To win 50 caps, you need to be committed and resilient and be seen to perform consistently well over a lengthy enough period, so to get there was very satisfying and a measure of what I had put into my rugby down the years.

"I hadn't set my sights on 50 caps at an earlier stage because in sport things can change so quickly and you can't predict the future. It might sound like a clichÈ, but I really did take it one game at a time and my target was always the next cap rather than a particular number. There are more matches these days and the introduction of substitutions means modern players will be able to run up significant numbers of caps in a shorter period of time, but when I got to 50, only eight Irishmen had done it before and it was nice to become part of a group which included such famous names as Mike Gibson and Willie John McBride."

In reaching 50 caps, Johns joined an exclusive club of Irish greats headed by the inimitable Gibson and the legendary Lions leader McBride, followed by Fergus Slattery, Phil Orr, Brendan Mullin, who had been a colleague earlier in his Test career, Tom Kiernan, his first Ireland captain Donal Lenihan and a fourth lock, Moss Keane. The family had bought him engraved Tyrone Crystal to mark the achievement and he had got a lot of congratulatory messages from old friends and colleagues, including Mark McCall in a letter which recalled the days when the pair had plumbed the depths of despair on the New Zealand tour of 1992. "No-one deserves the honour more" wrote Mark. "You are a great example to every rugby player in Ireland and have done a great job since being appointed captain."

But reminiscences on his first 49 caps and reflecting on what had got him to this milestone could wait for later. There was a job to be done as Ireland sought to break a barren spell at Murrayfield which stretched back to 1985. "It was a big emotional day for me and all the family were there watching, but apart from the personal landmark, I saw the game as a big chance to get the Murrayfield monkey off our backs. Having never won there before, it would have been great to do it on my 50th cap, but sadly it wasn't to be."

In rugby, it is customary to let a player lead the side out on their 50th cap but, as captain, Paddy was scheduled to be doing that anyway, giving the Irish camp a bit of a dilemma about how to make sure he stood out. So they sent him out on his own. "I thought maybe the boys would hang back a few yards so I would be running out a wee bit ahead of them, but they actually left a huge gap and I suddenly found myself standing in the middle of the Murrayfield pitch as the only Irishman in sight. I felt like the Lone Ranger!" recalls Johns. "We got off to a dream start with Dion scoring in the first minute or two and did well enough until just after halftime if memory serves me right before really falling apart in the last half hour."

Bell was back for Henderson and Miller for Costello but Scotland easily won a fast, open contest which painfully exposed the limitations in Ireland's game, with the backline, apart from Humphreys, looking woefully inadequate. At various times in the game, Ireland lost their shape, their nerve, their ideas, their discipline and even the ability to do the basics right. They lost their way, lost the plot and, of course, the upshot was that the lost the match itself. Most crucially, Gatland's greens kept losing the ball at critical moments on an afternoon they couldn't keep possession for half the length of time their opponents could . . . even though they would have needed the ball for twice as long to do as much damage. By contrast the Scots typically fought for every scrap and wasted little, allowing the man who taught them that parsimony pays in rugby, the great Jim Telfer, to sign off with victory in his final Murrayfield Six Nations match before retirement.

Several moments and passages during the game summed up the crucial difference between the sides on a day when Scotland made sure they cashed in their dividends while Ireland repeatedly squandered hard-earned gains. By not being able to score from sustained pressure either side of half-time, Ireland put themselves through a mountain of hard work to eventually get from 15-10 down to 15-13, only to promptly concede 12 points in the space of two minutes. That was a soul-destroying microcosm of Ireland's hapless plight, but there were other examples as Scotland showed how much more adept they were at playing a fluid game. When it came to effectiveness and penetration, their play was generally in a different league.

"My 50th cap will always be special, but the result certainly took a lot of the gloss off the occasion. It was deeply depressing to lose at Murrayfield yet again and to lose by that sort of margin when we genuinely felt we were capable of winning. I remember talking to Warren Gatland in the airport on the way home. Naturally enough we were both pretty gutted, but mystified as well. To this day, I still struggle to put my finger on why we had such a poor record against Scotland, with not a single win in the 1990s."

By not being picked for the 2000 Championship game between the countries at Lansdowne Road, Johns missed out on a win over Scotland to end seven years of famine and thus was condemned to never tasting victory against them at senior level. "Apart from the fact that we never stayed in an environment conducive to success, you have to hand credit to Scotland. They always had a few key players like the Hastings brothers, Gary Armstrong and Craig Chalmers. Those guys always produced something and everyone else chipped in."

In preparation for their entry to the Championship the following year, Italy played an international against the 'spare' side in each round of the 1999 competition. That meant facing Ireland on the fifth and final weekend of the series. The way the fixtures fell that year, Ireland had played their four Championship matches on the first four weekends, so Italy were tagged on at the end for Paddy's team rather than coming somewhere in the middle of the programme as they had for the other competing nations.

It was a match which Ireland could have done without at the end of a long hard season and, in recognition of the amount of rugby they had already played and what was to come before the end of the year with the Australian tour and the World Cup, Wood and Paul Wallace were left on the bench. Clohessy moved back to tighthead with Fitzpatrick coming into the team, while Nesdale wore the No 2 jersey. Trevor Brennan got his first start, at blindside in a remodelled backrow which featured O'Cuinneagain moving to openside in place of Ward and the musical chairs between Miller and Costello continuing, with the latter returning at No 8. Ciaran Scally and Eric Elwood took over from McGuinness and Humphreys respectively at halfback, while Henderson came in at inside centre for Bell, who had had a most unhappy time in Edinburgh. It proved to be a far from impressive Italian job.

Ireland eventually beat Italy 39-30, but some of the elementary errors and mediocre fare provided en route left a restless crowd bewildered and humiliated. Admittedly things did improve in the second period, but only after the most crass, dire 40 minutes of dross imaginable from the home side. It all began with an Italian try after 51 seconds and, as the visitors were generously assisted into a 23-8 lead by their blundering hosts, pre-match suggestions in some quarters of a landslide victory to cure the ills of Irish rugby soon looked well wide of the mark.

Ireland never led until 12 minutes from the end, but at least they won to finish their season with four victories from eight Tests, albeit including Georgia and Romania, and results elsewhere over the weekend bizarrely meant Gatland's greens ended up third in the Five Nations championship table ahead of Wales and France. Considering that placing was the coach's stated objective and that it was Ireland's highest finishing position in the table of the 1990s, it offered some consolation, but in the early stages of the game, the only thing to cheer the Lansdowne crowd was the Irish-trained Grand National winner they had just watched on the stadium's big screen.

Italy scored in the opening minute when Costello failed to deal competently with the kick-off, the hooker drove deep into the 22 and, from a quickly run penalty, veteran lock Walter Cristofoletto crashed over in the corner. Diego Dominguez converted superbly from the touchline and, although Ireland responded with a Bishop try, they dropped the Italian kick-off and were punished with a drop goal. That was cancelled out by an Elwood penalty, but the hosts again spilled a long restart and were put under more pressure which yielded six more points for Dominguez. The second half of those came from a drop goal and, within two minutes, Italy were 23-8 ahead thanks to a try which had every Irish rugby fan wincing as Conor O'Shea and Bishop both fumbled the ball under no immediate pressure and then a bad turnover allowed the winger to round off a huge overlap with Dominguez converting.

Elwood reduced the interval arrears with another penalty and, after O'Shea's try had given Ireland a good start to the second half, he completed his hat-trick of strikes before Gatland sent on Lions Wood and Wallace. Early in the final quarter Elwood kicked a penalty and then missed one, but his loop with Bell launched the move which led to a good try, scored by Dempsey, and O'Shea got his second touchdown to ease Ireland further ahead with seven minutes remaining, seizing on a loose ball which shot out of a scrum. Ireland had scored 26 points without reply, but Italy weren't beaten yet and grabbed a converted try in the 80th minute to make it 34-30. But a searing Scally break allowed Ireland the final word with a disputed try by Paddy himself and everyone breathed a collective sigh of relief.

"After three losses in a row to Italy, it was a relief to win that one alright, especially as we had been so far behind at one stage and because the game was in doubt right up until I scored on the final whistle. Italy were a team which we should have been beating every time, but it hadn't been happening before that, so a win was a win even though we didn't play particularly well."

When Paddy was back in Ireland for the Italian match, he had taken the opportunity to check out a couple of possible new homes for the Johns family, who were ready to return to Ulster following a three season sojourn at Sarries. That move would mark the end of his era in England, but another chapter was also about to close. He didn't know it at the time but, when the final whistle went against Italy in Dublin, Paddy's year long reign as Ireland captain was over. Dion O'Cuinneagain was selected as skipper for that summer's tour of Australia.

"I never really thought about continuing or not continuing at that point but it was a bit of a shock to be chopped for the tour after doing the job for so long. In fact it was only a year, but that covered 10 Tests and I'd got used to being captain. That's not to say you ever take the honour for granted, or that it means less, but you do settle into a role after a period. I'd have been less surprised to lose the captaincy after the previous summer's South African tour. Back then, I almost saw myself as a caretaker captain in a way, because the expectation was there that the captaincy would simply revert to Keith at the start of the next season. It seemed like I had only inherited it on a temporary basis and in the very specific circumstances of him having declared himself unavailable for the tour.

"Woody was probably our highest profile player and had been captain beforehand so, although I was fairly content that I had done the job I was asked to in South Africa, I didn't feel like it was an open-ended appointment and honestly expected him to be brought back. To that extent, I suppose I was a bit surprised to be asked to continue back then, but Warren seemed to be pleased with how I'd done on tour and was happy enough to let me continue. I don't know to what extent Keith holding off on signing his contract might have been a factor. Anyway, being asked to stay on was not something which I had counted on, just as I can also say that I didn't see the change coming when I lost the captaincy before the Australian tour of 1999.

"Donal Lenihan rung me up to tell me the news. I had mixed feelings about it. While I was naturally very disappointed to lose the captaincy, I'd never thought that I would be Ireland captain in the first place or even, having been asked to do it in South Africa, that I would keep the job for so long. Not many people get to captain their country, so I could consider myself lucky, could be thankful, could look on the bright side. I was also genuinely pleased for Dion, knowing that he would experience the same special feeling which I had had, starting with the euphoria of being asked to do the job."

His mum adds: "He'd captained his country 10 times and no-one could take that away from him. We knew he wasn't finished and that he'd bounce back, because that was his nature. It was disappointing for him, but the positive was that he could now really focus on his own game, for the captaincy did make extra demands on him especially because he took his role so seriously."

What softened the blow for Paddy was the fact that it was made clear both publicly and privately that the change was no adverse reflection on his leadership over the course of the previous 12 months. With three leading locks, Johns, Davidson and O'Kelly, in contention and a World Cup coming up in the autumn, Gatland understandably wanted a free hand in his second row selection rather than being tied to always picking one of the trio because he was captain. That meant finding a new skipper from another area of the team, but O'Cuinneagain, not born in the country and still fairly new to the Irish scene, was a bit of a surprise choice to replace Paddy even though he had been a shining star amid the Murrayfield malaise, was an outgoing and articulate individual and was an exciting player.

Characteristics shared by Wood, although the two people are also very different. But what of the man himself? Where had the Lions hooker gone in the equation? Why had Uncle Fester remained in the wilderness and, one year on from initially opting out of the South African tour, still hadn't returned as skipper? "That's a question for Warren Gatland" says Paddy, "but perhaps he thought at that stage that Keith was better without the added responsibility of captaincy. There was certainly a school of thought at one stage that that was the case."

How had captaincy affected Paddy's own game? "It's up to others to judge but, speaking personally, I certainly don't think it had an adverse affect. If anything, I think that I possibly played better with the captaincy." Responding to a suggestion in an Irish Times interview ahead of his 50th cap that the captaincy had brought out more aggressiveness, Johns had said: "Maybe sub-consciously, I doní't know. I always thought I was aggressive before I was captain!"

Ireland prop Justin Fitzpatrick offers: "Paddy was uncompromising as a player, and as a captain he pushed that even further. He was a captain who led by example and would not ask anyone to do what he wouldní't do himself first. The other big thing was his precision. He himself leaves no stone unturned with his personal preparation and as captain he made sure that the players around him were fully briefed."

Apart from any debate on whether Wood was better being left to concentrate on his own game while someone else led the side, there was an inevitable feeling that he was still being punished for his contractual dispute with the IRFU in the autumn of 1998. "It wasní't that we disagreed so much with Keithís issues" insists Gatland "as the fact that he backed us into a corner in terms of the timing. To come in and threaten a week or two before the squad was announced was probably intended to exert maximum leverage, but it left us in a difficult position. The Union had said to us that, if it came to a head, he should be left out and he left us with little option but to take that course. In any case, Paddy had done a great job and we were delighted to keep him on."

So Paddy had relinquished what he always saw as a temporary title, though after a longer period than expected and not to the man he had believed himself to be keeping the seat warm for. If people are asked to place the period in which Paddy Johns was Ireland captain, chances are that they'll mention that South African trip of 1998, not just because of the controversial Tests, but because leading a team on tour is more all-pervading than being a skipper for individual games on home soil.

Paddy hopes, however, that the South African tour doesn't come to define his time in charge, not from any strong sense of shame at what happened there, but because there were greater positives to remember his reign by. He unsurprisingly nominates the win over Wales at Wembley the following February, Ireland's solitary victory in the last ever Five Nations and hence the only Championship triumph under his captaincy, as the highlight of his period in charge.

He was only captain for roughly a year, but Ireland played 10 Tests in that period, four of which were won and six lost. Three of those were against a great Springbok side and the home defeat against France was very unlucky. The low point was the Murrayfield mauling which marred the occasion of his 50th cap. After that baptism of fire in South Africa, Paddy's first home international as captain produced a then record rout of Georgia, who were thrashed 70-0 in a World Cup qualifier, and he also ended his reign with a home victory, against Italy. Again demonstrating that sense of occasion referred to in an early chapter, Johns marked the Georgian and Italian matches by scoring a try in each, the two touchdowns accounting for half of his ultimate Test tally of four.

For the record, Ireland were in credit in terms of points difference over the course of his 10 Tests in charge, notching 254 with 252 against, and scored 27 tries. Gatland was the man who both appointed and removed him. Lenihan was manager throughout the period.

With the family remaining his abiding focus off the pitch and providing stability, neither gaining nor losing the Irish captaincy changed Paddy's life much. He saw it as an honour, enjoyed the job and gave it his best but, although he admits it gave him a buzz, he wouldn't pine for the status or control which he was now relinquishing.

Judging by the lack of lacy things in his mail, captaining his country may not have caused any rise in his stock as a sex symbol, nor indeed have led to much media intrusion, and neither had he particularly sought to exploit any increase in commercial value which resulted from his status as skipper. In the 12 intervening months he had done the job to the best of his ability and now handed on the baton with the same humility and grace which he had shown when accepting the honour and responsibility a year earlier.

27. BACK DOWN UNDER

A foot soldier again then, and heading off to Oz once more with the clear implication that his place in the team was, at the very least, under the severest of threats. Otherwise why would Gatland have removed him as captain in favour of a less than compelling candidate in O'Cuinneagain.

In the five years since he had previously toured Australia, a lot of water had, inevitably, passed under the bridge in the form of fatherhood, appearing in a World Cup, being in and out of the side, living in London during his three year Saracens sojourn, switching back permanently to the second row and captaining his country. Now he had returned to the ranks in the Irish set-up, serving under a man who hadn't even been born on the emerald isle and had only won his first cap on Paddy's tour of South Africa the previous summer.

The general view was that O'Cuinneagain only got exercised about his Irish roots when it became apparent that he wasn't going to make it with the Springboks and saw Ireland as a backdoor into international rugby. But Paddy didn't have a problem with Dion. For a start, the captaincy change had been no direct reflection on either man's perceived suitability for the job or on Paddy's performance while in post. It was more a case of Gatland wanting flexibility with his second row selections, so that meant appointing a captain from another area of the team. If, for that reason, it wasn't going to be Johns, he didn't really mind who it was. They weren't being appointed out of any sense that they could do the job any better than him.

Secondly, he wasn't too hung up about any 'plastic paddy' syndrome surrounding O'Cuinneagain or outraged that the captaincy had passed to a player who some regarded as not being a fully-fledged Irishman. There was no personal animosity towards O'Cuinneagain thanks to the circumstances in which the captaincy changed hands and, perhaps because the pair got on well, Paddy never thought of the athletic loose forward as an outsider.

"I suppose it might have been different if I hadn't liked Dion as a person, but I remember phoning him to offer my congratulations and feeling genuinely pleased for him. I had no problem whatever with being supportive of him as captain." Conscious that, having been around so long, won over 50 caps and been skipper for the previous year, he was a father figure, was Paddy particularly mindful of the danger of undermining O'Cuinneagain in any way by being seen as some sort of alternative leader? "Absolutely. I was happy to be a help to anyone, but was always careful not to undermine the new captain in any way and to let him stamp himself on it.

"In fairness, he did well. Dion and I would have had quite different styles, both as players and as captains. I'd have been quite abrasive and done a lot of unseen work, while he was a very skilful, exciting player with great pace who did spectacular things and caught the eye. He was laidback but engaging and took all the media stuff in his stride. Dion is very articulate and intelligent, not that I'm not intelligent, but he would definitely have been more comfortable with doing interviews and so forth than me. We are both involved in the same sort of professional area outside of rugby and I think I can safely say that we respected each other both as people and as players. I never had any problem with Dion as captain and we got on well."

So having a good relationship with O'Cuinneagain helped, as did the knowledge that his demotion hadn't been down to any failure of his captaincy, but how difficult did Paddy find it being back in the ranks after having been the main man? "It was maybe slightly strange at the start and a bit of a disappointment, but I get over things fairly quickly. As a sportsman, you have to get over things quickly and move on, to take setbacks in your stride as much as possible. If you can't deal with disappointment and just give up or let it eat at you, you'll be destroyed. Not many Irish internationals have had a smooth ride throughout their careers. Top level sport can be a bit of a roller-coaster and, by then, I was well used to it."

People perceived Paddy as being fairly level-headed and able to cope with the fluctuating fortunes better than most, but he admits to being as easily hurt as the next man and Kirsty would testify that some of the blows, especially his increasing marginalisation within the Irish set-up later, did hit him hard. Although a proud man, Paddy is also a humble one, so he didn't need to be Ireland captain to satisfy his ego and that helped him adjust fairly easy to his return to the rank-and-file, albeit a revered elder statesman.

In any case, Johns had enough on his plate without worrying about the lost captaincy. What's done is gone and his career had now entered a new phase. With Jeremy Davidson and Malcolm O'Kelly now both fully fit, competition for places in his department of the team was going to be fierce. With another World Cup looming large on the horizon a few months hence and media momentum building in favour of a possible 'dream-ticket' second row pairing of two younger men in Davidson and O'Kelly, the pressure was on him to perform. He was disappointed to lose the leadership but relished the challenge of fighting for his place as a player, with everyone certain that selection would be purely on merit and no-one able to claim that, as captain, he was going to get preferential treatment.

"I did feel that, although I had started the last 21 Tests, my longest unbroken run at any stage, this was another crossroads in my career, with Warren openly stating that he wanted to have the option of playing Jeremy and Mal together. It didn't unduly bother me though, for I backed myself to respond to the challenge and was determined to hold my place. There was a World Cup coming up before the end of the year and an awful lot to play for. I knew that I had to prove myself all over again and make sure that I came out of that tour still being a first choice second row for Ireland. My aim was to go out there and really focus on each game and play well in each.

"Starting both Tests was a big target and it was pleasing to achieve that. People may have felt that the tide had started turning against me and that the other two boys would be thrown straight in together now that I was no longer captain. By staving off that scenario, at least until another day, I may have proved some people wrong, but I don't know whether satisfaction is the right word. The bottom line was that I wasn't planning on missing out in the World Cup, and starting both Tests in Australia was a step in the right direction. I may have been taken off both times, but the fact was that I started two and Jeremy and Malcolm started one apiece. That was a positive."

Rob Henderson, who had started against Italy, effectively saw his World Cup hopes dashed when he was omitted from the tour party, while Conor McGuinness was ruled out by the injury which was to cut short his career. Brian O'Meara was included instead as one of the two scrumhalves alongside young Ciaran Scally, but had to withdraw due to a broken thumb, resulting in a call-up for the uncapped Tom Tierney of Garryowen. The party included several prodigious prospects in Jeremy Staunton, Brian O'Driscoll and Robert Casey along with a couple of new names on the Irish scene in Mike Mullins and Matt Mostyn, two men who had been born and grown up in the Antipodes.

Both selections caused considerable disquiet in the country at the time given that, apart from what people felt about the desirability or principle of picking 'outsiders' for Ireland, they had not really yet demonstrated that they were worthy of selection. Mullins, a Kiwi at West Hartlepool, and French-based Aussie Mostyn of Begles-Bordeaux had both featured in the A team's facile victory over the Italian second string in April, but fans of Henderson and Denis Hickie were not impressed by their inclusion.

"It wasn't talked about in the team" says Paddy "and, if the issue was even thought much about, I imagine the attitude would have been 'if they're good, then great'. Beggars can't be choosers and Ireland had a limited pool of players so we were always glad to utilise anyone who could potentially strengthen the squad. These guys were qualified to play for Ireland under the eligibility rules and the selectors had decided they were worth including, so that was alright. They felt Irish and fitted in fine. In general that has been the case with anyone who came in. There are natural checks and balances anyway in that, if someone doesn't fit in or isn't good enough, they won't survive anyway, or alternatively if they make a contribution, few people will question their right to be there."

As for the youngsters, the exciting Staunton had been making waves as a precocious teenage talent for Garryowen, while UCD midfield man O'Driscoll, a member of the Ireland Under 19 team which had won the FIRA Junior World Cup in April 1998, was earning rave reviews. The third highly-rated new boy originally selected was Blackrock lock Casey, still only 20 but already a giant physically and considered an even better prospect than O'Kelly had been at the same age. Did Paddy see Casey as being largely an investment for the longer-term future, or someone who would be emerging as a serious threat to his place sooner rather than later?

"When you're in the team, you must look all round you and treat anyone who is on the scene as a serious contender. At that stage, Casey was coming through and getting pushed forward as a big hope for the future, so he certainly couldn't be dismissed as a challenger. Robert was a big, heavy boy for his age but, unfortunately, had bad knees and ankles, which have subsequently held him back" said Johns, on whom the young O'Driscoll made a favourable impression. "Brian was young and had no experience at full international level prior to that tour, but he was very fast and keen and looked a class act. We knew that he would come through very quickly. Tours are good for bringing on a player quickly and integrating them into a set-up. They are an ideal opportunity to assess what someone can offer, what makes them tick and whether they've got what it takes in terms of talent and temperament."

In addition to that trio and the presence of Mostyn and Mullins, the call-up of Tierney meant there were half a dozen new caps in a squad which also, as well as 14 of the starters against Italy, featured the four men who had come on from the bench in that game, Bell, Paul Wallace, Wood and Ward. The party was completed by Humphreys, who had been first choice flyhalf throughout the Five Nations, a fit-again O'Kelly, who had missed the entire Championship due to injury, fourth prop Reggie Corrigan and flanker David Corkery, who had burst onto the scene on the previous tour of Australia five years earlier.

Rather than being a traditional tour with a significant number of fixtures outside the Test series, including midweek matches, this trip was a foretaste of the favoured format of the future and the itinerary tailored to assist Ireland's World Cup preparation. It was expected that the development of the young players would largely take place on the training ground with less opportunities to give fringe squad members gametime than, for example, in South Africa the previous summer. The present was now more pressing. The other sign of the times was the fact that Ireland took a back-up team of 10, headed by Gatland, his assistant and the manager Donal Lenihan, to support a 28-man playing squad, skippered by O'Cuinneagain with Conor O'Shea as vice-captain.

Ireland had a gentle enough opener against New South Wales Country Districts, a match which they won 43-6 but, five days later, the tourists went down 39-24 to the full NSW state side in Sydney. Paddy played in the latter and recalls that "we played some good rugby but lost." Gatland chose three new caps behind the scrum for the opening Test in Brisbane, in Mostyn, O'Driscoll and Tierney, the trio coming in in place of Girvan Dempsey, Henderson and Scally, with Maggs moving to inside centre. Humphreys was restored at outhalf for Elwood, with Clohessy switching to loosehead and Fitzpatrick and Nesdale dropping out of the front row to accommodate the return to the starting line-up of Paul Wallace and Wood following their rest against Italy. In the second row stakes, Johns and Davidson held off O'Kelly, while Ward pushed Brennan out of the loose forward unit, O'Cuinneagain reverting to blindside.

An Irish nightmare repeated itself under the lights at Ballymore as the men in green were hit for six tries by an increasingly slick and rampant Wallaby machine. Gatland must have felt heartily sick of South African debutants going on scoring sprees against his team after the spectre of Stefan Terblanche had followed them from Bloemfontein to Brisbane. Exactly a year earlier, Terblanche had marked his first cap with four tries as South Africa beat Ireland in the first of two Tests and there was more than a hint of irony that the main beneficiary in Australia's record victory here was a former Springbok captain.

Tian Strauss skippered South Africa five years previously before losing his place and missing out on his native country's tremendous World Cup triumph under Pienaar in

1995, but now the veteran could look forward to playing a prominent role for his adopted Australia in the next tournament. The 33-year old Strauss, who had recently qualified for Australia under the three-year residency rule having originally emigrated to Sydney to start a new rugby league career, was introduced to the action six minutes into the second half. He finished off a great phase of Wallaby continuity to register his first score early in the final quarter and then was up in support of fullback Chris Latham five minutes later as Australia produced an immediate response to Ireland's sole try of the evening from Maggs.

Brave defence kept an increasingly dominant Australia at bay for the next quarter hour but, with the game deep in injury-time, Strauss provided the extra man on the outside after a gallop from lock David Giffin to complete the rout and his hat-trick. The tourists had just about managed to keep their hosts' points tally to under the half century mark and narrowly avoid the 40-point margin of defeat which former Wallaby legend David Campese had predicted, but it was still a bad beating which didn't augur well for the following Saturday's second Test and, indeed, the coming World Cup.

"We played below par that night" says Paddy candidly. "We expected an awful lot more of ourselves than we produced in Brisbane and everyone was determined not to leave the country on a low note. As a team, we had let ourselves down and, given the history of second Tests overseas being a bit of a disaster for Irish sides, were determined to turn things around a week later."

Yet Ireland could so easily have gone in level at half-time in Ballymore instead of 13-3 down, even though they had ominously trailed 10-0 after 16 minutes to a penalty by debutant fly-half Nathan Spooner, later of Leinster, and his conversion of Ben Tune's try, created by George Gregan. One successful penalty strike from two attempts by Humphreys got Ireland on the scoreboard and then Gatland's greens came close to a try just before the break when debutant wing Mostyn was stopped inches short of his native country's line after being released by another new boy, O'Driscoll.

Ireland got nowhere from a series of attacking scrums and Spooner rubbed salt in the wounds with a stoppage time penalty and, although the tourists began the second half with a flourish, a powerful burst by big centre Daniel Herbert following a lineout saw him break several tackles before offloading to his supporting captain David Wilson, who went under the posts. Spooner's conversion made it 20-3 and left Ireland really facing down the barrel, but they didn't concede again until 55 minutes when Herbert scored following more visionary play by Gregan. The final quarter was all about Strauss waltzing through gaps in the Irish defence as Australia stretched them to the limit with some clever interplay, but Maggs' try, converted by Humphreys, at least took the tourists into double figures.

One casualty of the Brisbane bashing was vice-captain O'Shea, who had sustained a broken jaw, so Dempsey took over at fullback for the second Test, while Bell was selected on the wing for Ireland for the first time since the Five Nations match at Murrayfield in March 1995, when he scored a try. He took over from Mostyn wide on the left, while Paddy had a new second row partner with O'Kelly replacing Davidson. O'Cuinneagain moved to No 8 at the expense of Costello, allowing Brennan to claim the blindside berth.

The feeling was that Johns had played pretty well at Ballymore, his best display for a few games and enough to stave off the immediate threat to his place in spite of a poor performance by the team and a depressing result. "Brisbane was very disappointing from a team point of view, but I'd done enough to retain my place and be part of the side which had the chance to pull things back in Perth which, I must say, was a strange setting for a second Test." Perth is not a rugby town. One of the authors spent six weeks there the following summer on a medical placement with the local Aussie Rules team, the West Coast Eagles and was struck by just how relatively little interest there is in the sport.

In the event, Ireland restored lost pride and gave Gatland a base to build on for the World Cup with a plucky Perth performance against the Wallabies. It wasn't so much that these two Tests were dress rehearsals for the Pool meeting between the countries at Lansdowne Road on October 10, for Ireland could reach the quarter-finals of the tournament without actually beating Australia. More importantly, this tour Down Under was to provide a measure of Ireland's state of health with less than four months to go to the World Cup and, had they suffered a real Perth pasting to go with the previous week's Brisbane bashing, the prognosis would have been serious indeed.

Instead, this rousing display, albeit in defeat, was just what the doctor ordered and, when added to the good work done on the training ground during the four week trip, allowed the squad to travel home in good heart. They would reassemble in August to play Argentina and then go on an internal tour with warm-up matches lined up against the Irish provinces, giving them a chance to build on this performance and fine-tune their gameplan. It would all have been so different had the feared 60-point hammering materialised in the second Test, forcing Gatland to go back to the drawing board, but even in the opening exchanges, it was very apparent that the men in green had no intention of lying down and dying.

Just as their obituaries were being written, Ireland sparked into life by at last recapturing the old traditional underdogs' passion which had been sadly lacking against England back in March and in the first Aussie Test. The pack finally refound the fire which had been quenched in recent times and, allied to solid setpieces, reclaimed the reputation, established in three clashes with world champions South Africa in 1998, that they were capable of competing with the best. A continuation of the basic mistakes, particularly in relation to ball retention, which had let Ireland down against Italy and in the first Test, would have left Gatland with an insidious and extremely worrying problem, but his men showed pleasing improvement.

Porous defence had cost Ireland dearly against Scotland and New South Wales in recent months, but was pretty sound in Perth apart from wavering briefly in the second half as the brilliant Tim Horan ignited the Australian backs when he moved to stand-off, while the discipline also held up better than expected. It all contributed to the reduction of the defeat margin from 36 points the week before to a mere six point gap this time, an achievement put in context by the results of the Tests in New Zealand in 1992 when a 24-21 first Test loss became 59-6 in the second.

Admittedly, Ireland scored two tries late on at the Subiaco Oval when the game was effectively dead, but the fact remains that, in times past, instead of grabbing a couple of scores of their own, the men in green would have conceded another few. So this was further evidence of the spirit and, of course, the fact that this Ireland team now had the fitness to play for a full 80 minutes, unlike some of their predecessors. Even though the clock was showing 86 minutes when Maggs repeated his try-scoring exploits of seven days earlier, it was still a tremendous achievement for Ireland to cross the Wallaby line three times in an away Test.

Discipline, defence, passion and character were all central to this tour salvage mission, but there were also glimpses of the style which Gatland was trying to develop around his dynamic skipper O'Cuinneagain, Ulster fly-half Humphreys and young O'Driscoll. Several slick Irish attacks were a sight for sore eyes, while the tries were tribute to tremendous continuity by forwards and backs in the first instance, good vision by Bell for the second following an efficient backline move, and clinical execution in the case of Maggs' effort.

Ireland began brightly, with two Aussie turnovers in a match where they lost the ball far more often than the tourists, leading to a Humphreys penalty strike after five minutes, and Irish intentions were made clear when the Ulster flyhalf boldly ran the ball from deep in his own 22 two minutes later. Spooner, a future Leinster player, levelled the scores with 10 minutes gone and pushed Australia ahead before the end of the first quarter, but Ireland came close soon afterwards thanks to Ward grabbing loose ball three times in the space of 90 seconds.

Eventually the tourists had the try they deserved when Clohessy timed his run to perfection to finish off yet another wave of Irish attack from a lineout and although Humphreys missed the conversion, he extended the lead with a stoppage-time penalty. Huge tackles by Brennan and Ward helped Ireland hold their advantage until the interval, though it took one lucky bounce to preserve their line and limit the Wallabies to another Spooner penalty from the last kick of the half.

An angled punt by Humphreys almost brought joy for Bell early in the second period, but he edged Ireland 14-9 ahead with half an hour remaining when Australia were finally penalised for upending Paddy at a lineout. The Wallabies were under immense pressure, but finally got a lucky break when the otherwise faultless O'Kelly spilled ball in his own 22 and it was worked to Horan, who scored, with stand-in kicker Joe Roff - Spooner had gone off ñ converting. Roff then pushed a penalty before landing two as Australia began to pull away, and his conversion of Latham's try - which probably stemmed from a forward pass - had virtually made the game safe before his final penalty on 78 minutes.

At 32-14 and with Australia playing their most dangerous rugby of the series, the wheels could really have come off, but the irrepressible Humphreys twice saved the day and Ireland finally had their reward when Bell came off his wing and chipped perfectly for Justin Bishop to just about apply enough downward pressure by the corner flag. Finishing strongly, the tourists then launched wave after wave of attack in the next six minutes of injury time and the margin was cut to a highly creditable six points when the skipper and impressive young scrum-half Tierney set up Maggs to crash through following a scrum, with Humphreys converting. "I actually think we should have won that game"

Johns insists. "We had underperformed in the first Test, but improved massively between Brisbane and Perth, for the Wallabies played better too second time around and yet we generally held our own."

On our first go at chatting about Australia 1999, admittedly distracted slightly by Paddy keeping an eye on the telly on the last night of the Big Brother series, there were no anecdotes which readily rolled out about life on that tour. A later second attempt proved equally unproductive. Had these trips lost their novelty? Were the modern Test tours simply too serious to enjoy too much? Tours no longer represented a month away from the day job. Was Paddy getting a bit weary of life on the road as a pro player?

"The main things which I remember about that tour are the Tests. They were the focal point of the trip, why we were there, and also, from a personal point of view, extremely important in terms of my immediate future with Ireland. With the World Cup only a few months away, that tour was pretty serious stuff for everyone. As a team we were working towards that tournament and, individually, we had an awful lot to play for." So no crashing golf buggies or soaking The Claw like five years earlier.

His mum had a great time though. Having toured South Africa the previous summer, she was off on her travels again in support of her son and the Irish side. "It was the trip of a lifetime" says Mrs Johns. "South Africa was good but, naturally, there is less tension in Australia and we also had a different party of followers which gelled together better. I've got relatives in Australia and had been there before, but hadn't been to the Great Barrier Reef. It was a lot of fun snorkelling there.

"The trip ran without a single hitch and I made some very good friends. I got to know Frank and Geraldine O'Driscoll (parents of Brian) very well and it was nice to share with them the joy of seeing their son get his first cap. It brought back memories of Paddy starting out. Theyíre a delightful, charming couple. I can remember a very enjoyable dinner party in the top of the Centre Point restaurant with the O'Driscolls, Pat Bell (Jonny's mother) and Rhona and Joe Fanagan, the parents of the Ireland physio, Denise."

There's no rest for the wicked. It was all go for Paddy on every front when he returned from Down Under. He was back home, ready to link up with Ulster again and, on the international scene, there was a Test against Argentina coming up before the end of August, with the World Cup starting on October 1. And, although he didn't know it at the time, Kirsty was expecting twins!

28. RETURN TO RAVENHILL

It wasn't quite like he'd never been away. When Paddy rocked up at Ravenhill in the autumn of 1999, the old place, bless it, was little changed on the surface although it was now an inhabited home to a professional rugby team. There were also plenty of familiar faces around in the Ulster squad. And his first provincial coach more than a decade earlier, Harry Williams, was in charge again. Home, sweet home. It was like one of those spot the difference competitions, where the two pictures look the same at first glance, but when you look more closely, the subtle changes become apparent. For a start, there was someone sitting in Paddy's pew. Scrumhalf Stephen Bell had pinched his old peg. For years, Johns had sat in the same spot, through the door directly in front of the heater. Now it was taken.

"I was a few minutes late for our first day of pre-season training and, when I arrived, Stevie Bell was in that spot. I asked him if he'd mind moving and told him that was kind of my place. He said he had been there first. I said 'I don't think so'. We had a bit of banter about who had really had 'been there first' or had a call on that peg. He was maybe the man in possession as I'd been away, but I'd first played for Ulster more than 10 years earlier."

Bell gave in with good grace to the senior statesman, but Johns could have been considered the imposter given that, in the strictest sense, he was the new boy returning to a changing room full of European Cup winners. Paddy stresses that he was very well received by everyone, but that episode or exchange could be taken as a metaphor of how things had moved on, as life inevitably does, and the legacy of Ulster's famous triumph earlier in the year. He may have been an ex-Ireland captain with more than 50 caps for his country, but that success the previous season had turned the group of men he was now joining into local heroes wearing a continental crown. In spite of all he had achieved and his long service in a successful Ulster side a decade earlier, it could be argued that Johns was now almost the outsider and returning to Ravenhill at a difficult time when the team was in a no-win situation.

It was always likely that the 1999-2000 season would be something of an after-the-Lord-Mayor's-show sort of affair for Ulster and so it proved, spectacularly so, in the form of a whitewash in the Pool phase of their attempted European Cup defence. Much has been said and written about second season syndrome and the hangover effect associated with winning the trophy, something which had previously afflicted 1998 winners Bath and subsequently afflicted 2000 winners Northampton. Reality suggested that, especially with the English teams back in the competition, Ulster would find it extremely difficult to even come close to emulating the amazing achievement of the previous season, while certain other factors also counted against them.

While it was the same for everyone, the World Cup certainly proved a disruptive influence in the early part of the season and Ulster definitely didn't get the breaks this time around. It seemed that they had used up all their luck the previous term, not least with regard to injuries. Losing the massively influential pair of Andy Ward and Jonny Bell for the European Cup opener in Bourgoin was an enormous blow and, with Fijian prop Joeli Veitayaki proving a disastrous signing from the word go, Ulster were condemned to a season of struggle.

Paddy insists that he had no particular apprehensions about Ulster being on a bit of a hiding to nothing at the time he rejoined, but reveals that the atmosphere and attitude which he found in the set-up quickly had the alarm bells ringing in his head. At the Ulster Rugby Awards dinner the previous May, this writer had picked up a 'how-do-we-ever-top-that' sense of reluctance on the part of some players for a new season ever to start, what seemed like a natural hankering to keep wallowing in their wonderful achievement forever without having to put their crown back on the line. Johns, for his part, experienced what could perhaps best be described as a hint of conceit and complacency in the camp when everyone turned up to start a new term. Taken together, the two syndromes served as pretty powerful portents of an unsuccessful season.

"I remember the first couple of sessions and getting a bad feeling from the changing rooms" he recalls. "There were guys with false confidence that we were so much better than everyone else, that things would just be like the previous year or that for Ulster it would now simply be a case of turn up and win. From an early stage, I felt that there was an air of over-confidence with a lot of joking and bravado and so forth, the boast that anyone who comes to Ravenhill will get a good kicking. But to have that you must work doubly hard the next year and there is no doubt that, if you stand still, you will go backwards. Things were a bit lax among the players I felt. I just got a gut feeling that things weren't going to go well." It proved very prophetic.

In spite of his status, Paddy didn't look down on his less illustrious colleagues and they still treated him with due respect even though the European Cup had been won in his absence. Some of that summer's other signings didn't fit in so easily however. Coach Williams, realising that his panel lacked the strength in depth to sustain success in Europe, didn't take the easy option of sitting on his hands and sending the same squad into battle to defend their trophy the following season. Instead, he traded on the Euro triumph to attract a number of names to Ravenhill in a bid to bolster the squad.

Johns came home, as did former international Niall Malone, who had previously moved from Leicester to Worcester. Williams and the Ulster Branch took a bit of a gamble in giving Paddy's former Dungannon clubmate Tyrone Howe a professional contract. He had been sidelined for several seasons by injury, but was now playing again down the leagues in England and working as a schoolteacher. The return of Johns and, assuming he was physically fine, Howe, would have been widely welcomed, while Malone represented experienced, quality back-up to Captain Marvel David Humphreys at flyhalf.

Simon Best, the former Portadown College prop who had been making an impression on Rob Andrew at Newcastle, came home, while Bangor boy Mark Edwards, at university in Dublin, got a full-time contract in an expanded professional squad as did two bench boys from the European Cup winning team, Bryn Cunningham and Ritchie Weir. That left five outsiders, journeyman England A winger Spencer Bromley, a colourful character in 6'4" centre Riaz Fradericks, former Fijian captain Veitayaki, Johns' successor as national team captain, Dion O'Cuinneagain, signed from Sale, and another Ireland loose forward, Eric Miller.

The globetrotting dreadlocked Fradericks, born in South Africa, brought up in Australia and capped at international level by Hong Kong, was a bit of a crowd-pleaser with his long, loping strides and nonchalant air, and will always be remembered for scoring a spectacular length-of-the-pitch try against Munster at Ulster's temporary base at Upper Malone. But he broke his hand and spent most of the important part of the season sidelined while, although Bromley bagged a few tries, he kicked possession away down the wing far too often. Additionally, with James Topping fit again, his presence only served to limit opportunities for a fit and hungry Howe.

"I would have to say that Bromley and Fradericks weren't the most popular in the squad" he concedes. "They fitted in well enough at the start, but Ulster had a poor season and I suppose everyone suffered a bit. By the time they went, it was probably fair to say that it hadn't worked out." Veitayaki was an unmitigated disaster, O'Cuinneagain took a lot out of himself with his Ireland World Cup commitments and was seldom seen at his best by Ulster, while Miller appeared like a fish out of water.

He had been bought out of his contract at Leicester, where he had fallen out of favour under a new coach, but ultimately is a Leinster lad at heart and his switch to his native province a year later was a relief for all concerned. Miller, whose nickname was TZ (for Twilight Zone, on the basis that he was 'out there somewhere'), failed to impress in his early Ulster matches, he reacted badly to being substituted at Donnybrook in the second interpro and there were complaints about his attitude by both the media and fans. This writer got a bad first impression of him at the July reception at a Belfast hostelry to launch the new Ulster season and, although Johns asserts that his fellow players understood him better, he accepts that it was never likely to be a long-term relationship.

"I think people were pleased that Eric was coming here as he was a good player, but his move to Ravenhill was partly a case of Ulster being prepared to get him out of jail at Leicester and, longer-term, he was always likely to feel more at home with Leinster. Eric was a nice enough guy and did his best for Ulster, but he lived in Dublin and played his club rugby for Terenure, so I don't think it was a huge surprise when he linked up with Leinster the following season."

Apart from the creation of a gym under the stand and the advent of floodlit Friday fare for close-to-capacity crowds, Ravenhill hadn't changed much in tangible terms, but the whole Ulster set-up was, inevitably, much more professional than the one he had left to go to London. "When I returned, Ulster was becoming comparable with a Premiership club" he reflects. "Saracens were very switched on, but we were catching up and of course things have come on a lot further again in the three years since then." Going to work at Ravenhill every day was something Paddy could never have imagined but, now entering his fourth year as a professional player, the routine was familiar and so were the surroundings, so there was no real culture shock.

"Paddy fitted straight in as one of the boys" says Williams. "When he came back he was a big star and had captained Ireland, but was still a lovely big fella. He was always well-mannered and good with kids, but a hard man on the pitch, a man who took no prisoners and asked and gave no quarter. He's a fantastic guy and the ultimate professional. I suppose the best word to sum up him and his approach is 'honest'. He was clean-living and prepared well, so he was always in great shape. You certainly always got your money's worth and more out of Paddy Johns."

Justin Fitzpatrick recalls: "Paddy's a very honest, decent guy who always worked very hard at his rugby and had no airs and graces. Most of the Ulster squad had played with him before, either for Ireland or before he went to England, or at least against him. He certainly fitted in well and there was absolutely no problem. Paddy would be the last to create a hierarchy or stratas within a squad."

Following a friendly with Glasgow not far from Stranraer, Paddy's first competitive match back in the white jersey was an interpro against Connacht at The Sportsground in Galway, which was also to be the scene of his last ever away game for Ulster some 33 months later. Traditionally, the Sportsground has never been seen to constitute inspiring surroundings and conditions are often less than hospitable, but on this occasion, with the interpros kicking off earlier than ever on the first Saturday in August, the sun shone and Ulster made metaphorical hay. Half a dozen tries and another 20 points from the golden boot of Simon Mason made it a most satisfactory start to the new term for the European Cup holders as they eased themselves back into meaningful action for the first time since conquering Colomiers at Lansdowne Road.

Next stop for Ulster was Dublin, their first return visit there since European Cup final day, but this time they were very much the away team, against Leinster, and didn't dominate at Donnybrook like they had lorded it at Lansdowne more than six months earlier. In fact Leinster had the better of the game, but Ulster came away with a 26-15 victory which seemed to encapsulate the old adage that 'champions win matches'. In spite of not being at their best, the White Knights' winning knack and spirit carried them through. Thanks to Johns, the first half featured some sparring for Trevor Brennan ahead of his bout with Wallaby Toutai Kefu in the World Cup a couple of months later but, as on that occasion, the Mary's milkman got more than he bargained for as Paddy recalls with a titter.

"I had my back to Trevor at a ruck but knew he was going to break off and head for our backs. I swung my arm back to kind of block him, but actually connected quite well! He thought that I'd hit him on purpose so he threw a punch. I said 'that was uncalled for' and threw one back and he threw another." By that stage, O'Cuinneagain had come back to separate the pair but, seeing another white jersey, a now incandescent Brennan took a swing at him as well, leaving the mild-mannered Irish captain with little choice but to retaliate. Wild-eyed, Brennan stumbled clear of Paddy and Dion only to run into Ward, who was arriving on the scene to see what was happening and, after having a flail at the flanker, ended up getting another clout for his pains. When the dust settled, Brennan's face was a slightly sorry sight and, to add insult to his injury, Ulster had been awarded the penalty!

Ulster were barely out of their own territory in the second period but defended doggedly, including surviving a series of scrums on their own line before a wonderful break-out by O'Cuinneagain from his own 22 in the dying stages saw Ward put Mason over in the corner for a try which he also converted from the touchline. "Dion had a lot of pace and that try sealed the victory. That season though, I felt that we maybe fell into the trap of subconsciously playing for penalties, knowing that Mason wouldn't miss. Teams had watched Ulster the previous season and worked us out. They knew it was a big priority not to give penalties away, but too often we relied on them doing so and Simon doing the rest. We did well to get out of Donnybrook with a win that night, but got into a rut as the season went on."

Perhaps reflecting the concerns which he has outlined at the start of this chapter, Johns gave an interview ahead of that Leinster match, asserting that Ulster still had it all to prove domestically. He said at the time: "What the boys achieved in Europe last season was amazing, but it won't count for anything now as we face the other provinces, except perhaps making them even more determined to beat us this year. Until we prove ourselves by actually lifting the interpro title again, we can't claim to be the team to beat in Irish rugby - Munster are the champions and it's up to us to take that crown from them.

"We've got a lot of praise for our performance against Connacht and there was plenty of encouragement to be taken from it, but people shouldn't get carried away just yet. There's a long way to go in this competition never mind the season, and a lot of hard work to be done. Professional rugby teaches you the truth of the old clichÈs about taking one game at a time and only being as good as your next result. We need to stay focussed and keep trying to improve, for there will be a lot of tough challenges ahead."

Johns and his fellow Ireland squad members then went off to play a warm-up match against Connacht and international against Argentina before Ulster's next interpro, at home to Munster. A botched spraying job had rendered the Ravenhill pitch unplayable in the early part of the season, so a temporary stand was erected at Queen's University playing fields for Ulster's September matches against Munster and the Irish team. Munster had not won in Belfast for two decades, but all good things must come to an end and Mick Galwey's men proved to be kings at Queen's. The White Knights almost ambushed their visitors with one final flourish but by then it was too little too late, with the southern street-fighters having already won the war.

On the day, their battle-hardened forwards were simply immense and totally eclipsed Ulster's much vaunted pack, particularly in the lineout, where the home side had an uncharacteristic nightmare. Munster ensured that the wheel turned full circle as the Euro Cup winners were put to the sword by the side which had been the last to beat them, 11 months and 11 games previously. The result left Williams' warriors with a mountain to climb in their bid to avoid a seventh lean year in the interpros. With six minutes remaining, with Ulster 14-25 down and desperately struggling to keep Munster at bay as the visitors pounded their line, Fradericks brought the game to life with his scintillating try from near his own line, Mason converting and quickly adding a penalty to close the gap to a single point.

With four minutes left the match was, unbelievably, back in the melting point, but Ulster's chances of completing the steal of the century were terminally undermined by the loss to imperious Wallaby man-of-the-match John Langford of a lineout in the Munster half following a Mason penalty to touch. "Munster played well that day and Mike Mullins really made the difference between the sides. He cut us up a few times and had a huge influence on the game. Langford did very well at the lineout. I remember the last five minutes us desperately trying to force a penalty to get the winning points."

Johns scored a try for the greens as Ireland unimpressively saw off a vastly understrength Ulster in their final World Cup warm-up match at the same venue a couple of weeks later and then, following the national team's exit from that tournament, found himself on the bench for the Munster return in Cork at the end of October. European Cup winning locks Mark Blair and Gary Longwell were paired in the engineroom as Williams gave Paddy a post-World Cup rest.

Munster hammered home their pedigree as Irish champions by blowing Ulster away in the final quarter at Musgrave Park. On a miserable night, it was Galwey's men who finally seized a scrappy game by the scruff of the neck and pulled well clear of their visitors with tries at the beginning and end of the final quarter. Backed by a strong wind, Ulster led 10-3 after only 12 minutes thanks to a well-worked move which brought Bromley off his wing to create the extra man in the line, ending with his fellow wide man Topping crossing in the right corner and Mason typically curling in a touchline conversion and then kicking a penalty.

Mason and O'Gara, who finished with 26 points, traded penalties to leave Ulster 16-12 ahead at the interval and the visiting fullback landed his fifth kick from five to nudge his team back in front after two more strikes by the home outhalf within seven minutes of the restart. O'Gara gave Munster the lead again and then winger John O'Neill pounced on Topping's fumble of an Anthony Foley kick to score at the end of the third quarter. Even the introduction of Johns and Miller couldn't stem the tide as the hosts outscored Ulster by 18-0 in the final half hour.

Ulster had the consolation of a return to the restored Ravenhill turf the following Friday night, when Paddy was back in the starting line-up for the interpro against Connacht on the eve of Australia's victory over France in the World Cup final. He partnered Blair with Longwell taking a turn on the bench and Ulster's 42-22 victory, combined with Leinster's 13-30 loss to Munster, which retained the title for Galwey's men, was enough to ensure the White Knights' qualification for the following season's European Cup. Ulster celebrated their long-awaited Ravenhill homecoming - it was the first game there since the Stade Francais semi back in January - in some style, rattling up a 37-3 lead in the opening hour before rather taking the gloss off by leaking three tries to their unfancied visitors.

Bromley, who had his best match for Ulster, scored his team's first try, while Jan Cunningham bagged a brace and there were also touchdowns for Blair and McWhirter. Ward had the last word following an unexpected burst of 19 unanswered points by the visitors. "It was a fairly physical contest in which we started well and ended on top, but really let them back into it in between. That game showed us Connacht were getting stronger and that progress has clearly been maintained in the Celtic League both last season and this."

The result from Donnybrook spared Ulster a Euro qualification shootout with Leinster the following Friday and that was just as well, given that Fradericks, Howe, O'Cuinneagain, Bell and Fitzpatrick were all ruled out by injury. Williams took the opportunity to engage in a little rotation with Allen Clarke and Stephen Bell dropping to the bench to give Weir and Edwards starts, while the latest bout of musical chairs in the second row saw Johns make way for the return of Longwell. A baffling penalty on top of a try which seemed to stem from a forward pass denied Ulster the Euro send-off they wanted on a night when Williams didn't bother to introduce either Paddy or his old RSD mucker Clarke.

Although Hickie's disputed try with 10 minutes remaining gave Leinster a lead which had threatened to be decisive, Mason booted Ulster back in front in the closing stages, but the sickening knockout blow was still to come. Even after Mark McHugh's injury-time penalty, Ulster rallied and Ward came close with one last heroic charge, but the immediate long whistle ensured Williams' team would launch their European Cup defence in Bourgoin the following Saturday on the back of a defeat.

Although going to France is never easy, Bourgoin were by no means the most formidable of that country's clubs who were in the competition, while Llanelli were not quite the force then which they have become since. Veitayaki, who had done well for Fiji at the World Cup, had arrived and was handed his debut in the front row alongside Clarke, who had been passed fit in spite of being plagued by a recurring neck problem and Fitzpatrick, recovered from his toe injury.

Paddy was paired with Longwell in the second row and Humphreys gave Williams a boost by declaring himself fit to play, but there were major disruptions either side of the skipper, with his two minders, Ward and Bell, both being ruled out with a hairline foot fracture and wrist injury respectively. O'Cuinneagain, recovered from a shoulder problem, came back into the team out of position at openside, albeit that he had played there for Ireland, while Ulster's lack of depth was exposed by the choice of Malone at inside centre as Bell's replacement. The pack was completed by Miller and McWhirter, with Stephen Bell at scrumhalf, Jan Cunningham partnering Malone in midfield with Fradericks sidelined by injury, James Topping and Bromley on the wings and Mason at fullback. As luck would have it, Malone and Cunningham, neither of them in their natural positions, were up against the highest quality unit in the Bourgoin team in the form of their only two players to have featured in the World Cup, French international Stephane Glas and Scotland giant James McLaren.

If anyone had failed to grasp the enormity of Ulster's achievement in winning the European Cup the season before or to realise just how difficult it would be to provide an encore, they knew after this. The chill wind of second season syndrome left Ulster cold in the freezing south of France as a rugged, workmanlike Bourgoin team deservedly claimed the scalp of the visiting champions and added further to their formidable home record. In a poor match which featured a place-kicking contest for most of the first half and scoreless stalemate through a dire and dispiriting final quarter, the hosts struck with a decisive double whammy of tries in a seven-minute spell either side of the break.

As European champions visiting this Lyon's den, Ulster had expected a hot reception on the pitch in response to the sub-zero temperatures, but the White Knights produced an encouragingly pumped-up start, refusing to be intimidated either by their abrasive opponents or the partisan 9,000 crowd packed into the compact stands on all four sides of the ground. Indeed for long periods in the first half, the crowd were relatively silent and, following a few early skirmishes when Ulster refused to take a backward step, the Bourgoin players seemed to accept that their visitors could not be bullied out of the game. The couple of hundred Ulster supporters were making more noise than all their French counterparts put together, but unfortunately Humphreys' men were unable to really cash in on their superiority, though they still seemed set to hold a narrow interval advantage.

But then Bourgoin struck a major practical and psychological blow in the four minutes of stoppage time controversially added on by Scottish referee Rob Dickson, with a try which was unsatisfactory in more ways than one. The hosts surprisingly had the courage to go for touch instead of goal from a penalty on the Ulster 10-metre line and another award took them right into the corner, setting up the lineout from which scrum-half Laurent Balue sneaked over for the night's opening try.

Balue's halfback partner Alexandre Peclier, who had already contributed a hat-trick of penalties, just curled in a difficult conversion from the right touchline to ensure maximum reward for Bourgoin's bravery in taking the attacking option with little time available, but Ulster had every reason to feel aggrieved. Apart from questioning the seemingly excessive amount of injury-time given the lack of significant stoppages, there was a clear case for reversing the initial penalty award given that Clarke was gratuitously assaulted by three opponents after the whistle and there were also suggestions that the referee had missed a Bourgoin infringement before Balue touched down.

Earlier, Ulster could have been ahead after only two minutes, but skipper Humphreys - who had contributed a string of drop goals during the previous season's glory run - hooked a good chance well wide, though the men in white maintained their momentum until finally taking a deserved lead six minutes in courtesy of a Mason penalty. Peclier equalised and, although Mason put Ulster back in front following a miss from wide out on halfway, an over-eager Cunningham came up too quick to put in a crunching tackle on McLaren and it was all square again.

The next Peclier strike, early in the final quarter, put Ulster behind in a European Cup match for the first time in a year, but even more ominous was the telling fact that the penalty award came from a very poor Ulster scrum, starting an unexpected rot which was to feature a retreating visiting eight on several occasions, an increasingly irate referee and, eventually, almost a sending-off for Veitayaki. After all the hype surrounding the arrival of the massive Fijian and the build-up of hopes that he would instantly cure Ulster's perennial problem, it was deeply disappointing to see the visiting scrum still in apparent difficulties and this game set alarm bells ringing that Big Joe would become a marked man with referees.

Mason squared the score at 9-9 on the half hour and then edged his team ahead five minutes later for what proved the final time, as Bourgoin bagged their first try in injury-time before adding 10 unanswered points in the second half. Ulster withstood a series of scrums on their own line shortly after the break, but eventually Bourgoin spread the ball right and the visiting centres - how Bell was missed in midfield - appeared to collide in trying to stop Glas, who spun out of the tackle to score, with Peclier converting. Peclier's fourth penalty left Ulster needing two converted tries from the final quarter just to draw and, although he drew a horrible blank late on, by then Williams' men were barely threatening to score one try never mind two.

As European champions, this was a match which Ulster should have won against fairly ordinary looking opponents - albeit with a great home record and unbeaten to date in the season's French championship - but it was a bad day at the office for too many players, with only a rejuvenated Miller and the big-hearted McWhirter really emerging with much credit.

"I remember we started very well and the French backed off us, but when they saw the chink in our armour they went for it and the referee started hitting us. McLaren played well, but we missed a few chances. It was definitely a game we should have won. We had been very optimistic going into that match, for Bourgoin were certainly by no means the top side in France."

Williams had had to withdraw Veitayaki, who had already been yellow-carded for dropping the scrum, and although the coach denied afterwards that the south sea islander was now damaged goods, the writing was on the wall for the 22-stone veteran. Easy going and affable, Veitayaki admitted to this writer that he had spent the month following the World Cup 'eating and drinking' and, apart from being hounded by referees for suspect scrummaging, his all-round contribution was negligible. Put simply he proved a liability and Williams compounded the problem by persisting in playing him game after game as a face-saving exercise, rather than cutting his losses and admitting Big Joe was a bad signing. The other players weren't amused.

"If we'd scrummed well in Bourgoin, we'd have won that match" Paddy insists. "Ulster struggled in the scrum that season and were constantly under pressure in that area. When other teams recognise a chink they will try to exploit it and we were targeted. Big Joe came in and Harry kept playing him. To be honest, we had to carry Big Joe. I don't think it damaged the spirit in the squad, but we were definitely saying 'what's going on here'. Other players resented the fact that he was a bit out of shape, but if he'd at least been able to do his bit in the scrum, that would have been something."

This writer's abiding memory of Bourgoin, apart from the popular hot port tent, was of Veitayaki coming out for the pre-match warm-up from the changing rooms, which were situated at one end of the stadium. He had his headphones on and ambled as far as the 22 before turning and rolling back in again, not seeming to fancy the cold. It didn't augur well.

Ward and Bell were both thankfully back on board for the next game and Ulster also had home comforts when they faced Wasps the following Friday night, the first floodlit Euro tie at Ravenhill since the famous quarter-final win over Toulouse when the former had dashed from the pitch to the maternity ward. The return of Ward allowed Williams to give a complete break to Ireland captain O'Cuinneagain, who had been battling with little success against a shoulder injury, general burnout and then having to play in the No 7 jersey in Bourgoin. Not surprisingly he had failed to distinguish himself and had also picked up a knock on his 'good shoulder' towards the end.

The game was the first opportunity since Ulster won the European Cup to silence the English begrudgers and answer the apparent arrogant attitude of Lawrence Dallaglio and others towards them. However, on the night, an appalling decision by French referee Joel Jutge delivered a cruel sting to Ulster's hopes of retaining their trophy. Visitors Wasps were already leading the holders 12-6, but this Ravenhill tie was still balanced on a knife-edge until Jutge handed the Londoners victory on a plate. Ulster fullback Mason was blatantly taken out as he stretched for a Howe pass as the home side countered from deep, but play was allowed to continue and Wasps prop Will Green plunged over in the corner for a decisive try.

A combination of the pre-match hype and a super-charged atmosphere under the lights at a packed stadium made a fiery start inevitable and it was little surprise when Blair and the other Wasps prop Molloy were yellow-carded for second minute fisticuffs. Mason drew first blood for Ulster, his penalty being the only score of a fiercely fought half, but Kenny Logan crucially landed four of them in the third quarter before the home fullback replied with his second. It was little reward for six minutes of continuous pressure and Green's rogue try on 75 minutes unsatisfactorily settled the outcome.

Ulster had lost Jonny Bell on the stroke of half-time and when his replacement Malone was again painfully exposed, within a minute of coming on, Williams ruthlessly hauled the former international off, moved Topping to centre and brought Howe on out wide. For Johns, who gave way to Longwell just after Green's killer try, it was a first real taste of the Friday floodlit fare which had become synonymous with the new era at Ravenhill. The atmosphere was awesome, but the outcome naturally disappointing.

"That was quite a tough one" he recalls. "Wasps were strong enough and just had that bit more pace. They had a few quite sharp backs and managed to put on enough pressure to pick up their penalties in the first part of the second half. The way their try came about at the end was disappointing but I guess when you're in the rut, decisions go against you and you simply don't get the rub of the green."

After a two week break, facilitating Paddy's return to AIL action for Dungannon, Ulster faced a double-header with Llanelli in the space of eight December days, needing to bag a brace of victories to stay afloat. A good AIL performance for his new club Ballymena saw Edwards picked at pivot at the expense of Stephen Bell for the first of those clashes, at Ravenhill, while the mild nature of Jonathan Bell's concussion against Wasps allowed him to return a mere fortnight later. Williams revealed that he might have again made a change in the second row under his rotation policy but for the fact that Blair 'had such a good game against Wasps'. So he continued in harness with Paddy. O'Cuinneagain returned to duty with a place on the bench.

It was the first anniversary of the quarter-final victory over Toulouse, but this time the second Friday in December proved to be something of a night of shame for Ulster rugby, with the holders dumped out of the European Cup courtesy of a humiliating home hammering (6-29) by the Welsh and some mindless morons in the crowd abusing Williams. "It was very close at halftime, but they got a couple of soft scores and it was a very disheartening night overall" says Paddy. "There was a very flat feeling at the end."

For the return at Stradey Park, Williams recalled Longwell alongside Johns in the second row, picked little Sheldon Coulter on the wing in place of Topping and made three enforced changes, with Weir taking over from the injured Clarke and both McWhirter and Edwards being ruled out of the starting line-up by illness. O'Cuinneagain returned at blindside with Miller moving to No 8 and Stephen Bell was restored at the base of the scrum, but the disruptions didn't end there as Ulster's wretched luck continued. It's an ill wind though that blows no-one any good and the cloud was to have a silver lining for Paddy Johns.

Both skipper Humphreys and talisman Ward had to retire to their beds on arrival in Swansea on the Friday afternoon and, with a night's sleep failing to have the desired effect, the pair withdrew the following morning. More surprising than the decision by Williams to turn to Paddy to lead the side in Humphreys' absence was the fact that he had never actually done the job before, even on a one-off basis. In his younger days, Ulster had had leaders aplenty and then he'd been away for three years.

"I'd obviously captained my country by that stage, but never my province, so naturally I was thrilled when Harry asked me to be captain. By then we weren't going to qualify but everyone was determined to bounce back from the low of the previous weekend and it was good to get an immediate chance to make amends against the same opposition. It was a dark and dismal afternoon and we didn't win but didn't do badly, especially considering the disruption to the side and the reality that we were in a real rut and nothing was going for us. At least we got a lot of pride back that day at Stradey Park."

It finished 20-3, a late try by John Davies taking the Welsh side's eight-day aggregate against the Irish province to 49-9 and ensuring that Ulster would spend Christmas wondering just when, or even whether, they'd ever win again. When the Pool phase resumed in the New Year, Ulster faced a trip to Wasps, where a much weaker and injury-ravaged line-up had been hammered 56-3 on their last visit for a Euro Cup tie a couple of years earlier.

There were six changes from Stradey Park, with fit-again Fradericks getting a debut in the competition as Bell's centre partner, Humphreys and Ward returning, James Topping winning his place back from Coulter, Howe taking over on the other wing from Bromley, who had a hamstring strain, with the revolving doors bringing Blair back into the second row for Longwell. Clarke and McWhirter were again missing, albeit with different fitness problems to those which kept them out against Llanelli, while the under-fire Veitayaki held onto the No 3 jersey in spite of mounting criticism. The backline which had impressed at the start of the season was thus reunited and, although Ulster predictably suffered their fifth defeat in five group games, they finally broke their embarrassing try famine by getting their first two touchdowns of the competition.

The drought was ended in style by Humphreys in the first half and Mason doubled Ulster's try tally for the campaign when he went over in the second period. That touchdown broke a remarkable run of three matches in which Ulster had scored no second half points. Mason converted both tries and kicked a first half penalty to account for 12 of Ulster's 17 points, but Wasps scored 49 in coming from being behind as a result of the Humphreys try - made by centres Bell and Fradericks - to secure an ultimately comfortable victory.

Dethroned holders Ulster had one game left to avoid a Pool whitewash and, with home advantage against an average Bourgoin side showing nine changes from the November meeting, hopes were high that such an embarrassment could be averted. Williams made only one change, recalling Longwell, who had broken Willie Anderson's record of 78 Ulster caps when coming on as a substitute at Loftus Road, in place of Blair as Paddy's second row partner. But it was the same old story on the night, a sixth successive group game being lost as Bourgoin took toll of Ulster mistakes and injuries in rattling up no fewer than 36 points, leaving them nine clear of their hosts and Williams feeling 'utterly dejected'.

Ulster were hit for six in the shape of half a dozen Bourgoin tries after a good start by the home side which had seen them go 10 points up in as many minutes, with Paddy having a hand in the try. Mason, who had opened the scoring with a penalty, hoisted a high ball, made a perfect follow-up tackle and then did superbly to intercept as a Bourgoin player tried to flick the loose ball back on the visitors' side. Johns was up in support to take Mason's pass and send his Dungannon colleague Howe round behind the posts for a converted try. But it proved a false dawn and, by the end of the evening, Ulster were a sorry sight and the large home crowd left the ground deeply disappointed, a feeling shared by the players.

"That was another one we could have won," muses Paddy. "We were well in the game, but again struggled in the scrums and again problems stemmed from us knowing that Simon Mason could kick any penalty which we won in their half." A bad Ulster season was to cost a number of individuals dearly when the internationals came around a few weeks after the European Cup Pool phase finished and Paddy Johns suffered more than most.

29. LOSING OUT IN LENS

Hindsight is a wonderful thing. Resting Paddy Johns in preparation for a World Cup quarter-final which never happened proved to be a very bad call on Warren Gatland's part. For the second time in as many years on French soil, Paddy was left looking on helplessly as the clock ticked down to an Irish defeat, but this Lens loss to Argentina brought an awful lot more anguish and post mortems than the gallant near miss in Paris 20 months previously. On that occasion, when Paddy's late substitution had disrupted Ireland's lineout and arguably contributed crucially to the winning French try, Ireland won widespread praise for coming close in a game most had expected them to be sunk without trace in. But in Lens on 20th October 1999, Ireland had gone into the World Cup quarter-final play-off as firm favourites against an Argentinian team which they had beaten back in August in an international at Lansdowne Road.

The management obviously shared the general confidence that Ireland would progress. So confident were they that it was decided to give Paddy a break ahead of a potential quarter-final against the French at Lansdowne Road on the Saturday. Rather than even having him on the bench in case of emergencies, Gatland and whoever else may have had an input went the whole hog and left Johns out of the match 22 altogether, leaving rookie Robert Casey as the back-up to Jeremy Davidson and Malcolm O'Kelly.

So Paddy was left languishing in his blazer and, like those of us in the press box high in the steeply banked stand in that compact football stadium, watching in helpless horror as the nightmare unfolded and Ireland's World Cup dream died not far from Flanders' fields. He still recalls the despair and dejection, the empty feeling and the frustration. Paddy is not arrogant enough or foolish enough to claim he would have made the difference between defeat and victory.

But there's nothing much worse for a sportsman than being powerless to play your part. And, amazingly, after that tournament, he was barely called upon again by his country. For reasons best known to others, Paddy was practically pensioned off at that point. Considering how he had consolidated his place in Australia in the summer of 1999, done well in the World Cup warm-up games, including the Test against Argentina, and started the tournament superbly with a very fine performance in the match with the USA, it was all a bit baffling.

The international season had begun so well for him following that productive trip Down Under. It started with an impressive cameo as a sub for the Irish XV against Connacht in Galway as the national team began their tour of the provinces. A mix-and-match Ireland line-up had been struggling to tame the westerners at the Sportsground before a batch of substitutions made a major difference with Johns in particular having a real impact. "We were in danger of losing that one, but a few of us came on and fired into it and we gained the upper hand. It was a good game to come on in as the chance was there to make an impression when things weren't going well."

If Ireland had gone to Australia with the second row selection stakes being essentially a case of perm any two from three, it was now becoming more of a question of who would partner Paddy, with Davidson and O'Kelly going head to head. Did he feel himself that that was how it was shaping up? "I guess after losing the captaincy and being told the reason for it, I was always looking over my shoulder and very aware of the need to keep ahead of at least one of Jeremy and Malcolm. Although I was seen as the specialist front-jumper, either of those lads could have jumped at two as well as at four, so playing the two of them together was definitely a live option. I really preferred the front, largely because I was so used to it, but many players are comfortable with either and don't see it as an issue."

With every game a shop window, Paddy went into the August Test against Argentina every bit as conscious that he was playing for his place as he had been on the Pumas' last visit almost nine years earlier. "From losing the captaincy, I saw every game as being an important opportunity to cement my place, so it was vital to play against Argentina and to do well. The game naturally also brought back memories of my debut and I was determined to lay any ghosts from that day given that I was dropped following my first cap."

Johns was the sole Irish survivor from that last Lansdowne Road meeting, while Argentinian captain Lisandro Arbizu was the only common denominator in their team. Apart from Paddy having metamorphosised from novice new boy to seasoned, streetwise elder statesman, the other big difference between this game and the one in 1990 was that this time Ireland were able to assert their superiority in rattling up a 32-3 lead in the first hour against a side which had beaten Scotland at Murrayfield the week before. Ireland had made three changes from the line-up which had pushed Australia in Perth, with the fit-again duo of O'Shea and Mostyn returning for Dempsey and Bell respectively, while Davidson, who like Johns was one of the few players to impress in Galway, displaced O'Kelly. It was not clear whether the selection of Mostyn, who had made a mediocre start to the season for Connacht, indicated that he was a first choice or, alternatively, was still playing for his place in the squad. Either way, his hat-trick e ffectively put the issue beyond any doubt there may have been.

Wood got Ireland's first try following a lineout take by Johns, though he can't remember his contribution now, and four penalties from five attempts by Humphreys had the hosts 17-3 ahead by the time a magical move brought Mostyn's first score just before the break. A low skip pass by Humphreys found Bishop scorching off his wing between the centres and he linked with boy wonder O'Driscoll to put Mostyn clear down the left. Three minutes into the second period Mostyn was in business again after O'Driscoll, circling brilliantly out of defence, offloaded to his skipper O'Cuinneagain, who sent the left wing away for another try. He completed his hat-trick 10 minutes later after hacking on Wood's punt out of defence.

Naturally Gatland's team were aiming to peak at the start of October rather than the end of August and heavy legs as a result of being in the middle of an intense preparation programme cost them in the final quarter. Argentina cashed in with three converted tries, including a brace for pivot Pichot, to leave only eight points in it at the end, but Ireland had generally been superior enough to ensure that when they faced each other again in the World Cup second stage, the greens were firm favourites.

Following the match, Ireland's squad for the tournament was announced. The number of players which countries could bring to the World Cup had expanded from the 26 of previous finals to 30 and Gatland opted for a 17-13 split between forwards and backs. St Mary's No 8 Costello, paying a price for being off the pace in Australia, Munster skipper Galwey and his Shannon colleagues Foley and Quinlan had already been left out of Ireland's preliminary panel of 34. The uncapped pair of Jeremy Staunton and Shane Horgan were ruled out as a result of injuries sustained playing for Ireland Under 21's in the summer SANZAR tournament in Argentina, though neither may well have made the cut anyway.

With an ageing Clohessy being first choice loosehead, Gatland decided that he should carry additional tighthead cover for Paul Wallace, so the uncapped Angus McKeen of Lansdowne was included as a fifth prop along with the top two and Corrigan and Fitzpatrick. London Irish coach Dick Best had expressed surprise at the inclusion of his flanker Kieron Dawson in the preliminary panel given that the exiled Ulsterman had played very little rugby in 1999 due to a series of injuries. A broken ankle had kept him out for the second half of the previous season and two groin operations curtailed his preparations for the new term, but Gatland gambled on his fitness because he wanted specialist openside back-up to Ward.

Taking six loose forwards as well as five props meant that all 17 forwards initially named made the final squad so four backs missed out including, predictably, rookie third outhalf Ronan O'Gara and, unluckily, pivot McGuinness, Ireland's regular scrumhalf of the past couple of years. He lost out to O'Meara as understudy to Tierney, with the experienced Elwood getting the nod as second outhalf alongside Humphreys. Henderson and a slowly rejuvenating Hickie were the three-quarters to miss out as both Mullins and Mostyn were included along with Ulster winger James Topping, his provincial colleague Bell, first choice centres Maggs and young O'Driscoll and regular right wing Bishop. The fullbacks were O'Shea and Dempsey and the hookers were Wood and Nesdale, while young Casey completed a quartet of second rows as back-up to Johns, Davidson and O'Kelly. Captain O'Cuinneagain was joined in the loose forward department by Ward, Dawson, Miller, Brennan and Corkery.

After the Argentinian Test, the players split up and many found themselves opposing each other in the interpro between Ulster and Munster in Belfast, before the squad reassembled for another warm-up match, this time in Cork against the home province. Ireland fielded what would largely have been seen as a second string side and a depleted Munster claimed a prized scalp, giving the national team a bloody nose courtesy of a 26-19 victory. There are more ways that one to skin a cat. You can either consolidate your place through performing well or through your rivals not making the most of their opportunities. In the latter respect, that game in Cork also contributed to cementing Paddy's place in the first choice World Cup team.

The following week, the roadshow rolled into Belfast, with the brief stay there culminating in the final warm-up match, when Paddy found it a bit strange to be on opposing sides to Ulster. "It was difficult, the only time I'd ever played against Ulster, but I had to just try and block that out and be as competitive as I could be." In the event, he actually scored the first Irish try of a soggy Sunday afternoon. "I caught the ball in the lineout, they drove me on and I was able to pirouette and nip over from close range." But all didn't go according to plan for the national team as Ulster predictably raised their game in trying to follow Munster's example, albeit against a much stronger Ireland line-up than had featured in Cork.

"Ulster really got stuck in. People recognise that that sort of situation is always tough and a bit of a no-win scenario for the team who are in the position that Ireland were that day. By definition, Ireland should have been better, man for man, in every single position on the basis that we had all been chosen in the World Cup squad and those whom we were playing against hadn't, but games like this are not played on paper or in theory. To the Irish squad, the match was largely a means to an end as we prepared for the World Cup but, naturally, to the Ulster team that day it was a big opportunity to give the national team a bloody nose. That was always going to ensure a closer outcome than might have been expected if you just simplistically compared the two sides, but I always felt we would at least get the win."

It took a late try from skipper O'Cuinneagain to seal a 25-16 victory after a fine try by Tyrone Howe had given Ulster real hope going into the closing stages. Ireland weren't helped by Humphreys having a bad day with the boot, admittedly in difficult conditions, to go with his four failed conversion attempts out of four in the Argentinian Test. Naturally he suffered in the Ulster match in comparison with Mason, who had been overlooked in favour of uncapped teenage prospect Gordon D'Arcy as World Cup squad replacement for Dempsey, who had withdrawn due to injury.

So, the warm-up programme out of the way, Paddy was all set for his second World Cup. It would be hard for it to better South Africa 1995 which, as well as being special for being his first, was also, as he recounts in an earlier chapter, very successfully staged, helped by being contained in one country. The 1999 tournament was more fragmented, with games in each of the countries which made up the Five Nations, but set against that was the appealing opportunity to play in a World Cup on home soil, with plenty of support. The World Cup was poorly supported in Scotland, with embarrassing expanses of empty seats appearing on people's television screens, but Paddy feels that, while not perhaps emulating the buzz felt in South Africa, the event did catch fire in Ireland.

"I think it did" he insists. "South Africa 1995 was unique in so many ways and special for being my first World Cup, but I can remember there was plenty of interest in this country in 1999 and it was exciting to be involved in it. Although after 1995 I had realised my dream of appearing in a World Cup, you definitely do want to do it again. World Cups are special and, even though you've been there before, it still means a lot. It was good to be going into this one with the experience of 1995 under my belt. I felt good going into the tournament in 1999. I was more mature and felt I was playing pretty well. Four years is a long time and you don't know what happens from one World Cup to the next so, in 1995, I would have had no guarantees I'd be at another."

That said, Paddy didn't mentally make 1999 his final World Cup or see it as his swansong, even though he would be well past his 35th birthday when the next round. After all Davy Tweed had been that age in South Africa. In the event, ˰ was squeezed out not long after the tournament and will have been retired for over 16 months when the rugby world assembles again in Australia late next year but, back in the autumn of 1999, the outlook was very different. "I still thought I'd be playing until I was 40" he says with a grin.

Three days before the World Cup started, Paddy heard that he was going to be a father again, twice over. Kirsty was expecting twins! He also heard that he had indeed been selected in the side for the tournament opener against the United States. By then it was very much expected by the pundits that he would be chosen and he felt things had been going well, but also knew by now not to take anything for granted.

Although the Americans had just beaten all of Europe at golf in that infamously ill-tempered Ryder Cup clash, Ireland on their own were always fancied to be strong enough to down the Eagles in rugby. And, sure enough, the Irish greens did prove well too tough for the USA, who were spectacularly sunk thanks to what could perhaps be described as a famous 'four Wood' in the shape of a sensational scoring salvo by a certain bald hooker.

Against the United States, who were captained by Bath's Dan Lyle, Ireland produced enough ingredients to serve up an impressive World Cup start and then that man Wood put the icing on the cake of what, in the end, was a Yankee doddle. An accomplished performance which produced 50 points and a convincing win would have been exactly what the management wanted, but in writing himself into the record books, the cult hero hooker also ensured a public feel good factor.

He captivated the crowd with a pulsating hat-trick of tries in the final quarter which, added to his first half effort, saw him equal the mark set by former Ulster No 8 Brian Robinson, who bagged a quartet of touchdowns against Zimbabwe in the 1991 tournament. Irrepressible, instantly recognisable and irresistibly unique, crowd favourite Wood was the ideal man to steal the show and his tour de force not only sent everyone present into the streets happy, but created a wider buzz of excitement across the country. The happy hooker modestly insisted afterwards that he had only been in the right place to finish off the good work of others and described his own achievements as secondary to a fine Irish win.

"There was a bit of banter afterwards about Keith's poaching" recalls Paddy. "A couple of the tries were very good, but a couple he got cheaply. But he's quick, can finish well and scores a lot for a forward. The Americans though would have been disappointed with some of the concessions."

Every bit as important as those four tries was the goal-kicking form of Humphreys, who put his nightmare from the final warm-up match behind him to be successful with all six attempts at goal here. After five misses from seven against his home province in Belfast a fortnight earlier, an easy, early chance to strike helped settle the nerves and he never looked back. The history books will record that he kicked 14 points, but that fails to tell the overall story of an all-round performance every bit as polished as Wood's pate.

Even less recognition or acclaim went to Johns, but Paddy's personal reward for a mighty engineroom display would be a confirmed starting place against Australia eight days hence. The second row was one of Ireland's most competitive departments and, six months earlier, Johns' jaded Five Nations performances seemed to pave the way for the 'dream ticket' of Davidson and a fit again O'Kelly to come together sooner rather than later. But Paddy had produced the goods in the summer's second Test against Australia after justifying his selection in the first, showed up well in the August win over Argentina and then raised his game even further in the World Cup opener, stealing crucial American lineouts and getting through a mountain of donkey work round the fringes. "Yeah, I was pleased with how I played, including setting up a try for Kevin Maggs. It is always important to start a competition well, to stake your claim, to put down a marker if you like. I feel I did that."

Ireland had gone with the same line-up as started against Argentina for the United States clash but, for the second group game with Australia the following Sunday afternoon, there were two changes. Ulster prop Fitzpatrick and Leinster lock O'Kelly came in for Clohessy and Davidson, neither of whom had been able to take a proper part in training during the week due to injuries. Both were named on the bench, though Davidson's place there ultimately had to be taken by Casey.

The squad had spent most of the week in the idyllic surroundings of West Cork, a pleasant retreat and welcome break from being based continually in Dublin, but a place also equipped with some state of the art facilities in the form of the multi-million pound Inchydoney complex. "We went to Clonakilty and were based by the sea, which was very relaxing. The environment was very tranquil and they had a salt water recovery spa centre with lots of water jets. It was somewhere different and an ideal place to go to help the bumps and bruises." The place was renowned for its restorative effect and its reputation had already spread to the wider world. Southampton Football Club had visited the previous season, while England cricketer Darren Gough was arriving just as the Irish were leaving.

An intended spin-off of Ireland's internal tour both before and during the tournament was to spread a sense of ownership of the team around the country and plenty of well-wishers turned out in West Cork to watch the squad train. Ahead of this game, Gatland also revived the Paris ploy of encouraging the public to fax messages of support to the team hotel, while O'Cuinneagain praised the great atmosphere there had been at the American match and stressed the importance of the home crowd to Ireland in this tournament. "The faxing idea seemed to help at times when we were underdogs and, if used selectively, was something which I feel worked quite well and was worth having" says Paddy. "It was something different and Gatland was quite astute in that sort of thing, motivational methods and harnessing public support."

A fair bit was made in the media in the lead-up to the Australian game that it may not necessarily be in Ireland's best interests to win and hence top the group in that this would mean travelling to take on a resurgent Wales, who were on a great roll, at their new Millennium Stadium. Finishing second, providing Ireland could negotiate a play-off, would mean a quarter-final at Lansdowne Road, almost certainly against the fragile

French, who had started the tournament most unconvincingly, had nearly lost in Dublin earlier in the year and traditionally didn't travel that well. That was all fine in theory but, for the Irish camp, there was no dilemma, no agonising over whether or not they should beat Australia. As they knew from the summer, winning against the Wallabies wasn't exactly something which was in the whimsical gift of the Irish team! The thought that Ireland would give anything less than 100 percent effort or not be trying their hardest to claim such a huge scalp in front of a full house at Lansdowne Road was nonsense, but Paddy says the players were more amused than annoyed at the notion.

"It was certainly never an issue for us" he confirms. "We wanted to win every game we could and if beating Australia had meant ending up in Cardiff, we'd have been going to a place where we'd a great record with confidence sky high and real momentum going. In doing so, we'd have saved ourselves an extra round, avoided a banana skin which, as it happened, turned out to be lethal, and had more rest before a potential quarter-final. So, no, we didn't set out to try to lose!" Unsurprisingly, they didn't need to.

Australia, who had beaten Romania 57-9 in their tournament opener at Ravenhill the previous Sunday, recalled big guns Joe Roff, Stephen Larkham and Matt Cockbain, making for a most formidable Wallaby line-up also featuring the likes of Matt Burke, Ben Tune, Daniel Herbert, Tim Horan, George Gregan, Phil Kearns, John Eales, Toutai Kefu and David Wilson.

After having gone out of their way to play down suggestions that, strategically, it might be best to lose to Australia, Ireland could have done with that excuse at Lansdowne Road. The capacity crowd failed to set a new world 'roar' record, but they could hardly be blamed for, on the day, there was precious little to shout about from a home point of view. A dreadful first half set the tone for a disappointing afternoon but, because Australia were also well below par, Ireland turned round only 6-0 in arrears. Considering Ireland had been playing into a strongish wind, their scoreboard position was far from hopeless at the break, but their performance to that point gave little cause for optimism. Just as England had done in Dublin earlier in the year, the Wallabies strangled Ireland out of the game in a grim opening quarter and, as Gatland admitted afterwards, anxiety produced mistakes and the cumulative effect crippled his team.

The hoped-for rain arrived just before the start but was short-lived and, although Australia went too long with their kick-off, leading to a scrum back on half way, they virtually, in the words of the Irish coach, 'owned the ball' in the first quarter. Burke gave the Wallabies an early lead, but he then missed two before Eales took over the duties himself and also drew a blank. Remarkably, Ireland could have drawn level on 34 minutes, but Humphreys had just taken a bad bang on the thigh and stand-in kicker O'Shea was well off target. It took more bungling by O'Shea, who had a shocking afternoon, to help the Wallabies double their lead. Firstly he and the equally hapless Mostyn made a mess trying to run from a scrum near their own line and then the fullback gave away a penalty hightackling Larkham as Australia attacked from the lineout. Eales landed it and Humphreys, who finally gave way to Elwood on the hour, missed from long range with both a drop goal and a penalty attempt.

The rousing sight of the Irish players in a huddle singing along with the tannoy rendition of the Fields of Athenry just before the second half kicked off failed to produce the desired effect as relentless Australian attacking saw Burke stretch their lead to 9-0 with a penalty on 45 minutes. But then came the passage of play which just might have inspired an Ireland comeback as, firstly, the crowd were incensed by the sight of Toutai Kefu beating Brennan's face to pulp as a couple of colleagues held him defenceless. Ireland didn't get a penalty from that incident and Australia surged up field, but finally Wood found himself in possession behind his own line, dodged a Wallaby tackler and hoofed the ball upfield where the greens followed up so well they forced a penalty and Humphreys slotted over what proved to be the hosts' only points of the game.

The first Australian try came on 56 minutes when Kefu broke away from the base of a ruck and fed prop Richard Harry, who made big inroads, before O'Shea and Ward both missed Horan en route to the line. Ireland spent as much time in Australian territory as their own in the final 40 minutes, but a 17-3 scoreline for that period tells a tale of the visitors' greater potency. Home woes were summed up in the final 10 minutes when they made no impact at all from an attacking scrum five and then when frenzied but futile attempts to attack from the middle of the field yielded nothing but an eventual turnover. That led to Roff scorching through and linking with Horan, who sent the swallow-diving Tune in for the try which made the game absolutely safe for Australia and Ireland couldn't even manage a consolation try to send the fans away in better heart.

Gatland complained afterwards about the referee allowing uncontested scrums when both hooker Kearns and his replacement Jeremy Paul were off the field injured, but accepted he couldn't blame the defeat on that. "Australia were the best defensive team in that World Cup, with only one try against them in the whole competition. We just couldn't get into it that day" admits Paddy. "We felt a bit down afterwards because we had expected to do better. As in the summer, I think it would be fair to say that we still didn't really see them as likely tournament winners at that stage. We knew they were very hard to break down, but didn't necessarily think they had enough to win it overall."

Defeat left Ireland needing to beat Romania to progress to the quarter-final play-offs and, although the eastern Europeans had given Gatland's greens a good rattle in the qualifiers a year earlier, the match was seen as an opportunity for some experimentation without endangering the result. There was an expectation in some quarters that old hand Johns might be rested for this Friday floodlit fixture, which would hopefully be the first of three matches in less than 10 days for Ireland culminating in that prospective quarter-final against France the following Sunday.

As it happened, when the team was named on Tuesday, there were nine changes, with other leading lights such as Wood, Wallace, captain O'Cuinneagain, Humphreys, young O'Driscoll, his centre partner Maggs, and Ward among those rested. But, a shade surprisingly, Paddy was picked. "I wasn't really surprised myself, just pleased to play. I had played in all the games at the 1995 World Cup and was keen to do the same here. It was up to others to decide how best to use the resources at their disposal. I just took it as it came, but my desire would always have been to play."

The squad suffered a double back row blow that week, firstly with bad boy Brennan being banned for 10 days by the IRB along with his Aussie assailant Kefu after both had been cited for fighting. Then their other specialist blindside Corkery was forced out of the tournament with a back injury which, incidentally, was to prevent him playing for Ireland again and cut short his career, resulting in a call-up for Quinlan. To make matters worse, Miller, who was scheduled to start at No 8, had to withdraw from the team with a hamstring strain so, in addition to Ward being drafted back into the side in the unaccustomed blindside berth, O'Cuinneagain also had to play.

O'Shea had been named as stand-in skipper, but ended up being the captain of his country who wasn't, as O'Cuinneagain's return to the team meant him relinquishing the role without actually fulfilling it. Was Paddy surprised not to have been asked to lead the troops? "It would have been nice to do it again and, at the time, I might have thought that Warren could easily have given it to me, but maybe he didn't want to go back to the previous captain in a one-off situation. Anyway, in the end, Dion played."

Ireland put their Wallaby woes behind them, not missing the rested regulars in running riot against Romania with a more than satisfactory display featuring five tries. The disruption in the ranks had continued right up until match day, when Mostyn and Wallace were drafted in to replace Bishop and Clohessy. Topping, Bell and Mullins made their first starts in the three-quarter line, with Elwood partnering Tierney at halfback. Fitzpatrick continued at loosehead with Nesdale at hooker and Paddy was partnered in the second row by O'Kelly, with Dawson making his World Cup debut in the back row alongside the two men pressed into emergency service, Ward and O'Cuinneagain.

Johns had a hand in Ireland's first try, nearly scored one himself and helped the team into a 34-6 lead before being called ashore with half an hour remaining as Gatland sent on all seven subs during the second period. He gave way to Davidson, with Ward departing at the same time allowing Quinlan to become the first new cap of the night, followed by D'Arcy and McKeen on the hour just after Tierney had claimed Ireland's fifth try.

It was Paddy's lineout take just inside his own half on seven minutes which sparked the move that ended in Ireland taking the lead. The much-maligned Elwood broke enterprisingly and linked with Dawson before Topping sent the skipper over. Elwood's conversions of that try and another by Ward sandwiched a penalty and left Ireland coasting at 17-0 up, more than a point per minute. Paddy thought he had got on the scoresheet early in the second quarter but the 'try' was disallowed because he was adjudged to have been guilty of a double movement in grounding the ball.

O'Shea, having his third bad game in a row, was at the centre of something of a comedy of errors for much of the match, but bagged a brace of tries either side of the interval thus facilitating the procession of replacements. It was floodlit fun and Friday frolics as the final sub Wood had to come on in the back row when O'Cuinneagain bowed out injured towards the end and O'Driscoll, on at stand-off for a bloodied Elwood, rounded off the evening with a drop goal leaving the final score 44-14. "I think Romania had gone back a little from the previous year, but we were pretty satisfied. I hadn't played that great against them in the 1998 match so was determined to put in a performance."

Argentina's failure to score 48 points against Cardiff in their final group game condemned them to third place in that Pool and meant that they rather than Samoa would be Ireland's opponents in the quarter-final play-off the following Wednesday night. Gatland had expressed a preference for the south sea islanders but, considering Ireland had had a good win against the Pumas in August, confidence in the camp was high. High enough for thoughts to run ahead to the next round.

When the team to face Argentina was announced, Johns was missing from the 22 as was Clohessy, who was still suffering from his back problem. Paddy had jarred his knee in scrummaging practice at an earlier stage, but says that "by the time the side was selected, I was fit to play. But they told me that they wanted to keep me for the quarter-final. Clearly the management expected that we would win against Argentina. Whether you call it pragmatism or complacency, the management were clearly planning ahead on the basis of an Irish win. It was disappointing but I had to accept the decision."

In spite of what Gatland described as 'his best game for Ireland in two or three years', Elwood, who had landed seven goals from seven attempts against Romania, gave way again to Humphreys in the No 10 jersey. The regular backline was reunited, but Corrigan, the only player not to have got a taste of the action in the first phase of the tournament, displaced Fitzpatrick at loosehead even though the Dungannon prop had just been named in one newspaper's 'World Cup team of the weekend' on the back of shining in the Romanian match. Davidson and O'Kelly were paired in the second row with Ward remaining at blindside and Dawson keeping his place in the team on the strength of the pace and intelligent support play which he had demonstrated in the final group game.

Lens, a football town some distance outside Lille which seemed better served by defecating dogs than a regular train service, was an unlikely location for a World Cup knockout game but the aim was presumably to raise rugby's profile in the north of France where it is nowhere near as popular as in the south of the country. Much has been said and written about the undesirability of that particular tournament's format and the extra round imposed upon some sides, a flaw which has been eliminated for the 2003 event, but Johns says it would be churlish of Ireland to complain in retrospect.

"Everyone knew the format and we had no problem with it before the tournament" he insists. "We knew what was required to reach the quarter-finals, but we failed to achieve that. Nor would I have a problem with 20 teams being at the World Cup, providing the smaller sides are competitive. It expands the global game and it must be remembered that, without bottom teams there wouldn't be top teams. You don't want sides being beaten by 100 points, but Spain did quite well against Scotland for example, so I think the expansion was broadly justified."

For Gatland's greens, Lens was simply supposed to be a stop-off en route to a quarter-final appearance back in Dublin, but Irish eyes were left crying as Argentina dramatically dashed their World Cup dream in the dying minutes. A 73rd minute try by wing Diego Albanese, the only touchdown of the game, gave the Pumas the lead for the first time in a match hitherto dominated by Ulster skipper Humphreys. Humph kicked like a dream all night, landing seven penalties from seven attempts and slotting a drop goal for good measure, to win his head-to-head with the tournament's top marksman at the time, Gonzalo Quesada, but the 24 points counted for nothing as Ireland scrambled round in the frenetic final minutes searching for a saving score. It was ironic, with six minutes of injury-time already played, to see Ireland pile 14 men into a lineout, a mirror image of Gatland's trademark tactic with Connacht, where his success had largely earned him the Irish job. This time though it didn't do the trick.

Two Humphreys penalties had his team 6-0 up in the first seven minutes, but yet another World Cup mistake by O'Shea allowed Quesada to get the Pumas on the board and although the Irish outhalf made it 9-3, his opposite number had levelled matters by the 24th minute with two more strikes. O'Cuinneagain was obstructed from the restart, allowing Humphreys to nudge Ireland's noses back in front and he added another to make it 15-9 at the break before taking the greens 12 points clear early in the second period with his sixth penalty followed by a superb drop goal.

Two penalties from Quesada either side of a brilliant break out of defence by Humphreys, which went unrewarded, halved the deficit, but the Broughshane boy completed his magnificent seven strikes on the hour mark. It was now 24-15. It seemed inconceivable going into the final quarter of a game featuring penalties galore and Humphreys in fantastic form that Ireland would fail to score again but, to the Pumas' great credit, he never got another opportunity.

Ireland were left to rue the absence of Johns when Davidson had to retire after an hour with a thigh injury to be replaced by young Casey for, as things got tighter, Paddy's experience would have been an invaluable asset. Quesada brought the Pumas back to only a single score adrift on 64 minutes and suddenly it was Argentina who began to look more like getting the game's first try. A brilliant sweeping attack featuring a delightful reverse pass by captain Arbizu and a deft overhead effort by Pichot took Argentina deep into the Irish 22, where they got the scrum, and two long skip passes freed Albanese to the corner flag. Quesada converted superbly to put the Pumas ahead.

To find themselves behind for the first time so late on understandably induced panic in the Irish ranks and Quesada actually added a penalty before Gatland's greens regrouped for one last efforts to save their skins. It was sadly in vain, however, as a series of lineout drives and tap penalties close to the Argentinian line were repeatedly repelled, legally and illegally, until the delayed final whistle after an agonising eternity of injury time merely sealed Ireland's fate. This writer can recall bumping into shell-shocked Irish players in the corridors of the stadium that night as everyone struggled to come to terms with what had happened. It was a seminal moment in Irish rugby history and was to have major repercussions for many people, including Johns even though he had had no direct part in the game.

"It was very disappointing for everyone involved and, at a personal level, a very frustrating way for my World Cup to end. I certainly didn't think after the Romanian match that my tournament was over. The night before the Argentinian game, the guys who weren't involved in the match 22 had gone out for a meal to get out of the hotel, somewhere we could relax and have a glass of wine. We ended up having a few extra drinks at the restaurant and then going back to an Irish bar, where there was a big sing-song. No-one had planned to go out, it just sort of happened, but it was an enjoyable evening. It was all harmless enough and we got back in around 1am. We weren't going to be involved in the game, but there were high hopes that Ireland would win and that, as a squad, we'd have a quarter-final to look forward to at the weekend. Sadly it wasn't to be."

In the quarter-final at Lansdowne Road, Argentina put up a spirited display before falling to a French side which finally came to life in that game and went on to famously topple the All Blacks in a 43-31 sensational semi before being crushed by Australia in Cardiff. The Wallabies had won there against Wales in the last eight and, in an absorbing semi, beaten the Springboks 27-21. Jannie de Beer's famous batch of dropgoals had earlier helped South Africa to victory over England in the last eight, while New Zealand had seen off Scotland. But by then the World Cup was only a bad memory and recurring nightmare for Ireland, with the players having returned to domestic action while the post-mortems continued. In a significant move, Eddie O'Sullivan was drafted in as backs coach ahead of the inaugural Six Nations.

30. CRUMBS OF COMFORT

When Warren Gatland was shafted by the IRFU in late November 2001, one of those who picked up the phone to sympathise with the Kiwi about his shameful sacking was Paddy Johns. It was a generous gesture towards the man who had effectively consigned his international career to the scrapheap at a time when he felt he still had plenty to offer.

A walk-on bit-part role in the famous victory in Paris on St Patrick's weekend the previous year and captaining the A team to the shadow Triple Crown allowed Paddy to salvage something from the Spring of 2000, but for a man still as hungry as ever and who was used to full Test match fare, it really was a case of being asked to feed on the scraps. And after that autumn he was to be starved completely.

"I had been bitter and annoyed when I was dropped, of course I was, but when Warren was stabbed in the back, I rung him up to offer my commiserations. I said to him 'you made your choices', but told him that I still respected him. He was very much a players' coach, a man who put his players first and showed loyalty to them. Warren's priority was looking after us rather than trying to curry favour with the Blazers. Maybe that came against him eventually, but I certainly had a lot of time for him."

The coach giveth, the coach taketh away. Gatland was the man who made Johns captain, the man who replaced him in the role, the man who decided to phase Paddy out of the Ireland picture before his time. That's life. Johns realises as readily as anyone that that is what a coach is paid for. To make the decisions which he feels are right, without fear or favour. He accepts Gatland must have had his reasons for dropping him, but he didn't have to agree with them. Although Paddy had had a good innings, he didn't feel he was ready for the Test scrapheap. The end of the World Cup might have been a natural break, a time to bring down the curtain on an international career which had brought him 57 caps. But the thought never crossed his mind. He may have had a lot of miles on the rugby clock but, at 31, was still relatively young and about to embark on a new phase of his career, back with Ulster. The hunger was still as strong as ever.

"No chance" interjects Paddy adamantly when asked if retiring from international rugby at any stage of that season had been an option. "That was why I played the game and I'd never have voluntarily removed the possibility of playing for my country. I was available for Ireland until the day I retired partly because I needed that to aspire to and partly because I still believed I was good enough."

There is a great irony in the sense that Paddy sort of became one of the scapegoats for Ireland's Lens low and Twickenham trouncing either side of the turn of the millennium even though he featured in neither. In general terms he became part of the clearout of long-serving players, one of the fallguys with the likes of Conor O'Shea and Paul Wallace. Perhaps that's not strictly true. While several others bit the dust in the direct aftermath of Twickenham and were replaced by the new brigade, the circumstances surrounding Paddy's demise were slightly different. In that Johns wasn't chosen for the English game which opened the inaugural Six Nations of 2000, to some extent the decision to move on had already been made. Mick Galwey had already been brought back.

There was only going to be room for one veteran front-jumping second row and now, with the southern press clamouring for his return, Galwey was going to get another go. At Paddy's expense. Playing both men at that stage wasn't really an option. "Realistically, it was probably a case of either/or with myself and Mick in that we were both maybe seen as similar players and are of a similar age, though he is actually about 18 months older than me."

Back in the summer, Johns had done well in the joust with Davidson and O'Kelly for two starting places in the second row and earned himself a continued starting role through the World Cup, but now a new dimension had entered the equation. The goalposts had shifted. Part of the problem was that he was not simply competing with Galwey on the basis of their respective abilities as player, but up against a figure who, for various reasons, had become something of an institution and a folk hero, especially in Munster. Galwey was seen as a real man of the people, a great leader of men, an inspirational mentor for all the young Munster players who were blooded in the aftermath of Twickenham. When they were brought in and a fairly remarkable renaissance followed in the shape of three wins on the trot in the Championship, Paddy's goose was well and truly cooked.

Munster's run to the 2000 European Cup final, set against Ulster's earlier Pool whitewash in their ill-fated attempted trophy defence, compounded the situation. Paddy also admits that he wasn't playing particularly well in the struggling provincial side. "I'm sure my cause wasn't helped by the fact that Ulster didn't win any European Cup games in the period between the World Cup and the start of the 2000 Six Nations. We were in a rut and the harder we tried the bigger the hole seemed to get. I didn't have a great period myself, not helped by a knee problem."

The first Ulster fall-guy was Jonathan Bell, left out of a training squad of 45 in early January along with four other World Cup squad members in props Reggie Corrigan and Angus McKean, young fullback Gordon D'Arcy and Aussie wing Matt Mostyn. David Corkery was not considered due to injury. Munster supplied no fewer than 16 of that preliminary panel, with recalls for Galwey and Anthony Foley and the inclusion of eight uncapped players from that province, namely Ronan O'Gara, Peter Stringer, John Hayes, David Wallace, John Kelly, Frankie Sheahan, Marcus Horan and Jeremy Staunton.

But Ulster individuals really felt the chill wind of their collective lack of success at provincial level when the numbers were cut to 25 for the next session in the build-up to the Six Nations opener, with Johns, Andy Ward and Eric Miller all biting the dust. The three were all banished to the second string outfit, which had just been taken over by Declan Kidney and Harry Williams as coach and manager respectively, while Bell suffered the ignominy of being left out of even a 23-man A squad.

Humphreys was the only northerner among 11 senior squad backs as Ulster reaped the whirlwind of their Euro struggle, but Johns could feel hard done by in losing out to two men at opposite ends of the age spectrum, Bob Casey and Galwey, who joined Davidson and O'Kelly in a quartet of locks. The inclusion of Galwey could perhaps have been seen as a form selection but here was a player who had failed to establish himself in the past, was a couple of years older than Johns and hardly represented the future. In that O'Kelly was included in spite of an indifferent start to the season in terms of his personal form, Johns could have expected similar treatment as an established international who had a good recent record at Test level. Ulster may have been struggling, but surely having proved he could 'do it' for Ireland should have counted for more?

"You'd need to ask the coach that" he suggests. "I felt I'd done well enough for Ireland in the second half of 1999, but at the time the 2000 Six Nations came around, Ulster were not going good and I wasn't standing out from that. Current form is important. Munster were getting on top at the time but, having said that, nine of their players getting in was an awful lot. The decision was made though and, following Twickenham, results improved during that Championship, so I guess that could be used as justification.

"I can't remember if I was contacted directly to be told I wasn't in, but it did come as a bit of a shock as well as a massive disappointment. You always look at your competitors and, while Casey was a good prospect, I couldn't really rationalise his selection ahead of me and the same applied to Galwey. Mick came on a lot in his last few years with Munster playing beside John Langford, and I don't want to take away from his outstanding career, but I would always have fancied myself in a head-to-head with him and would also have won in the fitness stakes."

Gatland, now Director of Rugby at Wasps, admits that the respective fortunes of Munster and Ulster at that time did affect the second row selection situation, with Galwey gaining and Johns losing. "It was probably largely a culmination of that" says Warren. "I didn't always feel that Mick Galwey was the greatest player in the world, but he was playing on a winning squad and we looked to build the national team around the nucleus of that successful provincial side, something which frequently happens in all countries. I knew, however, that Paddy was training pretty well and knew what he was capable of. Whenever he came in too, you knew that he would give 100 percent and put the team first in the same way that he was supportive of Dion O'Cuinneagain after losing the captaincy. Paddy may not have agreed with a particular decision, but he showed loyalty."

There were five uncapped players in the 25, the Munster quartet of Stringer, O'Gara, Hayes and Sheahan plus promising Leinster three-quarter Shane Horgan. Ulster had five representatives in total including exiles Davidson and Kieron Dawson, with Humphreys being joined by Dion O'Cuinneagain and Justin Fitzpatrick in the home-based category. Wood was appointed captain again in place of World Cup skipper O'Cuinneagain and, when the squads were formalised for the English trip, Horgan and Hayes were released to the A party.

Ward was controversially left out of the A team's match 22, leading to a statement from IRFU Press Officer John Redmond which made reference to Johns, who had been named as the shadow side's captain. Defending Ward's omission, Redmond insisted that the purpose of the A set-up was "not necessarily to simply select the next best 15 or 22 players who didn't make the full Test squad. A teams are an opportunity for the management to look at a range of players and be a platform for development. They are unique in that they are not necessarily picked with merit as the only criteria."

He continued: "The statement released with the team announcement indicated that Andy Ward had not been 'considered' for selection, which was intended to indicate that this is not simply a case of him being passed over. There were five or six back row forwards in the A training squad named last week and the management were keen to look at less experienced players such as Quinlan, Easterby and Wallace in a match situation. Paddy Johns is a different case in that the management wanted an experienced captain for the A side and, as a former skipper of the Test side and someone with more than 50 full caps behind him, he fitted the bill perfectly." The same presumably applied to Eric Elwood's controlling presence at outhalf.

"Being A team captain was important to me" says Paddy. "If I wasn't going to be in the senior team, being skipper of the A side was the next best thing, another feather in my cap. I still saw it as an honour to captain an Irish representative side even though I'd won 57 caps at senior level over the previous 10 years. So I was pleased to be asked to do the job and it gave me a real focus.

"There was certainly no case of wandering about the A set-up in disillusionment not really wanting to be there. I took my role seriously and we had the satisfaction of being the first Ireland A side to win the shadow Triple Crown. That success and the fact that we also had good craic as a group made it a pleasure to be part of it all and went some way to making up for the fact that I was missing out at Test level."

The 23 retained in the senior squad included a surplus fourth lock but, in the event, that equation solved itself when Davidson withdrew due to an elbow injury, while O'Gara pulled out of a possible debut which secured David Humphreys' place at outhalf and saw Elwood promoted from the A squad to sit on the bench. It had been felt that, had Davidson not been ruled out, Galwey would have been the second row who missed out on a place in the final match 22.

Ultimately there were only four personnel changes from the line-up which lost to Argentina, one enforced by Davidson's injury. The others saw a fit-again Peter Clohessy take the place of the discarded Corrigan, Mike Mullins come in at centre with Kevin Maggs moving to the wing where Mostyn had been dropped and Foley getting a first Championship start in five years. Conor O'Shea, in typically hot form for London Irish, got another chance at international level in spite of his shocking World Cup campaign, while Justin Bishop, Championship debutant O'Driscoll, Humphreys and pivot Tom Tierney retained their positions in the backline. Casey, who had been having a good season with Leinster, came in to partner O'Kelly in Davidson's absence while, to accommodate the return of Foley, deposed captain O'Cuinneagain reverted to the blindside berth which the ditched Ward had filled in Lens. Wood, Paul Wallace and Dawson were the other survivors up front from that fateful night.

Johns, who had had a good World Cup and not even been involved in the Argentinian match hadn't been as lucky as some of those who were but, in the event, he wasn't able to pull on a green jersey at any level that first weekend in February. Paddy withdrew from the A side with a perforated ear-drum, so Mick O'Driscoll moved up from the bench to partner Leo Cullen in the shadow Six Nations clash with the English second string at Northampton. Mark Blair was added to the replacements panel rather than fellow Ballymena lock Longwell. Injuries to others had brought belated call-ups for Ward and Bell to the A bench, but the latter himself had to withdraw, leading to a first step back from the wilderness for a man who was to suddenly make a big impression on the big stage, Wasps centre Rob Henderson.

Kidney and Williams got off to a dream start in their capacities as Ireland A coach and manager with victory over their English counterparts at Northampton in spite of having been deprived of the services of Johns and Elwood. They were facing an England A team with more recognisable names than would normally be the case, probably a function of the full England side looking decidedly less settled than usual due to injuries and retirements. Consequently, the England management may have felt the need to look at what they felt were the next best alternatives rather than use the A arena mainly for the purpose of developing emerging talent.

Hence Ireland were up against a team containing the likes of skipper Tony Diprose and Lions Tim Stimpson, Will Greenwood and Graham Rowntree, but the second string greens hung on for a famous 31-30 victory, reprieved by the sight of a Stimpson conversion coming back off the woodwork in injury-time. Ireland had remarkably led 21-7 at the interval, with tries by Simon Easterby, John Kelly and Emmet Farrell, all of which the Leinster outhalf converted. But a pair of penalties by Stimpson and giant young winger Steve Hanley's second try closed the gap to three points, setting up a grandstand finish. Replacement flyhalf Paul Burke kicked a penalty and converted a Denis Hickie try and although England crossed twice late on through Paul Gustard and Greenwood, Stimpson missed the second conversion and the visitors had won.

It was a very different story in the senior game, however, where Ireland were trounced 50-18 on a depressing day when it was hard to leave Twickenham with any other view than that the gap between the English and the other home countries was widening. Over-run and trailing 25-3 at the interval following a relentless English first half bombardment, Ireland leaked another try straight after the resumption and an absolute massacre seemed on the cards. The visitors then scored 15 of the next 21 points, but their hosts finished strongly to hit the half-century mark and post a record score in the fixture.

Central to many Irish gameplans over the years and the basis of most of the effective performances produced had been disruption of the opposing team and causing general mayhem. More destructive than constructive, it had often been said that the greens were better without the ball than with it. But, to a degree, some of both the new and relatively recent law changes had sought to eliminate that sort of negativity (or pragmatism, depending on your viewpoint) and, combined with the introduction of the sinbin, could mean time was up for the tactics employed in the past. And if, from what had been seen in the previous decade, Ireland's realistic level against the Test best must be damage limitation, containment and respectable defeat, both the creation of new offences and new sanctions would make even those modest objectives all the more difficult to attain.

The dreadfully out-of-sorts O'Cuinneagain, who had captained Ireland at the World Cup, was axed completely from a 25-man squad named ahead of the next game against Scotland at Lansdowne Road, with Eric Miller being recalled and the uncapped Simon Easterby of Llanelli also being included. It was a remarkable fall from grace for a man whose performance in the last Championship game against the Scots, at Murrayfield some 11 months earlier, had had everyone waxing lyrical.

He was not the only casualty though, Gatland's patience having finally run out with O'Shea, O'Cuinneagain's vice captain at the World Cup, and Easterby's older brother Guy being brought in for another Twickenham flop, Tierney, as one of two pivots. The Leinster pair of Hickie and the uncapped Horgan were among 11 backs as was O'Gara, who had recovered from injury and reclaimed his place from Elwood. Hayes, who had played in the A side against England, was again included as one of four props.

Maggs and Bishop withdrew injured before the team announcement, which showed eight changes including five in the backline and featured five new caps in O'Gara, Stringer, Horgan, Hayes and Easterby. Gatland thus gambled on fresh faces for a game Ireland needed to win to keep him in a job, but also brought back Galwey to partner O'Kelly in the second row, so the fit-again Davidson had to settle for a place on the bench. The Munster captain took over from Casey, with Hayes getting the nod at tighthead over underachieving Lion Paul Wallace, who had been living on his reputation for too long.

Easterby for O'Cuinneagain was the only change in the back row, but it was a new order at halfback with Munster rookies Stringer and O'Gara displacing Tierney – who had already lost out to the former at provincial level – and Ulster captain Humphreys. It meant that Bangor boy Dawson, who had never actually played for the province, was Ulster's only representative in the starting line-up. Hickie and Horgan, out of position, were given starts on the wings in place of the injured Bishop and Maggs, with Dempsey taking over from O'Shea at fullback and Henderson getting a recall to the bench. The apparently over-rated Mullins held his centre starting spot alongside O'Driscoll. For a coach who had always erred on the side of continuity rather than change, this marked massive selectorial surgery.

The sweeping changes in the senior squad meant that Johns, fit to resume as A team captain, had plenty of experience in his pack to face the Scottish second string, with himself and fellow former senior skipper O'Cuinneagain being joined in the pack by Lions Wallace and Miller. Elwood and Tierney, among seven full caps in the side, had dropped down also to form the halfback combo, in place of Farrell and the promoted Guy Easterby. Little Ulster utility back Sheldon Coulter filled the wing vacancy left by Hickie's elevation, with his provincial colleague Tyrone Howe occupying the other wide berth.

Full international fullback Dominic Crotty and the slightly makeshift centre pairing of converted wing John Kelly and Connacht's Mel Dean, an A debutant, completed the backline, with Wallace exchanging places with Hayes in a front row completed by young Shannon loosehead Marcus Horan and experienced Blackrock hooker Shane Byrne, who had led the side in Johns' absence at Franklin's Gardens. Johns was partnered in the second row by Cullen, with Miller, O'Cuinneagain and the uncapped David Wallace of Munster forming a very exciting loose forward trio. All told it was an impressive side and Paddy thoroughly enjoyed his involvement in the A set-up that Spring.

"Of course every single player wants and aspires to be in the senior squad and I don't want this to sound like sour grapes, but there was a great atmosphere in the A squad that season and I found the whole environment much more enjoyable than the senior set-up at that time. Everyone got on very well as a group and it was a real pleasure to work with Declan Kidney and Niall O'Donovan, with Harry Williams obviously there too as manager.

"Both squads trained at the AASLA complex, but the atmosphere in the A squad was so much better. Declan made it fun and we all enjoyed meeting up for training and the matches. It was a real breath of fresh air being part of the A squad, whereas the senior set-up was very heavy and a bit of a closed circle. Whenever I moved up to the senior squad for the Italian and French games, it was progress in playing terms, but I didn't find the squad atmosphere as enjoyable.

"There were so many Munster players in the senior squad that I felt the whole thing had become very cliquish. We knew the Munster guys were always very tight with each other and Mick Galwey had a big influence as a father figure, but non-Munster players maybe ended up feeling on the outside. The whole nine or 10 of them would go out together, to the pictures or the Chinese or whatever and I guess the handful of Leinster and Ulster guys felt it was a bit of a closed shop. I'm not sure whether they wanted to just stick together with people from their own province or if they realised quite how obvious it was.

"We'd always got on well enough with the Munster lads but I suppose myself and the other Ulster players, maybe the Leinster lot to a lesser degree, were feeling sore after a poor provincial season and in those circumstances you maybe look for excuses or develop a bit of a siege mentality. The Munster players were always nice enough individually, but when they got together they were very parochial. I suppose I'd have been feeling sore about how Ulster had done in the season and also the way selection was working out, but there was definitely a feeling that they enjoyed being a big clique and kind of Munsterising the environment."

For the A game at Donnybrook, Scotland fielded eight full internationals to Ireland's seven, their team including the likes of Derrick Lee, Craig Joiner, Stewart Campbell, Cammy Mather and Simon Holmes. Ulster players may have been deemed surplus to requirements for the following day's main fare at Lansdowne Road, but it was two of the White Knights' finest who combined to snatch victory for Ireland in the shadow international. Howe's last minute try, created by a brilliant break by O'Cuinneagain, pulled the game out of the fire for the hosts as the lead changed hands for a fourth and final time only six minutes after a try by visiting hooker Steve Brotherstone seemed to have secured a Scottish steal reminiscent of several of their Lansdowne Road efforts of the previous decade.

Brotherstone's burst down the left wing to capitalise on a big overlap put the visitors 21-18 up and, on the basis of two tries to nil, it would have been churlish of an Irish side who, in spite of coming agonisingly close to the tryline on several occasions, had hitherto had to rely on the impeccable boot of Eric Elwood, to complain too much had it stayed that way. Ireland were actually down to 14 men with Horan sinbinned when Elwood landed his sixth penalty from as many attempts but it took some O'Cuinneagain magic and Howe's strong finish by the corner flag to snatch victory in an exciting finale.

Surprisingly it was nowhere near as close the following day. Gatland went into the game knowing that he was drinking at the last chance saloon but, by the end of a memorable Saturday afternoon, champagne celebrations might have been more in order for Irish rugby. The journos for their part would have needed something to wash down the large helpings of humble pie. But no-one could honestly have predicted that Ireland's Scottish famine would end in an astonishing try feast which brought a 44-22 victory. It was quite surreal but stirring stuff as the Irish side containing five new caps put on a five star performance and claimed five touchdowns en route to a record-breaking rout which ended a dozen years of drought in the fixture.

The Scottish bogey was laid to rest in majestic, magnificent fashion as Ireland registered their highest ever Championship score by far thanks to an unanswered and unforgettable 44 point blitz after falling 0-10 behind, easily beating the previous best, notched up in a 30-17 win over Wales in 1996. Ironically, Ireland had not won a single home game in the competition in the intervening four years. The most satisfying thing of all from an Irish point of view was contemplating the role reversal from Murrayfield the previous year when Scotland had won 30-13 by making the most of their chances on a day when Ireland's lack of creativity and cutting edge meant that they were frequently having to work twice as hard for half the reward. This time it was Scotland's turn to turn over the ball with regularity while it was Ireland who opportunistically and lethally latched onto every scoring chance which came their way. The visitors actually had territorial advantage in both halves.

O'Gara improved after a mixed start to his first cap, but Ireland really moved into overdrive when Gatland sent on Humphreys, whose kicking and general play was red hot as the hosts added tries by O'Driscoll, Hickie and Wood to the earlier scores from O'Kelly and Horgan. Two late Scottish touchdowns only served to lessen the margin of their still crushing defeat.

For those weaned on regular Scottish sickeners and dour dogfights which ended in defeat on dismal Dublin days, this scintillating show in glorious sunshine was a barely believable departure from the sorry script of the 1990s. For Paddy Johns though, the feelings were naturally mixed. As an Irish international throughout the past decade, he had suffered more than most at the hands of the Scots and had yearned for the tables to be turned. But for a team to win so well in your absence isn't exactly conducive to getting you back in the side. At a personal level the sense of 'the team is going a bit too well here' would be an entirely understandable, if selfish, reaction.

If the Twickenham trouncing hadn't helped Johns regain his place, this stuffing of Scotland certainly wouldn't, yet as it happened he was back in the senior squad, albeit on the bench and only as a result of injury, for the following Championship clash with Italy a fortnight later. He wasn't named initially for duty, Maggs and O'Cuinneagain being the only pair added to the 22 who had togged out against Scotland for training ahead of the Italian job. But Maggs and Davidson, the latter due to a knee injury, subsequently withdrew and, while the Bath centre didn't need to be replaced given that there had been 11 backs in the initial panel, the Lions lock's cry-off meant a call-up for Paddy.

Gatland unsurprisingly named an unchanged team for the game against Italy, so the only two alterations in the match 22 were on the bench where former Test skippers Johns and O'Cuinneagain replaced the injured Davidson and the dropped Brennan. In Paddy's absence, a Ward-inspired and Byrne-skippered A side beat their Italian counterparts 31-3 at Donnybrook to make it three wins out of three in the shadow Six Nations and keep the Grand Slam bid on course. Apart from the uninspiring patches of poor play, the match was also unsatisfactory for the disgraceful tactics employed by the visitors, including a vicious knee in the back on Howe by veteran lock Walter Cristofoletto.

Great expectations have traditionally rested uneasily on Irish shoulders, but the sense of a new dawn gained currency and gathered momentum with an Italian job clinically done on another record-breaking afternoon. For the first time since 1993, Ireland had won two Championship games in a row, burying bogey team Italy in splendid fashion by building a 33-0 interval lead and going on to break the half-century barrier. Wood, Horgan and Dawson touched down before the interval, with O'Driscoll and Dempsey following them onto the scoresheet in the second period before the Lansdowne centre bagged the second of his brace to take his tally to three in two Tests playing out of position on the wing. O'Gara had a dream day with the boot, converting all six tries and landing half a dozen penalties thus giving him a perfect 12 out of 12 and a record haul of 30 points. Unfortunately, like Humphreys, Paddy didn't get onto the pitch, but one man who did make the most of being introduced from the bench was Henderson, who d id superbly well in setting up O'Driscoll's try.

"I didn't get on and it's frustrating being on the bench at the best of times but, having been out of the squad altogether for the first two rounds of the Championship, it was a step in the right direction. I genuinely thought I was getting closer again. By the end of the season I may have had a sense that they weren't keen to pick me, but not at that stage. I felt I was back in the picture, that I would get my chance again and, that when I did, it would be up to me to take it. If the A set-up hadn't been so good to be part of, things would have felt worse. When you're in the A team, you need it to be going well and the senior team not so well to help your chances of getting promoted. By the middle of the Championship, the senior team were winning so that made it less likely that other guys would break in, but at least the consolation was that we were going well ourselves as an A team and having a lot of fun."

Paddy was again on senior duty though for the next Six Nations round, away to France. Davidson had recovered from elbow surgery, but was packed off with the A squad, so Paddy retained his place on the bench. Reversing the selection for Italy, again on the principle of horses for courses, the abrasive Brennan returned to the squad at the expense of O'Cuinneagain, while a fit-again Maggs was added to the 10 backs on duty for the previous game. Shane Horgan withdrew as a result of the knee injury sustained in an AIL match at Dungannon the weekend before the international, so Maggs took his place on the wing, while a rejuvenated Henderson was picked at inside centre in preference to Mullins. Andy Ward was added to the squad as cover for Dawson, who had a hip problem, and, although the London Irish openside played, the concerns over his fitness were such that Brennan was withdrawn from the bench and the Ballynahinch flanker togged instead.

How fitting that a glorious Sabbath day hat-trick by the man his team-mates had nicknamed God should finally end Ireland's 28-year famine in Paris. Three stunning tries by boy wonder O'Driscoll gave Ireland hope in the Stade de France and then Ulster captain Humphreys struck the killer blow with a clinically despatched penalty from long range three minutes from time. Like the authors, O'Driscoll was not even born the last time Ireland won in the French capital, but his dazzling display was as intoxicating as the sweet taste of success itself following almost three decades of drought. His hat-trick was the first by an Irishman in the Championship for almost half a century, the result gave the men in green three Six Nations wins in a row and, equally remarkably, it condemned the French to a fourth successive home defeat in the competition.

In so many ways, O'Driscoll's individual brilliance represented a crowning badge of honour for this emerging Irish team, which relentlessly battled back from behind to magnificently come of age in sun-splashed Paris on St Patrick's weekend. Full of the old attributes of pride and passion, but now with the panache and confidence to match, Ireland responded perfectly both to the sceptics and the higher level of opponent by going up a further gear from the record home victories over Scotland and Italy. This was indeed an altogether tougher challenge, but Ireland rose to it with spirit and skill, culminating in that beautifully struck match-winning penalty by Humphreys. That memorable moment will remain forever with those of us fortunate enough to be there to see it, but all the more so after being present for the Argentinian anguish on Ireland's last visit to France and also when Humphreys missed that crucial penalty against the French in Dublin 13 months earlier.

In so many ways this was a quite remarkable victory, not just because it was France in Paris, but considering that Ireland spent most of the match behind and had less possession or territory than their opponents. Over the years, France have had the reputation of being able to turn quarter-chances into seven points at the blink of an eye and Ireland of having to toil long and hard for the slightest reward. Times had changed.

A French side ahead on a sunny afternoon in Paris is usually bad news for the opposition, yet Ireland backed up with deeds their bold words about now, in this brave new world, being a team which wants conditions conducive to the playing of good rugby. For that huge credit had to go to the brilliant O'Driscoll, but honourable mentions at least to rejuvenated World Cup rejects Hickie and Henderson, supersub Humphreys and maturing fullback Dempsey. It had been universally accepted that, to end the long losing streak in Paris, Ireland would need to be at both their best and luckiest with every visiting player performing above himself on the day. In the event, almost everyone did have a very good match and Ireland undeniably got some rub of the green, but there were also several things which went against them that would normally have been enough to cost the chance of ending the French famine for another two years.

The opening French try originated from a wayward Wood lineout throw which fell into the hands of Benazzi just inside his own half, while the ball also appeared to go forward just before scrumhalf Christophe Laussucq finally scampered over from a tap penalty. Dawson came agonisingly close to a try late in the first half and O'Gara hit the bar with a penalty early in the second, yet Ireland still won without those points and in spite of the sinbinning of one of their subs in the final quarter.

The man who saw yellow was none other than Patrick Stephen Johns. His sinbinning seemed set to spell disaster for the gallant Irish team, so no-one was more relieved that the tale had a happy ending. Paddy was back on in time to have a big hand in O'Driscoll's crucial third try. But he readily admits now that it was a pretty dreadful moment when Kiwi referee Paul Honiss reached into his pocket and that the next 10 minutes felt like the longest of his life as he went through the caged tiger experience, bursting to return but trying to stay focused and not plumb the depths of despair. If the team could somehow keep afloat in the meantime, they'd certainly need a big finish from him when he returned.

But back to the beginning of the afternoon. It would be easy to forget later, amid the euphoria of one of Ireland's most famous victories, that France actually produced one of those great starts which had so often blown away the greens in Paris. Wood described the first 20 minutes as 'without doubt the fastest I have played in' and admitted to being 'relieved and delighted we weren't 30 points down at the end of the first quarter'. In many ways, the start was Twickenham revisited in terms of Ireland being dominated by the heavily-favoured home nation but, by weathering the storm this time, the visitors actually turned that unrewarded French pressure to their own advantage.

Irish hearts were in mouths inside the very first minute as France took a quick tap penalty and swept downfield for winger David Bory to touch down in the left corner after exactly 60 seconds of his debut. O'Gara's overcooked kick-off, one bad missed tackle and a nice break by Bernat-Salles had resulted in a four-on-two overlap, but the eagle-eyed Honiss had noticed that the final pass was marginally forward and disallowed the 'try'. With the first Irish scrum in alarming trouble, Stringer had to find touch himself and, from the lineout, the French forwards made major inroads before a three-man overlap was kicked away and Hickie touched down for the drop out.

The flying French start undoubtedly deserved some points and the first three duly arrived when rookie flyhalf Gerald Merceron slotted over a straightforward penalty to give his team the lead. The enigmatic Ntamack, playing fullback, had a causal clearance charged down by Maggs soon afterwards, but the hosts extended their lead 10 minutes in as Merceron punished an offside tackle by O'Driscoll. Great hits by Dawson and O'Driscoll, who injured a shoulder in the process, helped keep the French in check and, remarkably only 6-0 down at the end of the first quarter, Ireland finally got on the attack.

A long O'Gara pass put O'Driscoll into space and he linked with Henderson and Dempsey for Ireland to force a penalty on the 22, but the young outhalf pulled the ball across the face of the posts from wide on the right. It was only temporary respite for the French, however, as another brilliant break by O'Driscoll was carried on by Dempsey, Hickie and the lion-hearted Foley before Clohessy was stopped just short. But the ball was recycled quickly and O'Driscoll scythed over from the pass of O'Gara, who then converted. Astonishingly, in light of all the French pressure, Ireland were ahead, with strains of the Fields of Athenry drifting across the stadium.

Ireland seemed to have sabotaged the furious French onslaught which followed when Wood hacked a loose ball clear, but the skipper quickly spoiled his good work with a wayward lineout throw and the result was a converted try for scrumhalf Laussucq. France edged further ahead three minutes into the second half when Dempsey failed to release Maggs following a lovely flat pass by O'Driscoll and Ireland were turned over and penalised, with Merceron making them pay from far out on the left.

Then came a moment which summed up Ireland's resilience. Ntamack finally took a high ball, brilliantly, and steamed majestically out of defence before linking with Benazzi, who sent hooker Marc dal Maso away. He was tracked down and bravely tackled by Hickie who, in saving a certain try, sustained a bad gash to the head and had to go off for stitches with Dempsey switching to wing and Humphreys coming on at fullback. Dawson stole a French lineout and Ireland forced a penalty just over halfway, but O'Gara's long range effort came back off the bar before another Merceron penalty made it 19-7 after 53 minutes.

France now appeared to have the platform to really pull away but Ireland, with Hickie returning and Ulster warriors Johns and Ward replacing Galwey and Dawson, immediately stung back. Great runs by Henderson and Hickie put the visitors on the attack before the former made another big burst and fed nicely to O'Driscoll, who raced over by the posts for O'Gara to convert. But apparent disaster then struck on the hour mark when Johns was sinbinned for an illegal tackle in his own 22, with Merceron's resulting penalty rubbing salt in the wounds.

"I was very pumped up, delighted to get on and really keen to make an impact. I'd been out of the side for a while and this was a big chance in a big game. The referee had warned our captain Keith Wood that the next deliberate penalty would be a bin, but that hadn't been relayed to me. In any case, I genuinely thought the ball was out when I made the tackle. The French scrumhalf had his hands on the ball, so I went through the ruck. Later I read an article on video evidence and rules interpretation which said I shouldn't have been binned, so that was some consolation as well as the fact that we did go on to win.

"But all that was no good to me at the time and, whatever the rights and wrongs of the decision, I was off. I can't really put into words how devastating it felt to be walking over to the touchline but, suffice to say, it was a very, very long 10 minutes indeed. I needed to be strong for the good of the team, to be in a frame of mind that I could come back on and do a job, but I must admit I was pretty distressed. A sinbinning costs a side seven points on average, so I was just praying that France wouldn't score."

Following Paddy's yellow card, Ireland immediately replaced O'Gara with the much more experienced Humphreys and the 14 men in green did well to force a penalty which the Ulster captain hammered home superbly from long range wide on the right. Stringer spilled the long French restart deep in his own 22 and, although Merceron hit the post with a dropgoal attempt, the pressure continued until the Montferrand stand-off made it 25-17 with another penalty. One fantastic looking Irish backline move involving Humphreys on the loop came to nothing, but the visitors achieved parity in Paddy's period off the pitch and his timely return then galvanised the Irish challenge as their opponents seemed to tire.

Humphreys tracked across to nail Laussucq into touch just inside the Irish half, then express pace took Hickie deep into French territory and suddenly O'Driscoll was racing clear behind the sticks to complete his sensational hat-trick. The easy conversion from Humphreys closed the gap to a single point and everyone wondered if Ireland were going to suffer a third successive near miss at the hands of the French. But Gatland's gallant greens, no longer lacking self-belief, knew they had the winning of it and within two minutes had forced a long range penalty, giving Humphreys the chance to put his team in front and exorcise his French ghost of 1999.

He was a long way out, but distance proved no more of a problem than accuracy as the ball sailed sweetly between the sticks and the Irish contingent in the crowd began to dare to think the unthinkable. There was still what seemed an eternity of time remaining, and although Ireland spent most of it in the perfect place – the French half – one final foray took the hosts deep into Irish territory and within range of what would have been a match-winning penalty. But this was Ireland's day as the crucial turnover came, and then the long whistle, sparking sunshine celebrations and confirming a first victory in Paris in most of these players' lifetimes.

"It was strange for me in terms of being on for five minutes then off for 10, then on again for just over 10" Paddy admits. "I came back on with the bonus of knowing that we hadn't lost ground when I was off and I just tried to make sure that the card wouldn't be an issue in deciding the match. It was satisfying to contribute to O'Driscoll's third try. He was incredible really, just on fire and David Humphreys also played his part magnificently.

"Having been there before and been stuffed several times and also having the anguish of 1998, it was just great to be part of Ireland's first victory in Paris for so long. Even though, unlike Twickenham in 1994 for example, I was only a sub and also got sinbinned, the win is still a real highlight of my career. An awful lot of great Irish players never tasted victory in Paris and many guys would have traded a fair few caps to win there just once."

A remarkable roller-coaster week for Paddy continued with the birth of the twins on the Thursday, a joyous event to eclipse the disappointment of learning that he had lost his place in the 22 for the final Six Nations match against Wales in Dublin. Davidson, having proved his fitness in the A team's narrow defeat in France, was recalled, so Johns dropped down again to captain the second string in the final leg of their shadow Triple Crown bid. "In spite of the sinbinning, I'd enjoyed Paris and felt I made a contribution, including being involved in the third OíDriscoll try, so it was disappointing when Donal Lenihan rung with the news just after the twins were born. It was a worse feeling than losing the captaincy, as my priority was always playing for Ireland first and foremost. Going back into such a positive A set-up softened the blow."

Horgan returned to the senior side at the expense of Maggs, so Mullins dropped to the A team, with Henderson holding off the challenge of both men at centre. Gatland continued with the luxury of leaving Paris hero Humphreys on the bench in an otherwise unchanged team, with Ward retaining his spot among the replacements ahead of either Brennan or O'Cuinneagain. Paddy had seven fellow full internationals in an A side showing five changes from the last Triple Crown game against Scotland. His old schoolmate Allen Clarke was at hooker for the injured Byrne, while the exciting Geordan Murphy of Leicester and Mullins were now in the three-quarter line in place of Coulter and Deane, and Emmet Farrell and Brian O'Meara formed the halfback pairing instead of Elwood and Tierney. The last pair were on a strong bench which also included Casey, who hadn't displaced Cullen as Johns' second row partner, and two more capped players in Corrigan and Killian Keane.

The Irish second stringers clinched the Triple Crown with more comfort than a final score of 28-26 suggests, with two late tries flattering the visitors on a night when Paddy's team dominated the lineout in particular and rattled up a 25-7 lead before leaking three tries while only adding another Farrell penalty at the other end. The Blackrock outhalf, whose career has been blighted by injury in the intervening couple of years, was a real star for the Irish, contributing 23 of the home side's points courtesy of a try and half a dozen penalties.

He kicked a rapid fire hat-trick in the second quarter to put Ireland 12-0 up after half an hour and, although Wales got a converted try against the run of play before the break, tries by Farrell and Howe put the hosts well clear and they held out for a very satisfying victory. The senior side failed to give Donal Lenihan, who was leaving to take up his new role as Lions manager for the 2001 tour of Australia, a winning send-off the following afternoon, however, failing to reproduce their recent form and slumping to a disappointing 19-23 April Fools Day defeat.

Disappointingly, and somewhat alarmingly in terms of the signal it sent out for his future, Johns was left out of both the Irish XV for the IRFU's 125th anniversary match against the Barbarians at the end of May and the party for the summer Test tour of the Americas which followed. With Galwey missing the Barbarians' game at Lansdowne Road because of leading Munster in the previous day's European Cup final defeat by Northampton and Davidson consequently returning to the team, there was a second row vacancy on the bench, but young Casey was called up instead of Paddy and was also included in the tour party at his expense. On the tour, Ireland opened up by losing again to Argentina, 34-23, recorded a facile 83-3 victory over the United States in a game which featured Howe's first Test cap and a hat-trick for Mike Mullins among 13 Irish tries, but finished on a rather low note by only drawing with Canada.

There had, however, been good news for both Paddy and another out-of-favour Ulsterman, Bell, on the eve of the Barbarians' match, in which the Irish XV, captained by Humphreys, only went down 30-31 in an entertaining game against strong opposition featuring a host of quality internationals including Jonah Lomu, Agustin Pichot and Ian Jones. Johns and Bell both had their international contracts renewed by the IRFU in spite of speculation to the contrary. The pair were among 25 home-based players to be given contracts.

"It had been a frustrating few months in terms of losing my Test place and not even being a first choice for the 22, but I was able to salvage more from that Spring than had seemed likely at the end of January" says Paddy. "I picked up another cap, was part of an historic win in Paris and captained the A side to Ireland's first ever shadow Triple Crown, all of which were worthwhile achievements. Missing out on the tour was disappointing, but at least it meant seeing more of the twins in their first few months. All I could do was take a break and then work hard in the hope that my chance would come again. I certainly felt I still had plenty to offer."

31. PEARL HARBOUR

Irony of ironies for a man throughout whose long and distinguished rugby odyssey no quarter was asked or given, that his Ireland career of more than a decade should end in a sentimental gesture. A quarter of an hour into the second half of Ireland's facile romp against Japan in November 2000, Paddy Johns, who was winning his 59th cap, trotted off to allow his fellow Ulster lock Gary Longwell to win his first. In doing so, he unwittingly brought the curtain down on an international career which, although the caps had now slowed to a trickle, had him within sight of Willie John McBride's mark of 63 appearances and only 10 away from Mike Gibson's all-time Irish record.

When the team was named to take on South Africa eight days later, Paddy found himself sensationally dropped to the bench with Longwell elevated to the starting line-up in his place. It was a huge shock to most people, not least the man himself. Worse was to follow in that he didn't get on in that game and never set foot on the field for Ireland again. The wearing of the green was at an end. That was it, done and dusted with no fond farewell, no ceremony or circumstance, no time to cast even a parting glance around the arena. Unlike Peter Clohessy earlier this year, Johns was, even more so than Mick Galwey, ushered out by the tradesman's entrance. The circumstances of his departure have left a bitter taste until this day, compounded by a nagging sense that he contributed to his own demise.

Up until now, he still hadn't got over it, hadn't found closure, hadn't really moved on, hadn't forgiven himself, never mind anyone else. Those close to him were hoping that doing this book would have a therapeutic effect and contribute to the drawing of a line under these events. It would need to be so, both for his sake and theirs. Talking about how his Ireland career ended has been like opening an old wound, but you didn't have to scratch very far below the surface to touch the raw nerve. Mixing metaphors still further, we sense that until now Paddy has still privately picked at the scab too much and too often for his own good. Time is supposedly a healer, but the hurt has still been palpable in the past few months.

Initially it seemed that the book's role in helping him get over it would be in recording his feelings fully and frankly, putting his heartache out in the open. Instead, when he saw every spilled out emotion written down in black and white in the cold light of day, it struck him that he didn't want this position to be set in stone for all time. He knows he needs to move on and that the feelings of the moment, however real, could seem petty in print and prove divisive in the wider context of his attempt to move on.

This is Paddy's book and the authors have complied with his wishes to the extent that he has been allowed to rewrite key sections of this chapter and even re-name it. To some extent these are the green shoots of him moving on, an exploration on his part of the perspective he knows that he needs to develop, rather than a raw reflection of what he has felt up until this point. Because we are prepared to believe that what he has written represents the position he is genuinely trying to move towards, because we feel it will prove therapeutic for him and, in a sense, bind him to the position which he is outlining, we have decided to suspend author authority and instead give him his head. The initial draft was probably a more honest reflection of his feelings over the past two years, but it strikes us that, if he can hold to the position and version of events which he has outlined below, he will be all the happier for it.

So Paddy claims to finally have found closure and to have moved on, having learnt a valuable lesson. He was put under considerable peer pressure to come off in the Japanese game and, when it then proved to be his last, he blamed himself for taking his foot off the gas both in the weeks preparation and during the match.

One of the main reasons Johns was so amenable to the idea of accommodating Longwell, was that, like a lot of other people, he thought it might be his friend and Ulster teammates only chance of picking up a senior Ireland cap. Being close friends for many years, Paddy genuinely wanted Longwell's many years of service as a steady provincial player for Ulster to be capped, if you pardon the pun, by international honours. Having got as close as the bench, it was possible that he could 'miss the boat'.

South Africa the following weekend would be a full-on affair, a game with no scope for gestures and, thereafter, Mick Galwey and Davidson should be recovered from their injuries and back in business come the Spring. Under pressure, Paddy made a conscious decision to make sure his Ulster colleague would definitely get a run one way or the other.

Hindsight is a wonderful thing and he is adamant now that if he had sensed the danger of what was about to happen, he would have played his cards differently, and made it impossible for the selectors to leave him out. Longwell has since grown into international rugby, but his selection ahead of Paddy in the starting line-up to face the Springboks eight days after that Japanese game shocked the Irish rugby fraternity and surely delighted the South Africans.

Johns had been out in the cold at the end of the inaugural Six Nations and was not taken on the summer tour of the Americas, but the knee ligament damage sustained by Munster skipper Galwey in a European Cup tie at Bath opened the door for his inclusion in the squad to face Japan along with Davidson and O'Kelly. It was an encouraging sign for Paddy that he was named in the panel ahead of young Robert Casey, especially considering that he had missed Ulster's Euro double-header with Toulouse as a result of the neck injury sustained in the second group game against Saracens. Casey, Mick O'Driscoll, Leo Cullen and Donnacha O'Callaghan were all named in the Ireland Under 25 squad to take on the Japanese at Ravenhill.

Apart from any concerns over his potential lack of match fitness, Johns also had to contend with a throat infection which made him doubtful at the start of the Japanese match week, leading to Longwell being called into the squad on Monday as cover for his Ulster colleague. In the event, Paddy recovered and was actually named in the team the following day when Davidson withdrew due to a cracked bone in his hand which had been belatedly diagnosed several weeks after it was sustained. In the match programme, former Irish international Tony Ward wrote of a "welcome recall for Paddy Johns . . . one of the great servants of Irish rugby as well as one of the game's genuine nice guys".

It was a case of double delight for Dungannon with Tyrone Howe also being handed a first cap on home soil, the only player over the age of 25 in an exciting young back division which again featured Ronan O'Gara at the expense of David Humphreys in the No 10 jersey. Girvan Dempsey, who missed the tour with injury, gave way to the exciting Geordan Murphy at fullback with Denis Hickie on the right wing and the Leinster centre combo of Shane Horgan and Brian O'Driscoll being paired together for the first time at international level at the expense of the previous season's regular No 12 Rob Henderson. Peter Stringer's retention at scrumhalf was always likely even before Guy Easterby's leg break the previous weekend.

Up front, John Hayes held off the challenge of a rehabilitating Paul Wallace for the No 3 jersey to join Peter Clohessy and skipper Keith Wood in the front row, with Johns and O'Kelly reunited in the second. Andy Ward's series of storming displays for Ulster won him the nod ahead of Eric Miller to replace the injured Simon Easterby at blindside in a loose forward unit completed by Anthony Foley and Kieron Dawson.

Warren Gatland was well satisfied after his team rattled up a Lansdowne Road points record in putting the hapless Japanese to the sword, although they weren't quite able to match the 83-point mark which they had set against the United States in the summer or that the Under 25s had equalled against the tourists earlier in the week. A very rusty and disjointed first quarter performance allied to Japan's courage and commitment in spite of being outclassed and physically overwhelmed, ensured Ireland never really threatened the century some had been predicting.

Ireland actually trailed 3-6 at one stage, the first two of flyhalf Hirose's total of three penalties more than cancelling out one by O'Gara, who later kicked 10 conversions to equal the record set by Eric Elwood against Georgia in 1998. But Gatland's greens eventually managed a point for every cap which the captain Wood and fellow front row stalwart Clohessy had won between them prior to the match, enough to eclipse the previous Dublin best of 70 in that Georgian game.

The home country attempted to stretch the Japanese defence as wide as possible at every opportunity, a tactic which was ultimately fairly well executed, particularly by O'Driscoll and O'Gara, and which reaped dividends in that 10 of the 11 tries came from backs. Even the one exception, when Clohessy was driven over from a lineout with a quarter of an hour remaining, was a cause for celebration in itself, as it allowed the Claw to make his personal mark on an afternoon which began with his son Luke running out between himself and Wood as the Irish mascot.

Humphreys, deployed at fullback, and Henderson, who claimed a try, did well when sprung from the bench, while Howe scored two tries on his home Test debut in spite of remarkably not getting a touch for the first half hour. Hickie claimed a hat-trick, while O'Driscoll bagged a brace. The first two touchdowns came from Murphy and Stringer. In spite of his throat infection, Paddy had grafted as hard as ever for 55 minutes before giving way to Longwell.

"I was put under pressure by several people, who asked me 'are you going to let Boat on?' I felt a lot of pressure, almost to the point of coercion and the implication that it was something that I had a virtual duty to do. In my mind, I knew I was very sympathetic to the idea of helping Gary, so I think some of the lobbying was unnecessary. I was rooming with Gary and like him a lot and was genuinely as keen as anyone for him to get a cap. He had got on the bench because of a couple of injuries and there would have been a concern that if he didn't get on against Japan, the chance just might not come again. Maybe it was a false perception."

"At the time, although I had always taken any challenge to my place extremely seriously, I didn't see Gary as a major threat to my Irish place and couldn't have foreseen that he would be picked ahead of me the following week. Gary had little experience jumping at the front of the lineout and I expected Mal to be picked for the middle.

"Even though a team is winning comfortably, there is no guarantee that a sub will get on to win a first cap. Look at Paul Shields against Romania this autumn or Barry Everitt against Samoa last year. Maybe that's why I was asked the question, 'are you going to give Boat his cap?' I suppose being a fellow Ulster player it was going to be my arm that was twisted, but I doubt there was any similar pressure placed on Malcolm O'Kelly. I take the positive out of every life learning experience, and this was a big one. I am very conscious to teach each of my children to make their own choices in their lives and to turn their back on peer pressure if they feel it is the wrong thing to do."

"I'd gone into the Japanese game a bit under the weather from the throat infection and I also had missed a few recent games due to a shoulder injury I had picked up whilst playing for Saracens. For the opening 20 minutes we'd been playing as a collection of individuals, all greedy to get ball in hand and score tries. It wasn't working against the spirited Japanese, who were able to slow down our ruck ball in the tackle area. My lungs and legs felt fresh, so with the lack of quick ball for the ever increasing back line, I made the decision to hit as many rucks as possible. I felt I had plenty left in the tank when I was pulled off."

Gatland made four changes for the following Sunday's Test against the Springboks, the most surprising of which saw Longwell given a first Ireland start in place of Paddy. His Ulster colleague Ward was deposed by Miller, Dempsey returned at fullback for Murphy who had looked shaky against Japan, and Henderson was preferred at inside centre to Horgan, who dropped to the bench rather than displacing Howe on the wing. But the big talking point was the second row selection where, in spite of his relative lack of recent rugby and throat infection, everyone assumed Johns would get the vote to face a team against whom he had proved himself in the past. The game seemed tailor-made for someone of his hardness and experience.

"It was a huge shock to be left on the bench. I'd been out of the team for most of 2000, but to be honest I didn't expect to be out again so quickly. It made me question whether a decision had been made that the Japanese game would be the end of my International road. There are a lot of forward substitutions in test rugby these days, so after missing out on the starting line-up against South Africa, I was disappointed not to get on, especially as there were some very heavy legs in the pack going into the final quarter.

"The game was on a knife-edge and the second rows were plodding, out on their feet - I just watched them specifically - and yet I wasn't brought on even though by now I was fully recovered from the throat infection. It didn't make sense. My number just seemed to be up. Maybe someone in the IRFU had decided that Johns wasn't going to get 60 caps, so maybe I was only ever going to get on the pitch against South Africa in the event of an injury. Who knows? It sounds like the ultimate conspiracy theory, but had I simply become a bad player overnight?

"After being dropped I knew I would need to start playing really well for Dungannon and Ulster to have any chance of appearing in the 2001 Six Nations when Jeremy, Mick and Bob would be back from injury. However there was now this nagging in the back of my head that it might no make a difference how I played, as my services could be surplus to requirements."

Looking back, Gatland admits it was a close call between the two Ulstermen that autumn. "I've a lot of time for both Paddy and Gary and it was a difficult decision at the time. I knew Paddy would always give 100 percent, but towards the end his body was starting to break down as 10 or 15 years of top level rugby started to take its toll. Sometimes when he'd join up with us he'd be so battered and bruised that we'd need to man-manage what he did very carefully.

"I think, at the time, it was one of those situations where I just felt Longwell had a little more to offer because of his size, but it was always a very, very difficult decision to leave Paddy Johns out because of his experience and his commitment. A lot of people at that stage were surprised that Gary Longwell was in the squad never mind getting in the team ahead of Paddy, but I had been impressed with him in training and felt that he had learnt quickly."

The Irish A team had a great victory over the South Africans at Thomond Park to set up the Test at Lansdowne Road, but there was to be no pot of gold at the end of the rainbow as the Springboks finally killed off a spirited home challenge. Level at 18-18 with a minute remaining, Gatland's men were within touching distance of at least avoiding defeat for only the third time in 14 Test meetings between these nations, but the visitors regained the lead through a penalty and added a killer try in injury-time. As if scripted, a rainbow appeared over the stadium to greet the rainbow republic's victory and the combination of sunshine and rain which accompanied it seemed to sum up Ireland's mixed emotions following a mighty performance which left them so near but yet so far.

In spite of the expansive approach by both sides in the opening quarter, the game remained scoreless until Percy Montgomery, playing stand-off, landed two penalties in three minutes midway through the half. Buoyed by that six-point lead, South Africa sought to press home their advantage and produced one wonderful spell of continuity which took them from well inside their own half to the Irish 22, firstly through some excellent interplay and then by picking and driving powerfully from a succession of rucks. Centre Robbie Fleck was caught by Wood after a searing break, but from the second setting of the subsequent scrum, Joost van der Westhuizen dived over in typical fashion after his captain Andre Vos had been held up. Montgomery converted to make it 13-0 with less than half an hour played.

Following yellow cards for Clohessy and future Ulster prop Robbie Kempson, O'Gara kicked a penalty which was approved by the officials in spite of appearing to slide past the far post and Ireland almost immediately followed up with a try. The ball was spun out to O'Driscoll and he did the initial damage before passing to Tyrone Howe, who handed on to Henderson steaming down the left touchline. The Wasps centre had little space to work with, but produced a well-weighted and directed chip ahead and Hickie won the race for the touchdown, O'Gara's conversion rounding off an Irish purple patch which had yielded 10 points in three minutes.

Springbok fullback Delport was sinbinned for taking out Howe just before the break and, although Ireland couldn't capitalise on the numerical advantage, O'Gara levelled the scores five minutes after the resumption. Anthony Foley ran hard out of defence after taking an overcooked South African throw on his own 22 and O'Gara put in a diagonal which led to 1995 World Cup icon Chester Williams being trapped and penalised. But South Africa went ahead again with half an hour remaining, replacement van Straaten hacking on after O'Driscoll spilled in midfield and scooping the ball off the ground to Montgomery before centre Grant Esterhuizen's dive pass allowed Rossouw to send flanker Corne Krige over. The conversion attempt hit the post.

Humphreys came on for O'Gara with just over an hour played and within three minutes found himself lining up an attempt to give Ireland the lead following a brilliant equalising try. Yet again O'Driscoll was centrally involved, making the initial inroads from Humphreys' skip-pass before flipping up to Hickie, coming off his wing at full tilt on a perfectly angled run and putting fellow winger Howe away for a super score. Unfortunately Humphreys couldn't convert from out on the left, but with a capacity crowd raising the roof, Ireland still sensed real opportunity at 18-18.

A long kick downfield by Dempsey left Rossouw in two minds as he waited to see if the ball would go dead, but when the winger finally decided to pick up near his own corner flag, he made huge ground before sending what looked like a marginally forward pass to Krige. Little Stringer made a brave tackle but Ireland were penalised and although South Africa tapped it quickly and swarmed close to the tryline where they were given a scrum, another penalty from the original position was awarded following a touch judge intervention. Van Straaten slotted it over to put his team back in front in the 80th minute and then converted to make the final victory margin a flattering 10 points when Andre Venter crashed over in injury-time.

Wood, while angry that his team had "missed a great opportunity" could still take heart from the hosts' display on an afternoon of mixed emotions for Ireland, but one which left Paddy Johns with a flat feeling. "It was very disappointing and frustrating to not to get another crack at the Boks, to not even get on, never mind start. Gary played the full 80 and that taught me a valuable lesson: charity begins at home."

January 2001 began very badly for Johns when, in the course of the same week, he was left out of a pre-Six Nations Ireland training squad which included six locks and then only featured on the bench for Ulster in a European Cup tie in Cardiff. The fit-again duo of Galwey and Davidson were joined by the pair who had started against South Africa, Longwell and O'Kelly, as well as the previous summer's tourist Bob Casey and the uncapped Mick O'Driscoll of Cork Con. When the 44 was cut to 30, young guns Casey and O'Driscoll got the chop leaving Longwell in the frame along with the established trio of Galwey, Davidson and O'Kelly.

So although Paddy had been part of the match 22 in the most recent international against the Springboks in November, it was little real surprise when he was omitted from both the senior and A match 22s for the opening round of Six Nations action in Italy. Galwey, O'Kelly and Davidson made the main squad, with Longwell, Casey and O'Driscoll being included in the second string set-up. One of three players on duty against the Springboks to lose their place in the senior squad, Johns found himself squeezed out altogether unlike the other pair, Longwell and Fitzpatrick, who each reverted to the A team.

"Paddy has lost out in the shuffle with all the locks we have" explained assistant coach Eddie O'Sullivan at the time. "We have O'Kelly, Galwey, Davidson and Longwell. He could have probably got into the A team but the A team is not always your second choice team. We are trying to bring some young guys in and we have up-and-coming players in Bob Casey and Michael O'Driscoll. Paddy is not forgotten by any means. We know what he can bring to the party and if we need him at any time we can bring him in."

Bah. Cold comfort. For one thing, O'Sullivan's words made it clear that Paddy was now formally behind Longwell and, obviously, Galwey as well as his fellow big guns Jeremy and Malcolm in the pecking order in spite of still believing that he should at least be in the top three. For another, while he appreciated the theory about the purpose of an A team, he was concerned with how things would actually work out in practice.

"I can understand that an A team may be used to an extent for development purposes and that an older player may not necessarily be picked in the shadow side if they miss out on the senior squad even though they're still better than the young guys selected instead. The theory is that the two teams are picked on different criteria, so that if a vacancy arises in the senior squad, you may still supposedly be next in line for a call-up because of your experience and so forth even though you haven't been in the A team.

"But in practice, you're out of the loop by then, out of sight out of mind almost and all too often the tendency would be to simply promote from the A squad as a matter of course. A default pecking order emerges and, whether or not you were left out of the A squad for strategic reasons, it's all too easy to become number seven in the list in the case of a second row. All that said, like everyone else I did probably benefit on the way up by being given a chance in Irish subsidiary teams on the grounds of youth and potential, so I suppose one generation on I was getting the flip side of that."

It could be considered undignified for a man of Paddy's reputation and track record to drag himself round the A circuit, hoping for a call to even sit on the shadow side's bench in the autumn of a career which had brought 59 Test caps and seen him captain his country 10 times. He was better than that and many would like to have seen him draw a line under his international career at a certain point rather than simply drift further and further out of the picture. Johns could have called time on his international career at the end of the previous season when being left out of the Americas tour had sent out a very clear signal about his international future or lack of it. But he didn't see it that way and didn't consider the A side beneath him.

"I was always hungry to represent my country, whatever the level and that was the main reason I continued to play the game. My motivation in being available at A level was the desire to play Test rugby. I was available for Ireland until the day I retired and still believed I would have been good enough to make a contribution if called upon. If I'd given that aspiration up any earlier, I might as well have packed in playing rugby at the same time. But it was hard for the last while, knowing that realistically they were never going to pick me."

The way down is painful. If your international career is falling apart before your eyes for reasons best known to others, you need something to soften the blow. The previous season he'd captained the A side to the shadow Triple Crown and been part of the famous victory in Paris. But this time there was no redemption. He'd always been a bounce back sort of guy. But this time there was no way back. From here on in Irish terms, all his resilience, courage and determination, not to mention past exploits, would count for nothing. Those who made the decisions had decided to move on. The Australian cricket team have had a policy of dispensing with ex-captains, even if still worth their place in the side purely on playing criteria, but it hasn't really been an issue in Irish rugby. Anyway Johns had already proved he was in no way a troublesome ex-leader or focal point for dissent.

Ireland A, with Longwell and Casey in the engineroom and both the former and Mick O'Driscoll being among the scorers of 10 visiting tries, got their shadow Six Nations campaign underway by beating the Italian second string 68-16 at Viterbo the night before a Rob Henderson hat-trick helped the senior side to a 41-22 victory at the Stadio Flaminio. The Irish performance in the latter game, which featured a Championship debut for Howe, was flawed enough to confirm that, just like Rome wasn't built in a day, any true Irish rugby revolution wasn't going to be completed overnight.

The luckless Davidson broke his hand and damaged knee ligaments in captaining Castres to a defeat at Beziers in a French championship game the following weekend, so Longwell was called into the senior squad to face France at Lansdowne Road, with O'Driscoll moving up to the A starting line-up and Leo Cullen taking his place on the shadow side's bench. It was more disappointment for Paddy in that the A match was at Ravenhill and he would have loved to be involved. The Irish lost that game 23-55.

Next day at Lansdowne Road, however, Ireland recorded their second successive victory over France at senior level, winning 22-15 helped by a try awarded to Brian O'Driscoll by the video referee, with Longwell coming on for Galwey in the final 10 minutes and playing his part as the home side held out for another great victory. The outbreak of Foot and Mouth meant the rest of the Championship was postponed until the autumn, but there was to be an international against Romania in June.

In spite of leading Dungannon's charge for AIL glory and the absence of Lions squad members Davidson and Malcolm O'Kelly, Johns didn't make the match 22 for the Bucharest Test, losing out to young Mick O'Driscoll of Cork Con, who was chosen as bench back-up to Galwey and Longwell. Paddy may have had the better of O'Driscoll as Dungannon beat Constitution in the AIL final, but it was no longer going to change anything. Not only had the squad been picked for the Romanian match, which Ireland ultimately won 37-3 after a sluggish start. The die had irrevocably been cast. They'd simply keep picking the next best young guy from here on in.

And that was effectively that. Paddy's draining Donnybrook experience at the start of the new season in August put paid to any hopes, however unrealistic given the way the tide of selectorial opinion had tuned against him, he may have harboured of appearing in either the carried over Six Nations matches or the November internationals. Ireland's hopes of a Grand Slam evaporated in another Murrayfield mauling, rendering a record rout of Wales at the Millennium Stadium and victory over England after seven lean years as being slightly anti-climactic. Later in the autumn, a depleted side beat Samoa and then ran the All Blacks close, building up a 21-7 lead before ultimately going down 29-40 in a memorable match.

Galwey had been ditched for the Murrayfield match, Davidson and O'Kelly starting in the second row with Longwell on the bench on a day when the selections of Guy Easterby ahead of Stringer at scrumhalf, Shane Horgan at inside centre instead of Kevin Maggs in place of the injured Lion Rob Henderson and of two ring-rusty flankers in Simon Easterby and Kieron Dawson didn't work. Ireland slumped to a shock 32-10 defeat.

For the next match against Wales, Davidson was the only man dropped from the squad, to facilitate yet another recall for Galwey and Gatland then sprung something of a surprise in his team announcement by giving Longwell the nod to partner the Munster skipper at the expense of the under-achieving O'Kelly. In the event, however, Longwell fractured a finger in training, thus denying him a first Six Nations start and generating the famous amputation offer, so O'Kelly was restored with the versatile Trevor Brennan brought onto the bench as Davidson was now sidelined by a knee injury. David Wallace and Miller were recalled in place of Dawson and an injured Simon Easterby. Humphreys' sensational European Cup performance against Wasps the week before won him back the No 10 jersey from O'Gara and he kicked 19 points in a 36-6 victory.

An unchanged team recorded a famous 20-14 win over England at Lansdowne Road a week later, but Gatland then fielded an understrength side for the 35-8 victory over Samoa in November with several players not risked ahead of the All Blacks clash the following Saturday. Longwell started the Samoan game in the absence of O'Kelly, who had a wrist injury, but the summer's Lions tourist returned to face New Zealand. The Ballymena second row came on for Galwey on the hour as the tide turned against Gatland's greens.

Gatland was amazingly axed as coach less than a fortnight later, with his assistant Eddie O'Sullivan promoted in his place, but the change was never likely to make any difference to Paddy at this stage. On the Friday night of the first weekend of the 2002 Six Nations he was playing for depleted Dungannon in an AIL defeat at Cork Con and was consequently out of sight and out-of-mind as both the Irish A and senior sides sensationally gave their Welsh counterparts 50-point pastings. The second stringers, with Davidson partnering Leo Cullen in the second row and young Donnacha O'Callaghan on the bench, won 55-22 at Musgrave Park on Saturday and then the embattled Great Redeemer Graham Henry hadn't a prayer at Lansdowne Road on Sunday as an imperious Humphreys steered his side to a 54-10 walloping of the woeful Welsh.

In spite of injury to O'Kelly, Longwell had been leapfrogged for a place in the starting line-up by young Munster prospect Paul O'Connell, but was on after half an hour when the debutant sustained concussion shortly after scoring a try. A fit-again O'Kelly took the place of the sidelined O'Connell for the next outing at Twickenham, when Ireland were thrashed 45-11 to undermine the notion that they had now joined the ranks of world rugby's superpowers. A dental abscess sidelined O'Connell for the next match against Scotland sparing the selectors a difficult decision, the status quo being maintained among the locks for a game which O'Sullivan's side won 43-22 with another O'Driscoll hat-trick.

Galwey had been acting captain with Wood out of the side, but was dumped from the squad altogether, for what was to prove a final time, ahead of the Italian game, the management taking the view that O'Kelly, O'Connell and Longwell were now the top trio of second rows. Ulstermen were the main beneficiaries of Galwey's axing, Humphreys taking over as skipper and Longwell making his first Championship start, as did long-serving Leinster hooker Shane Byrne, in a game which Ireland won 32-7 and was memorable for two tries on debut by Cork Con three-quarter John Kelly. Clohessy, who had announced he would be retiring at the end of the season, got a standing ovation as he left the Lansdowne Road pitch for the last time near the end.

Wood was back for the final Six Nations game against the French, but there was to be no repeat of 2000 as Ireland were thrashed 44-5. Longwell started in harness with O'Kelly and was replaced by O'Connell with 15 minutes to go. So, in Eddie O'Sullivan's brave new world of raising the bar, Paris pastings, just like Twickenham trouncings could still happen. Raising the bar, how are you. When the IRFU got rid of Gatland five months previously days like this hadn't been part of the plan, especially for a side which now had specialist forwards, fitness and defensive coaches.

32. 'GANNON GLORY

The face of Paddy Greene said more than a thousand tribute words. Every club has its characters and, as the old man with the knitted blue and white scarf mingled in speechless excitement with his heroes, his namesake was reminded that part of the sweetness of success is in sharing it with those to whom it means almost more than words can say. That Johns knew so many of these people and had known them for so long made it all the more special. Magic memories for the whole 'Gannon family.

Even for a man who had played with and against the best in the world for over a decade and achieved what Paddy Johns had in the game, the last Saturday in May 2001 was as good as it gets. Standing there in his beloved blue and white jersey holding the All Ireland League trophy aloft with his old schoolmate Allen Clarke to the acclaim of the Dungannon faithful at Lansdowne Road was a proud and emotional moment which one of Stevenson Park's favourite sons will cherish forever. This triumph rates right up there with his international highlights and the Saracens Cup success three years earlier. There were shades of Sarries in that here too was a club trophy won in stunning style courtesy of a record rout in the final.

It's an ill wind that blows no-one any good and Paddy would be first to admit that the cloud which the outbreak of Foot and Mouth disease cast over the British and Irish farming industry in the Spring of 2002 had a silver lining for Dungannon rugby club. The resultant rescheduling allowed them to field a settled and star-studded side week after week, making the most of key men like David Humphreys in a glory run which took them from also-rans to All Ireland League champions in a couple of memorable months. It may have been a last hurrah for club rugby before the AIL was downgraded in the name of the representative rugby revolution, but Dungannon ensured that the old era went out with a bang rather than a whimper, playing some scintillating rugby and rewriting the record books in blowing away table toppers Cork Con in the Dublin decider.

Dungannon had started their league programme with a 16-14 defeat at newly-promoted but much strengthened Galwegians, Humphreys just failing to snatch victory with a long range penalty attempt. But the Irish flyhalf contributed 20 points as the Tyrone team trounced defending champions St Maryís 30-8 at Stevenson Park next time out (Gary Leslie becoming the first man from any club to make 100 AIL appearances), though they then slipped to a surprise and disappointing 33-20 defeat at Clontarf before recording a 22-14 home win over Lansdowne. Those games against the Dublin teams were the only two AIL matches missed by Paddy all season. Successive visits to Limerick saw Gannon go down 19-17 at Young Munster and draw 23-23 with Shannon.

"We were well down at half-time against Young Munster, you could say that we were still on the bus for that first half, but I feel that our second half revival was the start of the upward turn. We lost, but the team had gained a tighter bond that would count in the tough matches to come. The Shannon trip was also pivotal and one which still stands out. Going back down there after Young Munster and with a visit to Old Crescent ahead of us later in the season, we knew we would have to take points in Limerick.

"For the Shannon match, we went down on the Friday night and went to Eddie Rockettís, where we had a milkshake and a meeting. Everyone was fairly fired up and the environment was very close-knit and focused. We knew we would be up against a tough test and came out the next day and played very well. We let them back into it and were robbed of the win points at the death," recalls Paddy, who was involved in the unfortunate injury-time incident which led to Shannon securing a draw.

"I pulled the Shannon scrumhalf into a ruck and he turned around and punched me. The Munster touchjudge didn't raise his flag, so I tapped him on the shoulder to ask if had seen the incident. The flag promptly went up and I thought 'great, we're going to get a penalty here'. Instead, the referee calls me over and goes 'the touchjudge says you attacked him and verbally abused him'. I was flabbergasted. He cautioned me and Thompson kicked the penalty to level the scores."

Then came the enforced break due to the Foot-and-Mouth outbreak with Dungannon languishing well down the table thanks to a record of two wins, a draw and three defeats from their first six matches. When the competition resumed, they were to win eight of their remaining nine followed by victories in the semi and the final itself. It all started with a hard-fought 22-16 victory over league leaders Cork Con, who came to Stevenson Park with an unbeaten record. Allen Clarke had sadly been forced into retirement by injury, Paddy taking over as captain, but the bonus was that Dungannon would now have the rest of their big names available week after week.

After being told by the referee that a Dungannon penalty was the final play of the game, Humphreys belted the ball out of the far side of the ground before turning towards the home fans on the facing bank and leaping in the air, fists pumping in triumph even as the official raised the whistle to his lips. The Ulster skipper had been responsible for 17 of his side's 22 points, but it was the way in which his body language embodied the hunger of the representative stars for club success which augured well. Howe marked his first AIL appearance of the season with a well-taken try.

A week later, new Ulster coach Alan Solomons was in attendance to watch a free-flowing Dungannon drub DLSP 43-17 with a Jan Cunningham hat-trick being among six home tries. That maintained the teamís 100 percent home record but, until beating Blackrock 26-18 at Stradbrook next time out, Gannon hadnít won away from Stevenson Park since the old millennium. It was a great victory for the team, who responded superbly to losing their captain Johns to the sinbin for 10 minutes. On Easter Tuesday, however, there was what everyone hoped would not prove a costly slip-up in the form of a 17-12 defeat at Buccaneers, the only game which key figure Humphreys, who contributed a staggering 253 points overall, missed in the entire campaign.

From there though it was victories all the way, starting with a 62-3 thrashing of Terenure, a game which featured a hat-trick of tries for Constable, while Howe bagged a brace. The Tyrone team then picked up a couple of wins against the sides who went on to be relegated, Howe again getting two tries as Old Crescent were beaten 34-27 in Limerick and repeating the feat for the third game running in a 46-26 victory at Belfast Harlequins. That was the first of two Ulster derbies in three days as the fixtures came thick and fast to make up for the period of hibernation.

Old rivals Ballymena were soundly beaten at Stevenson Park, two superbly worked tries by Howe and Bryn Cunningham helping Dungannon into a 19 point lead in the opening half hour against another team in the running for a top four play-off place. The visitors improved, but Paddy's boys defended heroically and held out for a clearcut 25-12 victory. A win over Garryowen, who were now out of contention having lost the same night to Limerick rivals Young Munster, would guarantee Dungannon a semi-final spot and it was duly achieved thanks to more tries by the Cunninghams and Constable, though a sensational one man show by Irish international Killian Keane, who scored a hat-trick of second half tries and kicked three conversions and a penalty meant the scoreline was as close as 39-34.

Dungannon were in the play-offs and anything was now possible. They were in red hot form and would be a huge threat from here on in. The force was with them and, in spite of being away in the semis, few doubted that the Tyrone team could now go all the way. "At one stage we needed to get a few wins to be safe from the threat of relegation, but then we got the chance to play our strongest side every week thanks to Foot and Mouth and started stringing some victories together.

"Because we were well down the table earlier in the season, no-one took much notice of us or really gave us a chance, so there was little pressure of outside expectations and we were able to just get on with it. But the more wins we got, the more momentum we built up and after we beat Cork Con at home we were confident we could beat anyone on our day. Our pack could compete with anyone, we had the best outhalf in the country in David Humphreys and we also had some great finishers. We all got on very well with each other and were fortunate with injuries. Everything started coming together and we realized we were capable of going all the way."

In boldly going where no Ulster club team had previously gone in reaching the AIL final, Dungannon did it with the style their followers and the rugby public had come to expect. A converted try by the home side in injury-time meant the Tyrone team had only two points to spare over Galwegians at Crowley Park and their workmanlike hosts were left to agonise on how close they came to extending their excellent first season back in the top flight by one more week. Their outgoing coach John Kingston might even have had his departure to Harlequins delayed by a week had Eric Elwood not missed what, by his standards, was a straightforward penalty in the 79th minute of a pulsating encounter.

Both teams contributed fully to this being a closely fought contest, but Dungannon did more to make it a spectacle and most would have agreed that their presence in the following Saturday's final against table toppers Cork Con would be likely to enhance Irish club rugby's showpiece of the season. From the rumbling runs of Ireland prop Fitzpatrick to the classy counter-attacking of young full back Bryn Cunningham, Dungannon would bring plenty to the party and looked as capable as anyone of robbing

Constitution of their ultimate reward right at the end of a campaign in which they had set the pace.

By contrast, Dungannon had come from virtually nowhere, with Anderson admitting that the pressure was essentially off his team after a poor start in which they seemed utterly incapable of winning away from home and did themselves little justice. But the intervention of Foot and Mouth proved the ill wind that blew somebody good, with Dungannon able to finally get all their stars on the pitch at the same time and, helped by the lack of injuries and absence of the distractions of representative rugby, to field a settled side week after week in Spring conditions ideal for facilitating their expansive style.

They were behind within two minutes of the start, Connacht stalwart Elwood drawing first blood for Galwegians by slotting over a penalty from just to the left of the posts when Dungannon offended at the opening scrum of the afternoon. The cheers of a packed Crowley Park were quickly silenced however, Humphreys putting Dungannon back on level terms with a similar strike of his own before Elwood just failed to nudge the hosts in front again, making poor contact with an attempt from long range as two naturally nervous teams made their share of mistakes.

Galwegians then struck with the game's opening try, making the most of a Dungannon error when Constable couldn't hold onto a Humphreys pass he didn't seem to be expecting and Elwood made considerable ground down the left flank. He was hauled down by the cover, but Galwegians got a penalty which they kicked to the corner and, following the lineout, skipper Barry Gavin was nicely worked over for a try near the posts with Elwood adding the extra points.

Again Dungannon lost little time in responding, Humphreys making a delightful break before his lovely long pass released Constable, who had the pace to round the defence and score wide out on the right, from where the Ulster captain couldn't convert. It was 10-8 with only 12 minutes on the clock, the crowd having seen two more tries than in the 80 of normal time in the earlier semi-final at Temple Hill, though things settled down a bit after that and it took two more Elwood penalties in the space of four minutes midway through the half to ease the home side eight points clear.

Another wonderful long pass by Humphreys to Constable followed by a dangerous run from Bryn Cunningham finally led to a Dungannon penalty, but the Ireland fly-half's kick just veered off target in the gusting cross-wind. That was to be only a temporary reprieve for Galwegians, however, for 'Gannon soon launched a daring raid from deep and international winger Howe tore down the left touchline through the last attempted tackle to score in the corner. Humphreys' conversion remarkably rattled off both posts before dropping over for two more precious points to maximize the damage to Galwegians and reduce the arrears to one point with half an hour played.

Elwood, unsurprisingly, couldn't carry the distance with an extremely ambitious penalty from a few metres inside his own half after 35 minutes and Dungannon then went ahead for the first time at a psychologically important juncture just before the interval. Kearney won the lineout which resulted from a penalty to the corner, Jonny Bell took the ball up powerfully in midfield and Fitzpatrick proved unstoppable from close range as he

The victorious Dungannon team celebrate on the Lansdowne Road pitch (above) after captain Paddy lifted the All-Ireland League trophy

Pictures: Tyrone Times

Dungannon fanatic, Paddy Greene, celebrating the All-Ireland league success with man-of-the-match, David Humphreys

Picture: Tyrone Times

Paddy with mum, Wanda, (left) and good friend, Mrs 'Tilly' Devlin during the team's victory bus trip through Dungannon

Picture: Mark McCormick

Christopher and Emily join 'dad' on the Lansdowne Road pitch after Dungannon clinched the All-Ireland League title

Picture: Tyrone Times

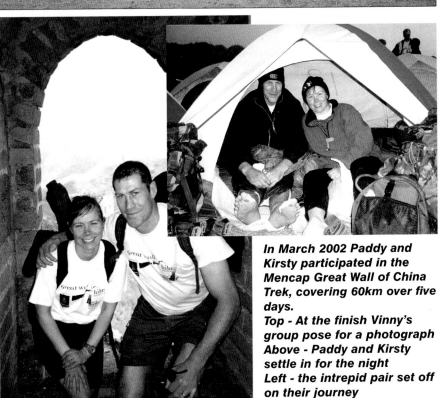

In March 2002 Paddy and Kirsty participated in the Mencap Great Wall of China Trek, covering 60km over five days.
Top - At the finish Vinny's group pose for a photograph
Above - Paddy and Kirsty settle in for the night
Left - the intrepid pair set off on their journey

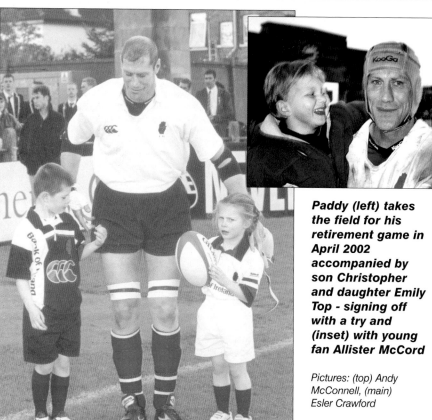

Paddy (left) takes the field for his retirement game in April 2002 accompanied by son Christopher and daughter Emily Top - signing off with a try and (inset) with young fan Allister McCord

Pictures: (top) Andy McConnell, (main) Esler Crawford

crashed over by the posts. The easy conversion from Humphreys put Dungannon 22-16 up and, although there was still time for Elwood to kick a penalty in injury-time before the break, it was cancelled out by one from his opposite number just two minutes after the resumption.

Dungannon couldn't capitalise on the temporary numerical advantage which they enjoyed as a result of the sinbinning of Galwegians' Kiwi lock Mark McConnell with half an hour remaining and, although Humphreys kicked a penalty following the New Zealander's return, Elwood almost immediately responded in kind. But Galwegians didn't appear to learn any lessons from their first reprieve, No 8 Swift getting himself yellow-carded for punching Paddy at the bottom of a ruck 10 minutes from the end, with Humphreys hammering over the penalty to complete their punishment.

There were two scores in it again, so the surprise was not that Gavin and Elwood elected to go for the posts with a penalty two minutes from time, but that the veteran Irish international missed from comparatively close range. That was a major let-off for Dungannon, who had had two chances to go further clear in that final 10 minutes, firstly a Humphreys penalty attempt from half way and then when former Portadown player Denvir Rumney produced a fine try-saving tackle following a brilliant weaving run by Bryn Cunningham. There was an extensive period of injury-time but, by the time the returned Swift ploughed over there were nearly 85 minutes on the clock and it was a mere consolation try. Elwood kicked the conversion with a resigned air and Humphreys grubbed the kick-off into touch to trigger the final whistle and spark sunshine celebrations for Dungannon.

"I will never forget our supporters, who seemed to be there in huge numbers, thronging in front of the Galwegians clubhouse in the sunshine that afternoon. I can remember our patron Bobby Mills, Paddy Greene, Will Taylor, Stanley Turkington, Kenny Wright, Johnny Gamble, Willie Dunne, Willie 'Brother' Neville and many, many others. We were a bit worried about Arthur Hamilton, who had a dodgy ticker and had had heart surgery but was jumping up and down with the rest. Luckily he survived! The realization that we were in the final started to sink in and it was a fantastic feeling, something which would have been beyond our wildest dreams just after Christmas."

Humphreys had been his usual influential self and contributed 16 points to the 31-29 victory, while the younger Cunningham shone, but Anderson rightly reserved special praise for his magnificent pack. Ulster No 8 McWhirter won the man-of-the-match award for a towering display, but one of the side's unsung players, flanker Ally Boyd, wasn't far behind him. Like their final opponents, Cork Con, this Dungannon side had few obvious weaknesses. It promised to be a cracker. On the eve of the Dublin decider, Anderson insisted that consistent Con, who had led the way for most of the season, must be considered favourites, but acknowledged that Dungannon had a great chance if they can maintain their red hot recent form. This was effectively Dungannon's last chance to cash in on the presence of all the star names Anderson had attracted to Stevenson Park, for the leading professional players would effectively be taken out of the club system from the following season due to an expanding provincial fixture list.

They appeared to have blown their chance of challenging with that poor start to the campaign, but had hit form in the past couple of months in making a strong surge into the play-offs. Having gone further than any Ulster club side had previously, the pressure was effectively off them, but the hunger was there on the part of the leading players to sign off in style and justify Anderson's claim that this was Dungannon's best team ever.

"We all met up at the club to leave for Dublin at lunchtime on Friday. Harold, Betty and Suzanne had put on a big spread for us. There were maybe a dozen people turned up to see us off. The numbers weren't huge, but it meant a lot to us. I remember, when the bus was moving off, them looking down from the door of the club and waving, like parents seeing their children off to school." That analogy is fitting, for the 'one big family' feeling was undoubtedly a contributory factor to Dungannon's success and a constant theme in the story of it. So too the Saracens parallels, not least the carnations.

"For the 1998 Tetley Bitter Cup final, we arrived in dark blue suits with button-holes and sunglasses. We treated it as our FA Cup final and thought we should look the part. Afterwards we felt it had given us a little edge, so I suggested to Willie that we wear suits with button-holes for the AIL final and, again, I think it worked to the team's advantage. It really brought home to everyone what a special occasion this was and ensured we would play as if our lives depended on it. I think when Cork Con, in their tracksuits, saw us in our suits, they were slightly taken aback as well. They knew we absolutely meant business. To our fans, this was a big day out, almost like when a county reaches an all-Ireland gaelic final. When you get this close, you must seize the moment and I had a good feeling on the day."

Anderson concurs. "At the meeting before we left the hotel, I showed the clips of some of the tries the boys had been scoring, of them singing the club song after the semi-final in Galway and also of what one of our great old stalwarts Paddy Greene had said after that match. There were tears in the eyes then, but after the journey to the ground with the motorcycle outriders and then seeing the boys walking into Lansdowne Road in their blazers and ties with the blue and white carnations that Paddy Johns had insisted we have, I knew we couldn't lose" says Willie.

"Apart from having the ability to play the game I wanted them to play, the other thing was the hunger the players showed. I've never seen emotion like the last couple of weeks. There's something about Dungannon which brings that out. I was pleased for the boys who came, or came back, to the club and believed in what we had. I was delighted that Paddy was one of the people to bring that through and no-one deserved more to be captain at the culmination of it than him. The team wanted to play in a certain style and he was a main character in that. He had considerable input and I was delighted that he could take some of the pressure off me."

Dazzling Dungannon duly rewrote the record books in gloriously living up to Anderson's assertion about this being the best team ever to represent the club. It was stunning, spectacular, scintillating stuff in the Saturday sunshine at Lansdowne Road as the memories came flooding back of that famous Ulster triumph there two seasons earlier. Cork Con, like Colomiers before them in the 1999 European Cup final, were simply swept away by a team delivering on its destiny and giving Anderson his finest hour to crown several decades of distinguished service at Stevenson Park as player and coach. The scale was smaller, obviously, but the parallels were inescapable. Admittedly the home heroes were wearing blue and white jerseys this time instead of red ones, but many of the same people were there, both on and off the pitch. Some of us will never forget this one either.

One uses the term 'home heroes' advisedly for, by their own admission, this game felt like a home tie for 'Gannon thanks to the fact that their support vastly outnumbered the Constitution following. Cork is a lot bigger place than Dungannon but, to borrow from the club song about when "Derry was a village and Belfast a little town', the southern city might as well be a mere hamlet measured in terms of Con's failure to bring anywhere near as many fans with them as the Tyrone team.

The ovation the Dungannon boys got when leaving the pitch after their pre-match warm-up had shades of Ulster two years previously and the effect on the Cork boys, as they trooped off virtually unnoticed, was palpable. When they came back out and lined up for the pre-match formalities, the Con players linked arms and looked rigid with tension while Dungannon seemed loose and relaxed in keeping with their laidback preparations of the preceding few days. A team secure in the knowledge that, if they played to their full potential, no-one could thwart them. The names of the Cork Con crew were greeted with barely a cursory cheer, but the reception for every single Dungannon player was superb and wonderfully egalitarian. Every man in blue and white got the same response regardless of size of reputation, length of service or place of birth. No outsiders, no second class citizens.

Anderson, himself the heart and soul of Dungannon rugby, had managed to mould a magical mix of talent, much of it attracted to Stevenson Park by his own personal appeal, while staying true to the club's ethos and identity. He had brought in the stars, but only men who would buy into the Dungannon way, and those who came found themselves richly rewarded both on and off the pitch. They had shown they cared about the club which in return took them to their hearts. They had great mentors of course, not only in Anderson himself, but proud senior pros in the ranks like Johns, Allen Clarke and Tyrone Howe and the AIL final victory wouldn't have come about solely as a result of the fact that this team could play a bit.

It also took passion and commitment, and it is surely no coincidence that in Leinster, where many of the contracted professionals simply seemed to bunk off early for their summer break, only one of the province's five Division One teams finished in the top half of the table that season. But, at Dungannon, the big names gave it their all for the club jersey and were rewarded with the sea of happy faces which greeted them and the trophy at Stevenson Park just before midnight that Saturday. From the local MP and new club President Ken Maginnis to the kids with blue and white painted faces to several senior citizens in wheelchairs, everyone was delirious with delight and the boys were tangibly touched by the size and warmth of the reception.

They included McWhirter, who had earlier had a simply immense game at No 8 and played with the same huge heart which characterized his role in Ulster's Euro triumph in the same stadium two seasons before. Then there was Australian international Constable, Dungannon's waltzing Wallaby Wizard of Oz and model professional rugby player, but obviously every bit as at home in what felt like one big family party as Anderson himself.

Unlike in the afternoon, when he struck fear and panic into the opposition every time he got the ball, no-one was uneasy about his presence.

McWhirter and Constable starred on a day everyone played their part and two more who deserve particular mentions are the contrasting cases of David Humphreys and Ally Boyd, one never out of the limelight, the other a classic unsung hero. Humphreys won the man-of-the-match award for another virtuoso performance, never mind 26 points, which again suggested that he, rather than his absent Cork Con counterpart Ronan O'Gara should have been heading Down Under with the Lions. He would have forgiven Dungannon fans though for being just a tad selfish in being glad that he wasn't unavailable for the final and, while denied the ultimate honour of becoming a Lion, David himself would have been genuinely disappointed to have missed out on Dungannon's big day. Be in no doubt that it meant an awful lot to him.

For the second week running, flanker Boyd produced the goods on the big occasion and it was fitting that he got on the scoresheet in the final quarter. His alternating fellow wing forwards Michael Haslett and Andrew Hughes also played their part in supporting McWhirter in the back row, while young Nigel Brady made a good fist of trying to fill Allen Clarke's boots. Giant young Dubliner Aiden Kearney came to Dungannon to further his education as a second row under Anderson and alongside Johns and was richly rewarded with an AIL winners medal as well as an Ulster contract for the following season. Fringe players who contributed to the campaign included Richard Mackey Clarke's brother, Ally, Alastair Redpath, Mark Bradley, Ralph Mercer, Keith Walker, Richard Stafford and Steven Elkinson.

It was great also to see Anderson's nephew Stephen Bell bag a try on his final appearance before heading off to Bedford. His excellent service gave Humphreys the time and space to run the show and it was an extremely mature and virtually faultless display. His namesake Jonathan had seen it all before in terms of big Lansdowne Road occasions, having won the man-of-the-match award in Ulster's Euro final victory there, but this one still meant enough to him to battle on in spite of injury, potentially jeopardising his prospects of an Ireland return the following weekend, and his commitment was rewarded with a try.

Ireland prop Fitzpatrick strolled onto the balcony at Stevenson Park that night to a hero's welcome, not bothered by the disgraceful attack on his credentials by Neil Francis the previous weekend. Now the southern press were ganging up on him, Fitzy could consider himself a true honorary Ulsterman. And with both a European Cup and AIL winners medal to his name, the guy had proved he was no patsy! "It was a brilliant campaign and a great day, as good as I've had in rugby" insists Justin. "The support went way beyond expectations. The club have always had a very loyal following, but it really struck me when we came out before kick-off. Dungannon is a great club and Paddy's whole attitude and approach sums up what it's about."

For his fellow prop Leslie, a Dungannon stalwart throughout the 11-year history of the AIL, the triumph was particularly sweet and many of the old guard who had been around when the team containing the likes of he and Paddy had begun the revolution with a string of Senior Cup successes, were around to support. The old front row of

Davy Millar, Hugh McCaughey and Leslie even got back into the old formation in the early hours of Sunday morning!

The Cunningham brothers, denied much of an Ulster show in the season just ended, had seized the shop window of Dungannon's AIL run superbly, forming a potent back three with Ireland winger Tyrone Howe. Between them that trio and outside centre Constable ran in nearly 40 tries. Howe, whose career had been in the balance for so long due to serious injury, was now living out his dreams on a daily basis, with a Lions tour call-up still to come as the icing on the cake of a dream season. He was one of the few members of the Dungannon team to have played alongside Anderson, as were the pair who collected the trophy, club captain Clarke poignantly being brought up for the presentation with Johns.

"I'd said to Sniffer 'if we win it, you come on up to the platform with me for the trophy presentation'. I never thought much in advance about the actual moment of lifting the trophy, instead just concentrating on what we needed to do to ensure we were ahead by the final whistle. I think I had in mind that we'd lift it together and then thought he might let it go, but the wee man wasn't for letting go! It was a wonderful moment, a great feeling, both because the sea of faces in front of us were Dungannon people and also because of the style with which we had won the trophy. I can still remember each of our tries clearly."

Clarke says: "When I broke my leg the previous August, I had three ambitions. I wanted to play again, to play for Ulster again and to lift the AIL trophy. The first two were achieved before I retired and, thanks to Paddy's gesture, I was able to tick that third box as well. He let me come up to lift it with him and, once I got my hands on it, I couldn't let go! When we won the European Cup, I was disappointed that Paddy wasn't there to be part of it, so I was delighted that he got the AIL as a compensation. As you'd expect, he did a fantastic job when he took over the captaincy from me."

Dungannon had got a rude awakening inside the opening minute when Conor Mahony, playing at outhalf in the absence of O'Gara, slotted over a drop goal to give Con the lead and himself a confidence boost, but it proved a false dawn for both he and his side. The Tyrone team quickly snapped into action with two penalties from Humphreys, the first after some great Gannon movement and the second the result of obstruction on him by Ireland hooker Frankie Sheahan. O'Meara and Humphreys traded penalties in the space of a couple of minutes midway through the half and Paddy's side then began to dominate with some slick passages of play.

The only unimpressive facet of the Gannon game was their inability to deal effectively with restarts, but elsewhere their class was starting to show and they threatened on several occasions with flowing attacks though, ironically, when the first try of the afternoon came, it was a scrappy affair. Stephen Bell charged down O'Meara's attempted clearance from the base of a scrum and pounced to score with Humphreys converting to give the Stevenson Park side a comfortable cushion. O'Meara sandwiched a successful penalty strike with two misses in the 10 minutes leading up to half-time, leaving Gannon grateful that there were still seven points between the sides at the break. They knew, however, they had plenty more to offer.

Dungannon's lead was extended to double figures within a minute of the resumption courtesy of another Humphreys penalty and then, after the Tyrone team gained a crucial turnover deep in defence, the Ulster captain cleared long downfield and soon added a dropgoal. Relentless recycling and probing attacks which stretched Con to breaking point finally created the space for Humphreys to take his pop at the posts as Paddy's boys noticeably stepped up a gear early in the second period.

A double tackle by the Brians, O'Meara and Walsh, cut Constable down after yet another dangerous run, but Howe's chip ahead forced the AIL table toppers to carry over their own line and concede a scrum five wide on the left. From the setpiece, Dungannon initially spread the ball right with Jonny Bell spinning out of a couple of tackles in midfield and skipper Johns typically being there to take it on a few yards further before Humphreys ran laterally and flung out a huge pass to McWhirter standing on the left wing. The big No 8, who had a magnificent game, did superbly well to stay on his feet in the tackle until he could pop the ball perfectly into the hands of Jonny Bell, who looped around his blindside and squeezed down the touchline before making good ground round towards the posts.

That made Humphreys' task of converting that bit easier and his kick put Dungannon a sensational 20 points clear with half an hour remaining, giving the stand-off the luxury of being able to finally miss a penalty on 56 minutes after notching a magnificent seven successes from seven attempts including the drop goal. Cork Con responded by throwing on club captain Ultan O'Callaghan for his return following injury and O'Meara pulled back three points with a penalty a quarter of an hour from time, but the force remained emphatically with Dungannon and, in the end, it became a stroll in the sunshine for the Tyrone team as the gaps opened up and they clinically added 17 points in the final five minutes.

Unsung flanker Boyd was rewarded for another good display by coming up with the ball following a surge to the corner by the Dungannon pack and Humphreys kicked an excellent conversion and penalty as Anderson threw on the rest of his subs to savour the occasion. It was fitting that Dungannon should have the final word and, when Con threw out a wild pass, Constable smartly scooped up to Howe inside his own half. He chipped ahead down the touchline, regained his balance to win the race to the ball and dribbled on expertly to dive over for a try which Humphreys duly converted with the last kick of the match to take his personal tally to 26 points. Anderson afterwards expressed his opinion that Humphreys should have been going on that summer's Lions tour rather than O'Gara, a view with which Paddy entirely concurs.

The triumph was similar to the Saracens Cup win three years earlier in that Paddy's team had again destroyed their opponents on the big day and won the trophy in stunning style. His boxes of newspaper cuttings contain a Belfast Telegraph piece, written after Dungannon had won the Ulster Senior Cup for the fourth successive season in 1996, criticising the way Anderson's team played then, so to ultimately win the AIL with such free-flowing rugby was sweet indeed. But which triumph meant more to him?

"Dungannon was on a smaller scale to Saracens, or to Ulster's European Cup win for the guys who were involved in that, but meant equally as much to me. Dungannon is my home club, where I started and learnt my rugby. Where you grow up and play the most of your rugby is very important to you and, if I had to choose between the two, I'd say the AIL win of 2001 was my biggest club highlight. In Irish club rugby terms, that Dungannon side was as good as you'll get and, by achieving a record victory margin in the final, I think we proved that."

Paddy acknowledges that Cork Con would have been champions under the old league only format, but points out that Dungannon did beat the Temple Hill team twice in the two meetings that season. "Under the old format, they would have been worthy winners of the 2000-01 AIL, but the play-off system gave us a second bite at the cherry and we certainly made the most of it." O'Gara was a big loss to Con in the final, though Johns believes Humphreys might well have "shown him up" on the day. It was still a more than useful line-up which Gannon had beaten, containing internationals O'Meara and Sheahan plus many players who had represented Munster including Walsh, John Kelly, Mahony, Mick O'Driscoll and Donnacha O'Callaghan. To crush them 46-12 was a wonderful achievement and worthy of a long night of celebrations.

"We met the supporters outside the Lansdowne clubhouse and our bus left at the same time as their buses left, but we stopped for a meal in Balbriggan, where there was also a free bar laid on. We had a good bite to eat, a bit of craic and some beers and then continued the journey. The wives and girlfriends were on the bus on the way home as were Willie's kids; my mum had taken ours on ahead. We had a fantastic singsong and then stopped at Stangmore, a few miles from Dungannon, to meet our incoming club President, Ken Maginnis, who had the trophy.

"I'll never forget the scenes as we arrived back at the club, with the balcony packed and people out on the steps to welcome us home. It was a great night for everyone associated with the club, a real family atmosphere. A girl called Karen Smith was having her birthday party in the club that night, but I'm afraid it was rather invaded! The tape of the game was played on the big screen and it was great to re-live what had happened that afternoon, to see how well we had played and to let it sink in. We finished up at nearly 4am on the Sunday. When the place was being tidied up on Monday, they found a set of false teeth and word was put around that these could be collected at the club. A night or two later, one of the alickadoos, a fella known as 'Black Bob', came down to claim them. He reckoned he'd fallen asleep and sneezed, causing them to fly out. But he'd had a great evening.

"As well as the trophy being a reward for us as a team, I was delighted that we'd won something for the likes of Paddy Greene and Harold Walker. Paddy's unbelievable. Dungannon Rugby Club is his life and he wears that scarf to bed. He was there every second of our campaign and you'd hear him shouting 'Gannon, Gannon, Gannon, Gannon, Gannon' wherever we'd be, backing us whether we won or lost. And every club needs someone like Harold Walker. Dungannon have a lot of people who backbone the club, but he definitely deserves a big mention. He's in charge of the bar and plays a big part in generating a bit of atmosphere in the place, ensuring there's never a dull moment." The President, David Wishart, also gave us great backing throughout the season.

Paddy was also pleased for the much-maligned Anderson, who had taken some flak earlier in the season when 'Gannon weren't going so well and had had the disappointment of losing out on the Ulster job. Anderson had his long-term future with Dungannon sorted a few weeks previously and didn't need the quick fix of an AIL play-off place, but winning the competition meant a lot to him and, like Johns, he rates it at the top of his rugby list. Big Willie and the club with which his name is synonymous had retaken their vows earlier that Spring, convinced that maintaining the marriage was still the best option for both parties and that mutual faith was richly repaid. Securing a play-off place for the first time would have brought breathing space in the form of a second honeymoon, but taking the final two steps to being crowned all-Ireland champions fully vindicated Anderson and the club in the choices they had made.

On the Friday night after the final, the team undertook a tour of the town on an open-top bus, though Paddy admits to having had a few reservations, perhaps paranoia that they would end up driving like pompous 'eejits' round empty streets, which would have been a real anti-climax. "It was something we didn't expect we'd be doing and I was very apprehensive because, well, we weren't exactly Manchester United and club rugby in Ulster isn't a big crowd-puller.

"Ulster did something similar when they came home with the European Cup in 1999, but that was obviously much higher profile. Saracens had a public celebration too, but it was tied in with Watford Football Club who had won their division and so that was certain to pull a crowd. Football always does. In the event though, it was fine. We got a good reception as we went round the town and stopped at three pubs, The Fort, Halliday's and Feeney's Bar. Local television presented their evening sports round-up from Halliday's. Looking back, I'm glad we did it. Dungannon can never win the AIL for the first time again, and of course we were also the first Ulster club to win it, so that was a special season for the club and why not take as much out of it as we could."

A big marquee erected in the club carpark hosted a banquet for some 300 people to round off the official celebrations. The players were presented with framed team photos and specially engraved plaques, but what Paddy and his colleagues would treasure most deeply of all were the memories which would last a lifetime.

"There are lots of specifics on and off the pitch which I'll never forget from those few weeks . . . us having our boots inspected and some confiscated at Shannon Airport (during the Foot-and-Mouth period) . . . the fantastic opening 20 minutes against Ballymena . . . the nervous final 10 minutes against Garryowen in the last league match . . . the delight of our supporters after the semi-final in Galway. . . the special send-off we received at the club when leaving for the final . . . being stuck in traffic on our way to the ground from our hotel in Lucan before the motorcycle outriders arrived to bring us through . . . Terry Jackson looking forward to being waterboy at Lansdowne Road and having a shower there afterwards (Terry's wife, Heather, was also pleased he had a shower!) . . . and, of course, bringing the trophy into the clubhouse a few hours later and the one mighty party that followed."

33. WISDOM OF SOLOMONS

Paddy pour Perpignan? Few people know how close Johns came to finishing his playing days with a stint in the south of France. When he saw the writing on the wall and realised his Ireland days were done, there was plenty to ponder in the spring and summer of 2001. A career crossroads and a pay-cut meant it was time to reassess his professional prospects.

But the fact that he gave such careful consideration to the Perpignan proposition was about more than earning potential. Strange though it seems after all he had achieved, Paddy perhaps felt he had a point to prove. He'd always taken pride in his performances and felt he still had a lot to offer any side. So, at a time when the IRFU had not quite demeaningly downgraded him to provincial player status but certainly devalued his contract, it was pleasing to receive an offer from France, never mind the fact that it was a potentially lucrative opportunity.

Five years earlier when he'd signed for Saracens, Kirsty would have been happy enough for them to relocate to France for rugby, had that been the best option at the time. The idea of playing there appealed to Paddy, encouraged by positive feedback from his good friend and former Dungannon and Ireland team-mate Jeremy Davidson, who was now Castres captain. Harry Williams had stepped down as Ulster coach and, rather than seeing the prospective infusion of a new regime as representing Ravenhill renewal and a fresh start, he saw it as a potential natural break, the end of an era.

The previous summer, Paddy had already made a major contribution to Ulster's 2000-01 season before it started, being instrumental in persuading two of his former Saracens team-mates, Ryan Constable and Brad Free, to join the Ravenhill ranks. As related in an earlier chapter, Constable, a player whose outside break reportedly îscaresî even Brian OîDriscoll, and Johns went back a long way, while the Wallaby wizard and his fellow Aussie were good mates who lived together during their time in London. Due to ancestry qualifications, Free had played for Ireland A against the touring Canadians at Ravenhill in November 1997, making one memorable searing break only to break his ankle and be sidelined for a long period.

"I rated Brad very highly, though he was never the same after that ankle injury," says Paddy. "There was a time when Kyran Bracken was injured that he got a run in the Saracens side and really established himself. Brad was man of the match against London Irish one week, but then Kyran was fit again and was brought straight back in. Obviously Brad was very disappointed and had words with Francois Pienaar, which effectively finished him at Saracens. He left the club in the summer of 1997, but we always kept in touch and he has spent at least a couple of Christmases with us.

"Initially I'd put him in contact with Bective where a friend of mine, Greg Lynch, was coaching. Brad joined them and got involved with Leinster, where he hoped to get a contract, but he hurt his neck, which required an operation, and that kept him out for another lengthy period. He came to Ulster the following season and played pretty well, but didn't play much last season and began to make other plans. He started to look ahead to his life beyond rugby and was released from his contract when we were knocked out of the European Cup in January of this year."

By remarkable coincidence, the very evening we were discussing the people Paddy played with at Saracens, including Free, our conversation was interrupted by Brad phoning his former colleague for a chat from his new home in the United States! "Brad is at Life University in Atlanta, which is where we played the United States in January 1996. He's studying to be a chiropractor and is enjoying married life with Jessie. A real new man!" grins Paddy after coming off the call.

"Ryan had finished his contract with Saracens in the summer of 2000 and was thinking of going back home to Australia. He was on holidays in Majorca with Brad and Brad emailed me. I emailed him back and asked about Ryan. I put them in touch with Harry Williams and Ryan ended up coming over as well, moving in again with Brad. I think he has been one of Ulster's best ever signings and I made sure that, at club level, he came to Dungannon."

Constable confirms: "After Paddy got in contact and asked if I would be interested, I came over to Ulster for a weekend and enjoyed the place so much that I signed after that. Without Paddy's recommendations, I don't think I'd be here today. Had it been an agent, I don't think that I'd have pursued it at all, but I knew that Paddy wouldn't be advising the move if he didn't think that it was in the best interests of both myself and Ulster. But thankfully I came, and have enjoyed every minute of it. There was never any doubt either that I wanted to join his club, Dungannon, and that too has been a great decision."

Fijian flop Veitayaki, Miller, Bromley and Fradericks had all departed as had reserve pivot Mark Edwards, while Mason had made a lucrative move to Stade Francais after effectively giving up hope on Ireland's call coming again. Ulsterman Clem Boyd came home after spells with Currie, Bedford and Bath, Ballymena's versatile Kiwi Shane Stewart was given a contract, young Dubliners John Campbell and Aiden Kearney were signed up and both Grant Henderson and Russell Nelson came from South Africa.

Henderson, a big former South African Under 21 international fullback, had failed to pick up a Super 12 contract back home and didn't really cut it in Ulster either, but Nelson, who has Irish ancestry, made more of an impression in the back row. Ulster were glad of him given that Miller had departed while O'Cuinneagain unfortunately broke his wrist in pre-season training and didn't play for Ulster again, helping out with coaching the forwards before returning to South Africa to continue his medical studies.

Humphreys was reappointed captain while Williams, entering the third and final year of his coaching contract, announced fairly early in the season that he did not wish to continue in the post, thus allowing the search for his successor to begin well in advance. The hope was that Harry could go out on a good note, with Ulster finding some form of equilibrium and consistency following the remarkable highs and lows of the first two terms of his second tenure.

The pre-season friendly programme resulted in four straight victories, over Leicester at Omagh, away to Coventry to round off a week spent in a training camp, and then at home to Rugby and Edinburgh. Unfortunately Irish hooker Allen Clarke broke his leg in the game against the Scots, but the wins set things up nicely for the opening competitive game of the season, an interpro against old rivals Munster at Ravenhill and Williams went for a fit-again Jonathan Bell at centre in spite of the impression made by new boys Stewart and Constable in his absence during the warm-up programme. Free was chosen at the base of the scrum with Nelson on the blindside and Longwell was paired with Johns in the second row.

Munster had not won at Ravenhill for more than two decades, their victory in September 1999 having been at Upper Malone when Ulster's headquarters was out of service, but the team which had reached the European Cup final three months earlier maintained their winning knack of the previous season. The visitors showed three changes from the Twickenham line-up, with Keith Wood and Eddie Halvey having defected to the English Premiership and John Hayes being injured, but were simply able to bring in three more internationals in their places, namely Frankie Sheahan, Alan Quinlan and Marcus Horan.

Two late drop goals by Ronan O'Gara to add to his five penalties finally sunk an Ulster side which had trailed for most of the first half but snatched the interval lead through a magnificent Andy Ward try and then edged five points clear in the second period to the delight of a five-figure crowd. Constable showed his worth, holding on wonderfully in the tackle to pick out his compatriot Free in support and Bell and Henderson maintained the momentum. Skipper Humphreys was collared as play then went left, but Constable came back right and found Ward, who had an awful lot to do but powered 20 yards to the line, bringing the crowd to their feet as Humphreys prepared to nudge his team in front with a fine conversion. Sadly though it was all in vain.

Boyd, who withdrew from the Munster match with injury, did so again after being intended to be the only change to the side for the following Friday night's game in Galway, where Ulster beat Connacht 39-15, with Williams preferring to look on the bottle as being half full rather than half empty in assessing a mixed performance. The White Knights were outscored in a stuttering second half when they lost Ireland prop Justin Fitzpatrick to the sinbin and subsequently lost their way. But they had done enough before the interval, in scoring 25 unanswered points, to allow themselves the luxury of easing up slightly.

Ulster got their interpro challenge back on track before the greyhounds took centre stage on the first ever Friday night of rugby at the Sportsground. Williams' thoroughbreds were fast out of the traps, showing their hosts a clean pair of heels before rather going to the dogs albeit without really giving the underdogs a sniff of victory. Paddy was driven over by the pack for the second of Ulster's three first half tries and they added two more in the final 40 minutes.

Williams had substituted Henderson at the Sportsground where he had again been shaky after a difficult debut against Munster, but gave his new South African fullback a vote of confidence by retaining him in the No 15 jersey for the third interpro against Leinster at Donnybrook. Boyd was this time ruled out before selection, so the side was unchanged, suggesting that the coach had abandoned his much-maligned rotation policy of the previous season.

"It didn't affect me as much as the other two second rows, Gary Longwell and Mark Blair, but I think in general the guys didn't like it. When you're a player, you want to play and to always be picked on merit. There's nothing worse than knowing that, virtually no matter how well you do this week that next week is someone else's turn, or equally that you'll continue to get a game every couple of weeks even if you're not really delivering. Most players would prefer to take their chance on being out of the side for a period with no guarantees if the converse meant that, providing you got in and took your chance, you could look forward to a good run in the team."

A 13-point scoring spree by Leinster midway through the second half left former continental kings Ulster facing a real dogfight to secure a place in the following season's European Cup. The White Knights led for most of the opening hour but then slipped behind for the first time and Leinster quickly followed up with a killer blow in the form of an intercept try, going on to win 19-6. With Leinster due at Ravenhill for the return fixture the following Friday, the final whistle at Donnybrook was always effectively only going to be half-time in a two-leg tussle between the sides likely to be locked in a straight shootout for the second Euro qualification spot on offer.

Ulster went into the return with £100,000 of pressure resting on them after Ravenhill boss Michael Reid revealed in the week that this would be the conservatively-estimated cost of not qualifying. And a rejuvenated home side passed the biggest test of the Williams era on an occasion reminiscent of the old European Cup glory nights as the White Knights came out in front of a near-capacity crowd and tore into the visitors with cult hero Ward leading the charge and skipper Humphreys running the show masterfully. They won 26-13 and it was a great triumph considering the repercussions of the result and the fact that Johns had been forced to withdraw on the day of the game due to a neck injury.

That took a lot of pressure off before the visit to Cork the following Friday, when Paddy was fit to return in place of his deputy Blair, and Ulster bravely threatened to spoil Munster's party at Musgrave Park. In the end, skipper Mick Galwey's 100th Munster appearance was crowned by the clinching of a third successive interpro title by his team, but up until late in the game the hat-trick celebrations had been firmly placed on hold.

O'Gara kicked an early penalty for Munster, but Free then charged down his attempted clearance and pounced on the loose ball to give the visitors the lead. The champions regained it with a try from Dominic Crotty, though Paddy came agonisingly close to winning what should have been an unequal race with the fullback to ground O'Gara's roll to the line. O'Gara converted, but Humphreys cut the gap to two points with a penalty at the end of the first quarter and then helped his team back into the lead in spectacular fashion a couple of minutes later.

A glorious sweeping move launched by the electric skipper finally yielded the try it so richly deserved. Twice the captain opened up the play coming left and then, following interchanging by half the pack, Ulster moved the ball right where big fullback Henderson broke the first couple of tackles. He was finally hauled down just short and, for an agonising moment, everything seemed to stop, but James Topping was on hand to pick up and dive over, Humphreys adding the extra points for good measure. O'Gara pulled back three with a penalty two minutes later but drew a blank shortly before the interval.

Munster predictably made a storming start to the second half, pulling Ulster across the full width of the pitch twice before Stewart put in a superb try-saving tackle on Ireland centre Mike Mullins. Swarming Ulster defence repelled Munster's follow-up surge but suddenly a clearly provoked Johns unleashed a flurry of punches at O'Gara and, following touchjudge intervention, the young No 10 made Paddy pay with a penalty which cost the visitors their lead. "He had pulled my headguard right down over my face and I just lost it. O'Gara has a bit of a reputation of doing little nasty, niggly things like that. I'd say a lot of the punches thrown at him aren't for nothing."

Two Humphreys penalties gave Ulster a 21-16 lead and real hope, but suddenly Munster struck from a lineout with Clohessy appearing and popping the ball to Foley, who went through a gaping hole and sent Anthony Horgan in for a try which O'Gara converted. Two minutes later he struck with a penalty as Munster quickly went from trailing by five points to leading by the same margin and the Cork Con outhalf duly had the last laugh when giving his team a two-score cushion with another three-pointer as the game entered stoppage-time.

Ulster's Euro qualification hopes got an unexpected boost the following day in the form of Connacht's shock victory over Leinster and they duly clinched their place in the 2001-02 Heineken Cup by beating Connacht 36-22 at Ravenhill a month later to clinch runners-up spot in the interpro table. Johns, who had been injured during October's Euro group games and was due to play for Ireland in their autumn internationals over the following fortnight, was given a break on the bench by Williams, though was introduced in place of Longwell at half-time on an evening when fellow lock Blair bagged a brace of tries.

In between, Ulster had had a real roller-coaster ride in their first batch of four games in the Pool phase of the Heineken Cup's so-called 'Group of Death', with a great victory over Cardiff and heavy defeat at Saracens being followed by a dramatic draw in Toulouse and then the anguish of seeing the French snatch a last gasp win at Ravenhill five days later. The Cunningham brothers, Jan through injury and Bryn due to Williams' preference for Paddy Wallace, missed out on a squad which included Ireland cricketer Neil Doak as third scrumhalf ahead of European Cup winner Andy Matchett. Ulster's hopes of signing ACT Brumbies hooker Tom Murphy to take the place of the injured Clarke were scuppered by ERC red-tape however. Their first opponents Cardiff, for their part, were unable to field Welsh prop Peter Rogers, just signed from Newport, but the Welsh could still boast 20 capped players in their star-studded squad.

Ulster brought back glorious memories and revived the famous Ravenhill roar by adding cosmopolitan Cardiff to their impressive list of European scalps by the end of an enthralling game of fluctuating fortunes where the lead constantly changed hands. Cheered to the rafters by the competition's best set of supporters, Humphreys and his magnificent White Knights held their nerve to come from behind and get their campaign in this toughest of Pools off to the perfect start, leaving special guest George Best applauding with the rest.

As thick smoke billowed towards the carpark end from the extravagant fireworks display which greeted the sides onto the pitch, the capacity crowd who had generated an electric atmosphere even before kick-off, willed their Red Hand Heroes to fire from the start. Neil Jenkins, record points-scorer in both Test and European Cup history, got the game underway for Cardiff, but Longwell gathered in the kick-off and Ulster cleared their lines as the sparks flew between Paddy and man mountain Craig Quinnell. Humphreys dropped an early goal and, although ginger goal glutton Jenkins cancelled it out with his first penalty of the evening, his opposite number landed two to make it 9-3 midway through the first half.

Cardiff went ahead in the third quarter courtesy of a penalty, try and conversion from Jenkins, but Ulster responded with a super score of their own. Constable's outside breaks had already caught the eye often enough since his arrival at Ravenhill, but it would be hard to better the sublime effort which burnt off the Cardiff cover and put Ulster back in front on the half hour. He went round behind the posts to give his captain the simplest of conversions and, after Jenkins hit the upright with a penalty, Humphreys landed one to make it 19-13 at the break.

Left wing Craig Morgan, the only uncapped player in the visiting line-up continued his long unbroken run of scoring in every match for Cardiff as the Welsh went on to win the third quarter 10-3, the lead actually changing hands three times in that period, including twice in as many minutes as Humphreys and Jenkins traded penalties. Ulster thus went into the final quarter 22-23 down.

Humphreys missed a penalty from long range, but he put Ulster back in front with his next effort on 67 minutes and the hosts were again reprieved when Jenkins completed a hat-trick of misses. The immense Longwell took a lineout in the final minute and Ulster drove hard before their captain slid a dropgoal attempt across the face of the posts. The ball was fumbled, however, and the ever-hungry Howe followed up to hack over the line for a conclusive try and Humphreys took his personal tally to 22 points as a capacity crowd raised the roof.

"Cardiff was a very big win" agrees Paddy. "It was a really tough group, but we had the advantage of starting with a home game and knew that if we really performed we would have a good chance. Beating them set us up nicely for the trip to Saracens which, as well as being a very important fixture for the team, was obviously a massive match for me because I was going back to where I had spent three happy seasons. Naturally I was very keen to do well, but it was a disappointing day as I got concussed and we ended up being heavily beaten after a good start."

Scottish second row skyscraper Scott Murray missed the match with injury, while new signing Tim Horan was neither fit nor eligible, but Saracens were still able to field 11 full internationals including Irishmen Paul Wallace and Darragh O'Mahony, England winger Dan Luger, little French star Thomas Castaignede, Scottish hooker Robbie Russell and some of Paddy's old colleagues, Bracken, Grewcock, Diprose and Hill.

Star-studded Sarries struggled to get the better of their brave visitors for an hour before breaking free and running riot with 31 unanswered points in the final quarter. Luger helped himself to a hat-trick as slick Saracens pulled away in a devastating scoring spree as the gallant White Knights were swamped after magnificently matching the tournament favourites blow for blow until midway through the second half, when they led 25-24.

Castaignede drew first blood for the hosts with a penalty, but a hat-trick of Humphreys strikes had Ulster 9-3 up by the half hour and, although Francois Pienaar's team hit back with a Hill try and Castaignede penalty, the visitors went in with their noses in front thanks to a stoppage time penalty from the soccer stadium's centre spot by their skipper. A dazed Johns had to bow out at the break, but his replacement Blair won a lineout following a long Humphreys penalty to touch and Stewart, a late call-up due to Jonny Bell's cry-off, ripped through with power and pace for a converted try which put Ulster two scores clear.

Hill was driven over for his second touchdown following a Grewcock lineout take, Castaignede converting and the two kickers then traded penalties to leave Ulster with that one-point advantage on the hour mark. But rugby league recruit Duncan McRae put Sarries in front with a converted try and from there it was sadly one-way traffic with Luger the main beneficiary. "We really took the game to them for the first hour, but they put together a great spell and the floodgates opened. I only actually remember the early part of the match though because I was concussed thereafter!"

Paddy, who had been damaged in a severe shoeing by his old colleagues, was diagnosed as having a trapped nerve in his neck and, frustratingly, had to miss the crucial double-header with Toulouse which would go a long way to deciding Ulster's fate in the group. Blair replaced him as Longwell's partner, while Bell and Nelson returned following injury in place of Stewart and Derick Topping respectively for the first, away, leg against a side missing Emile Ntamack, Xavier Garbajosa, Lee Stensness and Sylvain Dispagne.

Heroic Ulster breathed new life into their Group of Death campaign with a stunning late comeback which earned them a famous first ever point on French soil. Skipper Humphreys slotted over an ice-cool conversion after 85 minutes to level the scores for the third and final time in a remarkable match which brought back memories of Ireland's great last gasp triumph over France in Paris on another glorious sunny Sunday afternoon seven months earlier. All of Ulster's bravery had seemed set to count for nothing for a second weekend running as Toulouse pulled 14 points clear with eight minutes remaining. But the White Knights simply refused to lie down and Bell's 80th minute try set the scene for James Topping to juggle his way down the right for the crucial score following a storming run by sub Stewart.

An early Fabien Pelous try was cancelled out by Free's snipe down the blindside following a brilliant break by Constable and then Howe started and finished a move with Humphreys adding the extra points to cancel out Toulouse's second try, scored by Franck Tournaire and converted by Michel Marfaing. A great long-range penalty from Humphreys seemed set to give Ulster an interval lead, but they were then hit with a double blow in first half stoppage time, with Constable limping off and then pivot Jerome Fillol grabbing a converted try to make it 19-15.

Humphreys sandwiched a Marfaing penalty as Ulster took advantage of the sinbinning of two French forwards in the second half, but two more strikes by the winger edged Toulouse seven points clear and he then converted a seemingly decisive try by centre Cedric Desbrosse. Ulster rallied with wonderful heart and spirit, however, which brought a try for Bell, deftly converted by a Humphreys drop-kick in the final minute of normal time. There were five minutes of injury-time and Ulster gloriously continued to take it to the French before Stewart's gallop down the right was finished off by Topping, who did well to hold on and also showed considerable presence of mind to go round as far as he could to ease his captain's burden slightly.

The French crowd went ballistic, jostling this journalist and others whilst venting their wrath on the referee, and Paddy has his own abiding memory from that dramatic conclusion. "I wasn't fit to play in the game, but was there and on waterboy duty and can recall the French fans being very agitated at the end. But the thing I will remember is Davy Irwin's part in celebrating the Topping try. When Shane Stewart made the break, Davy was level with Jimmy on the touchline around halfway, but by the time Topper touched down there was The Doc round behind the posts to be first to hug him, still wearing the familiar green cap and carrying his bag. Mark McCall still has great fun playing the moment on tape. That David was there so quickly says a lot both about his fitness and his desire for Ulster to succeed."

But the tables were turned at Ravenhill five days later, when Toulouse left Ulster's Euro dreams in tatters by snatching victory with an injury-time try which would haunt a huge Halloween crowd for many a day. The French, behind throughout a gripping match, stole a sweet if unlikely victory right at the death to gain revenge for the previous weekend. Ulster, who needed to capitalise on that sensationally snatched draw, went behind to an early penalty but quickly struck when experienced visiting scrumhalf Jerome Cazalbou, recalled for this game and one of 10 internationals on the Toulouse team even with Christian Califano left on the bench, passed straight to Ward, who romped over by the posts for Humphreys to convert.

Yann Delaigue and Humphreys traded a pair of penalties apiece to leave Ulster 13-9 up after half an hour and Howe's fearless claim of a high ball led to his captain extending the lead still further right at the start of the second period. That was cancelled by another penalty for the French, but the Ireland flyhalf added two more either side of McWhirter being sinbinned for killing the ball. He then replied to a strike by Delaigue to leave Ulster 10 points up with as many minutes remaining.

Toulouse seemed to be losing their cool and Tournaire, now substituted after a bad-tempered display, was reprimanded by Dr Irwin for heckling Humphreys as he lined up a penalty and then had to be physically restrained from attacking the crowd. But his team-mates still on the pitch retained enough focus to drive over in the left corner with five minutes left, Delaigue converting to conjure the vision of the previous Sunday's scenario in reverse. And the nightmare duly materialised two minutes into injury-time when Toulouse mounted a typically French raid from deep to sneak Garbajosa over in the corner, Marfaing rubbing salt in the wound with a touchline conversion. Humphreys' magnificent seven strikes from seven attempts was an effort in vain.

The result left Ulster with little to look forward to when the competition resumed in

January and, apart from the deflation, their chances of hitting the ground running at Cardiff Arms Park were hardly helped by the inevitable ring-rustiness caused by not playing together competitively as a team for over two months unlike their opponents. Following the second Toulouse tie all Ulster had was an interpro against Connacht at the start of November and then a dire practice match against the westerners at Ravenhill just after Christmas, hardly ideal preparation for resuming a European Cup campaign.

Williams cut his losses with import Henderson and recalled Stan McDowell at fullback for his first Ulster appearance since the 1999 European Cup final and Allen Clarke, making a welcome return at hooker having battled back from his August leg break, but there was disappointment for Johns. Losing his Ireland place for the November Test against South Africa had been traumatic enough but now he found himself confined to the Ulster bench, failing to dislodge either new international Longwell or Blair, who had deputised well in Paddy's injury-enforced absence from the Toulouse ties.

Ulster's hopes of grabbing a Group of Death lifeline were buried beneath an avalanche of Cardiff tries as the hosts romped into the quarter-finals with an assured performance which swept the White Knights out of the competition on a tidal wave of relentless Welsh pressure. The only uncapped player in the home line-up, Jamie Robinson, bagged two tries in the opening quarter and then Craig Quinnell got a fortuitous score as Cardiff piled up a 20-6 lead before a long pass from Humphreys put James Topping over. Ulster desperately wanted to register the first score of the second period, but Jenkins banged over a penalty from five metres inside his own half and added two more by the 53rd minute, the last of them when Longwell was punished for a retaliatory punch on Quinnell. That was Williams' cue to send on Johns and Best for Blair and Boyd but, either side of a McWhirter 'try' being disallowed, Jenkins dropped a goal and then went over for a try which he also converted to make it 42-11 and although Topping bagged the second of his personal brace right at the end, it was of little consequence or consolation.

That put Ulster out of contention to qualify for the quarter-finals, but the squad were determined to give Williams a winning send-off against Saracens the following Friday night. For Paddy, the prospect of taking on his old club again provided extra motivation, especially after the events at Vicarage Road in the first meeting in October, which had left him sidelined for several weeks.

"Paddy had been well fired up for going back to Vicarage Road in the autumn, but had got caught on the wrong side after making a tackle and took an awful shoeing from his old team-mates" recalls Justin Fitzpatrick. "He was pretty sore and battered afterwards and actually ended up missing a couple of games. I remember when we watched the video, he kept rewinding it, playing it again and again in a bid to see exactly who the culprits were.

"He carefully marked down all the names for future retribution. The last person to ruck over him that day was his old mate Paul Wallace and it was like 'oh Wally, ok, you got to come to Ravenhill now mate' as he watched the tape. Sure enough when Saracens came to Belfast a few months later, Paddy hadn't forgotten. He said to me before the game that he was going to get even. So at the very first scrum, I moved my head to the left, Paddy dropped his bind and the big fist came through and made good contact with its intended target. 'That's one each, Wally,' he said.

Later that night, when visiting Wallace in hospital after his ankle break, Johns caused his old Saracens team-mate more consternation. "When I came in, he was sitting up in bed in an Ireland jersey," Paddy recalls. "As a joke, I told him that it mightn't be advisable to be wearing what he was wearing, for the guy in the next bed had a UVF tattoo on his arm and mightn't appreciate the green shamrock shirt. Broken ankle or no broken ankle, he managed to whip the shirt off pretty sharpish!"

"Paddy was a past master at the right hook in the middle of the scrum," continues Fitzpatrick. "That was neither the first time nor the last that I've felt his fist whistling just past my face to discipline a tighthead who was doing things he shouldn't!" laughs the Ireland prop, who the writer recalls joining Johns in dishing out retribution to the Ballymena tighthead during an AIL match between the Braidmen and Dungannon at Eaton Park the same Spring. Along with others the pair had spotted an indiscretion and dispensed swift justice at the next scrum where a Fitzpatrick left hook and a Johns haymaker from the second row left the home No 3 requiring the blood bin.

For that Saracens game, Williams had recalled Paddy in place of Blair as he sought to end his second stint as Ulster supremo on a high note. Johns, who had done well as a sub against Cardiff, admitted that he had been itching to get his place back. "It has been a bit disjointed and frustrating recently," he said at the time. "But I'm glad to be back in and playing against my old club in front of a big Ravenhill crowd. The crowds Ulster get these days have helped make playing here really special since I returned from England.

"We might be out of the European Cup, but every match at this level is a big one and it's always an honour to represent your province. I don't think we'd lack motivation playing in front of our own fans in our last Ulster game of the season, but when you add the fact that this will be Harry's last match in charge it becomes a very special occasion and every one of the players is determined to give him the best possible send-off. So far this season, we have only managed to win once and draw once in our five European matches, so it would be nice to improve on that record. We maybe feel we have played better than our results suggest, but that is what you are judged on.

"It has been a very tough group and I suppose our chance was lost when we let a lead slip in those last few minutes at home to Toulouse. No game is easy these days, but you must win your home fixtures and we slipped up badly on that occasion. Going to Cardiff last weekend needing a win to stay alive in the group was very difficult, especially after such a long lay-off since our last competitive match. We were caught cold, got them on a good night and ended up being well beaten. There can be no complaints about the result" said Johns in a pre-match interview where he also took the opportunity to counter speculation of possible retirement and confirmed his continuing availability for Irish selection.

In the event, there was to be no farewell victory for Williams, but skipper Humphreys at least managed to provide a fitting send-off for his retiring boss on a nostalgic night at a typically packed Ravenhill. The man who had captained Ulster to Euro glory under Harry two years earlier swooped to score six minutes into injury time when Saracens' last attempted counter-attack of the game broke down. Hopes of a first ever Euro victory over English opposition had already been extinguished, but at least it was a moment to savour right at the end of what had been the toughest of campaigns for the White Knights.

Williams' team had been given a rousing reception on a freezing night and things became heated in the opening minutes, presumably thanks to Paddy's intervention from the depths of the Ulster second row, though it was ultimately Wallace and Fitzpatrick who were lectured by referee Joel Dume before the former received treatment. To their credit, both sides showed admirable willingness to move the ball, the hosts seeking to treat their magnificent fans to some decent rugby, and the visitors in pursuit of the scores they needed to keep alive their hopes of quarter-final qualification.

Wallace and Clarke then had an angry altercation before the Lions prop was a central culprit in sparking a prolonged brawl 12 minutes into the game. A fracas took place in the middle of the pitch even though play had moved on to the right touchline and Fitzpatrick was glad of his colleagues streaming back to help out after finding himself outnumbered by half a dozen angry Saracens. When order was restored, Dume dispatched both Fitzpatrick and Wallace for 10 minutes in the cooler, but his award of the resulting penalty to the home side was a clear indication of where he apportioned the main share of the blame.

Saracens looked increasingly threatening as the pace became more fast and furious and the scoreless stalemate was finally broken just after the half hour when centre Tom Shanklin was brought through the middle at pace to cross by the posts with McRae converting, but Saracens suffered the blow of seeing Wallace carried off injured before the game restarted, thus ending his crazy evening. A Humphreys penalty deep in first half stoppage time got Ulster on the board before the break and was due reward for some sustained pressure.

Saracens pushed Ulster back right at the start of the second period, but Johns was spectacularly upended at a lineout in his own 22, leading to a relieving penalty though no yellow card for the culprit. That incident not only allowed Ulster to clear their lines, but lit the fires of a home revival, led by Johns charging at his former clubmates like a man possessed. Ulster suffered a major blow however eight minutes into the half when Jonathan Bell had to come off injured, his loss being compounded by the absence from the bench of the injured Stewart, so McDowell moved to centre with Malone coming on at fullback. A limping Clarke gave way to Weir and Stephen Bell took over from a largely anonymous Free at the base of the scrum.

Humphreys reduced the arrears to a single point courtesy of a second penalty with half an hour remaining, but Saracens cranked it up again to produce the perfect riposte within three minutes, McRae slicing through a gap to wriggle over by the posts and convert. Blair replaced Longwell just before the hour mark and there was plenty of drama in the next 90 seconds as Humphreys missed with a dropgoal attempt when Ulster were reduced to 14 men by the sinbinning of Constable, also well fired up against his old team, either side of the advent of a streaker.

Conscious of their need to chase tries, Saracens ran two penalties deep in Ulster territory, but another bout of fisticuffs which this time resulted in a yellow card for Chesney brought a relieving penalty for the hosts. There was real needle in the contest now and McWhirter was warned and penalised for an incident involving him and Luger. The pressure finally told and Hill crashed over on 76 minutes, McRae's conversion widening the gap to 15 points at 6-21. Ulster finished with a flourish, going on the attack during another lengthy period of injury-time, but just when they seemed to have been denied one last score for Harry, his Captain Marvel came up trumps.

Saracens coach Pienaar, revealing afterwards that he had seen the Ulster players "coming out for the second half with tears in their eyes," reckoned the Williams factor had been instrumental in his side being denied a quarter-final place. For Paddy and the rest of the squad, the brave though ultimately futile Pool campaign had "allowed us to get our self-respect back, but the consistency was still not there. Throwing away the home game against Toulouse was fatal. I wasn't able to play that night and watching from the stands is always more frustrating for it's out of your hands. That's why coaching must be difficult."

Speaking of coaching, the appointment of South African Solomons as new Ulster supremo had been announced at the end of the first week of January, the 50-year old former Springboks assistant coach having been chosen ahead of several other candidates, notably Willie Anderson, Harry's assistant Mark McCall and Ballymena boss Andre Bester. At the time of his appointment, he was coach of South Africa's most successful Super 12 side, the Stormers, and had been Mallett's assistant during the Springboks' great unbeaten run. A qualified barrister on a career break, Solomons was chosen by a six man panel comprising IRFU Chief Executive Philip Browne and President Eddie Coleman, Ulster Branch Chief Executive Michael Reid, Branch President Neil Jackson (a man with a background in personnel), Senior Vice-President Joe Eagleson and Cecil Watson, Chairman of Ulster's Provincial Management Committee.

Solomons was given what was reported to be a lucrative three-year contract, with McCall and New Zealander Adrian Kennedy as his assistants, but Reid vehemently denied that the bank was being broken, the pay structure busted or a proverbial king's ransom paid to secure the services of what he described as "top drawer . . . one of the world's best coaches." He cited Solomons' application, interview and references as all having been excellent. Although some people criticised the appointment of an 'outsider', at least the South African was making it clear that he was selling up back home and going to live in Ulster full-time. So how did Paddy feel about the appointment?

"To be honest I didn't really know anything much about Alan Solomons prior to his appointment even though he had been Western Province coach and Springboks assistant when we played both those teams in 1998. Obviously he had an impressive track record of being involved with successful sides and at a high level of the game. The feedback from Mark McCall, who went over to South Africa to meet with him, and Dion O'Cuinneagain, who knew him very well, was extremely positive.

"We knew Willie (Anderson) was up for it and no-one was too sure who else was really in the running. I'd say in general terms the Dungannon guys would have been happy enough with Willie but one or two of the Ballymena boys might have been keener on Andre Bester. Mark McCall would have been seen as having a genuine chance and in fact might well have been the players' preferred option. He'd done well as Harry's assistant, relating well to the squad but also managing to achieve the necessary distance the role demands between himself as a member of the management team and guys he used to play with."

Like the other players, Johns viewed the appointment of a new coach in Solomons with an open mind. It isn't something which players have a say in, but obviously a change of coach brings all sorts of changes in the environment, so it does have an effect. In any case, however, it was by no means certain that Paddy would actually be around to be part of the new era under the South African.

"That Spring, I had actually agreed a contract with Perpignan" he reveals. "Along with Beziers and Narbonne, Perpignan was in the region of France where I would have been keenest to go, so geography was clearly an attraction. With French clubs, everything is done through their President. The Perpignan President phoned my agent and agreed terms. I must say that I was very, very close to taking the offer. But before any written contract came over, things seemed to be getting a bit doubtful. In the meantime, Alan Solomons had phoned me to talk about his plans for the season and that had influenced me to think very hard about the option of staying. This was before he came over for his brief visit in April. Things were still in the balance at that stage, but he was very persuasive in making up my mind to stay even before the Perpignan deal effectively fell through. When it did, I was happy to be re-signing for Ulster."

Solomons visited the province for two days in early April during a break in the Super 12. As well as meeting officials, he sat down with four senior players from the Ulster squad, Johns, Humphreys, Ward and Bell, to discuss plans for the season. At the press conference and in a whirlwind round of media interviews which followed, the new coach went out of his way to stress publicly, as he had been doing privately to Paddy, the importance he attached to having Johns as part of his squad for the coming season. "Ensuring Paddy was on board was a major priority and he will be a very valued part of my plans. It's great for me and Ulster that he will be playing for us next season. You need the resilience and know-how of guys like that when the going gets tough" said Solomons that day.

Because of the misguided rumours of possible retirement which had been doing the rounds about Paddy in the preceding months, many put two and two together and assumed that the only doubt there had been about his continuation in the squad was the option of hanging up his boots. That, however, had never been on the agenda and Paddy who "noted what Alan Solomons said those days in the media," assumed the comments had been a reflection of the coach's relief that Johns was not heading for France. Both Solomons and Reid, however, insist that they were not aware at the time of how live an option Perpignan was, though the Chief Executive admits that "contractually, we did try to accommodate Paddy."

The other interpretation placed by the media on Solomons' remarks and clear public admiration of Paddy was that he was considering making him his new captain in succession to European Cup winning skipper Humphreys, who had done the job for three years and seemed keen enough for a break. That too, according to the coach was wide of the mark. "My motivation for talking about Paddy that weekend was neither an attempt to persuade him to stay, for the contract had already been signed, or as a signal that he was going to be the captain. It was simply a reflection of how highly I regarded him and how much of an asset I felt he would be in the squad. Having been mad keen to keep him, I was just delighted that he had signed up again" explains Solomons.

Paddy admits that he had noticed the media speculation, "but was used to taking all speculation with a pinch of salt." When Ward's appointment was revealed in the News Letter at the end of July, it was assumed that Solomons had initially been planning on Johns, but then didn't want to tie his hands to a second row as skipper in light of Lions lock Jeremy Davidson's decision to move home and the consequent increased competition for places which there would be in that department of the team. Again not so, says Solomons.

"In terms of the captaincy, I was taking a longer-term view and looking for some stability over the three year period of my own contract. Paddy, while still a great force, was definitely getting on a bit in rugby terms and, realistically, unlikely to play for three more years. To my mind, Andy Ward was the other guy who had stood out on Ireland's tour of South Africa in 1998 and, although there are no guarantees in life, was more likely to be around for subsequent seasons. But I knew that Paddy would be a great group leader, a very supportive senior pro and so it proved," continues Solomons. So Paddy was to be at Ravenhill for one more term. It proved to be his last.

34. CALLING IT A DAY

Hanging up the boots. That dreaded day comes to all players but, as with so many things in life, timing is crucial. Knowing when is perhaps the hardest bit. Thankfully, the foolish imploration of his mini rugby coach way back in the 1970s had not been heeded and, in the intervening years, Paddy sometimes felt he would go on for ever but, steered by the wisdom of Solomons, he finally made the decision to quit in January 2002 and announced that he would be retiring from all rugby at the end of the season.

Ironically, having had a most frustrating season on the back of that draining experience of playing at Donnybrook in August when ill, Johns had enjoyed a real renaissance in Ulster's European Cup ties in January and Dungannon's big AIL derby win at Ballymena a week later. Coming as it did in the wake of that game, his decision to call it a day took many people by surprise. But by then Paddy was starting to look at the bigger picture. In rugby, old soldiers do themselves no favours by hanging around long enough to fade away.

This writer received a call from the PR Agency, who handle media relations for the Ulster Branch, on the Friday morning (January 25), informing me that there would be a press conference at Ravenhill at lunchtime at which, among other things, the retirement of Paddy Johns would be announced. I immediately put in a call to a source who has represented Johns and other Ulster players commercially. The agent said he knew nothing about either the announcement or the press conference, but offered to get in touch with Paddy and ring me straight back. He did so, reporting that the player had no plans to be at Ravenhill a few hours later.

At that stage, it seemed to me that Paddy must have been pushed, given a conversation which I had had with the same source the previous Sunday afternoon following Johns' excellent performance in the Ulster derby at Ballymena the day before. The Ulster Branch had been briefing heavily for some time that Paddy was intending to retire but, a week after the Euro campaign was over, sources close to the player were still insisting that he was ready and willing to take up a new contract if one was offered.

Having seen a rejuvenated Johns play well for both Ulster and Dungannon in the first few weeks of January, the writer was disappointed, even angry, that the curtain seemed to be coming down on his career without his full and free consent. So driving to Ravenhill that day, one had traces of bitterness amongst the nostalgia and sentiment. Paddy had been part of the rugby furniture for as long as those of our generation could remember. As much a fixture as Ravenhill itself. I decided that, at the very least, I would pitch for the privilege of putting his story into print.

But, in the event, this retirement chapter is not the tale of a resentful Johns baring his soul about being forced out of the game. That wasn't the way it actually was. While it hadn't originally been his intention to quit so soon, he did ultimately make the decision himself. He had moved a long way in a few days after doing an awful lot of thinking. The good performances in January were not allowed to become a distraction or diversion from making what he and Solomons both ultimately agreed was the right decision. By the same token, the two victories over Munster later in the year didnít unravel his belief in having made the right choice.

Paddy takes up the story. "Retirement, although it was something which Kirsty and I had talked about in vague, general terms as a change which would come in our lives one day, had not been in my thoughts. I'd had a frustrating pre-Christmas, stemming from that Donnybrook game, but was getting back into it and doing fairly well. I assumed that I might be offered a new contract by Ulster but wasn't worried either way. I knew I could always play in France. As well as the sense of 'wanting to go on for ever', I felt I was still well capable of doing a job in professional rugby and was still, on balance, enjoying it.

"But, following some fairly intense discussions with Solly and consulting one or two others, I began to see the merits of making a decision to retire at the end of the season even though I used to think someone would need to shoot me to stop me. Realistically, my prospects of playing for Ireland had gone, Ulster had a couple of promising second rows who it was now time to bring through and it would be better to bow out at the top than potentially start to decline. I had no desire to become a fringe player. It would be better to make a clean break now and return to dentistry, to enter a new phase of my life. I hadn't yet turned 34 but had been playing at the upper end of the game for a long time and my body had taken a lot of traffic.

"Kirsty, while very supportive, knew that this was a decision which I must make myself and wouldn't have tried to influence me. My best friends would also have known better than to get involved - they wouldn't have dared - so it was very much a personal decision, obviously in conjunction with Solomons."

Solomons says: "I thought about Paddy's situation very carefully and, although he'd been getting better and better again after recovering from the post-Donnybrook fatigue and had cemented his place, his body was stuck with sticky tape. He was bloody marvellous and his bravery was second to none, but it is better for a player to go too early than too late. It is difficult for all human beings to know that time, but the obvious thing was that, if he retired at the end of the 2001-02 season, he was going to eliminate the risk of going on too long and his powers diminishing. So the decision was made and, in the event, what a fine way to finish, with victory over Munster and then a second one for good measure."

Ulster assistant coach Mark McCall, whose acquaintance with Paddy goes back over two decades since they first crossed swords as schoolboys, says: "Solly was very good with Paddy. It was important for himself that he didn't play one season too many. There is a time. I'm honoured to have played with Paddy and, in these last couple of years, to have had a hand in coaching him. He's definitely the easiest person you'll ever coach, the most professional professional. Paddy is a shining example to any young player, not least in how he has managed his bodies down through a long career at the highest level."

Although Ross Collins of the PR Agency hadsaid the Johns aspect to encourage this writer to make the unscheduled 40-mile journey to Belfast at short notice, that Friday press conference was called ostensibly to unveil Ulster's contracted squad for the following season. But, in light of the former Ireland captain's announcement that he would be retiring from rugby at the end of the current season, coach Solomons chose to concentrate primarily on the "more significant" closing of a chapter and ending of an era. Before leading the warm tributes, Solomons revealed that Paddy had reached his decision following discussions with him that week and described his departure as "a sad day for Ulster.

"Paddy Johns has been a magnificent servant of the game in general and, in particular, of Ulster and Ireland" said Solomons that day. "He has made an enormous contribution and it is true to say that one only appreciates the real length of the tree when it is cut down. This man is an absolute professional right to his fingertips, someone who gives everything on the pitch and is a fine example to the younger players. When I came here a year ago, he was someone I desperately wanted in my squad and his input this season has been invaluable.

"Today is tinged with sadness, but it pleases me that Paddy is going out at the top. No-one would want to see such a great player continuing beyond their best and that is why, just like John Eales and Mourne du Plessis, it is right that he should go when he is still good enough to perform at the highest level. Although I have only been here for a season, it will be very strange even for me not to have Paddy around next season, but I know that he will only be a phonecall away and that he will continue to be totally supportive. His heart will always be in Ulster rugby.

"Paddy Johns is a thoroughly decent man who, to me, typifies the best of what Ulster offers. He is an exceptional bloke, respected by opponents the world over for his honesty and modesty. I was assistant coach with the Springboks when he captained Ireland on their tour to South Africa in 1998. Little did I know then that I would later have the privilege of working with him, but what impressed me was how incredibly competitive and combative his team was. Paddy is an extraordinarily honest and committed player. He played international rugby for over a decade which, in the modern era, is a remarkable feat given the toll which the game takes on players' bodies. As a player who really puts his body on the line every time he plays, the physical demands have been immense and he has taken a lot of traffic during his career. Paddy has given superb service to the game and everyone in rugby will wish him well with his future."

It was not only a supremely fitting, but deeply moving address by the little South African, an unscripted oration of palpable warmth which clearly came from the heart. Paddy himself looked a little embarrassed and emotional, while even among the hardened hacks there was hardly a dry eye in the house. "It was like attending your own rugby funeral to be honest," he says. "I suppose at the time my attitude would have been 'it's no big deal a guy giving up playing a sport, why are we having all this hullaboloo'. But there were a lot of nice things said that day and they did mean a lot to me. I suppose the press conference, the making public of the decision, really brought home to me that I was quitting, but by then I knew it was right."

One man who actually wasn't surprised at Paddy's decision was his long time mentor and Dungannon coach Willie Anderson, in spite of that excellent performance against Ballymena. "It reminded me of the end of my own career in that you eventually get to the point of frustration and be ready to move on even though at an earlier stage you could hardly imagine not playing. Paddy had been there, seen it, done it and got the T-shirt and there was nothing more to achieve. He'd put himself about, his body had more rugby miles on the clock than most and he, correctly in my view, decided to make a clean break.

"There is another factor to consider as well. Like Paddy, I was married at an early stage of my career. When you have children and are an international rugby player, it does have an effect on the kids. With the best will in the world, no matter how keen a father you are or how supportive your family is, you will lose out a little on their early years. Eventually it comes to a point where enough is enough."

Preparations for the Ulster 2001-02 season had begun with Solomons' advance visit to Belfast the previous April, when the new coach struck Paddy as being "very direct, very workmanlike, very precise. He brought a lot of ideas with him to the extent that he was able to say in many areas 'here's what's going to happen', but also adopted a consultative approach and stated his belief in good communication. He had his team leaders, with the squad split into four groups of eight to 10 players and there were player reps and other mechanisms. I suppose it would be possible to overdo the whole democracy and structures thing, and there's no perfect approach, but certainly it's good to have communication and I would have welcomed the opportunity to obtain as much support and feedback at earlier stages of my career.

"There were no real teething troubles with the new regime, though it quickly became apparent that we would be pushed hard, not least by the new fitness coach Phil Mack, who reminded me of his equivalent when I was at Saracens, Mike Yeates, father of the international 800m runner. The two men have different personalities, but both would know a slacker if they saw one! "Although I had, and will always have, the utmost respect for Harry Williams, a new coach and change of personnel does freshen things up and Harry himself did identify three years as being what he felt to be a maximum stint in a job like this. Pre-season was very tough, with some very, very tough drills. I remember going to Peebles near the end of it for our training camp and working very hard, but it did pay off and Ulster did finish strongly in many games that season on the strength of superior fitness. Several matches were won late on, notably against Stade Francais. From a personal point of view, I've always enjoyed training, going to the gym, pushing myself; pro rugby has never been a chore and I genuinely relished the regime under Solly and Phil Mack."

Davidson's return to Ravenhill from Castres, just before he departed on his second Lions tour, was something which Paddy "genuinely welcomed" even though it would mean more competition for second row places. Of the previous season's squad, Allen Clarke had been forced into retirement by injury, Stephen Bell moved to Bedford and Grant Henderson was released. Adam Larkin, an Irish-qualified Kiwi who had previously played for Bristol and Castres and come to the attention of the then Ireland coach Brian Ashton in his earlier days, and a young Aussie flanker, David Allen, were the other incomers, while the promising pair of Bryn Cunningham and Paddy Wallace were given their first full-time contracts.

As reported in the previous chapter, there was also a new captain, Humphreys having handed over the baton to Andy Ward. A cult hero in the eyes of the Ravenhill faithful, Ward was sure of his place in the side and a senior figure in the set-up who was well respected by colleagues and someone who would lead from the front and shoulder the honour proudly even though born in New Zealand.

"Andy is certainly an adopted son of Ulster, who has fitted in very, very well" says Paddy. "He plays for Ulster like he was born here and the crowd like him. He is quick and has a good hand-off and generates the sense of something happening or being about to happen. Crowds have always liked eye-catchers and, especially in these days of people coming out to rugby who maybe haven't followed the game before, they will respond to that type of player.

"Having had to be a ball-carrier for Ulster, which is not ideally a role you want your No 7 to have to perform, may have been detrimental to Andy's Irish prospects in more recent times as well as being seen as neither a specialist blindside or openside, though I think he's good enough for both. I think the Munster success has also been a factor in him being overlooked by Ireland and maybe his face doesn't really fit there, but he seems to enjoy captaining Ulster and the profile which goes with it, and has done well, especially considering he hadn't really captained teams before."

In August, Ulster launched the Solomons era by beating Coventry and Sale in pre-season friendlies before getting their inaugural Celtic League campaign off to a winning start against an admittedly understrength Swansea, missing Lions Scott Gibbs, Mark Taylor, Colin Charvis and Darren Morris, at Ravenhill. The new coach opted to play young Paddy Wallace out of position at fullback, omitted Ryan Constable in favour of Adam Larkin and chose Shields at hooker ahead of the contracted Weir on the strength of his storming display against Sale.

Davidson, who had made his Ravenhill return as a substitute for Gary Longwell with half an hour remaining of the Sale friendly, was again left on the bench but this time came on for Paddy in the second period. Ulster put the visitors away in convincing style in front of a large and appreciative crowd, winning 30-13 on a night when the only downside was the sight of Brink leaving the field clutching his shoulder. Sadly, although his retirement announcement didn't come until some 13 months later, the Springbok was never to start another match for Ulster. There was more bad news when it was revealed that the signing of Kiwi hooker Matt Sexton could not be completed in time for the European Cup as Canterbury would not release him before the end of their NPC campaign.

Both Davidson, at the expense of his old Dungannon mentor Johns, and fellow Lion Tyrone Howe were included in the starting line-up by Solomons for the following Friday night's trip to Glasgow, Paddy being left out of the match 22 altogether to give Mark Blair a turn on the bench. In the event, Ulster did well to snatch a draw from a game in which they played poorly and had trailed 22-6 with half an hour remaining. Late tries by sub Constable and by Wallace brought the visitors back from the dead and former skipper Humphreys snatched a 25-25 draw with a cool conversion.

From not being in the 22 at Hughenden, Paddy found himself skippering Ulster against Llanelli at Ravenhill four days later, with Ward ruled out by the sprained ankle he had sustained in Glasgow and Solomons opting for a forward to lead the side instead of vice-captain Humphreys. It was only the second time Johns had captained his province, the first also, ironically, having been against Llanelli, in the European Cup defeat at Stradey Park just before Christmas 1999. Sadly his first home game in charge was to end in defeat against the same opposition.

Johns was one of eight changes, another of which saw uncontracted 20-year old former BRA captain Neil McMillan given Ward's No 7 jersey in preference to full-timer Allen and Dungannon's pair of development-contracted flankers Michael Haslett and Andrew Hughes. It was to prove a foresighted selection for the future. Solomons' sweeping changes were as much a reflection of the punishing schedule Ulster were undertaking as on the poor showing in the opening hour in Glasgow, though several squad members were rewarded for making a good impression as subs in that game.

Constable returned to partner Bell at centre, with Blair also getting a chance in the second row as Davidson was benched again and Longwell left out of the 22. Nelson returned at No 8 after injury, allowing Solomons to have another look at McWhirter in the blindside berth. Kieran Campbell got a run at scrum half in place of Free, who like Longwell was left out of the match squad with Neil Doak brought onto the bench. Coulter got a go on the wing in place of Topping, while both Harlequins props, Best and Boyd, were included as Fitzpatrick took a turn on the bench.

Welsh outhalf Stephen Jones broke Johns' and Ulster hearts as his curling conversion of an injury-time try by Paddy's old acquaintance Wayne Proctor gave Llanelli a last gasp victory and cost him his dream of a home win as captain. Illness had forced Ulster into three changes in the hours before the match, however, with Longwell coming in for Blair and both centres also withdrawing. They were replaced by Shane Stewart and Bryn Cunningham, with young Wallace moving to midfield to accommodate the latter at fullback. But in spite of the disruption and the strength of a Llanelli side comprised almost entirely of internationals, even in the absence of Ireland's Easterby brothers and Lions Scott Quinnell and Robin McBryde, the hosts made an encouraging start.

A two-handed lineout catch from Johns in the opening minutes led to a 20-metre trundle by the home pack and a hungry Coulter had a few eager darts before Ulster went ahead on eight minutes courtesy of a Humphreys penalty. But the former captain threw a suicidal pass in his own 22 a minute later and that mistake was compounded by poor defence from the subsequent scrum which allowed hooker Marcus Thomas to canter in by the posts, Jones converting. The stand-offs exchanged a pair of penalties apiece before Ulster scored with the final play of the first half for the third successive home game to get in front by the break, Cunningham hacking on and getting the touchdown.

Humphreys extended the lead with a penalty early in the second half, but it was the chargedown of his attempted clearance which led to a Llanelli try two minutes later. Johns did well to track back, but Ulster went offside in midfield and the visitors quickly spread left from the penalty for winger Garan Evans to cross in the corner. Jones converted, but Ulster regained the advantage with two Humphreys penalties in the space of a minute and stretched the lead to six points with four minutes left. But there was still time for Welsh heroics and so Ulster went to Donnybrook three days later on the back of a defeat.

The circumstances surrounding that Leinster game and the effects of a bug on the Ulster squad in general and on Paddy in particular have been well documented in chapter 20. Doak was given his chance at the base of the scrum for a game which trebled as a Celtic League tie and an Irish interpro with European Cup qualification points at stake while, although Ward was passed fit, he made his return in the No 6 jersey with young McMillan retained at openside. Longwell was ruled out by injury, so Johns and Davidson were paired in the engineroom and Blair, now over his illness, was named on the bench. Bell and Larkin, preferred to a weakened Constable, were back in midfield, while Fitzpatrick and Topping returned for Boyd and Coulter respectively. Leinster's line-up, their strongest of the season, included 13 full internationals.

Leinster would have been formidable opposition for a fully fit and firing Ulster, but the effects of the bug, which forced Topping out before kick-off and left Johns drained, injuries on the night and the visitors' malfunctioning lineout compounded by Paddy Wallace gifting Malcolm O'Kelly a try with a suicidal quick throw in his own 22, meant this game was over as a contest well before the end. But Leinster rubbed salt in the wounds by crowning their 31-9 victory with a try four minutes into injury-time which clinched a crucial bonus point.

Paddy Johns, always eager to take on ball, gave it all he had got in spite of being "pretty ill" and indeed almost grabbed a try, but inevitably had to bow out in the second period. Ulster had been 16-9 down at the break and had been hit with another Leinster penalty and the loss to injury of midfield rock Bell when Paddy's replacement Blair was sinbinned for an indiscretion. Gordon D'Arcy soon scored his second try to put the hosts two scores clear and all four of Solomons' Ulster group leaders were off the pitch by the end, skipper Ward and his predecessor Humphreys having hobbled off to join Johns and Bell on the sidelines well before Hickie went over from the final move of the match.

Ulster recovered quickly, bouncing back to reach the Celtic League quarter-finals with a hat-trick of victories over Welsh opposition, but the damage to Paddy was much longer lasting for, as our earlier chapter records, he suffered the after-effects for months, initially in terms of his physical state and, later, the difficulty of regaining his place in a, by then, settled side. Humphreys and Bell were ruled out of the next match in Ebbw Vale and Ulster were 20-3 down at half-time, but a fine fightback at Eugene Park finally yielded a 29-27 victory.

Humphreys and Ward each bagged a brace of tries as Ulster started and finished brilliantly in a 46-14 Ravenhill rout of Bridgend the following Wednesday, the day after the terrorist atrocities in America. Solomons' side's destiny was now in their own hands and they duly clinched a place in the knockout stages by beating Pontypridd 29-20 at Sardis Road, subs Constable and Blair scoring tries. The win was actually enough to earn Ulster second place in their group and a home quarter-final, against Neath a few weeks before Christmas.

Paddy, given a complete break from those final three Celtic League group games in order to recuperate, would have had hoped to regain a place in at least the match 22 for Ulster's European Cup opener in Treviso at the end of September, but Davidson and Longwell were retained in the second row with Blair again on the bench. Solomons explained Johns' absence as being at least partly a symptom of consistency in selection.

The signing of Aussie hooker Mark Crick and Puma prop Leopoldo de Chazal meant Ritchie Weir and John Campbell missing out on the Euro squad of 30, while exciting prospects Scott Young and Matt McCullough were included in the registered panel at the expense of full-timers Niall Malone and Aiden Kearney. Jan Cunningham missed out for the second year running, axed to facilitate the inclusion of three scrumhalves, Doak and the full-timers, while long-term injury victim Brink was also omitted. That meant room for both McMillan, who was making a major impact, and the anonymous Allen. For the Euro opener, however, Solomons reshuffled his back row, bringing back the more experienced McWhirter, with Ward reverting to openside. Doak was named at the base of the scrum, with Stewart preferred to Constable as Bell's centre partner.

It was a successful Italian job in the end for Ulster, but only after 23 points from the boot of former Ravenhill favourite Simon Mason, now in Treviso after a season at Stade Francais, had threatened to spoil the script. When the hosts pulled back to only 28-30 down entering the final 10 minutes, the nightmare scenario of ace marksman Mason burying his old buddies with yet another nerveless kick loomed large. But Ulster held on and went into their second game, at home to Wasps the following Friday night, in good heart. Solomons named an unchanged 22 for that game, so Paddy was left out in the cold yet again while Longwell was winning his 100th Ulster cap. Even in the absence of Lawrence Dallaglio, the visitors were able to field a dozen internationals including All Blacks greats Ian Jones and Craig Dowd.

A buzzing Humphreys sensationally stung Wasps with a stunning 37-point contribution which took Ulster to a first ever European Cup victory over English opposition. In atrocious conditions, the magnificent home pack swarmed all over their illustrious Wasps counterparts, roared on by a capacity crowd, and the magnificent Humphreys turned every bit of pressure into points. He kicked half a dozen penalties and banged over a record four drop goals, adding an opportunist's try and conversion for good measure before long-serving lock Longwell fittingly sent Howe clear for the final touchdown in an unforgettable 42-19 triumph.

The European Cup then took a break to accommodate Ireland's carried over Six Nations matches and Longwell had a break of his own, fracturing a finger in training ahead of the Welsh game. When the competition resumed at the end of the month, the Ballymena player had only just recovered, while Davidson was ruled out by the knee injury he sustained against Wasps, so Blair and Johns were paired in the second row for the first match of a double-header against Stade Francais. Paddy had looked sharp in Ulster's behind-closed-doors friendly against Leinster on the eve of Ireland's Welsh match and Solomons enthused that "it's fantastic to have someone of his calibre to bring back in. I think the break has helped him".

Unfortunately, Humphreys didn't recover in time from the ankle injury which had forced him off during the previous weekend's win over England and pulled out of the team, meaning Paddy Wallace had to be thrown in at the deep end opposite Diego

Dominguez. After talking all week about the desire to test themselves against the best, Ulster came face to face with the sharp end of European Cup rugby as a slick, strong and star-studded Stade side steamrollered them with a power-packed Paris performance. Ulster stepped into the fast lane at Stade Jean Bouin and were hit by a juggernaut in the guise of the previous season's finalists, who justified their tag as one of the competition favourites with a forceful and at times explosive display which left Ulster bruised and battered as well as soundly beaten in the shadow of that old graveyard of Irish teams, Parc des Princes.

A McWhirter touchdown pulled Ulster back to only 6-5 down in the opening quarter, but they were hit with a Stade scoring spree which brought three tries in 10 minutes and ultimately trailed 27-11 at the break. Johns gave way to Longwell a quarter of an hour into the second half, in which the hosts added 11 more points without reply and Ulster lost Bell to injury along with centre colleague Stewart, whose knee collided with Paul Shields' head. The absence of Humphreys had been acutely felt, as much for his authority and presence as for the loss of his sublime mix of skills, though young Wallace had kept his head up in a way which augured well for the future.

And Ulster famously turned round the 29-point drubbing five days later, stunning Stade and clinching victory with a dramatic injury-time try at a delirious Ravenhill. There were fully 86 minutes on the clock when Lions winger Howe went over in the corner for the match-winning touchdown as the ghosts of their semi-final defeat in the same stadium came back to haunt the French in Halloween week. Humphreys, who had been passed fit, missed several penalties but landed two to more than cancel out an earlier effort by Dominguez. A try scored, ironically, by former University of Ulster student Mike James, the Canadian international lock, put the French ahead, but Humphreys completed his hat-trick of penalties to give the White Knights a one-point interval advantage, just as they had had in the 1999 semi-final.

Stade struck with a try on 62 minutes by fullback Sylvain Jonnet, who got a lucky bounce chasing a chip from Dominguez, who had kicked a penalty earlier in the half. Young Wallace, who had taken over the place-kicking duties from a limping Humphreys, was successful with his second penalty attempt on 70 minutes just after Solomons had sent on fresh legs in the form of Boyd, McMillan and Johns, who had lost his place in the starting line-up to a fully fit again Longwell. Wallace, who started at centre, was now at fullback, Bryn Cunningham having been stretchered off in the first half after having his thigh sliced open, almost to the bone, a gaping wound which raised question marks about the legality of the Stade studs.

Then the French crucially went a man down on 77 minutes, an episode in which, as related in an earlier chapter, Paddy had at least a small hand. "I tackled their scrumhalf, Galthie, and then punched him on the ground. I can't really remember why, if it was in response to provocation or if it was to provoke retaliation, but anyway Auradou retaliated by kicking me in the back and the ref said to him 'off you go'. It's frustrating being a sub and I've never really liked it or completely bought into the notion of it being a squad game of 22 rather than 15, but the subs certainly did change the course of that match I feel. When we came on, Ulster urgently needed an injection."

For long enough the French held out, but Ulster were finally, dramatically, gloriously to make that numerical advantage count. Deep in injury-time, Wallace was tackled by an offside defender and when the penalty was finally given, Longwell won the lineout. After being stopped in the corner, Ulster opened out, eventually earning another award at a ruck. Doak and Humphreys moved the ball left and Howe made it over by the corner flag to give Ulster victory and send the crowd wild, with Wallace firing over the touchline conversion for good measure. Another great Ravenhill night and the opposite of the Toulouse sickener a year earlier. This time Ulster's Euro dream would still be alive over Christmas.

Ulster lost 22-16 to Connacht in dreadful conditions in a friendly in Galway the weekend before their Celtic League quarter-final against Neath at Ravenhill, but put both that and the distraction of Warren Gatland's sacking as Ireland coach on the afternoon of the match out of their minds to record a 38-29 victory over the Welsh All Blacks. Frustratingly for Paddy, he was again left out of the match 22, to accommodate the return to the bench of a fit-again Davidson, with the Ballymena pairing of Blair and Longwell retained in the engineroom. Solomons' side had to come from behind several times to shake off the visitors in an enthralling affair which was a great advert for the inaugural competition. Humphreys contributed 28 points, including a penalty from eight metres inside his own half, and produced a perfectly weighted cross-field punt for his skipper Ward to claim superbly for a crucial try with 10 minutes left.

That set up a semi-final against old rivals Munster at Lansdowne Road the next Saturday and Davidson's withdrawal after experiencing further discomfort in his now suspect knee allowed Johns to return to the bench as back-up to Blair and Longwell. Although the Ballymena pair had remained ahead of Paddy in Solomons' pecking order since Johns' draining Donnybrook experience, many felt at the time that it would have made a lot more sense to play Paddy from the start in what was sure to be a tight contest up front and then utilize Blair, whose loser style made him more suited to the role of impact sub, in the final half hour. Ulster, who also left the classy Constable languishing on the bench, were also without Ward and Topping, while Munster were missing internationals John Hayes and David Wallace.

Munster's 15-9 victory was widely expected and their first half territorial dominance may have served to underline many people's pre-match expectations but, by the end of the game, Ulster could just have nicked it. If Howe, woefully short of confidence in his post-Lions season and utterly lacking in luck, had been able to make more of two late opportunities, the White Knights would have been on their way back to Lansdowne Road for another final though that would, admittedly, have been a real steal on the day. Johns certainly tightened things up when he came on for Blair, but Solomons seems to accept that hindsight confirmed it would have been better had the roles of the two Armagh men been reversed.

"It's always easy with hindsight" admits the Ulster coach. "Paddy had generously played at Donnybrook back in August when he shouldn't have played and spent the rest of the autumn slowly coming back. In the first half of that Celtic League semi, Munster bullied us up front and we thought 'bugger this, we'll get Paddy on'. So on he went for the start of the second period and I think the Munster players spent half of the rest of the game worrying where he was! There was going to be no more bullying, that's for sure!"

"As always, I was disappointed not to start even though strictly speaking I had only been brought into the match 22 because of Jeremy's injury" says Paddy. "I would probably have suited a tighter, more abrasive, physical game than Mark, a player who is very skilful, has good hands and is quick. Like Keith Wood, he has a high try-count for a front five forward, but in a strange sense that could actually almost be an indictment. Blairso loves to get the ball in his hands and you could say he forgets to hit rucks at times. The boys nicknamed him 'Pick and Go' last year because he used to time his arrival to coincide with the ball coming back, but in fairness he has tightened up this part of his game greatly this season and is putting in the hard yards."

The interpro which had been rescheduled for the festive Friday night between Christmas and New Year was downgraded to friendly status by the IRFU and Munster, who had lost the Celtic League final 24-20 to a Leinster team which triumphed in spite of having Eric Miller sent off for kicking Anthony Foley, only brought a second string side to Belfast, but Ulster at least treated a superb crowd of some 7,000 to six tries and a total of 51 points on a freezing night. Constable, making a rare start, bagged a brace, while Paddy played the entire match in tandem with Davidson.

Unlike with the previous year, Ulster were still in contention for a quarter-final place when the European Cup resumed in January and also, thanks to the Celtic League knockout stages and that Munster friendly, were less rusty this time around. The only change from the CL semi was the inclusion of Paddy in the second row in place of Blair, who had broken a wrist in training and was to be sidelined for the rest of the season. Davidson was on the bench, as was Constable. Less than 48 hours before the Loftus Road game, a depleted Dungannon beat Ballynahinch 32-3 in the Senior Cup final at Ravenhill.

A glorious comeback, which yielded 20 points in a five minute purple patch, brought Ulster to the brink of a first ever Euro win on English soil, but they ultimately fell just short of a famous victory and thus lost control of their own destiny in the Pool on an afternoon when the White Knights gifted their opponents two tries and missed five kicks at goal, yet still only lost 36-32. Sadly their rousing rally was not quite enough to deliver a sensational sting in the tale as Wasps just about held on in a thrilling finale to this superb tie.

Ulster could though take great credit for the resilience shown in getting as near as they did, with skipper Ward leading by magnificent example, after losing key man Humphreys to injury in the first half and then falling 33-12 behind. With Wasps' interest in the competition already ended and their line-up understrength, the hope was that greater hunger would give Ulster the edge. Ward's warriors did get off to the perfect start, with a Humphreys penalty in the opening couple of minutes and, although Alex King replied immediately for the hosts, the Irish flyhalf nudged his team back in front with his second success from three attempts.

Wasps captain Mark Denney danced over for a try to give his side the lead, King converting, and Ulster were hit by an even bigger blow when ace card Humphreys hurt his ankle in a heavy collision with stocky Samoan hooker Trevor Leota. He soldiered on until nearly the break, but relinquished the place-kicking duties to young Wallace who was successful with the second of two penalty attempts in the space of two minutes. But King restored Wasps' four point advantage and then extended it with two more strikes either side of a shocking miss by Wallace. Worse was to follow for Solomons' side when they spilled the ball on the home 22 and saw their hosts break away to score through Roiser.

Another King penalty put Ulster 26-9 down as Humphreys hobbled off and, although Wallace pulled back three points with the last kick of the half, the young gun had an awful start to the second period, seeing his pass which was intended for Bell running wide picked off by Fraser Waters for an intercept try which King converted either side of two more penalty misses from the stand-in visiting kicker.

He did make it 33-15 following sub Constable's first delightful dart of the afternoon and Ward himself then launched the fightback in earnest at the end of the third quarter, touching down in the left corner after a couple of wonderfully weighted hacks ahead which even Humphreys would have been proud of, followed by a deft pick-up.

As well as Constable for Larkin and the enforced change of Bryn Cunningham for Humphreys, Davidson was already on for Longwell and Solomons introduced more fresh legs up front on the hour, with both McMillan and Crick joining the action as Ulster continued to take the game to their hosts. A couple of chances were squandered, but then the visitors struck, Bell doing the initial damage and Ward exhibiting great hands to put the speedy Constable away for a stunning try which Wallace converted. Now only four points behind, the force was with Ulster and that sense was accentuated by the sinbinning of All Black great Jones and a drop goal from Wallace.

King missed with a penalty but then landed another after an unfortunate passage of play where Wasps got fingertips to Wallace's attempted touch-finder from a scrum and then Coulter seemed to be obstructed as he tried to follow up a kick. Wasps ran it back and, although Doak made a great tackle, the hosts got the crucial penalty which left Ulster needing a try for victory. They got agonizingly close in injury-time, but were finally penalised on the home tryline and King booted the ball into the stand to prompt the final whistle. Heartbreak for gallant Ulster, so near but yet so far.

Constable, predictably, was recalled as the only change to the side as Ulster chased tries the following Friday night against Treviso at Ravenhill. He had produced another classy cameo at Wasps as the White Knights mounted that sensational comeback, but his return here was more a horses-for-courses selection than reward for red-hot form. Solomons noted that Davidson had "done particularly well at Wasps but was still in a rehab situation and we don't want to push him too hard at this stage."

With Ulster looking to run up a cricket score, the coach used a cricketing analogy by pointing out that, if you build a proper platform in a limited overs match, there is "no limit to the number of runs you can score at the end". So the plan was to really get on top of Treviso, who were incidentally fielding 14 internationals including the Dallans, Mauro Bergamasco, Moscardi and Checchinato, and the tries should come. In the end, Humphreys was passed fit, though Wasps coach Nigel Melville had, interestingly, suggested that Ulster were more fluid and dangerous with young Wallace at flyhalf.

The game marked the return to Ravenhill of former favourite Simon Mason, who received the warmest of ovations from the crowd as he stepped up to kick Treviso's only points of the night, which actually gave them the lead, but was to turn villain before the end of the first half when sinbinned by the Welsh referee. "Simon was a very popular man with the fans and got a great reception that night from the Ravenhill crowd. As a fullback, he was safe under the high ball and cleared his lines well. It was felt that lacked a yard of pace and was not really a threat in attack, but he never seemed to miss a kick at goal. It is a tribute to him that Ulster virtually based their game plan around him the season of the European Cup win and the following season, even though second time round, as I've said earlier, it may have been a counter-productive tactic. Ulster would kick for position, apply the pressure, force the penalty and Mason would do the rest."

Ulster ran in a total of eight tries, half a dozen of them in a 20-minute purple patch either side of the interval, but the hosts frustratingly couldn't cross the Italians' line again until deep into injury-time and were left fretting overnight that, in spite of a record 59-3 victory, they mightn't have done enough. In the end though it didn't matter for, although Northampton did them a favour by beating Cardiff, Ulster were undone by Leicester's surprise loss at Llanelli. It didn't make pleasant Saturday afternoon television viewing for the players ahead of that evening's dinner to mark Gary Longwell's 100 provincial caps.

To continue the cricketing analogy, in the opening quarter Ulster too often resembled the team who had sent in a pinch-hitter in an attempt to get off to a flier but fallen between two stools. It took a second Humphreys penalty midway through the first half to finally get their noses in front, leaving Solomons' side an hour to do some serious damage. After another penalty, Ulster did cash in on Mason's binning with tries from Longwell and Doak to lead 21-3 at the interval and then touched down three times in the first 10 minutes of the second period, Howe bagging a brace either side of the scrumhalf's second score. During that period, Paddy left the European Cup stage for what was to prove the last time, replaced by Davidson. Larkin got Ulster's seventh on the hour, but that was that until Constable crossed from the last move of the game.

Llanelli's victory left Ulster with no regrets about not scoring enough against Treviso, though the near miss at Wasps had proved costly, while the progression of Llanelli on the basis of the stack of tries they ran in against Italian whipping boys, the wonderfully named Fly Flot Amatori and Calvisano, rankled considerably.

"It's fine to encourage the lesser nations, but if you're going to have very weak teams in, there would need to be one in each group or else, with this 'best runners-up' format, it isn't a level playing field" argues Paddy. "The alternative would be four groups of six, though that would mean fitting in extra fixtures. We felt we had a good chance last season, that we could win in Treviso and all of our home games, which we did. That wasn't quite enough as it proved, but we came very close to winning at Wasps. Although we lost, that game showed that Ulster can be competitive on English soil.

"In the last match against Treviso, our aim was to keep a pattern and get to a magic figure of 15 points ahead before really trying to cut loose. Even though we didn't ultimately make the quarter finals and I didn't know at the time it would be my last match in the competition, being part of a big win at a packed Ravenhill was a nice way to bow out in the European Cup."

The following Saturday, back in harness with Davidson in the Dungannon engineroom for the first time in nearly six years, Paddy starred as the Tyrone team came from behind to register an excellent away victory in what was to prove his last Ulster derby. He got through a mountain of work in a vintage display reminiscent of his halcyon days as Ireland captain, proving to himself and the watching Ulster management that there was life in the old dog yet, that he would be good for another season as a professional if he wanted it. Within the week though, he was to announce that he didn't.

35. WALKING THE WALK

At the grand old age of 30, Paddy sat down to take stock of his life. In doing so, he made a list of all the places in the world he would like to visit. Amongst these was the Great Wall of China. Last Spring, opportunity came knocking, or rather calling across the airwaves.

"Dungannon were to play Belfast Harlequins in the AIL and I was travelling home from training one evening that week. I donít usually listen to the radio, but for some reason that night I did. A lady from Mencap came onto Cool FM and talked about the Great Wall project and my ears pricked up. I had done some charity work before and some PR stuff for learning disabilities, but always planned to do more. Obviously the location of the walk meant I could kill two birds with one stone. The project was a sponsored 60km walk along the Great Wall over five days and sounded fantastic. As soon as I got home, I told Kirsty all about it. She was very enthusiastic and thought it sounded like a great opportunity, but was a bit downcast as she thought, with four young children, she'd have to stay behind. I didn't want her to miss out and assured her that we'd overcome the obstacles."

In the end, grandparents undertook babysitting duties, and Paddy was given the all clear by Mike Reid of the Ulster Branch as he also "thought it was a great idea. I was so excited by it all that I contacted Mencap that evening. We filled in all the forms they sent us and then set about raising the £2,500 required, plus £300 for airfares". "We did everything," says Kirsty. "Quiz sheets, a quiz night at Dungannon, a bucket collection, an auctions, a calendar sponsored by companies, and my Mum ran a 'guess the name of the doll' competition." "People really rallied round us," recalls Paddy. "The workers at the club, Harold, Betty and Suzanne Walker, did breakfasts before the Lions games to raise money, and other friends helped no end."

In other circumstances, Paddy might, like Peter Clohessy, have been making his farewell appearance for Ireland against Italy at Lansdowne Road the third Saturday in March 2002 and bowing out as his country's most capped player. Instead, typically without any fuss, he and Kirsty were taking off for China in the early hours of the morning, having worked tirelessly in raising over £6,000, since swelled to around £10,000. They were helped in no small measure by the big man's former team-mates and opponents being prepared to donate items of memorabilia for auction. That is a legacy of the respect in which Johns is held throughout the rugby world and, although never one to trade on his name for personal gain, Paddy is pleased that his personal profile has helped his efforts on behalf of Mencap, a charity close to his heart.

"I treated special needs patients as a dentist in the community service before turning professional," explained Paddy before setting out. "There were patients who were autistic and others with Down's Syndrome. Before then I would have been a bit uncomfortable around kids with these problems because of not really knowing how to react, so it was good experience and I'm just pleased if, by doing this walk, I can be of help to those in that situation. The money raised will be spent on good causes, including helping out the Gateway clubs, which are effectively day centres where people with learning difficulties can go to socialise and engage in leisure pursuits, and sending young people on trips to the seaside, things like that. Mencap represents those with learning disabilities, giving them a voice as well as supporting them and their families."

Paddy and Kirsty spectacularly surpassed the sponsorship threshold of £2,500 in spite of finding that fundraising for worthy causes is "very competitive indeed. Businesses get maybe four or five letters per week asking for donations, so they have to be selective. But I had great support from a number of local companies, which was much appreciated and I'll definitely always make a point of going to them in future when I want to purchase certain goods or services. What goes around comes around" Michael Reid had given him clearance to get involved and also four Ulster jerseys, a couple of which he used to swap to get other items for an auction which raised over £2,000. Philippe Sella, David Humphreys and Jeremy Davidson were among those to donate items.

For some of the 70 people doing the walk, the physical demands were set to prove daunting, but Paddy was sure to take it in his stride. As a professional sportsman, he would find the actual walking bit easier than most, but no-one had worked harder on the fundraising front. He and Kirsty, although full of good intentions, never quite managed to get round to any of the specific training they'd planned. They also consciously decided not to research the places they were going to visit. "I didn't really want to know anything," explains Kirsty. "I just wanted to take it as I found it and let the whole experience educate me. I think I had enough preconceptions from television."

"My thoughts of China were mainly of good food!" laughs Paddy. "Seriously though, I expected a lot of poverty to be evident. My first impressions were that it was very mountainous and very, very barren. We went in the dry season and the whole landscape was very desolate and arid. Our group had quite a lot of contact with the people, as we stopped at several villages. The locals were always courteous and pleasant. They were very poor and survived on very little. They were very honourable people and, even though they didn't have much, they seemed to be very happy and were always very friendly towards us."

The tour party consisted of 71 people. Initially the group was 72 strong, but unfortunate Keith Elliott only made it as far as Heathrow. As the others embarked upon the 14 hour flight via Istanbul, Mr. Elliott was left on terra ferma when he realised that the back injury he had sustained only the previous day meant his trip was stopped before it could even get started. Most participants were in the 20-40 year age range, but including a 65 and 69-year old couple.

"It wasn't a race. We just took our time. Physically, Kirsty and I coped, no problem, but we weren't blasting it at all. Actually, I'd brought ibuprofen with me, as I was convinced that I'd need it for my knee, but it was fine and as it turns out, Kirsty twisted her knee on the first day, so she was the one on medication! We had natives who were caterers for us. The food was unbelievable. We had cooked breakfasts and dinners with a packed lunch. They even brought a bar, which suited our lot very well! The craic was fantastic and there was a really good mix of people from all walks of life. Getting onto the wall had some dodgy patches which required a lot of teamwork, and everyone was up to it.

"A lot of where we walked was not usually open to Westerners, so we had to get special permits. It made us all feel quite privileged. There was one point when we had to come off because we were entering a military zone – so there were some similarities with home! The land was fairly up and down with the highest tower 4,200m above sea level. It took us two hours to climb up there and was a very humbling experience. I can't put it into words really . . ."

"It really is the most amazing spectacle to be looking down on mountains, as opposed to up at them," adds Kirsty. "Though one thing the trip taught me was that I had a previously undiscovered fear of heights! I had absolutely no idea and had laughed at my dad over the years for being scared of heights. I got really angry with myself and there were lots of tears. I was basically petrified a lot of the time. At the highest tower, we had a two hour lunch break on a three foot platform with a sheer drop to one side and a severe drop with a few trees to break your fall to the other side – not fun. Otherwise, I found it all very manageable. Although there were moments like a stair-climber from hell!"

"On the last day, we all sat in a valley and had five minutes to reflect on what we had done, why we'd done it, and I guess what we'd got out of it all," recalls Paddy. "It was so peaceful and tranquil surrounded by mountains and terrace farms. I just thought about what's important and how lucky we are, and how thankful we should be for basics like health and running water." "It was a bit different for me," says Kirsty. "I didn't think so much about how lucky we are, but how greedy we are. You realise that you don't actually need all the things you couldn't possibly do without at home."

Time and space for Paddy to reflect on his lot in life and count his blessings. Both inside and outside rugby, he had worked hard to achieve what he had and get to where he was, but also felt grateful for God-given ability and the opportunities which had come his way. Just like the Great Wall walk had been fascinating and exhilarating, his rugby journey had been a rich and enhancing experience of peaks and troughs where he had put in a lot and got a lot back, tackling each new stretch with relish. Metaphorically, he had travelled a long rugby road and both this China trip and an earlier one to Canada following his retirement announcement had afforded time to reflect.

Of course there had been some disappointments; anything which means enough to you will cause you hurt at some stage and his relationship with the game had been a passionate one, but overall he had few rugby regrets. Any frustrations he felt have been dealt with elsewhere in the book, but overall he could reflect on a good innings in the game and how he had been able to leave it with his head held high, and at a time of his choosing, unlike those whose careers end suddenly and prematurely due to injury. Rugby had brought him a lot of places, made him a lot of very good friends and taught him a lot about himself and about life.

In Canada in February, partly on the advice of his brother Johnny, Paddy had begun to jot down some things by way of memoirs. It was part of the closure process and ultimately fed into this book which, incidentally, could never have been an autobiography, for Paddy would have downplayed himself too much. In fact, he often struggled to come to terms with just how good he was or the reality that people did look up to him as a sporting hero, icon or role model. Modest to a fault. "Maybe at times it has taken others to point out to me what I have been fortunate enough to have achieved in rugby in order for it to sink in properly. I've learnt that there are more important things in life than rugby, but the thing which I'm proudest of is that I've made the most of my God-given abilities by being honest and working hard."

Paddy's friend and former Dungannon team-mate Keith McGarry says: "I've followed Paddy's career closely and desperately hoped he'd get the record, so he might start to realise just how significant a figure he is in Irish rugby history."

It sounds like a ridiculous statement of the obvious to say that, no matter how well you play, you can only win one cap for any international appearance, but the point is that, while someone could earn rave reviews for performances over a 12-month purple patch but then disappear from the picture altogether, accumulating 59 caps requires additional qualities of resilience and the ability to maintain that necessary hunger year after year. To win 59 caps, you have to be fit enough and playing well enough to convince the selectors that you are the best option in the country for your position on 59 individual occasions. So what was the secret of Paddy's longevity?

"I looked after myself physically and always had a burning desire to pull on that green jersey but, being an Irish rugby player, it's also important that you learn how to deal with setbacks and the ups and downs which inevitably come your way. That means not letting yourself be destroyed by being dropped or taking a bit of flak. I just saw both criticism and selection as someone's opinion and knew that, if I proved them wrong, I would have the final say. You have to be stubborn and single-minded.

"The other big thing was that I never lost my hunger, was never content with a particular number of caps. Whether I'd won one or 10 or 30 or 50 or 59, I always wanted the next one. Equally, I never saw my 43rd cap, say, as a logical consequence of my 42nd. You take nothing for granted, just keep going, trying to be the best you can be. I was delighted and very proud to win 50 caps but, until Keith McGarry pointed it out then, had not really been conscious of the marks beyond that, or of Willie John McBride's record of 63 so reaching or passing that had never been a target in itself. I felt that I could have won some more caps in the last couple of years of my career, but to finish up with 59 and fourth on the all-time list is very satisfying indeed."

In getting to 59, Johns passed every Irishman of his own generation and, from any era, all but Ulster midfield man Mike Gibson (69), his hero and second row predecessor Willie John McBride (63) and Fergus Slattery (61). So he bettered the likes of Phil Orr (58), his contemporaries Brendan Mullin (55) and Peter Clohessy (54), Tom Kiernan (also 54), his first Irish captain Donal Lenihan (52), another of his early second row heroes Moss Keane (51) and long-time Irish colleague Nick Popplewell (48). For a modest man like Paddy, reeling off his name in such a distinguished hall of fame is a humbling experience.

"Modern players have the advantage of there being more internationals these days, so you have the chance of winning more caps in a given period, though against that it could be argued that careers are probably shorter now for a variety of reasons. The other thing which will distort cap tallies from now on is substitutions. In the old days when players could only be replaced if injured, there were many Test matches from which only the 15 guys who started won caps. Now you could have up to 22, especially with the 'bench clearance' tendency which has come in for some criticism lately.

"Take my position of second row, for example. In the old days two second rows were capped in any given Test, but these days the lock on the bench has a very good chance of getting on as a sub, so that's nearly a 50 percent increase in caps being won in that position. When you consider Ireland have something like 14 internationals this season, there are a lot of opportunities to win caps in the modern game. It must be hard for the older guys who maybe had to play for 10 years to get 40 caps to see the tallies mounting up so quickly for the modern players but that's life.

"I only won two of my 59 caps from the bench, but some players would have a very low percentage of starts in their cap tally. Their number of caps might be similar to those of their predecessors, but if you did a comparison of international match minutes, there would be quite a disparity" said Paddy. Perhaps, with modern players set to increasingly dominate the leading cap-winners' charts, there is merit in finding a new index to measure the magnitude of international careers.

One of those closing in on Paddy's caps tally, helped by substitute appearances, is flyhalf David Humphreys, who recently drew level with the great Dr Jack Kyle as Ireland's most capped player in the position. But, even though a considerable number of Humph's appearances have been from the bench in recent times, Johns will not begrudge his fellow Ulsterman if he passes him, not least because he believes that he should be starting for his country on a regular basis ahead of Ronan O'Gara anyway.

"I first encountered David at university level when he was playing for Queen's against Trinity and we've also been on opposite sides in the past for Dungannon and Ballymena and Saracens and London Irish. For the last number of years, I've played with him for Ireland, Ulster and Dungannon and there is no doubt that he has matured like a good wine. His confidence has improved, his defence has improved, his tactical awareness is excellent and his place-kicking as good as you'll get these days."

In the early days there may have been a tendency for Humphreys' head to go down when he missed a kick or two, but Paddy never recalls being concerned about any fragility on the part of the gifted flyhalf. "David's kicking has matured, just like his all round game. He has alternated with O'Gara in the Irish team for the past couple of years, often having to play second fiddle, though I can't see why myself. I know who I'd pick. Humph is mentally tough, is consistent and has a very good attitude, the sort of guy I'd always want in my team."

Each man has found the other supportive when captaining a team, Johns being Humphreys' skipper with Ireland for a year and then playing under him for Ulster for a couple of seasons. The role reversal never caused a problem and the pair, while quite different, are reasonably close and have certain things in common. "We're both married and settled, we've both enjoyed Sevens and both have thinning hair," says Paddy. "He's a better golfer though! David is very set in his ways; once he makes his mind up on something, that's it, but he is a man of his word and someone I respect."

As a very close personal friend of Paddy's, Humphreys' predecessor as Dungannon No 10, Keith McGarry, has a better insight than most into the drive and determination which helped Johns keep adding inexorably to his tally of Irish caps. "When he was left off the Ireland team around 1996 or 1997 having already won a stack of caps, I was sort of advising him to not get toosaid about it, but he was adamant that he was going to get his place back . . . and of course he did. I remember him getting on as a sub in one international and being like a bear with a sore head, a man possessed."

During Paddy's career, other players have burst onto the scene and disappeared again while he remained there or thereabouts for a decade and a half. "Players come and go, or have peaks and troughs for all sorts of reasons I guess" says Johns. "Personal circumstances can change, as players get married and have kids and so forth. In the old days, the demands of a player's day job came into that and some like Rob Saunders gave up rugby early to concentrate on their other career. A player's desire or motivation level can change and sometimes that is relative to the quality of rivals you're up against for a place. Maybe, for example, someone like Brian O'Driscoll comes along in your particular position!"

Whatever the contemporary threats or challenges, Paddy always kept plugging away but, by the end, the dice was loaded against him and, no matter how hungry he still was, the Irish management had decided to move on. To compound matters, he felt frozen out of the A set-up on the grounds of age and the Irish selection situation may even have had a knock-on effect in Ulster with Gary Longwell perhaps getting preferential treatment on the basis of his contemporary Ireland status. While he didn't play that fateful night against Argentina, Paddy became a major casualty of the early exit from the 1999 World Cup. For most of his last two years, he was confined to the international wilderness.

So, while Clohessy was having his curtain call at Lansdowne Road, Paddy was doing his bit for charity in China. The expedition raised around £500,000 for Mencap, including over £1,000 from a whip-around for a school the walkers stayed in one night. "The kids were absolutely delighted and raised a flag for us," Paddy remembers. "A thousand pounds isn't a lot for a school at home, but there it would go a long way."

After all the hard work, the trekkers became tourists for a day's sightseeing in Beijing. This included trips to the Forbidden City, Summer Palace, silk markets and Tiananmen Square, which was of particular interest to Kirsty. "My uncle was a correspondent for a Canadian broadcasting company and actually witnessed the massacre in 1989. It was quite surreal to be there and think of what had gone on when now it's such a big tourist trap." The overall experience must have been a good one, as the Johns couple are planning to do something similar trekking through rainforests in Brazil next March, also for Mencap.

Although this trip was unrelated to rugby, Paddy's pastime and then profession has taken him right around the globe. "Rugby has taken me to a lot of different countries. Unfortunately, when you're on a rugby tour, you don't get much of a chance to look around and everything gets kind of glazed over. Without rugby though, I wouldn't have travelled so much so quickly. I've definitely got the travel bug. There's a lot to see in the world and beach holidays don't appeal to me." His mum adds: "I've always encouraged the children to travel. Apart from Canada, Paddy and John Gamble went to Norway one year with the Peace People and had a good summer there."

"Also, coming from Northern Ireland, when you get away, you get a chance to look in and realise just how insignificant, on a global scale, much of it is" says Paddy. "There are quite a few places I'd like to go back to. I thought Sun City was amazing and I've got Kirsty on a promise to take her there. I'd also like to go back to Kruger National Park. I really loved that and I'd love to go on another safari. Our next family holiday's going to be to Egypt, and hopefully we're going to Canada soon and travelling down to Florida. Right now though, I'm looking forward to the Bermuda Classics in November."

It's a long way from Stevenson Park to the Caribbean and a quarter of a century has elapsed since Paddy's mini-rugby days at the former. Little did those who shared that small stage with him, the likes of Terry Sweeney, John Wright, David and Gerald Heffron, Pip McCord, Niall Campbell, the Shields twins, Scooby Shields, Chris Falloon, John McFaul, Barry and Robin Adair, Irwin McFarland, Conor Drayne and Ewing Morrow, realize that, in their midst, there was a legend in the making. The club which set him on his way has been richly repaid for the early encouragement he received from the likes of Willie John McKenzie and the Honorary Life Membership bestowed upon Johns last year was a well-deserved accolade.

It is no coincidence surely that Paddy's coming to prominence coincided with Dungannon's emergence as a major force under Anderson in the 1990s and the club dominated the Ulster Senior Cup in the middle years of last decade. Paddy and others are proud of the fact that, in spite of its rural location, the club has been able to recruit and retain quality players during the past decade, starting with the likes of McGarry (ex-Methodist College), Davy Millar (Belfast Royal Academy) and Gary Leslie (Belfast High School) in the early days followed by such as David Humphreys, Ryan Constable and Justin Fitzpatrick in recent years.

"Rather than drift complacently like some of the big Belfast clubs may have done, we always kept a step ahead in recruitment and the great thing is that 99 percent of the boys who came down never seemed to leave. People like Keith have stuck around to play down the club, while Fitzy and Ryan are now blue and white through and through though they weren't even born in Ulster. Players coming in have found the club very warm and hospitable and they've responded in kind. It really is a great place for club spirit."

Paddy himself has played his part in fostering that sense of oneness and belonging. In an article in the club programme for last season, following the AIL win, he writes. "Everyone will have their own memories of the club's first AIL championship, but I feel the most important thing about last season is that every team in the club took a step forward and Dungannon Rugby Football Club grew stronger together" and McGarry reveals how Johns paid more than lip-service to that desirable state of affairs.

"When he was captain, Paddy always wanted the club to train together so that the likes of Justin and Ryan would get to know players from the other teams and that it would inspire those players to improve. I also remember him coming down to help coach the Fourths and Fifths even though he had all his own commitments. It wasn't beneath him to do it and we ended up having an excellent season."

McGarry's team, containing many of the men who had played for the Firsts in the Senior Cup wins of the previous decade, remarkably won all 25 of their games that season, scoring 980 points in the process. Old familiar names included Paul Archer, Ronnie Carey, David Lewis, Alan Burns, Brian Smith, McGarry himself and his brother Neil, Richie Weir, Stanley Turkington, Johnny Boyd, Michael Beggs, Wilfie Nelson and Kenny Wright.

Among other to contribute to the great Cup run were Stan McDowell, Tyrone Howe, Ashley Blair, Millar, McCaughey, Leslie (who made a staggering 121 consecutive AIL appearances in a 10-year period), a young Jeremy Davidson, the Hastings brothers, John Gamble, Willie Dunne and Johnny Patterson. Dunne, a vet from Kildare who worked in Newry at the same time as Paddy, remains a close friend. The side played in a different style to the AIL winning team of 2001 and, indeed were sarcastically slated in the Belfast Telegraph for a limited and boring style of play after winning the Cup for the fourth year running, but those were special triumphs for the club at the time and laid the base for future success.

"Paddy was a big Dungannon man even when he was at Trinity" recalls McGarry. "The first time I met him was back in our Irish Universities days when he was known as Pat the Baker. We were at Queen's in those days, but came down to Dungannon and his enthusiasm about the club would certainly have been an influence in that migration. That was when Dungannon was really taking off as a force. Willie Anderson had brought in the Hastings brothers and then a few more of us arrived in 1991. I'll never forget my first ever training session at the club, with Stanley Turkington and Willie Milligan knocking bells out of everyone! One great thing about Dungannon is that there has never been any superstardom and Paddy sets a great example in that regard with his humility. Take this book even. He was kind of embarrassed the night he told me it was happening."

Before going to China, Johns had signed off from Dungannon with a couple of victories which guaranteed the AIL champions their place in the top flight for the following season. They beat Galwegians 32-12 in his last game at Stevenson Park and, although the mud and sleet represented very different conditions to those pertaining for the previous May's semi-final, it was an important result for the club. It was sad to see big Paddy trooping off the pitch he had graced with such distinction after allowing himself the indulgence of a few hugs with his teammates but, as was to be the case with Ulster at Ravenhill, at least he went out with a win.

Victory at Lansdowne Road, scene of some of his greatest rugby triumphs, a fortnight later provided a fitting finale to his long and distinguished Dungannon career. The Tyrone team were in front throughout against a Lansdowne side coached by former Ulster supremo Harry Williams, thanks in no small measure to the place-kicking of little flyhalf Mark Bradley. Big Paddy proved that he was bowing out at the top with a commanding personal performance, including making the first try for Seamus Mallon and admitted afterwards that it was a good way to go. "A lot of things were pleasing, including making my last appearance for Dungannon on the main pitch at Lansdowne Road where I'd played many internationals and where we won the AIL final. The Lansdowne game will be another special memory of it."

It really was the end of an era for Dungannon, with Anderson also leaving during the summer to take up his new post as full-time assistant coach to Leinster. The task of renewal has been entrusted to another man who should have a feel for rural rugby, former All Black Andy Earl, and Paddy is confident that there are some good youngsters coming through to maintain the club tradition. His own club career had been Dun and dusted, so to speak, before he went to China, but there were still a couple of big Ulster games to look forward to on his return.

36. PADDY'S NIGHT

As an understated way of bowing out, it would have been ssooooo Paddy Johns. Trotting off early in the second half as Ulster put Treviso to the sword in their final European Cup group game at Ravenhill on a chilly January night. Coming as it did before the retirement announcement, no-one knew at the time that it would be his last curtain call in the competition and, had that indeed been his Ulster swansong, the lack of fuss would have been typical of the man who was leaving the stage.

Yet it would have been totally inappropriate for such a giant of the game to leave unacknowledged. That's why, apart from the fact that he would still be available for the outstanding interpros later in the season, the Ulster Branch had the idea of staging a game to celebrate Paddy's outstanding career. Call it a benefit match, a testimonial or whatever you like. Branch Chief Executive Mike Reid and Ulster coach Alan Solomons rightly felt it was a gesture and recognition that Paddy richly deserved. Surely no-one could have any objections. Well, yes, actually. The IRFU.

Shame on the bitter old buffers in blazers who did their best to scupper the Ulster Branch's wish to hold a match in honour of the great Paddy Johns. It would have surprised and outraged many to learn in this writer's News Letter column the morning after the game that the IRFU opposed, tooth and nail at every turn, the concept of a game to celebrate one of the most distinguished careers in Irish rugby and mark the player's retirement.

Modest, honourable and self-effacing as ever, big Paddy retained his dignity by making no public comment on the slight at the time, but the Union's begrudging and mean-spirited treatment of him was nothing short of a disgrace. Totally exonerated from the criticism were the Ulster Branch, Reid and Solomons, the men who conceived the game and did their best to ensure it could take place.

Sadly the same wasn't true in Dublin where some of the great and the good apparently took the view that holding such a game would set a dangerous precedent and open the floodgates for similar exercises in the future. If there was a match for Johns, would something have to be done for Galwey and Clohessy? Where would it end? What a nuisance for the Union. How awful that a long-serving player might make a few quid. Furthermore, they would doubtless have said, it never happened in 'their day'. Obviously not, given that rugby back then was an amateur game. But jealously gets you nowhere and it is telling that some of England's World Cup winning soccer stars of 1966 have publicly come out and said they aren't bothered by the astronomical earnings of today's footballers.

Paddy Johns didn't bring in professionalism. He, along with contemporaries like Galwey, started out in the amateur game and had to juggle representing their country with other careers just as their predecessors did. He also didn't ask for a benefit game. It was the concept of the Ulster Branch and the idea even initially embarrassed him. He'd have happily gone without fuss and was never eager for the public to put their hands in their pockets to line his.

Initially, his inclination was only to agree to it if part of the proceeds could go to charity. If the Branch wanted to put on a sort of fond farewell for him, fine, but let others benefit. This from a man who the previous month had walked the Great Wall of China and raised more than £6,000 (with a further £6,000 subsequently) for Mencap. If there was going to be a game, he stipulated that half must go to charity and his half would be put into a trust fund to support his four children if and when any or all of them chose to attend university. But, Paddy being Paddy, he still wanted no fuss and didn't go public to promote his own generosity or highlight the fact that charities would benefit from his testimonial, unlike Republic of Ireland soccer stars Niall Quinn and Gary Kelly, who earned plaudits for similar gestures.

An irresponsible article in a Belfast evening newspaper which apparently claimed that Paddy stood to pocket £30,000 from a benefit match is alleged to have fuelled the fires of resentment in some quarters within the IRFU. For a while, in spite of the strongest possible representations in favour by Mike Reid, the match was more off than on and, eventually, only got the green light if several conditions were met. Apart from the granting of Ravenhill as a venue and the turning out of an Ulster Select XV, the Branch had to completely distance itself from the venture, leaving Johns' club Dungannon to front it.

It was a game he never sought and money he never craved, but that doesn't excuse the attitude and behaviour of the IRFU. They don't seem to have grasped that it is the norm these days for long-serving professional sportsmen to have benefit games, from relative journeymen county cricketers of much less distinction than Johns to famous footballers who are filthy rich already. Whether a player is granted one should be up to his professional club, in this case Ulster, and thereafter market forces, in the form of the public voting with their feet, will decide how much or how little money is made.

Both the dinner back in January to commemorate Gary Longwell reaching 100 Ulster caps and the proposed Johns benefit match embarrassed the other provinces who had done little to mark the achievements of their stalwarts, so the IRFU stepped in in heavy-handed fashion. So all credit to those at Ravenhill who were keen to do the decent thing for a decent man and shame on those who sought to scupper it. Paddy, for his part, stood above it all like the gentleman and giant of the game that he has been. Publicly, at the time, he kept his own counsel, but privately he was pretty hurt. It wasn't about money, but about respect. Disappointment that these powerful people could be so petty and small-minded.

"The game wasn't my idea, but the idea of Alan Solomons and Mike Reid and I'd still like someone from the IRFU, Philip Browne or whoever, to explain to me why it was such a problem, or else to admit they got it wrong and apologise. I reckon I'd wait a long time though. I've never bothered too much with the committee men, but I know Philip a bit and he had always been decent to me. At the end of the day though, I hold no grudges. People can make their own minds up and the IRFU can answer for their own consciences as to whether they feel they acted in a mean-spirited manner. I never had any direct contact with them about the match.

"While I hadn't sought a match or dwelt on the possibility of financial gain, the petty and begrudging attitude of the Union was disappointing and the uncertainty round whether the game would go ahead was frustrating in that my brother Marcus, sister Vanessa and many friends, including Nigel Wray, had booked flights home from Britain to be there and, in the week before the match, the whole thing was very much in the balance, on one day and off the next. In the end, I just thought 'if it's meant to go ahead, it will go ahead'."

The Ulster Branch were not allowed to be seen to be organising the game, so Dungannon stepped in to front the venture, though Ravenhill was available and Solomons, glad of the match practice anyway before the interpro against Munster, put out his strongest side available in the guise of an Ulster XV wearing plain white jerseys with a red hand and navy shorts. Paddy's injured colleague Jonny Bell enthusiastically took on the task of putting together a Celtic Warriors XV comprising of people who meant something to Johns and who would be able to at least give the Ulster side a good game.

"There was some suggestion of us playing an actual team, be it an English Premiership club or a southern hemisphere provincial side, but to be honest I preferred a match where those involved had some link or connection with me, a meeting up again of old friends for a good hard game and then a bit of craic with people who I knew well and whose company I enjoy. There are plenty of big name professional sides who come to Ravenhill these days in the European Cup, so this would be something different. Jonny put in a mountain of effort did a great job to get the calibre of side he did considering how hard it is to get guys released in the professional era and given that the competitive season was still ongoing across the water.

"Of the squad Jonny got together, there were only a couple who I didn't know, so it was great to be playing against guys who meant something to me. While they got well looked after, none of those boys got paid for turning out so it was a generous gesture on the part of everyone. Brian Robinson took a big chance in playing even though his career had been ended by injury and his knee ligaments are completely shot. It was good to see the likes of Alan Tait and Derek Stark coming over from Scotland. I knew Starky well and he and Denis McBride were good mates from the days when Ulster used to play the Scottish Saltires. I got to know him in Hong Kong, where he was actually playing for an English President's team and we had this chant 'there's only one English Starky'. He took a lot of stick."

With Tait and Maurice Field paired together, the Celtic Warriors were sure to be competitive in the centre, with Paddy's old Saracens and Ireland team-mate Richie Wallace and Northampton's Harvey Thorneycroft proven finishers out wide. "I'd have known Harvey from the Sevens circuit and found him a very friendly guy. He and Tim Rodber were good friends and those would have been two of the Northampton and England boys I'd have talked to." Ulster European Cup winner Stan McDowell was at fullback with Ballynahinch's Darryl Callaghan and James Grindle of Leicester at halfback.

Dungannon's former Ulster props Richard Mackey and Gary Leslie started either side of ex-Scotland hooker Jim Hay in the front row, with Welshman Tony Copsey and Keith Walker, former engineroom colleagues of Paddy's at Saracens and Dungannon respectively, paired in the second. Skipper Denis McBride was joined in the loose forward trio by Ben Wheeler, son of former England hooker Peter, and Scotland's Stuart Reid. The bench included more old Ulster favourites in Colin Wilkinson, Davy Tweed, Stephen McKinty, Robinson, Stuart Duncan, Derick Topping and Riaz Fradericks plus Stark, Dungannon front row stalwarts Davy Millar and Hugh McCaughey, and Malone player-coach Jacques Benade, who had played against Paddy on Ireland's tour of South Africa in 1998. Allen Clarke "found it very hard not being able to play" because of the injury which enforced his premature retirement and "even thought about reffing part of it, but decided that would be diluting the credibility of it too much".

McBride pledged that his assorted All Stars would do their best to ensure a memorable match in honour of Paddy and promised his side would enter into the spirit of the occasion as fully as possible. "We're obviously only coming together as a scratch side so, considering we're up against a professional outfit, will need to raise our game, especially as some of us haven't been playing on a regular basis." Denis admitted the night before. "But there's a lot of experience in the ranks and most of the guys are in pretty good shape and the sort of competitors who'll certainly not want to make a fool of themselves.

"Most importantly of all, it's a big night for Paddy and we're there because we want to mark his retirement and give him the send-off he deserves. That means doing our best to try and make a game of it and give people a bit of a spectacle. I'm sure Ulster will enter into the spirit of things as well, so that everyone on and off the pitch will enjoy their evening" said McBride, who paid tribute to the "application and attitude, determination and dedication" which had sustained Johns at the top of the game for so long.

The IRFU may be seen as a pretty powerful body and, on the day itself, a conspiracy theorist could have been forgiven for thinking that the powers-that-be in Lansdowne Road had even hijacked control of the weather, so great was their desire to piss on Paddy's parade. "There was wind, rain and hailstones that evening and a bomb-scare in the afternoon which gridlocked the Belfast traffic," recalls Johns. "I remember thinking to myself, fair play to anyone who would make the effort to get to Ravenhill in the circumstances. We ended up getting at least a couple of thousand people there, more than the old interpro days when I started off, even though the outcome of the match wasn't going to mean anything. Obviously a lot more came for the real thing against Munster in May, when it was great to bow out with a win in front of a full house."

Those who did brave the wind and rain to pay tribute to the retiring great were treated to 13 tries, 10 of them from Ulster in an entertaining charity match played in bitterly cold conditions. There were no shortage of household names in the invitation team line-up but it looked like these Celtic Warriors' best battles were behind them as Ulster literally sped into a commanding early lead. Wingers Jan Cunningham and Tyrone Howe raced clear for a long-range try apiece in the opening 11 minutes, though the real red faces for the All Stars came in between, when Ireland A prop Simon Best was allowed to waltz over by the posts. But Celtic captain McBride had vowed that his team were determined not to be made fools of and the skipper led a spirited riposte which brought tries before the end of the first quarter for himself and McDowell.

Ulster lost flanker Tony McWhirter with a shoulder injury midway through the half, but extended their lead soon afterwards when a long pass from Neil Doak put Wallaby Ryan Constable over in the corner. The game was inevitably disrupted by rolling substitutions akin to ice hockey as Anderson rotated his cast of thousands to give the lungs and limbs of his more venerable squad members a rest. As well as the blasts from the past such as McBride, Field, Tweed, Richie Wallace, Halpin, Tait and Copsey, the crowd were treated to a lively appearance from Fradericks, who showed he still had the flair if no longer the dreadlocks.

New Ulster hooker Matt Sexton was severely lectured by Rolland for an altercation with opposite number Hay on his first appearance at Ravenhill just before a Bryn Cunningham try converted by Paddy Wallace stretched the interval lead to 31-10. Substitute scrumhalf Kieran Campbell nipped over for an Ulster try within two minutes of the resumption, though McDowell quickly responded with his second of the night, Ballynahinch outhalf Darryl Callaghan completing a hat-trick of conversion misses.

The most popular try of the evening came on 52 minutes when Johns broke free and wrestled his way over, but kicking a first conversion of his long and distinguished career proved well beyond him, though he does claim there were mitigating circumstances in the form of distractions and even interference with the placed ball. "I knew my old mate Tony Copsey would move the ball, which he was holding to stop it blowing over in the gusting wind, and I'm sure that made all the difference," he smiles. "I'll have you know that I actually won the Irish team's drop-goal competition at the qualifying tournament in Portugal for the 1997 Sevens World Cup. We had to take pots at the posts from the 22 and when you missed you were out. In the end, it came down to a shootout between myself and Eric Elwood, and I fluked it!!!"

The Celtic Warriors had a very good period in the middle of the second half but finally dropped the ball on the Ulster 22 and Constable scooped it up to run the length of the pitch for his second touchdown, Wallace's conversion taking the score to 50. Campbell joined Constable and McDowell in the two-try club, but not before Paddy's younger brother Johnny had joined him in the second row, a poignant moment, marking his arrival on the field with a spectacular forward roll.

Anderson briefly threw on his entire squad, so it was 28 against 15 for a couple of minutes, but when normal service was resumed, Howe scorched away to score from the final move of the match, converting himself. It finished 64-15. The match was a warm-up for the mammoth autograph session which followed.

"Afterwards, there was food in the Ulster Branch, then a bus pulled up and took us to The Fly, a popular nightspot with the team. The top floor had been reserved for us and we had a massive party up there. I had friends who had come from Dublin and Donegal; there were about 30 of them staying at La Mon House Hotel and the bus came back at around 1am to take us there. We'd a good old singsong on the bus and, when we arrived at the hotel, Charlie had the residents' bar open and sandwiches laid on. It was a long night in there and two of my mates from Carndonagh, Papa and Curly, never made it to bed at all. When it got to 6.30 they decided breakfast was the best bet! The whole occasion was very enjoyable and I'm grateful to everyone involved in organising or supporting it."

In sharp contrast to the IRFU's attitude, Paddy's former employer at Saracens, Nigel Wray, had taken the time and trouble to be in Belfast for the game even though the club had a vital Premiership match that weekend. Paddy deeply appreciated his gesture, while Mrs Johns Senior recounts a funny episode which resulted on Wray's previous visit for the Ulster versus Saracens European Cup tie in January 2001. "After the match, Nigel couldn't be found" she reveals. "He was in one of the corporate tents but, by the time that was discovered, Paddy had left. It ended up that Ronnie Flanagan (the then Chief Constable of the Royal Ulster Constabulary and a big rugby man) got Nigel left back to Paddy's house in his official car!"

Paddy had been playing with and against his mates in front of a lot of people who knew him personally, with his two eldest children, Christopher and Emily, acting as mascots and the game being refereed by Alain Rolland who, by remarkable coincidence, won his first Ireland cap the same day as Johns, against Argentina in 1990. True to the way in which he had played throughout his career, the match had a very competitive edge, but essentially it was an emotional, enjoyable and entertaining evening and, in spite of all the advance wranglings and controversy, Paddy has no regrets that he didn't instead go for a corporate dinner and the chance to make a very substantial amount of money.

"I could have gone for a corporate dinner and made plenty of money out of charging an arm and a leg for a ticket or a table, but I preferred a game where people who actually knew me could come along if they wished, pay a few quid (it was £5 for adults, £3 for children) and see a game of rugby. You don't actually know most of the people at these dinners and many of them barely know who you are either for they've maybe just been brought along by a client. They come up and want to shake your hand and feel self-important or swarm you after they've had too much to drink. It isn't my scene.

"I'd also have been embarrassed to be lining my pockets in that way. I remember at a recent corporate dinner one of the boys saying to me 'When your time comes around Paddy, go for it', but I said 'no, I wouldn't feel comfortable' and 'how many people do you even know here'. I was happy with the evening which I had, even though the proceeds were a relatively modest £4,400 and I wasn't pocketing all of it. I'd rather have that than make maybe £20k by putting the arm into people who are either showing off or who feel obliged to be there and contribute. You can't buy memories."

While skirting round direct criticism of other testimonial occasions, Paddy has harsh words for the journalist who wrote the article about how much he supposedly stood to gain from the proposed testimonial. "I don't know how he got his figures and if he'd talked to any of us, we could have put him in the picture, but he seemed to write what he wanted to write. It was a bit annoying and I did ask him about the article, telling him he'd upset a lot of people and that the game might not go ahead as a result. When I came home from England, I quickly learnt from other players that we could talk to you and trust you, as with the guys I knew from before going away, Jim Stokes and

Michael McGeary. But the feedback on this fella, who I've only met a few times, is that he seems to be nice enough but needs to realise that you can't sh*t in your own nest or you won't last long."

Paddy's retirement game was typical of his career in that he more often sought to use his rugby status to benefit good causes than exploit it for financial gain. "I was never that big into speaking or personal appearances, so didn't proactively pursue commercial opportunities of that nature. I would have done quite a few things for people essentially as favours and might have got something to denote their appreciation in return, but didn't have a brass-necked, hard-nosed agent selling my services. I'm not sure that, even as Ireland captain, I would have been in huge demand anyway! "One of my personal appearances, for example, was for our next door neighbour in Enfield, Francois from Mauritius. He and his brother ran a computer business from home and, when they decided to open a shop in Enfield, he asked me to cut the tape for it. I think we'd have got our computer serviced free as a thank-you, but that was about it!" laughs Paddy, who cringes at the adverts which proclaim people can these days have lunch with his old Munster adversary Galwey for between 50 and 100 Euro. "I couldn't imagine having the face to do something like that, but I suppose everyone's different and if he finds there is a demand for it, that's fine. It's his choice."

Commercial considerations would certainly never have been allowed to get in the way of Paddy's actual rugby, so what was his attitude when, in the autumn of 1998, Keith Wood initially refused to sign a new contract with the IRFU because of a row essentially relating to intellectual property and image rights? The contract had already been signed by Johns, who had been captain on that summer's South African tour and was at Saracens in those days, nine fellow English-based players and Jeremy Davidson, who was with French club, Castres. Paddy was asked at the time whether any other player had considered taking the Wood line?

"The best answer I can give you," he had said, "is that we have signed, Keith hasn't. I just feel sorry for Keith and his family, because they're under a lot of strain. Keith came out to tour South Africa in the summer with his body in bits. He came because he was asked to and the amount of support he gave me as captain, I couldn't thank him enough for. It's important he sorts this out as quickly as possible, the team needs him." Wood's wrangle was resolved fairly speedily, though only after he had missed the World Cup qualifier against Georgia and Paddy, who had initially only expected to be stand-in skipper for the summer, was retained as captain throughout the season. What is his view of that episode now?

"I wouldn't have wanted to miss a Test match over not signing a contract, but everyone has different priorities and, anyway, you've got to take into account the fact that the stakes were a lot higher for Keith than most other people involved in that his commercial value was a lot higher and the opportunities open to him a lot greater and more lucrative than for the average Irish player. To most of the squad, signing the contract or not wasn't going to make much difference, but to him it was a huge factor." Why is Wood such big box office then, is it because he is a great player, because of the manner in which he plays or because he pushes himself forward?

"No matter who you are, if you're not a good player and don't make an impression, people won't want to know. Keith has skill, speed and ability. He does everything at 100 miles an hour and makes a real impact, really catches the eye. The media pick people out and Keith is an obvious choice, given that he is also very extrovert and recognisable. He didn't set out to invent himself as a marketable entity but has recognised the potential in his public appeal and made the most of his opportunities. Good luck to him.

"Making extra money out of the game has never been a major focus for me, so I was never jealous of Woody or sought to follow his example. I was more camera-shy and not proactive in that area, so you could maybe say that he was both more marketable and better marketed. But there was no resentment and, while I wouldn't have been prepared to miss an international on a point of principle through haggling over a contract, I didn't think any the less of him for it. He had a very strong view at the time and it was his choice. I had no problem with him returning to the side when the matter was resolved."

There appears to be a dramatic sliding scale of commercial value when it comes to the demand for Irish rugby players. Wood reputedly can earn up to £10,000 for a personal appearance, with Brian O'Driscoll rumoured to pocket a neat £1,000 for a ghosted column. Yet another notable player, who has over 30 Irish caps to his name, has informed this writer that he has barely been asked to open an envelope and hardly made sixpence out of rugby over and above his professional-player salary. A dramatic tail-off. Paddy's stock was enhanced by being Irish captain and, on the back of that, he was signed up by the clothing company, Rockport, "giving me my easiest wardrobe ever".

"They were trying to do something around the 1999 World Cup and got a player from each country to take part in a few adverts. I had got the contract in the Spring through Peter Deakin at Saracens when I was in England and was Irish captain, but had moved back to Ulster by the time the ads were shot. I remember flying across to London one morning, being picked up in a VIP limo and taken to Saracens where we had to run up and down the pitch and get a few photos taken. I remember seeing an advert with Tim Rodber and carrying a Rockport shoe. I also got a headguard and shoulder pads deal with Kooga."

Before the Wood stand-off, there had been one previous occasion on which professional player power had been exercised in the Irish game, as Edmund van Esbeck's book records. Agents had apparently travelled to an Irish training weekend in Kildare in August 1997 and, with the agreement of the Irish management, met with the players on Saturday night. The following morning the management were informed by the agents that the players would not train on Sunday as they were unhappy with the insurance element of their contracts. The players did not train and went home, though the issue was subsequently resolved and van Esbeck describes it as "a very poor demonstration of player power and agent power which backfired, but was indicative of the climate that now obtained in the game. An apology from the players for their precipitous and ill-advised action was later made to the IRFU."

A number of players have benefited financially from writing, or being interviewed for ghost-written, newspaper columns, an issue which came into sharp focus during last year's Lions tour, given the controversial offerings of Matt Dawson and Austin Healey.

Paddy's views on the matter are fairly clear. "If there's a demand for it, fine, but players must realise they will reap what they sow, particularly if they are being paid large amounts to be controversial. It is very dangerous to talk about others when you're a current player and I would certainly not have done a book like this one during my career. The only thing I really did of that nature in my playing days was a weekly column for a local paper, the Portadown Times, during the 1995 World Cup, but it was all very bland, innocent, weekly newspaper stuff about the whole experience."

It would be hard to imagine the loyal and cautious Johns generating the sort of column controversy which surrounded Dawson and Healey but, given Mark McCall's revelations about just how despondent Paddy had become on Ireland's 1992 tour of New Zealand, what are the chances he would have lashed out had such an outlet been available to him on that trip, especially if egged on by an enthusiastic ghost-writer who had no concern about him burning his bridges? "Very high I would say" he admits. "I was tired and emotional, naive and a long way from home, so I probably would have had a real go. That's why columns can be dangerous." Luckily Paddy didn't have the opportunity, for an outburst on that tour could conceivably have left him with 58 less caps than he ultimately won. A great career could have ended almost before it began.

37. WAY TO GO PUSDEY!

Paddy couldn't have chosen a better way to go. Down through his career, he could never imagine himself quitting, but time waits for no man and he'd come to share Alan Solomons' view that it is best to bow out at the top. Well, he did. And how.

From the decision to retire had been made public back in January, he had begun the long farewell, the relentless countdown to hanging up his boots. For his many fans, there was a series of priceless chances to watch the passing of this unobtrusive institution of the game. Although Paddy was at ease with himself and his decision, it was an emotional and nostalgic Spring as the 'games to go' tally became less and less and as he went through particular routines for the last time. Ever.

There was the final appearance at his spiritual home of Stevenson Park followed by his last ever game for his beloved Dungannon, which also happened to be an adieu to Lansdowne Road. There was his last trip with Ulster, to Galway, and a final away match for the province, against Connacht at the Sportsground. Like his Dungannon denouement, Paddy played well and finished on the winning side.

Now there was one to go. Just one more match. One last 80 minutes of honest toil at the coalface for this good and faithful servant. It would be in the famous white jersey with the red hand, and against familiar foes. A fitting finale. Ulster against Munster at Ravenhill. In recent years, Gaillimh's gang had held the whip hand and Paddy had paid a higher price than most. Munster's ascendancy over Ulster had cost him caps by elevating the Shannon stalwart to reign in his place. Johns hadn't been around the Irish team much for the past few seasons and, on his fleeting visits, hadn't found it much fun. The Munster mafia had taken over it seemed. And now they were coming to Ravenhill en route to another Heineken Cup final. The red army were on the march.

This concluding interpro may have been merely Munster's dress rehearsal for taking on Leicester at the Millennium Stadium but it was Ulster's own cup final. Some of Alan Solomons' new signings had already arrived, so it was a chance to begin building for the following season. Paddy of course wouldn't be around by then, but that made his motivation even greater. For him this really was the last chance to settle old scores and the team were fired up to send him off in style with victory over the old enemy. He'd always treated the next game as the most important and now, well, there weren't going to be any more, so this was it. The match meant everything to him. He'd remember this result for a long time. There'd be no chance the following week to get a defeat out of the system.

Leinster had clinched the interpro title by picking up a bonus point in beating Connacht in Galway earlier in the week, so there would be little resting on the result in tangible terms but there's no such thing as a meaningless match between Ulster and Munster.

Ravenhill's last big night of the season was an important stepping stone as Solomons looked ahead to his second term in charge and the anticipated bumper crowd would be hoping for signs that their team would be a force in the autumn. In that respect, it would be fascinating to see how the new southern hemisphere forward recruits, abrasive Kiwi hooker Matt Sexton and Springbok Warren Brosnihan, fared in the middle of the front and back rows respectively on their first big test in the white jersey.

Ulster were determined to give Paddy a winning send-off, while there was also incentive aplenty both for those included in Ireland training squad for the following week and for those omitted from the get-together in Limerick. The latter category included White Knights skipper Andy Ward and prop Justin Fitzpatrick, both of whom were sure to be well fired up to show what they had to offer as they sought a return from the international wilderness.

Munster, while hoping not to pick up any serious injuries, fielded their strongest possible line-up in a desire to get a rigorous workout before Cardiff, but Ulster were severely depleted by injury and unavailability. They would inevitably start as clear underdogs in the absence of Kempson, Boyd, Shields, Blair, Davidson, McCullough, Brink, Nelson, McMillan, Humphreys, Bell, Larkin, Stewart, Young and even Belfast Harlequins' South African Rhys Botha, who Solomons tried to call up in response to his centre crisis.

The coach had consequently turned to European Cup winner Stanley McDowell, by now a BBC pundit and dual status player with CIYMS and Ballymena, to partner Wallaby wizard Ryan Constable in midfield, whereas Munster could leave full international centre Mike Mullins on the bench. It was an incredibly long list of Ulster absentees, whereas Munster were missing only injured international back row men, Wallaby Jim Williams and Shannon No 8 Anthony Foley. Ronan O'Gara had recovered sufficiently from the nasty knee wound he sustained against Castres to be named at outhalf, where he would be directly opposite potential future Ireland rival Paddy Wallace, who was hoping to end a very promising first professional season on a high.

For the record, the teams were:

ULSTER: B Cunningham; S Coulter, R Constable, S McDowell, T Howe; P Wallace, N Doak; J Fitzpatrick, M Sexton, S Best, P Johns, G Longwell, T McWhirter, W Brosnihan, A Ward. Replacements: J Cunningham, J Topping, K Campbell; B Young, N Brady, A Kearney, A Hughes.

MUNSTER: D Crotty; J Kelly, R Henderson, J Holland, A Horgan; R O'Gara, P Stringer; P Clohessy, F Sheahan, J Hayes, M Galwey, P O'Connell, D O'Callaghan, D Wallace, A Quinlan. Replacements: M Mullins, J Staunton, M Prendergast; M Horan, J Fogarty, M O'Driscoll, C McMahon.

While Ulster were without key men like David Humphreys, Jonathan Bell, Robbie Brink, Jeremy Davidson, the still-to-arrive Robbie Kempson and other regulars in Paul Shields, Russell Nelson and Adam Larkin, Munster were fielding a dozen internationals and would start as clear favourites. But Ulster, who until the previous season had been defending a very long winning record against Munster at Ravenhill were determined to strike a blow against the suggestion that they were now condemned to being the 'third province' ad infinitum, lagging well behind both this lot and Leinster. Ever since losing the Celtic League semi-final to Munster back in December, Ulster had been hankering for some Ravenhill revenge and, although they had beaten Kidney's second string in a festive period friendly, it was victory here which would really count.

Johns relished the prospect of finishing with an uncompromising battle with old rivals Munster. Ever since he had decided to retire, he had had his sights set on this game. He knew very clearly just how he wanted to finish. It had always been the clearly-stated intention of Solomons and of Johns himself that he would play in these two interpros against Connacht and Munster, making the media's mistake of suggesting that he was coming out of retirement to do so rather bewildering. "I think Alan's idea was that I would start both matches, one with Jeremy and one with Gary, providing both were fit, but of course neither of them made the Galway game and Jeremy was still sidelined when the Munster match came around. I've no idea where so many journalists got the notion that I'd already finished."

So first up was a clash with Connacht at the Sportsground. Young Dungannon hooker Nigel Brady was handed an Ulster debut in the absence of Sexton, who had flown home to New Zealand following the death of his mother, and the injured Paul Shields, who was sidelined with torn ankle ligaments. Another young player from the Stevenson Park stable, Aiden Kearney, was in the second row with Paddy due to the injury-enforced absence of Davidson, Longwell and Blair, while Ireland Under 21 captain Matt McCullough was unavailable due to the imminent World Championships.

Johns was one of the few Ulster players to distinguish himself on a miserable evening when it took a Wallace penalty five minutes from the end to spare Ulster from an embarrassing defeat on a wet and windy night in front of only a few hundred spectators. Solomons' side had a fairly good first half but turned round only three points up and, by the coach's admission, "played so badly in the second period we could easily have lost. The venue and the elements were massive equalising factors as was the long break since our last game."

Connacht were without their lynchpin Eric Elwood, but still struck the first blow on a grim, grey Galway evening with a long range Mark McHugh penalty. It had, apart from two typically uncompromising hits by Paddy, been an undistinguished opening couple of minutes for the visitors on their first outing together in three months, starting with a messy kick-off reception. But waltzing Wallaby Constable blew away the cobwebs by dancing delightfully through the defence for a superb try to put Ulster in front 60 seconds after the McHugh strike.

Bryn Cunningham also scored a try, converted by Wallace, but the young flyhalf star was having a very mixed match and, thanks to the boot of McHugh, Connacht were in a position to take the lead three minutes into the second period courtesy of a try from Marnus Uijs. Wallace put Ulster back in front by landing the middle of three more penalty attempts, but when McHugh nosed the hosts ahead again 13 minutes from time a shock was on the cards. But the younger of the two Paddies finally got his radar working as the clock ticked down and even the sinbinning of Justin Fitzpatrick couldn't deny Johns a win on his last Ulster trip.

At the aftermatch meal in Galwegians, Ulster skipper Ward made his famous faux pas in thanking 'Galway' rather than Connacht for a tough match, home captain Dan McFarland cleverly replying in kind by congratulating 'Belfast' on their victory. Later the team went round to Elwood's pub, The Goal Post. "He's got a picture up on the wall of our 1993 win over England" says Paddy. "I'd a massive amount of hair then and the young Ulster guys were also teasing me that I must have played in the days of black and white film! It certainly looked like a long time ago. No wonder I was retiring!"

The order of the two interpros was perfect. Going out with a grudge game against the old enemy in front of a big crowd at his beloved Ravenhill was inestimably better than bowing out with a scrappy win over Connacht on a grey Galway evening with next to no-one there. "It can be tough in Galway" Paddy admits. "There's not much of a crowd or atmosphere, it's always raining, the pitch is covered in dog sh*t and you're expected to win easily. Connacht have also made major strides in the past couple of seasons as their results in the Celtic League have shown.

"Northampton have lost at the Sportsground and, just as Ulster would do in similar circumstances, Connacht really thrive on being underdogs on their own patch. It was a bigger game for them than for us and we were also a bit ring-rusty. But still, we came through, and overall my last Ulster trip was very enjoyable, not least for the beautiful hotel which we stayed in.

"But I think if I could have planned the fixture list, I couldn't have chosen a better last match than what I got" he acknowledges. "You'd pick a home game for starters and Munster were our biggest challenge. We hadn't beaten them for three years and, as well as dominating the interpros, they had done extremely well in Europe with two Heineken Cup finals and a semi in the space of three seasons.

"Ulster were underdogs and it was a huge test against a team very keen to win to maintain their momentum ahead of the European Cup final. It's always nice to beat Munster, but the fact that we hadn't done so for some time would make it very sweet if we could manage it. Quite a number of our squad were missing, so we knew that it would have to be a real team effort with everyone really pulling together. If we were going to win it, we'd have to really earn the victory."

The build-up was fairly familiar for Paddy as everyone went through their usual routines, but he does remember the others taking a moment for a special word in the changing rooms. "Before a game, everyone shakes hands or gives each other a hug or says good luck or whatever and, in this case, all the guys specially came over and wished me well. I was also very conscious that it was Stan's last game too. I got a good feeling that the team wouldn't let us down. I really wanted a win for Stanley as well. He hadn't been around the team for a long time, but went out and had a great match. Like myself, he's always been very proud to play for Ulster and it turned out to be a fantastic evening for both of us." Others remember Paddy's own pep-talk, typically short and to the point. It was basically along the lines of 'this is my last match and there's no way it's going to be lost'.

"From a wider Ulster point of view, there had been a lot of good in Alan Solomons' first season in that we had reached the semi-finals of the Celtic League before losing narrowly and also almost got out of our European Cup Pool. We couldn't win anything tangible in these end of season matches and it would have been easy to just drift through, draw a line under it and then those who were staying on could have their summer break and come back to prepare for a new season.

"But, as a squad, we decided to make something of these games, to set our own targets, to use them as a building block for the following season. Some of the new players had already arrived and it was, in a way, like a very early warm-up game for a new campaign. Individually, from the likes of Stan and myself being keen to go out with a win, to the new signings wanting to make a good first impression, to the Ireland squad members, to the boys who maybe felt hard done by being left out of the Irish stuff, to the guys who were getting their chance for Ulster that night because of others being absent, we all had plenty to play for.

"It was a good evening and there was a good crowd, which really lifted the team as well. Seeing so many people turning out at the end of a long season was a boost for everyone and we really wanted to win for them as well as ourselves. I'd known for about three months that, by the time this game came round, it would be my last. In ways it was strange, but it was nice to have planned how I would finish in the game rather than being in the position of some guys whose career ends with a short, sharp shock in the form of injury."

In the days leading up to the game, Solomons pumped up his players and the public alike with more eulogies to Johns and the tactic worked as a great crowd of over 10,000 turned out and a hungry Ulster started superbly to lead 9-0 at the end of the opening quarter. Young Wallace, deputising in the white No 10 jersey for Humphreys, sandwiched a low, skimming dropgoal with a pair of penalties to give Ulster due reward for their efforts.

Although the younger Paddy had missed with his opening penalty attempt early on, his excellent prod to the left corner immediately afterwards enabled Ulster to keep the pressure on until he got a second chance, with which he was successful, a few minutes later. A nice break by Constable, carried on by Tyrone Howe, resulted in another penalty, which Wallace couldn't quite curl in from wide on the left, but the confident youngster continued to steal the show.

His garryowen and then break after his skipper Ward had claimed the high ball kept Ulster on the attack and Wallace dropped a neat goal on 14 minutes after some great phases from the hosts around the Munster 22. Wallace landed his second penalty midway through the half and even better was to follow from him three minutes later when, ignoring the men outside him, he danced through for a delightful try by the posts, which he converted for good measure.

The crowd generously applauded visiting veteran prop Peter Clohessy as he left the field injured on the half hour mark, but it proved to only be a temporary absence and Ulster actually went a man down five minutes later when Ward was sinbinned for what seemed a most innocuous offence. Ulster by then had conceded an unconverted try to young Ireland lock Paul O'Connell, but only gave away three points, courtesy of an O'Gara penalty on the stroke of half time, in the 10 minutes their squad skipper was missing.

Visiting flanker Alan Quinlan was sinbinned just after Ward's return, but Munster ironically gained ground in his absence, O'Gara being successful with the first of two penalty attempts to reduce the arrears to five points. Clohessy, himself making a last appearance on Irish soil before retirement, turned villain in the crowd's eyes when he too was sinbinned on the hour and then so did earlier hero Wallace when Peter Stringer charged down his kick to score on 67 minutes, O'Gara's touchline conversion nudging Munster in front for the first time.

But it was merely a tantalising twist in the script and, in spite of that setback, big Paddy was to have the fairytale ending he so richly deserved as a brilliant breakaway try by Neil Doak four minutes from time followed by some heroic defence gave Ulster a famous victory over the European Cup finalists. Doak charged down a kick from O'Gara on the Ulster 10-metre line and deftly hacked on to win the race for glory, with Wallace converting and the brave White Knights then gallantly withstanding a sustained Munster siege until the long whistle of referee Alan Lewis ended the game and called time on Paddy's great career.

Talk about signing off in style. His final international had produced a record victory 18 months earlier, so too his last European Cup match for Ulster at the start of the year. He left Stevenson Park with a win and his last 'Gannon game, fittingly at Lansdowne Road, also ended in triumph. Now he had finished on the highest of high notes with the sweetest of sweet victories.

The way the game had worked out, with Munster going in front a quarter of an hour from the end and then still having time to win it again after Doak's try, added extra merit to Ulster's achievement. If they had maintained the two-score cushion of earlier on right throughout the match, their heart and character wouldn't have been so obviously tested and proven. But to come from behind against such a formidable and mentally strong side as Munster and then have to hold them out during a sustained siege meant Ulster really earned their success. This was a Munster team who had prided themselves on being able to deliver all over Europe, a side which could hang on in tight games or come from behind. They hadn't lost an interpro in 17 outings stretching back for several years and didn't intend that run to end here.

"The fact that we had to fight so hard at the end with all hands on deck and the game coming right down to the wire made it all the more satisfying" agreed Paddy. "To know we'd beaten a team which was only 80 minutes away from winning the European Cup was a great feeling. Stringer's try was a blow, but I remained confident because I felt we were fitter and stronger than them and that, if we kept position, kept possession and kept our heads, we could get the next score. There were only a few points in it and we did have time.

"For our try, I remember Doaky sprinting off after the ball. I was so far behind him, I couldn't see exactly where the goal-line was as he scooped it up and dived over, but the crowd reaction spelt good news. Paddy Wallace kicked a great conversion, putting us five points up and meaning they needed a try rather than a penalty. That was important, for there ended up being a lot of injury-time and it made things more difficult for Munster. The fact that there was so much play after Neil's try added value to the win and earned us more credit than if we'd snatched it with the last play of the match when they would have had no time to try to hit back."

At the final whistle, did Johns simply savour a great Ulster win as the crowd invaded the pitch, or was there a strong sense that 'this is it, that's it all over'? "Both probably. I knew I had made the right decision and I was happy with it, so there was no anguish. It was emotional, yes, but I was really able to enjoy the moment. It really couldn't have been much better. We hadn't beaten Munster since I came home, so to finally get the win in my last match was great. To retire without a win over Munster in my three seasons as a professional at Ravenhill would have been very disappointing."

Unsurprisingly, he'd been as abrasive and competitive as ever. "Munster were obviously keen to avoid injuries before the European Cup final and Mick Galwey actually said to me during the game 'Paddy would you ever leave us alone and take it a bit handy' or words to that effect. I laughed and said 'I'm having too much fun, Mick'. He should really have known me better!"

On the same basis that, when you win a Cup final, there's nothing more directly ahead of you to win, Paddy felt elated back in the changing rooms. This was THE win, the achievement. Not a means to an end but an end in itself. Naturally enough, the whole team were euphoric and skipper Ward still credits that victory for the boys coming back to pre-season training a few weeks later with a real spring in their step and genuine enthusiasm for a new campaign. For Paddy though, it was a parting of the ways. When he walked out of the oh-so-familiar changing room that night, up the short corridor and out the door, he knew that was it for him. But he was genuinely cool about it.

"I think when you're happy you actually can let go. I was happy that I was doing the right thing by retiring and I'd also got the finish I wanted, yet I suppose I was a little surprised at how well I was able to let go. But I'd built up to it properly. I think I knew back in January that I'd made the right decision to retire and the intervening three or four months had affirmed that. It was never about not still being good enough in the short-term, so the fact that we'd got a good win or that I'd felt good during the game didn't really come into it in that sense or make me have any doubts. Playing for Ulster, especially at Ravenhill, has been wonderful, but all good things must come to an end and this was the perfect way to leave." As it turned out though, we hadn't quite seen the last of him.

38. NEXT STOP BERMUDA

And so it was all over. The morning after the night before, the first day of the rest of his life. After the Munster match and the celebrations, a new day dawned with Paddy Johns now an ex-rugby player. Kirsty was a rugby widow no longer, but was her husband Pudsey at peace with himself or was he a bear with a sore head? It hadn't been sudden; he'd been reconciled to this for a few months now, had had a good innings and, unlike many whose careers had been curtailed by injury, was able to choose his time to go. Making the decision was the hardest bit and now, having gone out on a high, it was time to look forward. Time too for Kirsty and the kids to come first for a change.

Paddy had already proved a model husband and father in terms of his devotion to his wife and children, but the family's schedule had always, inevitably, revolved around his rugby, though he did effectively take paternity leave in skipping a Dungannon game the week the twins were born. Trips and matches are set in stone, with everything else having to fit around them. That's a fact of life for the partner and family of any professional sportsman or sportswoman, but Paddy is genuinely grateful to Kirsty for her understanding and support throughout his career. However good he was while he was there, the reality was that he also had to be away at times, be it a tour with Ireland or a weekend with Ulster, and she'd be left holding the babies. Nor were her own family close at hand to help out.

A lot has been written in recent times about the marital difficulties being experienced by a number of players in the England cricket team, often stemming from the sheer amount of time which they spend away from home, either when playing in other parts of the country during the English summer or on long winter tours. Rugby isn't quite so demanding in that regard, though the number of nights away in a given period is still significant, leaving the spouse to cope with loneliness or looking after children or, conceivably, both.

"Cricket is an exaggerated version of rugby in that regard, but it can certainly be stressful being married to a professional, international sportsman no matter how good the person is or how much you like them," says Kirsty. "In the professional era, players are moving more regularly from club to club, between countries and even continents and, when they sign up for a new team, the wives are simply expected to pack and go somewhere they know no-one and have no family support. It can be worse for the wives in that the players have the team around them and the buzz of a new challenge. At Sarries we were fortunate in that so many couples were in the same boat, so we formed our own circle. We had been thrown in together and made the best of it. Everyone made the effort and it worked really well there, but I'm sure that mightn't be the case everywhere you could end up.

"Coming from Canada to live with Paddy in Northern Ireland meant I would have been away from my own family anyway even if he'd stayed in Ulster all his days, or for that matter hadn't even been a rugby player, but in Enfield neither of us had our families around, so I was on my own with Christopher or, later, Christopher and Emily, anytime he was away. You need a very trusting and strong relationship. I had never any worries about Paddy straying or not being faithful and he was always very helpful and attentive when he was at home, but it's also about practicalities and coping with the day-to-day demands professional sport places on a player and his family."

Paddy and Kirsty had met before he had made the big-time in rugby, but inevitably some girls are initially attracted to sports stars by their fame and fortune, and those are the relationships which unsurprisingly prove the most vulnerable when the novelty wears off and reality sinks in. But, while there is inevitably a 'bimbo brigade' among the rugby wives and girlfriends and while Kirsty admits that the 'Footballers Wives' television series does have slight relevance, she points out that "there isn't the mad money in rugby that there is in soccer so that whole celebrity-chasing factor isn't as pronounced." And, although players are perhaps away more often and have more money these days than in the amateur era, Kirsty believes that is offset by the fact that "there were longer tours in the old days and more of a social side to them."

Those who know them best would point to Paddy and Kirsty as an enduring example of a strong and stable relationship between two people who complement each other. Romantic but practical, the pair are outward-looking and fun to be around, but know how to enjoy life's simple pleasures and clearly cherish their four children deeply. Since Paddy's retirement, they are enjoying being a 'normal family' again, free of the uncompromising structures of the rugby calendar. The withdrawal symptoms have, surprisingly perhaps, been little in evidence.

"We were fairly well prepared for Paddy retiring from rugby in that, from the day he turned pro we knew that there would, by definition, be a day where it would come to an end" says Kirsty. "Neither of us knew exactly when it would happen and of course he wanted to play for as long as possible, but we'd done a lot of talking about it as we knew it would bring a big change in our lives and be a stressful time for him, for our relationship, for everything. In fairness, I think that he, that we, have managed it pretty well.

"The day that he and Alan Solomons concluded their discussions, he phoned me and said 'we've decided on a one-year contract with a renewal option for a second year'. I said 'you're joking'; he said 'no'; I said 'what, you're playing again?' and then he told me that he was retiring. I said 'reality is going to set in now' at which point he hung up and turned his mobile off. I wasn't sure what state he was in or how he was going to come home, but he's been fine. He thought the decision through, made what he felt was the right choice and hasn't looked back."

Paddy says: "Giving up rugby has certainly been one of the biggest decisions of my life, but I believed in January that, in consultation with Alan, a wise man who has been around for a long time, I'd taken the right decision to hang up my boots and nothing since then has changed that; indeed I've probably become more convinced that it was the right thing. I was at ease with myself during the countdown to my last match in May and even when dipping in briefly this autumn, I never regretted the fact that I had decided to move on. Rugby has been great for me, but you can't go on forever. It was also time to do other things.

"As well as wanting to bow out at the top, a huge part of my decision was thinking about what was right for the family. They've stood by me and, while I've seen a fair bit of Kirsty and the kids, a lot of it hasn't been real quality time. That's also part of the reason I decided to retire completely rather than giving up professional rugby but continuing to play at club level for another season or two. If I'd kept playing for Dungannon, it would have been even worse in terms of time away from the family in that I'd have been working all day, training a couple of evenings a week and playing every weekend, with away games once a fortnight.

"Instead, we can do normal family things, like go away for the weekend in the caravan. I'm enjoying that and not really missing the rugby to be honest. I hadn't been at any of the Ulster games this season until asked to bench against Edinburgh. I meant to go to the Bedford friendly, but something came up. I don't think I'll go every week, but it certainly is a great way to spend a Friday night. When I go to Ravenhill, I'll probably stand on the promenade with friends rather than sit in the stand" says Paddy, who reveals that the phone "hasn't been ringing" with invites to be a celebrity-at-a-table in the corporate hospitality tents.

So it sounds like a real step back then in every sense, but does he envisage returning to the game in some capacity at some stage in the future or having a rugby role other than that of casual fan? "I will always love the game and certainly wouldn't rule out getting involved again down the line if I thought I had something to offer, but I have no plans or ambitions in that direction at the moment. My concentration for now is on my dentistry and on giving something back to Kirsty and the kids after all the support they've given me.

"Kirsty has been with me for virtually my entire rugby career and has been a pillar of strength, always supportive and sympathetic, but also good at helping me keep a sense of perspective, which has been very important for I'm the sort who would naturally be quite intense and turn things over a lot in my mind. If you've got the right person, marriage can be a stabilising factor. I'd never have been a big party animal anyway, but it is good to have someone who is close to you to share your feelings with, while the kids also ensured I would always have something at home to take my mind off the highs and lows of the rugby. Children want the same attention and affection whether you've won or lost. It helps you keep the sport in perspective, even if you are a professional and it is your livelihood. The kids keep the head on my shoulders, if you like."

Ryan Constable says: "Kirsty has been a rock for Paddy. He does take things to heart, but he cares and is very concerned for his family and that has balanced him. That's important, because he wouldn't by nature be the sort of guy who could simply clock out from the rugby and leave it alone. He's a perfectionist and very driven and could have become obsessive, but having a family has given him a healthy focus away from the game."

As well as enjoying spending more quality time with the family, Paddy's other abiding focus this year has been his dentistry. It will surprise no-one who knows him that he has immersed himself in his resumed career with the same thoroughness and dedication that were a hallmark of his days as a professional rugby player. "Because he was out of it for six years, he's worked his butt off since January to be totally up to speed when he took up his new job" reveals Kirsty. "He shadowed a dentist in his surgery, sat in on various sessions including on phantom headwork at the RVH and studied into the small hours preparing for interviews. Paddy does nothing by half and, just like he was as a rugby player, wants to be the best dentist he can be."

The practitioner he shadowed was none other than Philip McCarter, the Dungannon dentist he had done his work experience with 17 years earlier when he was half the age he is now. "He's as helpful as ever" says Paddy.

Again, Paddy's present job has strong links with the past. "When I worked in Larne, my dental nurse was a lady called Thelma Francis. We had a very good working and social relationship, and she and her husband came over to visit myself and Kirsty when I was at Saracens. After I had announced my retirement in early 2002, my old post became available again. The current dentist Gill McGrath was taking a career break. Thelma realised that I would be looking for a job and when the post became advertised as 'full-time temporary for six months', she rang me up to see if I would be interested in applying.

"I applied and was fortunate enough to be successful. It was great to get back into dentistry and really nice to have a familiar face around, plus we automatically understood our working relations and methods. In many ways it was like I'd never left. Being back in the dentistry has confirmed to me I'm happy with my decision to retire from rugby. It was my decision and it was the right decision. You can't keep looking over your shoulder, but have to keep moving forward. I'm 34. I can't play rugby forever.

"I've recently accepted a new permanent post in Whiteabbey and, ironically enough, just after I'd accepted the post, the place in Larne was advertised as a permanent position. However, Whiteabbey is closer to home and I'll be able to specialise more in working with children. Plus it's a relief that I now have a permanent job, which is definitely a weight off my mind."

As a community dentist, Paddy cares for a wide variety of patients with a variety of circumstances. One part of his job involves visits to nursing and residential homes for dental screenings. "These involve checking patients' dentures, any remaining teeth, looking for evidence of gum disease, ulcers or anything more sinister." He enjoys working with children and the gentle giant always tries to make the visit as tolerable as possible for the person in the chair. "When I was young, I didn't enjoy going to the dentist, so I really try to make the patient a little less nervous than they might be when they come in.

"I've also had a few amusing incidents during these consultations" he laughs. "I came to see one lady and said to her, 'I'm the dentist, come to look at your teeth. Can you take them out for me?' 'No, I don't think that's necessary' she replied. I was quite bemused at this and asked her again, about three times, at which point she said 'Oh, alright then' and proceeded to undo her blouse! The nurses who were in with me were absolutely creased over in laughter and had to leave the room.

"Another lady was quite confused and wouldn't let me look in her mouth. She was talking away, so I got down on one knee so I could try and have a glimpse as she was chatting. As I did so she said, 'Oh no, I don't think I want to marry you. I've been married once and that was enough!' One other time, I walked into the room and this frail, well-to-do looking lady said, "Look at the size of you! Your mother must have stood you in sh*te when you were a baby!"

Just as Paddy's rugby status goes before him in his job, it also seems certain to be a factor for son Christopher as he grows up, particularly if the mini-rugby which he has currently started leads on into playing seriously at school and even beyond. There will be an inevitable tendency for Christopher to be seen first and foremost as Paddy Johns' son, and comparisons with his famous father on the rugby field are inevitable, but the parents are naturally concerned that this will heap pressure on the lad as he grows up and are very keen for him to have his own identity.

"We're very conscious that he is himself, not 'Paddy's son' and are quite alarmed that they've been calling him Paddy at school" says Kirsty. "He's too young to really understand, though naturally he's been brought up around rugby and has been very interested in the game and the players. By being constantly around Saracens, he knew about three quarters of the guys in the team pic when he was two years of age" continues Paddy.

Being brought up with rugby, it is no real surprise that Johns Junior's favourite video is the Hong Kong Sevens. "Christopher knows every player and every move on that video," reveals his doting dad, "and has really been looking forward to starting minis this autumn. To be honest he has a bit of a ball fetish and can play any ball or racquet sport. When he started school he thought that you go to school to learn what you do when you're grown up and with me being a rugby player, he assumed that he was just going to learn how to play rugby like Daddy and there were tears when he realised that wasn't the case! He used to cry whenever Ireland lost as well, but it's only really this past year that he's been aware that it's a bit different for a dad to play rugby and be on television. It's a bit like a story I heard about the golfer Colin Montgomerie, whose son knew his dad was on the box, but just assumed everyone else's was as well!"

Paddy has moved seamlessly from proud rugby player to proud rugby parent but is determined not to put any pressure on Christopher in relation to the sport. If, for example, he proved equally good at a couple of sports and, like Liam Botham, chose an alternative to avoid the invidious comparisons, that would be fine. "I'm happy enough to see him starting mini rugby, but at this stage the main thing is that he has fun and enjoys rugby and any other sport he plays, for that is what it is all about. How good he is at rugby or how far he might want to go remains to be seen, but we'll be there to support him. He seems to be liking it alright so far."

Although tickled by the tape of Christopher mimicking Michael Lynagh's goal-kicking routine on television when he was a mere toddler, Mrs Johns Senior would "prefer to see him take up golf: I think he'd be a natural", but is confident that he will be fit to cope with any pressures that being Paddy's son place upon him. "Emily too is quite assertive and won't get lost in life" adds the proud granny.

"It's early days, but should Johns Junior prove a chip off the old block and emerge as a top talent, Kirsty and Paddy would naturally be keen for him to get a full education before any move into professional rugby and the attendant risk of dashed dreams and so forth. That prospect, however, is a long way away and the family will cross that particular bridge if and when they come to it. Emily is a couple of years younger than Christopher, while the twins "are not aware of any rugby stuff and when they do become aware of things like that, I'll be dad the dentist rather than dad the rugby player." Incidentally, if any of the Johns girls want to take up rugby, they'll have their mum's blessing "providing they play in the backs!"

Any sporting inclination which the children have is being facilitated at a basic level in their own backyard so to speak, Paddy having converted an old barn at their home into a serviceable sports hall. "It was a big rust bucket when we came here, but we've got it painted and kitted out as a kind of sports hall for badminton, football, hockey, you name it." There's never a dull moment and, as he really throws himself into family life and his long-neglected hobbies, Paddy has little time to think about missing the rugby according to Kirsty.

"He gave so much for so long that I think he's loving the change" she says. "Paddy was very absorbed in and totally committed to his rugby, no-one more so, but he's also always had so many other interests as well. He's big into cycling and likes painting (the old artistic streak coming through again) scenes in watercolours, though perhaps the home wine-making which he listed in one profile as being among his hobbies is a bit of a red herring! He is really enjoying being around the kids and doesn't like them going off elsewhere on a Saturday when he's at home."

Paddy is also wholeheartedly getting involved with school, church and youth activities and is actually County Armagh Ambassador for the Girl Guides. "You could say he's given up rugby and joined the Girl Guides" quips his mum. "He's a great believer in youth organizations and will take a keen interest in supporting them. Emily attends Waringstown Rainbows."

"Paddy has always been very interested in his children's education and supportive of the school" praises Gary Kennedy, principal of Waringstown Primary School. "He opened a garden fete for us a few years back and left an Ulster jersey, balls and posters for us to auction. He also helped with coaching at the school and we went on to represent mid-Ulster schools at Ravenhill. Not bad for a school which usually plays football and cricket, not rugby! Paddy's always been a normal Dad. No different to any other parent, not a celebrity" he observes. "Very quiet and unassuming, totally different to on the pitch. Just goes to show that he has a competitive nature when it matters." Keith McGarry adds: "Whatever school the children go to will get the benefits of Paddy as part of the package."

A regular church-goer, attending Waringstown Presbyterian Church, Paddy has found himself turning more to religion in latter years, or perhaps more accurately, returning to a lapsed love. It is something that is important to him as evidenced by the references to this aspect of his life in the personal statement at the start of this book. Johns isn't the sort to preach or ram religion down people's throats, but feels that he wants others to share in the sort of peace which he claims to have. Basically, he doesn't want to hide his light under a bushel and, you sense, perhaps wants to get the message across that believing in God is not something for macho young men to be embarrassed about. After all, if a guy as hard as Paddy can talk openly about a love for God, anyone can.

"I come from a Christian background" he says "and have always believed in God, but that has now got stronger and I am very at peace in my own mind about Christianity and know where I'm going. Looking back too, it would be right for me to acknowledge that I've only got this far because of the ability which God gave me. Part of realising that there is life beyond rugby has been coming to the understanding that if all I had in my life was my 59 caps, I would feel empty and would have found it very hard to cope with the rugby coming to an end.

"God has always been there throughout my career. Sometimes the door has been open and other times I have kept it blindly closed. In later times though, I've realised that whatever I could achieve in rugby or in life itself would mean nothing if I did not have faith in God. I think having young children has been a factor, for I realised that they need direction. I'd been a regular church-goer in England and knew I wanted to bring my children up as Christians, but I've got more actively involved in the church since I moved back to Ulster."

His mother says: "Paddy has a very strong faith, but he'd live his Christianity through how he behaves rather than preaching it. As in other ways, he would want to be more about actions than words. He has always had strong principles and fairly high morals. He was brought up in a church family and it was never a difficulty getting him to go to church. But his faith has come to mean a great deal to him in later years."

Paddy has found the strength to forgive and seek reconciliation for things which affected him deeply earlier in his life and insists that doing so has made him a happier person. "You must forgive and go on or you won't have any peace yourself and everyone has to get another chance or you will end up being judged harshly yourself. That comes right down to players you've had altercations with or journalists who have written things you didn't like. Sometimes people have to learn their lesson the hard way and I've come to realise that everyone is on their own individual journey.

"To that extent, I try not to see life as too black and white" says Paddy when probed about particular parameters which some may feel should apply to those claiming to be Christians, for instance whether it is legitimate to play sport on a Sunday, a live issue for a sizeable number of Ulster Protestants and indeed others. "There are different degrees and different perspectives and I don't think at the moment I would feel as strongly about that as maybe someone like Michael Jones (the former All Blacks flanker) did. I didn't have a problem with that during my own career and, even though I'm closer to God now than I was for all of that period, I would not be against Christopher playing on a Sunday if that was his choice. Other people do important jobs on a Sunday such as firemen and policemen and doctors and those who man power stations though I suppose you could argue they are providing an essential service and rugby players aren't. Some people will feel comfortable with things which others wouldn't; it's ultimately up to someone's personal conscience.

"I try to do what I think is right for myself and live as best I can, but I don't claim to be perfect or to have all the answers. I try not to use bad language, and have no problem having a few beers as long as it isn't a case of really drinking to access, though maybe I did have a few too many the night of my retirement match!" he confesses. "The bottom line is that I am able to pray and not feel phoney. To be honest, some of the biggest sins are in the mind and heart.

"I realise that there is a God and would like others to find the peace I now have, but it isn't up to me to ram stuff down people's throats or judge others on the basis of my perspective on 'right and wrong'. Everyone has their own journey and it isn't our business to judge - that's up to God" says Paddy, before expressing a similar view to that which got the Prime Minister's wife Cherie Blair into hot water some time back. "Take the Palestinian suicide bombers even. They blow themselves up with awful consequences for themselves and others but, y'know, I guess that's their own particular fate. It might be a controversial comment and not very politically correct to say so" he concedes, "but that is their journey in this life, their history. The loss of life though is terrible."

You imagine it can't be that easy to wear your faith openly in the slightly irreverent lads' environment of a rugby squad, but Paddy insists that he hasn't had a problem or been ridiculed or scoffed at by his colleagues. That might partly be out of their respect for a genuine guy and senior statesman, but he largely attributes it, again, to the fact that he isn't into the business of preaching at others. "I've done a few low profile things such as speaking at a youth club and an evening for Christians in Sport that was held at Malone RFC, but I don't know how aware the boys really have been of my beliefs and so forth. It isn't something which I would ever have rammed down their throats or made a song and dance about. I've more kept it to myself. While I'm not at all afraid to say that I go to church, I equally wouldn't be a 'bible-basher'!"

Probably a wise move. One former colleague, who himself is religious, expressed the hope that this bit of the book would not come across as a preaching platform or a crusading chapter. Almost on the same basis as Paddy's quote about not making cheques with your mouth which you can't cash, the ex-player, who would be good friends with Paddy, describes him as a "guy who is doubtless genuine in his zeal" but reckoned that too many old team-mates would be able to recall him "effing and blinding in the changing-room before a match" to wear too much heavy stuff in print here. Best not to lay it on too thick. The same thought occurred to this writer when Johns made his recent brief comeback against Munster. Had this book been out prior to that match and an altercation developed in it, the chances of Paddy following the Christian principle of turning the other cheek would, understandably, have been rather remote!

The good intentions regarding profanity would also surely be tested to the full if Paddy ever went into coaching, given all the emotion, stresses and frustrations which go with the job and considering that, with his full-on intensity and competitiveness, he would probably get more frustrated than most. What are the chances of him going down that route though? Before dealing with his own thoughts on the matter, it is perhaps instructive to set out the views of two former Ulster and Ireland team-mates of Paddy's, who have played with and against him as far back as his early teens, but who differ a little in their responses when asked about his suitability for a coaching future.

"I think it is essential that someone of Paddy's calibre is not completely lost to the game for good" says his long-time playing colleague Allen Clarke, now Director of Elite Development for the IRFU's Ulster Branch. "He may not want a full-time role, but if he could even be brought in on specifics, including mental approach and be utilized as a kind of mentor figure, it would be useful. One real strength which he would have is in analyzing opposition teams in that he has a very good rugby brain and is very thorough." Clarke, who is in charge of the Ulster Academy, uses Paddy as a role model for the province's emerging talent to follow, on the basis that "beyond his ability and achievements he is also a fine example of someone who remembered his roots and always put his family first."

Mark McCall agrees regarding Johns' analytical skills, while Paddy's friend and former Dungannon team-mate Keith McGarry adds: "His analysis of games is just unbelievable. Even when you're watching a match on television with him, he is forever pointing out little things. I think he learned a lot at Saracens. Paddy was around the game for a long time and is the sort of person to make the most of every learning opportunity."

Willie Anderson says: "I think that Paddy has the ability to coach and that the game will move more and more to specific coaches who have great expertise in particular areas of the game and will be used on a consultancy basis. On the other hand, professional rugby, while remaining the same basic sport, is evolving and moving so fast these days that it is hard to keep pace if you're not involved on a full-time basis. Paddy was a very deep guy and analysed everything meticulously. At times, I could have pulled my hair out with him and his stubbornness, but it is a lot better to have a player like that than one who thinks very little about the game. He came up with some very good and useful ideas and also had a good feel for the people around him.

"We understood each other pretty well and there was a basic mutual respect which sustained our relationship and allowed us to question, even agree to disagree on occasions without it diminishing the respect we had for each other. There was an interesting time in the season we won the AIL when, basically, the coaches wanted to take one approach and the players another. He'd have been very strong in his views, but we never fell out for long because we each knew that the other wanted nothing but the best for the team and for Dungannon Rugby Football Club."

Paddy's mum, however, feels that his professional future lies outside the sport. "Paddy has a very good profession in dentistry and is a professional in his own right. Dentistry is an honourable and noble profession, helping suffering humanity. He is a very caring person and he will give his dentistry career the same commitment as he gave his rugby career. Of that I am sure. His profile will also be of some help in his work."

"I'd never rule anything in or out for the future and I do believe that I have knowledge and experience of the game which would be worthwhile to impart to others in some capacity, but coaching certainly isn't what I want to do right now" clarifies Paddy. "I've had a long continuous run of being very heavily involved in rugby, physically, mentally and emotionally and I'm currently enjoying the chance to take a step back and put the family first, while professionally my big focus is on my dentistry career, re-establishing myself in that and seeking to be the best I can be in that field." You definitely couldn't see him as a jobbing rugby coach, dragging himself and the family around for say three years in Bedford, a season at Caerphilly, then two terms with Dolphin in the AIL. "No I won't be doing that" he confirms. "Coaching would be worse for family life than playing in that I'd definitely be bringing the team's problems home with me, going over and over stuff in my mind."

The perfectionist streak was also the reason why he didn't wind his playing career down gradually. On reflection, no-one is too surprised that he made a clean break rather than initially continue at club level and later drop down to perhaps play for Dungannon Fourths in his forties. Ulster coach Alan Solomons says: "I'm not surprised at all by the clean break decision. Paddy understood perfectly that, for someone of his calibre, when you get out, you get out. That's also why he was available for Ireland until the end. He believed that he was good enough to play international rugby and had to believe that or he would have stopped sooner. I would never want to comment on Irish selection, but the way that Paddy was playing at the end, I'm sure he couldn't help but think that if Mick Galwey could still play for Ireland so could he."

Ryan Constable opines that the concept of social rugby would have eluded the big man. "Paddy Johns playing rugby at social level would not be safe; his style of rugby doesn't lend itself to half measures or niceties" insists Ryan, while Justin Fitzpatrick points out that Paddy's personal preparations "for a pre-season friendly would have been as professional and precise as for a Test against one of the southern hemisphere big three", the implication being that, down the ranks, he would be driven mad by team-mates' more relaxed approach to training and playing. The man himself concurs.

"Apart from the fact that the combination of dentistry and amateur club rugby would have kept me away from the family more than being a professional player, the other reason why I didn't phase myself out by continuing to play at club level was because I'd only have been frustrated. I'd have trained flat out and played flat out, but would have had nothing to aspire to. If I'd played on I'd have wanted to be playing for Ulster and would have felt I was good enough, but the only way to have done that would have been to continue as a professional, so when I gave that up the only course of action was to hang up the boots completely. Never mind further down the club, I even found myself getting a bit restless with the AIL, frustrated with things that I wouldn't have previously. Maybe I'd got a bit tired and emotional by the end of my career!"

Roles in rugby other than playing or coaching? You sense he wouldn't make a natural 'blazer', while a role in the media would be very much a case of poacher turned game-keeper. "I have no great urge to go down that route. For one thing, I've never been big into getting my face or voice onto TV and, for another, I remember too well what the media can do. I don't think I'd like to go down the route of one or two ex-players and coaches and make money from knocking people." Some might question whether he'd actually say enough as a pundit, yet those who have been in teams with him point to how good he is tactically and his great knowledge of the game and cite his precise and analytical approach as reasons why he would have a lot to offer. It is for those same qualities that Clarke believes he would be ideal at compiling dossiers on opposition teams.

So a future role in rugby perhaps, but not for now. Mean-time, apart from an odd appearance in something like the Bermuda Classics, it's the family's time, no more than the long-suffering Kirsty deserves, having faithfully walked each step of the rugby road with him for more than a decade and been, to a degree at least, the proverbial rugby widow in spite of having a devoted husband. It's been a roller-coaster ride, but she wouldn't have missed it for the world. "I knew absolutely nothing about rugby the first day I saw Paddy play" she confesses, "but now I could referee a match! I got into the sport so much that I didn't just watch Paddy and where he was or what he was doing, but got totally taken over by the match as a whole.

"It was very nerve-wracking watch on television, for if you're physically there in the flesh, you can deal directly with the elation or disappointment. It was a bit weird and detached switching on the TV, seeing him appear out of the tunnel, play in the match, then disappear off camera again, though we'd obviously speak on the phone later that evening. For the Ireland tour of South Africa in 1998, I went back home to Newfoundland and had to rely on getting stuff off the internet. It was an explosive series but had no impact on people in Canada. Back home is the one place where Paddy is my husband and I'm not merely his wife, but I guess it's the same for his mum, for Christopher and for his brother Johnny too, probably; we're defined in relation to him."

While absorbed with the wider goings on, naturally enough though she did play it through Paddy's eyes and, on occasions, experienced anger, anguish and righteous indignation on his behalf. "Paddy worked for everything he got and, towards the end, knowing how hard he worked, it seemed very unfair that they weren't even considering him for Ireland though, to his credit, he wouldn't have been one to wallow in self-pity" insists Kirsty. "Most physios and doctors would have called him the perfect patient; if he was told to do something, he would do it to the word. Paddy's been very dedicated, very thorough. Sometimes I'd think 'oh go on Paddy, for goodness sake do something you're not supposed to for once'!"

To the authors, rugby without Paddy Johns is almost as inconceivable as rugby without Ravenhill or Lansdowne Road in that he has been part of the furniture for almost as long as we have been following the sport, while for Kirsty it is a case of getting her head round the converse notion: Paddy Johns without rugby. It had been a long farewell since the retirement route was sketched out in January, with Paddy feted each step of the way as his fans savoured each remaining appearance, but May's Munster match must have had quite an air of finality about it? "He really looked forward to that game and was determined Ulster wouldn't lose. They won and he felt ready to go. He has let go well and we have moved on as a family. In fact we seem to have adjusted fairly easily, maybe surprisingly so to some extent in that rugby has been his life, our lives, for so long and that he hasn't simply given up playing a sport but also had to change profession" muses Kirsty.

In the brave new world, Paddy can quite often be found down at his mum's on a Saturday afternoon, helping out with any heavy jobs which need doing. She has been at his side from the start even though "in the early days she didn't like going to games because she didn't want to see me get hurt." Throughout it all Paddy has simply been her son, 'Pads', so it must have been strange getting used to him being such public property? When did she begin to realize that he was destined for great things in rugby?

"Paddy would have been about 15 at the time, Royal School Dungannon were playing Methodist College and I was standing beside the late Ken Reid (legendary rugby administrator). He didn't know who I was, but commented to her that 'young Johns there' might just have a future in the game, based on his lineout prowess. "It was a gradual process of realization. Another time I was stood beside a priest at Blackrock, who said 'that guy will play for Ireland one day'."

How aware was she of Paddy's private pledge from his early teens that he would do exactly that or leave no stone unturned? "He would have made you aware of his ambition and of course he ate, slept and drank rugby, so there was time for nothing else. All of that contributed too and certainly nothing came about by chance. I can't say that I had any previous interest in rugby prior to Paddy's time in the game but now, having followed his career so closely, I wouldn't miss a match; it's almost become like a disease! It became a way of life and our lives were geared around rugby. As a parent, it is your duty to be supportive, but beyond that, there was a real buzz as well. My late mother used to watch it on the television too and loved it.

"Any sporting career is a bit of a roller-coaster and I suppose it is no different for a parent of the person involved. I've had a great time following his rugby and have enjoyed every minute of it. Each of the three boys is equally precious to me, so just because Paddy has had the public profile, I don't see him in any different light to the other two. He is my son and I am pleased for him and proud of his achievements, as I would be whatever he had done in life. It was strange to put on the radio in the office one day and learn that my son was being rushed from Dublin to Belfast with suspected appendicitis, but you'd have got used to him being on the television playing, or his name being in the papers, though naturally enough you are protective and I would have found it very hurtful whenever I saw him being criticized in print and felt it was unfair. No-one likes to see their son torn apart.

"There have been lots of highlights and we've made far too many memories to mention them all. I will always remember his first game at Lansdowne Road, against Japanese Schools, with their black heads and bright red tracksuits etched against the velvet green grass during the warm-up. That, for me, was the start of the big rugby. It was a thrilling experience to watch him play for Ulster against the 1989 All Blacks and of course his Ireland debut the following year was a very big occasion. In between it was a big shock to turn on the television and see him on the bench for that game in Paris when he wasn't even supposed to be involved at all! He was out of the team again for a while after the Argentina match, but I felt he'd bounce back because I had faith in him and he was always a guy who persevered. I supported him as best I could."

Mrs Johns has also got to know many of Paddy's playing colleagues to a greater or lesser extent, some of them almost assuming the status of distant nephews, but she has a particular soft spot for Jeremy Davidson. "Jeremy is a lovely big fella, and he and Paddy are great friends. I remember one year when Ireland were playing Wales away and we'd flown over from Dublin. Jeremy and Paddy were rooming together and, when I got up to the room, it was like a bombsite with all their stuff. After I arrived, Jeremy disappeared and I thought it was maybe to give me a wee while with Paddy which would have been considerate enough in itself. But when he returned, it was with lunch for me. That's typical of his kindness.

"It was annoying for Paddy towards the end of his career that he seemed to have been sidelined in Irish terms, but his picture hangs in Lansdowne Road as an Ireland captain along with a lot of rugby's greatest names and no-one can take his achievements away from him. By that stage, he had already made his mark. When he retired, there were feelings of relief, delight that he was still walking. It was good that he came back to finish with Ulster and Dungannon and nice that he won his last five games, six if you include Munster this autumn. Now we can all reflect happily on his achievements." Through it all though, before it and beyond it, he was, is and will always be her son, loved as much when he wasn't picked as when he was or regardless of whether his team lost or won.

39. LIGHTNING STRIKES TWICE

Only a phonecall away. Alan Solomons had used that expression at Paddy's retirement press conference in January in the context of lauding how supportive Johns would always be of Ulster rugby even now he was retired. Neither man could really have envisaged then though that when that call was made on September 1, it would be the Ulster coach asking the former Irish captain to make an emergency return to the colours. After some soul-searching, the gamble paid off for both men, with Paddy's reward being a second farewell win over Munster for the price of one and a final sweet little chapter in the story of a great career. A sensational tackle count of seven in 22 minutes was a fabulous footnote.

Most of Ulster's new recruits, notably Warren Brosnihan and Matt Sexton, had already been in place for the May match against Munster, the exception being Springbok prop Robbie Kempson, arguably the province's biggest name southern hemisphere signing of the professional era and described by Nick Mallett as 'a loss to South African rugby'. Still only 28 and capped 31 times by the Springboks, Kempson was regarded by Solomons as one of the world's best props and was certainly not coming to the northern hemisphere when over the hill.

Following the exit from the 2001-02 European Cup at the end of the Pool phase, Solomons had moved quickly to offload several foreign failures and strengthen his squad for his second season. Argentinian prop Leopoldo de Chazal, the most spectacular of the foreign flops in that he never actually set foot on the pitch for Ulster, got the boot along with Aussie imports Mark Crick and David Allen. Rising stars Paul Shields and Neil McMillan were rewarded for their performances in the white jersey with first full-time contracts, as was former IRFU Development Officer Neil Doak, while young guns Scott Young and Matt McCullough were promoted to the professional ranks.

Ritchie Weir and Niall Malone were the highest profile local lay-offs, while Dubliner John Campbell was discarded and of course Paddy had retired and Brad Free already departed for a new life in America. Dungannon lock Aiden Kearney later returned to his native Leinster, ultimately being replaced in the professional panel by promising former RBAI No 8 Roger Wilson. The enforced retirement of Robbie Brink early in the season due to his persisting shoulder trouble allowed Belfast Harlequins flanker Neil Best to be upgraded to a core contract. Andy Ward retained the captaincy for a second season.

While Paddy was relaxing, keeping in trim by doing a little running and swimming, Ulster were really cranking it up in a rigorous pre-season, culminating in a friendly away to Scotland's new, third, professional set-up, the Borders, which was won 31-0, with Lions lock Jeremy Davidson, making a welcome return to action, bagging a brace of tries in the space of four second half minutes. A routine 29-12 victory over Bedford followed and Solomons' side completed their warm-up programme unbeaten though were denied a hat-trick of wins when Glasgow grabbed a 19-19 draw at Ravenhill.

Ireland's failure to reach the knockout stages of the 1999 World Cup, which meant having to qualify for the 2003 event, had a knock-on effect for the provinces and, ultimately, Paddy, during the Celtic League. Ulster were not as badly decimated as champions Leinster, who paid a heavy price in the form of four straight defeats which cost them a place in the knockout stages, losing only David Humphreys and Gary Longwell to national duty.

The pair had both been in New Zealand in the summer, when Ireland did very well before going down 15-6 in the first Test, only to leak 40 points in the second, when Longwell, who started both matches with Humphreys benching, had the consolation of scoring his first try at international level. Along with several Ulster colleagues, they were then involved in training camps in Poland and Limerick, but were the only two northerners to make the cut for the three September internationals, a friendly against Romania in Thomond Park and the World Cup qualifiers against Russia in Siberia and Georgia at Lansdowne Road. Ireland achieved a hat-trick of victories over their eastern European opponents without really finding top gear.

Humphreys, who scored 14 of his side's points and created the game's only try for Paddy Wallace late on, and Longwell were available for Ulster's Celtic League opener in Ebbw Vale when Solomons' side produced a workmanlike performance to beat their unfancied hosts 19-0 on a miserable evening at Eugene Cross Park. Kempson showed all his scrummaging prowess in a game where he had been picked at loosehead with Simon Best at tight and Justin Fitzpatrick dropped for the first time in his Ulster career. Being benched had a silver lining, however, for the Ireland prop, who responded to the wake-up call by regaining his place and having an excellent autumn.

Davidson had had to leave the field in the opening half at Ebbw Vale after receiving a heavy kick to the hip, and what was an actual pain in the arse for him proved to be a metaphorical one for Solomons. With Longwell on Ireland duty, young Matt McCullough sidelined by the cheekbone fracture sustained in an early season Ulster A outing, the versatile Brink out of the picture and Kearney now at Leinster, Ulster's second row cupboard was suddenly looking very bare indeed. Young Dungannon back five forward Tim Barker was also out of action due to a facial injury. It must have crossed more than a few minds that it was a pity Paddy Johns had retired. He'd have been a bit useful to have around at a time like this. But he'd retired. Everyone had decided it was best that he hang up his boots. So that was that. He'd moved on, so had Ulster. Hadn't they . . .

Paddy rang this writer on the Tuesday evening to reveal that he had been asked to sit on the bench for Friday night's Celtic League clash with Edinburgh at Ravenhill. Solomons had asked him because of the second row crisis. He wasn't sure whether he was simply there as injury cover or would be treated as any of the other subs. No-one outside the squad had been told yet and Davidson had actually been named in the side that day with hopeful noises being made about his prospects of facing the Scots, but Paddy revealed that Jeremy had already been ruled out. As his biographer, he was letting me know out of courtesy, but asked that approval from Solomons be sought before running the story.

The following day, when at Ravenhill for a meeting with Ulster Branch Commercial

Manager Simon Wallace about one or two issues relating to this book, I bumped into Solomons, told him about the Paddy Johns biography and fairly bluntly asked whether there was another chapter still to be penned. The genial little South African seemed stunned and insisted that, under no circumstances, should I reveal the reality, not even in Friday morning's paper. Later that evening, at a Dungannon RFC reception, several Ulster players admitted that they'd been sworn to secrecy under threat that anyone who spilled the beans would be hunted down and disciplined.

In the end, although it went against journalistic instincts, I decided to respect Solly's wishes and not announce the news before the match rather than upsetting the coach by blowing his cover on something he was clearly hell-bent on keeping quiet so, with no other journalist rumbling what was going on, the public were kept in the dark right up until a few hours before the game, though the News Letter had carried a rather obscure hint in its back page preview where, ostensibly writing purely about Paddy Wallace, who was making his Ravenhill return after starring in the win over Munster in May, I concluded "Ulster are missing a number of leading players due to a combination of injury and Ireland commitments but, with rising star Wallace capable of magic moments and canny coach Alan Solomons likely to have one or two other surprises up his sleeve for the Scots, it really could be another case of 'Paddy's night' at Ravenhill . . ."

So complete was the cover-up that even the Ulster Branch's PR people, who release team news to the media, were not, to their considerable annoyance, informed until late on Friday afternoon that Davidson had been ruled out, even though apparently the decision had actually been taken the previous Sunday! As luck would have it, Jeremy was pictured on the front of the match programme, while the team-lists in the middle of it, although only finalised well into the week, did not include Paddy Johns. This cloak-and-dagger conspiracy reflected Johns' and Solomons' desire to avoid the distraction of the media hype which would, inevitably, have surrounded news of a Johns comeback and keep the focus on those who were taking the field rather than on a man who, however famous, was only there as an emergency.

"Our forwards coach Adrian Kennedy came up with the idea" reveals Solomons. "We were worried about our lack of second row options and he said 'Why don't you ask Paddy', for he had said he was there if we needed him in an emergency. He was initially taken aback, but agreed to help us out. Once he agreed, we knew he'd be fine. If it had been someone else, we'd have hesitated even asking, but everyone knew Paddy could do a job and he proved it in spades. The man would never hold back and only knows how to give everything. The Munster match was clear proof of that."

Paddy's role early on was simply to applaud with everyone else in a packed stand as his namesake Wallace gave Ulster a fourth minute lead, but it was a false dawn on an evening when a late penalty by Scottish fullback Brendan Laney stunned an 8,000 crowd and condemned Ulster to a first Ravenhill defeat in over a year since Llanelli had, ironically, similarly snatched a late victory to spoil Johns' home debut as captain in the inaugural Celtic League. For the second game running, a strike right at the death denied Ulster victory over Scottish opposition but, unlike the draw with Glasgow a fortnight earlier, this time there were priceless points at stake.

Some superb place-kicking by Wallace, who landed six penalties from six attempts, had ensured the White Knights were in front throughout an absorbing contest but, ultimately, the previously profligate Laney found his range, broke Ulster hearts and left them looking back in anger on what might have been on a night where Solomons admitted that Ulster had been the "authors of our own misfortune. We made far too many silly mistakes and although we improved greatly in the second half, had made it very difficult for ourselves by not making enough of having the wind behind us in the first. Our defence on their try was poor and overall the truth is that we blew this game."

Ulster's already depleted back five, missing Davidson, Longwell, Brink and Ward, suffered another blow after only 11 minutes when an injured Neil McMillan had to be replaced. Solomons chose to send on young Belfast Harlequins flanker Neil Best for his competitive debut rather than switching Tony McWhirter, playing second row for Ulster for the first time in years, to No 8 and risk trying to squeeze 70 minutes out of a retired and rusty Johns. Of course Paddy's spirit would have been willing, but Solomons' decision was sensible enough and had the spin-off of giving Best valuable experience at this level.

A hat-trick of Wallace strikes had Ulster 9-0 up inside the opening half hour and Laney then missed badly, but the kilted Kiwi still managed to make a mark before the interval with a well-taken try which he also converted before exchanging penalties with Wallace to leave Edinburgh only two points down at the break. A fifth penalty from Wallace soon after the resumption was cancelled out by a Duncan Hodge dropgoal in a third quarter which saw both Lions loose forward Simon Taylor and young Neil Best binned.

Just after the hour mark, Wallace nudged Ulster five points clear again with his sixth strike, but Laney immediately replied and a tight game went right down to the wire. With five minutes remaining Ulster elected, surprisingly in light of Wallace's superb long-range striking earlier, to go for touch from a penalty rather than the posts and, after nothing came of the lineout, the Scots got downfield to win the crucial penalty. One last brilliant break by Constable allowed Bryn Cunningham to chip through, but the visitors swept up, cleared downfield and stole the Ulster throw for good measure. That was that.

In those tense closing stages, as Paddy paced up and down the touchline, the authors exchanged frantic texts, hoping against hope that he wouldn't come on and finish up on the losing side, thus spoiling May's fairytale ending against Munster. As it transpired, he wasn't called upon, but reckoned afterwards that Solomons "must be kicking himself" and had missed a trick in not throwing him on. "Ryan Constable had told Scot Murray (the Scotland and Lions second row who had signed for Edinburgh from Saracens in the summer but was making his seasonal debut following injury) before the match that we had a little surprise for them, but when asked what it was just said 'you'll see'. Afterwards Murray said to Ryan 'it was Paddy wasn't it? . . . I was praying he wouldn't be on for the last 10 minutes as I was shattered' and seemed to be glad I hadn't been around to make a bit of mayhem! "Just after half-time Solly had told me to warm up, that things were too lifeless and that I would be going on with Fitzy, but Ulster did improve and he held me back and held me back. The whole experience was a bit strange to be honest and I felt like I was in a time warp, working in my job as a dentist all day until 4.30

and then coming along to Ravenhill for the game." One member of the great Ulster side of the 1980s had expressed concerns on Paddy's behalf that he was taking a big risk beyond the call of duty in making himself available, having "already done his time" and Johns admits himself that there were mixed emotions about the call-up.

"I could see two sides to the coin, one being 'great, lets get in here' and the other being 'what if I miss a tackle that costs us the game'. I'd played a match a couple of weeks previously, but it was only a charity game in Cookstown, and although I'd been keeping myself in shape, I wasn't in proper rugby training and hadn't been involved with the squad at all. I had to do the emergency relief of pain clinic in Belfast City Hospital on the Thursday evening and so couldn't even go along to the captain's run at tea-time. You worry that being away could take away your edge at that level and you don't want to let either yourself or the team down, but the over-riding sense was that I couldn't turn down a chance to play for Ulster. By the next game I was involved in, against Neath a fortnight later, I was much better prepared both physically and mentally."

In between, with Davidson back on board so Paddy was spared duty, Ulster had crashed to a 38-10 defeat on the darkest of days for Solomons in sunny Swansea where a rash of injuries rubbed salt in the wounds of long-range opposition tries. The sight of Lions winger Tyrone Howe pressed into emergency service as a flank forward and reserve hooker Paul Shields packing down at No 8 while the casualty list grew, summed up this wretched trip to west Wales. After losing Humphreys, Jonathan Bell, Wallace, Davidson, Russell Nelson and Brosnihan on the day to add to those already ruled out, Solomons claimed that he had never seen a side so afflicted by injuries in his two decades as a coach.

Ulster went into the game unable to call on the services of five of their core contracted squad in skipper Ward, the now retired Brink, Ireland lock Longwell, winger Sheldon Coulter and McCullough. Now the headache for Solomons would be so much worse ahead of the following Friday night's must-win match against Neath, with Brink gone for good, Wallace joining Ward on the long-term injury list and McCullough still sidelined. Davidson and Brosnihan were always likely to have recovered from nasty gashes which needed stitched, while the coach was left to sweat on the fitness of acting captain Bell, but it was the news that Nelson would miss the Neath game which prompted another call to Paddy on the Sunday evening. McWhirter would now be needed for No 8, so cover was required for second rows Blair and Davidson.

While Ulster were in Swansea, Paddy had spent a gloriously sunny September weekend with Kirsty and the kids in their caravan, with no hankering whatsoever to be playing at St Helen's but, when Solomons' call came, he again answered it. This time he was named on the bench at Tuesday's official team announcement, but it was to get a little heavy at home before the game came around while, for Solomons, things went from bad to worse. Of his squad of 35, including the development contracted players, only 21 were able to take part in training on the Monday and Ulster were then rocked by a double whammy on the eve of the game when Bell, due to skipper the side, pulled out with a combination of injury and illness while Springbok Robbie Kempson withdrew due to the latter. On the afternoon of the match Matt Sexton, named as captain in the absence of Ward, Humphreys and Bell, was struck down with tummy trouble and became the latest cry-off.

Meanwhile, neither Kirsty nor Paddy's mum were happy with the state of affairs which was pertaining, both feeling that he had given Ulster good service down the years, was now retired and should not have been prevailed upon to play again, whatever the second row shortage. In their view, that was not Paddy's problem but Solomons' and it was cheeky of the coach to ask him, knowing how hard Johns would find it to turn down a chance to pull on the white jersey. If the coach had led him towards the decision to retire at the top back in January in order to protect his legacy, was asking him to play now not endangering it and running contrary to what had publicly been said then?

For his part, Paddy was preparing better both mentally and physically than he had for the Edinburgh game. We met to discuss the book on both the Monday and Wednesday evenings of that week and he confirmed that it "feels like a proper match week this time." Paddy was out on a pre-arranged evening with some friends on Thursday and that night this writer got a call from a clearly distraught Kirsty, who confided her fears that things would all go horribly wrong.

Throughout his career, she had accepted the risks which went with her partner playing a contact sport and hadn't unduly worried about the possibility of him getting injured, but there must have been some sort of subconscious release of pressure in this respect after his final match in May and now she seemed to be dreading that his going back to the well just once more had the potential to turn their lives upside down. Without putting too fine a point on it, you get the impression she almost had a horror of him coming home in a wheelchair. There was also the (admittedly less catastrophic but statistically more real) danger of defeat spoiling some of the Munster memories, especially with Ulster so understrength.

"I'm sick in my stomach out of fear of Paddy getting injured, can't sleep at night and can barely swallow" said Kirsty that night, going as far as half-hoping aloud that Paddy would pick up food poisoning from his meal out or go down with the tummy bug which was afflicting some members of the Ulster squad. Anything which would prevent him from being on duty the next night. "I've even considered begging him to pull out" she said, with an air of desperation.

All I could say to that was 'do whatever you think is best' but pointed out that, as a man who never shirked a challenge, Paddy would surely take longer to get over a bogus withdrawal, especially if Ulster were let down by a raw substitute second row in the last few minutes of a tight game, than he would being part of a defeat. After all, he had played rugby for a quarter of a century and, while he hated losing, had learnt to cope with it. Two sides take the field and only one can win and all that. By the end of the conversation, Kirsty seemed resigned to Paddy benching against Neath, but would say enough was enough and ask him to draw a line under this saga if she got him home in one piece after the game.

Decimated Ulster, led for the first time by Lions lock Davidson, fought back superbly from 10 points down to get their Celtic League campaign back on track with victory over previously unbeaten Neath at a raucous Ravenhill, where 10,000 fans turned out to support their heroes in their hour of need. Making light of the absence of no fewer than 10 first choice players, the White Knights showed wonderful resolve and character in fighting back from 0-10 down to beat a side which had come to Belfast with three wins out of three under their belts, whereas Ulster by contrast were seeking to avoid a hat-trick of defeats.

The brilliant Bryn Cunningham and Howe each scored great tries on an evening when Davidson responded magnificently to the new responsibility of captaincy with his best game since returning to Ireland, Stewart similarly rose to the occasion in his first full match of the year following a long injury lay-off, McMillan was outstanding, McWhirter battled bravely against flu and halfbacks Larkin and Doak ensured the loss of Humphreys and Wallace wouldn't be catastrophic by filling in well in the No 10 jersey and place-kicking role respectively, the latter contributing seven points to a 17-13 win. A night for heroes in white.

After the match, Solomons, who had kind of promised Paddy some game-time, asked him to bench again against old rivals Munster the following Friday and assured him he would definitely get a run then. Although such a course of action would be fraught with risk, all Paddy's instincts were to play against the old enemy and he provisionally agreed, only to later have a full and frank discussion with Kirsty (who had attended the Neath game but looked pretty frazzled) which revealed the full extent of her concerns. His mother too was dead against this comeback, however temporary, pointing out that, as a dentist, he could not afford to injure his fingers. Unlike the other guys in the squad, he was no longer a professional, but was relying on a job as a dentist and had a wife and four small children to support.

We talked at some length about all of these matters on the Saturday evening, when Paddy sought my views, asking among other things what was 'best for the book'. Just as his friends 'wouldn't have dared' advise him on retirement, this writer shied away from presuming to suggest what he should do, but asked him to reflect on two issues. Firstly, could he package off these few weeks as separate from his career and, if the unthinkable happened and he was on the pitch when the whistle went on an Ulster defeat against Munster (and there are no guarantees in life), not allow that to take the gloss off his last official match in May. Secondly, could he be sure that he wasn't getting too much of a taste for the action again, with the potential of it making him regret his initial decision to retire and thus unravelling his conversion to 'civilian' life.

In response to the first point, he assured me that he had ended his rugby career on a high note in May and that nothing could unpick either that moment or the rightness of his decision to retire. He was merely helping out Ulster and Solomons and was pretty sanguine about how things worked out. If he played against Munster the following weekend, of course he would bust a gut in pursuit of victory. But a defeat wouldn't ruin his life. So both tests had been passed. Regarding the book, there was the danger of rather spoiling the script set against the advantage of him being back briefly in the limelight in the lead-up to publication. Either way though that should have been, and was, a very minor consideration.

Kirsty rang on Monday to say that, over the weekend, she and Paddy had done a lot of talking, both between themselves and with Solomons, and that a compromise had been reached, namely that the Munster match would be the last time he would be asked to bench and that he would only be brought on in the event of TWO injuries in the back five of the pack. She wasn't entirely happy, but fingers crossed nothing happened on Friday night and this would definitely be the end. Incidentally, Solomons was a little more vague about those commitments in a book interview on the eve of the match, only saying he 'hoped' this was the last time Paddy had to be asked and expressing his view that he would 'do a good job' if called upon! Bell, Kempson and Sexton returned but Davidson kept the captaincy and, while Humphreys and Longwell were on Ireland duty, Munster were missing Henderson, O'Gara, Stringer, Hayes, Foley and Quinlan for that reason, while David Wallace, O'Connell and Anthony Horgan were long-term lay-offs and both skipper Jim Williams and hooker Sheahan withdrew from the match due to injury. But the tables had been turned the other way in May when decimated Ulster beat a virtually full strength Munster. Anyway, the visitors still had eight full internationals in their starting line-up including Mick Galwey, who had resumed the captaincy he had relinquished in the summer with a view to taking a step back on the playing side, Eddie Halvey and Mike Mullins.

Doak had the night of his life as Ulster came back from 9-17 down to ensure Munster left Ravenhill empty-handed for the second time in five months. The Ireland A pivot, who had scored the winning try in the May match, bagged a brace of tries, converted them both and kicked four penalties to haunt Galwey's men along with Johns who rolled back the years to play his part and was rewarded with a second farewell victory over the old enemy in front of a capacity crowd. Paddy thought he had bowed out on the ultimate high in May, but this victory really put the icing on the cake for Ulster's stalwart servant. His impact on the last quarter helped tip the scales decisively in Ulster's favour on a night when the pack, with Fitzpatrick storming right back into Ireland contention, were magnificent.

Doak slotted over a penalty within two minutes of the start to reward Ulster's urgency and enterprise in attacking relentlessly in wave after wave right from kick-off until the visitors cracked. Things were looking very different 10 minutes later, however, Munster having suddenly rattled up 11 points without reply to reduce the Ravenhill roar to stunned silence. It all started when Halvey, a summer signing from London Irish and playing in the unaccustomed position of No 8 in the absence of Foley, Williams and Wallace, grabbed a bouncing ball at the second kick-off and surged into the 22. Ulster withstood the initial siege, helped by a great Howe tackle, and the ball finally came back on the home side, but precocious fullback Staunton fielded Larkin's rather aimless kick and dropped a goal.

On nine minutes, Munster again got the break of the ball, Killian Keane's chip ahead being allowed to bounce and sitting up perfectly for Jason Holland. He flipped it to Shannon youngster Mossie Lawlor, who crossed wide out for a try. The Munster scoring spree still wasn't finished, however, Staunton adding a long range penalty to extend the lead to eight points with 12 minutes played. Ulster tried to respond off some typical midfield magic by Constable, but the move perished on the rock of over-ambitious passing and it was not until midway through the half that Doak narrowed the gap with a penalty.

Ulster enjoyed a period of pressure but left the Munster half with nothing and were then hit by a double whammy in the shape of Holland's drop goal and McWhirter's sinbinning for repeatedly punching young Denis Leamy. Topping went off injured to be replaced by the emerging Young. Doak missed a very difficult penalty from long range near the right touchline but quickly reduced the arrears to five points with a successful strike from straighter. Again, frustratingly, Ulster immediately gave away points at the other end, Staunton knocking over a penalty, but there was still just enough time for the hosts to claim a much-needed try before the break.

The captain made inroads into the 22 and his fellow forward took it on until a chink appeared in the defence and Doak sniped through before stretching over for a try which he converted with the last kick of the half. Apart from the practical value of the seven points, the try couldn't have come at a better moment in terms of the psychological boost. Doak failed with an ultra-ambitious penalty from a foot inside the Munster half five minutes into the second period but some scintillating scuttling and scampering by the classy Constable constantly kept Munster on their toes and the crowd on the edge of their seats.

Davidson departed injured on 58 minutes, the curse of the captaincy striking again, but Ulster couldn't have summoned a more willing and able replacement to give heart and soul than the skipper's old mentor and accomplice Patrick Johns. Doak's dream night continued when he rounded off a great backline move by looping round to cross by the corner flag after a flat pass to Bell in midfield had originally set the White Knights in motion. He curled over a superb touchline conversion for good measure to put Ulster 23-17 up with 16 minutes left.

A clean catch by Johns, the mighty pack's 15 metre rumble and Larkin's half break in midfield was followed by the former Irish captain crucially getting there to hit a ruck and secure the hosts the put-in. They were penalised at the scrum, but the magnificent pack soon won back possession and Larkin popped the ball into touch in the corner. Ulster lost Bell to injury, but Doak hammered home another penalty to take his tally to 26 points and give his side a two score cushion with three minutes remaining. A magnificent cover tackle by big Paddy on Keane turned over possession in the Ulster 22 and the ball was laced downfield to touch. Doak missed with another very long range penalty attempt and there were nearly seven minutes of injury-time to endure, but the Red Handers held out heroically.

Another fairytale ending for Paddy Johns and, as Solomons said afterwards, no more than he deserved. From coming on with Ulster 16-17 down, his own contribution was immense and his match stats have become the stuff of legend in the squad. A tackle count of seven in 22 minutes was simply phenomenal. "You want to see Paddy's stats, mate" enthuses Constable. "For the 20 minutes he was on, he made seven tackles, which put him high up the team tackle count chart for the game as a whole. Everyone was embarrassed!"

No wonder Davidson had no concerns about the fiercely focused man he met before he had hobbled across the touchline. Paddy could hardly get the tracksuit off quickly enough as he chomped at the bit to enter the fray.

"You never like having to come off injured, but both myself and Alan Solomons had every confidence that if Paddy was called upon he would deliver in spite of having been out of it. We knew the hunger would be there and that he would still be good enough.

I was sat there with a smile on my face watching the way he was going and was delighted at the end that he had another win over Munster to his name. Both his willingness to help out at all and then his performance when he came on say an awful lot about the man. How many guys do you know who could have done what he did?" asks Jeremy in a manner which clearly indicates he sees it as a rhetorical question.

Justin Fitzpatrick too is full of admiration for how Johns carried the standards he set in his career into this little comeback cameo. "As a loosehead, you build quite a relationship with your second row, in that he is packing down behind you and you're lifting him at the front of the lineout. Paddy is an uncompromising scrummager and playing with him a few Friday nights back against Munster, it was like nothing had changed. He's as strong as an ox in behind you. I'd still happily pack down with Paddy Johns against anyone. Anytime. Anywhere."

Doak, one of a number of players to list Johns as their 'most respected opponent' in the squad's player profile forms, had done Paddy proud for a second Munster match running. "Over the last year Neil has really pushed himself forward and he was superb against Munster this time" praises Paddy. "When Alan Solomons came in, Brad Free was in possession, but he has forced his way in. Neil keeps his head down and works very hard and the goal-kicking is an extra string to his bow."

Paddy had enjoyed every minute on the pitch and, naturally, was elated with the result. He'd had his fairytale ending all over again, but for the rest of the weekend, there was a lot of anxiety that the price could be high and that his mother's fears might have been realised. Neither Mrs Johns had attended the game, his mum boycotting on a point of principle in that she didn't agree with him playing again, and Kirsty absent largely because she and Paddy were due to leave early the following morning for a wedding in Tipperary, though it must be said that she'd found the previous Friday night unbearably tense. So they tuned in anxiously to the live coverage on Irish language channel TG4, hoping and praying for the right result and that Paddy would walk away unscathed. Of course, as sod's law decreed, he had barely arrived on the pitch until he was needing treatment.

"After all the talk about my fingers, it was a remarkable quirk of fate that I should dislocate one about 30 seconds after coming on. Our physio, Gareth Robinson, came on and strapped it up, but I dislocated it again later in the game and was a bit worried that there was a break. It was quite sore on Saturday, but considering that we spent the day at a wedding in Munster, I think it would have been much more painful going down there if we'd lost! I went for an x-ray when I came back on Sunday evening and, although there wasn't a doctor there to read it, I had a look myself and couldn't detect a fracture so that was a relief. I found out for sure the following day when I phoned Lawrence Rocke (Rocky) that there was indeed no fracture."

Once that scare was cleared up, those close to him could sleep easily knowing that this time it really was all over after one last remarkable twist in the tale of a remarkable career. Longwell was available for the following weekend's 67-15 Celtic League rout of Caerphilly and then it was into the European Cup, for which Paddy was not a member of the registered squad. Davidson has had injury problems in the early weeks of that tournament and Nelson is still sidelined, as is Ward, but with young McCullough fit again and Best there as backrow cover, Ulster, who have again reached the quarter-finals of the Celtic League, are getting by.

At one level though, it is alarming that Solomons, while preaching youth policy and the future, felt he had simply no option but to drag Johns out of retirement this autumn. In truth the situation in the province is particularly bad in second row depth, but generally gone are the days when a mature club player could be pushed into the provincial side in the absence of a couple of regulars. Professionalism has widened the gap and, these days, the only options which seem to be considered beyond the core contracted squad are the cream of the young talent. It isn't a problem unique to Ulster though as Swansea's summoning of Robert Jones to sit on their bench last season or Toulouse's overtures to a retired Peter Clohessy this term confirm. A retired proven player is less out of the loop than the club journeyman.

And Paddy's comeback cameo underlined the point. Where someone else may have looked out of their depth and floundered, he made an immediate impact and also was able to bring his great experience to bear. Like at a lineout soon after he came on. "Everyone was getting a bit over-excited and there were about three calls came in" he reveals. "I said to Shieldsy, 'let's keep it simple here with a throw to the front and we'll drive it'. So that's what we did and we made a lot of ground." No wonder coaches return to the tried and trusted, especially when their backs are against the wall.

Yet it still seems remarkable that a player can slip so seamlessly back into such a high level of rugby after being out of the game completely, albeit just for a few months. "Just like knowing in my own mind that I could have pulled on a Test jersey right up until the end of my career and given a good account of myself, I knew that I had the ability and the fitness to not let myself down if called upon in these few games this autumn, even though I'd be up against guys who had done a full pre-season and been playing regularly. I wasn't fully prepared for Edinburgh, but did 21 50s without stopping on the Monday night of the Neath week and felt strong. For Munster, I did 10 150s and five 250s.

"Although it was a strange experience and a bit surreal, I enjoyed being involved and the adrenalin was there, but these last few weeks certainly haven't bred discontent about my decision to retire at the end of last season. It was nice to give a hand for the Red Hand, so to speak, and nice to be involved in the win over Munster, which was a very important result for the team, but I can honestly say that I felt retired and looking in. In fact, it has reinforced in my mind that I have indeed moved on and that playing on for another season would have been the wrong choice. Beating Munster was a high, but I was glad not to be going to Caerphilly the following weekend, instead doing some mountain-biking in the morning and then heading over to Dungannon with the kids. That's where I am now." All's well that ends well.

40. THE JOHNS OSCARS

It may surprise some people that Ireland's two superstars of the professional era, Keith Wood and Brian O'Driscoll, don't make it into Paddy's Select XV of all those whom he played with during his career. O'Driscoll loses out to the French master Philippe Sella, a Saracens stablemate of Johns in the late 1990s, while Paddy has gone for his tried and trusted fellow Dungannon stalwart Allen Clarke in the middle of the front row.

As sports fans, we all love to play at being selectors, but, having played with and against most of the world's top players at some of the best sporting venues for over a decade, Paddy is better qualified than most to nominate his 'Dream XV'. It was decided to restrict the eligible pool of players to those whom Johns has actually appeared on the same side as; otherwise it would effectively have been a World XV 1988-2002, for he has lined out against all of the leading nations. Rather than specifying what he thought was a theoretical 'Best XV' from those eligible, Paddy's emphasis has been on picking the line-up which he personally would like to take into battle. The assumption was that he would wear the No 4 jersey and captain the side, though he has chosen to defer that honour to Francois Pienaar.

The Paddy Johns XV reads:
Conor O'Shea (IRELAND)
Ryan Constable (AUSTRALIA)
Philippe Sella (FRANCE)
Scott Gibbs (WALES)
Simon Geoghegan (IRELAND)
Michael Lynagh (AUSTRALIA)
Gary Armstrong (SCOTLAND)
Nick Popplewell (IRELAND)
Allen Clarke (IRELAND)
Paul Wallace (IRELAND)
Paddy Johns (IRELAND)
Jeremy Davidson (IRELAND)
Francois Pienaar (SOUTH AFRICA, capt)
Richard Hill (ENGLAND)
Philip Matthews (IRELAND)

Selection is subjective and, as with all team selections, some of Paddy's choices may raise a few eyebrows or be vehemently disagreed with by others, but that only serves to generate yet more healthy debate as to the relative merits of one player compared with another. Johns says: "It's just my opinion and it may not be right, but out of all the people I've played with this would be my choice to take the field and has the best balance."

"Conor O'Shea had a gaelic upbringing and was always very safe under a high ball, he was also a solid player and a good last line of defence in a position where you need that. He perhaps wasn't as quick as some others like Jim Staples or Gavin Johnson, but as an overall package I think he had it. Philip Rainey was an important member of the great Ulster side of the 1980s, while Welshman Mike Rayer, who I played with for the Barbarians, Ireland's fullback of the early 1990s Kenny Murphy and Charlie Haly, who went to Canada with me in 1987 and with whom I played for a range of Irish representative teams, all deserve a mention.

"On the wings, Ryan Constable and Simon Geoghegan both have blistering pace. Ryan has a fantastic side-step and good hands. He is also a great team player. Simon has that unpredictability and enthusiasm which allowed him to squeeze in through the tightest of corners. I also rated others including Richie Wallace, Scotland's Tony Stanger and Denis Hickie, and was fortunate to have started before those two great Ulster and Irish wingers, Trevor Ringland and Keith Crossan, finished.

"Although I chose both my centres on their individual merits, I think that overall they also provide a great balance. All I can say about Sella is, '111 caps'. Nobody achieves that without being a special player. We've already talked about him in the book. I considered Ryan at 13, but Philippe just had to get it. Someone like Brian O'Driscoll could surpass him over the next few years. He definitely has a lot more still to offer, but Sella was an immaculate player and proved himself at the top level for such a long period of time.

"Scott Gibbs, with whom I played for the Baabaas, at his best was just what you want at No 12. He could crash it up with a few bodies hanging off him and was very, very powerful. Together I think they exhibit the qualities you want from your centres. Other centres at the forefront of my mind in an exercise like this are Scot Hastings, Wallaby Pat Howard, Small McCall, Maurice Field, Jonny Bell and the two Irish Triple Crown centres, Brendan Mullin and Michael Kiernan, who were still around when I made my Test debut. I also rated Philip Danaher and Mike Mullins.

"My outhalf was always going to be Michael Lynagh. He's one of those players that you can mention in any rugby circle and everybody knows who he is and respects what he has achieved. He just controlled games: awesome. I don't think that there's ever, and I know that's a big statement, been a No 10 as good. In any other circumstances, I'd be happy to choose David Humphreys or Eric Elwood, both of whom I rate very highly, while Brian Smith and Alain Penaud also merit a mention, but Lynagh was special." Indeed the Wallaby outhalf was once fittingly described by Bob Dwyer as 'the Don Bradman of rugby union'.

"I picked Gary Armstrong at No 9 because of all the problems he caused me against Scotland! You always had to watch what he was up to, but obviously he was great to play with, which I did when on Barbarians duty. A very gutsy player. The other scrumhalf nominations would be Rab Brady (the Ulster stalwart unlucky not to win an Ireland cap in the 1980s), Michael Bradley with whom I played a lot for Ireland, the current Irish pivot Peter Stringer, Ulster's Neil Doak, Andy Matchett and Ashley Blair, and former Saracens team-mate Kyran Bracken."

And so to the forwards . . .

"A few eyebrows might be raised at my back row, but basically, I just wanted all three of these players included in my XV. They are all very strong individuals both physically and mentally and they've all captained sides, which I think illustrates their mental edge. When you put them all together, you've got every quality you could want. Richard Hill was perhaps a bit quieter than the other two, but you could tell he was there mentally, and when he spoke people listened. Francois would be my captain. He was an excellent motivator and very intense. He was one of those people with an aura about them and where he led, you'd follow.

"There are no shortage of backrowers with whom I've been fortunate enough to play who merit a mention in an exercise like this. Had I not wanted to get a third flanker into the side, a pure No 8 contest would have been between Scott Quinnell, another Barbarians link along with All Black Aaron Pene, my Saracens colleague Tony Diprose, two Irish internationals from the earlier part of my career, Noel Mannion and Brian Robinson, Ulster's Tony McWhirter, and Barry Walsh with whom I played Irish representative rugby.

"My first choice partner in the second row would be Jeremy (Davidson). I feel he complements me best. For a start he's a natural number four jumper! He's very athletic, with great drive, determination and aggression. We trust each other and get on very well together and that always helps. I think my main qualities which I'd bring to this team are perseverance and work-rate. I'm a very bad looser, but I like to think that what I lacked in ability, I made up for in effort. Then again, that's for other people to say," Paddy says meekly. "You'd also have to be looking at Frenchman Olivier Roumat, Wallaby Rod McCall, my regular Saracens partner Danny Grewcock, Neil Francis, Willie Anderson, Malcolm O'Kelly, Mick Galwey and Gary Longwell.

"Again, my front row are all superb individuals, but I also think that they happen to provide an excellent mini-unit. When you were behind Poppy, it was like you didn't need to push at all. He was so strong I think he could have held the whole scrum up on his own! Paul Wallace was also very strong and solid as well as being technically a very good tighthead. Other props in the frame include Justin Fitzpatrick, Peter Clohessy, Roberto Grau, Jimmy McCoy, Gary Halpin and also Colin Ramsey, whom I played with at Dungannon.

"Sniffer's at hooker. Obviously we played together for a very long time and we had that relationship on the pitch. He is always on target with his lineout throwing and he played well beyond his weight and size. Keith Wood's exceptional abilities have been talked about in earlier chapters, but sometimes when he roamed about the field, popping up on the wing or at centre, it left the remaining forwards with a lot more tight work. Beyond those two, I'd look at Stevie Smith, Terry Kingston, John McDonald and Johnny Murphy, who won his only cap when I won my second, against Australia in 1992."

As well as playing alongside many good players as the above teamlist confirms, Johns has also faced some formidable opponents, including double Lions captain Martin Johnson. "When I talk to anyone they hate him" says Paddy, "but he and I get on ok. He's a fairly quiet guy and there is not much controversy around him. Dull is not the word, but he wouldn't be the life and soul of the party and neither would I. We were both No 4s and front-jumpers and I never played with him, but it was always a good battle between us at club and international level and I always played well against him. We had a bit of a row one day that we played Leicester at Saracens and there was a picture of me about to hit him. It seemed to be used in the papers anytime we played them thereafter!"

In spite of his jousts with Johnson, it is interesting that Johns cites Scotland's Doddie Weir as being his toughest personal opponent. In world terms, he has played against bigger names, but just like great Test cricket batsmen sometimes produce unexpected answers when asked which bowler gave them the most trouble, Paddy always found the Scot a handful. "When I was in my 20s I really rated Gary Whetton, but Doddy was someone I always had difficulty playing against. I don't know exactly why. There are just some people you always play well against and some you always struggle with, and I always struggled playing against him. I also always rated John Eales, John Langford, Mick Galwey, Frenchman Abde Benazzi and Springbok Mark Andrews as tough opponents in my position. At No 8, Scott Quinnell, Zinzan Brooke, Gary Teichmann and Mark Cecillon of France all stand out."

"The best team I've ever played against was the 1992 Auckland team. They were under Graham Henry at that stage and could have been the All Blacks. Actually, I think they were better that the All Blacks team of the time. Playing against them was like being hit by a tidal wave. They were just bigger, stronger and faster than anything I'd come up against. I'd rate them ahead of either the All Blacks of 1997, about whom so much was said and written, or the Springbok side of 1998 who equalled the record for number of consecutive Test wins."

When asked about his favourite ground, Paddy replies: "Oh, that would be Lansdowne Road, followed by Ravenhill, followed by Stevenson Park! Internationally, I really enjoyed playing at Ellis Park; all the South African stadiums are very impressive. Cardiff Arms Park always had a really good atmosphere whereas Twickenham was always dead, with no atmosphere at all. It was also a big thrill to play at Wembley as it was somewhere I'd seen so many times on television and held a lot of symbolism.

"For support, it's hard to beat a full house at Ravenhill on a Friday night while, at the other end of the scale, the most frenzied atmosphere I've ever played in was when Saracens faced Lydney from the Forest of Dean in the third round of the 1998-99 Tetley Bitter Cup the day after Ulster won the European Cup. Basically, this team was out to hurt as many of us as they could. They were way out of their depth and interested in damage limitation, not playing rugby. I've been spat at from Gloucester's notorious 'Shed' at Kingsholm, but the hostility, even raw hatred, at Lydney, was something else."

In a piece headlined 'Dean of iniquity', Ulster-born Daily Mail correspondent Peter Jackson carries Pienaar's accusations that Lydney fans had tried to "strangle Ireland captain Paddy Johns during an incident unlikely to have been witnessed at a major rugby match before. It happened four minutes into the second half when a touchline brawl involving at least 10 players spilled over into the crowd."

"A couple of spectators leant over the hoarding beside the pitch and grabbed Paddy by the throat" said Pienaar after the game. "They were trying to strangle him but then a couple of our players saw what was happening and got the spectators off Paddy. It all started when someone kicked me in the face. We didn't come here to get involved in any brawl and I wouldn't like to see that sort of thing happen again."

Johns is quoted at the time as saying: "I pulled one of their players towards the hoarding and some bloke grabbed me from behind by the throat. He pulled me back over the railing. Some woman in the crowd was screaming and I was pinned there for 20 or 30 seconds. It was the first time anything like that has ever happened to me." He now adds: "The supporters were getting really worked up and it was quite scary. I was probably only in the headlock for half a minute, but it felt like a long time."

Amazingly, the only player carded in the whole fractious affair was Constable. "A fight erupted around Pienaar" explains Ryan "and I went in to do what I could because he was badly outnumbered. Suddenly there were two of them on me and Paddy came in to help me out. It ended up with him being attacked by the crowd and me being carded, while their players escaped punishment. One of them was warned for punching Paddy early on but, unlike me, didn't get carded. But at least we won 40-0."

Paddy's nominates the 17-3 win over England at Lansdowne Road in 1993 as his greatest ever victory. "That was brilliant. We were such no-hopers going into that game with such huge odds against us and in the end we annihilated them!" The following year's repeat at Twickenham, ending the French famine by winning in Paris on St Patrick's weekend in 2000, leading Ireland to victory over Wales at Wembley in 1999 and taking part in the respective Cup final romps for Saracens and Dungannon would all be in a memorable top 10.

Paddy has been involved in a few 70-point wins, the first of them for Royal School Dungannon Under 14s against Royal School Armagh, alma mater of one of the authors, and then in Test matches against Georgia and Japan, but routine wins even by record scores are never as sweet as hard-fought victories, especially to as competitive a sort as Paddy. His most memorable try is the one which clinched victory for the Barbarians in the Dunblane International, as it came in injury-time and gave him his only win over the Scots, or at Murrayfield. He feels that, at a personal performance level, the win over Wales at Ellis Park in the 1995 World Cup gave him the most satisfaction.

At the other end of the scale, rugby disappointments would include the way in which his Ireland career ended, never beating Scotland in the green jersey, being taken off in Paris when Ireland lost narrowly in 1998, the Irish World Cup defeat against Argentina in Lens three years ago while he sat helplessly in the stand, not passing Willie John McBride's tally of Irish caps, Saracens not taking part in the 1998-99 European Cup and not being part of the Ulster side which won it that season, Ulster just failing to register their first Euro win on English soil at Wasps at the start of this year and, maybe to a degree, not playing club rugby in France. Overall though, the happy times and good memories far outweigh the negatives. He can also laugh at what was probably his most embarrassing gaffe, thanking Scotland in his speech at the Welsh post-match dinner in 1999.

Pienaar is rated by Paddy as his top captain from a list which includes Allen Clarke, Martin Higgins, Stanley Turkington, Willie Milligan, Willie Anderson, Hugh McCaughey, David Irwin, John McDonald, Denis McBride, David Humphreys, Andy Ward, Tony Diprose, Scot Hastings, Donal Lenihan, Philip Danaher, Michael Bradley, Terry Kingston, Nick Popplewell, Niall Hogan, Keith Wood and Dion O'Cuinneagain.

On the two main Ulster captains during the decade of dominance, Johns says: "David Irwin was basically very direct and determined, keen to get stuck in and lead by example. Although a centre, he had a wing forward mentality. There was a feeling in the Ulster team at that time of 'no surrender' and Davy epitomised that. Willie Anderson's teamtalks were blood-curdling stuff and generally involved an imploration to 'bate your opposite number about the scone at the first lineout!'

However Paddy can't, or won't, be pinned down to naming a favourite, or best, coach. "That's not fair!" he declares. "They were all different with different qualities. Declan Kidney was probably the most into the psychological stuff whereas Willie Anderson was an excellent motivator. Alan Solomons was very intense and lived and breathed rugby, so you ended up doing the same. Francois Pienaar was similar, but he was a player/coach, so it was slightly different. Harry Williams was possibly the best at man management and had a very good coaching philosophy. Warren Gatland was very quiet, but had a hard edge. His game plan was simple, but effective. He'd also played at the highest level, and in the modern game, so he understood where the players were coming from, and was very good at getting the best out of the players he had."

Elaborating a little more on some of the coaches he has served under, Johns observes: "Declan Kidney and Niall O'Donovan, as forwards coach, were a good team when I was involved with Ireland A. I found Declan very good on the mental side and player motivation. He will listen to players and there is a feeling of empowerment and being valued. That was a very enjoyable environment and, providing they realise you can't treat adults in quite the same way as children, schoolteachers will have certain skills which are well suited to coaching.

"Harry Williams, another coach from a school-teaching background, is a real gentleman and was a fantastic fella to have in charge of you. I had a lot of respect for him. He's an Ulsterman through and through and, although he didn't have a particularly scientific approach, he certainly knew how to get the most out of his players. He had a very good rugby brain, but liked to keep things simple and easy to understand. 'Get into them and bate all round you' was a bit of a favourite instruction, but he certainly knew what he was doing.

"I don't think either of us had changed that much from the time he was Ulster coach and I was a young player just coming into the squad to when I moved back home in the summer of 1999 and he was in his second spell in charge. He was still himself in spite of the European Cup win earlier that year, still always very nervous before games. Achieving what he did in the first year of his second spell made it difficult for him thereafter. Back in the 1980s, Jimmy Davidson was superb and ahead of his time in terms of approach, but Harry was less intense and undoubtedly got the best out of his players."

Of Willie Anderson, Paddy says: "People looking in from the outside will probably scratch their heads and wonder why Willie has not been used by Ulster. Obviously only one person can be head coach and Alan Solomons is doing a fine job, but surely Ulster rugby could have done with Willie somewhere. Of course there is politics around and the fact that he is very passionate and speaks his mind may have upset some people."

Both Anderson and Irwin were strong influences in the early days of Johns' Ulster career, while he says he also took example from Denis McBride and "would probably have modelled myself on him as much as anyone. He was that little bit older and we travelled together and socialised together during our time in the Irish team. We also trained together a fair bit and I always admired his dedication and resilience. Moss Keane and Ollie Campbell were probably my two rugby heroes, while I always wish I had been able to see the great Willie John McBride play in the flesh."

In additions to captains and coaches, there are other key roles around a rugby team, albeit that those who fill them are generally less heralded or acclaimed. Among those who provide for players' needs are doctors, physiotherapists, masseurs and baggage masters. Among the team physios Paddy has worked with are John Martin, Denise Fanagan, Gareth Robinson, Philip Glasgow, Pat Minder and Mary Shields, with masseurs including Joe Doran, Willie Bennett and Ron Holder. As well as Dungannon's kitman, Brian 'Maxi' Magowan, Ulster trio of Willie Wallace and 'Fast Ed' (Ed Grindle) and Kiwi Glynn Roberts, Paddy has had plenty of dealings with Paddy 'Rala' O'Reilly in his capacity as Ireland team baggage master.

"Rala is the Muhammed Ali of kitmen" insists Paddy. "He's No 1, simply the best. He is so comprehensive in what he has available; you definitely couldn't catch him out. Ask him for anything under the sun and he'll have it in his bag.He takes an awful lot of pride in his job and would do anything for any of the players. Any team which has him will be spoilt rotten. Rala is a fantastically funny guy and an absolute gent. He is very much at the heart of the Irish set-up and has been a real rock there since getting involved in the early 1990s. Definitely part of the furniture and an invaluable asset.

"In his day, Rala was a hooker. One day his team, Terenure, were playing against Garryowen and someone shouted out 'hit No 2' as the call. So Rala took aim and threw the ball against the back of Garryowen hooker Pa Whelan's head as hard as he could! Later, when he finally retired, he went out that night and dug a hole and buried his boots. Of course fate dictated that his team would come looking for him, so he had to go and dig them up again to play the following weekend!"

The closeness of the two Paddies is confirmed by Rala: "Paddy has also had myself and the wife to stay at his home, but before you gain access to the house, you have to go through Christopher's trial by football, cricket and netball in the barn. Only after he was satisfied, were you worthy enough to get into the house. In setting high standards and wanting things done properly, Christopher's a real chip off the old block."

As well as working with many different team officials in his time, Paddy has also encountered plenty of match officials, and rates Alain Rolland, with whom he made his international debut against Argentina in 1990, as being up there with the best. "I particularly rated Welsh official Clive Norling, while Frenchman Joel Dume was the best craic".

41. LET OTHERS DO THE TALKING

Let others do the talking. It could almost have been the title for this book. Paddy Johns has always been known around rugby as a man of few words, but whose actions spoke loudly. He is also someone about whom there is no shortage of volunteers to pay warm and genuine tribute. We could have filled a whole book in this way instead of a mere chapter, but there are probably only so many ways for people to say what a decent guy Paddy is and what a hard man he was on the rugby field. Pudsey and Dudsey and all that.

"Actually, Paddy has four personas," interjects Richard Wallace. "Pudsey, Dudsey, Funsey and Flirtsy. Flirtsy is long dead – since Paddy met Kirsty. Funsey wasn't around too much, but when he was, you knew about it. Paddy certainly knew how to party when he decided to. Funsey also took the children to the toy department in Hanley's and spent all day playing with the toys whilst pretending it was all for his kids' benefit! On the Irish tour of South Africa, there were the usual penpics in the programme on Paddy and the rest of us. At the end of his paragraph it said "Patrick is known to his friends as 'Paddy'," which we all thought was hilarious as Paddy was known by so many other names."

It's hard to find anyone with a bad word to say about Paddy. 'As hard as nails on the pitch and a gentleman off it' seems to be the general consensus.

"England were playing Ireland at Twickenham a few years ago," recalls the world's most capped forward Jason Leonard. "It had been a very feisty, but good-tempered match. I made a tackle on one of the Irish boys and ended up on the Irish side. To be fair, I didn't really try and move away. The Irish forwards saw this and basically rucked me out of the way, with Paddy being the most enthusiastic of the lot.

"I was wearing neoprene shorts and Paddy rucked me so hard that he tore one leg completely off. I was very lucky that the shorts took the brunt of it and not my actual leg. The ref, who was Derek Bevan, then awarded a penalty against me and gave me a stern look saying 'Don't you complain to me', which I had no intention of doing as I was on the wrong side. Anyway, Keith Wood came up to me after the game and said 'Have you seen Paddy yet? He wants to apologise for what happened on the pitch'. I told him not to be so silly, that it had been my fault and there'd been nothing illegal about it. Keith said that he'd told Paddy I'd be ok about it and knew that it was nothing personal, but that he'd got a bee in his bonnet and wouldn't be talked out of it. Apparently he said 'Jason's a decent fellow, I don't give a f*ck about most of the other English guys!'

"So we went back to the hotel for the post match function, and Paddy was waiting for me in the lobby with Kirsty. It took me five or 10 minutes to convince him that I was ok physically and ok generally with what had happened. The guy is an absolute gentleman; a very hard, uncompromising rugby player, but an absolute gentleman. Whether for club or country, he always gave 100 percent and you always knew Paddy was on the pitch, but come the final whistle, he would shake your hand and have a quiet pint in the clubhouse."

"We were talking about the book one day after Ulster training and laughing amongst ourselves" says another prop, Ireland's Justin Fitzpatrick. "Paddy's such an enigma. There are not enough words in the dictionary to describe what a quietly-spoken, likeable gentleman he is. Then there's Johns the rugby player: the ultimate competitor, the very force of nature.

"I mean, what stories there are which capture his hardness and how uncompromising he was. It is a side of rugby that's well known, but Paddy really stood out. Thankfully I've only played against him once, but still managed to get a smack for my troubles. It was just before the summer of 1998 when my team, London Irish, played Paddy's side, Saracens, away from home in the English Premiership. We were trying to avoid relegation and they were going for the double.

"Paddy had just been named Irish captain and I'd been named in the squad for the tour of South Africa. I was a young boy still to win my first cap, whereas he was a seasoned international of many years standing. I had met Paddy a few times, including the first time I worked with him properly, which was when I benched in Bologna for Ireland's Test against Italy earlier that season. It certainly wouldn't go down in history as a great Irish performance, but Paddy actually played one of the best games which I have ever seen a second row play. So anyway I knew him a little, but not that well.

"London Irish had a particularly good lineout at the time, with three Ireland second rows in Jeremy Davidson, Malcolm O'Kelly and Gabriel Fulcher. Jeremy was injured that day, so Mal and Gabriel were playing. We were very effective in those days in targeting the opposition throw and had been working hard on stealing the other side's ball. Paddy would have known this, because he studies hours and hours of tapes of games, really pouring over them and trying to work out every aspect of the opposition, including tactics, strengths and weaknesses.

"So at one stage Saracens had a lineout outside their own 22 and threw to Grewcock in the middle, leaving Paddy, who was positioned as usual at the front, free to make menace and mischief. Just before we went to put up Fulcher, I saw this fist coming. It smacked me on the side of the right eye, which proceeded to puff up and close. That was my welcome to the touring squad, my introduction to Paddy Johns! Fortunately it was my one and only time to play against him, though there's no REAL truth in the suggestion that the main reason Humph, myself and others joined Dungannon and Ulster was to make sure we were always on the same side as him!" laughs Fitzy.

As well as Richie Wallace's four persona versions of Johns, Fitzpatrick says that his colleagues have divided into three categories those who play against Paddy. "Firstly, there are his mates. That's almost worst, for he goes out to play very hard against them just to prove that he's professional enough to leave friendships on the sideline. Secondly, there are the guys who have annoyed him in previous games and who he goes looking for. They've nowhere to hide. Thirdly and finally, there's the biggest category, which is basically everyone else who wasn't in either of the first two, and he just goes bloody hard against them too! So no-one escapes Johnsie!"

"My first impression of Paddy is when I was an 18-year old and Queen's were playing Trinity at home in 1991" says David Humphreys. "Paddy ran over me three or four times and took lumps out of people all over the place! He is the hardest player never to get caught. I could not speak highly enough of Paddy as a player and a person," while Ulster coach Alan Solomons adds: "We've all known him to be an extremely feisty character, but off the pitch extremely different. He's one of the finest individuals I've ever come across."

Ireland flyhalf Humphreys also recalls an incident in Dungannon's AIL semi-final victory at Galwegians last year when Paddy came to his rescue after spotting him being held in a headlock by an opposing backrow forward, with some rough treatment about to be meted out. Johns arrived and hit Humphreys' assailant so hard that David, pinned against the Galwegians guy, winced when he felt the force of the punch through the body of his captor! "He is a psycho on the pitch" agrees Maurice Field, "but an honest psycho, not a Judas. He is prickly, all elbows and knees. A nightmare in defensive drills, and it didn't matter which side you were on. Half the time he took his own team out!"

Michael Reid, Johns' boss in his capacity as Ulster Branch Chief Executive, says: "I've never seen anyone more different on the pitch and off it. Years ago, when he was at Trinity and I was coach of Collegians, we went down to Dublin to play them. He rucked one of my players in the shoulder area and I was furious but, when I told my father (the late Ken), he just laughed knowingly." Johns' Dungannon mentor Willie Anderson concurs: "When Paddy crossed the whitewash he was a different guy and would have given anything for the cause."

A big admirer of Johns is long-serving Ulster stalwart Tony McWhirter who, growing up, was able to look to Paddy as a role model, both as a second row/No 8 and a dentist. "I always followed his career and, in these past few years, it has been an honour and a pleasure to play with him for Ulster. He came back and fitted in at Ravenhill like he'd never been away. But while I've been grateful for the chance to play with him, I can't say I regret the fact that, because we've both been Dungannon and Ulster, I don't get the opportunity to play against him. Thankfully I've never actually been on opposing sides in a match, but can remember as a young player attending my first Ulster squad session back just before he went to England. He was very nice and welcoming and all that, but at the end of the evening, we split up for a bit of opposed stuff and of course he was in the team and I was in the rabble. I remember trying to steal a ball from the back of a ruck and getting absolutely mullered!"

Although largely standard for a second row, the striking thing about Paddy for the rest of the population is his sheer size. Award-winning News Letter Travel Editor Geoff Hill was on the China charity walk with him earlier this year and memorably wrote, in the first of his series of articles, ". . . they included rugby international Paddy Johns, who was 6'6" in every direction you cared to look. Paddy was not so much built like an outside toilet as a whole terrace of them. I had arrived at the queue for the flight to Istanbul thinking there was a total eclipse, only to find it was because I was standing behind him!" Add his physical dimensions to that hard reputation on the rugby field and it is a pretty daunting combination, yet to children he really is the archetypal gentle giant.

"I took my daughter Rebecca to see him when he was working in Carrickfergus," recalls former Ireland colleague Maurice Field. "She was only three or four years old and was sitting in the dentist's chair with Paddy's huge hands in her mouth. He was being so gentle and yet the night before he'd been knocking the b*ll*cks out of people!" Adults, meanwhile, find him gracious, good-mannered, genuine and thoughtful in all his dealings.

"Paddy is a very warm and genuine guy," enthuses his good friend Greg Lynch. "If you needed anything, he'd help you out. He was a great help to me as a club coach with information regarding latest thinking in the professional game. I wouldn't ever want to cross him on the pitch though!" "I'd see him knocking people over and never taking a backwards step in matches," says Richie Wallace, "and then he'd come up and speak to you in his soft Northern Irish accent with no venom in his voice. His off the pitch persona just didn't match his playing one."

The contrast has often been written about. In a feature to mark Paddy's 50th cap, Irish Times correspondent Gerry Thornley tackled the apparent contradiction. "One of the great mysteries is how someone so correct and precise, so self-effacing and so soft spoken to the point where it seems he is whispering, becomes an aggressive, abrasive enforcer-type figure on the pitch" he wrote. "Apparently, within the team environment he's spitting venom by the Thursday. According to (Ireland manager Donal) Lenihan, this beast within the gentle giant was always there, it's only been noticed more of late.

Thornley then quotes Lenihan as saying: "He is a Jekyll and Hyde character, there's no question about that. I remember one Munster-Ulster interpro, going back 10 years, and taking a short penalty and this fella coming in and halving me. I remember catching my ribs and looking around to see who it was, and I couldn't believe it when it was Paddy Johns, because he certainly never had the reputation."

"So what comes over you, Paddy?" asked Thornley, to which Johns, who also points out that rugby is a good way of getting rid of adrenalin, replies: "What comes over me? I'm the same person on and off the field, but when I go to the restaurant or the pub, I'm not going to be in a contact situation unless someone spills a beer over me. And rugby is a contact sport. You can either be aggressive or not. You've got to be able to look after yourself."

And how! He could do that alright. Right from the early days it seems. "Paddy was never shy when it came to boots or fists" reveals his old Dungannon Royal team-mate John Gamble. "In general there is little fisticuffs or boots in schools rugby, but Paddy would have stuck the shoe in alright, and sorted out anyone. By the time we got into Sixth Form, he had grown into such a gentleman, but had also developed a very hard side on the pitch. A real Jekyll and Hyde."

His former Ireland coach Warren Gatland says: "Paddy's a great guy though, when it came to rugby, he did have a bit of a nasty, mean streak in him. I can remember when we'd be reviewing the tapes of games he would be adding up the opportunities which he had missed to shoe people!"

Keith McGarry, who as Dungannon outhalf in the old Senior Cup dominating side, received the same form of personal Paddy protection as his successor Humphreys did in more recent years, reveals that sometimes a look from Johns was sufficient to put the fear of God in either team-mates or opponents. "When he told you what he wanted, you did it, especially if it was accompanied by 'the look'. You only had to be told once. I'd have been his best buddy, but that wouldn't have got me off the hook.

"I remember us playing Cork Con one year. Jeremy Davidson had the flu and Willie Anderson had to come out of retirement and play himself. We won, but I remember Paddy admonishing Stan McDowell. Stan must have been on the Red Bull or something, for he was just bursting for the ball all the time, constantly coming charging into the line from fullback and dropping it more often than not. He finally spilled one from which they broke away and scored. Next thing you hear, right in the middle of Temple Hill is 'Don't give him the f*cking ball!'. Paddy's wishes were duly complied with! This writer can recall Gannon's impetuous scrumhalf Stephen Bell being reprimanded for taking a quick tap in one AIL game during the trophy winning run the season before last.

"There was another time we were playing Shannon, a fairly fractious game which we lost by a single point. I will never forget the fact that I hit the post twice in the match, but equally remember Paddy looking out for all of us and giving a guy an almighty dig on my half" says Keith.

But, while he can relate plenty of tales which strengthen the concept of Johns as a real enforcer figure, McGarry has even more stories which capture the thoughtfulness and generosity of Paddy and illustrate what a kindly, generous and considerate nature he has and what a gentleman he is.

"Paddy is a lovely big fella, totally straight in his dealings and without any hidden agendas. He's so kind and thoughtful. My wife, Lindsay, once spent a year in Australia and she absolutely loved the place. When Paddy was touring Down Under in 1999, Lindsay joked that she'd love to go with them as team nurse. He turned up at our house after the tour and gave her a Wallaby jersey. It was a real one which he had swapped his Irish one for after one of the Tests." Just as well Paddy won 59 caps, considering the number of jerseys which he gave away either to friends or to support good causes! "Talking of Australia, when Paddy had Michael Lynagh staying at his mum's house a few years ago, he invited me over to meet him because he knew that I regarded him as the best outhalf in the world and that I'd think it was wonderful" continues McGarry. "Paddy played with some fantastic outhalves such as Lynagh and David Humphreys and Eric Elwood, but would have worked as hard for me as his Dungannon No 10 as he would for any of them. He'd even wait behind after training when I was staying on to practise my kicking. Absolutely tremendous. On and off the pitch, he'd treat everyone exactly the same, rather than making a difference on the basis of how 'important' someone was.

"My mother recalls meeting a lady in Dublin who, when she heard where she was from, told her that her two teenage daughters thought Paddy was wonderful. Apparently he had been somewhere where these girls had been shoved out of the way and intervened. I also remember him clearing a path for a gentleman in a wheelchair in the foyer of the Berkeley Court one of those chaotic evenings following an international.

He is the sort of person who would have noticed a situation and would have acted.

"His manners too are legendary. For my dad's 60th birthday, we got Paddy to get a signed picture of the team. Naturally my dad, who loves his rugby, was absolutely delighted and wrote Paddy a thank-you letter. Paddy wrote back and thanked him for the thank-you letter! "Paddy doesn't suffer fools, but is totally loyal and would be as protective of you as a friend as he would of you as a team-mate. Nothing is too much trouble for you and you know that if any trouble befell you, he'd be there. It is genuine concern too. I remember him ringing me this summer when Jeremy Davidson's mum died and being really cut up about it himself on Jeremy's behalf. The man is extremely caring and sensitive.

"There are so many more stories which could be told. Everyone has similar examples of Paddy's behaviour. His friend Greg Lynch and I had a conversation along these lines the night of his retirement game in April. I also bumped into Rala, the Irish team bagman, in a hotel last February when staying in Dublin the night before going on holidays and we'd also had this sort of conversation, telling similar stories to each other and sort of nodding in recognition of the episodes being so Paddy" says McGarry.

"Paddy is a real gentleman's gentleman" confirms Rala, aka Paddy O'Reilly. "The morning after his 39th cap against France in Paris, he rang me in my room and asked me to come up to his. When I went up, Paddy presented me with his playing jersey, shorts and socks. I was really touched and dumbfounded for a long time. I thought 'this is a great man'. For me the 1998 tour of SA will be how I always remember Paddy. Our team song was Lucky Man by The Verve and it was the most enjoyable tour with a brilliant atmosphere, with Paddy as a great captain. He bought me two wooden elephants, like bookends, on that trip and they are on my mantelpiece at home."

Paddy's very close friend from schooldays, Andy Oliver, also admits to having often been on the receiving end of the big man's kindness and benefited from his thoughtfulness. "If Paddy had never been a rugby player, he'd still deserve to be talked about in a book as a great man" insists Andy. "I just can't speak highly enough of him. He's the most genuine fella I know and I've known him a long time, yet it still amazes you the bit extra he does.

"I travel a lot and, when I was away for six months earlier this year, he used to ring my parents every week or 10 days to check if they were alright. Like all of my generation's parents, they're getting on a bit in age, and it was good of him to keep in touch with them. Paddy is also very organised, unlike me, and persistent. He got himself a pension plan a while back and kept at me and kept at me that I should get one too. I didn't get round to it, so finally he made the appointment for me to see someone about it!"

Paddy's good at taking the time to call people. The story about Andy's parents isn't in isolation. Mark McCall says: "Paddy has a huge amount of humanity and is always thinking of other people. When I was at London Irish, he'd often be on the phone to me, just to ask how things were going. Paddy was always a gentleman and very polite from the first time I met him. He was quite conservative in his earlier days but, although he became more rounded the more he mixed, he never lost those good qualities or grew away from the basic decency he exhibited back then."

Meanwhile, Michael Reid relates how Paddy was the "first person on the phone" to his father Ken after the late, great rugby administrator was awarded the OBE a couple of years ago. Courtesy, saying thank-you, humility, modesty, thoroughness and attention to detail are all among Johns' good points. No wonder Solomons observes that he "obviously has been very well brought up."

"When he was doing his charity walk in China earlier this year, we gave him two framed jerseys to go towards his fund-raising and you'd think we'd given him the crown jewels" recalls Reid with a shake of the head. "He couldn't thank me enough and even bought flowers for my wife. He is so humble. Take his retirement game too. It was all about friends and family, not financial gain."

Another of those to encounter Paddy's good manners in the early days was Mark O'Donoghue, a flanker with whom he played for Irish Schools. "I had been used to the schools scene in Munster, so I didn't know quite what to expect when I was rooming with Paddy Johns before the Australia game" relates O'Donoghue. "I was sitting there and Paddy asked me if I'd like some tea. That was fine and he made me tea, although then it struck me that he wasn't having any himself. It was just for me. He was such a gentleman, so polite. I sat there drinking, wondering if Ken O'Connell had been there, whether he would have put the kettle on!"

The thank-you letters, the caring phonecalls and the appreciative gestures, as well as indicating Johns' decency, also signify his thoroughness and attention to detail. A lot of us have good intentions, but never quite get round to putting them into practice, whereas Paddy invariably does. His attention to detail has also been an underpinning theme of his rugby and a factor in him achieving what he did in the game.

"Paddy was a model professional" says Maurice Field. "The fact that he's only just retired is testament to this. He just soaked it all up and loved all the training. Paddy used to prepare for internationals straight after breakfast. He'd go and get taped and would emerge sometime later top to toe in the stuff. Before shoulder pads, this was topped with bubble wrap. It must have scared the opposition when he tackled them and 'popped'!"

"We had a team building weekend with the Irish Army in the Wicklow Mountains in 1999" recalls Denis McBride. "We were doing assault courses and such like and were on the go for about 22 hours solid, most of which David Humphreys spent on his mobile complaining! Anyway, bedtime had almost come and we were split into 8-man tents which we had to erect ourselves. The forwards had a few boy scouts, but the backs were a mess! Once the tents were up, we had to do one final assault course in the dark, camouflaged. We were then transported back to our tents and thrown out of the truck. It was pitch black and Paddy's sleeping bag had a knot in it. He was huffing and puffing because he couldn't open it and was exhausted. The rest of us fell asleep to the sound of Paddy swearing! It was funny, for he was usually the one who was properly sorted."

"Paddy analyses everything and is very precise in every aspect of his life" asserts Justin Fitzpatrick, a view echoed by Gatland. "You couldn't get a more honest and hard-working guy" says the man who made Johns captain of Ireland. "His preparation was always second to none and he left no stone unturned. Paddy is a man of actions, not words, and players saw and responded to the example he set. He was extremely loyal, something

I greatly respect about him, and I found him incredibly receptive to the methods we adopted in the Irish set-up. Whether it was embracing transcendental meditation or being prepared to try fake tan, Paddy was always ready to buy in."

McGarry supplies an amusing anecdote into Johns' questioning nature and constant desire to learn, to push new boundaries, to find ways to improve. "Paddy is very good at sharing new ideas or methods which he comes across and thinks are useful" says Keith. "He is quite evangelical in encouraging his friends to try things which he has discovered and thinks have merit. Even when he was in England and he'd have seen something he thought would be of interest to me in a book, be it on diet or positive thinking or whatever, he'd have bought it and sent it over.

"One day a psychologist Dungannon had hired was relaying a theory about there being six different types of personality and telling us which one he thought applied to each of us. Of course Paddy was right into it and fascinated by it. So when the guy said to him 'you'd be a Questioner, Paddy', he was listening so intently that his immediate response was another question 'why would I be that then?'. Naturally everyone roared with laughter. But that was typical Paddy; he has to get to the bottom of things, can't let them go."

David Hands, Rugby Correspondent of The Times, introduced a feature on Johns in late 1998 by writing: "You can tell a great deal from the study of faces. It does not mean you know the character behind them, but there is a surface quality that hints at the man within. Paddy Johns possesses a pale, slightly drawn countenance, the air of a man who does not have his troubles to seek, but will go to remarkable lengths to sort them out", while in Thornley's Irish Times article on the day of Paddy's 50th cap, former Ireland team doctor Donal O'Shaughnessy is quoted as saying: "Paddy worked with me as a dentist in my health centre and he's a model professional about his dentistry too. He's a very serious man, very diligent. He takes a fair bit of slagging from the other boys but he takes it in good spirit. All you get is a wry smile, nothing else."

A serious man maybe and diligent is his metaphorical middle name, but he can certainly see a joke and is by no means the dull or dour, rather monosyllabic character which may sometimes come across in television interviews. He is droll and, because of his serious image, he can get a lot of value out of telling stories which people don't expect to contain a punch-line until they actually hear it. Rala actually remembers Paddy as something of a prankster in the Irish set-up. "One of my first encounters with Paddy was in the changing room before a Five Nations match. He was strapping his fingers and asked me to cut the tape for him, which I did. At this point he let out a scream and clutched his hand. I thought I'd cut his finger off. Then about two seconds later he started laughing" recounts the long-suffering bagman.

"He also had this long running joke where he used to ask me in the lobby or teamroom or wherever 'What room are you in, Rala' and I'd say 'No 121' or whatever and he'd say 'no you're in the lobby'. The thing was, I fell for it every time. Paddy loves his practical jokes" admits a rueful Rala "Paddy's nickname is Pudsey and, once he gets tickled with something, there really is a childlike quality about him" grins Fitzpatrick. "He just can't stop giggling! Other people may have stopped laughing and the conversation have moved on, but if Paddy has really been amused, he'll still be sitting there chortling away quietly to himself, happy as a sand-boy."

On one occasion though, that inability of Paddy's to sober up again quickly after a fit of laughter had slightly painful consequences for an Irish Schools colleague, according to John Gamble. "Paddy's like a horse braying when he laughs" explains John. "Apparently one time he was away with Irish Schools there was some joke told at which everyone laughed and Paddy started to guffaw. When the laughter died down, Paddy was still guffawing and they then started laughing at him. He didn't take kindly to that and got up and smacked some guy!" Apparently something similar also once happened in New Foundland Pudsey and Dudsey again.

While Paddy may not always have got the public recognition someone of his standing and calibre merited, there was never any lack of respect for him within the game, as Lions prop Paul Wallace is quick to assert. "Everybody has the utmost respect for Paddy. He's a real diehard player and one of the least selfish players I've ever played with. He never really got the recognition he deserves and maybe that's because he's such a team player and is always willing to do the hard work rather than the glamour stuff" said his former Saracens and Ireland colleague. The other imagery which raises its head regularly when discussing Paddy with those he played with is that of him being an ideal man to be with in the trenches.

"When you go into the trenches you want to know that you can rely on the boys you're in with" says McGarry, sentiments echoed by Ryan Constable. "Paddy is the first guy you'd pick if standing in the trench with the whistle about to blow. He's held in very high regard in Dungannon and Ulster and likewise was at Saracens and much further afield. That wasn't just for his ability or achievements on the pitch, but for the way he has of making everyone feel included, fringe players, backroom staff, everyone."

"I cannot speak highly enough of Paddy and his family" says another former Ulster and Saracens colleague Brad Free. "They have always welcomed me to Christmas dinner in the five years I spent with them firstly at Saracens, and then at Ulster. Ryan Constable and myself would offer Christmas gifts to the children and we would always shop for the loudest and most irritating toys to annoy Paddy! The one disappointing thing is that when I came to Ulster I played for a rival team (allocated to Ballymena because Dungannon already had an Ulster-contracted scrumhalf in Stephen Bell) and playing against Paddy is not a thing I enjoy, either from a personal or professional perspective! He has shown enormous loyalty to Dungannon, Ulster and Ireland, and was constantly trying to improve himself."

Ryan adds: "There were a lot of overseas players at Saracens and Christmas caused a bit of consternation for us as it is very much a time to be with family but, Paddy and Kirsty being the people they are, they invited myself, Brad and Roberto Grau and his wife into their home and we enjoyed a traditional Ulster Christmas. It really was much appreciated and helped make the festive period a happy time rather than a lonely one."

Fitzpatrick uses the same metaphor about the trenches as Constable and McGarry, but extends it to lauding Paddy's willingness to lead by example and put himself on the line: "As a captain, Paddy certainly had the total respect of his players. The best analogy I could use is that of an officer at the bottom of the trench, who pushes other guys out of the way so that he himself can go over the top first and bear the brunt of the charge."

"Paddy wasn't very vociferous off the field" says his former Irish skipper and manager Donal Lenihan, "but he underwent a complete metamorphosis on the pitch, where he was a great leader. He is definitely one of the all time heroes of Irish rugby and the perfect gentleman, every mother's dream. He's very much a family man, now he's got the kids. His rugby and his family have been the two big things in his life." Another of Paddy's ex-captains, Saracens' Tony Diprose, adds: "You couldn't meet a nicer couple than Paddy and Kirsty, and he's been the model professional."

The undemonstrative manner but highly respected character of Johns is summed up in a piece by Sunday Life Rugby Correspondent Michael McGeary shortly after Paddy had led Ireland to victory over Wales at Wembley in 1999. "You won't find him backslapping, punching the air or giving the high fives" wrote McGeary. "Instead he will lead by example and, when he speaks with great passion and commitment, the players hang on his every word. If ever a skipper epitomised what was demanded of his team, it was Johns on the day the Irish made Wembley their home. With him, actions will always speak louder than words, leaving him reluctant to dwell on his contribution as captain . . . but unquestionably he has contributed enormously in the role."

So, we know that rugby people everywhere have held Paddy Johns in high regard and that his career stats, especially the 59 Ireland caps, are impressive. But how good was he and what marked him out from the ordinary player? Most pertinently, why did Paddy achieve so much more than most? As has been discussed at some length at various points in the book, determination, desire and dedication were all big factors, while Mark McCall also highlights "consistency: you could rarely have said 'Paddy didn't play well'."

"In Irish terms, he was as good as anyone and held in the utmost regard during my time at Northampton by guys like Martin Bayfield and Tim Rodber" says Allen Clarke, who played with Paddy off and on for two decades. "He was respected around the world as a lineout technician and a very competitive, combative player who would have galvanised any pack."

McWhirter points to Johns' mental and physical durability and how "even towards the end of his career when he had been left out of the Ireland set-up after so long and his confidence took a bit of a bang, it was testament to him that he didn't let his head drop, but kept up his standards, plugged away, continued to believe in working hard and still behaved like a model professional. He'd still have been the first man to arrive for training and the last to leave, while his outstanding comeback against Munster showed both his willingness to help out and what good shape he is keeping himself in since his retirement."

After suggesting that Johns may not have been the most naturally athletic lineout jumper in the world and quoting an un-named Irish player who suggested that 'you'd need a JCB to lift Paddy', Thornley's 50th cap Irish Times article offers a considered critique. "He wins his ball at the front . . . and with experience has become increasingly competitive and effective on the opposition throw" writes Gerry. "Also an honest toiler who hits more than his fair share of rucks and opponents. A trojan workhorse, and every pack still needs one, for it's his type who gives the modern boys some slack."

How does he see it himself? What would he like his legacy to be? "It really is up to others to judge" protests Paddy, "but I'd like to think that I never let my team down and that, while I never stood out like say Brian O'Driscoll or Keith Wood, I was always a sufficient cog in the wheel. As I player I would probably describe myself as 'physical, with a mixture of aggression and work-rate'."

A hard man? "If people wish to portray me as that, that's fine. It isn't a tag that I'd claim for myself, but equally it isn't a description which I would go to any great lengths to try to refute. I suppose the description can either be flattering or a little embarrassing, depending on the context in which it is used. I played the game how I saw it. When I was coming up, people tried to give me a cuff here and there to intimidate me, so I had to learn to look after myself. Starting off in the front five as a young lad, especially because I was coming in from an Irish Schools background, meant that people maybe dished out a bit in my direction, so you have to learn to stand your ground. You harden over the years. Being abrasive and physical were strengths of my game."

"Although a fantastic player by anyone's standards, Paddy would be the first to admit that he wasn't blessed with all the finest skills in the world, but he has been blessed with genuine combat skills and an inner strength and resolve which seems characteristic of people who overachieve" reflects Brad Free. "So to have had the career that he has had reflects the utmost credit upon him."

Gatland though sums up as well as anyone what it was that made Johns special and ensured that he would finish up with an even more exceptional record than his ability alone would have guaranteed. "You can measure how fast someone can run or how much they can lift, but you can't measure what is behind the breastbone or a player's mental approach or what you can get out of your body when you really want to. To my mind those were the things which set Paddy apart, along with a great work ethic" says the Kiwi.

Gatland and Johns appear to have understood each other pretty well and the same applies to the relationship between Paddy and Willie Anderson, another man under whom he enjoyed considerable success. His fellow Dungannon stalwart and predecessor as Irish captain pays warm and fulsome tribute.

"Paddy Johns deserved everything he got in rugby football" says Willie. "He always approached his rugby with a mindset of he owing the game and not it owing him. He had that very honourable attitude and maybe with too many players today, it's the reverse. Paddy would have died for the cause regardless of whether he was being paid for it or not. From his intuition he knew what he had to do in order to be successful and did it. He was forever asking, listening, learning and applying and that ensured he would also always be achieving. Paddy has the respect because he gives it. Honesty and respect are two key qualities and Paddy has both in abundance. He's the sort of fella you could always trust 110 percent, and for 110 percent."

One person who obviously knows Paddy for even longer than Anderson is his only sister, Vanessa. "My brother is a very strong character, consistent, reliable, predictable, very conservative, Paddy the unchanged" she says. "I suppose his weaknesses would be over-sensitivity and worrying about tramping on other people's toes." Well, one could certainly have a lot worse vices.

That sensitivity has led to Paddy pouring over the script of this book with a fine tooth comb, labouring long and hard in negotiating the removal of any little references which he feels would have the potential to be hurtful to his friends in the game. Modesty would have prevented him from doing himself justice had the book been written in autobiography form but, hopefully, as McGarry says, it will give him a glimpse of the affection in which he is held in the rugby world and serve as a reminder of all that he did achieve in his chosen sport.

Even in this case though, Paddy's modesty is writ large; McGarry says Johns was almost embarrassed to tell him earlier this year that his biography was being written.

"It's going to be fabulous for him to have the book and it is part of the process of drawing a line under his rugby career and moving on" says wife Kirsty. "The last 18 months have been difficult for him, but now it's all about the future. During his playing days he was always very wary of what he said to the media but, now that it can't hurt his rugby career, he has told his story and spoken about the things which he feels are important."

So there it is. Here we are at the end of Paddy Johns' rugby career and the end of this attempt to tell his story. His is a tale of achievement, with honour. A modest man who has made the most of himself and should prove an inspiration and excellent role model for any youngster with dreams of their own. By drawing together at least some of the strands which represent the fabric of Paddy Johns, this book hopefully brings to life the man in the green jersey as well as chronicling his achievements and setting them in context. For his family and friends, it will serve as a reminder that, as well as being a good guy, the man in their midst really is someone special for what he has achieved in rugby.

Keith McGarry says "my kids love him, they just think he's brilliant, and although they know they have seen him on TV, to them he's just Paddy, for the fame factor doesn't mean anything in their eyes. That's how he likes his friends to see him too rather than wanting to be put on a pedestal."

John Gamble says: "We've all known Paddy for that long, since we were seven or eight years of age and, because he is so unpretentious, it's so easy for us just to see him in the light of 'oh it's Paddy, we've known him all our lives' and forget that this man is a rugby legend who battled successfully with the biggest names in the global game for over a decade."

The authors have only known him for a relatively short time, but writing a biography is a fairly intimate business and we've got extremely close up in a few short months. Seeing what makes the man tick at first hand has been an enriching experience and working with an individual so honourable and humble in spite of his rugby status, has been instructive and inspiring. It has allowed us to humanise one of our rugby heroes.

We say amen to all the positive and warm things which have been said by others in this chapter and elsewhere. Saying familiarity breeds contempt would be to use the wrong expression, but we concur with John Gamble that it would be easy for Paddy's friends and family to lose sight of the sheer scale of his rugby achievements, while many fans of the sport will not have had the opportunity to know much of the man who won those 59 caps and captained his country.

Paddy Johns is a helluva lot more than a number, even a No 4! Hopefully this book has provided some flavour of both the man and the rugby player, both equally worthy, neither capable of being overstated. Much more than 'just Paddy' and much more than the standard description 'Johns, Ireland's fourth most capped player with 59 caps'. Doing this book with him has been an enjoyable journey for the authors, but all of us can be grateful that he didn't 'find another sport' as initially advised. Instead it's a case of thanks for the memories.